After Tamerlane

JOHN DARWIN

After Tamerlane

The Global History of Empire since 1405

ALLEN LANE
an imprint of
PENGUIN BOOKS

ALLEN LANE

Published by the Penguin Group
Penguin Books Ltd, 80 Strand, London WC2R 0RL, England
Penguin Group (USA) Inc., 375 Hudson Street, New York, New York 10014, USA
Penguin Group (Canada), 90 Eglinton Avenue East, Suite 700, Toronto, Ontario, Canada M4P 2Y3
(a division of Pearson Penguin Canada Inc.)
Penguin Ireland, 25 St Stephen's Green, Dublin 2, Ireland
(a division of Penguin Books Ltd)
Penguin Group (Australia), 250 Camberwell Road, Camberwell, Victoria 3124, Australia
(a division of Pearson Australia Group Pty Ltd)
Penguin Books India Pvt Ltd, 11 Community Centre, Panchsheel Park, New Delhi – 110 017, India
Penguin Group (NZ), 67 Apollo Drive, Rosedale, North Shore 0632, New Zealand
(a division of Pearson New Zealand Ltd)
Penguin Books (South Africa) (Pty) Ltd, 24 Sturdee Avenue, Rosebank, Johannesburg 2196, South Africa

Penguin Books Ltd, Registered Offices: 80 Strand, London WC2R 0RL, England

www.penguin.com

First published 2007
1

Copyright © John Darwin, 2007

Set in 10.5/14 pt Linotype Sabon
Typeset by Rowland Phototypesetting Ltd, Bury St Edmunds, Suffolk
Printed in Great Britain by Clays Ltd, St Ives plc

A CIP catalogue record for this book is available from the British Library

ISBN: 978-0-713-99667-8

For Caroline, Claire, Charlotte and Helen

Contents

List of Illustrations

Photographic acknowledgements are given in parentheses.

List of Maps

Preface

The death of Tamerlane in 1405 was a turning point in world history. Tamerlane was the last of the series of 'world-conquerors' in the tradition of Attila and Genghis Khan, who strove to bring the whole of Eurasia – the 'world island' – under the rule of a single vast empire. Within fifty years of his death, the maritime states of the Eurasian Far West, with Portugal in the van, were exploring the sea routes that became the nerves and arteries of great maritime empires. This is the story of what happened next.

It seems a familiar tale, until we look closer. The rise of the West to global supremacy by the path of empire and economic pre-eminence is one of the keystones of our historical knowledge. It helps us to order our view of the past. In many standard accounts, it appears all but inevitable. It was the high road of history: all the alternatives were byroads or dead ends. When Europe's empires dissolved, they were replaced by new post-colonial states, just as Europe itself became a part of the 'West' – a world-spanning league under American leadership. The aim of this book is partly to show that the passage from Tamerlane's times to our own has been far more contested, confused and chance-ridden than this legend suggests – an obvious enough point. But it tries to do this by placing Europe (and the West) in a much larger context: amid the empire-, state- and culture-building projects of other parts of Eurasia. Only thus, it is argued, can the course, nature, scale and limits of Europe's expansion be properly grasped, and the jumbled origins of our contemporary world become a little bit clearer.

This book could not have been written without the huge volume of new writing in the last twenty years both on 'global' history and on the histories of the Middle East, India, South East Asia, China and Japan. Of course, it is not only recently that historians have insisted on a global view of the past: that tradition, after all, goes back to Herodotus. Hidden in most histories lies a set of conjectures about what was supposed to have happened in other parts of the world. Systematic inquiry into the linkages between different parts of the world is, however, comparatively recent. 'The study of the past', remarked Frederick Teggart in his *Rome and China* (Berkeley, 1939), 'can become effective only when it is fully realized that all peoples have histories, that these histories run concurrently and in the same world, and that the act of comparing them is the beginning of knowledge.'[1] This challenge was taken up on a monumental scale in W. H. McNeill's *The Rise of the West* (Chicago, 1964), whose title belies its astonishing range and intellectual subtlety. But in recent years the resources committed to global and non-Western history have increased enormously. The economic, political and cultural impact of 'globalization' has been one of the reasons. But perhaps just as important have been the effects of diasporas and migrations (creating a mobile, 'anti-national' historical tradition) and the partial liberalization of many regimes (the greatest example being China) where 'history' was once treated as the private property of the state. New perspectives, new freedoms and new reading publics, wanting new meanings from history, have fuelled a vast outpouring of historical writing. The effect of all this has been to open new vistas on a past that once seemed accessible by only one route – the story of Europe's expansion. It has made it much easier than a generation ago to see that Europe's trajectory into the modern world shared many features in common with social and cultural changes elsewhere in Eurasia, and that Europe's attainment of primacy came later, and was more qualified, than we are often led to believe.

My debts to the work of other historians will be obvious from the notes that accompany each chapter. My first introduction to the fascination of viewing world history as a connected whole came as a pupil of the late Jack Gallagher, whose historical imagination was boundless. I have learned an enormous amount from my colleagues in imperial and global history in Oxford – Judith Brown, David

Washbrook, Georg Deutsch and Peter Carey – and have benefited from the expert knowledge of many other colleagues in the university and beyond, whose words of wisdom I have tried to remember. My thinking about the economic issues has been much improved by acquaintance with the Global Economic History Network, created by Patrick O'Brien as a forum for discussing the divergent paths of economic change in different parts of the world. Some of the ideas to be found in this book were prompted by arguments with James Belich and Phillip Buckner in several 'travelling seminars'. The stimulus of teaching so many talented students has been indispensable, and my historical education has been hugely extended by the supervision of many doctoral theses over the last twenty years. I am especially grateful to those friends and colleagues who commented on earlier versions of the chapters that follow: Richard Bonney, Ian Phimister, Robert Holland, Martin Ceadel and Andrew Hurrell. The errors and omissions I claim for myself.

I prepared draft maps using as a base the 'Mapinfo' program produced by Collins Bartholomew. I could not have done so without the instruction, advice and patient assistance of Nigel James of the Bodleian map department: it is a pleasure to acknowledge his help. The finished maps were drawn by Jeff Edwards. I am greatly indebted to Bob Davenport for his meticulous care in the copy-editing of the text.

The task of writing this book would have been much harder without the interest and encouragement of Simon Winder of Penguin. Faced with Simon's enthusiasm, no author could allow his efforts to flag. For this, and for his shrewd and timely advice at certain critical times, I am most grateful.

Lastly, writing this book over an extended period amid many other activities has largely been possible because of the extraordinary resources of Oxford's university libraries – embattled but unbowed – and because of the unrivalled facilities for research and writing that Nuffield College provides for its fellows.

A NOTE ON NAMES AND PLACES

Writing a book that ranges widely over time and space raises some awkward issues about the language of names and places. Not only do names change, but the changes reflect shifts of perception, status and often control. In many parts of the world, changing the names of cities, towns and streets – and even of countries – has been a way of symbolizing the end of the old (usually colonial) order and the reassertion of an indigenous culture and identity.

My practice has been to use the name most likely to be familiar to a predominantly Western and Anglophone readership, while drawing attention when appropriate to the alternative version. Sometimes this has meant using the name that gave a special contemporary meaning to a particular place. Thus I have used 'Constantinople' and not 'Istanbul' to denote the Ottoman capital. This was standard usage in the West long after the city was conquered by the Turks in 1453. I have retained it to signify its role as an imperial capital (quite different from modern Istanbul) and also its contested status as (in the eyes of many Europeans) an occupied Christian city that would one day be 'liberated'. This belief lasted until the Treaty of Lausanne in 1923.

Three issues deserve particular mention. Firstly, the romanization of Islamic names has always been somewhat arbitrary – perhaps inevitably so. When Europeans attempted to render the sound of Islamic names, they produced over the centuries extraordinary variations in spelling, some of which seem bizarre today. To complicate matters, some of these variations reflected the differences between spoken versions of Arabic, Persian and Turkish, the three main languages of Islamic Middle Eurasia. The most familiar of Muslim names can be found as Mahomet, Mehmet, Mohamed and Muhammad. Feisal can be found as Faisal or Faysal. I have used versions that I hope will be familiar and comprehensible, rather than those that might be more scholastically 'correct'.

Secondly there is the case of Iran. Until 1935 Iran was officially called Persia, the name by which the country was usually known in the West. 'Iran' was, however, the commoner usage in the country and the region, and I have chosen, for simplicity, to use it as the standard designation for the territorial unit and its people throughout the period covered by the book. But it is important to remember that 'Persian' (a word derived from 'Farsi') was the predominant language and culture, as well as describing the largest ethnic group in a land of several ethnicities.

Thirdly there is China. The Pinyin system is now widely used to romanize Chinese. However, since most of the references in this book are to Chinese persons and places, I have retained the forms most likely to be familiar to Western readers, following the older Wade–Giles system. The most obvious examples are as follows:

Ch'ing *not* Qing
Peking *not* Beijing (until Chapter 8)
Nanking *not* Nanjing
Canton *not* Guangzhou
Kiangnan *not* Jiangnan
Sinkiang *not* Xinjiang
Ch'ien-lung *not* Qianlong
Kuomintang *not* Guomindang
Chiang Kai-shek *not* Jiang Jeshi
Mao Tse-tung *not* Mao Zedong
Chou En-lai *not* Zhou Enlai

I

Orientations

1. Ptolemy's map of the world, the basis of European knowledge
   until the late fifteenth century

AFTER TAMERLANE

In 1401 the great Islamic historian Ibn Khaldun (1332–1406) was in the city of Damascus, then under siege by the mighty Tamerlane. Eager to meet the famous conqueror of the day, he was lowered from the walls in a basket and received in Tamerlane's camp. There he had a series of conversations with a ruler he described (in his autobiography) as 'one of the greatest and mightiest of kings . . . addicted to debate and argument about what he knows and does not know'.[1] Ibn Khaldun may have seen in Tamerlane the saviour of the Arab–Muslim civilization for whose survival he feared. But four years later Tamerlane died on the road to China, whose conquest he had planned.

Tamerlane (sometimes Timur, or Timurlenk, 'Timur the Lame' – hence his European name) was a phenomenon who became a legend. He was born, probably in the 1330s, into a lesser clan of the Turkic-Mongol tribal confederation the Chagatai, one of the four great divisions into which the Mongol empire of Genghis (Chinggis) Khan had been split up at his death, in 1227. By 1370 he had made himself master of the Chagatai. Between 1380 and 1390 he embarked upon the conquest of Iran, Mesopotamia (modern Iraq), Armenia and Georgia. In 1390 he invaded the Russian lands, returning a few years later to wreck the capital of the Golden Horde, the Mongol regime in modern South Russia. In 1398 he led a vast plundering raid into North India, crushing its Muslim rulers and demolishing Delhi. Then in 1400 he returned to the Middle East to capture Aleppo and Damascus (Ibn Khaldun escaped its massacre), before defeating and capturing the Ottoman sultan Bayazet at the Battle of Ankara in 1402. It was only after that that he turned east on his final and abortive campaign.

Despite his reputation as a bloodthirsty tyrant, and the undoubted savagery of his predatory conquests, Tamerlane was a transitional figure in Eurasian history.[2] His conquests were an echo of the great Mongol empire forged by Genghis Khan and his sons. That empire had extended from modern Iran to China, and as far north as Moscow.

It had encouraged a remarkable movement of people, trade and ideas around the waist of Eurasia, along the great grassy corridor of steppe, and Mongol rule may have served as the catalyst for commercial and intellectual change in an age of general economic expansion.[3] The Mongols even permitted the visits of West European emissaries hoping to build an anti-Muslim alliance and win Christian converts. But by the early fourteenth century the effort to preserve a grand imperial confederation had all but collapsed. The internecine wars between the 'Ilkhanate' rulers in Iran, the Golden Horde and the Chagatai, and the fall of the Yuan in China (by 1368), marked the end of the Mongol experiment in Eurasian empire.

Tamerlane's conquests were partly an effort to retrieve this lost empire. But his methods were different. Much of his warfare seemed mainly designed to wreck any rivals for control of the great trunk road of Eurasian commerce, on whose profits his empire was built. Also, his power was pivoted more on command of the 'sown' than on mastery of the steppe: his armies were made up not just of mounted bowmen (the classic Mongol formula), but of infantry, artillery, heavy cavalry and even an elephant corps. His system of rule was a form of absolutism, in which the loyalty of his tribal followers was balanced against the devotion of his urban and agrarian subjects. Tamerlane claimed also to be the 'Shadow of God' (among his many titles), wreaking vengeance upon the betrayers and backsliders of the Islamic faith. Into his chosen imperial capital at Samarkand, close to his birth-place, he poured the booty of his conquests, and there he fashioned the architectural monuments that proclaimed the splendour of his reign. The 'Timurid' model was to have a lasting influence upon the idea of empire across the whole breadth of Middle Eurasia.

But, despite his ferocity, his military genius and his shrewd adaptation of tribal politics to his imperial purpose, Tamerlane's system fell apart at his death. As he himself may have grasped intuitively, it was no longer possible to rule the sown from the steppe and build a Eurasian empire on the old foundations of Mongol military power. The Ottomans, the Mamluk state in Egypt and Syria, the Muslim sultanate in northern India, and above all China were too resilient to be swept away by his lightning campaigns. Indeed Tamerlane's death marked in several ways the end of a long phase in global history. His empire was the last real attempt to challenge the partition of Eurasia between the states of the Far West, Islamic Middle Eurasia and Confucian East Asia. Secondly, his political experiments and ultimate failure revealed that power had begun to shift back decisively from the nomad empires to the settled states. Thirdly, the collateral damage that Tamerlane inflicted on Middle Eurasia, and the disproportionate influence that tribal societies continued to wield there, helped (if only gradually) to tilt the Old World's balance in favour of the Far East and Far West, at the expense of the centre. Lastly, his passing coincided with the first signs of a change in the existing pattern of long-distance trade, the East–West route that he had fought to control. Within a few decades of his death, the idea of a world empire ruled from Samarkand had become fantastic. The discovery of the sea as a global commons offering maritime access to every part of the world transformed the economics and geopolitics of empire. It was to take three centuries before that new world order became plainly visible. But after Tamerlane no world-conqueror arose to dominate Eurasia, and Tamerlane's Eurasia no longer encompassed almost all the known world.

GLOBAL HISTORIES

In this book we traverse a vast historical landscape in pursuit of three themes. The first is the growth of global 'connectedness' into the intensified form that we call 'globalization'. The second is the part that was played in this process by the power of Europe (and later the 'West') and through the means of empire. The third is the resilience of many of Eurasia's other states and cultures in the face of Europe's expansion. Each of these factors has played a critical part in shaping the world that became by the twentieth century a vast semi-unified system of economics and politics, a common arena from which no state, society, economy or culture was able to remain entirely aloof.

No matter how detailed the subject or obscure the topic, histories are written to help to explain how we got where we are. Of course, historians often disagree with each other's accounts, and one of the reasons is the conflict of opinion about the nature of the 'present' –

the end product of history. To add to the difficulty, we constantly change our view of the present and 'update' it in line with unfolding events – revising as we do so the questions we ask of the past. But for the moment at least it is widely acknowledged that we live in an age that is strikingly different in many essentials from the world as it was a generation ago – before 1980. In ordinary language, we sum up the features that have been most influential in a catch-all term: 'globalization'. Globalization is an ambiguous word. It sounds like a process, but we often use it to describe a state – the terminal point after a period of change. All the signs are that, in economic relations at least, the pace of change in the world (in the distribution of wealth and productive activity between different regions and continents) is likely to grow. But we can, nonetheless, sketch the general features of the 'globalized world' – the stage which globalization has now reached – in a recognizable form. This is the 'present' whose unpredictable making the history in this book attempts to explain.

These features can be briefly summarized as follows:

1. the appearance of a single global market – not for all but for most widely used products, and also for the supply of capital, credit and financial services;
2. the intense interaction between states that may be geographically very distant but whose interests (even in the case of very small states) have become global, not regional;
3. the deep penetration of most cultures by globally organized media, whose commercial and cultural messages (especially through the language of 'brands') have become almost inseparable;
4. the huge scale of migrations and diasporas (forced and free), creating networks and connections that rival the impact of the great European out-migration of the nineteenth century or the Atlantic slave trade;
5. the emergence from the wreck of the 'bipolar age' (1945–89) of a single 'hyperpower', whose economic and military strength, in relation to all other states, has had no parallel in modern world history;
6. the dramatic resurgence of China and India as manufacturing powers. In hugely increasing world output and shifting the balance

of the world economy, the economic mobilization of their vast populations (1.3 billion and 1 billion respectively) has been likened to the opening of vast new lands in the nineteenth century.

This list ought to provoke a series of questions. Why, in a globalized world, should one state have attained such exceptional power? Why has the economic revival of China and India been such a recent development? Why until recently have the countries of the West (now including Japan) enjoyed such a long lead in technological skills and in their standards of living? Why do the products of Westernized culture (in science, medicine, literature and the arts) still command for the most part the highest prestige? Why does the international states system, with its laws and norms, reflect the concepts and practice of European statecraft, and territorial formatting on the European model? The globalized world of the late twentieth century was not the predictable outcome of a global free market. Nor could we deduce it from the state of the world five centuries ago. It was the product of a long, confused and often violent history, of sudden reversals of fortune and unexpected defeats. Its roots stretch back (so it is widely believed) to the 'Age of Discovery' – back, indeed, to the death of Tamerlane.

Of course, there have been numerous theories and histories without number explaining and debating the course of world history. The history (and prehistory) of globalization has always been controversial. Since most of the features of globalization seemed closely related to the growth of European (later Western) predominance, it could hardly be otherwise. The lines of battle were drawn up early on. Among the first to imagine a globalized world were the British free-traders of the 1830s and '40s, who drew their inspiration from Adam Smith. Worldwide free trade, so they reasoned, would make war unthinkable. If every country depended upon foreign suppliers and customers, the web of mutual dependence would be too strong to break. Warrior aristocracies that thrived in a climate of conflict would become obsolete. The bourgeois ideal of representative government, spread by traders and trade, would become universal. This cheerful account of how enlightened self-interest would remake the world to the profit of all was punctured by Karl Marx. Marx insisted that, sooner or later (he expected it to be sooner), industrial capitalism would drown its markets in goods. It could survive for a while by cutting its costs, driving wages below the cost of subsistence. But when the workers revolted – as revolt they must – capitalism would implode and the proletariat would rule. The world beyond Europe would be caught up in the struggle. In their hunger for markets, the European capitalists were bound to invade Asia (Marx's example was India) and wreck its pre-modern economies. The Indian weaver would go to the wall for the sake of Lancashire profits. India's village system and its social order were 'disappearing not so much through the brutal interference of the British tax-gatherer and . . . soldier, as [through] the working of English steam and English free trade'.[4] The saving grace of this work of destruction was its unintended consequence. It would bring a social revolution to Asia, without which (so Marx implied) the rest of the world would not reach its socialist destiny.

Marx had argued that a global economy would grow out of Europe's demands. Lenin insisted that capitalism depended upon economic imperialism, and predicted its downfall in a global revolt of colonial peoples.[5] The Marx–Lenin version, half-history, half-prophecy, seemed the key to world history. From the 1920s onward it exerted huge intellectual influence. It saw Europe's economic expansion as the irresistible force ruling the rest of the world. But, instead of creating the bourgeois utopia promised by the British free-traders, it had divided the world. The capitalist-industrial zone that was centred in Europe (and its American offspring) had become richer and richer. But across the rest of the globe, colonial subjection or semi-colonial dependence brought growing impoverishment. Capitalist wealth and Europe's imperial power had combined to enforce a grossly unequal bargain. 'Free' trade had been used in the non-Western world to destroy old artisan industries, block industrial growth, and lock local economies into producing cheap raw materials. Indeed, because those raw materials would get steadily cheaper than the industrial goods for which they were meant to pay (or so ran the argument), poverty and dependence could only get worse, unless and until the 'world system' they sprang from was demolished by force.[6]

For much of the twentieth century, this pessimistic view of the motives and meaning of globalization (though the term was not used),

sometimes combined with remarkable faith in its revolutionary outcome, was more than a match for the claims of the optimists who saw
the result of a fully global economy as being 'modernization' (i.e.
the replication of the West's social structure). Both attitudes had in
common the unquestioned assumption that Europe (or the West) was
the only real source of historical change. Both sides made use of the
astonishing insights (and even more astonishing industry) of the great
German sociologist Max Weber (1864–1920). Weber was fascinated
by the peculiar trajectory that Europe had followed compared with
India or China. While Marx had laid stress on the social revolution
that replaced Europe's feudal society with bourgeois-ruled capitalism,
Weber searched for the pattern of institutions and beliefs that had
made Europe 'different'. Capitalism had developed in other parts of
Eurasia, but Europe alone had made the transition to modern industrial capitalism, and the world pre-eminence that this had brought
with it. At the heart of Weber's explanation was the idea that modern
capitalism required above all an activist, rationalizing mentality.
Chinese Confucianism (rational but inactive), Islam (active but
irrational) and Hinduism (inactive and irrational) all discouraged
the vital combination. 'No path led from the magical religiosity of
the non-intellectual classes of Asia to a rational, methodical control
of life.'[7] But European Protestantism had created (accidentally) the
crucial psychology (and the institutional trappings) that allowed the
breakthrough.

Weber's insistence that Europe's peculiarity must be explained in
terms of a distinct socio-cultural complex inspired an enormous literature once his work became widely known (and translated) in the
1920s and after. It had a special appeal to those who rejected the
crude Marxian argument that Europe's wealth and success had been
gained by the plunder and pillage of the rest of the world. It encouraged the search for the critical factor(s) that had tipped the balance
in Europe towards productive investment and continuous technical
change. It seemed to confirm the belief (much older than Weber) that
European society was uniquely dynamic, and that other great cultures,
however magnificent, lacked the vital ingredients for material progress. Indeed, on this central issue, there was no real difference between the Weberian view and that taken for granted by the champions

of the Marxian 'world system'. For good or ill, from bad motives or none, Europe had energized a stationary world.

It is easy to see why in more recent years this Europe-centred account of modern world history has come under fire. The rapid dissolution of Europe's colonial empires after 1945 created a mass of new nations. Each needed a history that placed its own progress at the heart of the story. Each had its own heroes whose national struggle had been waged in the face of Europe's cultural arrogance. New 'nationalist' histories portrayed European rule (or influence) as unjust and repressive. Far from bringing progress to stationary parts of the world, European interference had blocked the social and cultural advances that were already in train. In the 1970s and '80s, 'subaltern' history dug into the fabric of many ex-colonial societies. It revealed complex peasant communities, fiercely resistant to control by outsiders, whose lives were disrupted by the clumsy if not brutal attempt to impose colonial 'order'.[8] 'Decolonized history' encouraged many different social, ethnic, religious or cultural groups to emerge from the shadows. The old colonial narratives in which Europeans stood out against the dark local backcloth now seemed like cartoons: crude and incomplete sketches of a crowded reality. The ambitions and projects of colonized peoples – teachers, writers, merchants, peasants, migrants and minorities – were described and documented. The 'stationary worlds' in which Europeans had posed as the sole 'dynamic' force were now to be seen as teeming with life. And, far from exerting a confident mastery, Europeans (in this new perspective) were often outwitted, exploited or simply ignored by locals busy with their own affairs.

This was not the first time that historians had argued that even colonized peoples had an autonomous history worthy of serious study. Before the Second World War, the young Dutch historian J. C. van Leur (1908–42) had denounced the writing of Indonesian history through European eyes – 'from the deck of the ship, the ramparts of the fortress, the high gallery of the trading house', as if nothing could happen without a European being present, or at his instigation.[9] Van Leur was killed in the war, and his ideas reached a wider international audience only in the late 1950s. But his work added a key new dimension to the historical attack on a Europe-centred world history.

It dismissed the idea that the arrival of Europeans by sea in the sixteenth century had transformed Asia's trading economy. Instead, Europeans were latecomers in a huge maritime commerce, pioneered by Asians, linking China, Japan, South East Asia, India, the Persian Gulf, the Red Sea and East Africa. Far from awaiting the Promethean touch of merchants from Europe, a 'global' economy already existed.[10] If global economic convergence was a dominant theme in modern world history, the part played by Asians (and other non-Europeans) could not be ignored. Indeed, 'globalization' – in the wider sense of the term – could no longer be seen as just a European project.

In the last twenty years, van Leur's original insight has been widened much further. The scale of global mobility, the growth of diasporas, the porous nature of frontiers, the limited power of most states, and the new distribution of industrial power (especially in Asia) have radically altered our sense of the past and what we want to know from it. For the moment at least, writing the history of nations and states seems much less important than tracing the origins of our world of movement, with its frenetic exchange of goods and ideas, its hybrid cultures and its fluid identities. A new global history has grown up in response. Its units of study are regions or oceans, long-distance trades, networks of merchants, the tracks of wandering scholars, the traffic of cults and beliefs between cultures and continents. Viewed from this level, the radical difference between Europe and Asia, the central assumption of older world histories, looks much less impressive. Instead, a chain of 'connectedness', both commercial and cultural, linked much of early modern Eurasia just at the time when (in older accounts) Europe's divergence from Asia was becoming decisive. Notions of universal empire, a new 'culture of travel', and millenarian rumours and fantasies circulated around the huge land mass between Spain and the Bay of Bengal.[11] Geographical location in Asia or Europe begins to look much less important for social and cultural change than a position astride Eurasia's trunk lines of trade, or in the arid belt where long-distance travellers did not have to toil through forest, jungle or marsh.[12]

A similar change of emphasis can be seen among historians writing the new 'global history of material progress'. As van Leur had suggested, the facile conclusion that Europeans had galvanized a somnolent Asia after Vasco da Gama's arrival in India in 1498 was a travesty of the facts. A dense mercantile network already linked ports and producers between the coast of East Africa and the South China Sea. Asian merchants were not passive victims of a European takeover. Whatever their shortcomings, Asian governments were more than the predatory despots of European mythology who crushed trade and agriculture by penal taxation and arbitrary seizure. In different parts of Asia, there were market economies where the division of labour, specialized trades and urban development (the hallmarks of growth as Adam Smith had described it) looked very similar to those found in Europe. In China, especially, the scale of commercial exchange, the sophistication of credit, the use of technology, and the volume of production (in textiles particularly) revealed a pre-industrial economy at least as dynamic as contemporary Europe's. Indeed, before 1800 what really stood out was not the sharp economic contrast between Europe and Asia, but, on the contrary, a Eurasian world of 'surprising resemblances' in which a number of regions, European and Asian, were at least theoretically capable of the great leap forward into the industrial age.[13]

Meanwhile, Europe's assumed centrality in accounts of world history had come under attack from a quite different quarter. From the late 1970s, an intellectual movement inspired by the Palestinian-American Edward Said denounced the classics of European writing on the history, ethnography and culture of Asia (and by extension elsewhere) as 'orientalist' fantasy. According to Said, European description was fatally flawed by the crude attribution of stereotyped qualities, almost always demeaning, and the persistent attempt to portray Asian societies as the slothful, corrupt or degenerate antitheses of an energetic, masterful and progressive Europe.[14] A huge literary industry sprang up to pick over the language and content of the various genres that transmitted the image of the non-Western world to an audience in Europe. The implication was clear. If the Europeans' reportage (whether fact or fiction) was intended to serve the ulterior aim of extending Europe's hegemony, or even if it did so unconsciously, it had no historical value except as a reflection of Europeans' own fears and obsessions. The comparative study of Europe and non-Europe was hopelessly compromised. It could even be argued (and some writers did so) that history itself was an alien enterprise that forced knowledge of the past into the concepts and categories invented in (and for) Europe.

Few intelligent people accepted the logical conclusion of this post-modern extremism – that nothing could be known and that all inquiry was hopeless. But the broader point held good: that European depictions of other parts of the world needed very careful decoding. The Saidian critique was part of a great sea change, a conscious attempt to 'decentre' Europe or even to 'provincialize' it. European accounts of other cultures and peoples should no longer be treated as the 'authorized version', however full or persuasive. Europe should no longer be seen as the pivot of change, or as the agent acting on the passive civilizations of the non-Western world. Above all, perhaps, the European path to the modern world should no longer be treated as natural or 'normal', the standard against which historical change in other parts of the world should always be measured. Europeans had forged their own kind of modernity, but there were other modernities – indeed, many modernities.[15]

RETHINKING THE HISTORY OF EUROPE'S EXPANSION

'Decolonized history' has cut Europe down to size. It has made it much harder to assume unthinkingly that European societies were inherently progressive, or that they were necessarily more efficient than other peoples in Eurasia – or on other continents. European definitions of 'progress', like European observations on the rest of the world, have lost their once unchallenged authority. Indeed, some modern writers reject the validity of any comparison between different cultures (because no one can be an insider in more than one culture), in the curious belief that a much-jumbled world is really composed of distinct and original cultures. Post-colonial history takes a generally sceptical view of the European impact and an even more sceptical view of the 'improvements' once claimed for colonial rule. It treats 'colonial' history as myopic and biased, perhaps even delusory, and its claims as so much propaganda aimed at opinion at home. Indeed, closer inspection has suggested an ironic reversal of the colonialist case. Far from dragging backward peoples towards European-style modernity, colonial rule was more likely to impose a form of 'anti-modernity'. Caste in India symbolized Indian backwardness. Yet British rulers, for their own convenience, struck a bargain with Brahmins to harden caste status into an administrative system (formalized in the census).[16] In colonial Africa a parallel process took place as clans and followings were reinvented as 'tribes', with chiefly rulers as their ancestral leaders.[17] Here, as in India, a political gambit was carefully packaged as an act of respect to local tradition. In the colonial version of history, caste and tribe were inscribed as immemorial features of the Indian and African past. In imperial propaganda, they became the genetic flaws that made self-rule for Indians and Africans impossible. But in 'decolonized history' the expansion of Europe appears as a vast conspiracy to reorder the non-Western world along pseudo-traditional lines, the better to hold it in check and exploit its resources – indefinitely.

On these and other grounds, Europe's place in world history now looks rather different from that in conventional accounts written a few decades ago. But histories that aim to 'provincialize' Europe still leave a lot to explain. The European states were the main force that created the 'globalized' world of the late nineteenth century. They were the chief authors of the two great transformations that were locked together in the 'modern world' of the 1870s to the 1940s. The first was the making of a world economy not just of long-distance trade in high-value luxuries but of the global exchange of manufactures, raw materials and foodstuffs, in huge volumes and values, with the accompanying flows of people and money. This was an economic revolution that was chiefly managed (not always well) from Europe or by Europeans, and fashioned to suit their particular interests. The second transformation was closely connected. This was the extension of European rule, overt and covert, across huge swathes of the non-European world – a process under way before 1800, but accelerating sharply in the nineteenth century. It was strikingly visible in the colonial partitions of Africa, South East Asia, the South Pacific and (later) the Middle East; in the great ventures of empire-building in North Asia (by Russia) and South Asia (by Britain); in the subjection of much of maritime China to foreign controls; and in the European occupation (by demographic imperialism) of the Americas, Australasia and parts of South Central Africa. In Africa, the Middle East, much of South East Asia, the Pacific, Australasia and even the Americas, it created the territorial units that provide the state structure of the contemporary world.

Europe thus engaged in a double expansion. The outward signs of the first were the spread of railways and steamships, building a vast web of connections much faster and more certain than in earlier times and capable of pouring a huge stream of goods into once inaccessible places. Harbour works, railway stations, telegraph lines, warehouses, banks, insurance companies, shops, hotels (like Shepheards' in Cairo or Raffles' in Singapore), clubs and even churches formed the global grid of Europe's commercial empire, allowing free passage to European merchants and trade and easing their access to a mass of new customers. The second mode was territorial. It meant the acquisition of forts and bases from which soldiers and warships could be sent to coerce or conquer. It meant the control of key zones astride the maritime highways that ran between Europe and the rest of the world: the classic case was Egypt, occupied by Britain in 1882. It meant a pattern of rule through which the products and revenues of colonial regions could be diverted at will to imperial purposes. Once their Raj was in place, the British taxed Indians to pay for the military power – a sepoy army – that they needed in Asia. Europe's commercial empire and its territorial empires did not overlap completely. But the crucial point about this double expansion was its interdependence. Territorial imperialism was a battering ram. It could break open markets that resisted free trade, or (as in India) conscript local resources to build the railways and roads that European traders demanded. It could promise protection to European entrepreneurs, or (as happened often in Africa) make them a free gift of local land and labour. But it also relied on the technological, industrial and financial assets that Europe could deploy. These might be decisive when it came to fighting – steam-powered ships and superior weaponry helped win Britain's first war in China in 1839–42 – though certainly not in all places.[18] The real advantage of industrial imperialism lay in scale and speed. Industrial technique and the supply of capital allowed

Europeans to stage a series of blitzkrieg conquests. They could lay down railways at breakneck speed to bring their force to bear hundreds of miles from the sea. They could flood a new zone with European settlers and transform its demography almost overnight, disorienting indigenous peoples and making resistance seem futile. They could transform alien environments with amazing completeness into a familiar European-style habitat: introducing wild animals, birds, fish, trees and flowers as well as crops and livestock. Above all, they could turn even the remotest parts of the globe into suppliers of the everyday goods like butter, meat or cheese once reserved for local producers at home. The gaunt freezing works with their grimy smokestacks that sprang up round the coasts of New Zealand after 1880 were the industrial face of colonization.

It would be wrong to suppose that Europeans lacked the support of allies and helpers; but they played the critical role in remaking the world. But how do we explain the extraordinary shift, which seemed all but complete by 1914, from a world of Eurasian 'connectedness' to a global-imperial world? Despite the libraries of writing that deal with the subject, much remains puzzling. Those magical dates 1492 (when Columbus crossed the Atlantic) and 1498 (when Vasco da Gama arrived in India) may have signalled the start of Europe's new era. But the pace of advance was spasmodic at best. Three centuries after Columbus had made landfall, most of the North American mainland remained unoccupied and virtually unexplored by Europeans. It took nearly three hundred years for the corner of India where Vasco da Gama had landed to fall under European rule (Calicut was annexed by the British in 1792). The rush started only at the turn of the nineteenth century. Not just the timing, but the form and direction of Europe's expansion need more explanation. Why did the Ottoman Empire and Iran preserve their autonomy long after India, which was much further away? Why was India subjected to colonial rule while China was able to keep its sovereign status, though much hedged about, and Japan had become a colonial power by 1914? If industrial capitalism was the key to the spread of European influence, why did its impact take so long to be felt across so much of the world, and with such variable consequences? Why were Europe's own divisions, periodically unleashed with such lethal effect, not more destructive of its imperial ambitions? And what indeed should be counted as 'Europe'? Why did some parts of 'non-Europe' succeed so much better than others at keeping Europe at bay, or throw off its grip more quickly? And how much was left, once Europe's empires collapsed, of the 'world Europe had made'?

To answer these questions, it seems wise to adopt a somewhat different approach from that of previous histories. Four basic assumptions have shaped the arguments advanced in this book. The first is that we should reject the idea of a linear change in the course of modern world history, in which Europe *progressively* rose to pre-eminence, then fell and rose again as part of the 'West'. It is more productive to think in terms of 'conjunctures', periods of time when certain general conditions in different parts of the world coincided to encourage (or check) the enlargement of trade, the expansion of empires, the exchange of ideas or the movement of people. The way that this happened might tilt the balance of advantage between different parts of the world, temporarily at least. One condition alone was rarely decisive. Producers and consumers might wish to do business. But governments and rulers also had to agree to permit free(ish) trade – or any trade at all. Politics and geopolitics were a vital part of the equation. The outbreak of wars and their unpredictable course could shatter one equilibrium and impose another. Thus the great expansion of trade in the late nineteenth century and the kinds of globalization it helped to promote came to a shuddering halt with the First World War. After 1929, 'deglobalization' set in with catastrophic results. Europe's original breakthrough to a position of primacy in its global relations is much better seen as the unexpected result of a revolution in Eurasia than as the outcome of a steady advance in Columbus's footsteps. The appropriate imagery is not of rivers or tides, but of earthquakes and floods.

The second assumption is that we must set Europe's age of expansion firmly in its Eurasian context. That means recognizing the *central* importance of Europe's connections with other Old World civilizations and states in Asia, North Africa and the Middle East. Of course, Europe's forced entry into the 'Outer World' and the 'neo-Europes' it created in the Americas, Australasia and Southern Africa were a key part of the story. Without the exploitation of American resources, and the commercial integration of North East America and North West Europe to form an 'Atlantic' economy, the eventual creation of a global economy in the late nineteenth century might not have happened at all. But the staggering scale of American wealth – the wonder of the world for more than a century – should not distract us. The centre of gravity in modern world history lies in Eurasia – in the troubled, conflicted, connected and intimate relations of its great cultures and states, strung out in a line from the European 'Far West' to the Asian 'Far East'.

Perhaps surprisingly, the most forceful statement of this 'Eurasian' view was made a century ago by a British geographer-imperialist, Halford Mackinder.[19] Mackinder was keen to remind his audience that the 'Columbian epoch', when European sea power had seemed to master the world, was only an interlude. The advantage of sea over land as a means of travel was temporary, not permanent: the invention of railways had seen to that. Before long the dominant influence in the world's affairs would revert to the power(s) that commanded Eurasia (what Mackinder called the 'world island') by controlling its 'heartland'. From this central position, and with a network of railways to mobilize vast resources, a Eurasian empire could drive any rival to the world's maritime fringe – the 'Outer World' of the Americas, sub-Saharan Africa, island South East Asia and Oceania – and even challenge it there. There is no need to follow Mackinder's geopolitical vision to its logical end (his aim after all was to puncture the complacency of the Edwardian Establishment), although the nightmare scenario of a 'heartland' super-empire became less far-fetched in the age of Nazi and Soviet imperialism. What we can see today, perhaps even more clearly than he, is that the shifting balance of wealth and power between Eurasia's main elements, and the different terms on which these elements entered the global economy and the modern 'world system', form the hammer and anvil of modern world history.

It might even be argued that Europe's annexation of the Outer World is only a part of this Eurasian history, and depended heavily upon Eurasian developments. In sub-Saharan Africa and in South East Asia, Europeans found themselves in competition with other Old World empires and their client states. After c.1870, fear of a 'peaceful invasion' by Chinese and Japanese settlers created racial paranoia all round the 'white' Pacific, in Australia, New Zealand and on the Pacific coast of North America. But it was also true that European efforts to create viable colonies in Outer World regions depended on co-opting or conscripting the resources of non-European Eurasia. India's taxes, soldiers, merchants and manpower (often in the form of indentured labour) helped throw open East Africa, parts of mainland South East Asia and the island Pacific as far away as Fiji to European (in this case British) enterprise. Chinese traders, miners and artisans were just as important in what became British Malaya and the Dutch East Indies (modern Indonesia). The critical fact was that Chinese and Indians came not as the agents of a Chinese or Indian expansion, but as the auxiliaries and accessories of one directed from Europe.

The third assumption is that we need to think out very carefully what that 'Europe' was. There are obvious objections to treating Europe as a unity when it was at best a loose and quarrelsome 'commonwealth'. Thus when we talk about 'European primacy', what we really mean is the collective primacy of the European states, especially those most active in overseas trade and empire. Part of the difficulty is that the word 'Europe' has acquired at least three different meanings: a geographical space; a socio-political community; and a cultural programme.[20] An easy solution, in writing of Europe's global expansion, has been to treat the continent's north-west corner as its centre of power. Britain, the Low Countries, northern France and western Germany become the 'quintessence' of Europe, setting the 'European' standard of economic and cultural modernity. Explaining Europe's successes is then a straightforward matter of invoking the strength and efficiency of its representative 'core states'.

In any long view of Europe's place in Eurasia (or in global history) this reductive approach is very misleading – for three different reasons. Firstly, the north-western states were not free agents who could disregard events in the rest of the continent – even after they had become Europe's richest section. Their wealth and safety were always dependent on the general stability of the European 'states system'. Turmoil in Central or Eastern Europe, or a major disturbance in the overall balance of power, could threaten their sovereignty or bring them windfall gains – in Europe or beyond. In fact in the period covered by this book no part of Europe achieved a lasting supremacy over all the others. The commercial prosperity of the north-western states was balanced by the military and demographic weight of the empires further east. The Europe of nations (in the west) might look down its nose at the Europe of empires (in the east), but it had to live with it. Coexistence was often explosive. The quarrels and conflicts of the European states, reaching a terrible climax in the twentieth century, were a constant limiting factor on their collective ability to impose Europe's domination on the rest of the world.

Secondly, too narrow a view of what Europe was ignores the problem of Russia. A long liberal tradition took a sceptical view of Russia's European credentials, seeing tsarist Russia as an 'Asiatic despotism', too crude and too poor to be 'one of us'. Some Russian thinkers returned the compliment by insisting that Russia was a separate (and superior) civilization untainted by Europe's amoral industrialism. A realistic view would see Russia, like Spain or the Habsburg Empire, as one of the frontier states that played a vanguard role in Europe's expansion.[21] The eventual predominance of the West European states across much of Southern Asia after 1815 was really achieved in a fractious involuntary partnership with Russia. Russia's huge inland empire, pivoted around Inner Asia, gradually absorbed much of the North Asian land mass. Ottomans, Iranians, Chinese and Japanese faced the British and French with Russia closing in behind them. The vast (but incomplete) encirclement of Asia by Europe was the great geopolitical fact of the nineteenth-century world. But, for all the pedantry of liberals and Slavophiles, the 'power supply' behind Russia's expansion was in fact its European identity: the leverage granted by its first-class membership of the European states system; the economic energy that flowed from Russia's integration into the European economy; and the intellectual access that Russians enjoyed, from the sixteenth century onward, to the general pool of European ideas and culture. Russians, like other Europeans, claimed their conquests as a 'civilizing mission'.

Thirdly, there is a powerful case for broadening our notion of 'Europe' to the west as well as the east. The importance of the Atlantic economy has already been mentioned. A vast economic space that included the West African coast, the Caribbean islands, the North American seaboard, Mexico, Peru and maritime Brazil was annexed to Europe commercially after 1500. The precise contribution of this mainly slave-labour zone to Europe's later industrialization has remained controversial, and may not have been large.[22] But the important point is that by the early nineteenth century, and perhaps even before, a significant part of this Atlantic world can no longer be seen as Europe's dependent periphery. The 'Old Northeast' of the United States, with its metropolis in New York, was functionally part of Europe's leading commercial region. It was an active – and became the dominant – partner in developing the agrarian lands in the American South and Midwest, its inland empire. By the 1870s it was financially and industrially on a par with Europe's richest countries. Although America's separate identity was loudly proclaimed by its politicians and writers, and fear of involvement in European quarrels ruled its diplomacy, America's relations with Europe were not cold or detached. Between the Old Northeast and North West Europe, the traffic of goods, technology, ideas and people was extremely dense. In culture and technology it was a two-way movement, with a strong mutual influence. By fits and starts, with retreats and advances, Old Europe and New Europe were being subsumed into a larger formation, the 'West'. It was a volatile process, on which the peculiar trajectory of American capitalism – with its huge corporate scale and aggressive protectionism – had a powerful impact. But it was one of the keys to Europe's place in Eurasia, and to both the duration and the mutation of Europe's leading place in the world.

The fourth assumption concerns our understanding of empire. Empire is often seen as the original sin of European peoples, who corrupted an innocent world. Of course its real origins are much older, and lie in a process almost universal in human societies. It was a human characteristic, remarked Adam Smith in *The Wealth of Nations* (1776), to want to 'truck, barter and exchange'.[23] Smith was thinking of material goods: it was the habit of exchange that allowed the division of labour, the real foundation of economic life. But he might well have extended his philosophical insight to the parallel world of information and ideas. The exchange of information, knowledge, beliefs and ideas – sometimes over enormous distances – has been just as typical of human societies as the eagerness to acquire useful, prestigious or exotic goods by purchase or barter. Both kinds of exchange bring consequences with them. A supply of cheap firearms (to take an obvious example) could shift the balance of power inside a society where firearms were scarce or unknown with astonishing speed, and unleash a huge cycle of violence against humans or nature. The spread of Christianity and Islam transformed their converts' conception of their place in the world, and their notions of loyalty to neighbours and rulers. As these cases suggest, at all times in history the exchange of goods and ideas has upset the cohesion of some societies much more than others, making them vulnerable to internal breakdown, and to takeover by outsiders. So a second propensity in human communities has been the accumulation of power on an extensive scale: the building of empires. Indeed, the difficulty of forming autonomous states on an ethnic basis, against the gravitational pull of cultural or economic attraction (as well as disparities of military force), has been so great that empire (where different ethnic communities fall under a common ruler) has been the default mode of political organization throughout most of history. Imperial power has usually been the rule of the road.

But if empire is 'normal', why has its practice by Europeans aroused such passionate hostility – a hostility still strongly reflected in most of what is written on the subject? Part of the answer is that so many post-colonial states found it natural to base their political legitimacy on the rejection of empire as an alien, evil and oppressive force. Some forty years on, this tradition is stronger than ever. Part of the reason is the far wider exposure to European empire-building than to that of (for example) the Mongols, the Ottoman Turks or the Chinese in Inner Asia. The constituency of the aggrieved is thus much larger. But the intensity of feeling also reflects the belief (expressed in much of the historical writing) that there was something qualitatively different about the empires that the Europeans made. Unlike the traditional agrarian empires that merely accumulated land and people, the arch-characteristic of European imperialism was expropriation. Land was expropriated to meet the needs of plantations and mines engaged in long-distance commerce. Slave labour was acquired and carried thousands of miles to serve the same purpose. Native peoples were displaced, and their property rights nullified, on the grounds that they had failed to make proper use of their land. Both native peoples and slaves (by different forms of displacement) suffered the effective expropriation of their cultures and identities: they were reduced to fragments, without hope of recovering the worlds they had lost. They became peoples without a history. And where expropriation by subjugation proved insufficient, European colonizers turned to their ultimate remedies: exclusion, expulsion or liquidation. 'If we reason from what passes in the world,' wrote the French thinker de Tocqueville in 1835, after a visit to America, 'we should almost say that the European is to the other races of mankind what man himself is to the lower animals: he makes them subservient to his use, and when he cannot subdue he destroys them.'[24]

This chilling account of the European version of empire (as practised outside Europe) seemed amply confirmed by what took place in the New World of the Americas, where Europeans (for reasons discussed in Chapter 2) were much freer than elsewhere to impose their will. Until c. 1800 it looked as if a variety of factors would prevent a similar pattern in other parts of the world. Distance, disease and demography would sustain much more determined resistance. Even where Europeans had established their bridgeheads, they would be forced to 'creolize' and make social and cultural peace with Afro-Asian peoples. But this is not what happened. In the nineteenth century, Europe's expansion was supercharged by technological and cultural change. Europe's capacity to intrude and interfere was transformed on two levels. Europeans acquired the means to assert their will on the ground – by force if necessary – over far more of the world. Most spectacularly in India, they imposed their rule directly on the conquered population, taxing, policing and laying down the law. At the same time, the growth of a Europe-centred international economy, the extension of a Europe-centred international system with its own laws and norms, and the spread of European ideas via Europe-owned media (like the telegraph, mail and steamship services) created a new environment at the 'macro' level. Europeans, it seemed, controlled all the lines of communication. Above the very local level, nothing could move unless it adapted to their ways. Trapped between these upper and nether millstones, it is hardly surprising that colonized peoples in Asia and Africa should have likened their condition to that of the Europeans' first victims in the Americas.

We shall see later on why this was too pessimistic, in some cases at least. Even supercharged Europe needed local cooperation, and had to pay its price. Some of what it offered was quickly adapted for local 'self-strengthening', building up the local capacity to build states and cultures. Some of it chimed with the aims of local reformers. Some of the claims of colonialism's fiercest antagonists now look less patriotic and more like the outcry of privilege displaced. Nevertheless, it seems unlikely that we will be able to take a detached and apolitical view of Europe's empire-building for a long time to come. In too much of the world its effects are too recent to be allowed to slip into the 'past' – that zone of time whose events we regard as having only an indirect influence on our own affairs. It may be an age before we regard it more coolly as a phase in world history – perhaps an inevitable phase – rather than as the result of the moral and cultural aggression of one part of the world.

There is one final complication that we may need to unravel. It is commonplace to talk of the 'modern' world, to describe the changes that made it as 'modernization', and to treat the attainment of 'modernity' as the most critical change in the history of a state or community. The intermeshing processes that we call globalization are usually thought of as part of modernity, since 'modern' societies supposedly interact more intensely with each other than did their 'pre-modern' counterparts. Modernization thus has a close and uncomfortable affinity with the expansion of Europe.

But modernity is a very slippery idea. The conventional meaning is based on a scale of achievement. In political terms, its key attributes are an organized nation state, with definite boundaries; an orderly government, with a loyal bureaucracy to carry out its commands; an effective means to represent public opinion; and a code of rights to protect the ordinary citizen and encourage the growth of 'civil society'. Economically, it means the attainment of rapid, cumulative economic growth through industrial capitalism (with its social and technological infrastructure); the entrenchment of individual property rights (as a necessary precondition); and the systematic exploitation of science-based knowledge. Culturally, it implies the separation of religion and the supernatural from the mainstream of thought (by secularization and the 'disenchantment' of knowledge) and social behaviour; the diffusion of literacy (usually through a vernacular rather than a classical language); and a sense of common origins and identity (often based on language) within a 'national' community. The keynotes of modernity become order, discipline, hierarchy and control in societies bent on purposeful change towards ever higher levels of 'social efficiency'.

It is easy to see that most of these criteria are really a description of what was supposed to have happened in Europe. Europe became modern; non-Europe stayed pre-modern – until modernized by Europe. The result is often a crude dichotomy that sees Europeans as the invariable agents of progress in a world elsewhere glued to 'tradition'. We have seen already that this view is hard to defend. There are three other difficulties. First, the elements of modernity (as listed above) were rarely all present in a single society. In much of Europe they were barely visible until very recent times. Even those countries that we think of as pioneers of modernity had strong pre-modern features. Slavery was lawful in the United States until 1863. The ruling class of Victorian Britain was largely chosen by birth, and religion remained central to social aspiration and identity. Twentieth-century America was a caste society whose marker was colour, used to exclude a large social fragment from civil and political rights until the 1960s or later. Post-revolutionary France confined the Rights of Man to men until 1945, when women gained the vote. Viewed from this angle, the threshold for modernity becomes very uncertain. Was Nazi Germany modern, or Soviet Russia? Are there objective tests for modernity, or is 'modern' simply a label for regimes we approve of? Second, some of the key features of conventional modernity were also to be found in parts of Eurasia far away from Europe. The classic case is China, which developed a 'modern' bureaucracy selected on merit, a commercial economy and a technological culture long before Europe. Was China modern, with some pre-modern survivals, or the other way round? Nor was Western-style modernity eventually taken up in the non-Western world without many local adjustments. How are these to be seen? Is there one modernity, or are there 'many modernities'?[25] Third, it may be the case, as the example of China suggests, that other kinds of modernity were not doomed to failure because their flaws were inherent. Instead it seems possible (some would say obvious) that Europe's expansion amounted in part to a deliberate assault on the modernizing ventures of other peoples and states. Perhaps it was not Europe's modernity that triumphed, but its superior capacity for organized violence.

Modernity is too useful an idea to be thrown away. But it may be wise to accept it as a fuzzy abstraction – as a rough-and-ready checklist of the social and cultural patterns that favoured the production of wealth and power at a particular time. For the term to be helpful, however, it ought to throw light on the relative success of different communities caught up in the greater regional and global connectedness that accelerated so sharply after the mid eighteenth century. Being modern was not an absolute state, but a comparative one – indeed a competitive one. The best test of modernity might be the extent to which, in any given society, resources and people could be mobilized for a task, and redeployed continuously as new needs arose or new pressures were felt. In principle, many different societies possessed this ability. In practice, and for reasons that we are far from understanding fully, for almost two centuries after 1750 it was North West European societies (and their transatlantic offspring) that mobilized fastest and also coped best with the social and political strains that being mobile imposed. Far-flung empires, and a global economy shaped to their interests, were to be their reward.

MEDIEVAL EURASIA

Before 1400, an observer who was able to survey the world would have had few accurate clues as to which of the main civilizations in Eurasia would eventually assert a worldwide pre-eminence. China, the Islamic realm in Middle Eurasia, and Europe had each attained a high degree of socio-political organization and material culture. They had all displayed a notable capacity for territorial expansion. But each was inhibited by internal divisions and weaknesses (as well as by the logistics of distance) from achieving predominance over the others.

Of these three great civilizational zones, fifteenth-century Europe was in many ways the parvenu. Since classical times (300 BC to AD 300), and earlier, culture and wealth in Western Eurasia had clustered round the coasts and river valleys of the eastern Mediterranean and the Near East. This was the nursery of city states and empires, where agriculture and trade had been most advanced and profitable. The great hinterland of 'Outer Europe' beyond the Alps was a barbarian region, to be explored, conquered and colonized by the civilized states to the south and east. The Gallic wars of Julius Caesar (58–50 BC) were the crucial stage in its annexation by the new power that had united the eastern Mediterranean and much (not all) of the Near East under the hegemony of Rome. But, despite their hunger for its treasure, commodities and slave manpower, the Romans could not incorporate the whole of Europe in their empire. Instead they partitioned it, keeping the 'barbarians' at bay beyond their frontier defences that stretched from Hadrian's Wall and along the Rhine and Danube into Illyria in the Balkans. Beyond the line lay regions too remote, rebellious and poor to repay the effort of conquest by an imperial system whose centre of gravity remained firmly fixed in the eastern Mediterranean.

By the 400s, Roman rule in the West was breaking down in the face of successive waves of migration pressing in from Europe's northeastern limits. The centre of the 'civilized world' retreated southeastward to Byzantium (Constantinople) to guard the wealthiest region in Western Eurasia.[26] In Outer Europe, towns dwindled to mere junctions on old Roman roads; society and economy became overwhelmingly rural and preoccupied with subsistence. Only where churchmen congregated or rulers established their emporia – licensed depots for the long-distance trade in luxuries – did any vestiges of urban life survive.[27] For much of the period between AD 500 and 1000, even parts of Europe that had once been Romanized became too poor and inaccessible to be of much interest to traders and rulers in the Mediterranean and Near East. After 600, the imperial heartland in Western Eurasia was itself convulsed by the rise of Islam and the amazing speed with which Muslim armies overran much of the Near East (including Iran), Egypt, North Africa and most of Spain. The Byzantine Empire, Rome's legatee, shrank to the point where its survival was doubtful. For a time it seemed as if the whole of Mediterranean Europe would be annexed as part of the Islamic world. Charlemagne's attempt to build a neo-Roman regime in the West had fallen apart by 843. It was the astonishing recovery of the Byzantine Empire in the ninth century, and the gradual consolidation of a feudal order in Western Europe in the eleventh, that marked the beginnings of Europe's emergence as a viable, separate world civilization.

The double-headed nature of medieval Europe was of profound importance. Historians have often written as though modern Europe descends from the empire of Charlemagne. In fact it was shaped by the impact of immigrant peoples in the European East (like Magyars and Bulgars), cultural imports (like Near Eastern monasticism), and the commercial stimulus of the Islamic Near East with its insatiable appetite for furs and other northern commodities.[28] But at the height of Islamic expansion before AD 1000 it had been the Byzantine Empire ('Romania') with its great fortified capital that had played the most important part in preserving a Christian Europe and defining its scope. Byzantine sea power helped to fend off the Muslim invasion of Italy (Sicily had fallen in the early 800s) that might otherwise have driven the medieval West beyond the Alps. Byzantine models of centralized, autocratic government, and of military and naval organization, inspired the post-Roman states in the European West.[29] The rise of Venice to become the great emporium for the West's trade with the East was closely connected with the Byzantine recovery; culturally, Venice was really an outpost of the great metropolis at Constantinople – as its architecture revealed. By 1400, of course, the Byzantine Empire had crumbled almost to nothing: the fall of Constantinople to the Ottomans in 1453 was the dramatic finale to a long collapse. The balance of power within Europe had long since shifted to the Latin West. But Byzantine influence endured. Liberating the empire's former (Christian) subjects from Ottoman rule became a European mania. An even more potent legacy was Byzantium's tie with Russia, for whose medieval states it served as a religious and cultural magnet.[30] The eastern, landward, Russian, face of European expansion (the ultimate expression of Byzantine imperialism) was to influence Eurasia's history almost as deeply as its western, oceanic, counterpart.

In the Latin West, unlike in Greek Byzantium, continuity with the Roman Empire had been decisively lost. What emerged instead was a distinctive 'Frankish' culture that drew in part upon Roman imperial precedents transmitted from Byzantium. But the real peculiarity of the

Frankish world was the social and political institution of feudalism. At its simplest, it meant the exchange of labour service for physical protection by a warrior class of nobles and their retinues. It may have derived from the freedom of great landowners to control their localities once imperial government caved in, taxation went with it, and the monetized economy contracted sharply. The age of invasions (by Hungarians, Norsemen and Muslims) that followed the collapse of Charlemagne's short-lived imperium may have strengthened the trend. By AD 1000 this seigneurial system had hardened into an elaborate structure of obligations and overlordship, and had become a powerful engine for exploiting land and labour to produce military power – in the characteristic form of the mounted knight. The resulting seigneurial units, with their heavy cavalry and their fortified strongpoints, became the building blocks for a new round of state-making that began after 1000. This was not accidental. The feudal kingdom, replicated across Central and Northern Europe, was the vehicle for an extended process of conquest and colonization by the Frankish aristocracy and its allies. It was the battering ram against the frontiers of Muslim expansion in Sicily, Greece, Cyprus, Spain and Palestine (the crusader kingdom of Outremer). East of the Elbe, it was consolidated by a tide of peasant migration, and the growth of towns and trade.[31]

In both Byzantium and the Frankish West, it was the fusion of secular with religious influences that created societies cohesive enough to withstand the aftershocks of imperial breakdown, barbarian invasion and Islamic expansion. In the West, churchmen had been the main repository of political tradition after the fall of Rome. They supplied the literati needed for any large-scale government. To rulers, they offered an invaluable source of divine legitimation and a wider vision of kingly ambition. The Church provided much of the ideological glue needed to bind the new feudal states together: Christianization was the basis of state-formation all over Northern and Eastern Europe after AD 1000.[32] Everywhere, institutionalized Christianity reinforced the ties of solidarity and obligation. With the priest, the parish and the hierarchy of territorial bishops, religious sanctions could be welded to the political order far more strongly than in China or the Islamic world. The close identification between the authority of Church and

State – the most striking peculiarity of medieval Europe – gave its ruling elites a depth of social control unmatched in other parts of Eurasia. With the gradual development of dynastic states, a process well advanced by the fifteenth century, these sources of social power became even more valuable.

Economic revival underpinned the achievement of social and political cohesion. By the fourteenth century, Europe had reached broad economic and technological parity with China and the Islamic Near East. Between AD 1000 and c. 1350 there was a long phase of economic growth. The population increased. Waste lands were colonized. Technical improvements like the mould-board plough (which opened up heavier lands) and the watermill increased productivity. The expansion of towns as centres of commerce and government reflected the increased sophistication of economic life: the specialization of crafts and trades; the extension of banking and credit; the use of new business techniques in partnership and accounting. A web of commercial connections now bonded together the trade of Northern, Eastern and Baltic Europe with the Atlantic coast and the Mediterranean.[33] A great 'double isthmus' ran from northern Italy to the Low Countries: one branch through southern Germany and down the Rhine; the other up the Rhône and across northern France to Flanders. Along these routes, and clustered thickly at each end, were the commercial cities of the medieval West, while the line of the isthmus was itself a reminder that the flywheel of commerce was still the exchange of products from Asia, the Near East and the Mediterranean for those of Northern Europe. It was this that explained the precocious growth of Venice and Genoa and the German port cities stationed north of the Alps.

Economic expansion ground to a halt amid the demographic catastrophe of the mid fourteenth century, when the Eurasian pandemic called the Black Death carried off perhaps 40 per cent of the population. The fifteenth century saw a slow recovery. By that point, certainly, Europe was no longer the backward hinterland of the Islamic Near East. Europeans enjoyed no obvious advantage over the rest of Eurasia, but they were coming to play a much stronger role in Near Eastern trade. More and more they were financing their purchases of Asian luxuries, Iranian silk or Syrian cotton by the sale of their own manufactures (usually cloth), exploiting the urban decline of Egypt and Syria.[34] Genoese and Venetian *fondachi* (trading depots) littered the coastline from North Africa to the Crimea. Meanwhile, to the west, a new maritime frontier had opened. The reconquest of Spain from Muslim rulers by the mid thirteenth century had encouraged the opening of a regular sea route between the Mediterranean and the ports of the English Channel and the North Sea. Lisbon, Seville and later Cadiz became the connecting links between the Atlantic and Mediterranean systems. Long before Columbus, Atlantic Iberia had become a springboard for marine adventure, a school of advanced seamanship, and the likeliest rendezvous between the maritime pioneers and the Genoese merchants and bankers on whose credit they leaned.

By 1400 a new Europe had been made: a loose confederacy of Christian states, with a common high culture, broadly similar social and political institutions, and a developed inter-regional economy. It was at one level an ingenious fusion of Roman and Frankish culture, while its Byzantine component, submerged politically after 1400, secured the continued attachment (however tenuous at times) of the Russian lands. But Europe had also been formed by its tense relationship with the Islamic world. Much of what was known in the Latin West about the intellectual life of the classical world was transmitted to it by Muslim scholars in Spain.[35] The commercial life of the Muslim world had been far more advanced than that in much of Europe. Prestige goods and luxury wares, as well as silver and gold, flowed west into Europe, not the other way round. Western Europe's recovery from economic implosion would have been much slower without this wealthier neighbour. But these ties of dependence were balanced by the sense of imminent danger from a Muslim invasion (in Southern Europe especially) and by savage resentment against Muslim control of the Christian holy places – the emotional fuel behind the crusades. Re-Christianizing the lands reconquered from Islam had been an uphill task. The threat from without and the pervasive fear of the enemy within (usually Jews or heretics) created an insecure and aggressive, rather than calmly superior, view of cultural outsiders. Hemmed in between Islam, the dark limitless sea, and the forests and tundra of the North, Europeans could not pretend to inhabit a serene 'Middle Kingdom', surrounded by tributaries and guarded by walls. For all the successes of the Frankish political system, it could make no headway in South East Europe against the Muslim advance in the fourteenth century. The hope of outflanking Islam by allying with the Mongol 'world-conquerors' had fizzled out after 1350.

At the centre of the old Eurasian world lay the realm of Islam. In 1400 it extended from Andalusia and Morocco in the west to the plains of North India and the islands of South East Asia, modern Indonesia. Its double heartland lay in the Fertile Crescent that linked the Nile and Euphrates, and on the Iranian plateau. It was in the Near East and Iran that Islam had been established by Muhammad's Arab armies in the seventh century over the ruins of Byzantine and Sassanid rule. By AD 750, most of Central Asia was Muslim. After 1000, Muslim Turks invaded North India, drawn by the 'gold rush' for Indian treasure[36] to create a series of conquest states. By the thirteenth century, Islam had reached Bengal and the trading towns of the Malacca Strait, the launching pad for its advance into the Malay archipelago. The Sudanic lands south of the Sahara were also being Islamized by the eleventh century.

Medieval Europeans were dazzled by the fabulous wealth and intellectual sophistication of the Islamic world. There were good reasons for this. Far more than the 'colonial' West, the Islamic Near East was the intellectual legatee of the Ancient World and home to an intellectual culture that had all but collapsed in the 'Dark Ages' of the West. Nor was the wealth and urban tradition of the Near East an accident. Here, where the earliest riverine civilizations had grown up, economic life enjoyed a double stimulus. In the Nile–Euphrates corridor, and scattered across the Iranian uplands, were agricultural regions of exceptional productivity. An agricultural revolution had introduced new crops;[37] hydraulic technique overcame the curse of aridity. An agrarian surplus sustained urban elites and their elaborate high culture. In the towns, an artisan class of legendary skill had sprung up to cater for these elites' material demands. But the Near East was also the great commercial crossroads of the world: the land bridge between China, Europe, Africa and India, and the portage for the seaborne trade of the Indian Ocean. Threaded between its mountain ranges and deserts were the caravan routes that brought Chinese goods across Central Asia and Indian goods up from the Persian Gulf: routes that

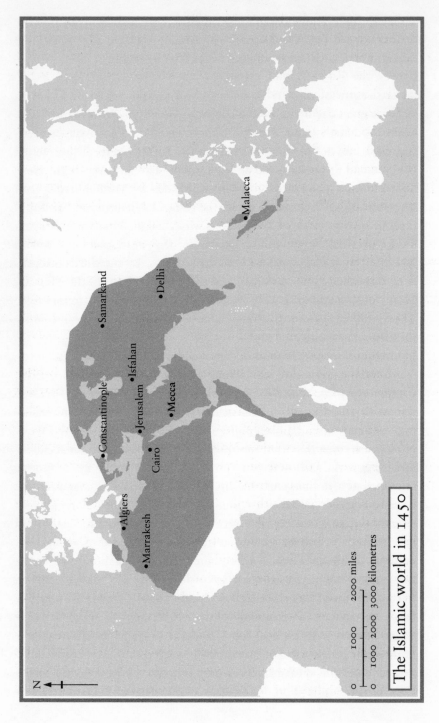

The Islamic world in 1450

ended at Syria's inland port cities (Damascus was the greatest), or further west at Bursa and Constantinople. Across the Isthmus of Suez ran another trunk route linking the Mediterranean to the Red Sea (where the Romans had maintained a naval squadron), with its onward connection to India.

These great channels of intercontinental trade with their local tributaries formed a stream of wealth tapped by the imperial systems that rose and fell in the seven centuries that followed the conquests of Muhammad. Near Eastern rulers were well aware of its value. For all his reputation as a tyrant of demonic cruelty, Tamerlane understood the point of commercial as well as military strategy. Destroying the trading towns north of the Caspian Sea was meant to enforce his monopoly over the trans-Eurasian trade that passed to its south. Other Near Eastern rulers took care to maintain the chief commercial roads, defend the merchants from tribal or nomadic predation, and build the great caravanserais – large fortified inns – that lowered the 'protection costs' of long-distance traffic. The ease with which it could be made to yield a revenue commended the golden goose of commerce to all but the most desperate or short-sighted of state-builders.

Tamerlane was the last of the great Mongol-Turkic 'world-conquerors' who swept into the Middle East from Inner Asia between the tenth and the fifteenth centuries. Their nomad armies, highly organized and fiercely disciplined, were composed of squadrons of mounted archers. They enjoyed the advantage of exceptional mobility and firepower.[38] For these empire-builders, the vast grassy steppe that stretched across Eurasia from Manchuria to Hungary was an open road to commercial wealth and almost limitless power. The trading cities of the Near and Middle East were a natural target. Each conquest left behind its deposit of migrants and reshaped the political and cultural landscape – like the periodic inundations of a mighty river. Dramatic as they were, these invasions from the East can be seen as part of a more general pattern of Middle East politics. The settled lands between the Nile and the Oxus where states had been made were exposed to disruption from their own desert frontiers, pressing in upon the pockets of the 'sown' and the towns they sustained. In his great philosophical history, the *Muqadimmah*, Ibn Khaldun explained how the inhabitants of the 'sown' slowly lost the will to defend

themselves against external depredation, until at last they were fair
game for an invading army of nomads, hardened by desert life and
the exploits of hunting and war. Ruthless, skilful and united by an
asabiyya (solidarity) long lost by the people of the 'sown', they formed
a new ruling class until they too succumbed to the corruption of
civilized life and were brushed aside in their turn.[39]

What Ibn Khaldun described was a political world indelibly marked
by the Arab conquest in the seventh century. Islam's triumph in the
Near East had turned on the capture of its towns and cities by the
Arab tribes that followed Muhammad. Islamic rule under the early
khalifas (caliphs) depended on tribal garrisons watching over the
unreliable townsmen. It was not a lasting solution. Under urban conditions, tribal unity weakened. There was no aristocracy to apply a
feudal remedy, and the problem of government was control of the
towns. The answer was found in recruiting military slaves, mainly
from Turkic communities in Central Asia.[40] These were slave soldiers
or Mamluks, hardy and untainted by the urban societies over whom
they stood guard. As slaves without kin or other ties of support, they
owed total loyalty to the amir or ruler. Their cost could be met
because the Islamic Near East, unlike the post-Roman West, had the
commercial economy and thus the monetary means with which to
buy them. Mamluk rule, sometimes by 'slave kings', became the
characteristic form of Islamic polity: in the North African Maghrib
and in Central Asia, North India, Egypt, Syria, the sub-Saharan Sudan
and the Iranian lands.[41] From the ninth century up till the death of
Tamerlane, the political history of the Islamic world had largely turned
upon the state-building (or empire-building) of Turkic tribal leaders:
founding dynasties, forming slave armies, and suffering overthrow in
their season.

The grand incursions into the Near East by Seljuk Turks from
Central Asia, the Mongol 'horde' of Genghis Khan and the followers
of Tamerlane must be set against this background. Each of these great
invasions brought destructive consequences whose scale is hard to
reckon, as well as the ferment of trade and religion that we noticed
earlier. For Genghis and Tamerlane, the aim was to unite the different
zones of the Islamic Near East under a Central Asian ruler, as the
prelude to fashioning a 'world empire' across the whole of Eurasia.

Both were frustrated by the logistics of empire-building in a region where the centres of cultivation and trade lay far apart, and distance dissolved the ruler's authority. The repeated cycle of mass military invasion, large-scale destruction, transient unity and imperial break-up gave the Islamic world a 'medieval' history starkly different from that of Europe or China. In Europe, the end of the great migrations permitted the gradual consolidation of territorial states whose people were subjected to ever-closer control by feudal lords, dynastic rulers and their clerical allies. In the Islamic world, the pattern was one of violent oscillation between the creation of 'world empires' and fragmentation into smaller tribal or dynastic polities whose rulers were usually men from the steppe, not the 'civilized' leaders of a home-grown elite.

By itself, a political tradition of such marked instability might have yielded economic and cultural chaos: a desert of futile ambition, not a civilization whose literature, science, philosophy, technology and art were more than a match for those of the medieval West. The vital elements of stability, continuity, identity and cultural cohesion were provided by Islam, a subtle fusion of religion, law and literary high culture.[42] Like Latin Christianity or Confucianism, Islam offered common observances, a common 'book', and a common language of learning. But in three important respects Islamic civilization was markedly different. Perhaps because of the distinctive ecology of the Near and Middle East, where agrarian society played second fiddle to long-distance trade, Islam was strikingly cosmopolitan. Muslims were first of all members of the *umma*, the great body of Islamic faithful, and only secondly subjects of their territorial ruler. Islamic religion was highly adaptable to alien cultures, and could coexist amicably with aspects of paganism. It was usually (not invariably) more tolerant of other faiths than medieval Christianity, though not to the point of treating their adherents as equals. Secondly, because it did not em-power a priesthood as the intermediary between the faithful and their god, Islam did not bind the individual so tightly into an ordered religious community. Its clerical elite, the *ulama*, were teachers, judges and scholars, not priests. Sufis and pirs, or holy men, exerted spiritual leadership, not religious *authority*. As a result, Islamic societies did not evolve one of the most important and characteristic features of

Christianity: a powerful ecclesiastical hierarchy under whose eye the individual communicant was firmly anchored in a system of territorial units – parish, diocese, state.

Thirdly, it followed from this that the relationship between religion and state in the Islamic world diverged from that found in Europe or China. The most that a territorial ruler could claim was to be the guardian of the faithful, or at best a *khalifa*, carrying on the work of Muhammad in uniting the *umma* and spreading the faith. Unlike the monarchs of medieval Europe, whose warrant from heaven was ritually conferred in a coronation ceremony, he enjoyed no special semi-sacred status, no heavenly blessing. The amir might command the *ulama*'s obedience. But it was always conditional, since their ultimate loyalty was to Koranic law (which they interpreted), and the alliance of Church and State had no meaning in Islam. Instead, Islamic states were usually marked by the disjunction between the ruler and his slave army and the agrarian notables (*ayan*), *ulama* and merchant guilds who formed the civilian elite. Since there were no territorial aristocracies with whom to share power, assemblies or parliaments were redundant. Nor would Islamic rulers grant the municipal autonomy conceded by European monarchs, usually for revenue. It remained to be seen how far the rise of 'gunpowder empires' in the fifteenth century would arrest the cyclical instability described by Ibn Khaldun, seal off the invasion routes of the steppe and desert, and promote the creation of dynastic states on the model of Europe and China.

If Islam was ill-adapted to the role of a state religion, Islamic law and theology, and the cultural aspirations of rulers in Egypt, Iran and the Fertile Crescent, had permitted a remarkable flowering of literature, art (especially architecture), science and philosophy. Islam's cosmopolitan individualism and the wide dissemination of its legal traditions also favoured the growth of a far-flung commercial economy – the outstanding feature of the Islamic world before 1400. Muslim merchants were the middlemen of world trade. Arab seafarers based in Oman, Hormuz, Bahrein, Aden and Jeddah plied the shipping lanes to Gujarat in western India, the Indonesian archipelago and Canton in southern China.[43] Muslims were pioneers in commercial institutions: the legal instruments required for mercantile credit or forms of partnership like the *commenda*, through which merchants borrowed capital in exchange for a share of the profits. The vast reach of their trade helped to make the port cities of the Near East centres of manufacture for high-value textiles and metal goods and great centres of consumption, information and knowledge. Fourteenth-century Cairo had a population of 600,000 – far larger than any city in Western Europe.

After 1400 there were numerous signs that the commercial dynamism of the previous two centuries was now in decline. The Mamluk empire of Egypt and Syria, the wealthiest economy in the Islamic sphere, was badly damaged by Tamerlane's invasion when Damascus and Aleppo were sacked.[44] A drastic population decline followed the Black Death. Venetian merchants tightened their grip on the maritime trade of the eastern Mediterranean. European textiles began to supplant locally made cloth.[45] A shortage of gold sharpened the pinch of commercial depression. But it would be rash to conclude from these signs of economic change that the Islamic world was about to cede pride of place to an insurgent Europe. For much of that world, European trade was of little importance. Its huge geographical scale dwarfed the Eurasian Far West. Its merchants were formidable agents of conversion. The foundation of a new entrepôt state at Malacca (Islamized by 1425) was the prelude to Islam's rapid spread in maritime South East Asia. Yet perhaps the starkest evidence for Islam's continuing dynamism was the forward movement of Ottoman power in South East Europe. The Ottoman state, the most vigorous of the Turkic principalities in Asia Minor, had crossed the Dardanelles into Europe in the 1350s. Independent Serbia was destroyed at Kosovo in 1389; Bulgaria was in Ottoman hands by 1394. At the Battle of Nicopolis (1396) a pan-European army of would-be crusaders was crushed. Ottoman power was resilient enough to survive defeat at Tamerlane's hands in 1402, and the capture of Constantinople in 1453 marked the consolidation of a new dynastic state militarily more formidable than any the Europeans had so far faced in the East. At the death of Mehmet the Conqueror in 1481, the whole Balkan peninsula south of Belgrade and the Danube estuary was under Ottoman rule. The 'gunpowder age' seemed to be signalling a violent new phase of Islamic expansion.

*

Around 1400, Islamic societies remained the most dynamic and expansionist element in Eurasia. But it was China whose wealth and power were pre-eminent. Despite periodic disruption by dynastic upheaval and external invasion, China displayed a political and cultural cohesion unmatched by Europe or the Islamic world. This cohesion had been severely tested. China, too, had felt the impact of Mongol imperialism. A Mongol dynasty (the Yuan) had imposed its rule for most of the century after 1260. The destructive fallout of the Mongol invasion meant the dislocation of trade, and the effects of disease (the Black Death) may have reduced the population from 100 million to 60 million. The Yuan era can also be seen in a more positive light as continuing the commercial expansion of the previous Sung period, opening China more fully to the trade and culture of Middle Eurasia. And after 1370, under the new Ming dynasty (whose founder was a Han, or native Chinese), the unity of the Chinese world was restored and strengthened.

The crucial ingredient of that unity could be found perhaps in China's social and cultural origins. China had been 'made' by the cumulative expansion of intensive agriculture from its beginnings in the north-west, where fertile, fine-grained loess soils had been exceptionally favourable to close cultivation. A continuous process of agricultural colonization carried this 'Chinese' culture across the plains of North China, and then to the Yangtze valley and into the south. Here the basis of agriculture changed, from the wheat and millet of the drier north to the growing of wet-field rice. This great southward expansion, absorbing new land and people into the Chinese world, was the crucial stage in the 'making' of China. It added the hugely productive rice-growing region (where double and triple cropping was possible) to the agrarian economy. It brought new crops and commodities from the sub-tropical south to stimulate a rise in domestic trade. 'The north in the past', claimed a contemporary writer, 'profited from dates and millet, neither of which southern China has had at any time. Nowadays, the south enjoys abundant profits from perfumes and teas, neither of which has ever existed in the north. The north benefits from its hares, the south from its fish. None of these things has been possessed by both north and south.'[46] The southward expansion also encouraged the relatively rapid emergence between

900 and 1300 of a commercial economy whose geographical regions were physically linked by a network of waterways. With these in place, specialization accelerated (because necessities could be brought from some distance away); an elaborate system of credit grew up; and the use of paper money eased the expansion of business. China assembled the basic components of a market economy earlier, and on a much larger scale, than any other part of Eurasia. It reaped the rewards from inter-regional exchange and the impulse this gave to technical change. Before 1300, a range of innovations in both agriculture and manufacture (cotton-textile weaving was by then well established in the lower Yangtze valley) had been widely adopted, and a culture of invention favoured the diffusion of new techniques.

This remarkable growth path, whose trajectory was quite different from the rest of Eurasia's, shaped China's political as well as economic history. To a much greater extent than anywhere else in Eurasia, the commercial economy that made China so wealthy needed the active support of public authority, mainly to build and maintain the waterways. China's communications, as well as the managing of its fragile environment – dependent on water, threatened by floods – required an unusual degree of bureaucratic liaison between centre, province and district. Secondly, it was brutally clear that without the union of north and south the pattern of regional exchange that drove the commercial economy would function poorly at best. That meant exerting effective control over a much larger land area than any other state in Eurasia was able to rule continuously. Thirdly, it was North China's acquisition of the vast, rich hinterland stretching away to the South China Sea that allowed it to meet its main geopolitical challenge – although not all the time. The Chinese Empire, with its highly evolved agrarian culture, confronted the nomad empires that erupted volcanically in the Inner Asian steppe. Indeed much of North China was dangerously close to the epicentres of nomadic energy – which usually formed where the steppe and the 'sown' came closest together. The primary role of a Chinese emperor was to safeguard the frontier against the nomadic irruptions that threatened to wreck (physically and politically) his complex agrarian world. The resources to pay for this eternal war of attrition against the Inner Asian invader depended heavily on the south's contribution in foodstuffs and trade. Thus,

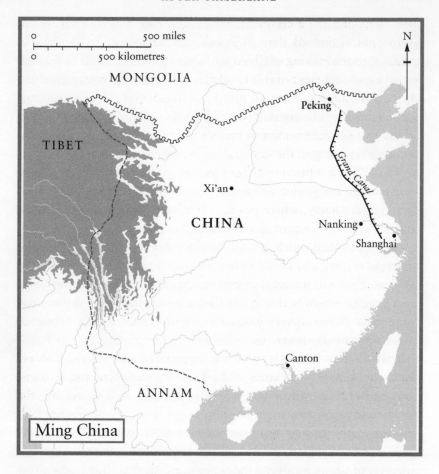

Ming China

although China, like much of Middle Eurasia, had felt the violent impact of Mongol imperial ambition, the blow had been softened. The steppe invaders had learned very quickly that they had to maintain the apparatus of imperial rule if they hoped to exploit China's agrarian wealth. They had to become 'Sinicized', corroding as they did so the tribal loyalties on which their power had been built. Mobilizing the south against the alien conqueror made it possible to maintain stable, continuous government far more completely than in Middle Eurasia, where Turkic tribes and military slaves were the main beneficiaries of political change.

But China's cohesion was not simply the consequence of commercial and strategic self-interest. It rested upon the achievement of a remarkable 'high culture', a classical, literary civilization, whose moral and philosophical outlook derived from Confucian texts. Just as critical, perhaps, to the making of China as the junction of its north and south was the entrenchment of this Confucian learning in a literati elite and their recruitment to form an imperial bureaucracy. Once Confucian scholarship and literary skill (writing the 'three-legged' essay required by the civil-service examiners) became the ticket of entry into imperial service, they enjoyed the devotion of the educated class in every part of China. The adoption by the provincial gentry of literati ideals (and bureaucratic ambitions) was a vital stage in China's transition from a semi-feudal society, where power was wielded by great landholders, into an agrarian empire. What made that possible was an imperial system that relied much less on the coercive power of the imperial centre (a clumsy and costly option in such a large state) than on the *cultural* loyalty of the local elites to an imperial idea with which their own prestige was now closely bound up. As a formula for the exertion of effective power at very long range, it was astonishingly ingenious and astonishingly successful.

It was hardly surprising that the impressive scale of the Chinese state, the wealth of its cities, the skill of its engineers and artisans, the quality of its consumer goods (like silk, tea and porcelain), the sophistication of its art and literature, and the intellectual appeal of its Confucian ideology were widely admired in East and South East Asia. In Korea, Japan and Vietnam (parts of which were ruled as a province of China for over a thousand years until AD 939), China was regarded as the model of cultural achievement and political order. Chinese merchants had also developed an extensive trade, taking their products to South East Asia.[47] The seafaring and navigational skills of Chinese sailors – including the first use of the magnetic compass – were comparable with, if not superior to, those of their Arab or European counterparts.

Around 1400, it might have seemed to any well-informed observer that China's pre-eminence in the Old World was not only secure but likely to grow stronger. Under Ming rule, China's subordination to the Mongols and their imperial ambitions all across Eurasia had been definitively broken. Ming government reinforced the authority of the emperor over his provincial officials. The use of eunuchs at the imperial court was designed to strengthen the emperor against the intrigues of his scholar-gentry advisers (as well as protect the virtue of his concubines). Great efforts were made to improve the agrarian economy and its waterway network. Then, between 1405 and 1431, the emperors dispatched the eunuch admiral Cheng-ho on seven remarkable voyages into the Indian Ocean to assert China's maritime power. Commanding fleets carrying over twenty thousand men, Cheng-ho cruised as far as Jeddah in the Red Sea and the East African coast, and made China's presence felt in Sri Lanka, whose recalcitrant ruler was carried off to Peking. Before the Europeans had gained the navigational know-how needed to find their way into the South Atlantic (and back), China was poised to assert its maritime supremacy in the eastern seas.

This glittering future was not to be. Instead, the early fifteenth century was to show that, while China was still the most powerful state in the world, it had reached the limits of oceanic ambition. There would be no move beyond the sphere of East Asia until the Ch'ing conquered Inner Asia in the mid eighteenth century. The abrupt abandonment of Cheng-ho's maritime ventures in the 1420s (the 1431 voyage was an afterthought) signalled part of the problem. The Ming had driven the Mongols out, but could not erase the threat that they posed. They were forced to devote more and more resources to their northern defence, a geostrategic burden whose visible part was the drive to complete the so-called Great Wall. Turning their back on a maritime future may have been a concession to their gentry officials (who disliked eunuch influence), but it was also a bow to financial constraints and the supreme priority of dynastic survival. The Ming decision reflected, perhaps, a deeper constraint. The Ming dynastic principle was the fierce rejection of the Inner Asian influence that the Mongol Yuan had wielded. It united China against the cultural outsiders. It asserted the exclusiveness of Chinese culture. A 'Greater China' of Han and non-Han peoples was incompatible with the Ming vision of the Confucian monarchy. The grand strategy of indefinite defence carried with it the logic of cultural closure.[48]

There was a further change, whose effects no contemporary observer could have fully grasped. The greatest puzzle in Chinese history is why the extraordinary dynamism that had created the largest and richest commercial economy in the world seemed to dribble away after 1400. China's lead in technical ingenuity and in the social innovations required for a market economy was lost. It was not China that accelerated towards, and through, an industrial revolution, but the West. China's economic trajectory has been furiously debated. But the hypothesis advanced by Mark Elvin more than thirty years ago has yet to be overturned.[49] Elvin stressed the advances achieved by China's 'medieval economic revolution' in the Sung era, but insisted that when China emerged from the economic depression of the early Ming period (a product in part of the great pandemic) a form of technical stagnation had set in. More was produced, more land was cultivated, the population grew. But the impetus behind the technological and organizational innovations of the earlier period had vanished, and was not recovered. China grew quantitatively, not qualitatively. Part of the reason, Elvin argued, was the inward turn we have noticed already: the shrinking of China's external contacts as the Ming abandoned the sea. There was an intellectual shift away from the systematic investigation of the natural world. And it was partly a matter of exhausting the reserves of fresh land, so that less and less was to spare for industrial crops (like cotton) after the needs of subsistence had been met. A subtler influence was also at work. China was a victim of its own success. The very efficiency of its pre-industrial economy discouraged any radical shift in production technique (even in the nineteenth century, the vast web of water routes made railways seem redundant). The local shortages, bottlenecks and blockages that might have driven it forward could be met from the resources of other regions, linked together in China's vast interior market. Pre-industrial China had reached a 'high-level equilibrium', a plateau of economic success. Its misfortune was that there was no incentive to climb any higher: the high-level equilibrium had become a trap.[50]

We should not anticipate too much. It was to be more than three centuries before anyone noticed.

2

Eurasia and the Age of Discovery

2. Constantinople in the
mid-sixteenth century

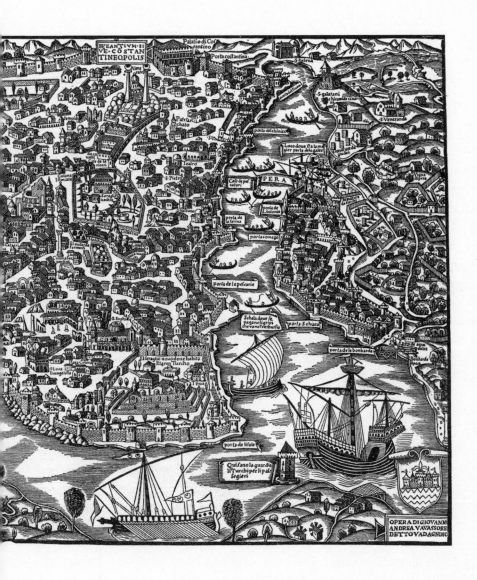

Labels visible on the map:

BIZANTIVM SI VE·COSTAN TINEOPOLIS

Palatie di Cost antino

Porta costantina.

S·helena

Alma teatro

S·galatani schiramide cinar

S·Veneranda

Patriarcato

porta del chinico

loco doue sta la mi gior parte de le galee

Teatro

PERA

Cale de pe scatori

S·Pietro

porta de S·Antonio

porta de la farina

porta conego

porta de le pescarie

S·Sophia

Schala doue se pagano li gripi che vano l'Verburso

porta S·chiara

Il seraglio nouo doue habita El gran Turcho

porta de le bonbarde

S·Luca Euangelista

Bonbarde meno

porta de lisole

Qui sano la guardia li Turchi per li pasegieri

OPERA·DI GIOVANNI ANDREA VAVASSORE DETTO VADAGNINO

In retrospect, we can see that the rough equality that existed between the three great divisions of the Old World was ultimately to be overturned by the events of the late fifteenth and early sixteenth centuries – even if their significance was to be largely hidden from contemporaries. With astonishing rapidity after the 1480s, Europeans voyaging from Portugal and Spain transformed the geopolitical relationship between the Occident and the rest of the Old World. Europe was no longer the Far West of Eurasia facing out over the 'Sea of Darkness'. It had become by the mid sixteenth century an emerging entrepôt for the oceanic trade of the whole world, the headquarters of a maritime enterprise that now extended from China to Peru, and the point of departure for a new transatlantic zone reserved exclusively for its exploitation.

Yet it is also important to keep this great change in perspective. It was not inevitable that the 'discoveries' should have led to Europe's global supremacy. We should not exaggerate the resources that Europeans mobilized for their voyages and conquests, nor mistake the means that allowed them to establish their footholds in Asia and the Americas. Least of all should we be tempted to read into the adventures of navigators and conquistadors a conscious design for a worldwide empire – even though Cortés tried to ingratiate himself with Charles V by claiming that Spain's American possessions were equivalent to the Habsburgs' European dominions. For all its drama, the Occidental 'breakout' of the long sixteenth century (1480–1620) had for long a limited impact. It depended heavily upon local circumstance and the gradual evolution of specialized subcultures of contact and conquest. It was not the working-out of an inescapable economic destiny (as some historians have argued), or the inevitable product of technological primacy.

One other temptation must be resisted. Europe's 'colonizing' history is often viewed in splendid isolation from the larger context of world history. It is as if from c. 1500 onward only Europe was dynamic and expanding: the rest of the world had ground to a halt. It is salutary to remember that, contemporaneous with the triumphs of Vasco da

Gama or Albuquerque in the Indian Ocean, or of Cortés and Pizarro in the Americas, were the consolidation of Ming absolutism, the emergence of a new world power in the Ottoman Empire, the reunion of Iran under the Safavids, the rapid expansion of Islam into South East Asia, and the creation of a vast new Islamic empire in North India after 1519. The significance of the discoveries must be seen against this larger picture of Eurasian expansionism: the Old World must be called in to balance the New.

THE OCCIDENTAL BREAKOUT

The Portuguese were the oceanic frontiersmen of European expansion. The Portuguese kingdom was a small weak state perched on the Atlantic periphery. But by c.1400 its rulers and merchants were able to exploit its one magnificent asset, the harbour of Lisbon. Europe's Atlantic coast had become an important trade route between the Mediterranean and North West Europe. Lisbon was where the two great maritime economies of Europe – the Mediterranean and the Atlantic – met and overlapped.[1] It was an entrepôt for trade and commercial information and for the exchange of ideas about shipping and seamanship.[2] It was the jumping-off point for the colonization of the Atlantic islands (Madeira was occupied in 1426, the Azores were settled in the 1430s), and for the crusading filibuster that led to the capture of Ceuta in Morocco in 1415. Thus, long before they ventured beyond Cape Bojador on the west coast of Africa in 1434, the Portuguese had experimented with different kinds of empire-building. Their geographical ideas were shaped not only by knowledge of the great Asian trade routes that had their western terminus in the Mediterranean, but also by the influence of crusading ideology.[3] Ironically, the crusading impulse assumed that Portugal lay at the western edge of the known world and that the object was to drive eastward towards its centre in the Holy Land. Perhaps it was this and Portugal's early forays into North Africa after 1415 (where it heard of Morocco's West African gold supplies) that pulled the Portuguese first south and east rather than westward across the Atlantic. The tantalizing vision of alliance with the Christian empire of Prester John (supposedly lying somewhere south of Egypt) encouraged the hope of navigators, merchants, investors and rulers that, by turning the maritime flank of the Islamic states in North Africa, Christian virtue would reap a rich reward.[4]

Prester John was only a legend, and so was his empire. Nevertheless, by the 1460s the Portuguese were pushing ever further south in search of a route that would take them to India – the goal triumphantly achieved by Vasco da Gama in 1498.[5] But it took more than navigational skill to carry Portuguese sea power into the Indian Ocean. Two vital African factors made possible their sea venture into Asia. The first was the existence of the West African gold trade that flowed north from the forest belt to the Mediterranean and the Near East. By the 1470s, the Portuguese had managed to divert some of this trade towards their new Atlantic sea route. In 1482–4 they brought the stones to build the great fort of San Jorge da Mina (now Elmina in Ghana) as the 'factory' for the gold trade. (A 'factory' was a compound, sometimes fortified, where foreign merchants both lived and traded.) It was a crucial stroke. Mina's profits were enormous. Between 1480 and 1500 they were nearly double the revenues of the Portuguese monarchy.[6] In the 1470s and '80s, they supplied the means for the expensive and hazardous voyages further south to the Cape of Storms (later renamed the Cape of Good Hope) rounded by Bartolomeu Dias in 1488. The second great factor was the lack of local resistance in the maritime wilderness of the African Atlantic. South of Morocco, no important state had the will or the means to contest Portugal's use of African coastal waters. Most African states looked inland, regarding the ocean as an aquatic desert and (in West Africa) seeing the dry desert of the Sahara as the real highway to distant markets.

In these favourable conditions, the Portuguese traversed the empty seas and then pushed north from the Cape until they ran across the southern terminus of the Indo-African trade route near the mouth of the Zambezi. From there they could rely upon local knowledge, and a local pilot who could direct them to India. Once north of the Zambezi, Vasco da Gama re-entered the known world, as if emerging from a long detour through pathless wastes. When he arrived in Calicut on India's Malabar coast, he re-established contact with

Europe via the familiar Middle Eastern route used by travellers and merchants. It was a feat of seamanship, but in other respects his visit was not entirely auspicious. When he was taken to a temple by the local Brahmins, Vasco assumed that they were long-lost Christians. He fell on his knees in front of the statue of the Virgin Mary. It turned out to be the Hindu goddess Parvati. Meanwhile the Muslim merchants in the port were distinctly unfriendly, and, after a scuffle, Vasco decided to beat an early retreat and sail off home.

But what were the Portuguese to do now that they had found their way to India by an Atlantic route that they were anxious to keep secret? Even allowing for the lower costs of seaborne transport, it was unlikely that a few Portuguese ships in the Indian Ocean would divert much of its trade towards the long empty sea lanes round Africa. In fact the Portuguese soon showed their hand. The Malabar coast, with its petty coastal rajas and its reliance on trade (the main route between South East Asia and the Middle East passed along its shores), was the perfect target. Within four years of Vasco's voyage to Calicut, they had returned in strength with a fleet of heavily armed caravels. Under Afonso Albuquerque, they began to establish a network of fortified bases from which to control the movement of seaborne trade in the Indian Ocean, beginning at Cochin (1503), Cannalore (1505) and Goa (1510). In 1511, after an earlier rebuff, they captured Malacca, the premier trading state in South East Asia. By the 1550s they had some fifty forts from Sofala in Mozambique to Macao in southern China, and 'Golden Goa' had become the capital of their Estado da India.

The Estado was neither a territorial nor a commercial empire. In part it was an attempt to force a monopoly over the trade in pepper, the most lucrative spice exported to Europe. But the Portuguese lacked the power to do this, and much of the spice trade remained outside their control.[7] Instead, the Estado became a system for extorting protection money from the seaborne trade between South East Asia, western India, the Persian Gulf and the Red Sea. Asian merchants had to buy a *cartaz* or safe conduct at one of the Portuguese 'factories' – Goa, Diu or Hormuz – or run the risk of plunder by the Estado's sea captains. In the Indian Ocean, after a crushing victory over the Egyptian navy at Diu, the Estado met no serious opposition, although it was not strong enough to block the Bab-el-Mandeb Strait and rule the Red Sea. None of the states that fringed the Indian Ocean had developed the naval technology that made the Portuguese caravel a deadly weapon of maritime warfare. Perhaps none, except Malacca, regarded oceanic trade as important enough to build a great warfleet. The major states of South Asia mostly looked inland. Maritime trade was left to coastal merchant communities that lacked social prestige and political influence.[8] So the Portuguese were able to enforce their naval supremacy in the Indian Ocean with comparative ease. East of the Malayan peninsula it was a different story. In the South China Sea or near Japan, the Portuguese were much more cautious. Here they found a niche as long-distance traders, convenient middlemen for a Ming Empire that disliked overseas activity by its own subjects and refused direct commercial relations with Japan.

As a result, the Estado modulated gradually from a crusader-predator into a loose-knit network of Portuguese communities, largely made up of *casados*, or settlers, and the local peoples with whom they intermarried. These Portuguese were not conquistadors carving out great inland empires. They lacked the strength, and perhaps the motive. Between Sofala and Macao, there were only six or seven thousand Portuguese in the 1540s, perhaps twice as many fifty years later.[9] Nor were they a dynamic commercial force, galvanizing the somnolent trades of Asia. Quite the contrary. The Portuguese had fought their way into Asia's trading world using the ship-handling skills they had learned in the North Atlantic. But their profits came largely from 'squeezing' the rich seaborne trade already there, until the development of Brazil after 1550.[10] As we shall see in a moment, it was the near-simultaneous venture to the Americas that allowed the Occidentals to establish themselves firmly in Asia's trading economy. Meanwhile, for the indigenous traders and shippers of the Indian Ocean and South East Asia, the Portuguese presence was a source of anxiety. For Malacca it had been a catastrophe. But for the larger states with whom the Portuguese came into contact they were at worst a nuisance, at best a convenience.

The puzzling question is how a far-flung chain of forts and 'factories' could resist the absorptive power of the societies around them. This is all the more surprising since by the late sixteenth century the

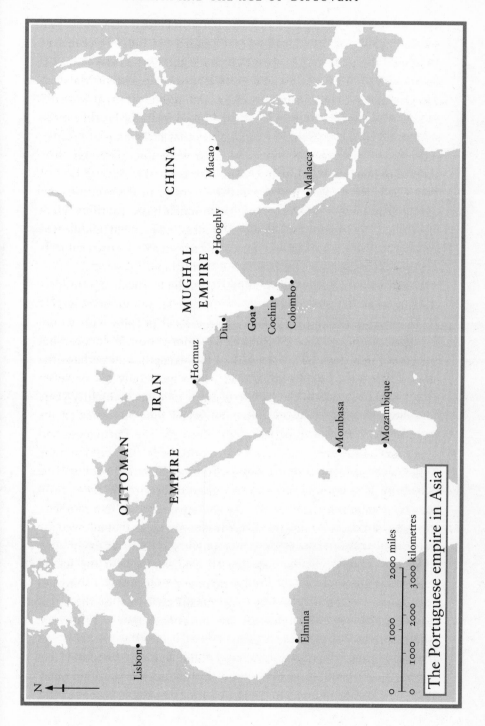

The Portuguese empire in Asia

OTTOMAN EMPIRE

IRAN

MUGHAL EMPIRE

CHINA

Macao

Malacca

Hooghly

Diu

Goa

Cochin

Colombo

Hormuz

Mombasa

Mozambique

Elmina

Lisbon

N

0   1000   2000 miles
0   1000   2000   3000 kilometres

local 'country trade' between Asian ports had become much more profitable than the thin stream of traffic dribbling round the Cape. It was not superior power or advanced technique that kept the Portuguese 'empire' together, but the more prosaic advantages of a merchant diaspora. The Portuguese were a network, held together by religion and language, and with better sources of market information in long-distance trades than their purely Asian counterparts.[11] Portuguese became the lingua franca of maritime Asia. The very marginality of the Portuguese as an alien maritime subculture helped to make them acceptable to governments mistrustful of their own commercial communities. Indeed, many Portuguese made their living as freelances. At Hugli, north of modern Calcutta, one enterprising merchant gained permission from the Mughal emperor Akbar to build a trading post to ship Chinese luxuries upstream to his court. Not far away, another band made their living as slavers and freebooters under the protection of the Arakan kingdom (now the coastal region of northern Burma), then struggling to keep the Mughals out of eastern Bengal. When the Portugese slavers carried off a high-born Muslim lady (who was then 'converted' and married to a Portuguese captain), it was the Hugli merchants who had to pay the penalty. That such 'sea people', occupying a niche in the maritime fringes of the Asian world, might be the harbingers of later Occidental domination would surely have struck most Asian rulers as risibly improbable.

At first sight a startling coincidence, the almost simultaneous entry of Europeans into both maritime Asia and the Americas after 1490 can be readily explained. The south-west corner of the Iberian peninsula was really a single oceanic frontier where Genoese banking, commercial and navigational expertise collaborated with local seamen, Portuguese and Spanish. Columbus, himself a Genoese, had learned his trade in Lisbon, and, like the Portuguese navigators and their backers, understood international politics and geographical exploration as a crusade to liberate the middle of the world from infidel rule.[12] His failure to win Portuguese, English or French backing for his transatlantic voyage may have reflected justifiable scepticism about his geographical assumptions (Columbus thought China lay some 2,500 miles west of Europe) or the belief that the African route was a safer bet. His eventual success in winning the support of Castile for his enterprise (Aragon, the 'other half' of the new Spanish kingdom, showed little interest) may have owed something to Castilian envy of Portugal's Atlantic ambitions and the wealth they might bring, as well as to the appeal that Columbus's crusading rhetoric exerted on the Spanish court with its *Reconquista* ethos. The capture of Muslim Granada in 1492 (the last corner of Spain to be ruled by the 'Moors') brought a high tide of fervour that helped carry Columbus to the West.

Like the Portuguese explorers, Columbus profited from the knowledge of winds and currents built up during the colonization of the Atlantic islands. In late 1492 he sailed from the westernmost outpost of the European world, San Sebastián de la Gomera in the Canaries, making landfall at the Bahamas on 12 October. Having reconnoitred Cuba and Hispaniola, he found his way back to Europe via the Azores. With astonishing seamanship, he established the sea lanes used for the voyage between Spain and the Caribbean for the next three centuries, and his sailing times were hardly improved upon for more than 150 years. As an expedition to find the sea route to China, however, Columbus's voyage had been a resounding failure. His second voyage, by contrast, was a colonizing venture bringing some 1,500 Europeans to settle Hispaniola, as the Azores and the Canaries had previously been settled.[13] On further voyages in 1498–9 and 1502–4 Columbus explored the coast of the Tierra Firme (Colombia and Venezuela) and Central America.

Thus far, the Spanish venture into the Americas could be seen as a bold addition to the Iberian settlement of the Atlantic islands: a marginal expansion of the European world. But, within thirty years of Columbus's first American landfall, the conquest of the Aztec Empire by Cortés and his company of adventurers signalled that European intrusion into the Americas held a different significance from the piecemeal colonization of Europe's oceanic periphery or Portugal's hijacking of Asian trade. It is easy to assume that the conquest of the Central American mainland was the logical continuation of the Columbian 'mission', and that the fall of the Aztec emperor Montezuma was the inevitable consequence of European technological superiority. A closer look at the motives and the means which transformed a tentative maritime reconnaissance into the overlordship of a vast interior plateau suggests instead that only a unique conjuncture of geographical, cultural and demographic circumstances permitted this first great conquest by a Eurasian power in the 'Outer World' of the Americas, sub-Saharan Africa and the South Pacific.

In large part, the key to Spain's transformation into a great colonial power lay in the Caribbean. The disposition of Atlantic winds and currents made it likely that the Caribbean islands – the geographic projection of the Americas towards Europe – would be the first land-fall for Spanish or Portuguese sailors. Unlike the great offshore land masses of Greenland and Newfoundland, these islands were hospit-able, colonizable and readily accessible to seaborne invaders. They could be conquered piecemeal and quickly reinforced from Europe. Their indigenous populations lacked adequate military organization and were tragically vulnerable to Old World diseases. Crucially, the islands lay out of contact with, and beyond the control of, the power-ful mainland empires of the Maya and the Aztecs, which had no advance warning of the alien invasion. Instead, they provided a vital springboard where the Spanish could acclimatize and from where they could reconnoitre the coast of Central America. Against the Arawak peoples of Hispaniola and the other islands, they could experiment with the techniques of warfare, control and exploitation later to be used on a grander scale. The occupation of several Caribbean islands – Cuba had become the main focus of Spanish activity by 1510 – also encouraged a decentralized pattern of sub-imperial *entradas* – armed forays to the mainland – rather than a single and perhaps disastrous continental expedition. They permitted the luxury of trial and error. Above all, the Caribbean brought gold.

The alluvial gold first found on Hispaniola was vital. The resulting gold rush brought some 1,500 Spaniards to Hispaniola by 1502, and whetted their appetite for further ventures on the islands and the mainland. It was gold seized from Amerindians, or extracted with slave labour, which helped to fund the *entradas* organized locally after 1508, rather than gold from Spain. The forward move on to the American continent was the work not of princes or capitalists at home in Europe, but of gold-hungry frontiersmen spurred on by the rapid exhaustion of the islands' deposits. Without the short-lived gold rush on the Caribbean islands and the nearby Tierra Firme, the impetus towards the territorial conquest of the mainland might have been delayed indefinitely, or certainly past the point at which the conquistadors could exploit the element of surprise and stupefaction which played such an important part in the victory over the Aztecs. Thus the Caribbean bridgehead supplied much of the motive and some of the means for this conquest.

Between 1519 and his final triumph in 1521 the first great conquistador, Hernando Cortés, was to capture an elaborate imperial regime of over 11 million people, rich in precious metals and based materially on the cultivation of maize. The colonial jackpot which Cortés's gamble brought him presents a stunning contrast with the well-merited caution which kept Europeans on the maritime fringes of Africa and Asia and warned against ill-fated schemes of conquest. Part of the explanation for Cortés's success may derive from the comparative novelty of the Aztecs' hegemony on the Mexican plateau and the hostility towards them of their subject peoples, who provided Cortés with allies and help; part from the technological superiority of the Spanish way of warfare.[14] But it would not be difficult to find other regions in Afro-Asia where similar conditions seemed to favour foreign conquest.

The real secret of the Spanish blitzkrieg was cultural and biological. What made the Aztec Empire so vulnerable to Spanish attack, it has been argued, was the inability of its high command to grasp the origins, aims and motives of their European enemy or to imagine the reasons for its sudden appearance. The result was paralysing mental disorientation which destroyed the Aztec emperor's capacity to resist.[15] Lacking any contact with the Old World and its wandering community of pilgrims, pedlars, merchants and mercenaries through whom news and rumour were carried to its remotest regions, Aztec civilization was baffled by a 'supernatural' event which no ritual, sacrifice or prayer could hope to influence. Military defeat was thus total and inevitable. But the rapidity and completeness of the Spanish military conquest and the collapse of any popular will to resist were also a biological phenomenon. After the cultural shock of inexplicable triumph came the biological shock of demographic catastrophe brought by lack of immunity to the diseases of the Old World. Between the time of Cortés's arrival and the end of the sixteenth century, the population of Mexico fell by 90 per cent from perhaps 12 million to just over 1 million.[16] The psychological impact upon the indigenous population is hard to imagine. At the physical level, the basic preconditions of administrative control were abruptly transformed in a way inconceivable in tropical Africa, India or China, as the ratio of rulers to ruled and settlers to natives lurched from one extreme to another.

It was in these bizarre circumstances – more like science fiction than history – that Spanish rule in Meso-America was rapidly extended over the central plateau (the Aztec heartland), Mayan Yucatán and the arid tableland towards what became New Mexico. This was the northern, or Cuban, thrust of Spanish imperialism, driven by settlers and adventurers from the local Caribbean centre of Spanish maritime power. Meanwhile, a more southerly movement had brought Spanish goldseekers to the Tierra Firme of the South American mainland – modern Venezuela and Colombia – and to the isthmus region known as Castilla del Oro. It was from here and the settlement founded at Panama in the early 1520s that the Spanish launched another blitzkrieg conquest (as it turned out) of the second great pre-Columbian empire.

In many ways the Spanish conquest of the Inca Empire in the Andean highlands was even more astonishing than the triumph over the Aztecs. The Inca dominions lay much further away from the Caribbean bridgehead. They were less accessible from the sea, and extended over a much greater area – from modern Ecuador into the northern part of modern Bolivia. The great interior plateau that the Spanish called the Altiplano formed the core of the empire. It was richer in minerals and ecologically more diverse than Aztec Mexico.[17] The Incas had successfully incorporated all the areas of stable peasant cultivation in the Andean highlands into their empire. Their system of taxation, designed to accumulate large quantities of produce as well as precious metals, sustained a standing army, rewarded local and regimental elites, and was more complex and efficient than anything seen in Mexico. The wealth that it yielded and the conscription of labour under the *mit'a* system enabled the Incas to construct a remarkable network of roads, fortresses, magazines, bridges, terraces and irrigation works, as well as a magnificent imperial capital at Cuzco with a population of between 100,000 and 300,000 people.[18]

This was the empire that Francisco Pizarro entered in 1532 with 167 followers – the 'Men of Cajamarca'.

Like some of the later *entradas* into Central America, Pizarro's expedition had been paid for by the profits from the looting of Amerindian treasure. This was how Gaspar Espinosa, Pizarro's main backer, had made his fortune and become the richest settler in Panama.[19] Pizarro, like Cortés, enjoyed the advantage of surprise and had weaponry unknown to his American opponents. Both these factors played a key part in the ruthless coup by which, with almost one blow, the Spanish were able to throw the entire Inca system into political chaos. On 16 November 1532 Pizarro met the Inca ruler at Cajamarca in northern Peru. Atahualpa may have believed that such a small band of strangers could be easily captured by his vast retinue, or that they were mere mercenaries who could be bought off with treasure. He was quite unprepared for the scale of their ambitions. Within hours of his entering the square at Cajamarca, he was a captive of Pizarro, his closest political followers were dead or dying, and some thousands of his army had been cut down by Spanish cavalry. This devastating onslaught virtually decapitated the empire. With the failure of the Inca counter-attack, the conquistadors were free to fight a fratricidal war for the spoils of victory before Peru was finally brought under the effective control of the Spanish authorities in faraway Madrid.

Like the conquest of Mexico, the conquest of Peru can be explained in part by the brittleness of the imperial regime that the Spanish had faced. Like the Aztec Empire, Inca rule depended upon the collaboration of many smaller ethnic units only recently subjugated or of doubtful loyalty. It may also be true that, at the moment of the Spanish invasion, both empires had reached a critical stage in their imperial expansion when adverse logistics and diminishing returns had begun to drive their rulers into new exactions and unpopular reforms. Prophecies of doom in pre-Columbian Mexico, and actual civil war in pre-Columbian Peru, were symptomatic of dangerous internal stresses.[20] But it was not these circumstances alone that made these empires so uniquely vulnerable to the aggression of a handful of seaborne invaders, whose predatory onslaughts elsewhere on the mainland yielded very mixed success or no success at all. What singled out the two great pre-Columbian empires was the very sophistication of their centralized political systems, pivoted upon an omnipotent, god-like emperor whose sudden capture disabled the whole imperial mechanism. What made this worse was the cultural isolation, which denied these omnipotent rulers sufficient knowledge of their alien invaders. With no advance warning, they failed to apply prudential rules of statecraft and self-defence. The Spaniards' weapons and tactics, especially their firearms and warhorses, inflicted the *coup de grâce*. The biological shock of Old World disease – a form of involuntary germ warfare – proved in both cases a deadly means of preventing the secondary resistance that might otherwise have sprung up as the effects of foreign conquest began to be felt. It was the combined effect of these different factors that turned the Spanish encounter with the two great mainland civilizations into blitzkrieg conquests of almost negligible cost. Perhaps any of the great Eurasian states would have enjoyed a similar success: Tamerlane would have made short work of Montezuma. It was the Occident's good fortune that its geographical position – closest to the Caribbean antechamber of the pre-Columbian empires – gave it a decisive lead in the acquisition of new lands in the Outer World.

It remained to be seen whether the conquistadors could transform the gargantuan pillaging expeditions that had wrecked the Aztec and Inca states into a more durable expansion of Spanish wealth and power. Would they be able to turn the fantastic windfalls of treasure into an economic system, and build a neo-Europe in the Americas? In economic terms, at least, the two great viceroyalties of New Spain (Mexico) and Lima (Peru) seemed a striking success. The cycle of short-lived gold rushes whose exhaustion had driven the Spanish beyond Hispaniola and Cuba was not repeated in Mexico and Peru. The early caches of gold, which had enriched the first conquistadors beyond their wildest dreams, were quickly supplemented by the discovery in the 1540s of large reserves of silver at Zacatecas in Mexico and at the great mountain of Potosí in modern Bolivia. By the later 1500s both viceroyalties were sending large quantities of bullion back to Spain in the great annual convoys of the Carrera das Indias. This stream of mineral wealth had important consequences. It sucked in new migrants from Spain and funded the import of slaves from Africa.

It paid for a colonial administration and a judicial system vastly more elaborate than the semi-feudal regime of the early conquest. It helped to pay for the massive presence of the Catholic Church, whose cathedrals, churches, cemeteries, ubiquitous imagery and public ritual were the most visible sign of the *conquista*.[21] In Mexico alone, the Church had deployed some three thousand priests amid a rapidly declining Amerindian population of about 1 million by the end of the century. By 1622 there were thirty-four dioceses in Spanish America. In short, it was gold and chiefly silver that turned the brutal fact of conquest into a structure of colonial rule.

But the extent to which this mineral bonanza had secured the economic and cultural integration of the New World into a 'Greater Spain' by 1620 should not be exaggerated. Vast areas of 'Spanish' America lay outside the enclaves of effective Spanish occupation: the *llanos* of Venezuela; the tropical lowlands of Central America; the deserts of northern Mexico; the dense forests east of the Andes; and the grasslands stretching away to the estuary of the Río de la Plata. There, unsupported by mineral wealth, Spanish influence was frail or non-existent. Nor was American silver a wholly reliable means of binding together the economies of Europe and the Americas. Supply and demand fluctuated. By the early seventeenth century, Mexican silver shipments to Europe (although not Mexican silver production) were in decline. Mexico's commercial links with East Asia, to which a large proportion of its silver was exported, were becoming more important. As Europe's population growth and commercial activity slowed down after 1620, its thirst for Spanish-American silver slackened: metropole and colony were drifting apart.[22] Culturally, too, the consequences of conquest were mixed. In both Mexico and Peru, the fury of the Spanish onslaught (both physical and biological) had quickly dismantled pre-conquest religious institutions. By 1531 the Spanish had demolished 600 temples in Mexico alone, and destroyed 20,000 idols.[23] The old priestly elite was dethroned. A wide degree of religious conformity was imposed upon the subject population, who adopted Christian cults and festivals with little resistance.[24] Amerindian notables were assimilated to some degree into the administrative structure. At a humbler level, Spanish clothes supplanted the traditional costume, on which the Church had frowned.[25]

Yet Spain's cultural impact was blunted by circumstances. Limited in numbers and concentrated in towns, Spanish settlers had only spasmodic contact with the Amerindian populations of the hinterland.[26] This tendency was reinforced by the decision of the Spanish government to segregate Amerindian communities from what administrators and churchmen saw as the corrupting and exploitative behaviour of the settlers. Combined with the remoteness and inaccessibility of much of the interior (especially in the Andean highlands), this helped to ensure that the landscape retained its old religious and magical significance for the indigenous peoples. Even where Amerindians were more directly exposed to Spanish colonial influence, the results were often ambiguous. To a large extent, the administrative divisions of New Spain re-created the old 'city states' of pre-Columbian times, with considerable continuity among the local ruling elite. Destroying the structure of pre-conquest religion did not mean the end of traditional healers, prophets and soothsayers, the *conjuros*, who continued to enjoy great prestige in the countryside.[27] Nor of course could Spanish supplant the pre-conquest languages. It was well into the seventeenth century, argues a recent study, before Spanish began to affect the grammatical structure of Amerindian languages: until then, its influence was limited to the use of certain borrowed nouns.[28]

If Spanish America remained residually and tenaciously Amerindian, it also became much more ethnically diverse. It was true that in both Mexico and Peru enough Spanish arrived – drawn from both sexes and a wide range of occupations – to create 'complete' societies, capable of preserving and reproducing Spanish communities along Old World lines.[29] But from the early days of conquest Spanish males had interbred with the indigenous population to create the 'mestizo' people. To supplement the dwindling and reluctant native labour force, they had introduced African slaves in the mid sixteenth century, and interbred with them as well, to form a 'mulatto' community. By the mid seventeenth century the population of New Spain consisted of some 150,000 white Spanish, 150,000 mestizos, 130,000 mulattos and 80,000 African slaves, as well as perhaps 1 million Amerindians. A similar pattern obtained in Peru; and throughout Spanish America there were perhaps 330,000 African slaves by the 1640s.[30] The outcome was the birth of complex, racially stratified societies in which occupation and status reflected ethnic origin, and where political and economic power was largely in the hands of the whites, whether Spanish-born or locally born '*criollos*'.

To an extent unthinkable in the Old World of Eurasia, Spain had wrought the dissolution of the most powerful societies in pre-Columbian America, and the virtual annihilation of some of the weaker. It had created the space in which a new post-conquest society could be created, potentially receptive to Spanish needs and ideas. But by the middle of the seventeenth century, after more than 150 years in the Americas, it had achieved the conquest but not the incorporation of its American possessions. New Spain would not be another Spanish kingdom, a replica of Castile. Instead, the outcome of conquest had been the creation of a new ethnic geometry, and a distinctive if still protean Spanish-American culture, a new Creole society.

Portuguese navigators and Spanish conquistadors were the most colourful agents of the Occidental breakout in the fifteenth and sixteenth centuries. No less significant for the future balance of power in Eurasia was the transformation by which in little more than a century the princely state of Muscovy – until 1480 a tributary state of the Mongol 'Golden Horde' – advanced over the steppe to the Caspian Sea and built a vast fur-trading empire through the Siberian forests to reach the Pacific in 1639. In a sequence of furious expansion, the Russians captured the greater part of North Asia before Chinese or Japanese influence could become predominant. They closed the northern gateway by which the steppe peoples of Central Asia had so often swept towards Eastern Europe, and seized the lower Volga before either the Ottomans or the new Safavid rulers of Iran could absorb the fragmented realm of the Golden Horde into their new imperial systems.

Even more than the Portuguese or Spanish, the Russians had been a frontier people largely cut off from the leading states of medieval Europe. 'Russia and Spain', remarked a Spanish writer, '[are] the two extremities of the great diagonal of Europe.'[31] The origins of Rus' lay in the eastern migrations of Slav peoples to the edge of the forest zone, where it met the steppe and its warrior nomads (the 'Tatars' as the

Russians called them). The first Russian state had been centred on Kiev, where a Viking or 'Varangian' ruling class had built an entrepôt to exploit the waterborne trading route that ran from Byzantium and the Near East to Baltic Europe. With the arrival of Orthodox Christianity in the ninth century, Kievan Rus' became a great cultural wedge of the Byzantine Occident, between steppe peoples to the east (Polovtsy, Khazars and Pechenegs) and pagan Lithuanians (or West Russians) to the west. Kiev became the headquarters of a vast missionary enterprise, which founded monasteries in the northern forests as far away as the White Sea. In the thirteenth century it was weakened by the rivalry of other Russian states, like Novgorod and Smolensk, and overwhelmed in the catastrophe of Mongol invasion. In 1240 the city was razed. The Russian states of the forest zone became tributaries of the Khanate of the Golden Horde, one of the four great successor states when Genghis Khan's world empire broke up in 1259. Russian rulers – and especially the exposed and vulnerable rulers of Muscovy, too close for comfort to the open steppe – found themselves acting as the agents and clients of the khanate's rulers in faraway Sarai on the Caspian Sea. Crucially, however, they retained a distinct occidental identity through the cultural influence of the Orthodox Church, which maintained its tenuous links with the Byzantine patriarchate.[32] Indeed the Mongols, who converted late to Islam, readily tolerated the Church and its doctrines.

The rise of Muscovy to a pre-eminent position among the several Russian states was due in large measure to the opportunism of its princes, who made themselves the allies and collaborators of the steppe khanate.[33] Mongol support secured them the title of grand prince after 1331; Mongol power drove back the rival Grand Duchy of Lithuania, the powerful West Russian state, Catholicized in the 1370s and linked in a union with Catholic Poland. Moscow earned the support of the Orthodox Church – a vital religious and cultural ally – through its influence with the Mongols and its leadership against Catholic Lithuania.[34] In the 1380s Muscovy exploited divisions in the khanate to assert a short-lived independence after the Battle of Kulikovo Pole. But the decisive influence on its fortunes was the vast geopolitical shock of Tamerlane's conquests from his original base in Central Asia – still the pivot of world history in the late fourteenth century. Though Tamerlane ultimately failed to build a new empire as far-flung as Genghis Khan's, he smashed the remnants of the Mongol system, including the Khanate of the Golden Horde, which gradually broke up into the separate khanates of Crimea, Astrakhan, Kazan and Sibir'. By the 1440s Vasily of Moscow enjoyed effective independence. In 1480 his successor, Ivan III (1462–1505), beat off the last attempt from the steppe to reimpose tributary status.

The hundred years after 1480 were the vital period of Muscovite expansion, and shaped the whole course of the Occidental invasion of central and northern Eurasia. With its territorial core on the upper Volga, Muscovy became the hinge between the vast forest empire to the north and east (eventually reaching the Pacific coast of Asia) and the hard-won steppe empire of the Caspian and southern Urals.[35] But the rulers of Moscow could scarcely have sustained these imperial ambitions had they governed no more than a petty East Russian principality, held in check by Catholic Poland–Lithuania and challenged as well by wealthy North Russian rivals like Novgorod, with its fur empire and Hanseatic trade. The rise of Russian power in Northern Eurasia required the consolidation of Muscovite rule over the Orthodox Russian states, and a forward movement to prevent their absorption by the dynamic joint monarchy of Poland–Lithuania that stretched from the Black Sea to the Baltic by 1504. Like it or not, the grand dukes of Muscovy could survive only by entering the European diplomatic system (to seek allies against Poland) and (no less important) by competing on cultural and ideological terms with the new-style monarchies of fifteenth-century Europe. Much of later Russian history would turn on the delicate balance between the distinctive Byzantine legacy, embodied in the Russian Orthodox Church, and the cultural borrowing from Central and Western Europe dictated by political and economic necessity.

The logic of political and cultural competition with Poland–Lithuania, where a rapid process of cultural 'modernization' was under way by the later fifteenth century (the first book was printed in Cracow in 1423),[36] was to transform Russian lands conquered by Ivan III into a dynastic state. The oligarchic traditions of 'Great Novgorod' were rooted out. Ivan projected himself as a grand monarch on the European model, blending Byzantine and Western styles of dynastic rule. In 1492 he restyled himself 'Grand Duke of Muscovy and all the Russias'. His marriage to Sophia Palaeologus, a Byzantine princess, was negotiated under papal auspices. His envoys fanned out across Europe. Italian artisans, builders and architects were brought to Moscow. The administration was reorganized around a system of 'chanceries', with elaborate record-keeping and bureaucratic hierarchies.[37] The accession of Ivan IV (the 'Terrible') was marked by a full-scale coronation carefully adapted from the defunct ritual of the Byzantine emperors. Perhaps to compete with the Catholic Counter-Reformation, Ivan IV promoted a monastic revival.[38] Hostility to the 'Latinstvo' – the 'Latin World', identified chiefly with Poland – was balanced by the opening of Russia to Germans, English and Dutch, who came as soldiers, settlers, engineers and merchants. A long series of wars was fought in the sixteenth century to keep Polish influence at bay in the West Russian lands, and prevent it from seducing Muscovy's restless boyars, the warrior-barons whose independence the grand dukes were determined to crush.[39]

The internal transformation goaded by Muscovite–Polish rivalry helps to explain the success with which the Russians held on to their startling territorial gains in forest and steppe. The foundations of a fur-trade empire in the northern forests had been laid by the republic of Novgorod long before its annexation by Muscovy in 1478. Moscow sent its first expedition beyond the Urals in 1483. By the 1550s a vigorous mercantile family, the Stroganovs, were building a business empire in Siberia to bring out the fur supplied by indigenous forest peoples. This brought them into conflict with the Khanate of Sibir', which also depended upon the fur trade and control of its supply. In 1582 Ermak, a Cossack adventurer hired by the Stroganovs, succeeded in capturing the Sibir' capital. The Stroganovs' private imperialism collapsed with his death in 1585. Instead, it was the Muscovite state, directed by Boris Godunov, which carried through the military conquest of western Siberia by the end of the century.[40] The way was then clear for the hectic rush of the *promyshlenniki* (private fur traders) across the continent, reaching the Yenisei river in 1609, the Lena in 1632, the Pacific in 1639, and the river Amur in the Manchurian borderlands of China in 1643. By 1645 there were some 70,000 Russians across the Urals.[41] The legacy of Boris Godunov's decisive

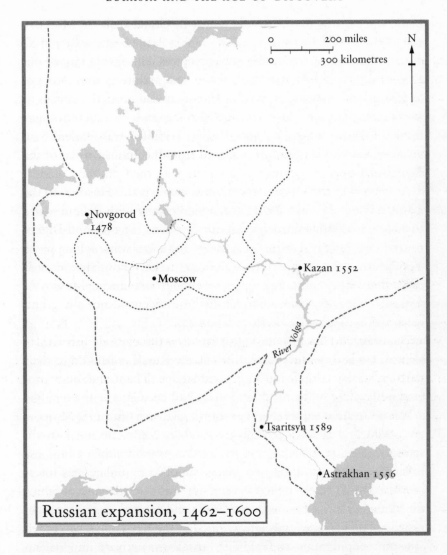

0 ____ 200 miles
0 ____ 300 kilometres
N

•Novgorod
1478

•Moscow

•Kazan 1552

River Volga

•Tsaritsyn 1589

•Astrakhan 1556

Russian expansion, 1462–1600

intervention was to be found in the administrative control which the reorganized Muscovite state fastened on its far-flung forest colony.

The comparative ease with which the Russian conquest of the North Asian forest was carried through was partly the result of the low level of political organization and technological capacity among the stateless woodland peoples the Russians encountered. Russian firearms conferred an important technological advantage. But, as the Stroganovs had found, it was only after the power of the Khanate of Sibir' had been broken that the Russians were free to trade and conquer. This was the crucial link between forest and steppe. By the 1590s the Russians had consolidated their hold on the neighbouring khanates of Kazan and Astrakhan, annexed to Muscovy in 1552 and 1556. Without the Ottoman backing and the trading network that propped up the Khanate of Crimea (which escaped annexation), the last survivor of the Golden Horde in Siberia was ill-equipped to resist the Russian advance.

At first sight, the Russian conquest of the steppe khanates suggests a parallel with the exploits of Cortés and Pizarro: almost at a stroke a vast swathe of hitherto unconquerable steppe – Gogol's 'golden-green ocean' of seemingly limitless promise[42] – fell under Moscow's control. Yet the Russians enjoyed few of the advantages of the Spanish conquistadors. They were well known to their foes, and could not be mistaken for gods. They could hardly hope to enjoy decisive tactical or strategic superiority on the open steppe – although Ivan IV took 150 cannon and his new musketeer infantry, the *strel'tsy*, with him to Kazan. A whole century later, the Russian attack on the Khanate of Crimea fell back in confusion, defeated by the logistics of steppe warfare.[43]

A more convincing explanation of Russian success can be found in the social and political crisis of the Volga steppe societies in the sixteenth century. The khanates were not dynastic monarchies, and never made the transition to a monarchical state already under way in Muscovy. They resembled loose-knit tribal confederacies in which the khans relied on the support of tribal chieftains. Their economies depended upon trade (especially with Central Asia), the taxing of their sedentary populations, and raiding by the dominant nomadic elements into the settled Russian lands to the north and west. By the sixteenth century, however, this political economy was in disarray. Tamerlane had destroyed the great trading cities of Azov, Astrakhan and Urgench on which the steppe depended.[44] The resulting impoverishment may have accelerated the process of sedentarization by which the old egalitarian order of the Tatar nomad tribe mutated into the divided world of landowner and landless peasant.[45] With diminished military power (as a result) and less internal solidarity, the political conflicts within the khanates became more intractable. Moreover, as successor states of the Golden Horde, Kazan, Astrakhan, Crimea and Sibir' were also engaged in mutual competition for control of the steppe. Muscovy (the fifth 'successor state') took advantage of this to play an active role in steppe diplomacy, and maintained peaceful relations on its vulnerable steppe frontier while it conquered the north in the 1470s.[46] By the early sixteenth century, as a result, Muscovy had grown considerably stronger than Kazan or Astrakhan: indeed, it imposed a form of protectorate on Kazan at various times before 1552, as well as nibbling away at its territory with new fortified settlements. By 1552 the Kazan khan Shah Ali was a Russian puppet. Many Tatar 'princes' had already defected to the Russians (and some had converted to Christianity), and some key tribal elements like the Nogai were intriguing with Muscovy to promote a new khan. Whether Ivan the Terrible meant to annex Kazan in 1552 is uncertain. But the city's resistance and its violent conquest ensured that result. It was with Nogai aid that the neighbouring Khanate of Astrakhan was subdued and annexed in a second lightning campaign.

Despite the drama of this steppe imperialism, it would be unwise to exaggerate its immediate significance. There was no treasure trove of minerals to finance the building of a great imperial superstructure, although Moscow merchants (and the Muscovy state) may have profited from easier access to trade with Iran and Central Asia.[47] The Volga lands were opened up to Russian peasant colonization. But beyond the river corridor Russian control was unsure, and the Volga remained a violent frontier region. Tatars continued to raid from Crimea. Even Moscow was raided as late as 1592, and its suburbs were burned. A huge effort was needed to build the fortified lines or *cherta* that were meant to deter the intruders or raise the alarm. One of these, the Belgorod Line, ran for over five hundred miles. In the early seventeenth century the Russians had to come to terms with the Kalmyks, who arrived in force in the North Caspian Steppe.[48] Further south in the Caucasus, Russian influence was checked by the new Safavid state.[49] The conquest of the Khanate of Crimea and the final closure of the Volga steppe frontier (the so-called 'Ural Gates' between the Urals and the Caspian Sea) had to wait until the late eighteenth century.

Nevertheless, Muscovy's struggle to transform itself into a dynastic regime able to absorb the North Russian states, resist Poland–Lithuania and overawe the Volga khanates marked a decisive phase in the eventual emergence of Russia as the engine of Europe's expansion into Northern Eurasia. Though far from safe by 1600 from Polish–Lithuanian efforts to drive it north and east towards the Urals, Moscow had made the key moves to connect itself to the European state system (Polish attacks in the early seventeenth century were beaten off with Swedish help) and to equip itself with the institutions needed to sustain three centuries of imperial expansion. Building on the legacy of Mongol favour and the support of the Orthodox Church, rulers in Moscow achieved a double revolution. They converted the old military system of boyar retinues into a gunpowder army of musketeers and artillery. They centralized control over landholding through the *pomestia*, by which noble estates were held on promise of military or administrative service. The boyars had been free to carry their allegiance wherever they chose. Now they were tied into a rigid structure of fealty and obligation, while new men – called 'state servitors' – were rewarded with conquered and confiscated land. The second revolution followed in consequence. In a poor agricultural economy, the burden of taxation and service to sustain Muscovy's military effort could be borne only if the landed class enjoyed close control over peasant communities hitherto mobile, free and often rebellious.[50] The counterpart to the fixing of boyar loyalty was the bonding of peasant labour through the institution of serfdom, enforced by a ruthless combination of state authority, noble power and Church influence. As the eastern vanguard of European expansion (rather than a weak buffer state between Poland and the steppe), Russia became a Eurasian Sparta, deploying an army of over 100,000 men by the end of the century.[51] But threatened to the west by wealthier European states, and harried to the south by its still open steppe frontier, Muscovy's transformation into 'Russia' or 'Rossiya' ('Greater Russia') was painful and traumatic. Its course was marked by internal terrorism (Ivan the Terrible's *Oprichnina*) and the 'Time of Troubles' (the anarchy preceding the Romanov accession to the tsardom in 1613). Moscow was overrun by Polish armies in 1605 and again in 1610.[52] In the Americas, the human cost of Europe's maritime imperialism was largely borne by the indigenous Amerindians and imported slaves. Overland expansion in the Old World faced tougher resistance and a harsher environment. So here the price of the Occidental breakout was a domestic regime of deepening social and political oppression, whose effects were eventually felt from the Baltic Sea to the Pacific.

THE ISLAMIC COUNTERPOISE

It is easy to overlook, in the drama of Europe's maritime expansion, the profound transformation that was occurring simultaneously in the Islamic lands. Two powerful trends converged in the sixteenth century to sharpen the Islamic challenge to the security of Europe, and to match the Occidental advance into the 'Outer World' beyond Eurasia. The first was the consolidation of stronger and more cohesive Islamic states. The great nomadic invasions from Inner Asia subsided as gunpowder revolutionized the art of war. The second was the expansive drive that carried Islam deep into South East Europe, sub-Saharan Africa, South India and South East Asia. If the Occident emerged richer and stronger from its age of discovery, so too did the Islamic world from its age of expansion.

The western vanguard of this Islamic expansion was formed by the Ottoman Empire. With the capture of Constantinople in 1453, Ottoman supremacy in the southern Balkans was crowned by possession of the region's great imperial capital, with its command over the maritime commerce of the Aegean and Black seas. Constantinople (to the Turks, Istanbul) remained the capital of the Ottoman Empire until its final dissolution in 1922–4. In the decades after 1453, Mehmet the Conqueror asserted direct Ottoman rule over the far south of Greece (the Morea, 1458), Serbia (1459), Bosnia (1463), Albania (1479) and Herzegovina (1483). Mehmet's successors secured the formal subjection of Moldavia and Wallachia (comprising much of modern Romania) to vassal status (1504), captured Belgrade in 1520 and, under Suleiman the Magnificent, added Hungary to their northern tier of protectorates. Only with the abortive assault on Vienna in 1529 did the Ottomans reach what can seen with hindsight as the limit of their apparently inexorable advance into Central Europe. To the Habsburg diplomat Ghiselin de Busbecq, who had seen Ottoman military organization at first hand, the outlook even in the 1560s was intensely gloomy. It was only Ottoman distraction with Iran, he thought, which delayed a final Turkish onslaught. 'Can we doubt what the result will be?'[53]

In the eighty years after 1450, the Ottomans had more than doubled their empire in Europe. No less astonishing were their territorial conquests in Africa and Asia. Having strengthened their grip in southern Anatolia, in 1516–17 they waged a lightning campaign that shattered the Mamluk empire that ruled over Egypt, the holy places at Medina and Mecca, and most of the Fertile Crescent from its capital in Cairo.[54] Having driven the Safavid rulers of Iran out of eastern Anatolia, the Ottomans were firmly established in Baghdad by 1534, and on the Persian Gulf by the end of the 1540s. With a naval base at Suez, they occupied and dominated the Yemen. By the 1570s almost the entire North African coastline from Libya to Morocco was under their control or suzerainty. While Spain at the western end of the Mediterranean was establishing its dominion in the Americas, the Ottomans had carved out, against much tougher opponents and on a far grander scale, a vast tri-continental empire, assembling in Busbecq's awed phrase 'the might of the whole East'.[55]

To a considerable extent these triumphs can be explained by the Ottomans' ability to maintain a large standing army,[56] their use of closely disciplined infantry (the janissaries), the skilful deployment of naval power,[57] and a ruthless diplomacy. The Ottomans were fortunate in the divisions between their opponents both in Europe, where they played successfully on dynastic rivalry and Catholic–Orthodox antagonism, and in Afro-Asia. Their two Islamic opponents, the Egyptian Mamluks and Safavid Iran, failed to combine, and the Mamluks' anxiety about Portuguese sea power may have added critically to their strategic indecision. But Ottoman imperialism was based on more than military and diplomatic opportunism. To the west, towards Europe, the Ottoman sultans could exploit the '*ghazi*' tradition (of religious war to conquer and convert the heathen) to encourage their followers. It seems more than likely that their general aim was to restore the limits of the Byzantine Empire (both their

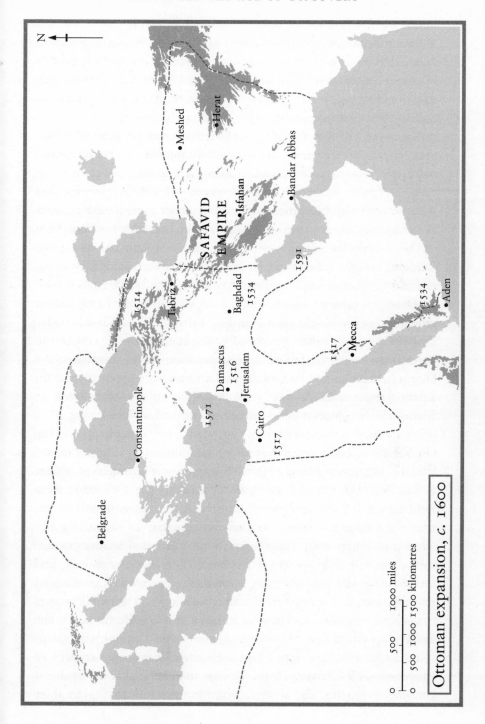

N

SAFAVID EMPIRE

Meshed

Herat

Bandar Abbas

Isfahan

Tabriz 1514

Baghdad 1534

1591

Aden 1534

Mecca 1517

Damascus 1516

Jerusalem

Cairo 1517

Constantinople 1571

Belgrade

Ottoman expansion, c. 1600

0   500   1000 miles

0   500   1000   1500 kilometres

model and their foe) at the height of its power. Indeed, their Byzantine 'inheritance' imposed its own demands. Like other great imperialists before and since, the Ottomans found themselves driven by the 'logic' of empire. A forward policy was needed to intimidate their numerous client states and collaborators; to avert hostile combinations; to impose direct rule where indirect control had broken down; to protect key agrarian and commercial zones by a firmer grip on strategic routes and fortresses. Nor were Ottoman rulers indifferent to commercial objectives. Their naval expansion into the Red Sea and the Persian Gulf, and their effort to assert sea power in the Indian Ocean, may have been intended to profit from the networks of trade just as much as the maritime enterprise of Portugal, Spain and later Holland.[58]

These methods and motives may help to explain the pattern of Ottoman conquest. But they cannot account for the successful implantation of Ottoman rule, or its remarkable durability. The inner secret of Ottoman power was its careful reconciliation between Islamic religious, legal and cultural institutions on the one hand and dynastic absolutism on the other, fashioned by the cosmopolitan statecraft of the ruling elite. Shared faith, and common acknowledgement of the Sharia or Islamic law, helped make Ottoman rule acceptable in the Fertile Crescent, Egypt and North Africa, while the sultan's role as Islam's champion against the Christian infidel gave him a strong claim on the loyalty of the faithful. In Ottoman Europe, Turkish Muslims and local converts formed the core of the political and administrative elite on which Ottoman authority ultimately depended. A shared Islamic high culture, promoting uniform values, played a vital role in binding the local and regional elites of a far-flung empire to the imperial centre. The genius of the Ottomans lay in reinforcing this Islamic solidarity with several shrewd innovations. The *timar* system in Europe and Asia Minor vested control over the revenues of rural estates in a local elite that was bound in return to provide military or administrative service to the Ottoman state. The *millet* system reconciled religious minorities, Christian and Jewish, by conceding a form of communal autonomy administered through clerical or religious leaders, appointed, like the Greek Orthodox patriarch of Constantinople, by the sultan. The most influential element in the conquered populations was thus firmly attached to the imperial system. The Ottomans made ruthless enforcement of the law and regular taxation (as opposed to arbitrary exactions) the hallmark of their rule, at least in the initial phase of their Pax Ottomanica.[59] To many of its Christian subjects in Europe, Ottoman rule offered the same imperial virtues of order and predictability on which the British were later to rest their claim to the loyalty of the Indian peasant. The imperial capital was a cosmopolitan city, where foreigners could expect to be treated reasonably.[60]

The real innovation of the Ottoman system was the *devshirme*. Until well into the seventeenth century, the Ottoman sultans balanced their dependence on the political and military service of the Turkish aristocracy by recruiting a slave army of Muslim converts (perhaps seven or eight thousand a year) separated in childhood from their Christian parents. *Devshirme* recruitment obliterated the ties of kinship and locality so feared by pre-modern rulers. It supplied the soldiers for the janissary force (a standing army of 25,000 men) stationed throughout the empire, as well as the clerks and officials from whom the sultans' most senior advisers were drawn.[61] It created the core of an educated, superior 'Osmanli' ruling class, the *askeri*, whose outlook was imperial rather than local, ethnic or religious, and whose loyalties were primarily dynastic rather than territorial. To Busbecq's eye, the meritocratic selection of the Ottoman elite made it greatly superior to its European counterparts. The Ottoman system seemed a masterly synthesis of religion and politics in an empire whose dynamism astonished and horrified European contemporaries. 'On their side', groaned Busbecq in 1560, '. . . endurance of toil, unity, order, discipline, frugality and watchfulness. On our side is public poverty, private luxury, impaired strength, broken spirit.'[62]

Yet the 1560s have often been seen as the climax of Ottoman strength, and the reign of Suleiman (1520–66) as the prelude to rapid decline as the Ottoman Empire sank towards 'backwardness'. Many standard accounts offer a kind of morality play. Ottoman 'decadence' is contrasted with the aggression and enterprise of early modern Europe, and ascribed to weak leadership, the growth of corruption, the institutional defects of the Ottoman monarchy, internal revolt, the erosion of central authority, lack of commercial and technical innovation, and a failure to adopt wealth-creating state policies.[63] A proper discussion of this must wait for a later chapter, but the diagnosis of decline is at best premature. It was certainly true that by the mid sixteenth century the Ottoman system had begun to change. The Ottomans had ceased to expand into Europe. Their feudal cavalry (*sipahi*) were replaced by a 'gunpowder' army. Ottoman military power was increasingly based not on the *timar* system but on the revenues of tax-farmers, whose provincial grip seems to have increased at the expense of the centre. The decline of the *devshirme* in the seventeenth century, perhaps under pressure from the ethnic Turkish elite, and the entrenchment of the janissaries as a hereditary caste – just what they were not supposed to be – may also have weakened the absolutism forged in the fifteenth century. The religious and social revolts in Anatolia at the end of the sixteenth century were perhaps symptomatic of an Ottoman 'time of troubles', not unlike that which accompanied the frantic expansion of Russia at much the same time. But the effect of these changes should not be exaggerated. It may be wiser to see them as signs of adaptation to a new territorial stability, more elaborate (and costly) forms of local governance, and a pattern of economic growth that benefited the class of provincial notables.[64] The so-called 'decline' of central authority may be a trick of the light.[65] Like most pre-modern states, the Ottoman Empire lacked the means to impose close administration on its subjects, and experienced alternating phases of centralization and devolution. Its real achievement in the sixteenth century was to create the basis for a decentralized but surprisingly cohesive Ottoman 'commonwealth' that stretched from the Maghrib to the Persian Gulf, and from the Habsburg frontier to the Safavid. The real legacy of Suleiman the Magnificent and his predecessors was not an absolutist state, but a network of Islamic communities ruled over by 'Ottomanized' elites, who enjoyed provincial autonomy while remaining loyal to, and dependent upon, the authority, prestige and legitimacy vested in the imperial capital in Constantinople. Less fearsome in European eyes than the aggressive despotism of the early sultans, the Ottoman 'commonwealth' was to prove remarkably durable. Its survival was scarcely in question before the mid eighteenth century.

If the Ottomans failed to achieve a decisive victory over the Christian states in South East Europe, and the Mediterranean, this was at least in part because their resources were strained by the hundred-years war waged against Safavid Iran to the east – an Islamic counterpart to the 'wars of religion' which afflicted much of early modern Europe.[66] From the Ottoman point of view, this struggle was much more vital to the stability of their empire than the pursuit of territorial expansion in Hungary or Croatia. The fluid borderlands of eastern Anatolia and Azerbaijan formed the bridge between the Turkic tribes who lay at the core of the Ottoman state and those who dominated much of the Iranian plateau. Ottoman rule in Asia Minor, and Ottoman supremacy in much of the Fertile Crescent, depended upon the tribal loyalties of this volatile region. It was hardly surprising that the Ottoman sultans reacted so fiercely to the rise of Safavid power in a zone that was the fulcrum of Turkic politics and culture.[67]

Ismail I, the founder of the Safavid Empire, was the son of the grandmaster of a militant Shia order based in Ardabil. The order became known as the Qizilbash, or 'Red-heads', from their distinctive headdress. The crucial feature of the Safavid system was the cementing together of a tribal confederacy through common allegiance to a religious leadership dedicated to Shi'ism, the dominant form of Islam on the Iranian plateau.[68] Shia hostility to the Sunni (orthodox) majority in Islam originated in the disputed succession to Muhammad in the early years of the Islamic caliphate, and drew much of its emotional intensity from the martyrdom of Hussein, the great Shia leader who was defeated and killed by Sunni forces, commemorated each year during Muharram. Shia Islam had its own scholastic and theological traditions, its own holy cities and centres of pilgrimage, at Najaf and Kerbela (in modern Iraq). There was also a strongly millenarian flavour to Shi'ism, with its belief in the 'Hidden Imam' (to whom prayers could be addressed) and its hope of ultimate triumph over an unjust Sunni world. Perhaps as a result, Shia Islam had historically been much less deferential to the authority of secular rulers than Sunni, looking instead to mullahs, or religious teachers.[69] The genius of Ismail lay in supercharging a tribal coalition (the usual means of state-building in western Iran since the death of Tamerlane) with personal devotion to himself and his successors as dynastic leaders of a religious fraternity engaged in a holy struggle.[70] Armed with this potent formula, he achieved astonishing success. In 1501 he made himself master of Tabriz, the greatest city of north-west Iran. By 1510 his armies had conquered Azerbaijan, Gilan and Mazanderan along the Caspian Sea, Hamadan, Isfahan, Yazd, Kirman, Fars and much of modern Iraq, as well as Anatolia as far west as Diarbekir (deep inside modern Turkey). In that year he also defeated the Uzbeks at Merv in Khorasan, and laid the foundations for absorbing much of modern Afghanistan, with its Iranian culture, into the Safavid Empire. But four years later, at the Battle of Caldiran in eastern Anatolia, Ismail was roundly defeated by the Ottoman army with its superior firepower. Although the Safavids continued to challenge Ottoman predominance in eastern Anatolia, the Caucasus and Iraq for a further century (the Safavids ruled in Baghdad between 1508 and 1534, and again between 1623 and 1638), defeat at Caldiran was to prove decisive in pushing the centre of Safavid power away from Anatolia and on to the Iranian plateau. In 1530 the capital was shifted from vulnerable Tabriz to Kasvin, and it eventually settled in Isfahan in 1598.

By that time the original basis of Safavid rule had been considerably modified. Under Ismail and his son Tahmasp, Turkmen tribal levies had provided the military muscle and Turkmen tribal chiefs – the 'amirs' – the military and administrative elite through whom the growing empire had been ruled. The distribution of conquered lands had been the means of preserving tribal loyalty to the ruling house. The price had been factional struggle, and at times open conflict, between tribes whose nomadic way of life was antagonistic to stable territorial administration. However, the accession of Abbas I, the fifth Safavid shah, in 1587 marked the onset of a political revolution. Abbas freed himself from dangerous dependence upon Turkic tribal support by a device very similar to the Ottoman *devshirme*. From Christian communities in Georgia and the Trans-Caucasus he recruited an army and bureaucracy of *qullars* (or *gholamani*), slave converts whose loyalty to him would be undivided.[71] By the end of his reign, in 1639, more than half the Safavid provinces were ruled by *qullars*. Abbas also created a royal army of musketeers (ethnically Iranian, not Turkic), and *qullar* cavalry and artillery, paid from the revenues of a growing number of directly administered 'Khassa' provinces.[72] This regime represented a deliberate dilution of the old Turkic character of Safavism, and an increasing reliance upon ethnic Iranians and foreign slaves, who adopted Persian not Turkic culture. The choice of Isfahan as the imperial capital, the lavish architectural programme which transformed the city, royal patronage of the ornamental, and the development of a distinctive Isfahan school of philosophy marked the appearance of a new Persian high culture which would command the respect and admiration (as well as influencing the thought and language) of the ethnically diverse elites of an empire which stretched at its height from Tabriz to Kandahar (conquered by Abbas in 1622).

The Safavid reunion of much of 'Greater Iran', together with (comparative) internal peace and order, also contributed to a commercial revival vigorously promoted by the ruling house. The Safavids used their increasing revenues to improve trade routes and build caravanserais. Under Abbas, Iran's principal export of raw silk was a royal monopoly (with Armenian merchants as his agents),[73] and Isfahan with its twin city New Julfa became a great commercial centre, with an Indian mercantile community of some twenty thousand by the end of the seventeenth century.[74] When John Fryer went there on commercial business in 1677 (wandering the streets in Persian clothes to avoid attention), he found a cloth market larger than the famous Blackwell Hall in London, and four Catholic churches. The shah had allowed Augustinian monks to build a church in 1598, and had even paid for its decoration.[75] Abbas was strong enough to destroy the Portuguese settlement at Hormuz in 1622 in favour of his own emporium at Bandar Abbas. Ultimately, as we shall see, the Safavid project of a great agrarian empire, with a flourishing commerce under royal control and a unifying high culture, was frustrated by the failure to subjugate completely the Turkic tribal elements – a reflection perhaps of the unfavourable balance between settled agriculture and nomadic pastoralism on the Iranian plateau.[76] Nevertheless, by their enforcement of Shia Islam, by institutionalizing it as the 'state religion'[77] and by restoring Persian as the language of government and high culture, the Safavids imposed on their far-flung dominions a remarkable degree of cultural unity. The extent to which they identified their rule with religious uniformity and popular religiosity is in striking contrast with the Ottoman model, and may help to explain why the ultimate territorial legacy of the Safavids was to prove some-what grander than that of their erstwhile Ottoman rivals.

The Ottoman Empire and Safavid Iran were both successor states of the short-lived world empire that Tamerlane had constructed between 1380 and his death in 1405. The Timurid *raj* had fallen apart in the fifteenth century, but its old imperial centre in Turan (Transoxiana or West Turkestan) continued to be the great cultural entrepôt of the Islamic world. Turan was still the launch pad for would-be empire-builders to the west and south, towards the Iranian plateau and the Near East, or on to the plains of North India. Its Turko-Mongol elite, with its prestigious high culture, its grand conception of monarchy and its command of a commercial and diplomatic network, was a ruling class in search of an empire.

By 1500, however, perhaps because the shrivelled remnants of Timurid rule could no longer defend the Turanian oases against the attacks of steppe warrior-nomads, Timurid power in its Turanian heartland had been broken by the Uzbeks. Among the defeated Timu-rid princes driven from Samarkand was Babur, who took refuge in Kabul.[78] But the Timurid instinct was strong. In 1519, with an army of some 1,500 men, Babur descended on to the North Indian plains like an Asian Pizarro to carve out a new Timurid kingdom. He entered Hindustan not as a predatory barbarian from the Central Asian steppes, but as the representative of the most advanced and cultivated society in the Islamic world. At the Battle of Panipat, near Delhi, Babur defeated the ruling Muslim dynasty, the Lodi sultanate of Delhi, and made himself master of North India. Behind this triumph lay personal courage, military skill and the technical prowess of Central Asian warfare, with its tactical mobility.[79] But the success of his con-quistador regime also built on his Timurid prestige and his control over the trade routes between North India and Central Asia, through which passed perhaps half of India's most valuable exports.[80] Babur himself, while relishing the wealth to be won in Hindustan, viewed its lack of civilized amenities with imperial contempt for colonial backwardness. When he arrived in Agra, he was disgusted at the state of the grounds where he wanted to create a proper '*char-bagh*' – an Iranian-style garden with running water and flowers. But the work was started: 'Then in that charmless and disorderly Hind, plots of garden were ... laid out with order and symmetry ... and in every border, roses and narcissus in perfect arrangement.'[81] It seems more than likely that Babur's real intention was to use North India's resources to restore Timurid rule in Samarkand, Tamerlane's capital. It was his early death (significantly, he was buried in Kabul by his own command) and the policy of his son Humayun which ensured that the Timurid enterprise would be focused instead on ruling North India.

The North Indian world which Babur's successors would rule had been dominated since the eleventh century by Muslim warrior elites of Turkic or Afghan origins. By 1500, much of the Indian subcontinent was divided between the great conquest states they had founded: the sultanates of Delhi, Bengal, Gujarat, Deccan (splintering into five successor states by 1500), Khandesh, Multan and Kashmir. Only in Mewa (a Rajput state in North India) and in Vijayanagar (in the far south) had Hindu states withstood the deluge. The Muslim colonial elites, the *ashraf*, were anxious to safeguard their group solidarity. They maintained an intellectual 'Establishment' of theologians, preachers and judges as a way of preserving their distinctive culture against the risk of absorption by the Hindu milieu.[82] To assert the permanence of their rule, they built mosques, colleges, shrines and emphatic monuments, like the impressive *minar* or tower at Chhota Pandua in Bengal.[83] Within the sultanates their power was based on a system of semi-feudal land grants in exchange for military service, and rested ultimately upon the agrarian surpluses of Hindu culti-vators, especially in the great North Indian 'fertile crescent' on the Indo-Gangetic plains.

Babur's dramatic *entrada* had been a false start. The Delhi rulers who had fled to eastern India revived under Sher Shah, who drove Humayun out of India in 1539–40. But Sher Shah's successors proved unable to build a cohesive North Indian empire, and the Timurids returned to Delhi in 1555. It was the reign of Akbar (1555–1605), who was Babur's grandson, that saw the real foundation of the Timurids' Mughal empire. Akbar embarked on a series of territorial conquests that brought almost all the subcontinent, except for the far south, under his rule by the early seventeenth century. This was not a transient despotism, a freebooter's empire that disintegrated as quickly as it had been assembled. Instead, Akbar drew upon Timurid traditions to fashion a grander and more durable imperial system than previous Muslim rulers in India had been able to create.

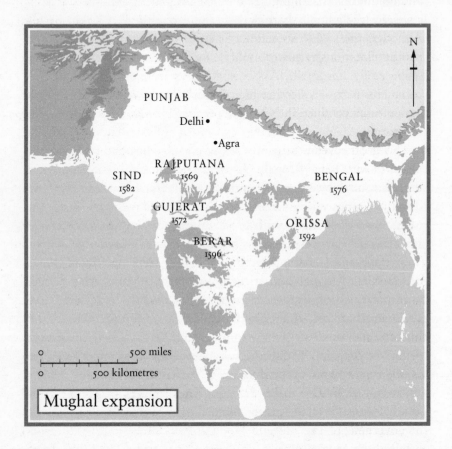

N

PUNJAB

Delhi•

•Agra

RAJPUTANA
1569

SIND
1582

BENGAL
1576

GUJERAT
1572

ORISSA
1592

BERAR
1596

0   500 miles

0   500 kilometres

Mughal expansion

At the core of Akbar's empire was a great service aristocracy of *mansabdars* or imperial rank-holders (most of them of Central Asian or Iranian origin)[84] who formed the amirs – the military and administrative elite. These men were rewarded (and their loyalty ensured) by the grant of large revenues drawn from the land. The ingenuity of Akbar's system lay in the careful distinction between the land revenues attached to a *jagir* (one of the landed estates which the elite held as *jagirdars*) and the exercise of administrative or judicial authority over its population. In any given locality a *jagirdar* exercised revenue rights but not political control, which was reserved to the official representative of the *padshah* – or emperor.[85] The imperial centre thus prevented the emergence of a decentralized feudal system. By instigating a new and ubiquitous rule of regular revenue assessment, it ensured that the state received a lion's share of the revenue that the *jagirdars* collected. Although they were sometimes obliged by political expediency to make concessions to powerful local landholders (those too entrenched to be easily uprooted), Akbar's ministers were able to apply their revenue system – collecting in cash perhaps one-half of the value of agricultural production[86] – with remarkable uniformity across his territories.[87]

This great revenue stream was the real foundation of Mughal imperial power. It paid for the army as well as a cultural programme that drew on the practice of Timurid Samarkand. In the Turko-Iranian tradition, followed by Tamerlane, Akbar projected himself not as a Muslim warrior-king, but as the absolute monarch of a diverse subject population.[88] His official genealogy laid claim to descent from both Tamerlane and Genghis Khan,[89] and thus to their legacy as 'world-conquerors'. Mughal court ritual – especially Akbar's daily appearance (*darshan*) on an elevated platform (*jaroka*) – emphasized the *padshah*'s supreme authority over even the greatest and wealthiest of his subjects. The court was the centre of lavish literary patronage. It promoted the study of the Muslim 'rational sciences' and the writing of poetry, the main literary medium in the Islamic world. But Mughal court culture looked to Persian or Central Asian models for its art and literature. Persian was the language of intellectual life as well as of government. The life and landscape of Iran (not that of India) inspired the Mughal poets, who evoked a world far away 'from the polluting influences of the subject peoples'.[90] Like Tamerlane, too, Akbar embarked upon a great building programme, of which the short-lived imperial capital at Fatehpur Sikri was the most astonishing product. Akbar's regime was cosmopolitan and eclectic, a tribute to Central Asia's influence as a great cultural entrepôt. It is even possible that his abortive attempt to impose a more centralized government in the 1570s and '80s (which led to the great revolt of 1580–82) was remotely inspired by the Chinese system of meritocratic bureaucracy refracted through Timurid Samarkand.[91] Famously, Akbar rejected the classic Islamic distinction between the Muslim faithful (the *umma*) and the unbelievers. He abolished the *jizya* (poll tax on non-Muslims) in 1579, and flirted with propagating a new religious synthesis of Islam and Hinduism.

The wealth and glamour of Akbar's imperium reflected the scale and productiveness of the Mughal economy. With a population of between 60 and 100 million, and a 'fertile crescent' of rich alluvial land, the Mughals presided over a larger and wealthier economy than the Ottomans or Safavids.[92] Exporting large quantities of foodstuffs, cotton textiles, tobacco, sugar and indigo, especially to its Ottoman, Iranian and Uzbek neighbours, Mughal India was a major trading power. Indian merchants maintained a far-flung network with Bukhara, Isfahan and even Astrakhan in Muscovite Russia. Artisan manufacture, especially of textiles, was widely dispersed through the countryside, and some estimates suggest that India's manufacturing capacity in early modern times dwarfed that of Europe. The Mughals were a stimulant to both internal and foreign trade. The efficiency of their revenue system created an ample surplus to be spent on luxury and manufactured goods by the privileged class of revenue-holders, the *mansabdars* and *jagirdars*, and the vast retinues that they kept. Inter-regional trade was made cheaper and easier by the Mughal pax and the convenience and safety of internal travel noted by European visitors.[93] In fact the Mughal rulers had brought with them the Central Asian tradition of protecting and promoting trade (Central Asian rulers were the guardians of the Silk Route). They built forts and caravanserais, founded new towns, and expanded old centres of trade. It was true, of course, that in certain respects Mughal India displayed 'backward' or 'colonial' characteristics by comparison with the Turko-Iranian heartland of the Islamic world and the rival civilizations in China and the Occident. It was less advanced technologically – the fantastic dexterity of Indian artisans compensated for the scarcity of tools. Although the state was active, there was little to show that the privileged elite of revenue-receivers was devoting its wealth to the increase of agricultural output or to improving the productivity of other kinds of enterprise.[94] A harsh and unstable environment may have discouraged them.[95] But at the death of Akbar there was little reason to think that the economic foundations of Mughal power would prove unequal to the task of sustaining a great imperial state and the Islamic culture that it represented.

THE LONG SIXTEENTH CENTURY
IN EAST ASIA

The long sixteenth century was also a period of exceptional dynamism in East Asia – the vast region occupied by China, Japan, Korea and the Inner Asian steppe. The early phase of Ming rule in China between 1368 (when the dynasty began) and the 1430s had seen the forceful reassertion of a distinctively Chinese political and cultural tradition after the long interlude of alien rule under the Mongol Yuan. The early Ming emperors reinvigorated the bureaucratic state and the examination system on which it rested. They swept away the chief ministers of the previous regime and created a personal absolutism. They proclaimed devotion to Confucian orthodoxy, and fostered the collection and publication of Confucian texts. In 1420 Peking was re-established as the imperial capital, once the completion of the Grand Canal assured regular supplies from the great grain-basket of the Yangtze valley.[96] In all these ways the Ming were the real founders of the system of government that lasted in China until the revolution of 1911. Their reaffirmation of Confucian cultural supremacy lasted almost as long.

Ming rule represented a vehement reaction against what was seen by its original supporters as the corruption, oppression and over-taxation of the Mongol Yuan.[97] In deference to Confucian beliefs, the Ming emperors embraced an agrarian ideology in which land was true wealth, and wealth was anchored in social obligations both upward and downward. Social order and cultural cohesion, the vital conditions of imperial stability, were locked into the system of agrarian production on whose food payments and land taxes dynastic authority depended. Fear of the disorders that had helped pull down the Yuan, and a watchful concern for agrarian calm, made the Ming reluctant to tax heavily, despite the huge burden of frontier defence. By the sixteenth century they had come to preside over an understaffed, underpaid and inadequate bureaucracy.[98] An over-narrow tax base, and the refusal to allow government agencies to engage in trade, produced a fiscal crisis. By the late sixteenth century the attempt to provide for defence by an army that paid for itself from its own agrarian estates had also broken down completely.[99] By that time, too, the level of rural disorder – relatively low during much of the Ming era – had begun rising sharply.

Ming diplomacy was intended to secure the external conditions for internal stability. From that point of view, the famous voyages dispatched by the emperor Yung-lo around the Indian Ocean under the admiral Cheng-ho were an aberration, prompted perhaps by fear of attack by Tamerlane and his successors. Yung-lo, the 'second founder', who reigned from 1403 to 1424, was an exceptionally determined and aggressive monarch. His naval imperialism, the protracted effort to incorporate Vietnam into his empire, and his military drive against the Inner Asian nomads may all have been part of an abortive strategy to assert China's primacy throughout East Asia.[100] But the strain was too great. His successors adopted a drastic alternative. The adventure in sea power was quickly abandoned. Private overseas travel and trade were forbidden. And to secure North China against invasion from the steppe, or unwelcome contact with its nomads, they preferred to rely not on military expeditions but on the Great Wall. Built to extend and reinforce earlier frontier defences, the Great Wall was largely constructed after 1470 and brought to completion in the following centuries. It was still being built when the Ming dynasty fell in 1644.[101]

Later Ming rulers thus chose to uphold China's place in East Asia by stressing its cultural unity and rejecting foreign commercial relations. That meant a deliberate withdrawal from Inner Asian politics, in which the Yuan had exerted a definite influence. It required a determined attempt to force both maritime and Inner Asian trade into the rigid framework of official tribute. By the early sixteenth century this had become unsustainable. Steppe-nomad demand for China's cloth and grain outstripped the supply through official channels of trade. Frontier warfare intensified.[102] For China's nomad neighbours, raiding and freebooting yielded the goods that the Chinese refused, or were forbidden, to trade. Along the sea coasts, the same restrictive policy bred a huge upsurge in smuggling and piracy, as China felt the early effects of Europe's commercial intrusion and, much more important, of the political and economic transformation of Japan.

Since the late twelfth century, Japan had been ruled through a compromise by which legitimate authority was vested in the emperor but actual power was in the hands of the shogun, formally acknowledged as viceroy or regent by the imperial court. The shogun or 'generalissimo' was – or tried to be – a hereditary military dictator, and usually rose from the ranks of the emperor's generals. However, the real basis of a shogun's strength was his coalition of allies among the feudal lords and their *bushi* or samurai, the warrior class. But under the Ashikaga shoguns this 'system' broke down in a 'feudal anarchy' of warring fiefdoms that lasted from the 1460s until the mid sixteenth century. At about the same time, fifteenth-century Japan experienced a phase of marked commercial expansion. New crops were grown and new commodities exported, including copper, sulphur and swords. Ming controls over trade meant that Japan's principal market was mainly accessible through a network of smugglers and pirates. But the collapse of the shoguns, who had also frowned on unofficial trade, and the rise of the *daimyo*, the local 'domain' lords, many of them with a direct interest in trade, encouraged an explosion of Japanese maritime enterprise. By the 1550s, Japanese traders, freebooters and *wako* pirates were ranging as far afield as Thailand, Burma and India. Japan's silver production made it an 'Asian Mexico', and a key trading partner for the Portuguese and Spanish who had entered the Pacific.[103] In 1567 the Ming emperor abandoned the struggle against illegal trade and threw open China's ports – although not to Japan.[104] Canton was opened to foreign merchants in 1578. Japan allowed in the Portuguese merchants, who settled at Nagasaki in 1571.

These moves in East Asia coincided with a remarkable phase of Christian missionary enterprise. Its headquarters was at Goa, the seat of Portugal's Estado da India. Portugal's claim to a European monopoly in the exploration and trade of Asia had been sanctioned by the Pope as part of the task of taking the faith to the heathen. Goa was the gateway through which dozens of missionaries made their way into Asia. St Francis Xavier, co-founder of the Jesuits, made his way ashore in 1542, barefoot and in rags. He died ten years later on the coast of South China. His body was brought back for burial in Goa, to be displayed once a year, miraculously preserved from physical decay. Its religious prestige was so great that the Pope insisted that at least one arm should be sent back to Rome. Other Jesuits went to the Mughal court and one, Roberto di Nobili, spent years in South India in the vain attempt to reconcile Hinduism and Catholicism to the satisfaction of the Brahmins. But perhaps the most remarkable of the Jesuit priests was Matteo Ricci. He went to China in the 1580s and, after years of patient diplomacy, was granted permission to go to Peking in 1601. Once there, his learning, shrewdly adapted to the style and bearing of a Confucian scholar, gave him an entrée to court. Ricci was able to draw the first map in China to depict the Americas. His skill in cartography, medicine and astronomy became the hallmark of the Jesuit mission, and its main source of prestige. Ricci's real objective – to persuade the Confucian intellectuals that their concept of heaven was really the same as his idea of God – proved much more elusive. But long after his death the mission remained the most reliable source of European knowledge about Chinese affairs, until European merchants arrived in numbers in South China after c.1750.

For the Ming, however, neither commercial concessions nor their attempt to appease frontier nomad hostility brought more than temporary respite. In Japan, the years after 1570 saw a dramatic struggle for reunification as first Nobunaga and then Hideyoshi imposed a ruthless personal supremacy over the warring *daimyo* – helped by the new gunpowder technology of muskets and guns. Hideyoshi was determined to win control over Japan's trade route with China, along the Korean coast. Frustrated by Ming delays, he formulated an astonishing plan to conquer first Korea and then China itself. In 1592 he invaded Korea with an enormous army of 200,000 men. When the Chinese intervened, he bartered for a measure of power in Korea and for freedom to trade with China. When China refused, he staged a second invasion in 1597, but it was quickly aborted when he died unexpectedly. Hideyoshi's ambition outran his military power. The Ming could not just be shouldered aside. But the real casualty of the Korean wars was Ming finance – and the Ming system.

The Ming had seen off the Japanese threat, but they still faced continuous pressure from the Mongol nomads along the Great Wall. Their most dangerous enemy was building up the frontier empire that overwhelmed them completely after 1620. During the 1590s, Nurhaci, a nomad generalissimo in the mould of Genghis Khan, had assembled a Manchurian polity that combined tribal elements from the forest and steppe with settled agrarian communities in the frontier district north-east of Peking. As Ming power dwindled amid fiscal crisis and growing internal disorder, Nurhaci strengthened his grip over frontier Mongols and Chinese, for whom his control was more real than that of their nominal suzerain. In 1601 he acquired a standing army using the 'banner' system, in which stress on Manchu ethnic identity was combined with division into military 'companies' as the key social and administrative units. In 1615 he sent his last tribute mission to Peking. Three years later he issued a manifesto denouncing the Ming and declaring his intention to overthrow the dynasty. By 1636, as much by winning over powerful Chinese as by military conquest, Nurhaci's successors realized this ambition – although their dynastic accession as the Manchu or Ch'ing (the Pinyin version is 'Qing') was delayed until the fall of Peking and is conventionally dated to 1644.

What was the significance of this change in the 'mandate of heaven', and of Japan's reunification after 1590? Together they cut short the experiment in 'openness' that was tried out in East Asia after 1550. In the later sixteenth century, the combination of Japanese commercial and maritime expansion, the opening of China and the trickle of European trade had stimulated the movement of people, goods and ideas.[105] Chinese and Japanese moved into South East Asia; Europeans arrived in Japan and China. In China, new overseas markets for porcelain and silk encouraged urban growth. The inflow of Japanese and American silver in payment monetized the economy and its revenue system – an important gain in a country without precious metals.[106] Japan, with its large population of maybe 12 million (three times that of contemporary Britain), its maritime sector and its reserve of bullion, may have been the vital agent in this opening-up. It was in the trading ports of south-western Japan that Christianity established a foothold when the Jesuits arrived after 1580. They skilfully exploited Christianity's appeal as a social adhesive in the age of disorder.[107] But Hideyoshi's supremacy, followed by the systematic repression of *daimyo* autonomy by Ieyasu (1524–1616), the first Tokugawa shogun, spelled the gradual end of Japan's 'Christian century' and the brief era of openness in overseas trade. Christianity was blamed for *daimyo* resistance, in Kyushu especially (where there was a major rebellion in 1638–9). Many Christians were killed, and Christianity was banned altogether in 1640. Ieyasu had tried to control foreign trade. His successors preferred to exclude Europeans completely. The Spanish were expelled in 1624. The English traders had already left. The Portuguese were confined to the island of Deshima in Nagasaki harbour, and then forced to leave in 1639. Japanese were forbidden to travel abroad after 1635. Chinese merchants and artisans continued to come: Nagasaki had its 'Chinatown'. China's cultural influence remained extremely strong. But against the rest of the world the seclusion policy (*sakoku*) was all but complete.

It ran in parallel with the systematic reassertion of Confucian ideology by the new Tokugawa regime, now based in Edo (modern Tokyo). Tokugawa rule maintained the outward forms of feudalism in the *daimyo* domains, but modified the substance. Feudal lordship was weakened by the grant of village autonomy and by transforming the samurai from a local warrior class into something more like a salaried service gentry paid (in rice) to administer the domains. To help legitimize this new dispensation, the early Tokugawa sponsored Confucian ideologues and educators. They preached the Confucian message of a four-class hierarchy (officials, peasants, artisans and merchants), and the need to pursue social and natural harmony in a well-ordered society.[108] In Ch'ing China it was a similar story. Dynastic change meant not the end of Confucianism, but its deliberate entrenchment as the official ideology of the new Manchu regime. Manchu rulers were less instinctively hostile than their Ming predecessors to foreign commercial contact. But they were deeply mistrustful of its political meaning in the coastal region south of the Yangtze, which was geographically remote, hard to control, and the refuge of Ming loyalists who were only slowly defeated.[109] But the most significant achievement of the Manchu dynasty was to reverse the ultimately disastrous introversion of Ming frontier policy. Manchu adeptness in steppe diplomacy helped to turn Inner Mongolia into a buffer zone, and to drive China's imperial power deep into Inner Asia. The northern inland threat to China's stability was efficiently neutralized. With a once-disruptive Japan now safety withdrawn into neo-Confucian seclusion, and Confucianism firmly in command in Korea and Vietnam, the Manchu accession heralded a remarkable restoration of the East Asian world order. European influence, based in faraway Java, was confined to its keyholes. Early Dutch interest in direct trade and diplomacy succumbed to the mood of mutual indifference: by 1690 the Dutch East India Company had stopped sending ships to China.[110] Meanwhile, imperial China reached the apogee of its power.

COMPARING EUROPE

Comparing Europe with other parts of Eurasia in the fifteenth and sixteenth centuries requires (for European readers) a certain mental adjustment. Our knowledge of Europe is so much more detailed that it is easy to see it as a cultural and political anthill that contrasts with the 'torpor' of 'oriental' societies. The existence of so many separate jurisdictions, with their own rulers, armies, laws and fiscal systems, all competing to survive, adds to the impression of a busy, energetic civilization. But we should not mistake all this activity (and the mass of paper it produced) for evidence that the European states had discovered the means to assert their predominance in the world at large.

Quite the contrary. The most dynamic elements in Europe's early modern culture promised not so much a great transformation as a syndrome of destructive instability. The intellectual revolt against late medieval scholasticism and the 'rediscovery' of a much larger body of classical literature formed the main ingredients of 'Renaissance humanism'. The history, politics and rhetoric of republican Rome had a particular appeal for the urban, bureaucratic and class-conscious milieux of northern Italy and Flanders.[111] But they also promoted a new conception of the secular state that undermined the claims of clerical privilege. They shaped a religious and intellectual climate in which the doctrines and institutions of the Catholic Church could be attacked far more systematically than by isolated heretics or social rebels. The astonishing success of the Protestant Reformation rested upon its rapid rise to intellectual respectability, its appeal to secular rulers (like the Elector of Saxony, whose protection was crucial to Luther's influence) and its association with the defence of urban or princely autonomy against the engrossing demands of dynasts and empire-builders.

In fact religious dissent could easily be seen as posing a devastating threat to social, political and moral order at a time when population growth and price inflation were sharpening social conflict. Alarm at its spread prompted the papal programme of church reform enacted at the Council of Trent between 1545 and 1563, and the urgency with which Elizabeth I constructed the Anglican *via media* in England. But there was no let-up in the savage ideological warfare between Catholics and Protestants after 1560, vented in the French wars of religion and the revolt of Dutch Protestants against their Catholic Habsburg ruler. If Renaissance humanism had created a new social type – the self-conscious, competitive, calculating individualists imagined by Jacob Burckhardt[112] – and transformed the state from a conglomerate of custom into a 'work of art',[113] the Reformation had injected a spirit of rebellion, intolerance and dogmatism which threatened to make the jostling polities of the Occident ungovernable.

Perhaps for this reason, the most attractive political idea of the age was dynasticism. The dynast was an ideal lawgiver, enjoying legitimacy through descent (by contrast with self-made despots) and commanding unstinting loyalty from his subjects. When fused with new notions of secular bureaucracy, and of the monarch as the glamorous patron of learning and the arts, dynastic rule was a powerful instrument for mobilizing social resources and imposing political order. In practice, European conditions sharply reduced dynasticism's potential. Local power still lay largely with aristocratic grandees and their networks of clientage. Their ambitions and rivalries were often more potent than royal decrees. They could evoke local patriotism and its attachment to custom against the centralizing schemes of the dynasts and call on the support of religious dissenters (or conservative resistance to a reformist regime). The grandest dynastic project of all, Charles V's plan for a universal empire uniting the Habsburg lands in Germany, Spain and the Low Countries under a single ruler, his son Philip, was wrecked by an alliance of German princes and Protestant reformers.

Dynasticism was also an unsettling force in a continent honey-combed with different jurisdictions. Dynastic prospects and policy turned on the accidents of birth and death, an endless source of claims and disputes. Dynastic 'logic' disregarded local autonomy or cultural identity. It ignored the balance of power. It provoked the bitter rivalry epitomized in the Valois–Habsburg wars in the first half of the six-teenth century. It also ruled out any united action against Ottoman imperialism in South East Europe or the Mediterranean. They would rather make peace with the Turks, declared the German princes in 1551, than accept the future Philip II as their ruler.[114] Horror at the infidel did not preclude a Franco-Turkish entente against the Habsburgs in 1536. Nor did it persuade Philip II to give up his struggle against the rebellious Dutch and concentrate Spanish power against the Turks in the Mediterranean after 1580.[115] Far from imagining a common supremacy over the rest of Eurasia, European statecraft was obsessed with intramural conflicts. Symptomatically, the wealth of the New World was used to finance the dynastic ambitions of the Old. The huge increase in his income of American silver after 1580 allowed Philip II to pay for his wars of dynastic hegemony – though even this windfall did not save him from bankruptcy in 1596.[116]

Thus much of the intellectual and political energy of sixteenth-century Europe was consumed by the religious and dynastic warfare that racked the continent until the peace of exhaustion at the end of the century. Set against this background, it is easy to see why European expansion was a meagre threat to the Islamic empires or the great states in East Asia. European thought and scholarship seemed mainly absorbed by the pyrotechnics of theological argument. Scientific in-quiry had yet to break free from the belief in witchcraft and astro-logical prediction to which most educated people subscribed. The great exception to this general rule of political and intellectual introversion was the spectacular growth of a maritime subculture.

It was hardly surprising that a 'peninsula of peninsulas' (one way of describing Europe) surrounded by numerous 'inland seas' – the Mediterranean, the Baltic, the North Sea, the English Channel and the Irish Sea – should have developed a dense system of sea communi-cations. Still less that the variety of maritime conditions, in Atlantic Europe especially, should have bred a wide range of ship types and techniques. In its combination of accessible hinterlands, ecological variety and population density, Europe was better endowed than other maritime regions like the western Indian Ocean (linking East Africa, the Persian Gulf and western India) or the island world of South East Asia. The result was the emergence long before 1400 of a number of powerful 'sea states': Venice, Genoa, Ragusa and Aragon in the Mediterranean; Portugal in South West Europe; Denmark, Norway, the Hanseatic League, England and eventually Holland in the north. In these sea states, maritime enterprise thrived on a profitable mix of fisheries, trade and piracy (to which traders resorted when their rivals used force to exclude them from commerce).[117] It won the backing of governments, who needed the revenues that seaborne trade created. It was no coincidence that mapping and navigational aids were the principal fields in which scientific experiment was translated most rapidly into technical practice. By the 1570s Ptolemy's world map (itself 'rediscovered' in Europe in the fifteenth century) had been replaced by the much more accurate map of Abraham Ortelius, based on the reports of European travellers and seafarers. By the end of the century a huge volume of knowledge about Asia and the Americas was in printed form, and the vogue for travel writing – sober, scientific or simply sensational – was well under way.[118]

By the sixteenth century it was clear enough that Europe's comparative advantage over other Eurasian civilizations lay in its precocious development of marine activity. The simultaneous growth of long-distance trade with the Americas and India was one sign of this. Another was the rise of the huge cod fishery in the North Atlantic, which already employed some 350 ships (Spanish, French, Portuguese and English) by the 1570s.[119] European sailors were especially adept in the use of force at sea, as an alternative to trade or as an auxiliary to it. The most striking case was Portugal's Estado da India. By the early seventeenth century Europeans were poised to assert a worldwide predominance in deep-sea trading and carrying, occupying (with much internal dispute) a profitable niche in long-distance trade. But, with the striking exception of their American conquests, there was little to show that they could move beyond the shallow coastal beachheads where this niche activity was usually carried on. Nor that the habits and ethos of such expatriate 'sea people' commanded any special prestige among the other Eurasian societies with whom they came into contact. Only on Russia's steppe frontier (in somewhat special conditions) had Europeans expanded successfully into the heartland of another Eurasian society. In South East Europe, by contrast, the advantage lay all the other way.

The nearest that the Europeans had come to building a world empire was the conglomerate of territories ruled over by Spain. Its span was tremendous. Spanish power reached across the Atlantic. It extended all the way from Chile to New Mexico. It stretched across the Pacific to the Philippine Islands, to where Mexican silver was being shipped after 1565 to exchange for the luxuries brought there from China. The long, lonely voyage of the Manila galleon, which set off each year between 1565 and 1815 on its six-month journey to Acapulco (on at least one voyage all the passengers and crew died of disease or starvation, while the ship sailed on like the *Marie Celeste*) was the thread that connected this remote outpost of empire.[120] Yet, for all its astonishing scale, this empire remained less than the sum of its parts. It was a windfall empire, called into existence by the demand for silver in Europe and China. It was built to enforce a global monopoly over American silver (which made up over 80 per cent of the world's supply from 1494 to 1850), but it lacked the means or the will to drive European trade deeper into the markets of Asia. There was no imperial 'grand strategy' to make Spain the centre of a world economy: indeed, such a plan would have been futile. Instead, Philip II devoted the 'royal fifth' – the monarchy's share of the silver stream – to the struggle to uphold Spain's pre-eminence in Europe against rivals and rebels. The resources of America, and of Spain itself, were harnessed not to a vision of global predominance, but to the insatiable demands of the king's 'messianic imperialism' – his mission to defend the Catholic faith against its Protestant foes.[121]

CONCLUSION

The American *conquistas*, Europe's seaborne trade with the southern coasts of Asia, and the Russian advance into the North Asian steppe were a huge enlargement of European horizons and a colossal stimulus to European ambitions.[122] But there was little sign by the end of the long sixteenth century (*c.* 1620) that they had triggered the emergence of a world economy or weakened the cultural autonomy of old civilizations in other parts of Eurasia. Europeans had woven a new mercantile web that linked the Americas with Eurasia. The supply of American silver gave them an entrée into Asian markets where there was little demand for purely European produce. It affected prices and money supply in the Ottoman and Ming empires as well as in Europe. But the commodities that circulated in this new global exchange were not staples but luxuries; their volume was tiny. In the sixteenth century, an average of fifty to seventy ships departed annually for the East from Lisbon;[123] and the traffic in manufactures like porcelain or textiles flowed mainly westward towards Europe and not the other way round.

Nor was there much sign that the balance of technical or cultural advantage had shifted significantly. In the sixteenth century, perhaps the most widely exported technology was gunpowder warfare, in which Europeans enjoyed a technical lead. Ottoman artillery used European experts. Japan's 'feudal' warfare was transformed by the import of European firearms. But neither in Japan nor in Iran nor in Mughal India was the social and political system unable to adjust to military innovation. Nor did a technical 'lag' create a real disparity between the military capacity of European states and those in the rest of Eurasia. On the contrary. The threat of further Ottoman expansion hung over Europe until the 1690s. In India and East Asia, Europe's remoteness made its mode of land warfare almost entirely irrelevant. In much the same way, patterns of consumption, codes of social etiquette and notions of hierarchy in the rest of Eurasia showed few signs of being influenced by Europeans' behaviour. The 'Columbian Exchange' between the natural products of the Old World and the New diversified Eurasian agriculture with novel plants like maize and potatoes, but created no dependence upon European suppliers.[124] European activity in the Americas aroused little if any interest in the rest of Eurasia.[125] Islamic and East Asian cosmology showed no loss of confidence in the face of European learning, or the violent upheaval in European religion and ritual.

In the two centuries that followed the death of Tamerlane, Eurasia remained divided between the three civilized worlds we have explored so far, and a number of others, Buddhist and Hindu, that we have passed over in silence. There was little to show that their cultural differences were narrowing. If anything, the energetic state-building that was taking place right across Eurasia and the wider diffusion of knowledge (through printed books in Europe and East Asia) were hardening the boundary-markers between them, and raising the stakes of cultural identity. Sometimes, of course, the meeting of cultures produced a mixture of feelings. The curious story of the Buddha's tooth showed how quickly the mood could change from casual indifference to religious zeal. In 1560 the viceroy of Goa led a raid against the Buddhist kingdom of Jafna (in modern Sir Lanka). Among the booty taken (so it turned out) was one of the holiest relics of the Buddhist world, the Buddha's tooth. Its fate quickly became known in the Buddhist states around the Bay of Bengal. The king of Burma made a huge offer for its safe return, and the viceroy accepted. But before the deal was concluded the Inquisition stepped in. The Inquisition in Goa was a very powerful body, waging constant war on (non-Christian) superstition and heresy. A few years later it forced the outlawing of Hindu rites in the Portuguese enclaves in India. Far from seeing the tooth as a profitable business (alas, for somebody else), it saw its deliverance into Christian hands as a providential victory – a chance to destroy one of the enemy's most powerful weapons (for the Church had no doubt about the power of relics). The viceroy was forced to give way. The tooth was removed, ground to dust and burned. Here, as elsewhere, the 'Age of Discovery' in Eurasia had brought greater physical contact but not a meeting of minds. It remained to be seen whether in the 'Age of Commerce' that followed it would be a different story.

3

The Early Modern Equilibrium

3. Batavia (modern Jakarta), colonial capital of the Dutch East Indies

The long sixteenth century of European expansion culminated in the founding of English and French colonies in the northern part of North America and the arrival of the Dutch and English in the trading world of the East Indies. But between the 1620s and the 1740s the expansive impulse of the Europeans lost much of its momentum. As we have seen already, the early modern European 'march to primacy' is in many ways an optical illusion, the deceptive product of hindsight. Europeans saw themselves as embattled against a triumphant Islam even while they plundered the New World and invaded the Indian Ocean. Their own achievements in political, military and commercial organization were matched or overshadowed by those of the Ottomans, Safavids, Mughals, Ming or Tokugawa. State-building and cultural innovation were striking features of Eurasian, not just European, history in the early modern era.

Of course it had been the Europeans who had made the most spectacular advance into the Outer World, who had captured the huge new resource base in the Americas, and who had opened up new long-distance trade routes linking South East Asia, India, West Africa and the Americas. But we should not assume that by these means they had created the basis for global predominance, or were now poised to encircle, isolate and subjugate other societies and cultures in Eurasia. It was far from clear, for example, that they had freed themselves from their long-standing dependence upon costly Asian manufactures; that their organizational skills – civil or military – gave them any special advantage over other Eurasians; that their high culture yielded greater material benefits than, or promised intellectual predominance over, other high cultures; or that the geostrategic weaknesses that had penned them in the Eurasian Far West since late Roman times had been decisively overcome by innovations in maritime transport and warfare. By enlarging Old Europe into a new Euro-Atlantic 'world', the Occidentals had acquired hinterlands as varied and extensive as those of the Islamic realm or East Asia. There was much less evidence in the later early modern age that this great enlargement in territorial scale would also bring about the internal transformation to which Europe's subsequent primacy is usually attributed.

Indeed, by contrast with the drama of discovery and conquest, with whose consequences Europeans had barely come to terms by the early seventeenth century, the century or more that followed was a phase of much more gradual change in Europe's relations with the extra-European world. The windfall gains of the 'discoveries' were not to be repeated. Political and economic conditions in the Euro-Atlantic world limited the scope for further expansion. Preoccupied with Atlantic rivalries, the European maritime powers showed little enthusiasm for empire-building in Asia. At the same time the states of the Islamic realm and East Asia displayed much greater robustness than might appear from many later accounts of European dynamism and Asian decay. The sphere of Islamized civilization continued to expand. The scope of Chinese imperial power reached its apogee in the second half of the eighteenth century. The prestige of Indian and Chinese manufactures in the West was at its zenith. Viewed in this light, the century and a half before the British conquest of Bengal after 1757 was not just a long prelude to the 'Eurasian Revolution' by which Europe overpowered the rest of the Old World. It was a period of near equilibrium between the dominant societies in Eurasia, and, in parts of the Outer World, between the invading Europeans and the native communities. What remained in question was how long this global pattern of competition, collaboration and coexistence, created by the geographical expansion and closer economic interdependence of Old World societies, would endure; and which societies, if any, would overcome the technological, organizational and cultural barriers to a more general predominance.

THE LIMITS OF AMBITION:
EUROPEANS IN THE WIDER WORLD

For much of this period, then, Europeans were intent more on consolidating their grip in the Atlantic world than on acquiring vast new tracts to occupy. The scope of geographical exploration, while evidence of remarkable individual tenacity, was comparatively modest overall. Vast areas of the globe remained a necessary blank on European maps – even in North America, where international competition between Europeans was fiercest. Although the location of Hudson Bay was known by 1610, it was only in 1682 that René-Robert La Salle travelled the whole tortuous river route from Montreal to the Mississippi mouth.[1] Until c.1700 California was widely thought to be a huge island.[2] Bering's confirmation that no land bridge connected Asia and the Americas was known only in the later 1740s. Until after 1750 it was generally assumed that a vast inland 'Western Sea' lay beyond the height of land that fringed Hudson Bay.[3] South America's geography was better known, but much of the more remote interior, especially in Amazonia and Patagonia, remained a *terra incognita* well into the nineteenth century.[4] In the Pacific, European geographical thinking was dominated until Cook's great voyages of the 1760s and '70s by the mirage of a great 'Southern Continent' – Terra Australis.[5] In West, East and South Central Africa, Europeans had almost no first-hand knowledge beyond the narrow coastal belts visited by slave-traders and other merchants. Consequently, in 1750 it was still believed that the river Niger flowed westward from East Africa, reaching the Atlantic via the rivers Gambia and Senegal – a delusion that invested both the latter with an undeserved significance.

This vast realm of geographical ignorance reduced European activity in the Outer World to an archipelago of settlements, mines and trading depots connected by a skein of pathways kept open only by constant effort. Wider exploration was impeded partly by technical difficulties: the high cost of overland travel; the obstacles of climate and disease, which destroyed human capital at an alarming rate; the reluctance of indigenous rulers to allow spies and interlopers who might infringe valuable monopolies of furs or slaves. In West Africa, European traders had to be careful not to offend local rulers, who readily disciplined them for misbehaviour. Nor were they a match for the armies that the rulers could muster – especially so in the case of Dahomey, whose soldiers were equipped with imported firearms.[6] Apart from a very limited amount of state sponsorship, it was usually the prospect of commercial gain or of new lands for settlement which funded exploration – a misleading term, which usually signified the 'mapping' of existing trade paths through local informants. But the propulsion of economic or demographic need was spasmodic at best. The Brazilian gold rush of the 1690s sucked in immigrants and encouraged the Sao Paulo *bandeirantes* (or frontiersmen) to roam the *sertao* in search of new finds.[7] But in Spanish America the inflow of European migrants fell away sharply after 1625.[8] English colonization of North America was slow. Not until the 1670s – a century and a half after Cortés had landed in Mexico – were the mainland colonies secure against economic failure and Indian counter-attack.[9] Migration to the English Caribbean was brisker, because economic prospects seemed better there. Whites in Jamaica, says a recent study, were ten times as wealthy as those on the mainland of British America. But a subtropical climate and its diseases, local and imported, exacted a fearful toll. Between 1700 and 1750, between 30,000 and 50,000 European immigrants arrived in Jamaica, but the white population in 1752 was a mere 10,000.[10] In 1700 there were perhaps 250,000 white settlers in Britain's American and Caribbean territories.[11] The pace of advance on the mainland was slow: not until the 1750s did the ubiquitous colonial land speculators and their friends in government begin to cast their net beyond the Appalachians. The number of French settlers in New France (Quebec), Acadia (now Nova Scotia) and Louisiana was tiny: perhaps 60,000 by the 1750s.

Altogether, by the middle of the eighteenth century there were between 3 and 4 million inhabitants of European descent in Spanish, French, British and Portuguese America – perhaps 5 per cent of the population of Europe including Russia. But of course the great majority of the transatlantic migrants to the Americas were not freeborn Europeans but enslaved Africans. An authoritative estimate suggests that by as late as 1820 four times as many Africans as Europeans had arrived in the Americas – some 8 million, compared with 2 million Europeans.[12] Their death toll in the tropical Caribbean was also enormous. Colonies like Barbados, originally reliant upon contract labour from the British Isles, rapidly converted to slavery after 1670.[13] Slavery had two important effects on European migration. Once introduced, it choked off the demand for manual labour from Europe in plantation economies, and through the spread of African diseases it probably increased the mortality of those Europeans who did come.[14] But, paradoxically, by promoting the development of those plantation economies, it eventually created the local markets (for foodstuffs, building materials and light manufactures) from which later European arrivals could profit. For it was only by concentrating upon a few subtropical commodities raised by slave labour that agricultural colonization in the New World could be made profitable. From the 1660s onward, sugar was king, with tobacco a distant second and cocoa and chocolate trailing behind.[15] But even sugar paled in comparison with the importance of silver mined in Peru (less and less) and Mexico (more and more). Silver remained the premier American export, despite a declining production through much of this period that was dramatically reversed after 1750.[16]

The sugar colonies of the Caribbean were the bizarre offspring of European expansion. Everything needed to make them profitable – except the soil itself – was brought in from outside: capital, 'management' (the European planters and overseers), labour (African slaves) and also the sugar plant itself, brought to the Caribbean from the Canary Islands. For masters and slaves alike, fear was ever-present: fear of attack by rival Europeans; fear of a slave uprising; fear of the punishment inflicted by vengeful or ill-tempered whites; fear of disease; fear of the climate, with its storms and hurricanes. In the British colonies, like Barbados, the Leewards and Jamaica, the planters pretended to be living in England. They wore wigs and woollens, ate much bread and meat (mostly salted and brought from America), and drank deeply for thirst and perhaps for oblivion. Well into the eighteenth century, the British West Indies were a true Wild West. One governor cut off the hair of a woman who resisted his advances. Another denounced the 'unnatural and monstrous lusts' of the planters, and patrolled the streets nightly to restrain their habits. Not surprisingly, perhaps, he was eventually besieged in his palace, and, after a battle that included the use of cannon, was murdered by the infuriated citizenry. His successor was jailed for stealing the church silver. It was little wonder that when the capital of Jamaica, Port Royal, was destroyed by an earthquake and flood in 1692, the disaster was widely attributed to divine displeasure.

Silver, gold (from Brazil), sugar and tobacco – commodities whose value was high enough to stand the costs of long-distance transport – were the lifeblood of transatlantic commerce. But their contribution towards improving the efficiency and productiveness of the European economy could only be limited and indirect. Sugar and tobacco were consumer goods for which demand in Europe grew quite rapidly (in sugar's case, much more rapidly after 1750).[17] Silver and gold extended the monetization of the European economies. Much silver, however, was re-exported eastward to pay for Asian textiles, porcelain, silks, tea and spices: Dutch and British exports to India in this period were overwhelmingly composed of 'treasure' – silver and gold.[18] American products did not supply the basis for new manufactures or new technologies: they stimulated the demand for Asian imports. Nor could the American economies in this mercantilist era of commercial regulation offer an export market dynamic enough to catalyse European commerce and manufacture, except in a few favoured localities and trades. American communities prospering on bullion, sugar and tobacco were a valuable market towards which British exports swung noticeably in the eighteenth century.[19] But Caribbean planters had to spend much of their income on slaves,[20] and a huge proportion of the American population was made up of slave or semi-servile labour living at or below subsistence level. Much of the indigenous Amerindian population was marginal or marginalized. In the Caribbean, the charges of shippers, commission agents and creditors, and the remittances home to absentee proprietors, ate into plantation profits and reduced local demand. The costly superstructure of mercantilist bureaucracy, with its horde of aristocratic placemen and pensioners and its privileged merchant oligarchies, may have been the chief beneficiary of this part of the American windfall. Colonial products were a useful supplement to trade within Europe: being in general demand, they helped smooth regional imbalances.[21] Until 1750 at least, it might be wiser to see the Atlantic trading world as the vital prop of a commercial *ancien régime* rather than as a dynamic element in the industrial transformation of even the most advanced European economies.

In reality, the pattern of Europe's overseas trade with Asia and the Americas reflected the unevenness of Europe's own economic performance in the 'Age of Crisis'. The underlying problem throughout the period was population: stagnation, worsened by the effects of war, in the seventeenth century; slow expansion after 1700. Deprived of the extra demand generated by a rising population, trade languished. The market for Eastern Europe's grain in the west and south of the continent fell away, and was further reduced by the adoption of maize and rice as home-grown substitutes. There was little evidence of any general rise in agricultural productivity, and famine remained a periodic menace into the nineteenth century. Inland communications away from river routes and artificial waterways remained uncertain, slow and expensive. Nor was there much sign before c.1750 of productivity gains in manufacturing through the systematic use of technological innovations – certainly not on a scale that could reduce significantly the cost of such goods to consumers at home or outside Europe. A large, perhaps growing, number of Europeans were trapped in rural immobility by the institution of serfdom, widespread in Eastern Europe as well as in Russia.

In this long phase of slow economic growth, it was the maritime states of Northern Europe that were best placed to enhance their prosperity. Cheap sea communications favoured specialization and the efficiency gains it made possible.[22] Access to the widest range of traded commodities, including colonial goods, allowed these states to maximize the benefit of a dense commercial network – the easy and frequent exchange of goods and paper credits with the largest number of destinations. As a result, a notable feature of the period was the rise of large port cities where these advantages were concentrated – London, Hamburg and Amsterdam. The English merchant fleet doubled in size between 1660 and 1690.[23] In general, urbanization increased as large cities – capitals as well as great ports – expanded at the expense of smaller centres. It was here, where new wealth and new styles of life grew up, that patterns of consumption were quickest to change and the vogue for imported foodstuffs, drugs, beverages, textiles and household goods was keenest.[24] It was also here that the commercialization of social life, labour and leisure was most visible.[25]

Partly for these reasons, it is tempting to see the most important change in this period as the rise of a group of commercial, maritime states to form an advanced 'core' surrounded by a European and colonial 'periphery' whose economic development was increasingly shaped by disparities in power, wealth and technical expertise. Among the 'core' states, meanwhile, a further struggle was being waged for outright hegemony in commerce and empire.[26] But though the 'sea states' coped most successfully with the economic conditions of the period, their strength and importance should not be exaggerated by hindsight. Much of their overseas commercial activity was risky and unprofitable,[27] as the misfortunes of the Royal Africa Company, the South Seas Company and the Dutch West India and East India companies revealed.[28] Commercial competition outside Europe, with its accompanying infrastructure of fortresses, convoys and mercantilist regulation, imposed huge, sometimes ruinous, transaction costs on them.[29] Commercial and military operations at long range were hazardous and often ineffective: despite naval and financial superiority, neither the British nor the Dutch were able to blast open completely the Spanish commercial system in the Americas. The financial apparatus of the maritime powers was also highly vulnerable to the effects of war and political uncertainty: as late as 1745–6 the invasion of the Stuart claimant to the British throne, Bonnie Prince Charlie, created a financial panic in London. Nor, despite their relative sophistication, did the maritime economies of North West Europe enjoy a clear predominance over the inland economies of the continental interior, with their manufactures, commercial networks and 'cameralist' ideas of state intervention and regulation. It would be better to stress the successful resistance of Europe's inland states to domination by the 'sea powers'. On the larger stage of Eurasian or global economic competition, the maritime sector of the European economy, for all its success in developing the commodity trades across the Atlantic, and in finding customers among the expatriate Europeans in the Americas, was simply too small, too restricted in economic and demographic capacity, to aspire to global economic hegemony in the pre-industrial age.

This slow-growing European economy was required to support an elaborate socio-political superstructure of courts, bureaucracies, churches and aristocracies. After the great wars and internal upheavals of the early to mid seventeenth century, the later part of the period saw a gradual consolidation of social and political authority over much of Europe. The incidence of peasant revolt and regional rebellion declined. As the political order dug deeper, and exerted more effective control, there was a steady rise in state expenditure and the burden of taxation[30] – especially indirect taxation, which fell disproportionately on the poor. But this trend towards more professional and systematic government was achieved only at the price of a radical compromise with the entrenched power of aristocracies. In France this meant careful cooperation with networks of aristocratic clientage in the provinces.[31] In England the aristocratic embrace of parliamentary government was built on a foundation of places, pensions and electoral corruption at public expense. In the Habsburg monarchy, the price of aristocratic loyalty to the Crown was dominance by a tiny oligarchy of great families and the state's underwriting of rural serfdom as the centrepiece of the social order.[32]

The gradual emergence of a more orderly *ancien régime* over a large part of Europe did not imply a neat division into unified nation states. 'Germany' remained a vast patchwork quilt of over three hundred states, most of trivial size. The Habsburg monarchy, combining territories in modern Belgium (after 1713), northern Italy, Hungary (after 1683), Central Europe and the northern Balkans, was hardly more than a loose-knit alliance of different kingdoms, precariously unified in the person of the emperor. Even in France, integrating the provinces acquired by marriage, diplomacy and conquest was an uphill struggle: as late as 1720 Paris had to crush a separatist conspiracy by Breton nobles enraged by economic hardship and the fiscal burden.[33] The unification of the British islands, insecurely based on a common monarchy, was tentatively begun in 1707 with the union of England and Scotland, severely tested by two Scottish rebellions, and constantly threatened by Irish disaffection. For the maritime states of the European Far West, as well as for the 'inland empires' of Eastern Europe, external policy still turned in large part on the loyalty of their peripheral provinces.

Two important consequences flowed from the limited degree of political integration that the main *ancien régime* states had achieved. Firstly, they usually lacked the means to exert real control over the activities of their subjects and citizens in the extra-European world. Their colonial policies were a battleground where mercantile lobbies, aristocratic networks and the court wrestled inconclusively: the result was often to leave settler or merchant outposts to their own devices in a form of 'salutary neglect'.[34] Secondly, to most Europeans the lack of any compelling sense of nationality meant that dynastic loyalty was the only practicable basis of political life. In reality, dynastic prerogatives were diluted by consultative or representative bodies that defended established liberties and privileges. But there was no *ancien régime* ideology, or political model, which could be exported else-where or easily transferred to exotic settings overseas. The balance of rights and prerogatives in every state (and every unit) depended upon local custom and precedent, inherited and defended by local interests. This way of thinking had been taken by Spanish and English settlers to the American colonies, and helped to explain the difficulties that faced every attempt to assert the authority of the imperial centre.[35] As a result, it was hard to see how any European state could drastically enlarge its territories overseas without jeopardizing the delicate politi-cal mechanisms on which its stability depended at home. Not surpris-ingly, it was a commonplace of political commentators to stress the importance of preserving territorial compactness so that the balancing of royal prerogative with aristocratic, mercantile, religious, municipal and regional privilege did not become completely unmanageable.[36]

Indeed, for all that it represented an astonishing extension of the European sphere, America also offered proof of the limits to the expansionism of the *ancien régime* states. In both English and Spanish America the price of imperial expansion had been de facto colonial autonomy.[37] When Nathaniel Bacon, a wealthy Virginia planter, led a rebellion against the governor in 1676 (accusing him of being soft on the Pamunkey people) and burned down the colony's capital at Jamestown, there was little or nothing that London could do. Luckily, perhaps, Bacon died of the 'bloody flux' before he could entrench his rebel regime.[38] For their part, imperial governments at home displayed a general reluctance to divert scarce military and naval resources to protect or expand colonial possessions, whose leaders had to compete (with all the disadvantages of distance) with the multitude of domestic lobbies, cliques and interests clamouring for the attention of monarchs and ministers. Of course governments in London, Paris and Madrid *were* deeply concerned to safeguard the revenues derived from their overseas trade, and willing to use force to prevent its disruption by rival states: tensions of this kind led to the War of Jenkins's Ear in 1739, when a long-standing dispute over the mistreatment of a British sea captain by Spanish coastguards in the Caribbean boiled over into war. But they usually showed little inclination to place territorial expansion at the centre of their grand strategy,[39] and were likely to regard their colonies more as a convenient extension of their patronage systems than as an addition to national strength.[40]

For all these reasons, the states of *ancien régime* Europe were politically ill-equipped to advance boldly towards the conquest of the extra-European world. With the significant exception of Russia, their aristocracies had little incentive to bear the burdens of territorial conquest. Yet it is sometimes argued that the competitive, pluralistic nature of the European states system, with its division into multiple states and antagonistic great powers, was a breeding ground for wars which spread inevitably to other parts of the world as well as prompting advances in military tactics and organization – so that Europeans acquired the motives and means to dominate the world almost despite themselves.

Ancien régime Europe certainly spent heavily on its armies and navies, and their use in war accounted for some 54 per cent of public spending in the European monarchies during the eighteenth century.[41] European armies had grown rapidly in size after 1660.[42] The French army peaked at some 400,000 men in the 1690s, and both Britain and the Netherlands (with far smaller populations) kept up armies of over 100,000 men during the War of the Spanish Succession (1702–13). Military organization also became increasingly professionalized, with the gradual introduction of common uniforms, drill and a regular officer corps.[43] Frequent combat and the widespread use of foreigners as officers and ordinary soldiers encouraged the rapid dissemination of new techniques throughout Europe. But before the 1750s, and even after, there was little evidence that this precocious development of warlike skills conferred a significant advantage on Europeans in most other parts of the world. There were several reasons for this. European armies had evolved into highly specialized machines to fight *each other* – but not to fight military forces whose 'strategic doctrine' was radically different. This was painfully apparent in the encounters between British troops and Native Americans in the 1750s.[44] When British troops under General Braddock (more a veteran of the gaming table than of the battlefield) marched into the woods and fought a battle near modern Pittsburgh, their close formation and brilliant uniforms (the secret of order and discipline in a European battle) turned into their death warrant. The wars of siege and manoeuvre characteristic of European conflicts could not be replicated elsewhere where geopolitical conditions were quite different – even if it had been possible to deploy the numbers required. European-style warfare had come to rely on an elaborate infrastructure of supply, and quickly ground to a halt where this was lacking. Even on the European continent, European armies performed poorly in marginal areas like Danubia[45] or the Pontic Steppe north of the Black Sea.[46] Not least significant were the terrifying effects of tropical disease, which destroyed European armies overseas more efficiently than any military resistance. When the British sent an expedition to capture Cartagena in the Spanish Caribbean in 1742, more than three-quarters of the troops were soon out of action. 'A bilious fever . . . raged with such violence', wrote the naval surgeon turned writer Tobias Smollett, 'that three-fourths of those it invaded died in a deplorable manner; the colour of their skins being, by the extreme putrefaction of the juices, changed into that of soot.'[47] Even naval power was subject to some of the same limitations. Naval vessels were extremely expensive items of capital equipment whose value deteriorated rapidly in adverse conditions. Naval warfare too was dominated by caution and manoeuvre. The stakes were high: outright defeat might mean invasion or the destruction of the merchant fleet. Hence navies were usually kept close to home. Even the occasional foray to the Caribbean, where sailing conditions had been known since 1500, posed extreme risks from weather and infection, while fear of hurricanes or adverse wind conditions made it dangerous to linger on Indian coasts when the northern monsoon began in October.[48] Of course, European warships usually enjoyed a significant advantage over their extra-European counterparts in armament, and sometimes in speed and handling. But they could rarely be deployed in force, and inland empires or land-based states elsewhere in Eurasia were largely immune to the naval harassment that played so large a part in European warfare.

All this limited the extent to which European conflicts could spill over into areas of the world that had not already been colonized. In practice, Europe's international politics were usually too introverted to pose much of a threat to other parts of Eurasia. They were also compulsively unstable, since European diplomacy was dominated by two dynamic forces which reacted explosively with each other. The first was the struggle to maintain a rough equilibrium between the numerous and unequal members of the European states system.[49] The second was the dynastic factor – an unpredictable mixture of dynastic ambition and the accidents of birth and personality. Disputed dynastic claims unleashed war on a massive scale between 1702 and 1713, lay behind the Great Northern War between Russia and Sweden (1700–21) and provoked the War of the Austrian Succession (1740–48) when Frederick of Prussia seized Austrian Silesia. And, although the anarchy of dynastic politics was offset to some extent by the tendency of the dominant European powers to construct conservative diplomatic 'systems' (a Spanish 'system' until the 1680s, followed by a French one),[50] any settled pattern was constantly threatened by events in the large zones of instability: the rickety Habsburg Empire; the frontier lands of South East Europe; anarchic Poland and the Baltic; and (in the later seventeenth century) the turbulent British islands. But the crucial fact of the equilibrium age was that no power in Europe was strong enough to dominate the others completely, or to embark upon a career of overseas conquest safe from the challenge of its European rivals.

The costs of this endemic instability, and the cockpit mentality it bred, were high. Whatever stimulus war may have given technically and commercially was likely to have been outweighed by its destructive effects, the waste of scarce resources, and the accentuation of economic uncertainty – in pre-modern conditions, already a huge barrier to investment and enterprise.[51] European rivalries also worked to the advantage of extra-Europeans: the Native Americans of the trans-Appalachian interior; and most of all, perhaps, the Ottomans, who skilfully exploited European conflicts to protect their embattled imperial frontiers up until the 1760s. It was the urgent need to redeploy his army against Louis XIV that forced the Habsburg emperor to settle with the sultan in the Peace of Carlowitz in 1699. The technological and commercial expertise of the Occidentals was counterbalanced by the fact that their aggression and competitiveness were so largely turned in upon themselves.

These limits to European capacity and ambition are strikingly reflected in European thought and wider culture. A fundamental distinction was drawn by most contemporaries between Europe's relations with the Americas and those with Africa and Asia – the rest of the known world. America exerted a powerful fascination for the European imagination, even if one strand of scientific thought regarded this 'new' continent as a harsh and hostile environment in which human physique displayed strong degenerative tendencies.[52] What excited Europeans was the belief that they had both the right and the means to 'make' or remake America in Europe's image, or even as an improved version of the old continent. This intellectual imperialism derived in part from the ease with which European rule had been established, and the completeness of the native collapse. But it was also founded upon a set of social and cultural assumptions famously expressed by John Locke. It was the Amerindians' failure to develop a system of property that Europeans could recognize, so Locke argued, that justified the Europeans' colonial land grab.[53] But although Locke evidently regarded the Ottoman Empire as a hateful tyranny, and hoped for a revolt by the Christians it had conquered, he displayed no similar assurance that Europe had any title to the conquest and occupation of Africa and Asia – even if it had the means. In this, Locke, who was exceptionally widely read in the travel and geographical literature of his day,[54] was probably reflecting the respectful tone of the most influential contemporary writing on the Ottoman, Safavid, Mughal and Chinese empires. Rycaut, de Chavannes, Bernier and Du Halde described states and civilizations which Europeans might dislike or even despise; but they gave little warrant for thinking that European conquest was morally justified, let alone practically feasible. The Jesuits, who virtually monopolized sources of information about China, purveyed the image of a beneficent orderly regime presided over by scholar-administrators.[55] Eighteenth-century critics held up Safavid Iran and Ch'ing China as a mirror to expose European bigotry, militarism and misgovernment. In *The Spirit of the Laws* (1748), Montesquieu, who had earlier expressed fashionable reservations about American colonization in his *Lettres persanes* (1721) – 'empires were like the branches of a tree that sapped all the strength from the trunk'[56] – portrayed China as an efficient, powerful despotism where religion and the social order were far too closely integrated for any outside influence (including Christianity) to penetrate successfully.[57] Indeed, much of Montesquieu's argument embodied the influential view that topography and climate had a decisive impact on the social and political order – a doctrine that implicitly stressed the danger and artificiality of European intrusion into the non-European world. 'Those who are established there [America]', he thought, 'cannot conform to the manner of living in a climate so different from their own; they are obliged to draw from the mother-country all the conveniences of life.'[58] Others put it more simply. 'Villainy is inherent in this climate,' wrote a British naval officer in Jamaica in 1731.[59] Meanwhile, the optimistic belief of the early Renaissance in the possibility of a universal Christian culture had long since been replaced by an emphasis on the entrenched diversity of religions and civilizations.[60]

INLAND IMPERIALISM:
FROM MUSCOVY TO RUSSIA

Thus the main achievement of West Europeans in this period was the fuller development of their Euro-American maritime economy. But European expansion had two faces: towards the sea and towards the land. Between the 1620s and the 1740s, the most dynamic overland expansion by Europeans lay along the frontiers of Russia.

Russia's part in the overall history of European expansion has always been controversial. To Russian historians of the later nineteenth century, like Solov'ev or Kliuchevskii, the whole history of Russia was bound up with its colonizing endeavour and its heroic transformation into a great imperial state equal to the greatest powers of Central or Western Europe. To many West European observers, on the other hand, Russia often seemed a semi-barbaric 'Asiatic' state, where a thin veneer of 'Westernization' barely concealed the oriental roots of tsarist autocracy and completely failed to hide the backwardness of rural life.[61] In more recent times Russia has been assigned an ambiguous role in the project of European world domination. One influential account of the origins of the 'modern world system' argued that, in the course of the seventeenth and eighteenth centuries, Russia was transformed from an autonomous economic zone into part of the 'semi-periphery' of European capitalism: the collaborator, instrument and victim of the drive for domination by the European 'core', and eventually (after 1917) a rebel against it.[62] Calling Russia a 'semi-periphery power' usefully highlights its very partial economic and social transformation along Western lines, its persistent sense of difference, and the endemic struggle between 'Westernizers' and 'modernizers' in one camp and the 'Old Believers', Slavophiles and *narodniks* (populists) who at various times denounced Russia's subordination to an alien (Western) culture. But it is also deeply misleading. However partial its 'modernization', Russia was – perhaps after 1700, certainly after 1762 – always one of the five or six great powers of Europe who made up the quarrelsome management committee of the continent's affairs. It became, after Britain, the second greatest imperial power in Asia, and a colossal colonialist. Its official culture proclaimed a sense of the imperial civilizing mission that was just as strong as anything found in Britain or France – where there were also dissident movements that rejected the aggressive expansionist message of imperialist modernity. Above all, there can be no doubt that imperial Russia played a crucial role alongside the Western maritime states in securing the European domination of Eurasia in the nineteenth century: helping to encircle the Islamic realm, sapping the political fabric of the main Islamic states, and assisting in the demolition of the old China-centred world order in East Asia. As the terrestrial vanguard of European expansion in Asia, Russia's part in creating the 'modern world system' in place by 1900 was second to none.

There is a further reason to resist a view of world history that relegates Russia to a secondary role as part agent, part victim of a capitalist juggernaut masterminded in the capitals of the European 'core'. Europe – even 'political Europe', as opposed to the 'geographical Europe' that would have to include the Ottoman Balkans – cannot be reduced at any period to a hierarchy of capitalist 'top powers' and their dependent 'peripheries' and 'semi-peripheries'. Europe was almost always a loose-knit 'confederation' of culturally similar states in whose mutual relations economic strength was only one of several important variables. Religious affiliation, dynastic allegiance, ideology and ethnic cohesion interacted unpredictably with economic forces to ensure the survival of some political and cultural units and the amalgamation or disappearance of others. The result was a pattern of markedly differentiated states whose competition and conflicts were driven not simply by the urge to be the 'top power' or to dominate the 'core', but by the periodic (perhaps endemic) incompatibility of their dynastic, religious, strategic and territorial, as well as commercial, interests. This diversity repeatedly proved too deeply entrenched to be forced into continental homogeneity – even by the genius of Napoleon. Time and again it was a powerful check upon Europe's collective impact in the extra-European world. Ultimately, perhaps, the most persistent strand of intra-European conflict to affect the extra-European world was that between the great landward imperialist and its seaborne rivals. Thus Russia not only shaped European domination of Eurasia, but also subverted Europe's would-be world supremacy at crucial moments and in crucial ways.

Recognizing Europe's diversity means rejecting the argument that Russia was (as some Europeans and Russians have always believed) a separate, distinct and alien civilization – so that the 'real' Europe becomes northern Italy, France, western Germany, the Low Countries and Britain: a sort of proto-European Community. In reality, late medieval Russia had been, like late medieval Spain, an important cultural province of Christian Europe. Like Spain, sixteenth-century Russia embarked on a massive process of colonization. Like the Spanish monarchs, the rulers of Muscovy were eager to keep the spoils of conquest in their own hands for personal and dynastic advantage. There were crucial differences, however. Russia's religious distinctiveness and the intense antipathy with which the Russian Orthodox Church regarded the Catholic meant that the powerful channel of reciprocal influence linking Spain to the rest of Catholic Europe hardly functioned in Russia's case: not until the later seventeenth century were European Catholic ideas a major cultural force there.[63] Secondly, Russian colonization did not yield the glittering wealth that helped fund the ambitions of the Spanish Habsburgs. However, commercial seclusion did mean that Russia's colonial gains in Siberia and the lower Volga were not easily plundered or penetrated by the European maritime states. It also made it easier for the tsars to keep a tight grip on the mercantile and territorial profits of empire. Relative cultural and commercial isolation reinforced the individuality of Russia's expansionist path.

The scale of that expansion in the seventeenth and eighteenth centuries was dramatic. By one calculation, Russia's land surface increased from 2.1 million square miles in 1600 to some 5.9 million a century later.[64] Having established themselves beyond the Urals by 1600, Russian fur traders controlled the river routes and portages into the Yenisei basin by 1620 and reached the Lena in the following decade. In 1639 their advance guard reached the Sea of Okhotsk and the Pacific.[65] At the same time other traders reached the region beyond Lake Baikal ('discovered' in 1643) and the great Amur river in 1643. The Amur led down through Manchuria into the Yellow Sea, and the arrival of the Russians there coincided with the Manchu conquest of China. In forty years the Russians had thrown a skein of influence across North Asia. But it was hardly more than a fragile network of trade routes. Even in western Siberia, Russian occupation was confined to the northern forests: the steppes were still the preserve of the Kirghiz nomads. Needing food supplies from Russia and penned in their forts, the settler population expanded very slowly until the 1660s, when their strengthening military grip allowed the gradual colonization of the open plains. Even so, the male population of Russian Siberia amounted to no more than some 400,000 as late as 1760.[66] Further south it was a similar story: the slow occupation of the open steppe by Russian gentry and their serfs migrating east from old or exhausted lands. The foundation of Orenburg in 1725 marked a crucial stage in this process of armed colonization.[67] The old society of the steppe was slowly strangled as a series of defensive *limes*, fortified barriers constructed with enormous labour, blocked the routes of the nomads' trade and raiding. Even so, on the Russian side, poor communications and the shortage of manpower made rural settlement painfully slow. On Europe's Inner Asian frontier, demographic expansion long seemed as hobbled as it was in mainland North America until the 1750s.

For Peter the Great (1689–1725) and his tsar predecessors, the great strategic problem lay to the west and in the sparsely populated Ukraine ('Borderland') to the south. The great Polish–Lithuanian

Commonwealth had threatened to crush Muscovy in a bear hug during the Time of Troubles between 1598 and 1613. After 1613 the Romanov tsars faced both the territorial rivalry of Poland and the new threat posed by the copper kingdom of Sweden, which was now carving out a wide Baltic empire. In the same way as the Poles, the rise of Swedish power threatened to drive Muscovite Russia away from Europe, destroy its claim to 'reunite' the Russian peoples, and, in an opportunistic alliance with discontented Cossacks, uproot Moscow's influence in the Ukraine. Peter's great achievement was to smash this Swedish imperialism. He seized the rich Baltic Estland, an important granary and the defensive outwork for the new imperial capital at St Petersburg, to which his government was transferred in 1716. The Treaty of Nystad (1721) at the end of the Great Northern War signalled Russia's definite entry into the ranks of the European great powers and the elimination of Swedish and Polish rivalry as a serious threat. Peter himself abandoned the old name of 'Muscovy' and adopted instead the grander title of 'Russian Empire'. An address from his senate proclaimed that Russia 'had joined the community of political nations'.[68]

Victory in the Ukraine was especially crucial to Russia's eastward imperialism. After the Treaty of Pereslavl in 1654, the tsars had enjoyed a special relationship with the autonomous 'Hetmanate', the part of the Ukraine that lay beyond the frontier of Polish control in this semi-colonial region. In the Hetmanate an emergent landowning class, the *starshyna*, fearful of further Polish expansion and nervous of the turbulent Cossack frontier to the south, looked to Muscovite Russia as the most promising model of social order.[69] With the elite so divided, the efforts of Ukrainian leaders, like the charismatic Hetman Mazeppa, to maintain their autonomy by alliances with the Ottomans, Poles or Swedes were bound to be risky. Peter's crushing victory over Mazeppa and an injured Charles XII of Sweden at the Battle of Poltava in 1709 marked the effective absorption of the eastern Ukraine into his imperial system. It offered fresh land for the colonizing nobility and (in the Cossack population) a valuable reservoir of military manpower. As a stage in Russia's advance towards Eurasian empire, the acquisition of the Ukraine, opening the road to the Black Sea, might be likened to the British conquest of Bengal after 1757.

What lay behind the emergence of this imperial conglomerate, which had now created on Europe's eastern wing such a powerful engine of territorial expansion – a 'Turk of the North' as the philosopher Leibniz nervously put it? Russia's aggrandizement was driven by the fears and ambitions of the Romanov tsars, who skilfully exploited the dread of invasion and anarchy in the Orthodox Church and the service nobility. After 1650, tsardom strengthened its grip on both Church and aristocracy. It abolished the Orthodox patriarchate. A new standing army on the European model and Peter's 'Table of Ranks' (which formalized the link between noble status and military and bureaucratic rank) emphasized the power and the claims of the monarch. Territorial expansion and economic growth were successfully harnessed to the centralization of power. Noble obedience was assured, in part, by the prospect of land grants in the zones of conquest – the source of many aristocratic fortunes, and one reason for persistent Cossack discontent in the Russian Ukraine. Through the *gosti* or official merchants, the tsars also controlled and exploited profitable sectors of foreign and internal trade, including the salt trade,[70] while Peter also constructed state factories and arsenals to supply his armies. Finally, territorial acquisitions swelled the taxable resources of the empire, allowing Peter to triple his revenues, while adding the Estland and the Ukraine to Muscovite Russia almost doubled its productive capacity.[71] Like the Spanish *conquistas* in the New World, therefore, Russian expansion fed on itself, fuelled by the windfall gains of conquest.

Even so, this can only be part of the answer. Seventeenth-century Muscovite Russia was also responsive to cultural and intellectual influences from elsewhere in Europe. Peter's famous incognito tours of shipyards in Holland were anticipated in the eagerness of earlier tsars to adopt the bureaucratic and diplomatic methods of the grander European monarchies. Russia's rulers and churchmen drew on ideas of the magnificent and spiritual from the baroque art and architecture of Central Europe, and adapted them to local tradition.[72] Orthodox fears of Catholic influence also prompted new interest in Greek and Byzantine liturgy, and encouraged more sophisticated and regimented forms of worship. It was this 'Russian reformation' of the 1650s and '60s that provoked the schism with the Old Believers. The importance of these changes lay in the way that they endowed the emerging Russian (as opposed to old Muscovite) state with the cultural prestige, literary resources and ideological sophistication to hold the allegiance of the Germanic barons of the Estland, the half-Polonized aristocracy of the Ukraine and its own nobility. The alternative – a retreat into Old Russian traditions of primitive community and customary worship (hallmarks of the Old Believers) – was incompatible with territorial expansion, the absorption of other cultures, and the claim to great-power status in Europe, for all of which a powerful vested interest now existed.

Finally, like previous tsars, Peter the Great understood that the survival of his regime depended upon membership of the European states system and the diplomatic leverage it could be used to secure – like his useful alliance with Denmark against Sweden. To be driven out of 'political Europe' by Poland or Sweden would have been a catastrophe. Fear of this was behind his furious impatience to adopt the administrative, technical and even sartorial practices of Western Europe: to outperform his European neighbours in the struggle for geopolitical survival. Peter's 'symbolic reforms' were meant to drive home the terrible urgency of political change. After his European tour in 1698, he imposed a ban on beards and personally cut off those of his leading nobles. Russian traditional dress – a loose robe or kaftan – was also outlawed, and 'German dress' was imposed. Ladies at court were instructed to adopt the plunging décolletage that Peter had admired on his travels, although the older custom of painting women's teeth black seems to have survived rather longer than old-fashioned modesty in female attire. Even in death, Peter pointed the way. In Western style, he lay in his coffin in a crimson coat, wearing boots and spurs, his medals and his sword.

Peter had great talents as an organizer and strategist; but he also profited from the incoherence of Poland's political system, the exhaustion of Swedish resources by c.1700, and the reluctance of the Ottomans to intervene against him at crucial moments.[73] Indeed, the dynamic behind Russian expansion is not to be found in any single factor, but in the remarkable combination of favourable circumstances in the century after 1613: the consolidation of a social order whose savage discipline reflected the mentality of the 'armed camp';[74]

its receptiveness to cultural innovation from elsewhere in Europe; Russia's profitable role as an entrepôt between Europe and the Middle East;[75] its open land frontier, which helped fuel expansion and lubricate the rise of autocratic power; its pivotal role in 'steppe diplomacy'; and the geostrategic fortune that allowed the exclusion of its European rivals from the whole of Eurasia north of the Black Sea after 1710. Here was a model of European expansion to set beside that of the maritime West.

RENOVATION IN EAST ASIA

Viewed from the West, the most striking feature of East Asian history was the retreat into seclusion after the upheavals that had convulsed the first half of the seventeenth century. In both China and Japan, the installation of new political regimes led to the search for political and cultural consolidation at home and to the deliberate shrinking of diplomatic and commercial contacts abroad. At first sight, then, a sharp contrast appears between East Asia – drifting into cultural stasis and economic stagnation behind the political barrier of xenophobic diplomacy – and Europe with its cultural openness, vigorous overseas trade and competitive politics. It would be easy to conclude that the check imposed on European expansion by the long economic downswing after 1620 was only a 'loaded pause' that concealed the widening gap between a dynamic West and an unprogressive East, trapped in its conservatism and introversion.

Before reaching such a verdict, we need to look carefully at the consequences of the great renovation brought about by the Tokugawa shogunate and the Manchu (or Ch'ing) dynasty. Both created polities that lasted some 250 years. Both presided over a period of rapid population growth, extensive agricultural colonization, widening internal commerce and rising demand for books. We should react sceptically to grand generalizations about stasis and stagnation. Nor should we be too quick to assume that China's very limited participation in international trade after c.1690 signalled its incorporation into the subordinate 'periphery' of a European 'world system'.[76] Indeed, closer inspection may suggest that the reconstruction of East Asia after c.1620 played a crucial part in strengthening East Asian civilizations against the full impact of European expansion that was felt across much of the extra-European world after 1750.

The gradual collapse of the Ming dynasty in North China culminated in the seizure of the imperial capital by the Manchus in 1644 and, nominally, the beginning of a new dynastic era – that of the Ch'ing, as the Manchus styled themselves.[77] But the real founder of the Ch'ing empire was K'ang-hsi (b. 1654, r. 1661–1723), whose long reign had the same importance for consolidating Ch'ing rule as Akbar's had had for the Mughals in India. At K'ang-hsi's accession, the prospects for a stable imperial regime were poor. The Manchus as a ruling elite had not yet made the transition from the clan system characteristic of steppe nomad societies.[78] The idea of dynastic succession – vital for the continuity of imperial rule – was alien to them. Clan politics meant a continuous competition for power and influence, and a sharing (and resharing) of captured wealth and land among the dominant clans and their leaders. It was profoundly at odds with the Confucian system of empire consolidated in the Han era (206 BC–AD 220) and brought to its autocratic apogee under the Ming. Partly for this reason, large parts of South China, and large segments of the literati elite, remained unreconciled to Manchu authority. It had been this state of affairs, and their original dependence upon ethnic-Chinese allies to overcome Ming resistance, that had forced the Manchus to delegate wide powers to the Chinese generals responsible for subjugating the southern and south-western provinces. Indeed, by the 1670s three of these generals – the so-called 'Three Feudatories' – enjoyed practically complete autonomy from Peking, with the tempting prospect of establishing their own dynastic claim. To add to this catalogue of difficulties, the Manchus faced new threats to their authority in Inner Asia: from the Kalmyks; from the theocratic empire of the Dalai Lama in Tibet; and, in the region south and east of Lake Baikal, from tsarist officials and Russian fur traders. Meanwhile, on the maritime frontier overlooking the South China Sea, the breakdown of Ming rule and the opportunities created by seaborne trade had spawned the trading and privateering state of the freebooter Koxinga (Cheng Ch'eng-kung), securely based, as it seemed, on the impregnable island of Taiwan.[79]

The most immediate threat to the Manchus' survival was their lack of real control in South China. Anticipating K'ang-hsi's determination to crush them, the Feudatories rebelled openly in 1673–4. General Wu, the most powerful of the three, contemptuously offered the Manchu court a territorial partition that would have left it only Manchuria and Korea.[80] A more real possibility was the division of China along the Yangtze, denying North China and the imperial government its vital foodbowl, and reducing Peking to a rump state precariously balanced on the flank of Inner Asia. After a prolonged struggle, K'ang-hsi had gained the upper hand by the early 1680s, partly because Wu had died (of dysentery) in 1678[81] and partly, perhaps, because the feudatory generals held little appeal for Ming loyalists in the south and the scholar-gentry preferred imperial continuity, even under the Manchus, to warlord rule. By 1683, too, K'ang-hsi had finally liquidated Koxinga's rebel state, and the drastic policy of evacuating the coastal belt[82] (to deny the rebels its resources) that had been pursued for more than twenty years could now be reversed. Foreign trade, closely restricted for the same reason, was opened up once more.[83] In the later 1680s, with South China more or less pacified, K'ang-hsi was able to turn to Inner Asia.

No Manchu emperor was likely to underestimate the danger of a new steppe challenger repeating the Manchu gambit: building a frontier state based on the fusion of steppe and agricultural economies and strong enough to subvert the loyalty of the ethnic-Chinese population. In the 1670s the Kalmyk (or Oirat) ruler Galdan began to assemble a steppe empire of menacing size. From his original base in Dzungaria, lying west of Mongolia, he conquered the oases and trading cities of eastern Turkestan. In 1688 he invaded Outer Mongolia and threw down the gauntlet to Peking.[84] At the same time, the Russian presence along the northern edges of Mongolia and in Amuria (north of Manchuria) foreshadowed a profitable alliance between these interlopers in the Chinese realm. Perhaps K'ang-hsi was fortunate that this double Inner Asian challenge came too late to coincide with the struggle inside China proper. But no Chinese emperor could have been better prepared for the mental and physical stress of a frontier war. K'ang-hsi was a passionate hunter, and claimed to have killed over a hundred tigers, dozens of bears and leopards, and nearly a hundred wolves. He regarded the chase as practice for war, and his frequent expeditions to the frontier zone, in search of sport and to visit his troops, gave him first-hand knowledge of the theatre of conflict, and of the tactics and logistics needed for Chinese victory.[85]

Neither the Russians nor the Manchus had at first much idea of each other's strength or objectives. In the mid-1650s, Moscow had begun to grasp that the mysterious eastern potentate 'Prince Bogdoy' was more than just a minor ruler and must be treated with as much respect as the Ottoman, Iranian or Mughal emperor.[86] The Russians persisted in hoping that the Manchus would agree to diplomatic relations and the opening of trade. There was already a growing Russian commerce with Central Asia and India through Astrakhan at the mouth of the Volga. Embassies had been exchanged regularly with the Kalmyks and Mongols since the 1630s. K'ang-hsi was willing to sidestep the rigid protocol governing Chinese diplomatic relations and meet the tsar's envoys informally; but he was also determined to expel Russian influence from East Asia. In 1684 he warned the Mongols to cease trading with the Russians. In 1685 his army razed Albazin, the most advanced Russian outpost in the Amur valley. The Russians returned, and Galdan's conquest of Outer Mongolia in 1688 threatened Peking with a long, exhausting frontier war. But the Russo-Kalmyk alliance failed to materialize, and in 1689 at Nerchinsk in south-eastern Siberia K'ang-hsi surrounded the Russian negotiators with a large army and forced them to renounce the whole vast area north of Manchuria – a defeat for Russian expansion that was not reversed until 1860. In 1690, Manchu armies used artillery to defeat Galdan in battle.[87] Six years later, after a further shattering defeat, Galdan committed suicide. The final consolidation of Chinese overrule in Inner Asia, with the conquest of Sinkiang or East Turkestan, was not completed for some sixty years. But K'ang-hsi had restored Peking's authority in mainland East Asia. This great triumph, followed up by the Yung-cheng (r. 1723–35) and Ch'ien-lung (r. 1735–96) emperors, was the vital geopolitical precondition for the domestic achievements of Ch'ing rule and, in the longer term, for its tenacious resistance to European diplomatic and commercial demands in the nineteenth century.

Indeed, this grand strategic victory opened the way for an exceptionally dynamic period in Chinese history. The Yung-cheng emperor
completed the transition from the clannish regime the Manchus had
brought with them to a revived and strengthened version of Ming
absolutism. The Manchu 'bannermen' – the private princely armies

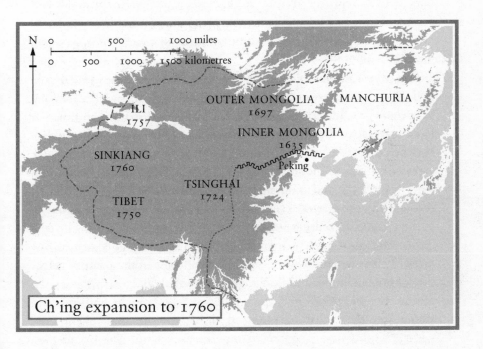

Ch'ing expansion to 1760

that had played a key role in the seizure of power – were brought
under imperial control or pensioned off.[88] This averted the threat of
factional warfare at times of dynastic succession. A new and more flexible Grand Council supplanted the Grand Secretariat and the censorate
as the centre of decision-making.[89] A third innovation, the 'palace mem-
orial' system, encouraged a stream of confidential information about
the misdeeds of provincial authorities. Careful renovation of the examination system was part of K'ang-hsi's reconciliation with the
Chinese literati. It was the crucial bond between the imperial centre,
the scholar-gentry of the provinces, and the county magistrate (*hsien-
chih*) whose *yamen* (or office) was the eyes and ears of the imperial

government. So long as the scholar-gentry aspired to bureaucratic advancement through the examination system, with its classical syllabus and Confucian ideology, and while China was governed from walled cities with an ultra-loyal Manchu army in reserve, rebellion was unlikely to spread far or last long. The early emperors also insisted upon frugal expenditure to ease the weight of taxation. With large tax surpluses, and having beaten, cowed or reconciled their enemies, the Ch'ing emperors had found the formula for external security and internal peace.

This was a favourable setting for economic progress and cultural revival. By some estimates, China's population increased threefold between 1723 and 1796 under K'ang-hsi's successors. There was a large increase in the area under cultivation, which may have doubled between 1650 and 1800.[90] Ethnic Chinese (Han) settlers colonized forested regions in the south and south-west. The state repaired damaged waterways and built new ones.[91] New food crops like maize (brought by the Portuguese) and sweet potatoes (brought to Fukien in the eighteenth century) supplemented rice; and cash crops like tea, indigo and sugar were grown for export, especially in coastal provinces like Fukien and Kwangtung. State officials in the frontier province of Hunan on the middle Yangtze promoted double-cropping with advice, tax incentives and the supply of seed.[92] Eighteenth-century China saw the end of serfdom, abolished by the Yung-cheng emperor,[93] and a new freedom to buy and sell land. The number of market towns rose steadily. In the Kiangnan region on the lower Yangtze, where water communications had favoured the growth of large commercial cities, cotton cloth was manufactured on a large scale by village-based artisans. Shanghai exported textiles to inland regions up to 800 miles away, and iron goods, silk and porcelain were widely traded.[94] This was a sophisticated mercantile economy in which paper money was supplied by private enterprise and credit was based on the sale of contracts for the future supply of salt to the government – a commodity for which demand was exceptionally stable. China's part in international commerce may have been relatively small, but its internal trade may have been as large, if not larger, than that of contemporary Europe.[95]

But perhaps the most striking feature of Ch'ing rule was that it promoted an exceptionally vigorous phase of cultural renewal. K'ang-hsi himself liked to converse with the Jesuits at court (their mission had survived the dynastic upheaval). He even learned how to play the harpsichord. But he rejected the idea of a regular traffic between China and Europe. 'China has no matters of common concern with the West' was his crisp conclusion.[96] Westerners, like the Jesuits, were welcome to come. But they had to stay and adapt themselves to Confucian ethics: they could not expect to come and go as they pleased. And when the Pope sent a message asking him to send back Europeans suspected by Rome of heresy, K'ang-hsi refused – adding sarcastically that he would cut off their heads and send them instead, so that the Pope could see that they had been 'reformed'.[97] The Pope's response is not known. K'ang-hsi's main concern was with Chinese culture. He and his successors sponsored the collection and publication of classical literature; K'ang-hsi himself commissioned an encyclopedia. Literacy levels rose, and the volume of printed literature increased to meet the demand.[98] Novels, poetry, histories, biographies, gazetteers, encyclo-pedias, anthologies and works of antiquarianism were published. This was a gentry culture that propagated the values and traditions of the Confucian classics: the search for harmony within society and with nature; the importance of hierarchy (especially between generations) and ritual or codes of behaviour for preserving social order and cohesion; the need for self-control and the subordination of personal desires. Through literature and art, and the state's provision of official 'cults' and sacrifices as a focus for local popular religion, the influence of Confucian culture was diffused more widely and deeply than ever before.[99] China's political and economic integration was thus matched by a growing cultural unity achieved in the last era before the more intense and then violent engagement with the West.

But there were limits to the Ch'ing achievement. Much of China beyond its great system of waterways remained locked in localism – though no more so, perhaps, than large parts of contemporary Europe. More serious was China's notorious failure to revive the naval power renounced some three centuries earlier. Chinese merchants and settlers in South East Asia had no claim on imperial protection, and savage massacres of Chinese in the Spanish Philippines drew no response from Peking.[100] European fascination with China – however ignorant and ill-informed – had no counterpart in Chinese intellectual circles, a measure perhaps of cultural self-confidence and the prestige of an unbroken classical tradition of exceptional range and subtlety. In some respects eighteenth-century China was turning even more markedly inward: the Yung-cheng emperor reversed in 1727 the limited toler-ance granted to Christian missionaries since Mongol times.[101] Even when European ideas were imported, they appeared unworkable or irrelevant in the Chinese context.[102] A good example is the idea of perspective in painting. Chinese artistic theory did not 'fail' to invent perspective: it rejected as invalid a single fixed perspective, stressing instead the multiplicity of viewpoints from which an object or land-scape might be viewed.[103] But perhaps a deeper problem (from the point of view of technological and scientific change) was the under-lying conservatism of Ch'ing society, which vested enormous social power in its bureaucracy and in corporate bodies like guilds and lineage or clan authorities, who played a key role in maintaining a hierarchic social discipline. Ch'ing rule may have added an extra twist to what were, no doubt, entrenched social tendencies. After all, for all its championing of Confucian culture, this was at bottom a 'Manchu *raj*' – imperial rule by an alien dynasty and its racial hench-men, who were segregated by residence and marriage laws from the Han majority. Like other colonial regimes in world history, the Manchus found that the price of stability was alliance with those who enjoyed local dominance, and the careful avoidance of social or political risk. Thus the *timing* of Manchu consolidation between 1680 and 1750 was highly significant. On the eve of the close encounter with the West, China's distinctive political trajectory (still dominated by its symbiotic relationship with Inner Asia) propelled it not towards an all-powerful oriental despotism (imagined by Europeans) – which might have permitted drastic change in the face of external challenge – but instead still further towards a 'limited *raj*' in which central government abandoned almost all initiative to local (and usually conservative) forces. When China's eighteenth-century 'economic miracle' turned sour, the scope for political change was correspondingly narrow.[104]

Like China, Japan experienced a remarkable period of political con-solidation and economic growth in the seventeenth and early eighteenth century. The shogunate, or regency, was made hereditary in the Tokugawa clan. The imperial court, reduced to symbolic importance, remained in the old capital at Kyoto, where the shoguns also maintained a splendid palace for their periodic visits. The key to political stability was the supremacy that the Tokugawa exerted over the clans and clan domains into which Japan was divided, and over the *daimyo*, or nobles, who ruled them. Military dominance was supplemented by the notorious system of *sankin kotai*, which required the *daimyo* to leave their wives and children at the shogunal capital at Edo and to reside there themselves in alternate years. While in Edo, *daimyo* were obliged to attend the shogun's court twice a month, and to perform administrative duties in and around the city. At the same time the hereditary warrior class, the samurai, were gathered in domain castle towns, like Himeji or Nagoya, or attended Edo as retainers of the resident *daimyo*. By degrees, they were transformed into a gentry service class, dependent on their clan stipends and increasingly attracted to the gentlemanly ideals propounded by Confucianism, whose vision of the social order was a useful buttress to their novel status.

Internal peace was accompanied by rapid growth in the population, which increased from 12 million in 1600 to some 31 million by 1721 – a figure half as large again as that of France, Western Europe's demographic giant.[105] There was considerable urbanization, and Edo (*c.*1 million), Kyoto (350,000) and Osaka (360,000) were all major cities by world standards. In 1700 Edo was twice the size of London.[106] The area under cultivation doubled between 1600 and 1720.[107] There was a large and sophisticated base of artisan production in textiles, metalwork, ceramics and publishing.[108] Regional economic specialization increased, promoting internal trade. Large commercial entrepreneurs managed this internal trade, which centred on Osaka. This was the 'kitchen of Japan', with its great rice market, fertile hinterland and proximity to Kyoto – still the cultural capital and a focus of manufacture especially in silk. By contrast with Western Europe, early modern Japan was still a 'wooden world', perhaps because in an earthquake zone this allowed cheap and rapid rebuilding. Its cities were vast agglomerations of low-rise wooden structures. But visiting Europeans were in no doubt that Japan was an advanced and wealthy civilization, and they were eager to trade with it.[109]

As we have seen, Japan had played a dynamic role in the expansion of East and South East Asian trade between *c.*1540 and *c.*1640, which coincided with the arrival of Europeans in the region. Japanese traders and buccaneers (*wako*) exploited the new commercial opportunities of a triangular trade between Japan, China and South East Asia, while Japan's huge silver boom helped fuel the commercial expansion and pay for foreign imports.[110] By some estimates, Japan was producing one-third of the world's silver by 1600[111] – one reason why Europeans were so eager to trade there. Japan's south-western ports, especially Nagasaki, grew rapidly, sprouting 'Chinatowns' where Chinese artisans and businessmen settled[112] – some 200 in Nagasaki alone by 1618.[113] Famously, however, the attitude of the *bakufu* (the Tokugawa government in Edo) towards this expanding foreign trade was deeply ambivalent. The regime was new, and its control over distant clan domains was likely to be compromised by unregulated external contacts. Catholicism, in particular, became identified with rebellion and subversion, and was vigorously persecuted. In the 1630s and '40s Chinese and Dutch trade (the Dutch were the only Europeans permitted) was restricted to Nagasaki and the artificial island of Deshima built in its harbour. The prolonged turmoil in China and the closure of its ports to legitimate trade after 1661 helped stifle East Asia's foreign trade. But when it revived, after 1685, the *bakufu* became increasingly alarmed by the outflow of Japanese silver and banned its export in 1688. The control system at Nagasaki was reinforced after 1698 to monitor the flow of commerce and intelligence even more closely.[114]

Japanese 'seclusion' was motivated in part by the 'bullionist' fears familiar enough to European governments, and in part by unease over relations with China, the regional superpower, whose East Asian 'world system' was a denial of Japan's independence. Isolationism was the solution by default of the problem of Sino-Japanese relations, and may have been calculated to dissuade the Ch'ing rulers from an invasion of the kind only narrowly defeated four centuries earlier. But seclusion was not complete. Chinese ideas and culture exerted a powerful attraction, and were deliberately fostered by the Tokugawa regime. China was the great model of a settled, stable, imperial state. Chinese literature and art set the tone in polite society: mastery of the Chinese language and the Chinese style of painting were highly prized.[115] Great efforts were made to adapt Confucian teaching to Japanese conditions. Thus Nagasaki was not so much a closed door as a narrow gateway and a listening post where the *bakufu* collected information from visiting ships (whose captains were required to write 'news reports' for transmission to Edo) and through which it imported books. 'Dutch knowledge' percolated slowly among the samurai, teachers and savants.

The regime of political seclusion did not mean economic stagnation. Japanese economic growth after 1600 was driven by a remarkable double revolution. Firstly, the political system created a large new urban economy as *daimyo* and samurai settled in castle towns. The most spectacular case was Edo itself. The *sankin kotai* rules brought to Edo hundreds of *daimyo* and their families and vast retinues of samurai.[116] By 1700 half of Edo's 1 million people were samurai retainers living in the great clan compounds that made up nearly three-quarters of the city area. Together the *daimyo* and the samurai formed a huge concentration of elite consumption for the services and manufactures of the urban merchants, artisans and day-labourers. Their purchasing power came from their domain revenues, sometimes rendered in kind and kept at the great storehouses along the Edo waterside, and sometimes remitted in cash once the rice tithe had been sold in the Osaka market, from where much of Edo's food came. This system was a powerful stimulus to internal trade and banking, and promoted a large integrated economy producing foodstuffs and manufactures for a central market. In turn, the demand of elite urban consumers for the revenues they needed was a spur to productivity in the rural domains. And the counterpart to *daimyo* residence in Edo was their regular journeying to and from their provincial homes. *Daimyo* processions, sometimes up to 2,000 strong, encouraged the growth of inns and a regular network of routes by land and sea.

Secondly, this pattern of elite consumption was not dependent (as it became in Europe) upon foreign trade. The Japanese were able to practise a policy of mercantilist self-sufficiency with remarkable success once foreign trade had become less rewarding. Unlike England, for example, the Japanese had their own supply of silver, and had no need of trade to obtain the basis of their currency – the problem that obsessed economists in early modern Europe. The Japanese also responded in a highly original way to the domestic demand for luxuries and new foodstuffs. Korean ceramics had long enjoyed prestige in Japan. After Hideyoshi's invasion in the 1590s, Korean artisans were brought to Japan and a native industry was established. Japan's wide range of climatic conditions allowed the indigenization of new cash crops: cotton, silk, tobacco and sugar. Silk and cotton were manufactured in Kyoto and Osaka, and self-sufficiency was achieved in sugar. Fishing too became of much greater importance in the seventeenth century. In all these ways the Japanese successfully exploited an exceptionally rich and diverse natural environment and developed a wealthy mercantile economy comparable with Europe's but without the costs and risks of colonialism. Even after 1720, when economic growth was checked by resource depletion and the lack of new land, and population ceased to grow, an 'industrious revolution' of more intensive agriculture, promoted in part by the state (through experimental farms and the import of Chinese botany), helped to preserve the economic achievements of the previous century and safeguard the political and social unification that the Tokugawa shogunate had engineered.[117]

The economic dynamism of early modern Japan and its subsequent turn towards 'mercantilist isolation' were both in large measure a consequence of Japan's position in the East Asian world order. The recovery of Chinese power and the reinvigoration of China's old diplomatic tradition offered little scope for Japanese influence on the continental mainland, which was, anyway, comparatively remote (by European standards). Fear of a dominant continental civilization was coupled with strong attraction to its cultural products and social values: it was a difficult relationship to manage successfully. Once Japan began to run short of silver and the domestication of foreign produce became practicable, there was good reason to look for economic and social stability in an insular commercial policy rather than run the extreme risks of oceanic expansion. Ironically, the Japanese imposed restraints on the import of foreign textiles at the same time as the British, but with much more success. The real threat to Japanese stability and independence lay less in the penetration of foreign ideas or technology – both of which could be gradually assimilated and nativized – than in some environmental or external shock. Famine, which, after a century, had returned in the 1720s, might wreck the economic system or enforce drastic change. Equally, renewed instability in the East Asian world order, which had sucked in outsiders in the sixteenth century, might upset the carefully guarded integrity of the Japanese world. But of this ominous prospect there was in the 1750s little sign. On the contrary, with the Ch'ing conquest of the further reaches of Inner Asia in 1759–60, the advantages that Japan reaped from its exceptional geostrategic location seemed greater than ever.

THE ISLAMIC EMPIRES UNDER STRAIN

In the later early modern period (1620s–1740s) the Islamic world was far more exposed to influence and competition from Europe than were the states and civilizations of East Asia. At innumerable points between South East Asia and the Atlantic coast of Africa, European soldiers, sailors, traders, missionaries and diplomats confronted their Muslim counterparts, since both the Islamic realm and Europe had expanded with the growth of long-distance trade between the fifteenth century and the seventeenth. As we saw in the previous chapter, the period celebrated in European history as the 'Age of Discovery' had also seen the consolidation of the three great Muslim empires: the Ottoman, Safavid and Mughal. It saw a rapid and powerful wave of Islamization in South East Asia after 1500, with the strengthening of that region's commercial ties with India and the Middle East and the attractiveness of Islam as the religion of trading states and more extended forms of kingship.[118] In West Africa, another vast sphere of Islamic influence since the eleventh century, the rise of the Songhay empire in the middle Niger after 1468, the reinforcement of Islam further east in the Hausa states like Katsina and Kano[119] and the consolidation of Bornu under Mai Idris Alawma (r. *c.*1571–*c.*1603)[120] asserted the continuing dynamism of religious, cultural and political ideas flowing south and west from the Islamic heartlands.

By contrast, the later early modern period (after *c.*1620) is often portrayed as an era of stagnation and impending decline in the Islamic empires and Islamic culture, whose introversion and conservatism are compared unfavourably with the innovative currents in European thought.[121] It is easy to race to the glib conclusion that European societies had adopted the scientific mentality needed for material progress, leaving their Muslim neighbours stuck in the religious mud. In fact the importance of the scientist, as opposed to the humble craftsman, in Europe's technological and commercial life was marginal, at best, before the later eighteenth century.[122] Nevertheless, there were some signs in the seventeenth and earlier eighteenth century that the great Islamic states and the Islamic culture they supported had lost the dynamism of the previous phase. Commercial depression and the Dutch conquest of the main Islamic states in South East Asia (Makassar, Banten and Mataram) after 1660 were major setbacks. In the West African Sahel the fall of Songhay in 1591 (ironically, at the hands of Moroccan invaders) inaugurated a long period of political disintegration in the middle Niger unfavourable to the deepening of Islamic influences.[123] And each of the three great Muslim empires experienced powerful centrifugal tendencies whose effect was to weaken its internal solidarity against external attack. But, for all that, there was little sign before the mid eighteenth century that these changes amounted to an irreversible shift in the relative strength of Islamic and European societies, rather than a more subtle adjustment in the global equilibrium.

At first sight, the history of the Ottoman Empire offers ample proof that Islamic states and culture were condemned to inexorable retreat and progressive decline. Between 1683 (when they failed dramatically to capture Vienna) and 1739 the Ottomans suffered major losses of territory, throwing into reverse the expansionist drive that had carried them into the heart of Europe in the sixteenth century. At the Peace of Carlowitz in 1699, after sixteen years of war, the sultan was forced to surrender Hungary and Transylvania to the Habsburg emperor. Renewed conflict between the two empires between 1716 and 1718 cost the Ottomans dearly at the Peace of Passarowitz in 1718. Western Wallachia, the Banat (or 'border region') of Temesvar (modern Timişoara in Romania) and Serbia were handed over to Vienna, together with the great frontier fortress of Belgrade, commanding the approaches to the lower Danube valley. The military elan and superior fighting technique that had carried the janissaries to so many victories in the previous century seemed much less effective against Habsburg armies trained in new methods of drill and led by generals like Montecuccoli or Prince Eugene of Savoy. Worse still, perhaps, from the Ottomans' point of view, after 1700 they faced not one enemy but two in the Balkans–Black Sea region. Faced with the threat of both Habsburg and Romanov expansion, the Ottomans lost their privileged status as an early modern 'superpower' in South East Europe, enjoying splendid isolation from the web of intra-European diplomacy. By 1740 the price of Ottoman survival was much fuller participation in the European states system, with all the costs, risks and compromises that this was bound to entail.[124]

Failure on the battlefield and in the conference chamber can be seen as the symptom of less visible failings in the political and economic life of the defeated state. Not surprisingly, perhaps, Ottoman political 'decline' after 1600 has been subjected to a keen historical scrutiny. Weaknesses of leadership, policy and institutions have been freely attributed to a variety of causes: the unhealthy seclusion of the sultans and their heirs in the harem and the growth of a secretive and intrigue-ridden court politics; the abandonment of the *devshirme*, which had staffed the sultans' government and armies with loyal slave dependants immune to local influence; the takeover of both the janissary corps and the bureaucracy by Muslim notables hostile to the sultans' authority and much more concerned with the profits of patronage; and the growing decentralization of revenue collection and provincial government that conceded more and more control to local notables (*ayan*) and tax-farmers. As central authority decayed, so runs the argument, local disorder and insecurity increased: *deys* (provincial viceroys), Mamluks and rebellious *derebeys* ('lords of the valleys') built up their armed retinues and battled for the spoils of provincial power.

Political incoherence was compounded (to continue this theme) by a deepening sense of economic languor. While the transit trade remained important to Ottoman cities on or near the Mediterranean, seaborne trade passed almost completely into the hands of European merchants. Increasingly the Ottoman economy became geared to producing raw materials and commodities for the European market, especially cotton. The trend towards relying upon European manufactures (like textiles) grew stronger and stronger. Craft industries declined. To make matters worse, the Ottoman government conceded trading privileges to European merchants which exempted them from taxes and tariffs and were widely abused. Instead of pursuing a 'mercantilist' policy of protecting their own producers and merchants, the Ottomans seemed, perversely, to favour foreign interests.[125] The result was to expose the empire to deeper and deeper economic penetration by European merchants, to erode craft industries and the urban communities they supported, and to Balkanize the empire as an economic unit.

Predictably, these classic symptoms of 'peripheralization' have been seen as part of a pervasive cultural malaise. Intellectual failure closed the vicious circle of political failure and economic decline. Gripped by an intense scriptural conservatism, accentuated by the growing political dominance of the Muslim educated class, intellectual life showed little interest in empirical inquiry or the systematic adaptation of foreign ideas. The level of curiosity about Europe remained modest – a relic, it has been argued, of the low cultural esteem in which Europe had been held in the Ottoman age of expansion and of the linguistic difficulty that Europe's polyglot culture imposed on Ottoman scholars.[126] Official ignorance of European geography was dire: as late as the 1770s, the Ottoman government imagined that the Russian fleet had reached the Mediterranean via a waterway in Central Europe.[127] Without the means or the will to adapt education to a new syllabus, empirical in spirit and technological in bias, the Islamic culture of the Ottomans had become a regressive backwater of illusions.

All this amounts to a formidable indictment of Ottoman failure. But it rests upon two dubious assumptions. The first is the contrast implied between the 'backwardness' of Ottoman life and the order and progress of Europe's. But Europe was not a uniform landscape of smiling fields and bustling towns. In the east and south it was a region of serfdom, periodic famine and the savage repression of rural discontent. Travel in the interior of Spain, southern Italy or the Scottish Highlands was always difficult and was often dangerous. Rural banditry was rife, especially in regions affected by the wars of the seventeenth century. Even in Western Europe, a provincial economy within a hundred miles of Paris was a precarious balance between subsistence and dearth, with its agricultural technique hardly changed at all since medieval times.[128] The religious intolerance of French and English governments (to take two Western European examples) contrasted strikingly with Ottoman attitudes. Secondly, as Ottoman historians have pointed out recently, much of the argument of Ottoman decline assumes that in its age of expansion the empire had enjoyed a regime of centralized efficiency ruined by the misgovernment of later years.[129]

Even when judged by the acid test of war, it is far from clear that by 1740 the Ottoman Empire could be written off as a case of terminal decline. The Ottomans had lost Hungary and Transylvania. But at the Treaty of Belgrade in 1739 they recovered what they had lost at Passarowitz in 1718, including Belgrade itself. Ottoman armies showed remarkable powers of recuperation, as Montecuccoli – the wisest of Habsburg generals – had warned. In 1711 they inflicted a stunning humiliation on the Russian armies led by Peter the Great in the Pruth campaign on the (modern) Romanian border. Facing a well-supplied Ottoman force, with much more artillery and a huge cavalry corps, the Russian invaders (inferior in number and badly in need of fodder and food) lost their nerve completely. They surrendered Azov, and Peter abruptly withdrew from the war.[130] The sultan's government in Constantinople (often called the 'Porte', after the great gate where the ministers had their offices) continued to preside over a vast tri-continental empire whose European 'front' was only one of its geostrategic burdens. But the largely successful defence of its territorial integrity suggests that Ottoman society was more flexible, resilient and cohesive than 'declinist' histories would have us believe.

That resilience rested in part upon a strong geopolitical position, much of which lasted into the 1760s. With the loss of Hungary and Transylvania, the Ottomans fell back upon the physical barrier of the Carpathian Mountains. Recovering Belgrade (in 1739) restored their control over the strategic funnel between Habsburg Europe and the Ottoman Balkans. Because they controlled the Black Sea as a maritime highway, the Ottomans and their clients, the Crimean Girays, could frustrate the Russian advance towards the Black Sea – despite the tsars' furious efforts to capture Perekop and Azov. The logistical nightmare of supplying an army marching across the Ukranian steppe meant that the Black Sea remained a *mare Ottomanicum* – an invaluable asset. Taken together, the fortress at Belgrade, the Carpathian wall and the interior lines that the Black Sea provided secured the Ottoman *limes* against the West. It was further entrenched by strong cultural defences. Apart from the Muslim communities to be found in the Balkans, the Ottomans could also rely on the loyalty of Greek Orthodox churchmen, who had little to gain from the triumph of Catholic Austria. On the most remote and vulnerable maritime frontier of the empire, in North Africa, fear and loathing of Catholic Spain, and economic dependence on piracy, shored up the loyalty of the Maghrib provinces to the distant capital.[131]

It was geostrategic security that really permitted the decentralization of government after 1600. The larger role played by urban notables in provincial rule and in revenue collection (as official tax-farmers) now appears less like the empire's collapse into widespread kleptocracy than as the timely recognition of newer provincial elites whose cooperation was needed to maintain social order and collect the taxes.[132] In the Arab provinces and Egypt, a similar pattern of devolution conveyed much local power to hereditary janissary garrisons and to the Mamluks in Cairo.[133] Greek 'Phanariots', drawn from the wealthy Christian elite of Constantinople, governed the Romanian territories. In the Maghrib, local dynasties with wide autonomy established themselves in Morocco, Algiers, Tunis and Tripoli. But until after 1750 there was little evidence that the imperial centre at Constantinople had lost control over these local interests, whose authority and legitimacy still depended upon their loyalty to the Ottoman system. The prime task of the Ottoman government was to maintain the prestige of the *daulat* (the sultan's authority) by resisting foreign intervention and avoiding military defeat.

Nor was the economic scene one of unrelieved gloom. Craft industries decayed under European competition, but Constantinople, Izmir and Cairo remained great commercial cities – in Cairo's case as a result of the huge new trade in coffee from Yemen.[134] The production of commodities like cotton, wool and tobacco brought a new prosperity to some regions at least, reflected in a great burst of new building.[135] The internal trade that supplied most consumer demand remained in local hands.[136] It was clear by 1740 that the Ottoman Empire could not match the most prosperous parts of Europe in artisan production or agrarian improvement. It also lacked the means to transform itself into a nation state or a national economy along the classic lines of European mercantilism. Nevertheless, by accident or design, Ottoman governments had devised a surprisingly successful formula for imperial survival in the more difficult conditions that they faced from the mid seventeenth century. After 1739, their strategic defences against the West looked more secure than they had for several decades. They had learned to play the European diplomatic game, exploiting French antipathy towards the Habsburgs to help regain Belgrade. The reform policies of the 'Tulip Period' may have ended in acrimony, but Ottoman rulers could still buy the military expertise and technology that they needed 'off the shelf' in Europe, without risking the cultural and social upheaval that a more ambitious programme of change might bring. Nor were the commercial privileges that they granted foreign merchants under the 'Capitulations' system a purely one-way bargain. They encouraged foreign trade while segregating foreign merchants and reducing the West's gravitational pull upon Muslim society. With their sovereignty unimpaired, with their unchallenged status as guardians of the holy places (in Mecca, Medina and Jerusalem), and as the overlord of Cairo, the cultural and intellectual capital of Islam, the Ottomans had been able to keep the delicate balance between the different elements of their extraordinary system: a multi-ethnic empire perched on the flank of Europe, and the political embodiment of orthodox Islam in its Near Eastern heartlands.

In the middle of the seventeenth century, the wealthiest and most dynamic part of the Islamic realm lay under Mughal rule. The core of the Mughals' empire was the 'fertile crescent' of North India: the Indo-Gangetic plains that stretched from the far north-west to Bengal and the Ganges delta. Its strategic centre was the Delhi 'triangle', which commanded the passage between the two great river systems and the 100-mile-wide 'corridor' between the Himalayan foothills and the uplands of the Deccan. It was to Delhi, and the purpose-built palace-city of Shahjahanabad, that the Mughals moved their capital from Agra in 1648,[137] a feat that reflected the colossal wealth on which the rulers of this plains empire could draw. By the 1650s this new imperial metropolis, with its countless aristocratic households clustered round the imperial court, was as large as Paris.

The rise of Mughal power had been a key factor in early modern world history. Mughal rule had unified and pacified northern India. It promoted India's overland trade into Central Asia and beyond. The Mughal conquest of Bengal had quickened the agrarian colonization of its jungle and marsh[138] and its trade in textiles up the Ganges to the inland plains of Hindustan.[139] Trade with 'Mogor', as the Portuguese called the sphere of Mughal rule, drew European merchants to the great port city of Surat in western India, from where the trade routes led north and east to Delhi and Agra. The skill with which Akbar had fused Muslim warrior nobles from Central Asia, Muslim scribes and clerks from Iran (still the cultural magnet of the Islamic world), Hindu Rajput warlords and Brahmin literati into a stable political system favoured the empire's economic expansion. As local 'dynasties' of land-holders consolidated their control, and tapped agricultural wealth, they increased the consumption of manufactures and luxury goods and encouraged the building of towns and *ganjs* or markets. With its large population (the Indian subcontinent was at least as populous as contemporary Europe), rich farmlands and accessible raw materials, India became the world's greatest centre of textile production, exporting cotton cloth to the Middle East and West Africa as well as to Europe. The range and quality of Indian cottons and their relative cheapness (by one contemporary estimate, Indian labour costs were one-seventh of Europe's)[140] conferred an enormous advantage in European markets. By the later 1600s the English East India Company had long since given up its old obsession with buying eastern spices to concentrate on the import and resale of Indian textiles[141] – increasingly from Bengal, which was becoming the main centre of its operations and the most dynamic of Indian regions.

In these ways, Indian merchants and artisans played a large role in the growth of international trade that was an important feature of the early modern centuries. Though detailed records are lacking – except for those kept by the Portuguese, Dutch and English companies – it seems likely that the bulk of India's maritime trade with the Middle

East – its most important market – was in the hands of Indian merchants and shipowners.[142] Without the dynamic response of Indian producers, the thickening strands of seaborne trade along which Europeans moved so profitably would have remained tenuous and fragile.[143] Politically and culturally, the result of this vigorous participation in the expanding networks of international trade was the subcontinent's receptiveness to foreign influence. This was true of the coastal regions of South India where Mughal authority was only partial or never fully asserted. But it was also the case in North India, where Mughal power was concentrated. In the seventeenth century, Europeans could be found in all the large cities of the empire as merchants, physicians and artisans.[144] European artillerymen served in Mughal armies. Jesuit missionaries were licensed to preach and convert – though their efforts seem to have been chiefly directed towards the wandering Europeans[145] and their few converts were drawn from the poor or outcaste. Mughal taste, especially in literature, still prized Persian models above all else. But the religious imagery and portraiture introduced by the Jesuits had a striking influence upon Mughal art.[146]

India's openness to commerce and culture from Iran and Central Asia, and to seaborne influence along its vast peninsular coastline, when combined with the rugged impenetrability of the Deccan, may be the key to the failure of any single ruling power – even one as skilful and sophisticated as the Mughals – to unify South Asia and impose the cultural and administrative uniformity achieved by the Ming in China. Muslim elites dominated the main states in the south after the fall of Hindu Vijayanagar in 1565. But the struggle to subordinate the Hindu gentry of the Deccan and to impose the Mughal system of land grants in exchange for administrative and military service provoked a gathering revolt centred on the Maratha region around Satara and Poona. It was led by Sivaji, a Hindu soldier of fortune – a man of 'meane stature . . . of an excellent proportion . . . distrustful, seacret, subtile, cruel, perfidious' in the judgement of an English observer, the Revd John L'Escaliot.[147] In 1674 the English East India Company sent an embassy from Bombay (modern Mumbai) to attend Sivaji's coronation at his castle at Rairy, where he was weighed in gold in the tradition of Hindu kings.[148] Indeed, by the

1670s Mughal alarm at Sivaji's revolt was enough for the emperor Aurangzeb to abandon the court city at Shahjahanabad and spend the rest of his long reign (1658–1707) in endless peripatetic campaigns to bring the Marathas to heel. Aurangzeb achieved a short-lived victory in 1690 (Sivaji had died in 1680). But by the time of his death, in 1707, Mughal power had been driven out of western India[149] – a defeat that was eventually formalized in the *farman* or imperial declaration of 1719. Aurangzeb's reign came to be seen by later historians as the climax of the Mughal era, and his death as the signal for a new dark age of imperial collapse, from which India was rescued by British intervention after 1765. Humiliated by the Marathas, unable to staunch the haemorrhage of power to their provincial governors or *subahdars*, and challenged by the rise of Sikhism in the Punjab, Mughal prestige was finally shattered by the invasion of Nadir Shah, the ruler of Iran. Indeed, Nadir's victory in 1739 was the starting gun for chaos. Maratha, Rohilla (Afghan) and Pindari (mercenary) armies, and those of lesser warlords, ravaged North India. In this predatory climate, trade and agriculture declined together. Economic failure echoed political disintegration. Small wonder, then, that Mughal India was the first of the great Eurasian states to fall under European domination after 1750.

In recent years, this simplistic 'black' version of India's pre-colonial history has been largely rewritten. The late Mughal period no longer makes sense as the chaotic prologue to colonial rule. India's conquest was a more complex affair than the foredoomed collapse of an overstretched empire and the pacification of its warring fragments by European rulers with superior political skill. A realistic account of the half-century that ended at the Battle of Plassey in 1757 (the opening salvo of Britain's colonial conquest) would stress the part played by Indians in building new networks of trade and new regional states. It was this that helped to set off the crises that overwhelmed them unexpectedly in the 1750s.

Indeed, behind many of the changes of the late seventeenth and early eighteenth centuries can be seen the effects of expanding trade, rising population and a growing rural economy. Urban prosperity and the rising wealth of the rural elite made provincial interests less willing to put up with central direction from Delhi. The Maratha revolt was

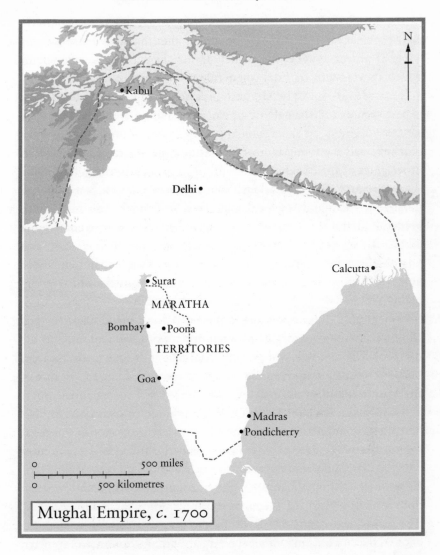

Mughal Empire, *c.* 1700

a symptom of this. The Maratha confederacy has long been portrayed as a predatory horde that reduced northern India to anarchy. But behind its rise can be seen something more interesting than an alliance of freebooters. The Marathas' territorial conquests were marked not by scorched earth but by their elaborate revenue system, whose voluminous records are preserved at Poona (modern Pune).[150] Maratha leaders aimed not at general devastation but at the gradual absorption of the Mughal domain into the sphere of their *svarajya* or 'sovereignty'. Their object was not so much the absolute overthrow of Mughal power as its enforced devolution: hence the eagerness with which they sought to cloak their rule with the authority of Mughal grants and decrees.[151] The Maratha enterprise, suggests a modern study, is best seen as the struggle of an emerging Hindu gentry, under their *sardars* or chiefs, to share Mughal sovereignty and revenues in ways that reflected the rising importance of new landholding groups.[152] In other parts of the Mughal dominions a similar pattern can be seen as the *subahdars* tried to slacken Delhi's grip as part of their effort to manage the demands of local magnates. In Bengal, Awadh (Oudh), Hyderabad and the Punjab (where *declining* trade was strengthening Sikhism), weakening Delhi's grip meant not so much a slide into anarchy as a new phase of state-building by local rulers who were anxious to pose as the legitimate representatives of the old imperial regime.[153]

Conceivably this trend might have led to a more decentralized Mughal 'commonwealth' as Mughal institutions were adapted to the needs of different regional powers. Maratha influence, based on formidable military power, might have become as widespread as that of the Mughals had been. Instead, two great destabilizing forces interacted to make Mughal 'decadence' the prelude to a revolution. The first was the impact of a new round of invasions from Central Asia, the traditional source of new hegemonies in India. In 1739 a huge Mughal army surrendered at Karnal in the approaches to Delhi. 'The Chagatai [i.e. Mughal] empire is gone,' groaned the Maratha ambassador, who fled from the scene, 'the Irani Empire has commenced.'[154] The subsequent capture of Delhi by the Iranian ruler Nadir Shah (he entered the city on a magnificent charger, with the humiliated emperor in a closed palanquin), followed by the Afghan incursions in the 1750s, wrecked Mughal prestige and devastated the old trade routes between Bengal and Upper India. A vital part of the Mughal heartland west of the Indus and around Kabul was wrenched away by defeat.[155] In a further battle at Panipat, in 1761, the Afghans crushed the Maratha army and killed the *peshwa*, chief minister of the confederacy.

The second great source of subcontinental change was the rapid integration of maritime India into international trade. In Bengal, the breakneck conversion of marsh and forest into ricelands and the huge workforce of cotton weavers and spinners (perhaps 1 million or more) created an exceptionally dynamic economy, whose growth was fertilized by the inflow of silver with which Europeans paid for their purchases of cotton and silk. Along the Coromandel coast south of Madras, in modern Tamil Nadu, a similar pattern of agrarian success and textile production created a flourishing mercantile economy in a region that was also the crossroads for trade in the Bay of Bengal and the Indian Ocean.[156] Here, as elsewhere in coastal India, a distinctive type of mercantile capitalism had grown up to finance and manage the production, sale and distribution of textiles and other commodities.[157]

From the late 1500s onward many Europeans came to India to try their luck in its courts and commerce. However, it was maritime India's trade that was the main attraction. By the eighteenth century, European warehouses (or 'godowns') and 'factories' dotted the peninsular coast from Surat to Calcutta. Some Europeans, like 'Diamond' (Thomas) Pitt, came to India as 'interlopers', defying the monopoly claimed by the chartered companies. Some, like 'Siamese' (Samuel) White, turned into freelances. White arrived in Madras in 1676. But he soon crossed the Bay of Bengal and made his way to Ayudhya, then the Siamese (Thai) capital. He made his name first in the elephant trade – the dangerous business of bringing elephants by sea across the bay to India – before becoming the king's chief commercial agent.[158] But most European traders were company men. The high costs of long-distance trade, as well as large armed ships (the 'East Indiamen'), shore establishments (with their garrisons to guard against attack by other Europeans or disorderly locals) and the diplomatic apparatus required for dealings with regional rulers and the Mughal court, had long made it necessary for European traders to be organized as joint-stock companies. These were forerunners of the modern corporation (with shareholders, a board and a management structure), and enjoyed a monopoly in the direct trade between their country and India. But their superficial modernity did not, of course, mean that European merchants were heralds of the open economy or the rule of the market. Indeed, they had little to sell, and they were forced to import bullion on a massive scale to pay for the Indian goods that they wanted to buy. Their commercial policy was to drive down the price and increase the quantity of the Indian textiles for which an insatiable demand existed in Europe. Hence the rival European companies (mainly after 1720 the English and French East India companies) were engaged in a constant effort to entice Indian weavers into their trading towns (like Madras or Pondicherry), where they had been allowed to build their 'factories' and exert their control over weavers and merchants in order to regulate the price, type and quality of the cloth produced.[159] This led them into close but often quarrelsome relations with local rulers, whose wealth and power also depended upon the profits of trade and the shuffling of tax revenues between commerce and credit. By the early eighteenth century, the threat of a boycott or a blockade of a port had become a powerful counter in the companies' diplomacy. Yet they still found it wise to show studious deference to the Mughal emissaries who arrived periodically, taking care to dress up in their Mughal robes – for wearing the robes that the ruler had granted was the symbolic affirmation of obedience and loyalty.[160] The Mughal defeat in 1739 sent a shock wave across South Asia. But at the moment when the young Robert Clive landed at Madras, in 1744, the idea that any of the European companies, let alone the English, with their dilapidated fort at Madras, could become a territorial power in India, let alone ruler of the whole subcontinent, was almost absurdly improbable.

South Asia in the first half of the eighteenth century should not be seen as a region that was drifting from stagnation to anarchy. In the northern interior the triangular conflict between Marathas, Mughals and the transmontane invaders was also a struggle between 'gentry' groups, who were striving to build a stable and sedentary order of towns, markets and settled agriculture, and 'warrior' groups who were part of the old tradition of nomadic pastoralism on the upland plains connecting northern India and Central Asia.[161] The economic and social change of the long Mughal peace brought that conflict to a head. Similarly, in maritime India, commercial expansion was rapidly transforming the economic and social order and relations with both the Indian interior and the outside world. Here then was a double revolution in the making: a 'coincidence' that was to hurl South Asia into its modern, colonial, era. But only the most visionary of prophets could have forecast in 1740 that the outcome of that revolution would be the conquest of the whole subcontinent by just one company of those European traders who seemed to find mere physical survival in the Indian climate an often fatal challenge. For such was the lottery of death and disease that one in every two who arrived from Europe could expect to die in his first year in India.

The invasions of North India in 1739 by the armies of Nadir Shah and in the 1750s by his former henchman Ahmad Shah Durrani (Nadir had been murdered in 1747) were something more than random tribal incursions of the kind that had disturbed the Indian plains for centuries past. Together they formed the last great effort at empire-building in the tradition of Tamerlane, tearing down in the process the Mughal and Safavid states. The Safavids were the first victim. Squeezed between Ottoman-dominated Mesopotamia and Anatolia in the west and a vast tribal hinterland stretching east and south to Herat and Kandahar in modern Afghanistan, Safavid Iran had always represented an uphill struggle to impose the authority of the city and the sedentary world on the steppe and the desert. Georgia, the main recruiting ground of its slave army and bureaucracy, was especially vulnerable to Ottoman and Russian pressure.[162] Politically, the Safavid system had been a precarious amalgam of a Turkic tribal alliance with the Iranian literati: but no real fusion had taken place. By 1700 this unstable coalition was coming under increasing external and internal strain.

Safavid rulers based in Isfahan had been no more successful than the Mughals in achieving an empire of fixed territorial boundaries. They had won and lost Baghdad. Their grip on Khorasan, Herat and the city and region of Kandahar had never been secure. Kandahar had been conquered by Uzbeks in 1629, captured by the Mughals in 1634, and recovered by Shah Abbas II in 1650. In 1709–11 the Safavids lost control of it to the Ghilzais, the dominant tribe in the southern Afghan lands. Herat and Khorasan had slipped from their grasp by 1718–19. In 1722 the Ghilzai leader Mahmud shattered the Safavid army at Gulnabad, captured Isfahan, and seized the throne abandoned by the shah. Both Russia and the Ottomans, perhaps mutually fearful, rushed to exploit the Safavid collapse. Peter the Great took Derbent, Resht and Baku along the Caspian Sea. The Ottomans grabbed Tiflis

(1723) and, with Hamadan, Erivan and Tabriz, much of western Iran. In a chaotic decade, the imperial legacy of Abbas I had been summarily dissolved.

But, at the moment of dissolution, a new political force appeared to drive off the Ottomans, Russians and Ghilzais. The Safavid claimant Tahmasp recruited Nadir Kuli (1688–1747), a Khorasan warlord of humble origin (a former shepherd), to his cause. Nadir was a general of Napoleonic talents and aspirations.[163] He was a careful strategist, but skilled in the use of shock tactics and light cavalry, and alert to the value of light artillery, drill and musketry.[164] By 1730 he had reconquered the cities of Meshed and Herat, smashed the Afghan tribes at Mehmandost, reoccupied Isfahan and Shiraz, and inflicted a devastating defeat on the once-triumphant Ghilzais. By 1735 he had recovered Tiflis and Erivan from the Ottomans, and forced the Russians to disgorge Mazanderan, Astrabad, Gilan, Derbent and Baku. In 1736 he declared himself shah. In 1737–8 he captured Kandahar, and in the following year Mughal Delhi. Kabul and the right bank of the Indus were annexed to his new Iranian empire, and in 1740 Nadir turned his attention to the Uzbeks in Bukhara and Khiva. This astonishing career was prematurely terminated by the madness and irrational cruelty (perhaps exacerbated by the effects of disease) that provoked his assassination in 1747. But a new imperialist appeared in Nadir's image. Ahmad Shah Durrani, one of his Afghan lieutenants, carved out an inheritance from Nadir's Indian and Afghan conquests. At its height his Durrani empire stretched from Khorasan to the Ganges and from the Amu-Darya to the Sea of Oman.[165] Not until the loss of Multan (1818), Kashmir (1819) and Peshawar (1834) to the British was it pressed back into the Afghan highlands.

What lay behind these two great ventures in empire-building that dominated the vast Indo-Iranian borderlands for half a century and had such a seismic impact on the politics of the whole subcontinent? One explanation might be that they were symptoms of a 'tribal revolt' against the encroachment of the bureaucratic sedentary states: Russian, Safavid and Mughal. But the persistence of the enterprise and the imperial aspirations of its leaders suggest that some deeper force was at work. It has been argued that the careers of Nadir and of Ahmad Shah coincided with the dramatic rise in the economic importance of the commercial corridor that stretched between North India and Russia and far away westward towards Meshed and Iran.[166] North India, as far south as modern Karachi, was part of a trading system newly invigorated by the buying power of Russian silver. If this was the case, then this new round of empire-building was aimed at controlling the commercial wealth of the region and was fuelled by the hope of exploiting it further. It may have been primed by the social tensions of the nomad economy, with its secular tendency towards overpopulation. Militarily, it made use of the old nomadic advantage of tactical speed and strategic mobility, adapting handguns to cavalry warfare[167] and, under Nadir Shah, also using artillery and even sea power.[168] On this view, neither Nadir nor Ahmad Shah could be described as a throwback to a barbaric era. Instead, they were state-builders in search of a new formula. They combined an imperial style with the brutal discipline of tribal politics. It is even possible to imagine the scenario of which they may have dreamed: a Greater Iranian Empire along Manchu lines, in which a nomadic warrior elite was transmuted into the hereditary administrative class of an agrarian state.

It was not to be. The imperial project failed – perhaps because its agrarian base was much too narrow to sustain its scale; perhaps because of the inherent instability of the tribal confederations on which it still depended; perhaps because external pressure (not least the advance of British power in India)[169] allowed too little time for the vital transition to a more settled government. Nevertheless, a significant legacy remained: the Afghan state first organized by Ahmad Shah in 1747, and the eventual reconstruction of Iran under the Afshar dynasty of the Qajars, whose rule lasted down till the 1920s.

EUROPE'S PLACE IN EURASIA

Historians have often been tempted to see the later part of early modern times as the grand prelude to the supremacy of Europe, and to imagine the imminent triumph of a global economy dominated by commercially advanced 'core' states in North West Europe. In fact there are few grounds for taking so deterministic a view of a period whose most striking feature was the limited influence that the European states could muster across most of Eurasia. From a European perspective, the most significant change was to be found not in Europe's relations with the Indo-Islamic world or the civilizations of East Asia, but in the consolidation of a huge region of settlement, trade and slavery in the Euro-Atlantic: West Africa, Brazil, Peru, Mexico, the Caribbean, and the French and English colonies in eastern North America. While the enlargement of European settlements was comparatively slow, the new slave-based plantation economies built up after c.1650 created valuable new markets for European exports and shipping. Exotic produce from the Americas whetted the appetites of European consumers. The spectacle of America had a similar impact on the European imagination. It is hard to exaggerate the intellectual and cultural impact of sudden mastery of an entire 'new world' on hitherto embattled subcontinental societies. As a source of knowledge, innovation and experience; as a treasure trove of bullion; as an employer of mercantile capital; and as a vast zone of navigation: its transatlantic provinces had helped to make Europe perhaps the richest and most dynamic of the Old World civilizations by the early eighteenth century.

But we should be cautious about assuming that this wealth and dynamism were sufficient to drive European power deeper into Eurasia. As we have seen, except in parts of the Near East, Europeans had made little headway in carving out new *markets* in Asia, and still less in asserting their physical domination apart from in a few favoured locations. The great vanguard of European power in Asia, the mighty Dutch East India Company (the 'VOC'), was staggering under the burden of its administrative and military costs after 1720, lurching into deficit and 'profitless growth'. By contrast, the volume of Indian textile exports threatened to overwhelm the cloth industry in Britain, which sought commercial safety in protective tariffs. European consumption, rather than European production, regulated the trade between Europe, India and China. And if Indians and Chinese were intrigued by aspects of European art and technology, the traffic in the opposite direction was just as heavy.

Still, we might be swayed by the claim that the most prosperous regions in Europe had established by 1740 an unbeatable lead over the rest of Eurasia in the 'modernity' of their economic and social institutions – a lead that would be translated sooner or later into a form of global hegemony. After all, the Netherlands had pioneered the 'modern economy', and Britain and France were following in its wake. Here could be seen the generic features of economic modernity: 'reasonably free and pervasive' markets for both commodities and the factors of production (including land and labour); a scale of agricultural productivity capable of supporting a complex division of labour; a state that promoted property rights and the freedom of movement and contract; and levels of technology and commercial organization capable of supporting sustained development, a rich material culture and the diffusion of market-oriented consumer behaviour.[170] Yet none of this saved the Netherlands from economic decline in the eighteenth century. Rapid development had unforeseen environmental consequences that affected water quality and agriculture. Urbanization and internal migration upset marriage patterns and checked population growth. High costs of production and the loss of export markets, as trade rivals raised tariffs, damaged manufacturing and drove capital towards public lending at home and abroad – a strategy shipwrecked by the political and diplomatic crises at the end of the century. Altogether the Dutch experiment in pre-industrial modernity was aborted by three forces endemic in early modern Europe: the 'mercantilist' tendency towards closed markets and commercial autarky – the trade-suppressing policies castigated by Adam Smith in *The Wealth of Nations* – the high costs of pre-industrial manufacturing, coupled with the environmental limits on agricultural growth; and the drastic consequences of intra-European conflict for the fiscal systems of European states. Dutch experience suggested that the limits of pre-industrial modernity would soon be felt for Britain and France also, and that it would require a technological, political and geostrategic revolution before the European style of economy could successfully colonize the rest of Eurasia – and the world.

4

The Eurasian Revolution

4. The defeat of Tipu Sultan

Between the 1750s and the 1830s the long equilibrium of cultures and continents was swept away by the Eurasian Revolution. During these years the European states gained for the first time a commanding lead over the rest of Eurasia and acquired the means to project their power into the heartlands of the great Asian empires, and not just their maritime fringe. Looking back at this change, historians have usually been struck most of all by the great transformation in economic potential from which the Europeans had profited. The 'Industrial Revolution' in technology and economic organization seemed the obvious source of the Europeans' new power. In fact it was not the only or sufficient explanation of European expansion. The Eurasian Revolution was in fact three revolutions: in geopolitics, in culture and in economics. It did not impose an era of universal European dominance. In the 1830s European mastery of the world was still partial and limited: the scope for resistance still seemed to be wide. In the deep interiors of Afro-Asia, it was scarcely a rumour. But it opened the road for an imperial order in which European control was riveted on the rest of the globe.

These three revolutions were closely connected and mutually dependent. Each reinforced the others' effects, extending their range and increasing their force. Commercial expansion sharpened the rivalry of Europe's maritime states. It increased the importance of European trade with other parts of Eurasia, especially with India, but made Europe more vulnerable to its sudden disruption. By increasing the stream of Asian commodities (especially cottons, silk and porcelain) into Europe, it may also have helped to spread the 'industrial' methods through which European manufacturers hoped to copy these desirable products in order to compete and survive. But Europe's overseas trade could not look after itself. The European traders' advantage lay in their system of credit and their command of the sea lanes. But before 1750 across much of Eurasia their position was far from secure. Without 'industrial' goods, their competitive position was weak. With little to tempt the Asian consumer, they were forced to pay for the goods that they wanted in silver or gold, a practice frowned on by governments at home. To make matters worse, the cost of their over-heads (mainly their fleets and fortresses) was cripplingly high, mainly because of intra-European rivalry. Thirdly, in both India and China, the two greatest markets for European trade, commercial access depended upon the agreement of rulers who might choose to reject it as a political danger (as happened in Bengal) or restrict it drastically (the 'Canton system' in China).

As a result, a great geopolitical shift was required before the Euro-peans could reverse the commercial imbalance of their Asian ex-changes. In turn, the effects of European coercion and conquest were widened and deepened by the machine technologies that revol-utionized transport and textile production. In a similar way, the visible benefits of scientific inquiry and technical innovation reinforced the impact of the cultural changes that allowed Europeans to imagine, explain and justify their claim to moral and intellectual as well as material ascendancy. But the making of maps, the charting of coasts, the gathering of ethnographical data, the collecting of plants, the viewing of monuments and the purchasing of curios – the vital pre-requisites of a universal thought-world – all required access to inform-ants and places, an apparatus to process the information accumulated, and an immediate motive to make the effort required. These were theoretically possible without a 'geopolitical' presence. But, without the military and political leverage that the British enjoyed in India after 1760, British knowledge of Indians would have been much smaller in volume as well as different in kind. Cook's three voyages in the Pacific Ocean would have proceeded more slowly had he been forced to depend on the cooperation of Maori and Aboriginal peoples, or encountered the sea power of a non-European state. Here, as in India, it was geopolitical strength that shaped the production of knowledge as well as the enhancement of trade.

This is the argument that shapes much of this chapter. Disentangling the threads of such a complex upheaval as we are here concerned with is a hazardous business. But the immediate cause of the revolutionary change in Europe's relations with the rest of Eurasia was not greater economic efficiency, since industrialization had barely set in before the turn of the century. Nor did it spring from using science and tech-nology more dexterously than Asians. Before the arrival of steamships,

European technology conferred little advantage, even on the battle-field, as the British found in India. Europe's sudden acquisition of a Eurasian pre-eminence was the result not of commercial success or scientific prestige, but of a series of forced entries or forcible over-throws. Each instance can be traced to a quarrel between interlopers and locals. Together they formed a vast Eurasian frontier of friction from the Crimea to Canton. But this too must be placed in its larger context. For the really astonishing feature of this revolutionary age was the geopolitical earthquakes that occurred not just in Eurasia but all over the world. They reached a pitch of intensity in Europe itself (where wars were fought for nearly half the whole period from 1750 to 1830), but some were triggered by pressures that had little to do with European activity. Nor was it obvious that their cumulative impact would be to Europe's advantage. In the most violent phase of the European conflict after 1790, the reverse seemed more likely. But when the pattern emerged by the 1830s (as many contemporaries believed), what it revealed more clearly than anything else was the colossal enlargement of Europe's zones of influence, occupation and rule. It was not just a matter of Europe's place in Eurasia: the whole global balance had been shifted as well.

Why and how had this happened?

A GEOPOLITICAL REVOLUTION

In the mid eighteenth century, an uneasy equilibrium still charac-terized the relations between the states and empires of the European, Islamic and East Asian worlds. That was also true of the balance of advantage between all the Eurasian powers on the one hand and the indigenous societies of the Outer World – in the Americas, sub-Saharan Africa, South East Asia and the Pacific – on the other. That is not to say that the position was static. The frontier between the European powers and the Ottoman Empire had moved backwards and forwards since the early years of the century. But, although the Ottomans had been forced to fall back since their last great invasion of Europe, in the 1680s, they had recovered ground lost before the 1730s and had stabilized their defence against Austria's advance in the Balkans. In the north, where they faced the endemic expansion of Russia, the approaches to the Black Sea – still an Ottoman lake and the strategic shield of their northern provinces – remained in the hands of their Muslim clients the Giray khans of the Crimea. On the coasts of North Africa and the Levant, the European maritime powers showed little desire (or lacked the means) to upset the Ottoman paramountcy that still survived there. Further east, around the Caspian Sea, Russian moves south from the Volga delta had made little progress, although there was a vigorous commercial traffic connecting the Russian towns with Iran, Central Asia and North India.[1]

The 1740s were a turbulent period in India, when Iranian, Afghan and Maratha invasions struck at the heartlands of the Mughal Empire, while its old coastal tributaries – especially Bengal – asserted increasing autonomy. The chartered companies of the British, Dutch and French had forts and 'factories' scattered round the coasts of South Asia, and had come to blows with each other in the 1740s. But in 1750 it would have seemed absurd to predict that the struggle for empire on the plains of North India would end in the triumph of a European rather than an Asian imperialism. A far more likely outcome appeared a division of the spoils between Afghan and Maratha empire-builders, while maritime India followed a different and more cosmopolitan trajectory. In the greatest empire of all, the threat of geostrategic upheaval looked less likely than ever. The Ch'ing monarchy was preparing the final destruction of nomadic military power on the steppes of Inner Asia, the oldest and deadliest threat to the East Asian 'world order'.[2] When this was accomplished (Sinkiang, or East Turkestan, was conquered by the end of the decade), the Celestial Empire would be still more massively impervious to external disruption, less willing than ever to make any concession when importunate visitors knocked at its maritime back door. Or so it appeared.

In the Outer World, too, there was little to hint that a decisive shift towards European hegemony was about to take place. The stand-off between the French and the British in North America (a function in part of their European relations), and the French alliance of convenience with the interior Native Americans, had halted the line of European settlement along the eastern foothills of the Appalachians. The advance of the Spanish from their Mexican base had also been stalled. The semi-arid Great Plains and their mobile, warlike peoples blocked one line of expansion; the remoteness and apparent inhospitality of the California coastline discouraged the other. (The Spanish did not occupy the San Francisco region until the 1770s.) In South America, vast regions of forest and pampas – in Chile, Argentina and the Amazon basin – resisted the feeble assault of Creoles and (Spanish-born) *peninsulares*. In sub-Saharan Africa, Muslim influence diffused into the western savannahs, and drifted up the Nile towards the Coptic redoubt of Ethiopia.[3] It drew the East African coastlands towards the Persian Gulf and India. But Europeans scarcely ventured beyond the beachheads of the slave trade in Atlantic Africa. In the far south, the Afrikaner 'trekkers' in the Cape interior were hemmed in by San (the old word is Bushmen) to the north and west and by Nguni communities to the east.[4] Most striking of all, in 1750 surprisingly little was known of the geography of the Pacific, though it had been traversed many times by European navigators. The shape and ecology of Australasia, the location and culture of the Pacific islands, and the Pacific coast of what is now Canada were blanks or fantasies on the European map. As late as 1774, an authoritative map declared Alaska an island.[5] The frontiers here had yet to be found.

Eurasia's equilibrium had not meant peace. Between 1700 and 1750, as well as the wars between Iranians, Afghans, Marathas and Mughals, there were major wars between the European states, between Europeans and Turks, and between Turks and Iranians. But after 1750 the geopolitical scene was doubly transformed. The scale and intensity of Eurasian conflicts became much greater, and their 'knock-on' effects outside the Old World much more disturbing. The reasons behind this remain somewhat mysterious. But part of the answer may perhaps be found in the explosive convergence of two longer-term trends. Both were connected to the quickening pace of the commercial economy in the mid eighteenth century. The first was the pressure to secure and extend the markets and trades whose value was rising and protect them from rivals, or predatory intruders. This pressure was felt (and transmitted) by Asian merchants and rulers, by American traders and settlers, and by European monarchs and ministers. A spate of short wars over land and trade might have been the result. But commercial growth sparked the critical phase of a more insidious trend. In eighteenth-century Eurasia it was fiscal strength and stability that determined the scale of state military power. This was not just a matter of a large revenue base and the collection of taxes. It presupposed also a close (and mutually profitable) connection between the public officials and the interests that managed the financial market, where the state was usually much the largest client. Possessing a well-developed financial system, able to mobilize funds quickly and cheaply, was the key to maintaining a loyal and well-equipped army. The expansion of trade thus contributed directly to war-making power, and financial resources became the ultimate arbiter of military fortune. 'A financial system . . . constantly improved, can change a government's position,' remarked Frederick the Great, who knew a thing or two about both. 'From being originally poor it can make a government so rich that it can throw its grain into the scales of the balance between the great European powers.'[6] By 1815, governments in London had ten times the revenue enjoyed by their predecessors a hundred years earlier. The 'fiscal-military state' did not by itself create conflicts and crises. But, by changing the rules that governed success, it opened the way for a new pattern of power.

There were two epicentres of geopolitical turbulence in mid-eighteenth-century Eurasia. The first was in Europe. The immediate causes of European tension seem obvious enough. Most European states were instinctive expansionists. In a pre-industrial age, power was equated with the possession of land and the population it carried, or with a trading monopoly in tropical produce with its glittering promise of a surplus of bullion. Dynastic ambition and mutual suspicion raised the territorial stakes. In Western Europe, the four-cornered struggles of France, Spain, Britain and the Netherlands over the previous century had turned on the question of whether Britain or France would be the dominant power in Atlantic Europe, with effective control over the maritime access to Europe's Atlantic extensions in North and South America. The other great pole of European antagonism was an 'inland America': the vast open frontier of Eastern Europe.[7] This region was notionally shared between four sovereign states: Russia, Austria, Poland and the Ottoman Empire. But the impression of Polish and Ottoman weakness sharpened the land hunger of their stronger neighbours and fuelled their mutual suspicions. Until the mid-1750s, the precarious stability of a quarrelsome continent was chiefly maintained by the primacy of France, the strongest power in the European world. If France had been denied an outright hegemony under Louis XIV, it remained the arbiter of Europe's diplomacy. It had the largest population, the biggest public revenue and the strongest army of any state in Europe.[8] Together with great cultural prestige, a well-developed commerce, an impressive navy and the most sophisticated apparatus of diplomacy and intelligence, these made up an apparently unbeatable combination. Even if France could not dominate Europe, it could hope to regulate the continent's affairs in ways that secured its own pre-eminence.

This aim was pursued through a careful diplomacy of checks and balances. France supported a party in Poland to blunt the incipient domination of Russia and the European ambitions of the Romanov tsars. It allied with Prussia to maintain pressure on Austria, and with the Ottoman Empire to frustrate the expansion of both Austria and Russia. The Bourbon 'alliance' between France and Spain (both of whose monarchs were Bourbons) was meant to defend the status quo in the Mediterranean and Italy. Since the French and Spanish fleets together usually outnumbered the British, it also served to limit Britain's maritime prospects in the Atlantic basin. Thus the 'conservative' primacy of France served unwittingly to uphold the larger equilibrium in Eurasia and the Outer World. It helped to guard the Ottoman Empire against an overwhelming combination of European enemies. It checked the influence of the English East India Company in South Asia. It blocked the way to the North American interior from the coastal settlements of the British colonies with an 'Indian' diplomacy directed from the impregnable fortress at Quebec.

The French system was far-flung, but its burdens were great. France had to be the greatest military power in Europe and maintain a standing army poised to intervene in Germany against Austria or Prussia. It had to compete with the British navy to preserve the Atlantic 'balance' and protect its colonial empire in the Caribbean, where its valuable sugar colonies rivalled the British. France must also be a Mediterranean power, with a fleet at Toulon to watch its interests in Italy, and keep the Near Eastern balance between the Ottomans and Austria – France's main rival in Europe. Financing this huge apparatus of naval, military and colonial power was a constant strain on the Bourbon monarchy and the state it had fashioned. After 1713 the massive army that Louis XIV had deployed (over 400,000 men) had had to be cut back to no more than half that number. By the mid-century years it was already a question whether France's real future lay in Atlantic trade and the growth of its colonies (the lifeblood of ports like Nantes, Bordeaux and La Rochelle), or in preserving and strengthening its continental position – and whether the revenues of the Bourbon state could bear the burden of both.

In the mid-1750s the precarious stability that French power underwrote began to break up. The French 'system' was challenged simultaneously in both west and east. The disruptive force was the rising power of both Britain and Russia, at a time when French military strength had reached its practical limit under the old regime. Russia could no longer be excluded from Europe; while Britain's financial muscle was now sufficient to fund a war-winning navy, two American armies and the subsidies needed for its allies in Europe. The result was a continental and maritime war that broke the back of Bourbon diplomacy. The Seven Years War of 1756–63 smashed French primacy, but replaced it with nothing. It set off instead a geopolitical explosion. The age of war and revolution that followed in its wake lasted more than fifty years, until a new and experimental five-power 'concert' (of Britain, France, Russia, Prussia and Austria) emerged at the Congress of Vienna in 1814–15.

The cracks appeared first in France's Atlantic defences. In the War of the Austrian Succession (1740–48) France had upheld its overall position. But in North America there were obvious signs of weakness. The great French fortress at Louisbourg, which guarded the naval approaches to the St Lawrence, France's main access to the American interior, was captured by a colonial army of Anglo-Americans with the help of the British navy. At the end of the war, the British (who were forced to hand Louisbourg back) constructed a new base at Halifax in Nova Scotia. Further south, British traders from the thirteen colonies competed energetically for the trade of Native Americans in the interior. Shorter lines of supply (compared with the river labyrinth that connected the Ohio valley to Montreal and Quebec) and cheaper credit and goods gave them the advantage. By the early 1750s the

French were worried enough to construct Fort Duquesne (on the site of modern Pittsburgh) to shore up their influence over the Ohio tribes and keep British traders at bay. But the pressure from the British side of the frontier was also growing. A war of maps had already broken out, with a British map of 1755 claiming the land west as far as the Mississippi. Traders, settlers, land speculators and even missionaries were determined to contest France's claim to the interior,[9] resting on the seemingly flimsy support of their alliances with native peoples

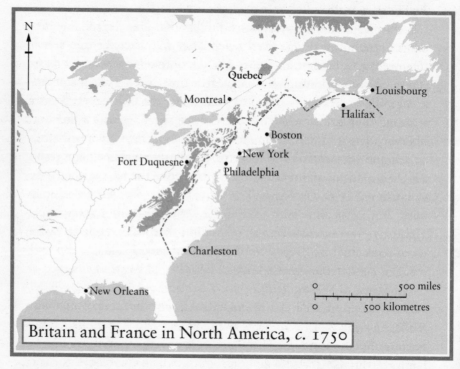

Britain and France in North America, c. 1750

and on a skeletal force of soldiers, priests and French Canadian woodsmen. In the British colonies, where elected assemblies and local interests were extremely powerful,[10] westward expansion seemed the only escape from economic stagnation, a view shared by many of the London-appointed governors. Probing the weaknesses of France's ill-defended monopoly became an irresistible ploy. It was just one of these expeditions, led by the young Virginian surveyor George Washington, that lit the fuse for an Atlantic war.

Washington's venture ended in disaster. His small force was surrounded by the French and their Native American allies. Some of his followers were killed. He was sent back to Virginia. But both sides reacted sharply to this frontier incident. To the French it seemed proof that the British intended a renewed assault on their inland empire and its headquarters at Quebec. So reinforcements were dispatched the following year (in 1755). But in London the French attempt to tighten their grip on the inland routes, the building of Duquesne and the treatment of Washington were regarded as provocative and threatening: a direct challenge to Britain's colonial future on the North American continent. An outcry arose from 'American' interests and their political friends. A fleet was dispatched to intercept the French reinforcements before they could cross the Atlantic. It failed to do so. But the naval skirmishing that followed began a new Atlantic war.

By itself such a war might not have endangered France's general standing. The British attempt to capture Quebec – the grand citadel of French North America – might have been foiled, as so often before, and the British disconcerted by the threat to their interests in Europe. But the American quarrel between Britain and France ignited a second explosion, in Eastern Europe. 'The turmoil in which Europe finds itself', wrote Frederick the Great in 1757, 'began in America ... Thanks to our century's statecraft, there is now no conflict in the world, however small it may be, which ... does not threaten to engulf the whole of Christendom.'[11]

The heart of the problem was the political disintegration of Poland, a vast ill-organized aristocratic republic stretching from the Baltic to the Black Sea. Poland was the key to French diplomacy in Eastern Europe. Its survival placed a limit on the power of Prussia, and reinforced its dependence on France's goodwill. It kept Austria in check, and limited Russia's capacity for interference in Europe. By the 1750s, however, Poland's elected kings were the puppets of Russia – a trend that encouraged a growing rebelliousness in the Polish nobility. The temptation for the Prussian king to embroil himself in Polish rivalries, and renew his challenge to Austria as the great German power, became almost irresistible.[12] He might have hoped to rely on his grand ally, France. But the Bourbon government was determined to keep the status quo in the East, and especially keen to prevent Austria from joining the Anglo-French struggle on the side of

Britain, its traditional ally.[13] In an astonishing reversal of historic antagonism, the Bourbon and Habsburg monarchies reconciled their difference and joined forces to repress an insurgent Prussia. This was the 'diplomatic revolution' of the eighteenth century, an event as stunning to contemporaries as the Nazi–Soviet pact of August 1939. The Franco-Austrian alliance brought together the two most powerful states in Europe. It should have secured a 'conservative' peace, helping France to settle her colonial differences with Britain. Instead, by tenacious resistance and a series of remarkable victories, Frederick the Great humiliated his great-power enemies. The militarist bureaucracy he had created proved a match for a distant France and an ill-organized Austria. Frederick could not win outright. But, with British subsidies and the damage the British were doing to France's Atlantic interests, he held out long enough to force his enemies to the conference table.

Now French primacy unravelled in earnest. While Frederick had held his own in Europe, the British had slowly assembled the force they needed to conquer New France in North America. In 1759, 'the year of victories', they won naval control of the Atlantic, cutting off the French in Canada from reinforcements. In September – in the nick of time before winter set in, the St Lawrence froze and the British fleet had to withdraw – General Wolfe captured Quebec, the key to French power in the American continent. It was a staggering blow. For (though they nearly lost the city to a French counter-attack in the grim winter of 1759–60) the British could now roll up the French system of influence in the continental interior. And, with France on the ropes in the Atlantic, the British began to threaten its junior partner, Spain, whose American empire was painfully exposed to their naval and military power. The year of decision was 1762: the British captured Havana, the Gibraltar of the Spanish Caribbean. Spain was desperate for peace. France was close to bankruptcy – indeed, it had been technically bankrupt since 1759, when it defaulted on its loans. Russia changed sides. A new tsar, star-struck by Frederick the Great, abandoned the war against Prussia.

The peace that followed in 1763 was really a truce of exhaustion. The French were driven from the American mainland, keeping their sugar-rich Caribbean islands and their fishing platform (the islands of

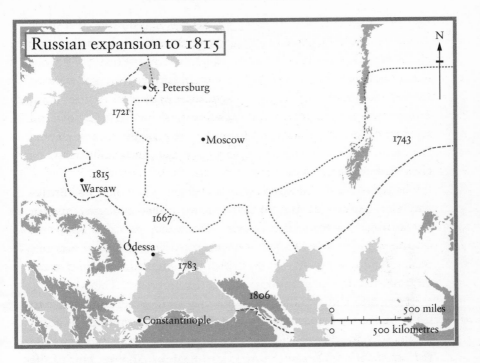

Russian expansion to 1815

St. Petersburg
1721
Moscow
1743
1815
Warsaw
1667
Odessa
1783
1806
Constantinople

500 miles
500 kilometres

N

St-Pierre and Miquelon) near Newfoundland. Louisiana went to Spain, which lost Florida to Britain. But the real decision of the Peace of Paris was that France was no longer the arbiter of Europe. The French 'system' had been broken. The next thirty years saw the progressive demolition of the old geopolitical equilibrium in Eurasia and the Outer World alike. The aggrandizement of the British could no longer be checked. In Eastern Europe and in Middle Eurasia, the main beneficiary of France's decline was the imperial Russia of Catherine the Great (r. 1762–96). Without the shadow of help from its usual protector, the Polish republic was eaten alive – in stages. The first partition was in 1772, when Russia, Austria and Prussia each took a bite. The Russian share was the eastern borderlands. What remained of Poland was now de facto a Russian protectorate under a client king, Stanislaus Poniatowski (one of Catherine the Great's lovers). The Polish agreement left the Russians free to complete their war against the Ottomans (1768–74) and gain their long-cherished objective: a firm foothold on the Black Sea at Kherson, under the Treaty of Kuchuk Kainardji in 1774. In 1783 they annexed the Crimean peninsula and made themselves masters of the Black Sea's north shore. Grigori Potemkin (Catherine the Great's favourite and lover) unleashed his furious energy as viceroy of 'New Russia'.[14] Another war against the Ottoman Empire (fought by the Turks in a vain attempt to reverse their losses) brought a new round of prizes. Odessa was founded in 1793 to be the metropolis of this new southern empire. The road had been opened to conquer the Caucasus, and perhaps even Constantinople. It was a critical phase in the ascent of Russia as a global power.

The course of British expansion was much less heroic. The British had felt the strain of war, and the pressure to compromise was strong. In this mood of financial stringency, the burden of a new American empire was almost an embarrassment. The thought of new commitments there was horrifying. So British ministers made haste to tranquillize their new acquisitions, not to develop them. They appeased the French Canadians in the new province of Quebec, and refused to set up the elective assembly demanded by incomers from the thirteen colonies. Quebec was to be governed as a military colony to supervise the old French sphere in the American Midwest. To the fury of the American colonists, a 'Proclamation Line' was drawn along the Appalachian mountains. Far from being the spoils of American victory, the interior was to remain an 'Indian' country, closed to American settlers and policed by imperial officials in the interests of peace, and financial economy. As if this was not enough, the British were also determined to force the American colonists to meet some of the costs of imperial defence. The colonists were to pay imperial taxes – like the notorious stamp duties. Colonial trade was to be more closely regulated to enforce the navigation laws prohibiting foreign trade where it bypassed ports in Britain and to suppress the widespread practice of smuggling.

The sequel is well known. The settlers rebelled. The British mismanaged what was anyway a difficult war with a long and uncertain supply route across the North Atlantic.[15] When they failed to deal quickly with the colonial revolt, their Atlantic triumph of 1763 became increasingly frail. Their maritime rivals, eager to restore the Atlantic balance, seized the chance for revenge. In 1778, three years after the beginning of the colonial war, France, Spain and the Netherlands joined in. Isolated, and outnumbered at sea, the British lost control of the Atlantic for a crucial period, sealing their fate in America. At Yorktown in 1781 their main army in the colonies surrendered. Though their naval defeats were reversed – frustrating the hopes of the French, Spanish and Dutch – the British were forced to accept American independence at the Peace of Versailles in 1783 – though they kept control of Canada.

On the face of it, the great British victory of 1763 had been almost completely reversed in just twenty years. But if we think in global terms we can see that the successful revolt of the British white settler societies against imperial control was really a final confirmation of the 'provisional' triumph of 1763. Now at last the American interior was fully thrown open to the 'neo-Europeans' of the Atlantic seaboard. As soon as the war was over – indeed even while it continued – the colonists began to swarm across the mountains. One of the earliest acts of the 'United States' was to lay down a programme for territorial expansion in the Northwest Ordinance of 1787. As the tide of settlement flowed into the Ohio valley and the Old Southwest (modern Alabama and Mississippi), the inevitable friction with indigenous peoples detonated a series of frontier wars. Divided, outgunned and increasingly outnumbered, the Native Americans were driven steadily westward while the land they left behind was filled up with white men and their slaves. By 1830 the tide of white settlement had raced ahead to reach and cross the Mississippi.[16] In fifty years a 'neo-Europe' on the American continent had emerged from the struggling colonies of the Age of Equilibrium.

In North America, the richest region of the Outer World had now been prised open for European occupation. But the most dramatic invasion of the Outer World after 1750 took place on the other side of the globe. In the flush of victory, and with a novel sense of its (worldwide) supremacy, the British navy launched a systematic drive to chart the oceans, winds and currents: the vital intelligence of maritime power in the age of sail. One of those chosen for these mapping expeditions was James Cook, who had made his reputation as a skilled navigator in the attack on Quebec in 1759. Nine years later he led the first of his three voyages into the Pacific, to observe the transit of Venus and also to verify whether 'a continent, or land of great extent, may be found to the Southwest'.[17] A decade of exploration followed before his death in Hawaii after a quarrel with the islanders. Cook's reports (and those of his scientific passengers, such as Joseph Banks) were sensational. They revealed a vast Pacific world of which Europeans had had barely an inkling. The societies and cultures of the Pacific islands struck the European public as a tropical Eden, a paradise of leisure and innocence. But Cook's revelations had more than a cultural significance. His voyage to the Pacific coast of modern Canada hinted that a new trade route could be opened between the fur-bearing regions of North America and a lucrative market in China. His greatest discovery, however, lay in the South Pacific. Cook exploded the myth of a Great Southern Land stretching south to the bottom of the world. Instead, he accurately charted the island continent of Australia, and on 22 August 1770 claimed its eastern half for Britain. He had already circumnavigated New Zealand. Within ten years of Cook's death the British government had established the first of the convict settlements in eastern Australia, perhaps partly to tighten its grip on the southern sea route that ran between the Indian Ocean and China. By the 1790s, European and American whalers, sealers, traders, missionaries and beachcombers were beginning to arrive in force in the Pacific islands, including New Zealand. Settlement was slow in what was still a region remote from Europe, subject to the 'tyranny of distance' and the threat of interference by France. But by the 1830s the colonization of Australia was fully under way, carried on the back of the wandering sheep. In 1840, British settlers arrived in New Zealand. A second 'neo-Europe' (perhaps to rival the Americas) was in the making.

The thirty years after 1763 thus saw a huge extension of Europe's grip on the territorial resources of the world, although the wealth of the 'new lands' was as yet more prospective than actual. What made this all the more significant was that it coincided with a no less dramatic shift in the balance of power in the Old World of Eurasia, forming the double foundation of European supremacy in the nineteenth century. This shift could be seen in the Islamic realm, in India and, by the 1830s, in East Asia as well. The arrival of Russian power (in strength) on the northern shores of the Black Sea in the 1770s and '80s marked a crucial stage in the opening of the Islamic Near East to European political and commercial influences.

It was some time before the full effects were felt. But losing the Crimea was a strategic catastrophe for the Ottomans. Until then the Black Sea had been a Turkish lake, part of the Ottomans' imperial communications. With a monopoly of power on its waters, they could guard the northern approaches to their empire with remarkable ease. Without seaborne supplies a Russian invasion into the Ottoman Balkans was difficult if not impossible, as Peter the Great had found. On the other side of the Black Sea, an advance into the Caucasus along the western edge of its mountain chain was even more arduous without maritime support. The Black Sea was the naval shield of the Ottoman system. It narrowed the strategic frontier which the Ottomans had to guard against their European enemy. Invasion must come through the western Balkans – an inhospitable region, where all the advantage lay with the defence. It reduced their great-power rivals effectively to one – the Habsburg Empire, with which they shared a border. It allowed the Ottoman navy to concentrate in the eastern Mediterranean, where it could guard the Aegean Islands, the approach to Constantinople and the shores of Egypt and the Levant with little to fear from the faraway naval powers of Europe – Britain, France, the Netherlands and Spain. Most of all, perhaps, the strategic benefit of the Black Sea was felt politically. The security it gave had permitted the decentralization of power in the Ottoman realm, a vital ingredient of its stability and cohesion in the eighteenth century.

With the sea gate to the north wedged shut, the Ottoman government in Constantinople had weathered the storms of the earlier eighteenth century. The Ottomans' prestige as imperial rulers had been battered, but not broken. Their value as allies in the Machiavellian game of European diplomacy had been real. But in the 1780s the keystone of Ottoman power was torn out. The effects were magnified by the decline of France. A new resurgence began in the Christian communities in Greece and in the northern Balkans. Almost imperceptibly, the empire began to change from a great power of acknowledged (if resented) strength into a region of contestation, a vast territorial prey round which a whole pack of European predators began to circle.

This transformation into the 'Sick Man of Europe' was, however, mainly a feature of the second phase of the geopolitical revolution after 1790. But long before that the effects were being felt of the other great centre of geopolitical turbulence in eighteenth-century Eurasia. In the last chapter we saw how by the early 1750s a 'double revolution' was under way in India. The old shell of the Mughal Empire, which had provided a framework of political unity for much of the subcontinent, was being cracked. In the inland heart of the empire, Mughal power was assaulted from two sides. Iranian and then Afghan adventurers pursued the old Inner Asian tradition of empire-building using the 'tribal' manpower of Inner Asia to impose their rule on the agrarian plains – just as the Mughals had done before them (or the Manchus in China). Their aim may have been to control the commercial traffic between northern India and Central Asia, still one of the world's great trade routes. Their attacks coincided with the decisive advance of Maratha power in western India: a Hindu confederacy of 'gentry' states bent on extending its rule and land-revenue system into the Mughal heartland on the North Indian plains.[18] Under the stress of social and economic, as well as political, change, Mughal power was breaking down (or mutating) into a looser regime, coexisting with the new 'sub-empires' scrambling for territory, trade and revenue. In maritime India there was a similar threat. Here the agent of change was the rapid expansion of the commercial economy and overseas trade. New wealth and new revenues gave regional sub-rulers more and more freedom from Mughal supervision, and made them less and less willing to pay the tribute they owed. But this growing autonomy came with a price. Would-be state-builders had to keep a close watch on the merchants and bankers who funded their power – and to keep a sharp eye on the European interests who had tightened their grip on India's overseas commerce. This was all the more vital when the Europeans showed signs of importing their quarrels into the Indian subcontinent. Getting themselves ready to fight each other turned the French and British into local military powers, and injected an explosive new element into a volatile political scene.

The main theatre of conflict was found in Bengal, the most dynamic and prosperous of the coastal economies. Here a vast output of cotton textile production had sprung up to meet a soaring world market. The riverine network of the Ganges and its delta and the foodstuffs grown in the newly cleared forests were the vital ancillaries of this export economy. Political power was in the hands of the *subahdar* –

formally the viceroy of the Mughal emperor – and his fellow Muslim magnates: the expectant legatees of Mughal decline. But stability was elusive in this parvenu world. In 1756 the *subahdar*, or nawab, Suraj ud-Daula was a new and nervous incumbent. He had political rivals. The financial power of Hindu merchants and bankers, such as the great Jagat Seth, checked his freedom of action: they managed the trade on which rents and revenue depended. They were closely connected with the European traders, especially the English East India Company with its fortified 'factory' at Calcutta – 'a large irregular place, something bigger than Deptford and Rotherhithe' is a contemporary description[19] – and its theoretical freedom (with its imperial *farman*) from the nawab's control. When the nawab suspected that the Company was sheltering those plotting against him, Bengal's jittery politics were plunged into crisis. The Company's refusal to yield brought a trial of strength.[20] In June 1756, the nawab seized Calcutta, and the Company officials who failed to escape were thrown into jail (the famous 'Black Hole'). For a moment it seemed as if this *coup d'état* signalled the rise of a new South Asian mercantilist state – an oriental Netherlands that could hold its own.

Suraj ud-Daula's misfortune was that the Company had the means to retaliate. It had a powerful motive for revenge: the loss of Calcutta had cost it more than £2 million. Six months later a squadron of ships arrived in the Ganges bringing troops from Madras under Robert Clive. Clive quickly recovered Calcutta and made contact with the dissident magnates eager to see the nawab brought down. After Clive's show of force at Plassey near the Bengal capital in June 1757, the nawab's army broke up and his rule collapsed. Clive was now the kingmaker. 'A revolution has been effected . . .', Clive told his father, 'scarcely to be paralleled in history.'[21] But Clive was reluctant to assert the Company's rule in Bengal. 'So large a sovereignty may possibly be an object too extensive for a mercantile company . . . without the nation's assistance,' he thought.[22] Instead it seemed wiser to install a Muslim noble as the new nawab. The experiment failed. The Company servants, pursuing their private trade, refused to acknowledge the nawab's authority or pay the duties they owed him. By 1764, friction had boiled over into armed struggle. At the Battle of Buxar, the Company army defeated the nawab and his ally, the ruler of Awadh.

The following year, the Company took on the *diwani* for Bengal, Bihar and Orissa: now it, not the nawab, controlled the taxes and revenue – 'Nothing remains to [the nawab] but the name and shadow of authority.'[23]

These events were astonishing. But the revolution in India was far from complete. Clive himself was fearful of overstraining the Company's power, and resisted the idea of a march to Delhi. The British were not the sole beneficiaries of Indian change. In the west and centre of the subcontinent, the remorseless rise of Maratha power seemed just as impressive. In 1784 it was the Marathas who took Delhi. In the south of India, Hyderabad and Mysore showed that new states could be built from the debris of Mughal decline. In Mysore, especially, a Muslim soldier of fortune, Haidar Ali, began after 1761 to construct a new-style fiscal-military state, with a revenue and an army that was more than a match for the Company at Madras. Under his son Tipu Sultan (r. 1783–99), these changes were carried much further. The state practised trade, subsidized shipbuilding, and funded a large standing army with artillery and infantry whose training and tactics were as 'modern' as the Company's.[24] Haidar and Tipu fought wars of attrition against the Company's influence and brought it to the verge of financial collapse. Without the resources it had seized in Bengal, with which it built up its armies from 18,000 men in 1763 to more than 150,000 by the end of the century,[25] without naval and military help from Britain, and without the loans advanced by Indian bankers, it is doubtful whether the Company would have retained its power in South India. And, though they defeated (and killed) Tipu in 1799, it is equally doubtful whether the British could have forced the Marathas to acknowledge their rule had they not been triumphant in the second great phase of European conflict to which we will turn in a moment. By the 1790s, indeed, the two main theatres of Eurasia's geopolitical upheaval had all but fused into one.

Already, however, Clive's Bengal revolution was beginning to lever an even more remarkable shift in Eurasian relations. Long before Europeans had entered the Indian Ocean, maritime India had served as the hinge between the trade of East Asia and that of the Middle East and the West. In the eighteenth century, Europeans had increased their commerce with China, strictly confined though it was to brief visits on sufferance to the port of Canton. The English East India Company dominated this trade, carrying mainly bullion to China in exchange (mainly) for tea, the growing craze of the British consumer.

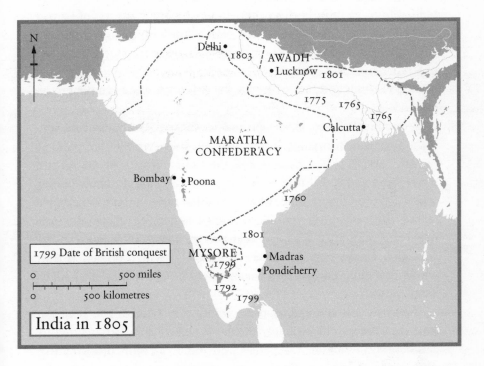

But it lacked the means to expand the traffic, extend more generous credit, or attract Chinese customers with more tempting products. The conquest of Bengal solved all three problems. With its new revenue stream, the Company could pay for the Indian produce that Chinese purchasers wanted – raw cotton, cotton textiles and opium – without resorting to silver or sending more exports to India. But the Company's means were only part of the story. Of growing importance was the 'private trade', tolerated by the Company for its own convenience. A small army of Europeans – soldiers and civilians employed by the Company in India – exploited its rise to make fortunes from plunder or privileged trade. (These were the 'nabobs', whose return to Britain roused much hostile comment.) The most profitable way to remit their winnings was to invest in a cargo to be sent to China.

When it was sold, the credit it earned was given to the Company (which held the monopoly for the purchase of tea) in exchange for a claim on sterling in London. Private trade was also the medium through which opium was sold, since the Company itself was forbidden to trade in it. In this roundabout way, the conquest of Bengal opened the way for a commercial revolution with huge geopolitical consequences.[26] As its exports grew by leaps and bounds, the economy of South China was drawn deeper and deeper into the triangular trade between Britain and India. The biggest fish of all was beginning to be hooked.

Geopolitical change in Europe and South Asia thus opened the way for a huge transformation in the relations between different parts of Eurasia, and between Eurasia and the Outer World. In the second phase, after 1790, the full extent of this shift became gradually clearer and the glimmering outlines of a new global order, faintly observable in the late eighteenth century, assumed a definite shape. But this happened only after a second eruption in European politics, and a new global war, had settled the question of which power, if any, would dominate Europe, and which would be free to take the path to world power.

The crisis was sparked by the revolution in France. The Bourbon state had become increasingly brittle. It lacked popular backing; its aristocratic and middle-class allies were more and more discontented; its intellectual and cultural prestige had been sapped by the pamphlet war of the *philosophes* and the earthier onslaught of popular writers. These were not unusual weaknesses in an eighteenth-century dynastic state. 'At present every power is in a state of crisis,' wrote the tsarina Catherine the Great in 1780.[27] What made them so dangerous to the Bourbon regime was the simultaneous collapse of its historic role as the guardian of French greatness in Europe and the world. By the late 1780s the 'grand nation' of Europe had lost its pre-eminence. For the monarchy's prestige this was bad enough. But the immediate danger was a financial breakdown. After a brief period of peace, France had gone to war in 1778 to reverse the verdict of 1763 and restore its Atlantic position in alliance with Britain's rebellious colonies. It was an expensive gamble, and yielded little. The price was a further accumulation of debts. It was true that the French public debt was smaller than Britain's. The critical fact was that it was far harder to manage, and far more expensive. On the eve of the revolution, just paying the interest consumed half the state's spending.[28] In 1789, with its prestige at a nadir, and its treasury bankrupt, the monarchy fell into the maelstrom of constitutional change, ceding effective political power to the self-proclaimed leaders of the 'Third Estate', reconstituted in June as the 'National Assembly'. As financial chaos grew deeper and social order unravelled, the threat of foreign intervention by the conservative powers, headed by Austria, loomed larger and larger. Fear that the king was conspiring with them to tear up the constitution he had signed in September 1791 radicalized French politics. By the spring of 1792 France was at war with Austria. Military disaster and the popular fear of invasion destroyed the influence of more moderate reformers and brought the monarchy's abolition in September 1792.[29] When Louis XVI and Marie Antoinette were executed in January 1793, France's transformation was complete. The pillar of the *ancien régime* in Europe, the archetype of the dynastic state, had become a militant revolutionary republic, bent on exporting its subversive doctrine of the 'Rights of Man'.

The immediate result of France's political turmoil was further to weaken its claim to influence in Europe and the world beyond. In Eastern Europe, French weakness made it easy to finish off the Polish state, partitioned to death in 1793–5. When the armies of Austria and Prussia marched into France in 1792, the army of Russia marched into Poland.[30] The spoils of victory included the western Ukraine, a vast new addition to Russia's Black Sea empire. But by the mid-1790s the French revolutionary state had developed extraordinary powers of mobilization, levying the men and the means for war on a scale that the hidebound monarchies could hardly match. The patriotic fervour of its citizen armies and the resort to talent in the choice of generals helped turn France once more into a great military power. Territorial conquest paid part of the bill.[31] Under Napoleon Bonaparte, this transition was crowned with charisma and genius. His victories in Italy made him a military hero. As first consul (1799–1804) and emperor (1804–14), he was dictator of France. Part of his aim was to restore the social discipline and administrative order that the revolution had dissolved. But he was also determined to revive and extend the European primacy that the Bourbons had lost. The effect of this on Europe's relations with the Outer World – in the Americas, sub-Saharan Africa and even the Pacific – was bound to be large. The Eurasian implications in the Near East, Central Asia and India (and thus China) hardly less so.

The first round of this struggle was fought over Egypt. In 1798 Napoleon and Talleyrand, the French foreign minister, framed an extraordinary plan for the conquest of Egypt. For Napoleon, whose military idol was Alexander the Great, the appeal was obvious. 'Europe is a molehill,' he is said to have exclaimed; 'all the great reputations have come from Asia.'[32] But his and Talleyrand's reasoning suggests how far they had grasped the scale of geopolitical change since mid-century.[33] Control of Egypt would allow France to revive the Suez route between Europe and India, and counter the ever-growing dominance of Atlantic-borne trade. An Egyptian empire would compensate France for the loss of its American colonies – Quebec and Louisiana, lost in 1763. It would help check the forward movement of Russia towards its ultimate object, the Ottoman capital at Constantinople – a movement that seemed to be accelerating sharply. And it would raise the stakes for the British in India at a crucial time. With France lodged at Suez, at the head of the Red Sea, and French influence radiating towards the Gulf and Iran, the diplomatic and military position of the British East India Company would be drastically weakened. Overawing the Sikhs, the Marathas, Hyderabad and Mysore would become much harder, perhaps even impossible. If its costs and risks became too large, the British experiment in oriental imperialism might collapse altogether.

In July 1798 Napoleon landed in Egypt with 40,000 troops – an enormous force. He also brought with him a 165-strong team of astronomers, mathematicians, chemists, physicists, mechanical, constructional and civil engineers, surveyors, architects, zoologists, artists, composers, economists, antiquaries, printers, surgeons, physicians and pharmacists. Their task was to record the past and plan the future of Napoleonic Egypt. On 21 July, at the Battle of the Pyramids, Mamluk rule was shattered. Napoleon insisted that the French had come to liberate the people from Mamluk tyranny, and promised respect for the Islamic religion, even discussing with the leading *ulama* the terms on which a mass conversion of his army might be considered (circumcision proved a stumbling block). He dispatched friendly messages to the Muslim rulers along the North African coast as far as Morocco, to the sultan of Darfur, and to Tipu Sultan in India. Muscat in the Gulf was suspected by the British of being under French influence. Plans were laid for the march into Syria, so that France would control the whole Levantine coast, as well as the western half of the Fertile Crescent. The ultimate scope of Napoleon's aims remains unclear. He must have intended that the geopolitical shock of his blitzkrieg invasion would rebalance the scales in favour of France, drawing the Ottomans back to their old alliance against Russia and Austria. But the odds were against him. Within days of his arrival in Cairo, Nelson's victory at Aboukir Bay destroyed the French fleet and cut him off from France. Egypt was too poor, too weak and too vulnerable to bear the burden of French rule and carry an army without overseas supplies. Revolt and resistance increased. The Ottomans declared war. The Syrian expedition failed. The 'Muslim' diplomacy came to nothing. By the time of Napoleon's secret departure for France in August 1799, Tipu Sultan was dead, defeated and killed by the British in May. The French army clung on, but there were no means in Paris to come to its aid. In June 1801 Cairo was captured by troops sent from Britain and India. The eastern project was finished.

This was not the end of the struggle, although the roof soon fell in on Napoleon's hopes of challenging the British at sea. In the decisive battle near Cape Trafalgar off the Spanish coast in October 1805, his nemesis, Nelson, shattered the French and Spanish fleets beyond hope of recovery. Napoleon had already abandoned the American mainland: Louisiana, recovered from Spain in 1800, had been sold for cash to the United States. St Domingue (modern Haiti), France's richest colony, was lost to a black revolt by 1804. Command of the sea allowed the British to seal off their empire in Asia. They captured the Cape in 1806, and the French Ile de France (modern Mauritius) in 1810. The Indian Ocean became a British lake. In 1811 they seized the Indonesian empire of Napoleon's client kingdom in the Netherlands.

Napoleon may have dreamed of renewing a French-led alliance with the Ottomans and Iran, partly to neutralize Russia in Europe,[34] but little came of this. His main object was still European hegemony.

In the same month as Trafalgar, his triumph at Austerlitz brought this prospect closer. The Austrians and Prussians were crushed. Napoleon redrew the map of Germany for a new client state, the Confederation of the Rhine, and reinvented Poland as the Grand Duchy of Warsaw. In 1807 at Tilsit, he and Tsar Alexander met on a raft and pledged Russo-French friendship. With Europe subdued, Napoleon turned the screws on Britain. Decrees at Berlin in 1806 and Milan the next year closed the whole continent to trade with the British. A reverse blockade was declared, to wreck the British economy, suck out its bullion, and force London to terms. If the British wished to be masters at sea, Napoleon seemed to be saying, he would drown them in their own element.

Had he succeeded, he might have recovered the ground France had lost since the failure in Egypt. But it was almost certainly too late. The 'continental system' that was meant to exclude British trade leaked like a sieve. It also destroyed any chance that Europe would accept Napoleon's version of empire. 'To ensure its success', wrote his former secretary caustically, 'it was necessary to conquer and occupy every country, and never to withdraw from any.'[35] Despite the magnetic appeal of his name for those discontented with the arthritic regime of the European dynasts, Napoleon's empire became intolerably burdensome. Russia rejected the commercial yoke, and demanded a promise that the Poles would never regain their kingdom. By 1812 Napoleon had reached the conclusion that only Russia's conquest would guarantee peace. Catastrophe followed. In the 'battle of nations' at Leipzig in October 1813, Napoleon's Grand Army, ravaged by its winter retreat from Moscow, was decisively beaten by the Austrians, Russians and Prussians. As France itself was invaded from the east and the south (by a British army from Spain), he went into exile (on Elba). His empire collapsed. Once his last bid for power (the 'hundred days' in 1815) had failed on the battlefield at Waterloo, the Vienna peace conference could reach its conclusions. In fact the decisions it made were Eurasian – if not global – in scope. The peacemakers grasped that there was no going back to the dynastic free-for-all of the *ancien régime*. Twenty-five years of revolution and war made the prospect unthinkable. Instead they constructed a territorial settlement to preserve a balance of strength between five great powers – Austria,

Prussia, Russia, France and Britain – designed to ensure that no single one could dominate the others. They invented the 'Concert of Europe', a process by which the five were to arbitrate differences and preserve the new distribution of power.[36] The Vienna settlement proved remarkably durable: Europe avoided a general war for nearly a century. Partly in consequence, it secured the conditions in which the two 'flanking' powers, Britain and Russia, were left free to pursue their extra-European ambitions except where they threatened the European peace. Vienna opened the door to Asia's encirclement from the north and the south.

The defeat of Napoleon and of his project of empire had a wider significance. It was the real culmination of the great geopolitical shift whose course we have traced, and whose radical impact he had failed to deflect. Once the British were free from the threat he had posed, they quickly made themselves masters of the Indian subcontinent. The commercial penetration of China, under way already before 1800, began to speed up. Although they handed the Indonesian archipelago back to the new Netherlands kingdom (designed as a barrier to French expansion in Europe), the British retained Singapore island and made it into the entrepôt for much of South East Asia. In the west, Spain's share of naval disaster in 1805 soon cost it control of its Spanish-American empire, whose trade was thrown open, mainly to Britain. Thus the cumulative effect of Napoleon's failure and Britain's success was to smash what remained of the old mercantilist system. The rival empires of trade, with their fleets and fortresses, their chartered companies and commercial monopolies, had been made obsolete by Britain's 'command of the ocean'. Even the British East India Company was forced to open up India to non-Company merchants in 1813 – although it kept its China monopoly until 1833. The most powerful check on the expansion of trade – the huge overhead costs of rival mercantile empires – had melted away. It remained to be seen how soon private trade – 'free trade' – would exploit the new opportunities that this great change presented.

THE GREAT DIVERGENCE

The geopolitical revolution had three major effects. Through the occupation and settlement of Outer World regions, it broke down the barriers to Europe's physical expansion. The North American interior and the South Pacific would soon be annexed as demographic extensions of North West Europe: they would become 'neo-Europes'. Secondly, in the critical stage after 1803 (when the European war was resumed after the briefest of respites) British sea power demolished the mercantilist zoning that had subdivided world trade into exclusive blocs, by destroying the naval balance of power on which it depended: the combined strength of the Spanish, French and Dutch fleets. The overhead costs (and risks) of long-distance trade, the excuse for commercial monopoly (justified in the past on grounds of the high price of protection) and the bar to new entrants were all cut away. Thirdly, the great transition in South Asia, carried through in stages between 1757 and 1817 (when Maratha power was broken), had offered the British huge windfall gains. By seizing control of the revenue and trade of Bengal, India's wealthiest region, the British acquired at a stroke the lever they needed to force open the door into South China's economy. With India as the base for their shipping and credit, the regional trades of East and South East Asia could be hooked up more easily to the long-distance traffic between Asia and Europe. The commercial seclusion of the East Asian world could at last be challenged.

It was unlikely, however, that these striking advances would have yielded much more than a temporary gain without a further great change in the economic relations between the European states and the rest of Eurasia. The great limitation on Europe's commercial exchanges with most of the rest of Eurasia had been the miserably small scale of the trade. It was almost entirely confined to luxury goods, tiny in bulk, and with a limited market. A year's worth of imports from Asia (so Jan de Vries has calculated) would scarcely fill up one modern container ship. Part of the problem had been that Europeans had little to sell that appealed to Indian or Chinese customers except bullion: that was why cotton and opium from India had been such a boon to the East India Company's agents buying tea in Canton. The only sure way of wedging open their access to the Asian consumer was to find European products in general demand, and discover some means of distributing them widely. Unless they did that, the growth in trade volume and value would soon level off: the doors they had pushed open might be closed again by more resolute rulers, and the Indian windfall be soon eaten up by the costs of conquest and rule.

What this meant in practice was that the enlargement and reordering of Europe's Asian trade that geopolitics had made possible would have to be supercharged by technological change if this trade was to escape stagnation. A technological transformation would be needed before European producers could overcome the historic advantage of their Asian competitors: the much lower costs of production in their artisan industries. The technology of travel required a similar change in Asia (and elsewhere) if the scale of exchange was not to be crippled by the costs of transport that isolated inland regions. Last, but not least, if the natural reluctance of indigenous rulers, whether Asian, African or even Latin American, to admit foreign traders and trade on more or less equal terms was to be overcome, or 'discouraged', then the ability to project power at very long range and at reasonable cost would have to be found. Since Europeans hitherto had enjoyed no obvious military advantage over other Eurasian (or African) states, except on the high seas, this also implied a technological solution.

We know, of course, that these 'solutions' were found – though not all at once, nor with universal success. Although historians differ over precisely when (not to mention how), it is clear that from about 1800 what has been elegantly termed 'the great divergence'[37] began to set in between the economic trajectory of the Euro-Atlantic world and that of most of the rest of Eurasia and Africa. For much of the next two centuries (longer in some cases), the disparities of wealth grew wider and wider (except in privileged regions). The reason lay, so it seemed, in Europe's unique capacity to industrialize its economies, achieving increases in output far above those that pre- or non-industrial economies could manage. Europeans exploited the flow of incremental improvements to their first innovations in mechanized production, increasing the pace of technical change and steadily widening the gap between their productive efficiency and that of non-industrial competitors. To reinforce this effect, which made Europe much richer than the rest of the world, the new industrial technologies conferred two other benefits of enormous importance. They supplied (at relatively low cost) the technological means for European domination in places where that had previously seemed hopeless, and on a scale unimaginable in the pre-industrial era. Advances in armaments (repeating rifles, machine guns, long-range artillery, steam warships) extended the radius and multiplied the impact of European or European-led armies and navies. Mechanized transport on land and sea projected military force over far greater distances and (in pre-industrial terms) at almost lightning speed, allowing comparatively small numbers of soldiers to be deployed and redeployed in campaigns that might be thousands of miles apart. British troops could be shuttled between South Africa, India, China and even New Zealand. Steam-engined troopships and 'strategic' railways, like those built in India after 1860, economized on the size of the garrisons needed to safeguard foreign control. The electric telegraph and the submarine cable played a similar role, enabling instructions to be sent, warnings to be issued, help to be summoned in a matter of hours not weeks. Information became the invisible weapon in the European arsenal, worth thousands of troops and millions of pounds. The other great benefit that industrialism gave was also a product of speed. The extraordinary rapidity with which invaders appeared, migrants rushed in, new trade routes were traced, and new port cities were constructed – all in various ways quickened by industrial technique – lent the European expansion into the Afro-Eurasian world, slow and hesitant as it was from some points of view, a blitzkrieg-like quality. With little time to react, and often poorly informed about their intentions, it was no wonder that sometimes the Europeans' involuntary hosts found it hard to contain them.

Of course, as the idea of divergence suggests, while the symptoms of change could be sudden and violent, it was decades before the economic transformation assumed an overall shape. What had begun to appear by the end of our period (in the 1830s) was, nonetheless, a set of economic relations radically different from those that existed before c.1750. Europe's industrialization was not a private affair: it altered fundamentally the exchanges it made with all other world regions, the volume and content of long-distance trade, and the circulation of goods and people all over the globe. What emerged from this was a new division of labour as parts of Europe assumed a set of specialized functions for a market that was, at least potentially, global. Already, in fact, Europeans had a virtual monopoly of the seaborne trade between Europe and Asia. When that trade was enlarged, its 'command and control' – shipowning, insurance, export–import and credit – was easily concentrated in European hands and reinforced further by Europeans' comparative advantage in commercial 'intelligence' – insider knowledge. But the real revolution lay in Europe's new role as the prime source of manufactures for the world as a whole, based in the main on the huge increase in output and the huge fall in real cost that mechanization brought. By 1810, calculates Paul Bairoch, a British operative using a spinning machine produced ten to fourteen times as much cotton yarn in an hour as his Indian competitor using traditional methods, a figure that rose to as much as four hundred times for the finer qualities.[38] Since textiles made up an enormous proportion of the manufactured output of non-industrial economies (perhaps 80 per cent), it is easy to see why industrial Europe became the global supplier of what was in almost every society the most widely consumed manufactured product. By the mid nineteenth century this industrial lead could also be seen in a huge variety of other consumer goods (especially metalware) that Europe could offer, as well as in the colossal expansion of machinery-making and industrial processes. To an extent inconceivable before 1800, Europe's industrial districts had become the workshop, factory and technical laboratory for the world as a whole.

Perhaps implicit in this, but as yet (in 1830) barely visible, was Europe's third global function. Industrial Europe (and above all Britain) became the world's main supplier of capital. The networks of trade and mercantile credit, the profits of industry and the gains to be made by constructing an industrial infrastructure (such as railways and harbours) to increase the volume of traffic made this a natural progression when savings had reached an adequate level. Once they had done so, Europe's commanding position in long-distance trade, industrial production and the export of capital became an *almost* irresistible force, combining systemically to reshape the whole pattern of global exchanges. Industrial Europe possessed, so it seemed, the transformative power to create a new global economy that turned most of the world into suppliers of raw products, consumers of manufactures and borrowers of capital. In this great reconstruction, Asian producers of artisanal manufactures for export (cloth above all) would go to the wall. Instead, the future of non-Europe would be emphatically rural: hard-working peasants growing raw materials for export, and buying (for example) cotton cloth in exchange. The commercial production of a huge range of commodities – cotton, silk, tea, sugar, coffee, tobacco, opium, cacao, rice, cinchona, jute, rubber, gutta percha, palm oil, gum Arabic, pepper, vanilla, indigo, gamboge, ivory, shellac, guano, hides, gambier – shipped in large volume to be processed in Europe, would be *their* engine of wealth, the means to improvement, and the vital incentive to social order and discipline. Or so ran the theory. In 1830 most of this lay in the future. As we shall see, its advance was resisted and was often slow and erratic. But the die had been cast.

This was the 'great divergence' that transformed the relative fortunes of the wealthiest societies in Europe and Asia. But how was it to be explained? What had happened to allow the richest parts of Europe to draw so far ahead of the richest parts of Asia? The favourite answer among Western historians has been to invoke the 'Industrial Revolution'. It was the unique capacity of certain European communities to invent and apply technological solutions that gave them the breakthrough. As a simple statement this is undeniable. But almost immediately the questions pile up. What made Europeans so technologically precocious? After all, in inventive capacity (as we have seen already) they had often trailed behind China. Nor was it obvious that the institutional setting for technological change was much more favourable in Europe than it was elsewhere – in China, for instance. Moreover, Europe's industrial transformation was not the result of a single 'big bang'. The growth of Britain's economy was relatively slow, suggesting a path of cumulative change, not a jackpot win in the technological lottery.[39] One influential account, drawing inspiration partly from Weber, stresses the unpredictable, almost random, conjunction of the crucial ingredients that allowed Europe to evade what had hitherto been the iron law of diminishing returns and resource exhaustion. The competition between states (allowing dissent and free thought), the restraints on state power (making property safer), a market economy that rewarded efficiency, a benign natural environment with ample reserves of food and fuel, and a staggering windfall (in the Americas) on which Europe could draw made up the elements of the 'European miracle' – unique and unrepeatable.[40] An alternative view radically shifts the balance of the argument. Here there is little to choose between North West Europe and the most advanced economies elsewhere in Eurasia, down to 1800. Europe's advantage lay not in its social or political structures, or even its progress in scientific thought. It derived instead from its dowry of coal (the result of geological chance) and colonies (the fruit of predation): they alone allowed its escape from the invariable fate of pre-industrial growth.[41] A third line of inquiry sees Europe's 'divergence' less as a result of its peculiar endowments (in resources, mentality or institutions) than as a reaction to global forces and trends. In this perspective, Europe's industrialization can even be seen as a defensive tactic with extraordinary unintended consequences.[42]

We might begin by acknowledging that in late-eighteenth-century Eurasia two regions stood out. One was in Europe. Of course not all Europe, since much of the continent in the south and east was poor and backward even by contemporary standards. Primitive agricultural technique, the lack of 'improvements' (like fencing and draining), bad roads or none, the shortage of artisan skills, very low levels of literacy, the absence of financial institutions to offer credit or capital, insecurity of person and property, the persistence of serfdom: conditions like these were still to be found in large parts of Europe's rural interior. The most prosperous regions could be seen in France, mainland Britain, the Low Countries, the Rhineland, northern Italy and parts of Catalonia, and among the commercial towns of southern and eastern Germany and the Austrian Empire. These were the places where an advanced commercial economy of the kind that Adam Smith described in *The Wealth of Nations* had taken firm root. Economic growth was driven by increased specialization and the division of labour, allowing productivity to rise and the market to grow in a virtuous circle. Incremental improvements in manufacturing technique and the use of the land pushed in the same direction. Added to this were the benefits derived from trade, both intra-European and also intercontinental. Though they are hard to measure, the effects of long-distance trade may have accelerated progress towards a mass consumer society (by promoting the taste for tropical products like sugar, coffee and tea) and stimulated innovation in marketing, management and the collection and use of commercial information. However, many if not most of these favourable conditions could also be found in China. Kiangnan (the Yangtze delta) was a great manufacturing region, producing cotton cloth for 'export' to the rest of China. With a dense population (a thousand people to the square mile)[43] of over 30 million, numerous cities, and a thick web of water communications connecting it with the middle and upper Yangtze (a colossal hinterland), as well as the rest of China (via the Grand Canal), Kiangnan was comparable to Europe's commercial heartland. A powerful case can be made that as a market economy it was as wealthy and productive as North West Europe. Textile production was similar,[44] while the consumption of items like sugar and tea may well have been higher. Technical ingenuity was widespread. Moreover, China benefited from laws that made buying and selling land easier than in Europe, and from a labour market in which serfdom had practically vanished (unlike in Europe). In an orderly, well-regulated society, with low levels of taxation and a state that actively promoted better practice (usually in agriculture), there seemed no obvious reason why material progress along Adam Smith's lines (what economists call 'Smithian growth') should not continue indefinitely, on a scale comparable with Europe.

Elsewhere in Eurasia, the barriers to material progress were higher. In the Ottoman Empire and Iran, no 'core' regions emerged along the lines of Kiangnan. With the exception of Egypt (where much of the Nile delta was still to be drained), the areas of dense and productive cultivation were scattered and few. Huge areas remained the preserve of nomads, in Anatolia and Iran. Population was scanty in a relatively harsh environment, sometimes subjected, like mid-century Iran, to violent disruption. The bulk carriage of goods, except in maritime zones, was extremely difficult. This helped to protect local suppliers of manufactured items from outside competition. But by the mid eighteenth century Europe's proximity had already begun to push the Ottoman lands towards the exchange of agricultural commodities for manufactured imports.[45] Iran's exports of silk had fallen away: it had few export commodities, let alone manufactures.[46] In India the position was different. Indian manufacturing was highly productive. Perhaps 60 per cent of global manufactured exports in the eighteenth century were produced in India, the textile workshop of the world. India's muslins and calicoes were in huge demand as luxury items in contemporary Europe, while its cheaper cottons were re-exported to West Africa to be exchanged for slaves.[47] Gujarat, Malabar, Coromandel and Bengal were commercial regions with strong international links. Cultivable land was abundant. But, unlike in China and Europe, the scope for building a large integrated economy was severely limited. In much of the subcontinent, inland transport was hampered by lack of navigable waterways. Trade routes in North India were badly disrupted by Mughal decline. Of course trade and traders survived, and perhaps even flourished, but the unstable geography of political power – shifting elite demand and protection from place to place – worked against the emergence of a stable 'core'.[48] The diffusion of technical skills – a crucial element in technological progress – suffered from the barriers of an occupation-based caste system. An unforgiving ecology discouraged long-term investment, as did the political turbulence that set in generally after 1750. It may also be true that Indian society at the level of peasants and weavers was too unruly and mobile to accept the 'labour discipline' imposed, for example, upon factory workers in Britain.

The question becomes: why did Kiangnan (and China) fail to match the economic expansion of Europe, and check the emergence of a Europe-centred world economy? The best answer we have is that it could not surmount the classic constraints of pre-industrial growth.[49] By the late eighteenth century it faced steeply rising costs for food, fuel and raw materials. Increasing population and expanding output competed for the produce of a more or less fixed land area. The demand for food throttled the increase in raw cotton production. Raw cotton prices probably doubled in the Yangtze delta between 1750 and 1800.[50] The demand for fuel (in the form of wood) brought deforestation and a degraded environment. The escape route from this trap existed in theory. Kiangnan should have drawn its supplies from further away. It should have cut the costs of production by mechanization, enlarging its market and thus its source of supply. It should have turned to coal to meet the need for fuel. In practice there was little chance for change along such lines. It faced competition from many inland centres where food and raw materials were cheaper, and which could also exploit China's well-developed system of water-way transport. The very perfection of China's commercial economy allowed new producers to enter the market with comparative ease at the same technological level. Under these conditions, mechanization – even if technologically practical – might have been stymied at birth. And, though China had coal, it was far from Kiangnan and could not be transported there cheaply. Thus, for China as a whole, both the incentive and the means to take the industrial 'high road' were meagre or absent.

The most developed parts of Europe did not face these constraints. Even if we exclude the much debated question of whether commercial institutions, the supply of credit and capital, and the dissemination of useful knowledge were more efficiently organized than in China (making technological progress more likely), it seems clear that the rising demand for food, fuel and raw materials was more easily met. Europe's 'resource frontier' had not been closed. New land was available (in southern Russia for instance), and agricultural improvement had raised the productivity of existing farmlands. And where the demand for fuel was at its most intense, it could be met by ample supplies of accessible coal. Europe also enjoyed the additional benefit of colonial trade, whose profits depended in part upon the fruit of slave labour. It had its windfall of 'free' land, especially in North America. Both may have contributed (though not decisively) towards Europe's escape from the fate of Kiangnan. The result overall was that the European 'core' had more time in hand to exploit the opportunities of technical progress, and a far better chance to make the technological leap to the use of steam power with its reliance on coal.

If this parting of ways had begun to occur, as the evidence suggests, around 1800, then a great revolution was indeed in the making. The story in fact is much more dramatic. One part of Europe experienced a supercharged version of economic change. This was in Britain, whose economic trajectory was considerably steeper than that of comparably prosperous regions on the European mainland. Here three features were crucial. Firstly, in the eighty years after 1760 there was a huge shift of employment from agriculture to manufacturing. At the beginning of the period industry employed around 24 per cent of the male labour force; by 1840 the figure was 47 per cent. This redeployment took place without raising the cost of agricultural produce, the vital condition for industrial expansion. Instead, while one agricultural worker could feed one industrial worker in 1760, eighty years later he could feed nearly three.[51] Secondly, while this massive enlargement of the industrial workforce, rather than any sharp rise in overall productivity, was a striking feature of Britain's Industrial Revolution, equally so was the great concentration on the production of textiles, especially cottons. Productivity gains were heavily concentrated in the textile industry. Machine-aided production using Arkwright's roller (1769) and Crompton's 'Mule' (1779), adapted for water power, allowed stronger, finer yarns to be produced at far lower cost than old forms of hand spinning,[52] and the industry converted in stages from skilled to unskilled labour. Yarn was exported, but it was also the raw material for the production of cloth, and brought down its cost. By 1801 cotton goods alone made up almost 40 per cent of British exports; thirty years later they were over 50 per cent. A vast new market was being carved out abroad.

Thirdly, the British pioneered the application of steam power and the use of coal on an industrial scale. Of course the principle of steam energy had long been known. Steam engines had been used since the early eighteenth century, but were of cumbersome size and gargantuan appetite. Not until 1775, when Boulton and Watt produced their model, was a more efficient version available. Steam power and coal formed a critical partnership. Steam engines pumped the water from mines, and without them coal production in Britain would have stagnated at the levels of 1700.[53] With them it grew by 1800 to 11 million tons a year – the equivalent of using the annual growth of wood from half the surface area of England. Steam released Britain from the constraint on fuel that (as we saw) had afflicted China, and opened the way for industrial processes with large energy needs. Coal and coke were the indispensable means to increase the supply of pig iron, which rose more than threefold between 1788 and 1806.[54] Steam and iron together produced more durable tools, artefacts and machines than could be made from wood. They helped to create a new 'engineering culture', whose incremental advances helped to transform the material world after 1800. Steam power was also applied to textiles by the 1790s, in the spinning of yarn, helping to drive down its cost even further. And by the 1820s it was beginning to be used for transport by water and land – an innovation that soon conferred enormous commercial and strategic advantages on its users.

These gains from steam power and coal meant an extraordinary increase in Britain's economic capability beyond that of any competitor in Eurasia. Of course, we should note that even by 1830 many of these gains had yet to be realized. The benefits of a steam- and coal-based economy may have become general only by the 1850s.[55] But well before 1830 the first great phase of Britain's industrialization had already transformed the most important commercial relationship between Europe and Asia. Europe's insatiable appetite for Indian cottons, and the competitiveness of Indian cloth in third markets elsewhere, had been the central fact of East–West trade since the seventeenth century. But by 1800 British manufacturers had largely replaced Indian goods in their own market at home and surpassed India in the export of calicoes, and they soon drove its cheaper varieties from other markets abroad. More remarkably still, by 1817 Indian weavers were importing British-made yarn on an ever-increasing scale. By the 1820s India had become a net importer of cottons.[56] With the arrival of power-weaving after 1830, Britain's advantage in yarns was extended to cloth. By the mid-1830s cotton goods made up more than half of British exports to India, and India had become Britain's second largest market for cotton manufactures.[57] It was an astonishing reversal. By demolishing India's long primacy in the world market for textiles, the British could drive their trade into any market in Asia whose door could be opened. India's was wedged open by British imperial power. It remained to be seen whether that power could be used on other markets as well.

It was, perhaps, more than just a coincidence that the European state that had played the most active role in colonizing North America, in extending the slave trade and in asserting European control in India should also have been in the vanguard of industrialization. The British had been able to extend their overseas trade on a massive scale during the eighteenth century – by as much as five times.[58] The surging demand for Caribbean sugar made the West Indies a buoyant consumer of British manufactures and of other supplies from the North American colonies. American earnings were also spent in Britain, swelling the volume of Atlantic trade. British exports to America and Africa rose ninefold between 1700 and 1774, overtaking the value of those sent to Europe.[59] The Caribbean was also – and infamously – a huge market for slave labour, and in the 1780s perhaps a quarter of British cotton exports were being sent to Africa to pay for slaves.[60] The importance of all this lay partly in the stimulus it gave to the networks of credit and finance in Britain, not least in Liverpool, which had become the principal port for American and West African trade. It created a ready-made network for the growth of new trades based on industrial processes: the supply of raw cotton came first from the West Indies, and cotton manufactures were sent to well-established markets. No barrier or bottleneck prevented the rapid expansion of the new manufactured exports or impeded the supply of the raw-material imports they needed. The sheer scale of Britain's foreign trade even before industrialization had other important effects. No government in Europe was more attentive to the needs of trade and manufacturing, more sensitive to the necessity to safeguard the financial system against the failure of confidence, or more willing to use its naval power in the interests of commerce. With the exception of the Netherlands, no other state had a ruling class so deeply involved in commercial investments, or so dependent for its income on commercial expansion. Finally, there is the Indian connection.

We saw earlier on that one intriguing possibility that might help to explain Europe's industrial transformation was its origins in a defensive response to Asia's global predominance in manufactured exports. Already by 1700, Indian chintzes and calicoes were all the rage among English consumers. 'We saw our persons of quality dressed in Indian Carpets,' said Daniel Defoe in 1708.[61] Imports of printed textiles from India were repeatedly banned to protect the woollens industry, but the demand was insatiable. The cotton industry in Britain began as the effort to capture this market with home-produced versions, importing plain Indian calicoes and adding coloured designs. It was 'the child of the East Indian trade',[62] and its products were called by Indian names.[63] After 1770, the new machinery for the spinning of yarn made Lancashire calicoes and muslins competitive. 'The Object they [the textile-makers] grasped at', so the London agent for Samuel Oldknow (the leading manufacture of muslins) told a government inquiry, 'was . . . to establish a Manufacture in Brittain that should rival in some measure the Fabrics of Bengall.'[64] But one of the results of the British conquests in India (Bengal especially) was a deluge of imported cottons by the East India Company, driving down prices and threatening to ruin the new home industry.[65] Competition from India (and also from cheap-labour Scotland), says Oldknow's biographer, gave 'a stronger impetus towards the adoption of the factory system, not only in spinning and the finishing processes, but also in weaving'.[66] To keep Indian goods out, duties were raised threefold in the 1790s and ninefold in 1802–19:[67] indeed, Indian imports declined sharply after 1802. Thus, in what became the leading sector for European penetration of the Asian market, imitation, protection and mechanization had been forced to advance together. Without the power to exclude competitive goods from India, while forcing open the door for British exports there, it might have been a different story.

COMPARING CULTURES

Territorial conquest and industrial technique were the most obvious features of Europe's novel assertiveness over the rest of Eurasia. But there was a third dimension to the new disequilibrium. It was in this period that Europeans first advanced the claim that their civilization and culture were superior to all others – not theologically (that was old hat) but intellectually and materially. Whether this claim was true need not detain us. Much more important was the Europeans' willingness to act as if it were. This was shown in their eagerness to collect and categorize the knowledge they gleaned from other parts of the world. It was revealed in the confidence with which they fitted this knowledge into a structure of thought with themselves at the centre. The intellectual annexation of non-European Eurasia preceded the imposition of a physical dominance. It was expressed in the ambition by the end of our period (earlier if we include the French invasion of Egypt) to 'remake' parts of Afro-Asia as the 'New World' had been 'made'. And it ultimately rested on the extraordinary conviction that Europe alone could progress through history, leaving the rest of the world in a 'stationary state' awaiting Europe's Promethean touch. We shall turn in a moment to look more closely at this 'mental revolution'. But what was happening in other parts of Eurasia?

In China between the 1750s and 1820s there was to be no great change in cultural direction, no drastic reappraisal of China's place in the larger world, certainly no repudiation of the cultural past. Nor was there any obvious reason why there should have been. This was a wealthy, successful and sophisticated gentry society.[68] The Ch'ien-lung (Qianlong) reign (1735–96) was one of political stability, prosperity and (in China proper) peace. In the slogan of the day, it was the 'Flourishing Age'. Their conquests in Inner Asia, the final victory over the turbulent steppe, crowned the Ch'ing's achievement in pacifying, reunifying, consolidating and securing the Chinese realm. The perpetual threat of dynastic collapse in the face of barbarian attack – the great constant in China's long history as a unified state – had been lifted at last: confirmation, were it needed, of China's cultural and technological superiority where it mattered most. It was, after all, a triumph which, in geographical scale and geopolitical importance (if not economic value), matched Europe's in America.

There were of course social and cultural stresses. Military failures against Burma and Vietnam; symptoms of growing bureaucratic corruption; popular millenarian uprisings like the White Lotus movement: all hinted at the onset of dynastic decline, the gradual decay of the 'mandate of heaven' on which dynastic legitimacy was thought to depend.[69] But the Confucian tradition remained immensely strong. Its central assumption was that social welfare was maximized under the rule of scholar-bureaucrats steeped in the paternalist and hierarchical teachings of K'ung-fu-tzu. The Confucian synthesis, with its Taoist elements (which taught the need for material simplicity and harmony with the natural world), faced no significant intellectual challenge. Religion in China played a role quite different from that of its counterpart in Europe. While 'pure' Taoism had some intellectual influence, and its mystical beliefs attracted a popular following, it had no public status and was regarded with suspicion by the Confucian bureaucracy. Salvationist beliefs were officially frowned upon.[70] Buddhism was followed mainly in Tibet and Mongolia. The emperors were careful to show it respect, as a concession to the Buddhist elites co-opted into their system of overrule. In China proper it was marginalized. Buddhist monks, like Taoist priests, were seen as disruptive and troublesome.[71]

The scholar-bureaucracy, and the educated gentry class from which it was drawn, thus faced no competition from an organized priesthood. No challenge was made from within the social elite by the devotees of religious enthusiasm. Nor was the bureaucrats' classical learning threatened by new forms of 'scientific' knowledge. For reasons that historians have debated at length, the tradition of scientific experimentation had faded away, perhaps as early as 1400. Part of the reason may lie in the striking absence in Confucian thought of the 'celestial lawgiver' – a god who had prescribed the laws of nature.[72] In Europe, belief in such a providential figure, and the quest for 'his' purposes and grand design, had been a (perhaps *the*) central motive for scientific inquiry. But the fundamental assumption that the universe was governed by a coherent system of physical laws that could be verified empirically was lacking in China. Even the scholarly *kaozheng* movement in the eighteenth century, which stressed the importance of collecting empirical data across a range of scientific and technical fields, rejected 'the notion of a lawful, uniform and mathematically predictable universe'.[73] It should be seen instead as part of the long tradition of critique and commentary upon 'classical' knowledge, not an attack upon its assumptions.

All this is not to say that scholarly debate was absent in China. The literati elite existed to write. The administrative system depended upon a stream of reports and inquiries, compiled, transmitted and then filed away. Scholar-gentlemen wrote papers and essays on matters of public interest to attract powerful patrons and advance their careers. The Confucian literati were especially numerous in the rich and urbanized Yangtze delta (Kiangnan) region, long seen as a hotbed of anti-Manchu feeling. From here criticisms circulated of the emperor's costly campaign to conquer Turkestan in the 1750s. But debate was constrained by the nature of China's political system. Unlike in Europe, there were no 'free spaces' on the political chessboard where a dissident intellectual could hope to find refuge. Public opposition to the emperor's authority was dangerous. A writer suspected of fomenting unrest could expect no mercy.[74] This was, after all, a Manchu *raj*, where key positions of civil and military power were carefully reserved to the Manchu minority. Manchus lived separately in special quarters of the towns; they were discouraged from intermarriage with the Han majority; and vigorous efforts were made to preserve their language and literature. The great imperial triumphs of the mid eighteenth century served, if anything, to reinforce the 'Manchu-ness' of the dynastic regime. His vast Inner Asian domain made the emperor more than a Confucian ruler: his claim was now to be a universal monarch.[75] The effect may have been to reinforce the conservatism of Confucian culture. Whatever their grumbles, for the scholar-gentry standard-bearers of the classical tradition the world seemed safer than in any previous era. The 'high-level-equilibrium trap' (things are too good to make change worthwhile), which explains so plausibly the technical conservatism of economic life, had its cultural counterpart. Outside influences were not excluded. But, as in the case of the court's Jesuit map-makers, they were neatly tailored to a monocentric world-view. The official version of the Jesuit maps removed the lines of latitude and longitude, to preserve the image of a China-centred world.[76] Official knowledge of European geography after 1800 remained grotesquely inaccurate.[77] It was a striking paradox that, on the eve of Europe's arrival in force on the shores of East Asia, Chinese intellectuals saw less reason than ever to concern themselves with imprinting their culture on the outside world, or with predicting its impact on their own moral universe. When Lord Macartney visited China in 1793, hoping to persuade the Ch'ien-lung emperor to allow diplomatic relations with Britain, the Chinese rejected his proposal outright. The gifts and gadgets he had brought, hoping to impress the court with British ingenuity, were dismissed as valueless toys and baubles. 'I set no value on objects strange and ingenious,' ran the emperor's message to King George III, 'and have no use for your country's manufactures.'[78]

In the Islamic lands, there was much less reason for cultural self-confidence after 1750. Politically, Islam seemed under siege. Both the

Ottoman and Iranian empires suffered military defeats and territorial losses, mainly at the hands of Russia. Egypt had been occupied by the French in 1798, until they were chased out by the British. The Mughal Empire had become a shell after 1760. Muslim Bengal became a British province. Muslim-ruled Mysore was crushed by the British in 1799. In Central Asia, Chinese rule was riveted on the Muslims of Sinkiang. In South East Asia, the British invasion of Java in 1811 paved the way for the later reassertion of Dutch colonial power (when the colony was handed back) over the Muslim states of the Javanese interior. The Islamic world seemed to be bearing the brunt of imperialism from both ends of Eurasia.

The greatest Islamic state was also the most exposed to European empire-building, commercial expansion and cultural influence. Ottoman officials and *ulama* – the scholar class that included imams or prayer-leaders as well as the learned interpreters of Islamic law and theology – were alarmed at the signs of imperial collapse revealed by defeat in the Russo-Turkish war of 1768–74.[79] European experts, like the military engineer Baron de Tott (the author of entertaining *Memoirs*), were already being employed to strengthen the Ottoman defences and instruct the army in European methods. Ottoman writers began to pay more attention to European politics and the military resources of the European powers. Some European books on geography and military subjects were translated. There was a trickle of Muslim travellers, some of whom wrote up their itineraries for the Ottoman government. How much impact this made is uncertain. Few Muslim scholars were familiar with European languages – perhaps none before the eighteenth century.[80] There was little up-to-date knowledge of European affairs.[81] In fact the cultural life of Ottoman Muslims in the late eighteenth century seemed largely unaffected by the contemporary ferment in the West. The intellectual inheritance of classical Islam remained extremely powerful, and was deeply entrenched in the central concerns of the learned class, theology and law. This was especially true for literary culture, and was also reflected in the continuity of indigenous motifs in architecture and design.[82]

This might be disparaged as a sign of 'decadence': the failure of a once-dynamic tradition to respond to the intellectual challenge posed by Europe's aggression. This would be a shallow judgement. Europe's geopolitical assault was sudden and violent. But the deeper nature of the European 'threat' was only gradually unfolded, and its 'meaning' could hardly be grasped by contemporary European 'insiders', let alone Muslim observers staring in from outside. With the benefit of hindsight, historians have often complained that the Ottoman Empire, like other Muslim societies, was very slow to adopt the cultural pattern of its European rivals: the outlook and ethos of the nation state; the ethics of liberalism; and the 'technicalistic' mentality of an industrializing economy. In reality, embracing such dogmas – still deeply controversial among Europeans themselves – would have struck Muslim thinkers not just as a leap in the dark, but as the surest route to self-destruction. Collapse from within would have hastened the work of attack from without. It seemed much wiser to continue the long-standing practice of borrowing piecemeal from European expertise, adapting foreign techniques to Ottoman or Iranian needs – as Safavid and Mughal rulers had done in their day.

It is easy to see why this should have been so. The cultural life of Islam (in the Ottoman Empire and beyond) was strikingly cosmopolitan. An educated man might seek his fortune anywhere between the Balkans and Bengal. The historian 'Abd al-Latif (1758–1806), born in Shustar at the head of the Persian Gulf, acquired his learning from scholars in Iran. But the hope of advancement took him to India, where his brother was already a physician in Awadh. He became the *vakil* (agent) of the ruler of Hyderabad to the Company government in Calcutta. His view of Indian history was Islamic not 'Indian'.[83] For the Islamic intelligentsia, the idea of territorial patriotism to an Ottoman, Iranian or Mughal 'fatherland' was deeply alien. The nation state as the unique focus of loyalty was simply meaningless. In the Ottoman Empire, Muslims (like Christians and Jews) drew their identity from their script and religion, not from their language or a concept of race.[84] Muslims enjoyed first place in a composite empire, as its soldiers, officials, lawyers and landowners. A Muslim nation state, a territory inhabited only or mainly by Ottoman Muslims, would have meant the end of the empire – indeed, it became possible only with the end of the empire in 1918. Nor were the guardians of culture sympathetic to the idea of a stronger state where that meant increasing the ruler's power. In an Islamic polity, there was always a tension between the *ulama*'s role as the exponents of the law and the ruler's duty to enforce and uphold it. 'Reforms' that shifted the weight of authority in the ruler's direction were bound to be suspect. From this point of view, the *nizam-i jadid* – the 'new army' created on the European model by Sultan Selim III (r. 1789–1807) – looked more like a weapon against his domestic opponents than against the external aggressor. A *fetwa* issued by the *sheikh ul-Islam* (doyen of the *ulama*) denouncing the sultan's new force was the signal for his deposition in 1807. In Iran, where the *ulama* looked back to their legal pre-eminence in the Safavid regime (1501–1722) and regarded the Qajar shahs after *c.*1790 as illegitimate upstarts, this mood was still stronger.[85] Abbas Mirza, the crown prince, who also established a *nizam-i jadid*, was forced to learn military drill in secret. He was unfit to succeed, said his *ulama* antagonists, 'for he has become a Farengi [i.e. Frank or Christian] and wears Farengi boots'.[86]

Even if the nature of Europe's 'divergence' had been better understood than it was, and 'reformist' elites had exerted more influence, there were multiple barriers to radical change. There was no secular 'public opinion' whose support could be mobilized. Learning and culture were widely decentralized in the numerous madrasas where the scholars held court. Outside the scholarly class, literacy levels were low. A printing press (in Arabic) had been introduced into the Ottoman Empire in the 1720s, but then suppressed until the 1780s. The first newspaper in the empire was not produced until 1828, and was published in Cairo, by then the capital of an autonomous viceroyalty. Since very few Muslims had travelled in Europe or commanded its languages, Ottoman and Iranian rulers often relied for their dealings with European states on agents who were drawn from their Christian minorities, Greek or Armenian. As their own communities seemed likely to profit from more European influence and the wider use of European methods, the loyalty of these agents could not be above suspicion. Under these conditions, Muslims alarmed by contemporary happenings were far more likely to look for guidance within Islamic tradition. Those who undertook the haj (the pilgrimage to Mecca) went home to urge stricter conformity in their own localities or to distribute the texts of the scholars they had met.[87] The Wahhabi movement in the Arabian peninsula (whose followers captured Mecca and Medina in 1803–5) was an extreme rejection of all non-Koranic influence as the source of corruption and evil. Its adherents were active as far away as Java. The Sufi brotherhoods, with their mystical rites, patron saints, relics and charms, were the main expression of popular religiosity. Regarded with jealousy by the *ulama* elite, they could not be ignored as the potential vehicle for mass discontent with the direction of change.[88] Even sophisticated observers of Muslim defeat at European hands, like the scholar-historians in late-eighteenth-century India, largely explained it away as a *moral* failure by decadent rulers. Restoring a state based on the sharia remained their common ideal.[89] Nor did it help that Muslims experienced European methods amid the shock of invasion. The great historian of late Ottoman Egypt al-Jabarti (1753/4–1825) was deeply impressed by the speed and efficiency of the French occupation regime, but revolted by its brutality and atheism. It 'established . . . a foundation of godlessness,' he wrote, 'a bulwark of injustice and all manner of evil innovations'.[90] Outrage, not curiosity, was the dominant feeling.

Of course, we should not discount altogether the ability of Muslim societies to reorganize their defences against European intrusion, or to adopt new ideas. In 1826, at the height of the Greek revolt, the Ottoman sultan Mahmud II liquidated the janissaries, the traditional corps whose alliance with the *ulama* had destroyed his predecessor. A series of reforms was then set in motion with the acquiescence if not the blessing of the most senior *ulama*, including the banning of the turban in favour of the fez. But before 1840 the impetus behind cultural and intellectual change was comparatively small – perhaps because of the lag in perceiving the radical challenge that Europe now posed. Nor should we imagine that Islam itself was in general retreat. In West Africa, for example, the late eighteenth century was an age of triumphant advance. Muslim warlords and Sufi brotherhoods extended the frontier of rule and religion. The timing was crucial. When Uthman dan Fodio founded his jihad state of Sokoto (in modern Nigeria) between 1786 and 1817, he and his counterparts in western Sudan (modern Mali) built a barrier against the Christian missionaries that were soon to arrive, and the Western colonialism that followed on later.[91]

*

The cultural worlds of China and the Islamic lands, for all their differences, had several features in common. They were not static or 'decadent'. Scholars debated. Architects designed. Artists drew. Poets mused. Townspeople sought entertainment. Students sought knowledge. Lawyers and doctors were trained. The rich desired objects of conspicuous consumption. Changes in social or economic fortune stirred moral or religious anxiety. Divine revelations or millenarian prophecy challenged intellectual orthodoxy. The worlds in which Sufism, Wahhabism or the White Lotus movement could flourish were not stagnant. But three great constants seemed to frame this scene. Firstly, in both the Islamic world and China, classical, literary civilizations were dominant. Conformity with their aesthetic and ethical precepts remained the basis of cultural life. Explaining how knowledge of the natural world confirmed their metaphysical truths was the real test of intellectual ingenuity. Secondly, in both of them cultural and intellectual authority was heavily concentrated in scribal elites, whose privileged status was effectively underwritten by political power. Open dissent from intellectual or religious orthodoxy was correspondingly limited. Thirdly, with certain trivial exceptions, both were largely indifferent to Europe (and each other) and not much interested in the Outer World beyond Eurasia.

Europe's distinctiveness should not be exaggerated. Europeans, too, were culturally introverted and heavily preoccupied with their own religious and intellectual concerns. They remained for the most part in thrall to their religious beliefs, and deeply intolerant of the beliefs of others. Clerical corporations (Churches) commanded great wealth and controlled education. Church and State were like Siamese twins. To most Europeans it seemed perfectly obvious that neither could survive without the other. The sacred elites governed with the secular, and monarchs were legitimized by the incantations of clerics. Nor were science and religion yet the sworn enemies that they seemed to become by the twentieth century. Isaac Newton, whose physics had swept the intellectual board, thought that the natural world was regulated by God, whose interventions adjusted the imperfections of nature. For most European thinkers, the natural order was fixed: adaptation (in Charles Darwin's sense) was unimaginable or unneeded. Much the same went for the socio-economic regime. The impact of technological and industrial change registered only faintly with the great minds of the Enlightenment. They were just as inclined to believe in a cyclical process of advance and decay as in the march of progress. They lived, after all, in a world in which serfdom still prevailed over large parts of Europe, in which political rights were closely restricted, and in which the wealthiest states were the most ardent practitioners of the slave trade and slavery.

Nevertheless, by the 1750s Europe was launched on a cultural trajectory that was sharply different from that in other parts of Eurasia. Within the intellectual elite, religious doubt could be openly voiced. The 'corrosive scepticism' of Pierre Bayle (1647–1706)[92] and the ridicule heaped by David Hume on Christian belief in miracles had little effect upon popular attitudes. Adherence to Christianity (in its various versions) remained a condition of social acceptance. But religious belief was gradually becoming a matter of opinion, to be sustained by argument not imposed by rule. After 1750, a flood of publications revealed the seriousness with which the challenge of unbelief was taken by churchmen. Ninety books were published in France in a single year (1770) to defend Christianity.[93]

This tolerance of scepticism reflected a deeper change in cultural assumptions. The huge intellectual influence of John Locke's *An Essay Concerning Humane Understanding* (1690) in Western Europe signalled the appeal of his individualistic psychology and philosophy. Famously, Locke rejected the notion that men understood the natural world by means of 'innate ideas' implanted by God. They relied instead on 'sense impressions' to build a picture of the world, and on reason to sort their impressions into a coherent pattern.[94] It was men's duty, said Locke, to withhold consent from truths that conflicted with reason and experience – an intellectual habit that education should foster.[95] They should not take on trust beliefs handed down from the past, and they could discover new truths by experience and experiment. Indeed, Locke was convinced of the value of 'rational and regular experiments', the practice to which the intellectual milieu in which he spent much of his life was deeply committed. By the mid eighteenth century this practice had become a central activity in European culture. Close observation of the natural world to test empirically the 'laws of nature' became an intellectual habit, a fashionable hobby among the educated. This was not to say that religious accounts of creation had lost all force. Much scientific inquiry was predicated on the role of a divine creator and the need to unravel the providential plan. But even creationist theories required constant updating to square with the results of observation. The oracular status of 'classical' knowledge had been demolished for good.

To scepticism and experiment we can add a third peculiarity: the European attitude towards space and time. Intense curiosity about the rest of the world had been a well-developed feature of European culture since the late Middle Ages. It may have derived from the pervasive sense that Europe lay at the edge of the world and not at its centre. Oceanic travel after 1400, and the reports it brought back, brought a huge expansion in literature reflecting this curiosity. The practical interests of merchants and colonizers swelled the demand for geographical data, while commercial controversy (for example, over the wisdom of exporting gold and silver) gave hard information on Asian and African trade a topical value. Maps and map-making assumed a growing importance, intellectually, commercially and also strategically. By the mid eighteenth century the systematic collection of geographical knowledge was a major preoccupation of European thought. 'Scientific' travel, with the careful observation of human and natural phenomena, acquired enormous prestige. The sensation caused by Cook's reports of the South Pacific, the founding of the African Institution (in 1788) to promote the exploration of the continent, the lavish scale of Napoleon's project for the 'Description of Egypt' (in 1798) and the intellectual impact of von Humboldt's account of his South American travels (1799–1804) showed how deeply the making of a 'global' world picture had become embedded in the European imagination. As we will see in a moment, this fascination with space may have helped to produce a new view of time.

A 'great divergence' between European culture and the culture of most of the rest of Eurasia was thus in the making by the mid eighteenth century. What is often called the European 'Enlightenment' was an intellectual movement whose roots have been traced deep into the seventeenth century.[96] Its crucial feature was the progressive collapse of the scholastic monopoly of 'classical' knowledge that remained so immensely powerful in Islamic and Confucian culture.

Why this should have happened in Europe is a historical puzzle of a thousand pieces. Europe's division into sovereign states, the rise of printed vernacular languages, persistent religious schism, the 'late' arrival of the European Renaissance, and the growth of a 'reading public' (itself a product in part of religious debate) may have created conditions in which the intellectual dominance of a unified scribal elite became impossible. To these we might add the other great difference in European history. Europeans alone acquired a 'New World'. How far this changed the direction of Europe's economic development remains debatable. But the impact of the Americas on the European mind is surely hard to exaggerate. They presented a huge intellectual challenge. It was not simply a matter of acquiring and organizing a vast bank of knowledge as the precondition of commerce and rule. It was in the Americas that Europeans discovered their capacity to impose radical change upon other societies – through enslavement, expropriation, conversion, migration and economic exploitation. It was there that they saw the devastating effects that one culture or people could have on another – an impact without parallel elsewhere in Eurasia. It was there, above all, that they found peoples who were living in what seemed an earlier age, following modes of life that, conjecture suggested, might once have prevailed in Europe. 'In the beginning,' said Locke, 'all the world was America.'[97] The result was a great backward extension of the historical past (far beyond the limits of biblical creation) and a new mode of speculative inquiry into the stages through which European society must have passed to reach its contemporary form.[98]

America revolutionized the European sense of time. It encouraged Europeans to devise a historical framework into which they could fit the states and peoples of the rest of the world. It helped to promote a conjectural history of progress in which Europe had reached the highest stage. In the later eighteenth century this sense of Europe's premier place in a global order was reinforced by three hugely influential ideas. The first was the virtue of commerce as a civilizing agent, on which Hume and the writers of the Scottish Enlightenment insisted.[99] In *The Wealth of Nations* (1776), Adam Smith pressed the case for commercial freedom as the surest route to material progress, and the idea of unfettered trade as a means to global harmony was taken up by Immanuel Kant in his *Perpetual Peace* (1798).[100] It was a short step to argue (like the Victorian free-traders) that Europe should lead the rest of world into universal free trade, and to see the world itself as a vast single market. The second was the extraordinary confidence displayed by Enlightenment thinkers that human institutions and even human behaviour could be reconstructed along 'rational' lines. No one carried this further than the English philosopher Jeremy Bentham, whose utilitarian calculus (the greatest happiness for the greatest number) supplied a measure against which laws and institutions anywhere in the world could be tested.[101] Armed with the calculus, the enlightened legislator (from Europe) could frame better laws than benighted locals mired in superstition and antiquated prejudices. To his follower James Mill, the history of India revealed that 'the manners, institutions and attainments of the Hindus have been stationary for many years' (since about 300 BC he suggested),[102] a savage indictment he extended to China.[103] Europe's Promethean touch offered the only hope for a resumption of progress. The third proposition was just as startling. It was the growing conviction by the end of the century that there rested on the Christian societies of Europe an urgent obligation to carry their gospel throughout the world. What was especially significant was the force of this evangelizing urge in Protestant Britain, the richest and strongest of the European maritime states, and by 1815 the dominant sea power throughout Southern Asia.

The second half of the eighteenth century thus saw the crystallization of a new and remarkable view of Europe's place in the world. The sense of the limits and peculiarities of European civilization characteristic of the Age of Equilibrium had been replaced by a conviction that Europe's beliefs and institutions had a universal validity. This confident claim drew strength from the expansion of dominion, trade and influence, strikingly symbolized in the conquest of India. It rested on the conviction that European thought had explained the stages of history, and that European science could provide – systematically – all the data that were needed to understand the globe as a whole. The vital ingredients for a new mentality of global preponderance had now been assembled.

PERSPECTIVES

We can now take the measure of the Eurasian Revolution in its three dimensions. We can see that it set in motion the great reordering in the relations of states that led eventually to the age of empires on which the sun never set and an apparently invincible European hegemony. That had yet to happen by 1830. But the huge new bridgeheads that Europeans and neo-Europeans had pushed out, and the unpredictable pattern of their conflicts and conquests, had already produced two important results. The first was the blasting open of the North American interior, whose rapid occupation by (neo-)Europeans and their slaves brought a colossal extension of the European economy by the mid nineteenth century. The second arose from the closely linked outcome of the wars in Europe and the wars in South Asia. The effect was to shatter the old system of mercantile empires that had raised the costs and flattened the growth of Europe's trade with Asia. Once the British commanded the sea road to India, South East Asia and China, closing the long phase of maritime struggle in the Indian Ocean, a swarm of new hopefuls arrived to try their luck at promoting commerce, Christianity and colonization in the world east of Suez. The era of 'free trade' was about to begin.

Part of the reason was the mysterious dynamism of the European economies, especially Britain's, and the advantage this gave them commercially and technologically. Supplanting Asian producers in their export markets, and then on their doorstep (when the British sold their yarn in India), pushed former manufacturing rivals towards the humbler position of raw-material providers – though not all at once, and never completely. Technological change, especially in steam power and high-energy processes, began to confer a whole set of advantages: in easing access to inland regions (rubbing out the old safety of non-maritime states); in the speed of movement (especially of troops); and in transmitting information. By the 1840s, no states that lacked this new communications technology could hope to match the long-range exertion of power by those who did possess it. The result was to place them on the constant defensive: to encircle them strategically, much as the new pattern of commerce had begun to box them in economically.

Indeed, the transformation at work could almost be summarized quickly and crudely as Europe's gradual occupation of an imaginary 'central place' from which the diplomacy and commerce of the rest of the world could be prodded and moulded into convenient shape. The great highways of international exchange (for goods, ideas and people) fell under the surveillance of European agencies – like the British navy. In the last section we saw how this intoxicating sensation of being at the centre of things – the principal source of cultural energy, the headquarters of knowledge, the entrepôt of world trade, and (for the evangelicals) the great depot of truth – had become almost a given in European thought by the end of the century. Not even China could retain its mystique. 'The Empire of China', wrote Lord Macartney at the end of his abortive mission in 1794, 'is an old crazy first-rate man-of-war [i.e. battleship], which a fortunate succession of able and vigilant officers has contrived to keep afloat for these one hundred and fifty years past, and to overawe their neighbours merely by her bulk and appearance.' But with lesser men at the helm her fate would be to be dashed to pieces on the shore.[104]

How was this great change in the balance of Eurasia – and hence of the world – to be explained? Had some overarching cause decided the fates of Western Eurasia (and its North American annexe) and the rest of the 'world island'? A plausible case might be made for the growth of trade as the critical factor. Not just long-distance trade, but the increase in commercial activity found right across eighteenth-century Eurasia as a result of the division of labour, specialization and the widening of the market. Commercialization was a political and cultural as well as an economic phenomenon. It unsettled old habits, promoted new tastes, created new discontents, disempowered old rulers, and advanced new interests. It stretched and strained the social fabric. It was a source of alarm as well as of complacency, most of all, perhaps, in the richest of states. Dislike of new wealth and its dubious origins created a new moral climate in late Hanoverian Britain in which the slave trade (reaching its peak in the 1780s) came under ever-fiercer attack from conservative as well as radical opinion.[105]

According to this argument, what really mattered was that some parts of Eurasia were more successful than others at adapting to the demands of commercialization and exploiting its benefits. In fact the critical issue for the survival and cohesion of states and societies can be described more precisely. It was whether their rulers were able to control the new flows of wealth to reinforce the power of the state against external attack. Four different cases may suggest how this worked. In North West Europe, British governments were able, by the ruthless deployment of maritime power and commercial regulation, to suffocate Dutch competition in the Atlantic trade and to tax Britain's new wealth to finance the costs of globalized warfare. In Middle Eurasia, the Ottoman Empire rejected the mercantilist doctrines favoured in Britain, allowing shipping and trade (and the revenues they promised) to fall into the hands of foreign merchants and the Christian 'Levantines', who gained foreign 'protection'. The fiscal resources with which to finance the stronger state needed by the 1780s were thus absent or lacking. In India, there were two different places where mercantilist states might have flourished. The first was Bengal, but it collapsed in the crisis of 1756–7 and became the East India Company's economic colony. The second was Mysore, whose political leaders were much more astute. It took the British thirty years and three wars to batter it to death. In the last case, East Asia, the verdict was still open until the late 1830s. For here, with far greater success than elsewhere beyond Europe, the rulers (of China and Japan) had preserved their control over foreign trade. What was much more uncertain was whether their grip on domestic sources of wealth would allow the courts in Edo and Peking to keep up their guard against Western intrusion.

Yet it should not be thought that non-European states had lost all room for manoeuvre. The Ottoman Empire passed through a terrible crisis in the 1830s, and came close to breaking up in 1833 and 1839. On both occasions it was saved mainly by the intervention of the European powers in a tacit admission that its survival (as both guardian of the Straits and governor of much of the Balkans, Anatolia and the Arab lands) had become an essential prop of Europe's post-war balance of power. Mahmud II (r. 1808–39) and Abdul Mejid (r. 1839–61) used external pressure to force through the changes intended to strengthen their grip on the imperial system and recentralize a decentralized empire.[106] Ironically, the greatest threat to Ottoman rule had come not from the Europeans, but from a rebellious vassal, the pasha of Egypt. Mehemet Ali (an Albanian Mamluk), who had arrived in Egypt in 1805 as the Ottoman governor, exploited the wrecking of the old regime at Napoleon's hands. He smashed the remnants of Mamluk power, took back the land revenue from the tax-farmers, and turned Egypt's exports (of cotton and grain) into state monopolies. In 1816 he started a textile factory.[107] Like Tipu Sultan in Mysore, his aim was to build a fiscal-military state that could master the region. In 1820 he invaded the upper Nile valley (modern Sudan) and founded Khartoum in search of black slaves to man his new army.[108] By the 1830s he had a huge conscript army of Egyptian peasants, and had forced the sultan to acknowledge the autonomy of his Greater Egypt, including Syria, Crete and the Sudan as well as Egypt itself. Without European intervention in 1839–40, it is more than likely that this tough adventurer and his garrison state would have absorbed most of the Ottoman Empire in Asia.[109] Checked though he was, he had turned Egypt into a dynastic state, with the most dynamic economy anywhere in the region.

In Iran, too, there was a surprising recovery from the chaotic conditions after the death of Nadir Shah in 1747. A rump state emerged to rule the west of the country under a Zand tribal leader, Karim Khan, who governed (at least nominally) as a Safavid viceroy.[110] The north and east (Khorasan) remained beyond his control. A new period of disorder broke out on his death, but by the mid-1790s another Turkic clan from the north had recovered most of what the Safavids once ruled. The first Qajar shah, Agha Mohammed, was crowned in 1796. His successor, Fath Ali Shah (r. 1797–1834), was forced to surrender the suzerainty of Georgia and part of Azerbaijan to the aggressive imperialism of the Russian generals in the Caucasus. The attempt to resist ended in the humiliating treaties of 1813 and 1828. But by a cautious rapprochement with the suspicious *ulama*, the careful refurbishment of ancient imperial tradition, Machiavellian tactics against the refractory tribes who controlled much of Iran,[111] and increasing skill in playing off the British against the Russians, the Qajar shahs reversed the drift towards internal collapse and bought time for reform.[112]

On the South East Asian mainland, the age of European dominance seemed still more remote. The Burmese Empire, with its capital at Ava on the upper Irrawaddy, had been plunged into crisis in the mid eighteenth century (at about the time of Plassey) by the revolt of its subject peoples, the Mon and the Shan. But, far from falling apart, it staged a dramatic recovery under the Kon-baung kings.[113] Its northward expansion towards the Himalayas, not British aggression, was the cause of the First Anglo-Burmese War, in 1824–5. In Siam, a similar pattern of consolidation could be seen after 1750. Like the Burmese kings, the Chakri monarchy skimmed the profits from the 'country trade' between India and China to fatten their patronage and cultural prestige. Most striking of all was the reunification of long-divided Vietnam under the Nguyen emperors in 1802. In all these cases, the local divisions and conflicts that had favoured the Europeans in maritime India and the Indonesian archipelago were conspicuously lacking.[114]

Nor, of course, was Europe's advance always a barrier to non-Europe's expansion. Europe's markets and merchants could be turned to advantage, and so could its politics. The imam of Muscat, whose Omani domain guarded the entrance to the Persian Gulf, put them all to good use. Omani sailors and traders had an old connection with the east coast of Africa. By the 1820s they had stolen its slave trade from the Portuguese in Mozambique and had turned Zanzibar into an emporium attracting British, German and American shipping. The rising demand for slaves (in the Middle East) and ivory (in Europe) fuelled the rapid enlargement of a mercantile empire on the East African mainland. By the 1840s, Zanzibar had become so prosperous that the imam had moved his capital there.[115] But why did the British – committed since 1807 to destroying the slave trade at sea – exempt the imam from their general ban? He was too useful an ally of their sea power in the Gulf, the chief source of their influence on the shah of Iran. Too brusque a suppression of his profitable trade, warned the Indian viceroy, might cause 'even our old and faithful ally, the Imam of Muscat . . . to be estranged from us'.[116] It was an ill wind that blew no one any good, the imam might have reflected, as he pondered the growth of his monsoon empire.

Finally we should cast a glance at the most intriguing case of all. One great Eurasian state had remained almost untouched by the expansion of Europe. The Tokugawa shoguns had preserved Japan's

seclusion far more rigorously than the Ch'ing rulers had protected
China. They allowed a handful of Dutch traders to come to Deshima,
in Nagasaki harbour, and permitted an occasional visit to Edo, partly,
it seems, for the fun of seeing the barbarians walk and talk in their
peculiar fashion. They also permitted some trade with China (there
was a Chinatown in Nagasaki). Despite their extreme hostility to the
subversive influence of Christianity, they allowed the limited circulation of 'Dutch (i.e. Western) knowledge' among the scholarly class.
But they remained vigilant to the point of paranoia against the activity
of 'spies'. One scientific visitor who was caught with maps of Japan in
his baggage was imprisoned for a year; his Japanese contacts suffered a
drastic penalty.

Under seclusion, Japan had become very largely autarkic. Foreign
trade was tiny. The domestic economy was divided into separate *han*
or princely domains, although the demands of Edo (whose million
people made it perhaps the largest city in the world) had created a
massive internal trade, especially in foodstuffs. In the eighteenth century, a stable population (unlike China's great surge) and an 'industrious revolution' – more intensive farming and the use of household
labour for spinning and weaving – had allowed a modest rise in
prosperity. But there were warning signs that agricultural production
was now close to its limits. Bad weather brought famine in the 1780s
and, after a brief remission, again in the 1830s. Rural hardship provoked rural unrest on a growing scale. The impoverishment of the
samurai and the decline of the shogun's revenues (both arose from
the difficulty of raising the land tax against peasant resistance) stirred
a debate on the social and political order. To make matters worse,
from the 1790s there was a series of alerts that Japan's long immunity
from European interference had come to an end. A Russian expedition
appeared on Hokkaido in 1792. Ten years later the Russians returned
to ask for admission to the trade at Nagasaki. Still more alarming was
the unexpected arrival in Nagasaki harbour in 1808 of a large British
warship, which departed only when its menacing demand for supplies
had been met. This was the shogun's first warning of the changes in
the Euro-Atlantic world since the 1770s. Other casual visitors, whal-
ing ships seeking water and food, were an unwelcome reminder that
Western shipping had come to stay in the North Pacific and that Japan

lay across the main sea lane between America and China. Until the 1840s, however, the impact of all this was surprisingly limited. The dominant view among Japanese scholars fiercely affirmed the innate superiority of the 'Divine Realm' over the Western barbarians and their insidious thoughts. The prohibition on foreigners' landing was enforced even more strictly.[117] And, as it turned out, Japan's geopolitical niche, at the furthest remove from European power, and shielded by China (the primary object of European attention), preserved the country's seclusion for two further (perhaps crucial) decades. But the race against time was coming even to Nippon.

5

The Race against Time

5. Commodore Perry's entry into Tokyo harbour, 1853

THE EURASIAN MOMENT

The Eurasian Revolution had signalled the onset of a seismic change in the relations of continents and civilizations. It transformed the geopolitics of the early modern world. When the Russians took control of the Crimea, they opened up the Ottoman defences like an oyster and won a springboard for the Romanov annexation of Georgia in 1804. Georgia was the gateway to the Caspian provinces of Iran, soon wrenched from the Qajars' grasp in the treaties of Gulistan (1813) and Turkmanchai (1828). With their defences off balance, the Ottomans saw Egypt occupied first by the French and then by the British, before escaping into virtual independence under their rebellious viceroy Mehemet Ali. This drastic shift in the geostrategy of the Near East made both the Ottomans and the Iranians much more vulnerable than before to the rival ambitions of the European states. But their fate was not peculiar. A comparable revolution had occurred in South Asia, where a British 'company state' based mainly in Bengal, had become the dominant military power by the 1830s after a half-century of war. From their port city of Bombay, the British could now drive their influence into the Persian Gulf and across the Indian Ocean into southern Arabia (Aden was seized in 1839), Zanzibar and East Africa. It was from eastern India and its South East Asian outposts (the 'Straits Settlements') that they dispatched the forces that broke the historic seclusion of the Chinese Empire and compelled the Ch'ing to open their ports in 1842.

The Europeans' invasion of the Asian states, their breakthrough into the North American interior (once the settlers had thrown off British imperial control in 1783), their beachheads in the South Pacific and the spasmodic advances into West and Southern Africa showed how far they had broken free from the constraints of the early modern world. We have seen how their opportunism was stimulated by consumer demand in Europe for Atlantic commodities and Asian luxuries. The increasingly universalist claims of European religious and intellectual culture offered a justification for these conquests, an explanation

for their success, and a programme for advance. Technological innovation made (some) Europeans more productive than Asians and freed
them from dependence upon the imported luxuries of the Asian world,
especially textiles and porcelain. By the 1830s, Europeans were assembling the means for the physical, commercial and cultural domination of regions that had been beyond their reach only sixty years
before, and whose civilizations had once seemed awesome and impregnable to European communities wedged at one end of the Eurasian
land mass.

Yet even in the 1830s, such a European pre-eminence was not a
foregone conclusion. The second round of discoveries and invasions
and the technical innovation behind the Europeans' commercial and
military expansion might have counted for little had European societies not adapted in ways that maximized their leverage in the non-
European world. It is not difficult to imagine an alternative scenario in
which Europe's new wave of expansion was slowed down or checked
altogether. The most likely obstacle was the renewal of conflict within
Europe itself. The peace of 1815 had sealed the defeat of Napoleonic
imperialism. But a restless superpower, whose defeat had required a
continental coalition; the ideological legacy of a violent revolution;
gimcrack states (like the Netherlands); submerged nationalities (like
Poland); and the fragile apparatus of dynastic overrule across Central
and Southern Europe (the Habsburg Empire) together made up an
unpromising recipe for continental peace. A new round of open warfare, or even an armed peace (a cold war), would have had far wider
consequences. It would have blocked the channels of trade and encouraged a general return to the mercantilist self-sufficiency that the economist Robert Malthus predicted, choking off the British experiment
in industrialism. ('No great commercial and manufacturing state in
modern times . . .' said Malthus, 'has yet been known permanently to
make higher profits than the average of the rest of Europe.')[1] It would
have delayed the diffusion of capital and technology that set off
Europe's railway age after 1830.[2] It would have stopped in its tracks
the flow of immigration from Europe that was feasible only when the
sea lanes were safe and conscription was light. Indeed, any general
war in Europe would have changed the face of the nineteenth-century
world. As in earlier conflicts, the European states would have carried

their quarrels into the other continents. The temptation to seek allies among the great Asian states would have been irresistible. Even when they were at peace with each other, Britain, France and Russia competed fiercely for the favours of the Ottomans, Egyptians, Iranians and Chinese. With European allies, it might have been much easier than it proved for Asian rulers to modernize their armies and manage the pace of political change. In the meantime, the growth of the overseas 'neo-Europes' in the Americas and Australasia would have been stalled as the flows of trade, capital and manpower on which they depended were dammed or frozen. After the upheavals of 1750– 1830, the world would have drifted towards a new equilibrium. Sheltered by the bitterness of European divisions, the rest of Eurasia and many indigenous peoples in the Outer World would have gained a breathing space: to reconnoitre, rearm and reform.

Instead they found themselves in a race against time: a race to 'self-strengthen' before European power and wealth could overwhelm their defences. Far from renewing their internecine quarrels, European societies recoiled from war and embarked instead upon an uneasy experiment in political and economic cooperation under the ideological banner of a wary, limited and contested liberalism. A 'Greater Europe' emerged to include both Russia and the United States in a vast zone in which political and cultural differences were moderated by a sense of shared 'Europeanness' ('Americanness' was merely a provincial variant) in the face of recalcitrant nature, hostile indigenes or 'Asiatic' competitors. It was a crucial if unexpected evolution, a huge accretion of strength by default, a vast material reinforcement. For if Europe was to transcend its old Eurasian limits and command the centre of the world, it had to become something more. It had to be reinvented as the 'West'.

INVENTING THE WEST

It might seem strange to argue that across the vast expanse of the Northern world from the American West to the Russian East a form of pax prevailed during the middle decades of the nineteenth century. Half a dozen exceptions would spring to mind. There were wars between the European states: the Crimean War (1854–6), in which Britain, France and the Ottoman Empire fought Russia; the wars of Italian (1859–60) and German (1866) unification, involving France, Piedmont–Sardinia, Naples, Austria and Prussia; the War of the Danish Duchies (1864); and the Franco-Prussian War of 1870–71. There were wars on the borders of Europe between Russians and Ottomans in 1877–8, between French and Muslims in North Africa, between the British and Egyptians in 1882. The longest and bloodiest conflict of all was fought on the American continent in the civil war between North and South (1861–5). But, numerous and bloody as these conflicts were, none of them led to a *general* war between the states and societies of Greater Europe. The Crimean War, which involved three great powers, and nearly a fourth (Austria), was practically localized in the Black and Baltic seas. The wars over Italy, Denmark, and German unification, and the Franco-Prussian War, were short, relatively limited, campaigns in which the great powers not directly concerned refused to participate. The Russo-Ottoman war of 1877–8 was concluded without blood being spilt between the European powers. The American Civil War involved no other power, although the North's blockade of the South came close to provoking intervention by the British.

More to the point, the result of these wars was not to instigate a wider struggle for continental or hemispheric supremacy. In Italy, Germany and the United States, their main effect was to demolish the regional barriers that obstructed the building of more cohesive nation states. Devastating as they were to the combatants and civilians caught up in them, the limited character of these 'Western wars' may have contributed to the widespread belief that armed conflict was an acceptable, perhaps necessary, means of resolving international differences and 'building the nation'. But what force restrained Europeans from the unlimited wars of mutual destruction in which they had engaged before 1815, and to which they resorted, even more catastrophically, after 1914?

The most important influence was the memory of the great war that had swept across Europe for a generation after 1792. The endless cycle of campaigns and conflicts, the seeming impossibility of any lasting peace, the experience of revolutionary turmoil and military despotism, and the terrifying fragility that the wars revealed in nations' social fabric made a huge impression on European opinion. It discredited the *ancien régime*, which had failed so dismally to keep the peace, and the old diplomacy, which now seemed so cynical, opportunistic and irresponsible. It demonstrated the urgent need for collective action against any great power that seemed to threaten the general peace. And it highlighted the importance of reconstructing Europe in the interests of its geopolitical stability. The Vienna settlement of 1815 and the 'concert system' that was meant to uphold it were the handiwork of statesmen whose watchword was 'never again'.[3]

Organized collective action against infringements of the Vienna treaty broke down soon enough. But the main principles of the concert system had a much longer life. They outlawed any unilateral act that would upset the overall balance of influence among the five great powers of Europe, the 'management committee' of its public affairs: Austria, Britain, France, Prussia and Russia. Change in the control of Europe's lesser states, or in the provinces of its dynastic empires, required the collective consent of the powers in conference. Of course, even this provision fell into disuse when the great powers quarrelled among themselves: their disunity was exploited by the French and Piedmont against Austria in 1859, and by Bismarck against Austria and later France. But the underlying convention was remarkably tenacious. Even Russia, often cast as the uncivilized bear of European diplomacy, with an insatiable appetite for control of the Straits, deferred to the concert idea, and its Balkan diplomacy was much less adventurist than was often portrayed by its critics in Britain and France.[4]

The strength of the concert system derived from self-interest: not just the fear of war, but nervousness about geopolitical change. British leaders were sometimes inclined to play to the domestic gallery and denounce the politics of their European neighbours. Austrian repression in northern Italy and Hungary was a favourite target. But even a minister as pugnacious as Lord Palmerston usually preferred rhetoric to action.[5] A bond far stronger than the concert principle united Austria, Prussia and Russia in an unspoken conservative alliance. All three ruled over vast tracts of Eastern Europe in defiance of any national principle. All three had reason to fear (especially after the 1848 revolutions) that any falling-out between them would set off a general explosion in which subjugated Poland (of which each had a share) would sound the first and loudest blast (the Polish revolt of 1863 was a timely reminder). This was why Bismarck (a Prussian *Junker* from east of the Elbe), for all his talk of 'blood and iron' and his reputation for *Machtpolitik*, stopped well short of any drastic reordering of the European map. His 'German Empire' of 1871 carefully preserved the old states and monarchies of the Germanic Confederation and repudiated the *Grossdeutsch* ideal of uniting all ethnic Germans (including those under Habsburg rule) in a single state. Indeed, the main challenger to the Vienna order up to 1870 was not Prussia but France. It was Louis Napoleon, the nephew of Bonaparte who had proclaimed himself emperor in 1851, who plotted the downfall of Austrian hegemony in the Italian peninsula. But even the French (least of all the peasants on whose votes Louis Napoleon depended) had no appetite for revolutionary warfare, and the paradoxical result of their intervention was not the client state in northern Italy that they wanted but an all-Italian Mediterranean rival. Ten years later, in 1870, the hollowness of France's claim to continental primacy was brutally exposed at Sedan.

Thus it might be too much to claim that peace prevailed across the 'Western Zone' from the 1830s to the 1880s. But it would be reasonable to conclude that a broad geopolitical stability – a pax – was maintained. This stability had several important results. Firstly, although Britain's maritime primacy was never wholly secure,[6] the sea routes within Greater Europe (especially the North Atlantic) as well as between Europe and the rest of the world remained open and safe throughout the period.[7] This had a huge bearing on the cheapness, reliability and speed of intercontinental connections and the gradual extension of Europe-centred trade. The large investment in new fleets of steamships from the 1840s onwards would have been unthinkable in conditions of maritime disorder. Secondly, the careful balance the continental states maintained among themselves, combined with the maritime strength of Britain, ruled out intervention in either North or South America, and allowed the United States to develop *as if* it really was isolated, unburdened by the need for external defence. This enormous benefit permitted the single-minded pursuit of economic growth and a local settlement of the violent disputes that constantly threatened to tear the Union apart right up to the final solution of 1865. Thirdly, the structure of European diplomacy conferred a wide freedom on Russia, France and Britain (the three 'world' powers up to the 1880s) to pursue their interests outside the continent, but simultaneously restrained them from an imperial free-for-all. The careful preservation of the Dutch colonial empire in South East Asia after 1815 and the equal trading and consular rights enjoyed by most European states in China after 1842 (mainly secured by British force) were symptomatic of the concern of metropolitan governments to avoid a violent clash of interests in Asia or the Outer World. Fourthly, geopolitical stability in Greater Europe favoured the growth (gradual, erratic, contested) of a minimal common ideology of 'limited liberalism'.

This too may seem a strong claim to make of a group of states whose institutions ranged from popular democracy (in the United States), through parliamentary government on a limited franchise, all the way to the quasi-theocratic tsarist despotism at the other end of the political scale. It was certainly true that European political thinkers waged ideological pamphlet wars denouncing (or extolling) monarchism, republicanism, socialism, capitalism, anarchism, imperialism and much else beside. Histories of Europe in this period graphically convey the frustrations of liberals, radicals and socialists faced with the entrenched conservatism of kings, emperors, aristocrats and peasants. In the failed revolutions of 1848, liberal, radical and nationalist movements were defeated by their conservative enemies, who had the backing of soldiers, bureaucrats and clerics. But by the 1870s scarcely any state in Europe (not excluding Russia) lacked at least the rudiments of a liberal constitution.

European liberalism had a long lineage. But as a practical programme it owed its appeal to Europe's great political crisis between 1789 and 1815. The violent upheavals of this period contained a double warning. They showed that even the most powerful of *ancien régime* states could be overthrown by a movement welling up from below. Old-fashioned absolutism was a feeble breakwater against popular unrest. Social and political stability required something more than simple-minded 'legitimism' – a return to the past. The second warning was just as dire. Revolutionary violence in France had been brought under control – but by the despotism of Napoleon Bonaparte. The Napoleonic legacy was mixed. In France and Italy, particularly, it was admired for the creative genius of Napoleon's state-building: the legal code; the administrative symmetry; the educational reform; the vision of an ordering and improving state; above all, the career open to the talents. But across the rest of Europe, and even in France, it was the terrifying force of Napoleonic ambition, the brutal erasure (and just as brutal invention) of rulers, states and institutions, the appalling ease with which the self-crowned emperor had demolished his enemies and imposed his continental domination, that left the deepest impression.[8] If *ancien régime* Europe had been vulnerable to popular unrest, it seemed practically helpless against a 'modern' despotism.

The core beliefs of mid-nineteenth-century liberalism sprang from the contemplation of this fearful period of European history. Escape from the cycle of war and revolution required political institutions that would defend the state equally against popular revolt and parvenu despotism. Rulers must be more 'legitimate'. They needed the loyalty of a wider range of communities and interests. Their servants and officials must be kept in check, ideally by a representative body. That raised the question of who should represent whom. Most of all it raised the question of how far a government should regulate the social and economic life of its citizens. Liberalism's answer to this was the key to its position, the fundamental premise of its political theory.

It was brilliantly sketched by the Swiss-born Frenchman Benjamin Constant, whose political writings were a fierce rejection of revolutionary violence and Napoleonic tyranny. Constant argued that ordinary people were bound to resist interference in their private and social lives and that arbitrary acts by the state destroyed the mutual trust between individuals on which all social and commercial relations depended. He distinguished between the proper (and narrow) sphere of authority and the wider realm (what would now be called 'civil society') in which the self-regulation of private interests should prevail. Modern societies, he suggested, were too complex to be ruled politically after the fashion of an ancient city state – the model to which many earlier writers (including Rousseau) had appealed. Diversity, pluralism and localism were the secret of stability and freedom. Secondly, the legislators, to whom the executive should answer, should be drawn from those least likely to favour the extension of arbitrary power or to be seduced by a demagogue. Politics should be the preserve of the propertied, who would exert a wholesome (and educated) influence on the 'labouring poor'. The propertied were the true guardians of the public interest. Thirdly, it was necessary for property rights and other civil freedoms to be protected by well-established rules – an ideal that implied the codification of the law and its machinery.[9]

Constant advanced a further crucial justification for his liberal system: it alone was compatible with social progress. All forms of arbitrary government tended sooner or later to impose uniformity. Yet without freedom of thought all societies were condemned to stagnate, since the expression and exchange of ideas was the means of advance in every sphere. Indeed, without the free circulation of ideas, governments themselves would scarcely know what course to pursue. Neither Constant nor the liberal thinkers who followed him intended to promote an anarchy of ideas. Their real concern was with the intellectual freedom of the educated, enlightened and propertied. For (or so they assumed) it was these who were the real political nation, the defenders of freedom, the engineers of improvement. Under their tutelage, civil society would be free, but also dynamic.

Of course, a sea of arguments swirled around these beliefs. Could a hereditary monarch be trusted as head of state, or was a republic the only safe form of representative government? Could women be part of the political nation, or was their 'physical frailty' a decisive bar? Did commercial and industrial wealth confer political virtue on its possessors, or did this spring only from property in land? Was religion the enemy of freedom of thought or the vital prop of social morality? Should the laws embody the 'custom of the country' (and become the subject of historical inquiry) or (as the 'utilitarian' followers of Jeremy Bentham believed) emancipate society from the 'dead hand' of the past? Then there was the question that vexed liberalism more perhaps than any other: was the achievement of 'nationality' – a shared ethnic, linguistic and (sometimes) religious identity – the essential precondition for liberal institutions to function properly?

And what if the pursuit of nationality conflicted with the central tenets of the liberal programme: freedom of thought and the strict limitation of government power? Was nationalism a forward-looking ideology or (except in a few favoured and 'progressive' places) a creed of the backward and benighted?

To this quarrelsome accompaniment, the main ideas of the liberal programme were diffused widely across Greater Europe between the 1830s and 1880s. That is not to say that they were uniformly adopted. Representative government was most firmly rooted in Britain and France, though not without an Indian summer of aristocratic privilege in the former and bouts of revolutionary and Napoleonic enthusiasm in the latter. In the German states, Prussia and Austria, liberal ideas helped sweep away the remnants of serfdom in 1848 and entrench forms of parliamentary government in the two great Central European states that emerged from the wars of 1866 and 1870–71: the German and Austro-Hungarian empires. The new Italian nation state, founded in 1860, with its elected chamber, limited monarchy and secular ethos, exemplified the hopes of bourgeois liberalism. To its critics, the new Europe of the 1840s, '50s and '60s seemed dull, selfish, commercially minded and vulgarly materialist. Thomas Carlyle and Karl Marx denounced the ruthlessness with which bourgeois capital treated proletarian labour. To other writers, impeccably liberal in outlook, the rise of 'public opinion' as the formative influence in national life threatened to crush the individual beneath the deadweight of popular prejudice.[10] The historian Jacob Burckhardt, a member of Basle's patrician elite, regretted the disappearance of 'Old Europe' and denounced the unreflecting, fact-grubbing and bureaucratic mentality of the new, with its complacent belief in inevitable progress.[11]

In the eyes of many European liberals, Russia was the grand exception in a happy story, and the absolutist claims of its tsarist monarchy were the enemy of freedom not only in Russia but wherever in Europe its influence prevailed. But even Russia was not immune from liberal ideas. To an influential group in the aristocracy, the war against Napoleon had revealed the shortcomings of absolutism and the urgency of grounding the imperial state in the loyalty of the peasant masses whose devotion had saved it in the terrible emergency of 1812. They imagined a regime in which the educated and enlightened among the noble-gentry class would guide the government and transform the subject masses of serfdom into a loyal nation. When a premature attempt at reform collapsed in the failed 'Decembrist' coup of 1825 (Sergei Volkonsky, a leading Decembrist, had briefly been a member of Benjamin Constant's salon in Paris),[12] the new tsar, Nicholas I, embarked on a thirty-year regime of reaction. Decembrist sympathizers were exiled to Siberia, or retreated into the coded and allegorical literature that was to be a long tradition in Russia. Censorship and surveillance were intensified among the gentry. Membership of radical or revolutionary groups was savagely punished. In 1849 the writer Fyodor Dostoevsky was sentenced to death for belonging to a socialist group – a punishment commuted at the very last moment to prison-exile in Siberia. But below the political surface the pressure to remake Russia as a 'national' community with its own national literature, music and art – in place of the old caste society in which the educated spoke French or German, and Russian was a peasant dialect – was growing apace. Its great literary inspiration was the poet Alexander Pushkin (1799–1837), whose writing exemplified the desire to conceive Russia in European terms, but with its own distinctive culture and character. The same ambition lay behind Tolstoy's *War and Peace*, originally titled 'The Decembrists' and eventually published in 1865.[13] When Russia was defeated in the Crimean War, the new tsar (Nicholas had died in 1855), Alexander II, embarked upon a programme of reform.

The centrepiece of reform was the abolition of serfdom, decreed in February 1861. Serfdom had become the symbol of a backwardness that had been punished by defeat in 1856. The serfs were liberated and granted lands on their masters' estates, but on a communal tenure in the village collective or *mir*. As part of the remaking of rural society, elective bodies or *zemstvo* were created through which the gentry were meant to play an active and 'improving' role in local life. Judicial reforms brought a 'modern European system of justice'.[14] Jury trial was introduced, along with Justices of the Peace to disseminate modern notions of law in the countryside.[15] The university statute of 1863 gave Russian professors as much freedom as American.[16] Censorship was lightened, and the more draconian restraints on personal freedom were lifted. After 1865 it was even legal to smoke in the street. In literature and music, the natural sciences, law and political theory, Russia converged more and more with the rest of Europe, even if – in European fashion – many Russian writers and artists asserted the aesthetic particularity and moral superiority of their native tradition (an English habit as well). Even the so-called 'Slavophiles', who rejected the 'cultural cringe' of the 'Westernizers' towards European thought and manners as alienating and atheistic, imagined Russia as a Christian Slav nation whose reforming elite would be in spiritual and political sympathy with the peasant masses. With liberal reform came the spread of newspapers, the rise of urban literacy (by the 1860s literacy levels in St Petersburg exceeded 55 per cent),[17] a flowering of Russian literature, a dramatic rise in Russia's cultural prestige, and a huge increase in the intellectual traffic between Russia and the rest of Europe.

By many standards, of course, Russia was still a profoundly illiberal society. It remained an authoritarian bureaucracy, in which the freedom to criticize could be withdrawn as quickly as it was granted. But the reforms of the 1860s signalled the tsar's recognition that a partial mimicking of the freedoms extolled by European liberals was necessary if Russia was not to fall behind the other great powers and abandon the Europeanizing project with which the Romanov dynasty had been associated since Peter the Great. Both tsarist reformism and Decembrist liberalism reasserted Russia's claim to be a European state whose historic role was to colonize and civilize its vast 'Asiatic' interior – the grand theme of Vassilii Kliuchevskii, Russia's greatest nineteenth-century historian.[18] It was no coincidence that, while Alexander II 'liberalized' at home, his soldiers and diplomats were driving forward the imperial frontiers in the Amur basin in East Asia and into trans-Caspian Central Asia. Here was a paradox in the making. Russia's part (and it was a very large part) in the expansion of Europe was energized and facilitated by the dynamic social vision of European liberalism: its sense of continuous progress; its emphasis on economic freedom; the contrast it drew between the liberty of the West and the 'stultifying uniformity' of the East. Yet the multi-ethnic nature of the Russian Empire, the fragility of its social bonds and its feeble infrastructure were a constant reminder that without the 'steel frame' of autocracy the grand imperial edifice might fall apart at the first sign of trouble. Russia, it came to seem, could be a nation state on the liberal model, or an empire, but not both.

The United States was the western wing, just as Russia was the eastern, of this liberal world. In conventional (and American) versions of the American past, it is America's isolation and detachment from Europe that are stressed: the forging of a separate political tradition; the making of an American 'exceptionalism'. Europeans were trapped in their history, condemned to work out the consequences of dynastic, class and ethnic struggles to their bitter and turbulent end. But Americans were free to create their own future, to pursue freedom without the shackles of Old World inequalities and antagonisms. In large part this story is merely a grandiose version of settler myth: versions of it can be found in most settler societies in the nineteenth century, and in most of their 'nationalist' historiographies in the twentieth. The American reality was more prosaic. America was the western extension of Greater Europe.

Ideologically, of course, America had certain peculiarities. Its constitution had been framed before the great upheavals of 1789–1815 that marked European liberalism so indelibly. The notorious American suspicion of executive power owed more to the 'country party' tradition of eighteenth-century Britain than to the liberalism of Constant. In European eyes, the United States, with its colossal scale (even before the huge increase of territory brought by the annexation of Texas and the Mexican War of 1846–8) and extreme decentralization, was hardly a state at all. It had no foreign policy, no army or navy worth the name (between 1815 and the civil war), and virtually no government. The British, who had kept control of nearly half of North America after 1783, feared not so much a deliberate assault on their possessions as a filibuster by a frontier warlord that the president of the day would be too feeble to prevent. Europeans were also puzzled and alarmed by American populism – the very wide suffrage (for white men) and the universal tendency towards elective office, even for legal or judicial officials. The English radical Edward Gibbon Wakefield condemned the rootless mobility of American society, its lack of any sense of place, tradition or history, and most of all the vulgarization that was inevitable (he thought) without a leisured and educated elite to set the tone. 'I saw a people without monuments, without history, without local attachments ... without any love of birthplace, without patriotism ...'[19] Alexis de Tocqueville, who had visited the country in the 1830s, admired the astonishing vigour of American self-government, but doubted whether its populism was ultimately compatible with intellectual independence.[20] But the most paradoxical feature of the American democracy was its tolerance of black slavery. This was a major source of Anglo-American tension before 1863 (when slavery was abolished). It fuelled the suspicion across the Atlantic that American populism was a coarse and degraded version of European liberalism: violent, racist and unstable. The American West, remarked the English historian T. B. Macaulay, was like the wilder parts of seventeenth-century Britain, where justice was administered with the gun and the knife.

Of course the shortcomings of populism were widely noted by Americans too. 'Whig' politicians denounced 'Jacksonianism' for its reckless expansionism, its disregard of treaties with Native Americans, its crude agrarianism, and its antagonism to the commercial and financial establishment of the Old Northeast.[21] In the 1850s the rise of abolitionism and the competition between slave and free states for control of the West (a struggle whose flashpoint was in Kansas) created a new popular ideology of 'free soil' and 'free labour'. On the eve of the civil war, the 'republican' coalition forged by Abraham Lincoln united the Northeast and Midwest sections against the South and destroyed the remnants of Jacksonianism. With the victory of the North in 1865, American politics no longer diverged quite so vividly from European models of the liberal state. The crushing of the slave South confirmed the pre-eminence of the Old Northeast, the heartland of industrial and financial America, and its huge port city of New York. The rise of the Wall Street banks and the concentration of financial power in trusts and cartels created a new class of tycoons wielding enormous political and social influence. Plutocracy – aristocracy's parvenu cousin – had arrived. In the 'Gilded Age' after 1865, the corruption of American politics became legendary. 'We have', said Mark Twain with his tongue in his cheek, 'the most expensive legislators in the world.' At the same time the scale of industrial employment, the rapid growth of large cities, the emergence of a recognizable working class and the imminent end of the old frontier of 'free' land – hitherto the safety valve (in theory) of the social tensions of the industrial East – drove home the point that, while America was still different from Europe – freer, richer, safer – it faced political and social issues that were comparable if not similar. An echo of this can be seen in the gradual change of American attitudes towards the imperial expansion of the European states. American 'anti-imperialism' was rooted in the universal hostility of settler communities towards imperial authority and the fear of exploitation by merchants, bankers, shipowners and suppliers in the metropole. Until the 1860s, it was supercharged by Southern resentment at British anti-slavery and by the fierce competition between the Old Northeast and Britain for commercial and financial predominance on the American continent. But by the 1880s the Old Northeast had won that struggle, and its elites were cultivating imperial attitudes and a social ethos much more in sympathy with their counterparts in Britain. The ground was being prepared for the 'great rapprochement'.

It would be reckless to deny that wide differences separated the political attitudes of Americans and Russians, British and French, Germans and Italians in the fifty years between 1830 and 1880. But these differences must be kept in perspective. For all the variations that sprang from local tradition and separate histories, the striking feature of the period is the steady convergence of all parts of Greater Europe towards a kind of 'generic liberalism'. The benefits were huge. After 1815, nineteenth-century Europe escaped the violent religious controversies that had torn it apart in the seventeenth century, the grandiose dynastic visions so productive of conflict in the eighteenth, and the genocidal ideological warfare that was its terrible fate in the twentieth. Ideological convergence – hesitant, partial, grudging – allowed the countries of Greater Europe – a 'proto-West' that extended by the 1860s across the northern half of the globe – to contrast their lot with that of the rest of Eurasia and the Outer World. It vindicated their sense of progress and dynamism – on which generic liberalism laid such stress – and heightened the difference with the 'stationary states' of Asia. Vitally, it equipped all the numerous communities of an expansionist Greater Europe with a 'road map' that could be applied almost universally to interpret, organize and justify their relations with non-European peoples. The 'civilizing mission' (not the mission to convert the heathen) was a liberal doctrine that appealed (in however crude a form) as much to imperial officials in Russia as it did to the frontiersmen of the American West. Unlike previous ideologies espoused by European expansionists – crusading imperialism, mercantilism, dynastic absolutism – generic liberalism proved remarkably attractive to some at least of the colonized. Its values were, or seemed, universal: they appealed to Indian, Chinese, African and Arab elites almost as much as to Europeans. Here was an astonishing and unprecedented third dimension to the expansive powers of the Europeans. It endowed them (that is, the more skilful practitioners of ideological politics) with a flexible new weapon in the search for allies in the non-Western world. It helped to prise open societies closed to all their other threats and blandishments. It was – or later seemed to its embittered foes – the Trojan Horse of European imperialism.

TOWARDS A WORLD ECONOMY

Much can be said for the view that in the middle years of the nineteenth century the most powerful force for change across the world was the ability of Europeans to penetrate the economies of Asia, Africa, South America and the Pacific far more deeply than ever before. The drive to exchange more, to seek out new markets, to find 'new' products and commodities, and to draw the commerce of the world into one vast network centred on the great port cities of the West – London, Liverpool, Hamburg, Bordeaux, Marseilles and New York – was the main dynamic behind the gradual formation between the 1860s and the 1880s of a 'world economy' – a single system of global trade. This was an era of steadily rising prices after the depression of the 1840s until the major slowdown in the mid-1870s, and of rising demand for raw materials. Of course, vast areas of the world remained outside the pull of international commerce because they were too inaccessible, too poor, or too insulated by political or religious controls from external contact. The hallmark of the 'world economy' was not the ubiquity of international trade but the way in which older regional systems of exchange, regional systems of pricing and credit, and regional hierarchies of mercantile power (like that which gave such wealth and power to Arab traders on the East African coast) were being broken down. It was no longer just a matter of luxury goods. By 1880 the cost of basic commodities (like food grains) was set by their price on the world market.[22] The supply of credit and commercial investment reflected the level of international, not merely local, demand – a change that could be seen in the spread of Western-style commercial banks to parts of Asia and Latin America. Western-based shippers, merchants, bankers and insurers were tending to displace, or subordinate, local mercantile elites in international trade.[23]

General peace and a significant degree of ideological convergence were vital elements in the ability of the emergent West to assert its economic dominance and to fashion a world economy to meet its needs. But the third crucial factor was the progress towards economic integration between the Western countries themselves. Without it there could scarcely have been the huge increase in the volume and value of international trade. The volume of trade grew by twenty-five times between 1820 and 1913, with the fastest rate of growth between 1840 and 1870. The wider integration of international markets was largely possible because of the extent to which the West itself had become a single economic space.[24]

The reasoning behind this claim will be explored in a moment. But first we should notice that, even in a period of astonishingly rapid growth in world trade, it was the volume of trade between Western countries that was the outstanding feature of the international scene. In 1876–80, Europe and North America supplied 76 per cent of the exports and took 77 per cent of the imports circulating in international trade.[25] Britain was much the largest trading nation in the nineteenth century. In 1850, 1860 and 1880 over 60 per cent of British trade was conducted with continental Europe and North America, leaving the remainder to be divided between Asia, Africa, South America and the Pacific.[26] Britain's trade with the United States alone was larger by a fifth than its trade with the whole of Asia: in 1880 its imports from the United States had a value equal to the whole of British trade with Asia.[27] Nor is this pattern surprising. It can partly be explained by proximity: it would have been strange if the British had not traded more with their nearer neighbours. Yet Britain traded more with the United States, 3,000 miles away by sea, than with France, Belgium and the Netherlands combined, though they were comparable in population and commercial development. What promoted trade and shaped the pattern of commercial relations was specialization. Maximizing production in the most profitable sectors was the engine of wealth, but it required a high degree of mutual dependence between trading partners. The active agent in making specialization possible was the speed, reliability and cheapness of communications. It was here that the countries of Greater Europe built up a decisive advantage over the rest of Eurasia and the Outer World.

The rapid spread of the telegraph (carrying commercial information, especially prices) and the steamship (at first mainly for mail and passengers) helped to unify the whole vast region from the Mississippi to the Urals from the 1830s and '40s onward. With the telegraph came the rise of press agencies: Havas (based in Paris) from 1835; Associated Press in New York from 1848; and Reuters in London from 1851.[28] But the most powerful agent of economic connection was undoubtedly the railway. As railways became more efficient, they galvanized the zones they entered. They could drive down the cost of inland transport (where no waterway existed) by up to 80 per cent. Regions where self-sufficiency had been the rule, because bulk transport by road consumed all profit after twenty miles or so, could now send their produce to far more distant markets. Dependence and specialization (the Siamese twins of economic growth) became feasible. Railway mileage is thus a revealing index of economic integration and its benefits. Here the contrast between the West and Afro-Asia becomes overwhelming. In 1850, when Western countries had 24,000 miles of line, Asia, Africa and Latin America combined had scarcely 250.[29] In 1860 the figure was 65,000 miles to 1,800. Even in 1880, when railway-building was well under way in British-ruled India, the Western countries still had (at 210,000 miles) ten times as much line as the rest of the world together. Russia, the least developed of the large countries of Greater Europe, had more miles of track in 1870 (and by 1890) than India, which had three times the population. In 1890 there were virtually no railways in China.

The ability to shift goods rapidly and cheaply between the countries of the West was matched by the creation of a financial infrastructure. More and more merchant banks and finance houses sprang up to provide the funds needed for long-distance trade. The credit instrument supplied in London (the 'bill on London') became the common currency of international commerce. Bankers in London and Paris (the Rothschilds operated in both) became the intermediaries for the raising of foreign loans – at first mainly for governments in Europe and America, but increasingly, by c.1860, for private enterprise, especially railways. After 1856 the Russian government turned to the foreign (mainly the French) investor to fund the modernization the reformers demanded. A stock exchange was established, and commercial banks appeared.[30] Beyond Europe and North America, these kinds of financial relations seemed possible only in certain favoured enclaves whose trade connections were particularly strong, or in colonies like India, whose financial system was supervised by an imperial power.

This precocious development in transport and finance helps to explain why so much of the world's trade was conducted between the countries of the West. But there was a third element that helped to make Greater Europe the most commercially dynamic part of the world: the returns on its human capital. After 1830, the trickle of migration out of Europe swelled gradually until by the 1850s it had become a flood. Over 8 million people left Europe between 1850 and 1880, almost all of them for the United States. This great migration had a double effect. It relieved the Old World of the worst of its rural overcrowding and transferred its population surplus to a region where impoverished migrants could become producers and consumers on a larger scale. Secondly, the transmission in human form of Europe's artisan skills (since not all migrants were poor) to an exceptionally benign environment supercharged the growth of what had become by the 1880s the largest economy on the globe.

It was the peculiar pattern of American economic growth that made it such a valuable extension of the European world. The most striking fact about America was its vast reservoir of 'free' land waiting to be exploited by a mobile army of white settlers and (in the South until 1865) their black slaves. The cost of obtaining this land by force or purchase from other claimants (French, Mexicans, Native Americans) was astonishingly low. The returns from agricultural land that had aeons of 'stored fertility' to use up and required only minimal inputs and husbandry (by Eurasian standards) to make it productive were so high that American agricultural productivity even in the 1830s was 50 per cent greater than Britain's (the home of capital-intensive 'high' farming) and three times greater than continental Europe's.[31] The rapid takeover of this landed booty poured a stream of exports across the Atlantic and paid for an equal stream of imports. Seventy per cent of American exports went to Europe after 1840; 60 per cent of imports were drawn from there.[32] This trade played a vital part in the growing prosperity of Europe's richest region, its Atlantic fringe. Britain, Europe's richest country, had a larger trade with the United States in 1860 than with the wealthiest countries of either Northern or Western Europe.[33] It was from 'Atlantic Europe' (Britain, France, Belgium and the Netherlands) that capital and skills, especially in engineering, were radiated east and south to the rest of the continent.[34] But what made the American 'windfall' so exceptionally beneficial for Europe was the contribution that Americans themselves could make to the speed and scale of their own growth.

In theory, the opening up of such a vast agrarian frontier (land costs aside) required a heavy burden of investment (in transport), a large supply of manufactured goods (both tools and consumer goods) and a sophisticated commercial network to bring credit to the farmer and his goods to market. The economic history of Latin America down to the 1880s showed how slow and uncertain the development of 'new countries' could be. But the story in the United States was entirely different. From the earliest days of independence (indeed, even before it), American commercial life – centred on the ports of Philadelphia, Boston, New York and Charleston – was comparable in sophistication and efficiency to its opposite numbers in Western Europe. After the revolution, as much as before, American merchants maintained very close contact with their trading partners in Britain. They were as adept as their British counterparts in lending and borrowing, and the speculative climate of the new republic may have spread the habit of financial risk-taking even more widely than in the Old World. As a result, of the large amounts of capital needed to build a modern economy (whose land area increased threefold between 1790 and 1850) more than 90 per cent, perhaps 95 per cent, was supplied

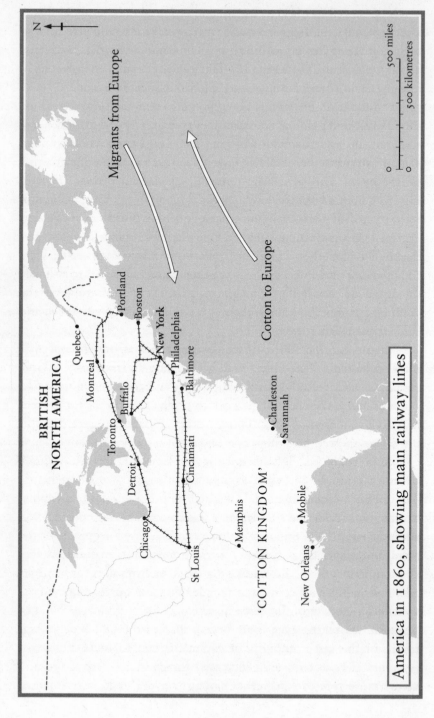

Migrants from Europe

Cotton to Europe

BRITISH
NORTH AMERICA

Quebec

Montreal

Portland

Boston

New York

Philadelphia

Baltimore

Toronto

Buffalo

Detroit

Cincinnati

Charleston

Savannah

Chicago

St Louis

Memphis

Mobile

'COTTON KINGDOM'

New Orleans

N

500 miles

500 kilometres

0

0

America in 1860, showing main railway lines

by Americans themselves, although foreign capital (mainly British) played a key role in the financing of railways.[35] The emergence of New York as the country's premier port, taking (by 1860) two-thirds of imports and dispatching one-third of exports, created a grand commercial metropolis, the centre of market intelligence and (with the proliferation of banks) financial power. By the eve of the civil war, its population had grown to over 800,000, and began to rival London's in size. With its self-confident mercantile elite – including immigrants like August Belmont, who had excellent overseas connections – its canals and railways stretching far into the interior, and its shipping lines up and down the Atlantic seaboard, New York had the expertise, the information and the resources to use domestic investment to the greatest advantage and gain maximum leverage from its overseas credits. The rise of New York City meant that much of the commercial and financial needs of a large and dynamic economy could be supplied from within.[36]

Secondly, for all that its economy was predominantly agrarian, the United States was far from being wholly dependent on Europe for its manufactures. From its beginnings, it had a significant industrial capacity, although much of it was organized in workshops rather than factories until the 1860s. Even in 1830 the United States ranked second (alongside Belgium and Switzerland) in industrial output, behind Britain but ahead of France.[37] By 1850, some 22 per cent of American gross national product came from manufacturing and mining (in Britain the equivalent figure was 34 per cent).[38] The Old Northeast, including New England, New York and Pennsylvania, became an American Lancashire, Yorkshire and Midlands. More and more it could service the demands of the huge agrarian sector (by 1851 Cyrus McCormick was producing a thousand reapers a year in his Chicago factory)[39] and those of a booming population that grew from under 15 million in the 1830s to over 44 million in the 1870s, while drawing relatively less and less on the industrial capacity of Britain and Europe. While British imports from the USA rose by £77 million to £107 million between 1854 and 1880, exports there rose more modestly, from £21 million to £31 million.[40]

It should now be possible to see the importance of America for the larger story of Europe's rise to dominance in Eurasia, and 'Greater

Europe's' advance towards global primacy. Conventionally, America has been left out of the narrative of European imperialism in the nineteenth century, entering the stage only in 1898 with the Spanish–American War. In fact America's peculiar growth path was extremely influential. For all the scale of its farming frontier, America's industrial and financial capacity made it a part of the Atlantic 'core' which drove the expansion and integration of Europe. Its trade helped enrich its Atlantic partners, but without consuming too much of their available capital. Its innovations in agricultural, mining, hydraulic and railway technology were readily diffused to other frontiers of European expansion. The telegraph was an American invention. So were three other devices that played a not unimportant part in the European conquest of Afro-Asia: the revolver (invented by Samuel Colt) and the Gatling and Maxim guns. In communications and weaponry, American ingenuity added hugely to the arsenal of Europe's colonizing technique. But perhaps one key aspect of America's economic history was even more decisive.

For almost all the nineteenth century, raw cotton was America's largest export, making up half the total from 1830 to 1860, and as much as a quarter as late as 1913.[41] After 1830, with the rounding-out of the 'Cotton Kingdom' in Georgia, Alabama and Mississippi, production rose sensationally under the regime of plantation slavery. The cotton trade was the lubricant of the American economy and the secret of New York's commercial ascent. Much the largest market for the cotton crop was Britain, in the mills of Lancashire. Cheap, reliable and abundant supplies of cotton and the invention of power-weaving made Lancashire the textile factory to the world, with a product that was highly competitive in almost every unprotected market. Cotton textiles were the battering ram with which the British first broke into the markets of Asia – though with opium as its steel tip in China. Once the age of plunder had subsided, it was the demand for cotton goods that turned India into a huge economic asset, a captive market that could not be trusted with self-rule lest tariffs follow in its wake. With India in their hands, the British became the greatest military power from Suez to Shanghai, and all round the rim of the Indian Ocean. The 'Cotton Kingdom' and its slavery system, Lancashire industry and British rule in India were thus bound together by an extraordinary symbiosis. In this respect, as in so many others, however 'anti-colonial' their political views, Americans were the indispensable sleeping partners of Europe's expansion into Afro-Asia.

THE FRONTIERS OF GREATER EUROPE

Its geopolitical, ideological and economic characterstics helped to make Greater Europe a grand expansionist conglomerate after 1830 on a far larger scale than in previous centuries. The voyages of discovery had been sensational. The Europeans' irruption into the trading world of the Indian Ocean was a triumph of naval and military technique. The capture of the mineral-rich states of pre-Columbian America was an astonishing reward for a daring filibuster. The building of an Atlantic economy based on slaves, bullion and the production of sugar had shown how the precocious development of long-distance trade and long-term credit in Atlantic Europe could create a highly profitable annexe to the European economy. But, until the Eurasian Revolution after 1750, none of this had made a decisive difference to the Europeans' influence in the world at large, least of all in the rest of Eurasia. In the Asian seas they had carved out a niche as 'merchant warriors', cruising aggressively along the maritime margins of the Asian states. On land they battered at the gates of the Ottoman and Iranian empires. In almost all of Africa, their direct presence was negligible, even if the commercial and human impact of their slave trade was felt far inland in West Africa, Angola and the Congo basin.

In the age of upheaval after 1750, many of the physical and some of the commercial constraints on European expansion began to give way. Huge new vistas of opportunity were glimpsed in India, China, the Pacific and even tropical Africa, revealed to British audiences by the West African travels of Mungo Park. The Americas, familiar in outline but mysterious in detail, were traversed systematically by Alexander Mackenzie (who crossed modern Canada), by Meriwether Lewis and William Clark in their epic journey from modern Pittsburgh to the Pacific Ocean in 1803–6[42] and by the great German geographer Alexander von Humboldt in South America. Enormous intellectual excitement was generated. Dreams of avarice multiplied. But it was after 1830, and not before, that Europeans began to strengthen their grip on the other continents and pave the way for the global supremacy that seemed theirs for the taking by the 1880s.

This great expansionist drive was fuelled by three sources of energy: cultural, commercial and demographic. As we saw in Chapter 4, the era of the Eurasian Revolution had seen a remarkable florescence not so much in the curiosity of Europeans about the rest of the world as in their apparatus of information-gathering and their marshalling of an intellectual framework into which new knowledge could be fitted. The plausibility of the new universalistic models of social, commercial and cultural progress proffered by (to take only British examples) David Hume, Adam Smith, Jeremy Bentham and James Mill (whose *History of India* appeared in 1817) removed old doubts about the Europeans' ability (and right) to reshape drastically the alien societies into which they had crashed or crept. Even in the late eighteenth century, the early British conquistadors in India had still been over-awed by the longevity and sophistication of the subcontinent's cultures. After 1800, this attitude was replaced by a bullish confidence that Indian thought-systems and the social practices they supported were decadent or obsolete, to be ignored or rooted out as circumstances allowed. And behind the new intellectual fervour with which Europeans were prone to denounce the beliefs of non-European peoples was a force which, if not new in European history, was in the throes of a radical revival: missionary Christianity.

By 1830 the missionary had become an active if not ubiquitous agent of European influence, but in some ways a contradictory one. Missionary enterprise in Europe had been rekindled by an emotional reaction against the rationalism of the Enlightenment, the horrific experience of revolutionary war, and (most obviously in Britain) the moral unease awakened by rapid social and economic change. Religious anxiety was sublimated in the evangelical duty to save the heathen by direct action or through the efforts of missionary societies. But, as well as being religious emissaries, missionaries were the eyes and ears of Europe in the African interior, along the China coast (where Charles Gutzlaff was a pioneer evangelist) and in remote New Zealand. Their messages, reports, pleas for help, fund-raising tours, missionary 'newspapers' and propagandist memoirs goaded opinion at home into action: to raise more money and to press their politicians to intervene or even to annex. Often, as in New Zealand, the motive was to protect a flock of new or promising converts from the predatory activity of degraded Europeans – selling rum or buying sex – or (as in East Africa) against Arab slave-traders. The greatest of all the missionary-publicists was David Livingstone. His heroic status in Victorian Britain showed the enormous appeal of this externalized religiosity.

Even missionaries rode the wave of commercial change, and without it their influence, activity and resources would have been much smaller. Indeed, missionaries like Gutzlaff or Henry Williams (in New Zealand) happily combined their religious and business activities, Gutzlaff by selling opium as he preached. European – especially British – merchants and their industrial suppliers demanded entry to the once-closed markets of Africa, Asia and the Americas, and put pressure on their governments to force it if necessary. A merchants' lobby had overthrown the old East India Company monopoly of trade with India in 1813 and with China in 1833. Merchant pressure drove London into the First Opium War (1839–42) and, through the Treaty of Nanking in 1842, secured the first real opening of China's trade to European commerce. Armed with the products of industrializing Europe, especially its machine-made textiles, European traders at last had a cargo of near-universal appeal, since cheap cotton cloth was a consumer good that could be sold almost anywhere, even against local artisan competition. The one requirement was an 'open' market in which European goods could be sold without the barrier of tariffs or prohibitions. For the European merchant it was 'free trade' that mattered, not conquest or political rule.

This commercial priority helps to explain the distinctive pattern of the West's expansion after 1830. Across much of the world, the Europeans' desire to 'globalize' markets, sell their manufactures, and fill their ships with homeward cargoes created a new form of commercial imperium that fell well short of colonial rule. Frequently, merchants and their governments gained commercial entry by agreements with local rulers and elites on terms that were, or seemed, mutually profitable. The merchant, after all, could sell only if he also bought.

What he offered to those who controlled the land was a market for produce they could not sell nearby – because land was abundant and its produce cheap. Landowners who had once been condemned to a subsistence economy could now be consumers – of clothes, furniture, iron goods, groceries (like tea or coffee) and tools – if they could grow the crops that Europeans would buy. Where this commercial understanding worked best, as in parts of Latin America, there was little incentive for the European states to scheme about conquest. Where local cooperation was not forthcoming and the ruler was determined to exclude foreign trade or regulate it closely (the most notorious case was China), the merchants' programme demanded government action. But even in China (where the British government obliged) this forcible intervention – in the opium wars of 1839–42 and 1856–60 – created little more than a maritime condominium in a series of 'treaty ports' scattered along the China coast and up the Yangtze. Here Europeans enjoyed privileged freedom to trade. But penetrating inland China still seemed dauntingly difficult in the 1870s.

In fact in many parts of the non-Western world European traders were forced to accept a rough and ready division of labour. Where they were barred from the interior – frozen out by native merchants, or baffled by the complications of currency, credit and distribution – as often happened in inland China and Africa, they had little choice but to rely on local middlemen. The European merchant stayed at the coast in his 'godown' (or warehouse), or cruised along it – a common practice in West Africa.[43] In India, where colonial rule *was* rapidly extended before 1850, the detail was different but the pattern similar. British merchants in their 'agency houses' (there were forty-seven in Calcutta in 1835) concentrated on the export–import trade in the main port cities and supplied the needs of the tiny foreign population in the interior. But they made little attempt to penetrate the up-country trade or the vast agricultural economy. Almost everywhere the danger of commercial failure was high. Extremes of climate, unreliable information, volatile currencies, losses at sea or political turbulence multiplied the ordinary risks of long-distance trade so that 'mortality' among European firms in India and China was heavy. This was the age of the mercantile pioneers, so brilliantly evoked in Conrad's tales, plying the Eastern seas in search of cargoes, and luck.

Even so, Europe's trading frontier made a steady advance into Afro-Asia in the fifty years after 1830. In East Asia, the first great rush of merchants had been to Hong Kong, seized by the British in the First Opium War and kept as a safe haven on the China coast. By 1860 more than forty British firms had set up in the port, attracted by quick profits in the opium trade.[44] Parsi merchants from Bombay and a sprinkling of other Europeans and Americans were also there. After the Second Opium War, the number of treaty ports grew rapidly, and small European-style towns with parks, esplanades, banks and offices were built as enclaves within (or close to) the main Chinese cities. By then Shanghai had already become the real entrepôt for the trade of China, the main port of entry from Europe and America. It lay at the end of what was fast becoming the great trunk highway between Europe and Asia that ran via Bombay, Colombo, Rangoon (growing quickly as a centre of the rice and timber trade) and through the maritime crossroads of Singapore, founded as recently as 1819, but with over 100,000 people by the 1870s.[45]

Symptomatic of this commercial growth was the network of more or less regular and rapid communication between Europe and Asia that appeared after 1840. In that year the Peninsular and Oriental Steam Navigation Company (the 'P&O') gained a royal charter for a mail monopoly between London and Alexandria. Two years later it had a contract to carry mail between Suez, Sri Lanka, Madras and Calcutta; and by 1845 its service was extended to Singapore and China. In the 1860s and '70s, India and China were linked to Europe by telegraph. But the greatest change came with the opening of the Suez Canal in 1869, cutting weeks off the sea route to India, speeding the transit of passengers and mail, and breaking down the barrier (as much psychological as physical) that once seemed to separate Europe from the 'Eastern World'. 'The piercing of the Isthmus of Suez, like the breaking of a dam', wrote Joseph Conrad in 1902, 'let in upon the East a flood of new ships, new men, new methods of trade.'[46] Easier access to Europe awakened the merchants' interest in neglected backwaters off the main sea lane. The Persian Gulf and the East Africa coast, once the preserve of Arab dhows, began to attract the attention of Bombay-based British merchants.[47] A new commercial front had been opened.

But there was as yet little sign that this buzz of economic activity would mean any large extension of European *rule* in Afro-Asia. Europeans, with the British in the van, acquired enclaves, bases, strongpoints and emporia for trade – such as Aden, Singapore, Saigon, Hong Kong, Lagos or St Louis in Senegal. Their commercial activity and political influence was radiated out from these and other bridgeheads. Treaties were made – or imposed – to prohibit slave-trading or to extirpate piracy. Quasi-protectorates propped up pliant rulers – often with ambiguous or unsatisfactory results. But no general scheme of imperial partition seemed desirable, necessary or practicable until the 1880s. The main exceptions were found in India (where special conditions applied), parts of Central Asia close to Russia's Caspian provinces, in the far north-west and far south of Africa, and in South East Asia, where the British, French and Dutch advanced uneasily into the Malay peninsula, Indochina and the 'Outer Islands' of the Indonesian archipelago. It was the huge enlargement of these 'uncertain empires' in the new global conditions of the 1880s that triggered the highest stage of Western dominance before the crash of 1914.

 In many parts of the world, the frontiers of Greater Europe were vague and imprecise – zones of interaction with Africans and Asians, rather than of purposeful incorporation. The missionary's and trader's frontiers depended on the cooperation of locals, whether in pursuit of god or mammon. But they were far from being the sole or most important theatres of European expansion. Up until 1880, and long thereafter, Europe's most dynamic frontier was demographic – its frontier of settlement. Here the scale of advance was startling. In 1830 white settlers in the United States had settled up to the Mississippi. By 1880 they had conquered or occupied almost the whole of what became the forty-eight states (excluding Alaska and Hawaii). In Canada, they had filled up the eastern farmlands and were poised (the delay proved considerable) to press on into the prairies. In Australia, 2¼ million settlers had fanned out over most of what could be used for agriculture or sheep-raising by the 1880s, leaving only a vast, dry empty interior. In New Zealand, where settlement had barely started in 1840, most usable land had been occupied by 1880, except for the redoubts of Maoridom in North Island. In all these places, the flood of white settlement had driven all before it: removing or excluding the native populations, fencing them into 'reserves', often destroying their livelihood and making them dependent on white charity. After 1880 only four zones were left for large-scale colonization by Europeans: the Canadian prairies, the Argentine pampas, the temperate lands of southern Brazil, and Siberia. In a fifth zone, Southern Africa, turned by main force into a 'white man's country', whites could dominate, but were too few to exclude, the black population, or live without its labour. In a sixth, Mediterranean Africa, European settlement was the sickly stepchild of French military power from start (1830) until finish (1962).

This great forward movement permanently altered the economic, cultural and political geography of the globe. By the end of the century, even sober commentators could assume that the future of the world was European. The population of 'New' and 'Old' Europe in 1800 had been 170 million, calculated the eminent British statistician Sir Robert Giffen. By 1880 it was 400 million. By contrast, apart from India, 'the non-European races have been stationary . . . The forces of civilization, as against those of the black and yellow races, have become practically irresistible.'[48] He thought that by AD 2000 'Europeans' would number 1,500 to 2,000 million, the Chinese a mere 400 million. Giffen extrapolated too much, but the demographic explosion of Greater Europe was real enough. Yet in 1800, except in parts of eastern North America, the great European land-grab was barely more than a series of claims to territory whose actual peopling was a dream. Why and how did this peopling happen, and so quickly?

The precondition of Europe's demographic imperialism was that so many Europeans wanted to leave their homes and were free to do so. It was no coincidence that most migrants up to 1880 came from regions with easy access to Atlantic ports. But this cannot be the whole explanation, since very few migrants came from France, or even from Spain until late in the century. What pushed people into moving was their expected life chances at home and imagined opportunities abroad. The British Isles were the main source of migrants until the last decades of the nineteenth century, and the largest source overall up to 1914. They were also the part of Europe affected first and most by the social and economic changes of industrialism. Changes in land use – like the conversion of marginal farmlands in Scotland into sheep runs – drove people off the land and into the towns – or abroad. In parts of England, the decline of old rural industries had a similar effect. There was no vast hinterland of small peasant farms (as in France) that could soak up the un- or under-employed. The extreme case was Ireland, where the terrible subsistence crisis after 1845 killed perhaps 2 million people and drove millions more into emigration, some of it to mainland Britain. It was relatively easy for those on the move to continue their journey beyond urban Britain to America (most) or Australia (a few). The sea lanes were peaceful. No legal barrier prevented emigration. And there were now transport systems that could carry large numbers of passengers to the ports and ship them quickly and cheaply across the Atlantic.

In this way, the physical consequences of industrialism pushed people into moving and then helped them to do so. The social and cultural effects of industrialism also had a role to play. Many of those who were uprooted stopped first in British cities. If urban conditions had been different, and the safety nets stronger, more might have stayed there. Instead, what grew up was a culture of mobility, fed by the eager propaganda of the emigration agents, shipping lines, migration societies, land companies and religious enthusiasts, and disseminated cheaply by the printed word – another consequence of industrialism. The urge to emigrate, originating in poverty and economic fear, was supercharged by the belief in migration as the means to a better life. Skilfully inflated by a host of emigration 'entrepreneurs' (migration was a business), it took root with amazing speed in the social imagination.

But migration was not just a matter of wishes and dreams, nor even of the cheapness of the one-way ticket. Much migration was paid for with remittances sent home by the 'advance guard'. 'Chain migration' was (as it is now for Third World migrants) the only practicable way for large numbers of poor emigrants to make the journey. But 'chain migration' also assumed a favourable report on the preferred destination, and the economic success of those who had travelled first. For movement on the scale that occurred after 1840, it was vital for the receiving societies to accept the incomers, and for their economies to be able to absorb them. Had economic conditions been unfavourable, poverty at home would have been replaced by destitution abroad (where the safety net was even smaller) and the chain would have broken. The prospect of a horde of indigent migrants, driving down wages and swamping the labour market, would soon have turned the 'old inhabitants' against an open door to new arrivals. The great migration would have come to a shuddering halt.

America was where most migrants went, and America's remarkable economic history explains why the great migration succeeded. What made America so attractive? More to the point, what made its economy so absorbent? Its astonishing natural wealth forms an obvious part of the answer: the huge reserve of fertile land; vast tracts of timber; deposits of iron, coal, lead, silver and gold; and a river system that opened up the interior and carried out its produce. But what made America so receptive was not the gradual exploitation of these natural riches, but the amazing speed with which they were harnessed to a market economy. It was speed that was critical in enabling America's population to grow so quickly and to accommodate so many Europeans without more signs of social stress. What made the peopling of America (by natural increase as well as by immigration) so swift and this frontier of Greater Europe so dynamic was (once again) the impact of industrialism: the transplanted industrialism of America itself.

We can see this at work in a number of ways. Large-scale agricultural settlement required tools, social organization and a variety of services (not least financial services) if the settlers were not to remain isolated, ignorant, and dirt-poor subsistence farmers. These needs had to be met locally if they were to be suitably 'customized' and not prohibitively expensive. Just as a fighting army needs a large 'rear' to service it with supplies, intelligence and direction, so an army of settlers needs an urban 'rear' nearby for farming equipment, market information and cultural amenities. Without these it quickly slips into a slough of stagnation. The remarkable feature of the American frontier was not so much the torrent of farmers who moved west, but how rapidly towns followed in their wake. Towns grew much more quickly in size than the population as a whole.[49] Town sites attracted artisans with industrial skills. In the 1820s and '30s, foundries, mills and smelters could be found in the new western cities, busily serving their local hinterlands. Steam power was early on the scene. Well before 1830, hundreds of steam engines were being built in the West, many for use on the steamboats that plied the Ohio and Mississippi. With engineering and industrial skills at hand, it was little wonder that railways spread quickly, bringing the means of industrial transport directly into the frontier regions. Railways and steamboats not only brought people in, they also moved people on to new opportunities, accelerating the demographic mobility on which industrialized settlement depended.

The deeper roots of this success story – the virtuous circle of incessant growth – can be found in the benign conditions that America enjoyed as part of Greater Europe. The absence of external threats, making a decentralized 'enterprise' culture rather than a regulated bureaucratic economy much easier to sustain,[50] was one. The colonial legacy of transatlantic trade was another. Together they had helped to make the Old Northeast a commercial and industrial region on a European scale and extremely efficient (partly for linguistic reasons) at importing and redeploying skills and the skilled from the most advanced regions of Atlantic Europe. The American frontier was thus not a pure dependency of the Old World. It needed (as we have seen) only small amounts of European capital. It enhanced its imports of goods and capital with the 'added value' of home-grown skills, output and institutions. It was the dynamic fusion of Old and New Europe that underlay its success. In Australia and New Zealand, the furthest-flung frontiers of European settlement, the same stimulants can be seen at work, but on a much more modest scale. These countries' natural endowments were less generous. Both were far further away than America, and distance was costly.[51] They lacked the head start America enjoyed before 1800. They were more dependent on inputs from Europe. But in other ways they drew upon the same industrial toolkit to tailor their environments for alien settlement. They introduced plants and animals and changed the landscape with ruthless energy (often by fire) to meet their needs. A box of matches, it was cynically said, was the pioneer's most useful tool. They did not adapt themselves so much as adapt the environment to a European community. To have done so much so quickly, at such vast distance from 'home', and on the scale required to keep up the momentum of settlement, would have been inconceivable without the apparatus, physical and intellectual, of an industrial civilization.[52]

There was another similarity of huge importance in the frontier story. The frontier was usually a place of steady, grinding economic advance. But it was also frequently the setting for a 'rush': for gold and silver, as well as for land. It was a place of feverish, cash-driven speculation, more the result of manias and crazes than of sober economic calculation. This was the manic tendency in the industrial culture of mobility, and it had important results. Rushes changed the direction as well as the pace of settler expansion, creating new and unpredicted lines of advance. The demographic effects could be electric. The discovery of gold doubled Australia's population in the 1850s and New Zealand's in the 1860s. In America, the westward drift of pioneer farmers towards the Pacific became a torrent in 1849 when gold was found in California's Central Valley. San Francisco boomed as the mining metropolis of the Far West.[53] Its commercial, financial and technical influence soon radiated up and down the Pacific coast and inland as far as Nevada, Utah and Idaho.[54] California's new wealth speeded the arrival of the telegraph in 1861 and the Union Pacific railway (by 1869). When gold was found in the Rockies in 1858, 600 miles west of the settler frontier, 100,000 people poured into the Colorado territory in little more than a year.[55] Another stream of hopefuls raced north to Montana when gold was found at Virginia City in 1863: 30,000 arrived in a year. The consequences were not simply economic.

So far we have ignored one crucial influence on these frontier histories: the resistance of indigenous peoples to displacement or conquest. Though there were minor variations, by the 1880s indigenous opposition had been largely brushed aside in the United States, Canada, Australia and New Zealand. The epic victory of the Lakota over Custer at the Little Big Horn in 1876, or that of the Nez Perce at Big Hole a year later, made no difference. But why was the resistance of Native Americans, Australian Aborigines and New Zealand Maoris overwhelmed so completely in a space of forty years or less? Weaponry is part of the answer,[56] though sophisticated firearms were acquired by native peoples and used to good effect – strikingly so against Custer's army. On the American plains, sudden environmental change (the destruction of the bison herds by commercial hunters and modern rifles) destroyed much of the basis of native livelihood and culture.

255

But the underlying reason almost everywhere was the frantic pace of the whites' forward movement: there was almost no time for native peoples to reorganize politically, redeploy socially, form wider alliances, or develop more effective military tactics. This was where the rushes were so important. The whites did not advance at a steady pace. They lunged forward unpredictably in crowds, leaping over vast distances at the lure of gold, silver or 'free' land. It was a gold rush in Dakota that drove the Native Americans from lands they occupied under treaty and led to the showdown to which Custer's defeat was the dramatic prelude. Elsewhere, speculative rushes constantly outflanked indigenous peoples or confronted them with an irresistible enemy whose numbers, organization, resources, equipment and transport bore the hallmarks of industrialism. In the temperate lands of settlement, the Europeans had decisively won the race against time by the 1870s.

UNCERTAIN EMPIRES

Elsewhere, the verdict was much less clear. The Eurasian Revolution allowed Europeans to force their way into parts of Afro-Asia where before 1750 they had had a beachhead or a 'factory' at best. As new technologies, more attractive trade goods, and better information became available, they could venture into the interior with greater confidence. In the right conditions, obstructive rulers and their armies could be pushed aside, bought out, or pensioned off – a process that went furthest (for reasons discussed below) on the Indian subcontinent. By the 1830s and '40s, Europeans were hammering on the gates of China, forcing entry into the Ottoman Empire for their trade, infiltrating the Iranian sphere in the Caspian and the Gulf, pushing Christianity in Indochina, and even reconnoitring Japan. There were schemes to colonize the Niger valley, a French invasion of Islamic Algiers (the germ of a vast North African empire), and a private empire on the island of Borneo won by the English adventurer James Brooke. In 1839 the British seized the barren rock of Aden.

But, despite this frenzy of commercial, political and philanthropic activism, the imposition of effective European imperial control over

THE RACE AGAINST TIME

the states and peoples of Afro-Asia remained the exception not the rule until the 1880s. In much of Afro-Asia, the years between 1830 and 1880 were a 'loaded pause' before the growing disparity in power, wealth, weaponry, mobility and information between (most) Afro-Asians and Europeans reached its widest point. It was only then that a new form of 'world economy' and a new system of 'world politics' combined to produce a Eurocentric world order and the near-universal extension of formal and informal colonialism.

In the meantime, the forward movement of European control showed recurrent signs of hesitation and uncertainty. There was plenty of pressure to push deeper and wider and expand the bridgeheads of European influence. Merchants complained of restraints on trade. Missionaries wanted to save more souls, or to save the souls they had won already. Soldiers wanted a strategic hill, sailors yearned for a deeper anchorage. Proconsuls claimed that a larger colony would mean cheaper rule. Each of these groups could count on lobbies at home to harry its government into intervention or conquest. Each could deploy the seductive rhetoric of free trade, the 'civilizing mission', religious duty, 'imperial defence' or the threat of rebellion to boost its appeal in the press, in Parliament or to public opinion. Sometimes European governments found it easier to bow to these demands than to resist them. But they were just as prone to pull back if a military failure or financial difficulty undermined the support for a forward policy. In hindsight, this looks like a waiting game before the full-blown imperialism of the 1880s. But to contemporaries the bounds, the scale, the stability and even the point of Afro-Asian empires seemed speculative, controversial and uncertain.

The most important reason for this was a widespread scepticism as to whether the cost of such empires would be justified by their benefits. The cost might arise from the need to defend them against European rivals. But the immediate cause for doubt usually came from the difficulty of imposing European authority on rulers and peoples who were determined to resist it. The period of the loaded pause was, across much of Afro-Asia, an age of resistance. In the North African Maghrib the French effort to conquer the hinterland behind Algiers lasted for decades, although Algiers itself was reinvented as a European city. In West Africa, Governor Faidherbe pushed France's influence up the Senegal valley and along the coast. But expansion stalled after 1860, and was not resumed until the 1880s.[57] In the Gold Coast (modern Ghana), the shrivelled British colony on the coast was so much at risk from the inland kingdom of Ashanti that its abandonment was mooted in the 1860s. Even in South Africa, where the Boers had conquered the highveld interior after 1840, a real white supremacy was delayed until the 1880s. The Transvaal republic was bankrupted by its unsuccessful war against the Pedi in 1876, while the Zulu 'menace' loomed over the British colony of Natal until the Anglo-Zulu war of 1879.

In many parts of Asia, attempts to assert European rule suffered a similar check. In the northern Caucasus (modern Chechnya), the Russians fought a long and bloody war before 'Circassian' resistance was broken in 1864. Only then was their road to Central Asia opened up. Russian rule was gradually imposed there, but not until the 1870s and '80s. Two British invasions of Afghanistan (1838–42, 1879–80) were aborted. The Burmese kingdom lost its coastal provinces to the British in 1826 and 1852, but the inland state survived until its overthrow in 1885. In Indochina, the French intervention in 1858 to protect the Tonkin Catholics ended with the occupation of Cochin China (in the Mekong delta) and a nominal protectorate over neighbouring Cambodia. But a real French imperium over the rest of Vietnam, the Lao states and Cambodia could not be achieved until the 1880s and '90s. In island South East Asia it was a similar story. The Dutch had control over Java and much of Sumatra. But in Acheh (in northern Sumatra), Bali, eastern Borneo, Sulawesi and the island chain stretching out towards New Guinea their paramountcy was delayed until the end of the century or even after it.

What made this resistance so effective? It could not usually exclude all European influence (or try to do so), but it did stave off European rule. In some cases, of course, a little resistance went a long way against European interlopers who lacked the means, the manpower and the motive to persist. Remoteness and poverty might be the best defence. But usually resistance required Afro-Asian states and societies to maintain a critical level of solidarity and cohesion in the face of European intrusion or attack. In fact many of these states were surprisingly well equipped against the European style of colonial warfare. Colonial armies – British, French, Dutch, Russian, American – had certain advantages. They were (more or less) professionals. They usually had greater firepower. Where access from the sea was possible, they could arrive suddenly (like the French off Da Nang in Vietnam in 1858) and achieve surprise. Sometimes they could use their naval firepower to intimidate the defence, as the British did in the First Opium War against China. But colonial campaigns were radically subject to the law of diminishing returns. None of the imperial powers could afford to keep many of its soldiers tied up indefinitely in frontier regions. It was costly, and they were needed elsewhere. Secondly, the longer that foreign troops stayed, the harder it was to ensure their supply and keep up their fighting strength. Right through the nineteenth century, disease continued to ravage the health of European troops in the tropics. Thirdly, the downside of surprise was often the lack of essential intelligence. Afro-Asians may not have known that the Europeans were coming: but the Europeans knew little of what they were coming to. With little to go on about the plans of the local ruler, his strengths, weaknesses, supplies and manpower, an invading force was often reduced to blind man's buff. Hence the pattern of so many colonial campaigns: the staging of a symbolic victory – the wrecking of a palace or the burning of a capital – before a retreat to the coast in dignified impotence. Joseph Conrad's description (in *The Heart of Darkness*) of a French cruiser aimlessly 'firing into a continent'[58] is an ironic comment on this undirected violence.

The defeat or containment of colonial invasion highlighted what was needed if an Afro-Asian state was to resist a European takeover. The real key was to maintain, more or less intact, the state's own network of communications, allowing the movement of people, goods, ideas and information. Only the most primitive and impoverished of societies did not need or had not developed such a system. Almost everywhere, it was essential if rulers, elites and their towns were to be supplied with food and revenues, if more than the most localized government was to be maintained, if the economy was to rise above subsistence level. All the most important, wealthy and powerful of Afro-Asian states (as well as many that were not) depended on elaborate networks to collect and distribute taxes, foodstuffs, luxury goods and essentials like salt. The prestige of the ruler and the extent of his rule were often a matter less of territory than of control over the paths of trade, tax and (sometimes) pilgrimage. The circulation of goods and money supported a class of wealthy traders whose self-interested loyalty helped prop the political regime. What was vital was that this network should preserve its hinterland, a 'security zone' where it did not have to face external competition or risk dislocation.

The states that fended off the Europeans after 1840 were those that were able to maintain a security zone – a hinterland large enough to support the superstructure of political rule. Of course, most states had other resources with which to strengthen their solidarity against European outsiders and deny them the collaborators on whom they almost invariably depended. Perhaps the most important was religion. Scholar-gentry loyal to the Confucian monarchy rallied Vietnamese resistance to the French on the Mekong in the 1860s.[59] Popular Buddhism helped the Burmese Empire fight off British control. In northern Sumatra, the Acheh struggle against the Dutch fell to leaders who preached a pan-Islamic jihad against the Christian invaders. Charismatic forms of Islamic belief sustained resistance to French advance in the Muslim lands of North and West Africa. Coptic Christianity gave the Ethiopian Empire a solidity against outside attack that belied its ramshackle administrative structure. In harsh environments, where almost any form of external contact posed a dangerous threat to social cohesion, the incentives to collaborate might be even weaker. Such places were, by their very nature, usually marginal to European interests, except where they fell across the road to a richer sphere.[60]

If a security zone and a network were the twin essentials of survival, they were also (potentially) two hostages to fortune. If the Europeans could disrupt the network, they could unravel the state and unpick the loyalty of its most powerful elements. If they could deploy their arsenal of steam-powered mobility, industrialized consumer goods and cheaper credit to break the links that bound the local economy together, the effect would be like an electrical short circuit. In the native state, ruthless action would be needed to repair the damage. But the 'cure' might be so drastic that it destabilized the polity and changed the nature of the resistance itself. We can see this process at work in the 'middle years' between 1830 and 1880. As the scope of

European settlement, commerce and religion grew wider, the points of friction with Afro-Asian states were bound to multiply. In many cases, as we have seen, the interventions that followed were indecisive. But often, whether by accident or design, the Europeans were able to dislocate the polity they had targeted by indirect means. This was most obvious in a case like that of the maritime states of the Malayan world, whose seaborne trade (the prime source of wealth and revenue) was swept away by Western competitors. The consequence was not a walkover for European imperialism. When the power of rulers crumbled, those they had kept in check grew stronger. If the ruler's network frayed, local men or the social predators that he had kept at bay quickly moved in. Religious cults – like the Buddhist messiahs in Burma – smuggling, piracy or slave-raiding (as in East Africa) might become the basis for a new social order. It might be more decentralized than the old regime. It was often more xenophobic and more violent. It confronted Europeans with a different kind of resistance. It confirmed their suspicion that much of Afro-Asia was dangerous and barbaric. But in the end it was usually too fragmented and unstable to withstand the ever-tightening grip of the Europeans on the routes, links and connections that bound region to region and place to place, or to frustrate the local coalitions that command over movement allowed the Europeans to build. In the end, a purely localized resistance could be overcome in detail or left to rot on the margins of a colony.

However, this 'endgame' only gradually became obvious. Across much of Afro-Asia, that meant after 1880 or even after 1900. In the meantime, in all those places where the Europeans had not yet assembled the means to break up local networks and substitute their own, the prospects for empire looked poor. Some form of Muslim imperium was much more likely than European rule in much of West Africa, thought the philosophical traveller Winwood Reade. 'Should the Turks be driven out of Europe,' he wrote, 'they would probably become the Emperors of Africa, which in the interests of civilization would be a fortunate occurrence.'[61] The French naval officer who explored the Mekong river wrote bitterly of the 'profound indifference' of French opinion to the vision of empire he had revealed.[62] Fighting endless 'native wars' against elusive enemies without the means for a rapid victory or local support for permanent rule held little appeal for European governments. They might license piecemeal advances from established bridgeheads and try their hand at a knock-out blow. But across much of Afro-Asia they were resigned to the survival of the great indigenous states, and forced to tolerate the resistance of the small.

The great exception was India, perhaps the most remarkable case of imperialism in modern history. By 1820 the British had made themselves the dominant power on the subcontinent. By 1856, on the eve of the Mutiny, they had conquered Sind and the Punjab and annexed Awadh. They seemed bent on taking direct control of every part of India, including those states whose princes acknowledged their paramountcy. Yet the conquest of India was neither swift nor uncontroversial. It was pursued at heavy cost in an age of depression caused in part by the weight of taxation on new colonial subjects. It was disliked in London, where the risk that the East India Company (still the embodiment of British power in India) would go bankrupt under the strain awoke fears of a parliamentary crisis on the scale of the 1780s. The tensions it provoked in Indian society eventually burst forth in the Great Mutiny of 1857. To many British radicals, India was a despotic encumbrance that corrupted British politics and seemed certain to drag Britain into an endless round of Asian wars.

Yet, despite all objections, the momentum of expansion had rarely faltered. London grumbled, but dared not disavow its hyperactive proconsuls. When the Mutiny was suppressed, and the Company discredited, the British government assumed the role of overlord of India. This willing attitude was all the more striking because the strategic burden of defending India against rivals from north and west had already become a major obsession in British diplomacy. Matters were made worse by the military reorganization that was needed in the aftermath of the Mutiny. In the interests of 'never again', up to 70,000 British troops were to be permanently stationed in India: one British soldier for every two Indian. This was between a third and a half of the British army – perhaps three times the pre-Mutiny garrison, and a colossal strain on the military defence of the rest of the empire. So two questions need answering. Why was India conquered earlier and more completely than almost any other part of Afro-Asia? And why were the British willing and able to assume the large risks and heavy costs of its rule?

To answer the first is to return to the circumstances in which India underwent a double revolution and British power was first established on the lower Ganges. In that double revolution, the Mughals, the nominal rulers of North and Central India, were disabled by an inland invasion led first by the Iranian Napoleon, Nadir Shah, and then by his Afghan legatee, Ahmad Shah Durrani. Almost simultaneously, the maritime regions – most of all the dynamic textile economy of Bengal – had become more dependent on their foreign trade and more at odds with the foreign traders. When the East India Company pushed aside the Bengal nawab Suraj ud-Daula with the help of local allies and installed a puppet ruler, it found soon enough that the old imperial rule from Delhi had all but collapsed. By the early 1800s the Company had forced its way up the Ganges, occupied Delhi, and turned the Mughals themselves into a puppet dynasty. The Company's servants, as its officials were styled, had much to gain personally from the extension of its power, since its control over trade created a stream of fees and its growing bureaucracy a flood of jobs. The Company state crushed any ruler that threatened its interests. It soon became commonplace to attribute its triumph to the assertion of British will over the chaos and lethargy of native India. In fact the key to British power could be found not in India's backwardness and indolence, but in its openness and accessibility, and in the sophistication of its financial and commercial life.

India's openness helped the British in several ways. It was part of the reason for the double revolution. Unlike China, no Great Wall had barred the approach from Central Asia to the plains of Hindustan. Nor were foreign merchants confined to keyhole ports like Canton. It was far easier for Europeans to gather knowledge about India than about China. It was far less difficult for European merchants to deal with their Indian counterparts. India's commercial economy – the hub of the world's textile trade in the eighteenth century – was far more outward-looking than China's, and its bankers and merchants were far freer from their rulers' control. In maritime India the British met trading states, not a hostile bureaucracy answerable to a distant emperor. When their interests were threatened, they found it easy to combine with the disaffected subjects of maritime rulers. Their limited reserves of organized force leveraged a large investment by local men for whom the Company's trade was too valuable to lose.

But that by itself would hardly explain the relative ease with which the British marched into the subcontinental interior. Here they could exploit three other benefits of India's early modern 'modernity'. Firstly, much of India was already connected by a credit system that shifted balances across the subcontinent. In their multiple wars the British could combine their profits from trade with the financial services of Indian bankers to survive the setbacks of military failure and outlast their enemies.[63] Secondly, starting with Bengal – the most prosperous region – they could draw on the income of a long-established system of land taxation – the 'land revenue'. They could pay the swollen ranks of their armies, and then annex fresh revenues to fund new wars. Here was a self-propelling colonialism that could hardly function in the less-developed regions of Afro-Asia, and not at all in non-monetized economies without revenue systems. Thirdly, partly because lowland India had already developed occupational castes and mercenary armies (the contrast is with clan-based loyalties and feudal levies), it was easy for the Company to recruit (just as it was possible to pay for) a professional army of sepoys loyal to its foreign paymaster. By 1835 the Bengal army had some sixty-four regiments of 'native infantry', and the Company's Indian armies were much larger than the whole British army, at home and abroad.[64] With this standing army as a battering ram, the Company could knock down all but the most determined opponents.

Thus India provided its European invader with the resources that could be turned to the task of conquest.[65] Astonishingly early, therefore, the Company created its own 'security zone' and made itself an Indian or 'country' power, competing on Indian terms with Indian rivals. It could use the fluidity of Indian society to its own advantage. Western India had long been open to foreign merchant elites, especially the Parsis, who originated in Iran and came to dominate the western port city of Bombay. They were natural partners of the Company 'firm'. In Bengal a new Hindu elite, the *bhadralok* ('respectable people'), quickly sprang up to replace the Muslim old guard and supply the educated collaborators on whom the Company *raj* depended. With allies like these, the Company could assemble the local networks it needed to squeeze – and eventually suffocate – the trade and revenue of any Indian rival. The effect was to shift the balance of cost and risk away from Britain, the ultimate beneficiary of Indian empire, and towards the hybrid 'Anglo-Indian' polity that first emerged in the Bengal 'bridgehead'. It was Anglo-India, not Britain, that financed the wars of conquest. When London sent troops to help out, the Company paid for their hire – one reason why their use was begrudged less at Westminster than the smaller forces sent to impoverished colonies in New Zealand or South Africa.

The size and wealth of the Company state had another consequence. From early on it was an eldorado of opportunity for those in Britain (and especially Scotland) who could win a nomination to its commercial and civil service or the officer corps of its armies. By the 1830s, these men and their families were a formidable vested interest, with much to gain from the Company's rise. Their writings and memoirs formed the basis of an Anglo-Indian myth in which India's centrality to British power became the ruling motif. Most remarkably of all, the dramatic spectacle of India's conquest, once excoriated by Edmund Burke, was now justified by utilitarians and liberals as the grand example of rational reform. The debris of ignorance and superstition was being swept away by civilized modernity. India was a project, not an abuse. Indeed, two of the most powerful writers of mid-Victorian Britain were eager to beat the Indian drum. Both had taken the Company's shilling. The historian T. B. Macaulay had been Law Member in the Company's Indian government. His essays on Clive (1840) and Warren Hastings (1841) depicted them as progressive empire-builders in the tradition of Rome. John Stuart Mill, the prophet of liberal individualism, was an official in the Company's London headquarters. In his *Representative Government* (1861), British rule was fiercely defended as the only path to social progress.

These influences help to explain why London was so tolerant of the Company's imperialism. Perhaps just as telling was the fact that by the 1840s India had become a major asset for a trading empire. By 1850 nearly 12,000 Britons lived in its largest port cities of Calcutta and Bombay.[66] After 1830, British exports to India consistently outstripped those to the British West Indies, the previous jewel of imperial trade. Indian soldiers were used to force open the ports of China and protect British trade in South East Asia. As the golden eggs piled up, it was easy to forget the health of the goose. But in 1857 the accumulated tensions of empire-building at this frantic pace burst out in a great revolt.

The revolt began as a mutiny of Indian sepoys (soldiers) at Meerut, some forty miles north-east of Delhi, against the use of ammunition defiled by animal fat. Behind this outbreak lay a widespread conspiracy among the Indian officers of the Bengal army. Low pay, the poor quality of the white officers, the decline of plunder, and bitter resentment at the dilution of a high-caste army by low-caste recruits had pushed them towards rebellion. Their aim was to throw off British rule and return to service under Indian rulers.[67] But the rebellion spread with sensational speed because a much larger mass of discontent took heart from the apparent collapse of British military power. Three different kinds of grievance lay behind the wider revolt. Among the Muslim elites of the old Mughal heartland, the declining prestige of the Mughal emperor – a puppet ruler since 1803 – was widely interpreted as a threat to Indian Islam, and the Mutiny became in part a Muslim reaction against an infidel overlord. When the mutineers marched into Delhi in May 1857, they promised the revival of Mughal power. Secondly, for a number of regional magnates, the sudden implosion of British control in the Ganges valley offered the chance to regain the power they had lost – or expected to lose – to the tightening grip of the Company *raj*. This was especially true in the kingdom of Awadh, annexed by the Company the previous year, and among local rulers in the uplands of central India. In Kanpur, power was seized by Nana Sahib, who dreamed of restoring the Maratha confederacy, broken by the Company in 1818. Thirdly, the weight of the Company's land taxation and its efforts to regulate landownership and title worked to the benefit of some local interests but embittered many others. The result was an uneven and unpredictable agrarian revolt. Across a vast swathe of northern India these three elements were jumbled together in an ill-coordinated anti-colonial front.

This was a massive emergency for British rule. The Company faced a long and costly war of reconquest, complicated by external dangers and furious political criticism at home. The Mutiny showed dangerous signs of spreading among the remaining princely states, whose forces also revolted against their European officers. In practice, although the Mutiny rumbled on into 1859 in the outlying hills and forests, it was

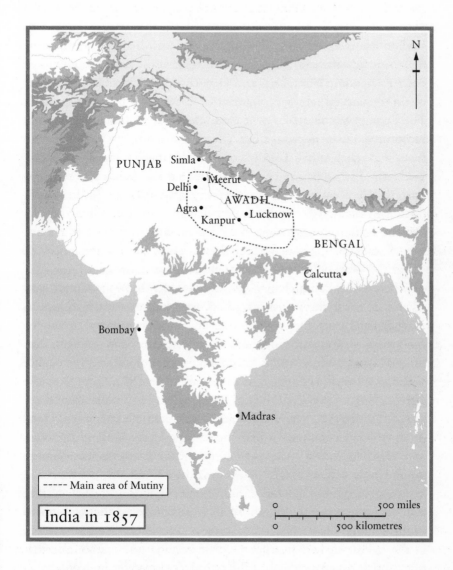

N

PUNJAB Simla•
    •Meerut
Delhi•
Agra• AWADH
  Kanpur• •Lucknow

BENGAL

Calcutta•

Bombay•

•Madras

----- Main area of Mutiny

India in 1857

0   500 miles
0   500 kilometres

crushed in its heartland in little more than a year. Awadh had been reconquered by July 1858. By April of that year the British had some 90,000 white troops and as many loyal Indians against rebel forces that were at most 60,000.[68] Despite the scale of their revolt, the rebels were thwarted by four critical weaknesses. The Mutiny was confined to North India: it did not spread (despite some alarming signs) into Bengal, Bombay and Madras, the core regions of British rule. The British could draw troops and supplies from these 'loyal' zones and summon help from home. Secondly, the British clung on by their fingertips to some vital outposts in the rebel zone, including Agra and Benares (modern Varanasi), and kept control of their new province of the Punjab (where they were warned by telegraph just in time). The Punjab was vital. From it came the (mainly Indian) army that recaptured Delhi in September 1857, destroying the only credible focus for rebel unity. Thirdly, once the British began to return in force, the divisions among the rebels, and the lack of a common purpose, ideology or leadership, allowed resistance to be broken down district by district. Fourthly, the rebels had too little time before the British counter-attack to smash the Company's network and replace it with their own. No neo-Mughal state could have arisen in North India: the rebel governments in Delhi and Lucknow could not even pay their sepoys. Though many Indian notables threw in their lot with the rebels when the British vanished, they had too much to lose to struggle hard when they reappeared. The uncompromising ferocity of the British reconquest, visible in the sack of Delhi and the expulsion of its Muslims, left no room for political compromise.[69]

Yet there was no doubt that the shock of the Mutiny profoundly affected Britons' views of their Indian empire. They were taken completely by surprise. The revolt had spread with electric speed. Hundreds of whites had been killed, including a large number of women and children (more than 200 in the Kanpur massacre). Despite innumerable acts of loyalty and humanity by Indians, a miasma of mistrust inevitably soured Anglo-Indian relations. Race feeling became more virulent. Many British were convinced that the source of the Mutiny was a Muslim conspiracy: 'The sepoys are merely tools in the hands of the Mussulmans.'[70] It became fashionable to argue that British rule depended on the sword.[71] Thereafter, mutiny scares were never far from the official mind. British rule became more cautious and conservative. The imperial burden of guarding India against attack from within and without seemed heavier. But there were massive compensations. After 1860, with the spread of railways, India developed much more rapidly as a source of raw materials and the greatest market for Britain's greatest export, cotton textiles. And if the burden of garrisoning India was heavy, it cost the British taxpayer nothing. Indeed, after 1860 two-thirds of the standing army of the British Empire (a total of some 330,000 British and Indian soldiers) was a charge on Indian not British revenues, and the forces in India could be (and were) used everywhere from Malta to Shanghai. As the partition of Afro-Asia speeded up after 1880, India's geopolitical, as well as its economic, value became an axiom of British policy. An uncertain empire had become indispensable.

THE RACE AGAINST TIME

What had happened in India was a warning, if warning were needed, of what could follow elsewhere in Eurasia and Africa once the Europeans arrived in the neighbourhood with their range of new weapons – commercial, cultural and military. More or less consciously, the rulers and elites of the Afro-Asian world found themselves in a race. They had to find ways of binding together their often loose-knit states; to reinforce the feeling of cultural cohesion; to encourage more trade and extract more revenue. And they had to do so in time. Again and again they faced a dilemma. If they tried to 'self-strengthen' using 'European' methods – European-type armies, bureaucracies, schools and technologies – they ran a huge risk. The social cohesion that they desperately wanted might dissolve in disputes with the old guardians of culture: the teachers, clerics, and men of letters and learning. The drive for political unity might affront existing power-holders who relished their provincial autonomy. More regulation of trade might enrage the merchants and also their customers. If they let more Europeans in, as traders, advisers and experts, they might suffer a backlash, bringing accusations of weakness or even betrayal. Nor could they be sure that these licensed invaders would not do them harm and be a source of disruption. But if they tried to exclude them, the self-strengthening project might run out of steam. Worse still, they might provoke an attack before they were ready, and bring on a catastrophe.

They had to run two races at once: a race to self-strengthen before Europe arrived in force; and a race to 'reform' before internal dissent wrecked all hope of success.

Of the great Eurasian states beyond Europe, China (above all) and Japan had always been the richest, strongest and least accessible to European influence. Until the 1830s, they seemed almost invulnerable to European attack. By 1840 that old immunity was dead in the case of China and dying in Japan. Instead, both states came under growing pressure from the Europeans. Britain, Russia and the United States took the lead. They demanded free access to the ports of East Asia, freedom to trade with Chinese and Japanese merchants, and an end to the diplomatic protocols under which Westerners had the status of barbarians, culturally and politically inferior to the Middle Kingdom and Japan. They accompanied these demands by the demonstration and use of military force, and by territorial demands – coastal and modest (though far from trivial) by the maritime British, much larger by continental Russia. Not surprisingly, this traumatic alteration in their international position had far-reaching political, cultural and economic consequences in China and Japan. By 1880, both had undergone a series of internal changes that were revealingly described by their makers as 'restorations': the T'ung-chih ('Union for Order') restoration in China, the Meiji ('Enlightened rule') restoration in Japan.[72] Both were the result of the convergence of internal stresses and external threat. But, as we shall see, their trajectories were very different, and so was the scale of the transformation they promised.

China was the first to feel the weight of European displeasure. The occasion was the breakdown of the old 'Canton system' for China's trade with Europe. Under this system, Canton was the only port through which the trade – confined to a closely regulated guild of Chinese merchants (the 'Hong') – was lawful. Europeans (who were allowed to maintain warehouses – 'factories' – on the quay) were forbidden to live permanently in the city, departing for Macao at the close of the trading season. The end of the East India Company monopoly of British trade in 1833, and the rapid increase in the number of 'free' British merchants selling opium – almost the only commodity that the Chinese would accept for their tea, apart from silver – brought on a crisis. When the Chinese authorities, alarmed by the flood of opium imports and the outflow of silver (the basis of China's currency) to pay for them, as well as by the widespread flouting of the rule that all foreign commerce must pass through Canton, tried to reimpose control, driving away the British official sent to supervise the trade and confiscating contraband opium, the uproar in London led to military action. In February 1841 the Royal Navy arrived off Canton, the Chinese war fleet was destroyed, and an invading force landed in the city. When the Chinese prevaricated, a second force entered the Yangtze delta, occupied Shanghai, smashed a Manchu army, and closed the river and the Grand Canal (the main artery of China's internal trade). By August 1842 the British had arrived at Nanking, the southern capital of the empire, and prepared to attack it. The emperor capitulated, and the first of the 'unequal treaties' was signed.[73]

Under the 1842 Treaty of Nanking, five 'treaty ports' were opened to Western trade, Hong Kong island was ceded to the British, the Europeans were allowed to station consuls in the open ports, and the old Canton system was replaced by the freedom to trade and the promise that no more than 5 per cent duty would be charged on foreign imports. It was a staggering reversal of the old terms on which China had dealt with the West. But its significance (at this stage) should not be overstated. Irksome as the treaty was to the Chinese authorities, it had certain merits. The foreigners were kept well away from Peking, could not travel freely, and, under the system of consular jurisdiction, would be carefully segregated administratively from the Chinese population.[74] To a great inland, agrarian empire, the snapping of barbarians on the distant coast was a nuisance to be neutralized by skilful diplomacy.

But the treaty was not the end of the matter. It was followed by continual friction between Chinese and Europeans. By 1854 the British were pressing hard for its revision, to open more ports and allow Europeans to move freely into the interior and widen the scope of their trade. In 1856, the '*Arrow*' incident, when the Chinese seized a ship allegedly flying the British flag, became the excuse for a second round of military coercion. When the Chinese stalled the implementation of a new treaty agreed in 1858, an Anglo-French expedition arrived at Tientsin and marched on Peking, burning the emperor's summer palace in revenge for their losses. The second great treaty settlement, the Convention of Peking, threw open many more ports, as far north as Tientsin and far up the Yangtze, and gave Europeans (including missionaries) the right to roam in the Chinese interior. Moreover, the old fiction of Chinese diplomatic superiority was to be firmly scotched by forcing the emperor to permit European diplomats to be stationed in Peking. China, it seemed, had been forcibly integrated into the Europeans' international system, on humiliating terms and as a second-rate power, at best.

To the more thoughtful of Chinese administrators and scholars (and Chinese officialdom was recruited from the ablest classical scholars), these startling events required explanation. Their conclusions were uncompromising. Their methods had failed: urgent reform was needed. Better ways had to be found to deal with the barbarians. Western knowledge would have to be systematically translated and disseminated. Transport and communications must be improved. Above all, China must acquire the modern weapons needed to prevent the ability of the West to attack the vital points of the empire almost at will. 'We are shamefully humiliated by [Russia, America, France and England],' complained the scholar reformer Feng Kuei-fen (1809–74), 'not because our climate, soil, or resources are inferior to theirs, but because our people are really inferior ... Why are they [the Westerners] small and yet strong? Why are we large and yet weak?'[75] But, by the time that Feng wrote, the empire was beset by an internal crisis that seemed far more dangerous than the spasmodic coercion inflicted by the Europeans. In the 1850s and '60s, huge areas of central and southern China, some of its richest and most productive regions, were in the grip of rebellion, paralysing trade, cutting off the imperial revenue, and portending the withdrawal of the 'mandate of heaven': the source of dynastic legitimacy.

Much the most serious of these great upheavals was the Taiping Rebellion. It began in South West China with the visions of a millenarian prophet, whose preaching combined elements of Christian teaching picked up from the missionaries with the bitter outcry of peasantry oppressed by economic misfortune. Hung Hsiu-ch'uan declared himself the younger brother of Jesus Christ, and in 1851 proclaimed a new dynasty, the Taiping T'ien-kuo, or Heavenly Kingdom of Great Peace, with himself as Heavenly King. With astonishing speed, his movement gathered recruits into a peasant army, picked off the isolated garrisons of the Ch'ing government, and swept into the empire's Yangtze heartland. By early 1853 it had captured Nanking. Hung's aim, however, was to replace the dynasty. By 1855 his troops had reached Tientsin and seemed poised to capture the ultimate prize, the imperial capital. This was the high tide. From there his army was forced gradually back to the Yangtze valley, but its eventual defeat was delayed until 1864, with the death of Hung and the fall of Nanking to imperial troops.[76]

The Taiping Rebellion, the great Nien Rebellion that spread across a vast region north of the Yangtze and lasted until 1868,[77] and the Muslim revolt in the west (1862–73) were symptomatic of a drastic breakdown in the political, social and economic order. This may have had its roots in the plight of the agrarian economy, which was battered by a series of misfortunes after 1830. China had achieved a remarkable growth in agricultural production in the eighteenth century. The clearing of new land, and the more intensive farming of old, had kept food supplies well abreast of a surging population that had reached c.430 million by 1850. Commercialization and the rise of internal trade enabled farmers to increase their output by specialization and exchange. Increasing supplies of silver (as foreign trade expanded) lubricated this prosperous pre-industrial economy with a stream of money.[78] But well before 1850 these sources of economic expansion had dried up. The inflow of silver was replaced by a massive outflow, as opium imports soared:[79] perhaps up to half of the silver accumulated since 1700 was lost in a few years after 1820.[80] The sharp contraction of money supply forced down prices and dried up commerce. The supply of new land could no longer meet the pressure of population. The struggle to extract even more food from old lands reached its limit and may have triggered an ecological backlash, with deforestation, soil erosion, the silting of rivers and declining fertility. In north-central China, the shift in the course of the Yellow River in 1855 was an environmental disaster on a massive scale. With these multiple setbacks came rising social tension: between tax-collectors and payers; between landlords and tenants; between locals and newcomers in regions where earlier prosperity had drawn in people from

elsewhere; between ethnic and religious minorities and the Han majority, who had poured into the western lands in the colonization movement of the previous century. The state officials, who struggled to
keep order, collect the land revenue, maintain the waterways and
manage the grain reserves, faced increasing resistance from a discontented population. Their authority and prestige had already been

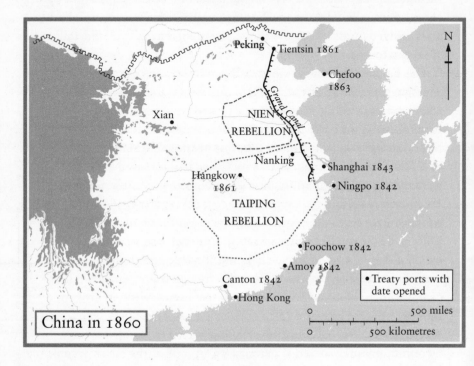

China in 1860

undermined by the 'privatizations' in the era of commercial expansion
as licensed merchants took more control over tax-collecting, water
conservancy and the grain tribute system – a change that was readily
equated with the growth of bureaucratic corruption. It was no accident that the Taiping programme demanded more land for the peasants, and the return to a more frugal and self-sufficient age. Nor that
it denounced the use of opium – a stance that ensured the furious
hostility of Western merchants and their governments.

By 1860, then, the scholar-gentry officials who governed the Ch'ing
Empire faced disaster. Their prestige and self-confidence were being

hammered by the demands of the British, French, Americans and Russians (who had wrung the vast Amur basin out of Peking in the Treaty of Aigun in 1858). Their domestic authority, and the revenue base that sustained the whole superstructure of imperial rule, were imploding as rebellion spread across the eighteen provinces of China proper as well as the outer provinces. In these desperate conditions, their achievements were remarkable. New generals like Tseng Kuo-fan (1811–72) and Li Hung-chang (1823–1901) contained, squeezed and eventually suffocated the great rebellions. They raised new-style armies in the provinces, equipped with Western weapons. They mobilized the provincial gentry, who officered these new regional forces. They levied new taxes on commerce and foreign trade (through the Western-managed Maritime Customs Service). As the rebellions petered out, Tseng and Li looked for ways to 'self-strengthen' China. They encouraged the import of scientific knowledge. Two great arsenals were built to produce modern weapons. Chinese merchants were encouraged with subsidies and monopolies to invest in modern enterprises, especially shipping and mining. There was even an abortive attempt to buy a modern navy in the West, complete with European officers. These 'modernizing' efforts were accompanied in rural China by the drive to resettle land devastated by the rebellions, repair the waterways, and restore the authority of the gentry officials.[81]

What this great effort could not achieve (and was not meant to achieve) was the transformation of China into a modern state on the Western model. The limits of Tseng's and Li's 'self-strengthening' were humiliatingly revealed in August 1884, when French warships blew China's new (but wooden-hulled) fleet to pieces in a quarrel over Vietnam.[82] Though state–merchant cooperation might have found ways of promoting industrial enterprise, this was a far cry from industrializing the economy more generally. The mid-century combination of agrarian crisis and political upheaval made the task even harder. There was no prospect, for example, of building a new China round the core of its most prosperous region in the Yangtze delta, the heart of its eighteenth-century commercial economy. It had been badly damaged in the Taiping Rebellion, and was too vulnerable to Western penetration to serve this purpose. It might even be argued that the real priority of the 'restoration' was precisely that: to restore the authority of the Confucian state and its ethos of frugality and social discipline, not to break the Confucian mould.[83] But if industrial transformation had eluded the scholar-gentry reformers, the importance of their state-building should not be underestimated. Of necessity, the mid-century reforms had devolved considerable power on the provinces and provincial gentry. The recovery programme in the countryside helped to revive the unwritten compact between the peasant and his scholar-gentry rulers. But the gentry were also bound more tightly to the empire by the progressive displacement of the high Manchu officials by ethnic Chinese: with a more unified elite, China was gradually becoming more completely a Chinese state – although recent research suggests that Manchu predominance remained a bone of contention.[84] China might not have been able to match the industrial output or modern firepower of the European states, but her cultural and social solidarity had been strengthened just in time for the crisis years after 1890.

Nor in the meantime had the European states been able to turn the Middle Kingdom into a mere semi-colonial periphery. The treaty ports had been meant as bridgeheads into the Chinese economy, opening it up Indian-style to Western manufactures. But, though foreign trade expanded (to the considerable benefit of the rural economy), Chinese merchants resisted the entry of foreign business into the domestic economy. Foreigners were forced to deal with their Chinese customers through a middleman, the comprador.[85] In a fiercely competitive and uncertain market, there were few easy pickings. The turnover was rapid. By the 1870s, all but two of the largest foreign merchants, Jardine Matheson and Butterfield Swire, had gone to the wall, or made way for new entrants.[86] Compared with India, China (with twice the population) was a far smaller and more difficult market, consuming only half the level of India's imports. When a crash came in the early 1880s, the commercial eldorado the Europeans had imagined seemed to have vanished almost completely.[87] But the real test of China's political and economic independence was yet to come.

In the 1850s and '60s there was every reason to think that Japan would suffer the fate of China, in an even more drastic form. Since the early 1800s the gradual opening of the North Pacific had brought more and more shipping to the seas round Japan, from Russia (whose 'Wild East' lay only a few hundred miles to the north), Britain and the United States. In 1853 the Japanese shogun had nervously welcomed the American Commodore Perry, accepting that the era of *sakoku* (seclusion) was over. Five years later, in the 'unequal treaties' of 1858, the main Western powers were granted similar privileges of access to those they had extorted from China in 1842. Foreigners would be free to come and trade in a number of 'treaty ports' (the most important was Yokohama, near Tokyo), where they would remain under the protection of their consuls and be exempt from Japanese jurisdiction. Here land would be set aside for their offices, warehouses and residences. Japan would not be allowed to levy customs duties except at a modest rate, to encourage 'free trade' and the diffusion of Western manufactures. With its old isolation once broken, Japan seemed far more vulnerable to Western domination than its vast continental neighbour on the Asian mainland. Its population (*c*.32 million) was much smaller, though far from negligible in European terms. Its main cities were desperately exposed to Western sea power (Japan had no navy). Russians had invaded Sakhalin (their first landing was in 1806) and threatened sparsely populated Hokkaido, the second-largest island in the Japanese archipelago. And in the early 1860s Japan's political system was on the verge of collapse as a civil war broke out between the Tokugawa shogun and his most powerful vassals in the south and west.

The arrival in force of the Euro-American powers (as a sideshow of their joint coercion of China after 1856) had coincided with and massively aggravated a crisis in the Tokugawa system that had governed Japan since the early seventeenth century. Formally the shogun, who was always chosen from the large and powerful Tokugawa clans, was the viceroy of the emperor, who lived in dignified impotence in his Kyoto palace, several days' journey from the seat of government in Edo. In practice the shogun's power was based on the submission of the numerous and semi-autonomous 'domains' (*han*) and their clan rulers to his authority in a form of vassalage. The *han* were required to pay a tax tribute to the shogun's *bakufu* (literally 'tent government'), and their ruling elites were forced to live in alternate years in their great clan compounds in Edo, as so many hostages for good behaviour. Ultimately the shogun's control rested upon the loyalty of the Tokugawa clans and the support of his other hereditary vassals against the *tozama* or 'outside' clans.[88] But the *bakuhan* system also drew strength from the Confucian ethos that pervaded the samurai caste and emphasized loyalty to the emperor, as well as from the extensive commercial integration that bound the domains into a single market centred on Osaka and Edo.

In the 1820s and '30s this *ancien régime* entered a phase of exceptional strain. The underlying cause may have been that agricultural production was now pressed up against its environmental limits. The clearing of forests and more intensive cultivation no longer yielded significant gains: marginal farmlands were dangerously vulnerable to climatic chance.[89] The 'Tenpo' famines in the 1830s, severest in the north-east, affected the whole of Japan. Domain rulers were squeezed between their obligations to Edo and their local burdens, especially the 'rice stipends' to the samurai elite, now largely civilized as a bureaucratic class. In several large domains, the ruling group took vigorous measures to restore its solvency, repudiating debts, attacking monopolies, encouraging new crops and manufactures, and hoarding bullion.[90] These groups also showed increasing interest in foreign trade, especially in Satsuma (whose long island tail in the Ryukyus stretching far away towards Taiwan had long been the avenue for trade with China), and in the more systematic acquisition of 'Dutch' knowledge – information about the West and its civilization that leaked through the keyhole port of Deshima, the Dutch trading station in Nagasaki harbour. At the same time, the leading domains in the south and west, Choshu and Satsuma, were acutely aware of the growing threat of Western intervention, to which they were most exposed. By the 1850s, both were buying modern firearms, cannon and steamships, and experimenting desultorily with Western metallurgy to make their own weapons.

These changes were bound to set them on a collision course with the *bakufu* in Edo. The balance of power within the *bakuhan* system was shifting. The 1858 treaties and the shogun's appeasement in the face of foreign pressure divided and weakened the *bakufu* and exposed it to xenophobic demands to 'close the country'. The *bakufu*'s own efforts to rearm were timid and indecisive, but it opposed the full opening to the West urged by some reformers, fearing the collapse of its ideological prestige. As the Western presence loomed larger, the political mood grew anxious and violent. Both Choshu and Satsuma came to blows with the West in 1863–4 and discovered at first hand its strength and their weakness. The next three years saw a rapid decline towards civil war as Choshu and Satsuma, with other domain allies, tried to win the emperor's support against the Tokugawa, and the *bakufu* in turn waged war on Choshu.[91] No compromise could be reached between *han* demands for greater autonomy and the shogun's determination to reassert his control. In 1866 the leading clans in south-western Japan formed an alliance against him. By January 1868, Choshu–Satsuma forces, better armed and better led, had over-whelmed the Tokugawa and driven the shogun into abdication. To fill the vacuum, and legitimate their revolt, the rebel leaders pro-claimed the restoration of imperial rule.

Thus far, the Japanese crisis had followed a familiar enough pattern. Close contact with an outside power, and the seductive appeal of its trade and technology, had unsettled local politics and discredited the ruler. As new men struggled for mastery, and the old regime fell to pieces, the time became ripe for foreign intervention: annexation, a protectorate, or yet more onerous 'unequal treaties'. Japan was saved from this fate partly by the reluctance of the several Western powers to interfere in its civil war[92] – perhaps because none of them could be sure to gain from its uncertain outcome – but even more by the speed and determination with which the new regime set about the building of a modern state.[93] The pace and scale of the change were astonishing. The charter oath of the emperor (6 April 1868) promised government by public discussion (a promise long deferred) and the search for knowledge 'throughout the world'. Government departments on the Western model were established, including a foreign office. Much more significant was the end of vassalage, transforming the hereditary domain rulers into removable governors, a step followed in 1871 by the outright abolition of the *han* and their replacement by 'prefec-tures'. The feudal conglomerate had become a unitary state with a single capital at Tokyo, as Edo was renamed in 1869. In 1872 the old system of tribute was swept away in favour of a uniform land tax, to be paid in cash, and in 1873 universal military service was introduced in place of the samurai and the feudal levies. The samurai were pensioned off, in money not rice. In a blizzard of reform between 1870 and 1873, legal equality, freedom of occupation, the right to sell land, and even the Western calendar transformed the social landscape of the Tokugawa era. The halting steps before 1868 to transform Japan along Western lines had given way to a headlong rush towards European-style 'modernity'. In the race against time, the Japanese had become the champion sprinters.

Two questions arise. Why did the new government follow such a dramatic course, and how was it able to impose such drastic change on a deeply conservative, not to say xenophobic, society? It had seemed more than likely that the rebel domains would seek merely to replace the Tokugawa shogunate with one of their own. In fact they could not do so. None of the rebel clans was strong enough to replace the Tokugawa by itself, and the attempt would have prolonged the civil war indefinitely. Dissolving the *han* was the only guarantee of political peace. Secondly, the leading figures in the rebel alliance were determined to 'self-strengthen' Japan against the West, and came from domains where the advantages of foreign trade, foreign knowledge and foreign methods for this purpose were widely acknowledged. The most urgent need was for a single army along European lines. To pay for it meant a unified system of taxation and revenue. Thirdly, in ways that remain partly obscure, the reformist samurai who led the new regime sympathized with the demands of the merchant class for an end to the stringent regulation of economic life and status. But it was one thing to embark on so ambitious a change, quite another to impose it on doubters and dissidents. The huge samurai caste (more than a million people) in particular might have been expected to resist the abolition of its hereditary status and military function. The peasant majority, upon whom fell an ever heavier tax burden, had even less to celebrate. The Western powers waited in the wings, determined to punish any ill-treatment of their nationals or their trade.

In fact the transition was far from peaceful. Many of the new regime's leaders fell victim to samurai vendettas. For many years, recalled Yukichi Fukuzawa, the most famous exponent of Western learning, he was too fearful of assassination to venture out at night.[94] The Satsuma rebellion in 1877 brought 30,000 samurai and their followers into the field before it was crushed by Tokyo's new army. There were numerous peasant risings. But the Japanese reformers enjoyed much more favourable conditions than their counterparts in imperial China. The new government controlled from the start the Tokugawa domains, extending over a quarter of Japan, and a vital reservoir of money and men. Secondly, the huge social power of the samurai caste, potentially so dangerous, was turned to the government's advantage. More than anything, this was crucial to success. The prestige of leaders like Saigo Takamori and Yamagata Aristomo[95] disarmed samurai fears, and large numbers took service in the Meiji state as soldiers, bureaucrats, policemen and clerks. The social discipline they had traditionally exerted, especially in the countryside, helped keep in check the peasant unrest that came so close to unseating the Ch'ing government in Peking. Thirdly, to a far greater extent than was possible in China, the long-secluded emperor could be reinvented as a powerful symbol of the new regime, the focus of a civil religion, complete with its shrines and state priests.[96] Finally, Japan's remarkable degree of ethnic unity neutralized a potential source of internal division and solidified the new state against external influence.

This political strength would have counted for little had the reformers failed on the second front. Economic self-strengthening was as vital as political. Economic failure would have been the Trojan Horse through which foreign influence turned into foreign control. This could happen in several ways. Western merchants might demand better access and bully their home governments into intervening more. More insidiously, a modernizing government in Tokyo might borrow heavily abroad, becoming financially dependent upon Western lenders. Worst of all, the difficult entry into the volatile world of international trade carried a heavy risk of bankruptcy, and a bankrupt regime, discredited at home and vulnerable abroad, had few defences against foreign intervention. The Japanese evaded these hazards with remarkable success. Of course their achievements should not be exaggerated. Industrialization was relatively slow. In 1880 two-thirds of Japanese exports were made up of raw silk and tea. In 1887 perhaps 90 per cent of Japan's overseas trade was managed by foreign merchants.[97] As late as 1890 it was easy in the West to see Japan as a picturesque oriental state whose solvency depended on a narrow range of commodity exports. In fact the main foundations had already been laid for economic independence and industrial advance. In the key industry of cotton textiles, domestic output matched imports by 1880, and exports began in 1883.[98] The key institutions behind commercial and industrial success – the specialized foreign trade banks, the large trading houses (*zaibatsu*) that combined manufacture and commerce, and the system of government subsidy – were all in place. The wild inflation of the 1870s (the result of too much paper money) was savagely checked in the deflationary 1880s and a stable currency was established. In the crucial transition phase, the Japanese borrowed almost no money abroad. The Cape Horn of modernization – financial collapse and social revolt – had been rounded.

Superficially, the Japanese had followed the same prescription as the Ch'ing reformers. The state had encouraged merchants into industrial enterprises and shipping, and had subsidized their efforts. It had given huge priority to making modern weapons. It acknowledged that foreign merchants would demand reasonable access, commercial security and moderate taxes. But the Japanese had already been more successful than the Chinese by the 1880s, and the difference in performance had become spectacular by 1914. To some extent this may have been the result of Meiji Japan's favourable inheritance from the Tokugawa past. 'Traditional' Japan had been a society with high levels of literacy and artisanal skills. It also had a remarkably centralized economy centred on Osaka and Edo. There was a long tradition of big banker-merchants, like the famous house of Mitsui, which dated back to the early 1600s, out of which the *zaibatsu* evolved. Some large domains had pursued foreign trade and Western technology well before the restoration. But these arguments can be overdone. Tokugawa Japan was not a free-market economy. Its income levels were 'far below' the initial levels in other states that industrialized successfully in the nineteenth century.[99] The travails of economic change might have easily forced a retreat or led to chaos. For a latecomer like Japan, entering the international economy required both a strong state and an unusually disciplined social order. It was this that made Japan exceptional. The samurai caste, whose leaders had made the restoration, dominated the new state. Samurai-led governments borrowed from the great banker-merchants and paid

them back with the knock-down sale of government-funded enterprises.[100] It was an alliance of necessity against two enemies: the West
and the threat of upheaval at home. The loser was the peasantry. With
its new 'national' army and police, the Meiji state could repress rural
discontent, tax the peasants as never before, and concentrate economic
power in the countryside in the hands of landlords.[101] It was the
peasants who paid when the fierce deflation of the 1880s drove down
prices. The Japanese embrace of Western methods, rules and institutions was real enough. But at the heart of 'samurai capitalism' was
the ruthless exploitation of the peasants to subsidize the struggle for
industrial and commercial independence.

These features of Japan's transition may have made it unique. An
advanced pre-industrial economy, the exceptionally strong social and
political order forged at the restoration, comparative remoteness from
the West and its firepower, and the fortune of timing that allowed
'self-strengthening' to begin before the full weight of Western power
was felt in the Asian Pacific after 1890 were crucial determinants
of its success in the race against time. In the third case, that of the
Ottoman Empire, these features were conspicuous by their absence or
worked to its disadvantage. The result by the late 1880s was subjection
to a form of economic tutelage and the deepening prospect of disintegration and wholesale partition among the Western powers whose
quarrels over the 'Sick Man of Europe' sometimes seemed the main
reason for his survival. It was true, of course, that Ottoman governments had a much less favourable geographical inheritance than the
Chinese or Japanese. The Ottoman Empire was neither compact like
Japan nor endowed with the vast, productive agricultural heartland
that was China proper. Spreadeagled across three continents, it was
(by the 1830s) exposed at many points to the sea power of the Europeans. As well as its 'external' frontier with Europe in the Balkans, it
had to defend a series of 'inner' frontiers against tribals, nomads and
desert-dwellers: in Anatolia (against the Kurds), in the Jezireh (modern
Iraq, with its Shia majority), in Syria (where desert Arabs were pressing
more and more strongly against the cultivated fringe), and in faraway
Yemen, the empire's southern pole. Arguably, by the 1830s its geostrategic equilibrium had suffered irreversible damage.[102] But Ottoman

leaders had accepted much earlier and more completely than Chinese and Japanese that the survival of the empire depended upon the deliberate grafting of Western technique on to the social and political structure of their Islamic empire.

This process had already begun in the 1820s with the liquidation of the overpowerful janissaries and their gradual replacement by a more European-style army. It was the terrible crisis of the 1830s, when the combination of Russian aggression from the north and the French-backed attempt at imperial takeover by the Ottoman viceroy in Egypt came close to overthrowing the empire, that made drastic change seem much more urgent. To conciliate the British – a vital ally – Constantinople agreed in 1838 to throw open its markets to foreign trade. Then, in 1839, wide-ranging reforms that became known as the *Tanzimat* or 'reorganization' were announced – partly, no doubt, to improve the empire's image abroad and win support from the European powers. Under the Edict of Gulhane, all Ottoman subjects were to have equal rights (ending the old distinction between Muslims and unbelievers), protection of their person and property was guaranteed, and sweeping changes were proposed in taxation and in the administration of the army and of the legal system, more or less on the model of an 'advanced' European state like France. In the '*Tanzimat* era' that followed, from 1839 to 1876, the Ottoman sultans (Abdul Mejid 1839–61, Abdul Aziz 1861–76) seemed committed to a systematic 'self-strengthening' that would safeguard the empire against the economic, political and ideological pressures that emanated from Europe. Four reformer-statesmen, the pashas Reshid, Fuad, Ali and Midhat, were determined to give the central government and its officials far more control over what had become a decentralized and unruly realm. They reorganized the army and (through conscription) hugely increased its size (from some 24,000 in 1837 to over 120,000 men).[103] Through the *vilayet* law of 1864, they imposed a more uniform system of provincial rule and cut down the power of local notables. They promoted secular education, to train new generations of bureaucrats and army officers in the scientific, technical and legal methods of the West and reduce the influence of Muslim clerics. They set up a finance ministry and a budget system, and founded the Ottoman Imperial Bank to serve some of the purposes of a central bank. Above all, they struggled to promote a new conception of Ottoman citizenship to replace the old regime of non-Muslim *millets* or religious communities, grouped around and inferior to the 'core' population of Muslims on whose loyalty the sultan's power had always depended. It was a heroic programme.

By 1880 the benefits of this great effort at reform seemed meagre, and the costs prohibitive. In 1878 the empire suffered a devastating series of territorial losses. Almost all the European provinces where there were substantial numbers of Christians were ripped from its grasp. Wallachia and Moldavia, autonomous since the 1820s, became independent Romania. The province of Nish was added to Serbia. Bulgaria became autonomous, and was allowed to merge with its southern third, so-called Eastern Roumelia, a few years later. Tiny Montenegro became a sovereign state. Even Bosnia and Herzegovina, where there were many Muslims, were placed under Habsburg tutelage. To add to these injuries, the island of Cyprus, Ottoman since 1571, was occupied, though not formally annexed, by the British, as the price of their support against Russia, while Russia seized the districts of Kars and Ardahan in eastern Anatolia. Before this territorial catastrophe, the Ottoman government had already been forced to concede a special regime under foreign surveillance in the Christian district in the Lebanon ('The Mountain') and in Crete, where an uprising of Greek-speaking Christians had raged between 1866 and 1869. And not long after it, Egypt and Tunis, both technically under Ottoman rule, were occupied by the British (who took Egypt in 1882) and the French. Nor was the great crisis of the 1870s solely political. Its effects had been worsened by financial disaster. In 1875 the Ottoman government defaulted on its foreign loans and became bankrupt. The price of its return to financial respectability was acceptance of a draconian regime of inspection and control. After 1881, the Ottoman Public Debt Administration, staffed and supervised by European bankers and officials, had first claim on Ottoman revenues to repay the creditors, doling out the residue to the sultan's government. Materially and symbolically, it seemed, the empire had been reduced to a virtual dependency.

On the face of it, the *Tanzimat* had led not to self-strengthening, but to self-mutilation or worse. In reality, the *Tanzimat* reformers had faced a combination of internal and external pressures far more daunting than those confronting their counterparts in East Asia. Strategically, the Ottomans were desperately vulnerable to the military power of Russia – unless the tsar could be restrained by his European rivals – and their position was made all the worse by the drastic decline of their naval power.[104] It was the Russian invasion in 1877 that led to the territorial losses at the Congress of Berlin in 1878. But the underlying weakness was the rejection of Ottoman rule by the Christian minorities and their insistent appeal to the European states to intervene on their behalf. As the century wore on, this problem became more and more acute. The spread of the 'national idea' through the rest of Europe was bound to infect the Ottoman minorities, who maintained close contact with their ethnic brothers outside the empire. Economic change, from which Greek merchants (for example) profited more than their Muslim fellow subjects, created a larger and more articulate constituency for political rights and tended to undermine the higher clergy through whom the sultan had ruled the Christian *millets*. Identity, said these new 'nationalists', must be sought in territorial statehood rather than church membership. *Tanzimat* reform itself had brought greater reliance on educated Christians. In these conditions, the reformers' hope that Christians would accept a shared Ottoman or 'Osmanli' citizenship and sink their differences in common loyalty to the sultan was unlikely to be realized. Indeed, when Midhat Pasha tried out this programme in Bulgaria in the 1860s he found himself attacked from all sides.[105] To many Muslims, the dilution of the empire's Islamic character was deeply offensive. It meant sidelining the *ulama*, the local scholar class, the repositories of legal and theological expertise. It meant shifting the empire's foundations from the bedrock of Muslim loyalty to the shifting sands of Christian cooperation. Anti-reform feeling was sharpened by resentment against the *Tanzimat*'s bureaucratic centralization, and by outrage at the fate of the hundreds of thousands of Muslim refugees driven out of the Caucasus by the Russians.[106] Indeed, the settlement of these refugees in the Ottoman provinces seems likely to have raised the temperature of ethnic and religious antagonism to fever pitch in the 1870s.

Conceivably, a powerful and well-financed administration might have won the battle for local control and deterred its foreign enemies more forcefully. But on this front, too, the reformers were defeated. They were driven into foreign borrowing by the soaring costs of the Crimean War (1854–6), and then badly mismanaged their loan operations. By the 1870s, the annual charge on these loans amounted to some two-thirds of state revenues, and on some borrowing they were paying up to 30 per cent interest a year.[107] Although they increased their revenue by some 50 per cent, they failed to drive out the old practice of tax-farming and control collection directly. They gambled on the growth of trade to fill the state's coffers, but Ottoman trade increased much less than the global average,[108] while political turbulence damaged both Ottoman commerce and the empire's credit rating. State-led efforts at industrialization languished, and the export of raw materials encouraged enclave development round the ports – a tendency that was reinforced by poor inland communications.[109] Hardly any of the government's borrowing found its way into the building of infrastructure like railways. The contrast with Meiji Japan could hardly be more striking. Ethnic diversity and the lack of a samurai-like caste to maintain social and political order was compounded by a pattern of economic development in which foreign control became 'overwhelming'.[110]

Yet, despite the pounding it had taken, the Ottoman Empire did not fall to pieces or slide weakly under European rule. The loss of the bulk of its European provinces made the empire much more fully a Turkish, Arab and Muslim state. Under the sultan Abdul Hamid II (r. 1876–1909), Ottoman rule became more sympathetic to pan-Islamic movements and more conscious of its international role as the guardian of the holy places, to which an ever-growing stream of Islamic pilgrims was brought by steamship and railway from India and South East Asia. At the same time, the old programme of the *Tanzimat* was pressed forward. The state machine was slowly modernized. The railway network was enlarged. Military and administrative control was pushed deeper into the Arab provinces. The Ottomans had lost the struggle to keep the great multi-ethnic empire they had built in the sixteenth century. After 1880 they entered a new race to solidify their remaining territories before a further confrontation with Europe, or the growth of an Arab nationalism, could tear Abdul Hamid's empire to pieces.

*

Two other Middle Eastern states were also drawn into the race against time. Their fates would be different. The first was Egypt, formally still part of the Ottoman Empire. Under its Ottoman governor Mehemet Ali, sent by the sultan after the expulsion of its French invaders, the practical autonomy of the Mamluk era became more definite. Mehemet Ali constructed an authoritarian state around his new army.[111] His real ambition was to build an Egyptian empire from the Sudan to Syria, and to make himself master of the Arab lands. Twice he came close to unseating the sultan; twice he was thwarted by the European powers. Instead he was forced to open his border to European trade, and give up his costly experiment in state-managed manufactures. Mehemet Ali died in 1849, but under his successors Said (r. 1854–63) and Ismail (r. 1863–79) part at least of his grand design was pushed steadily forward.

For both these rulers, the ultimate aim was to win for their dynasty a formal equality with the Ottoman sultan, and sovereign independence, free from the claim of the Ottoman government to control foreign relations, determine the size of their army, or (in the very worst case, which actually happened in 1879) to dismiss them from office. Both had in mind not a 'nation' state but a monarchical state, in which the ruler's power was paramount. The 'Turko-Circassian' elite (a mixture of the old Mamluk ruling class and Mehemet Ali's Turkish and Albanian followers) would be made to pay for its privileged status in an overwhelmingly 'Arab' society by loyal support for its patron and protector. Both rulers understood that their chances depended upon a rapid increase in agrarian wealth.

The omens were favourable. The demand for Egypt's long-staple cotton in industrial Europe seemed almost insatiable, but to meet it required an agricultural revolution. The area of cultivable land grew by 60 per cent between 1813 and 1877.[112] The delta marshlands below Cairo were drained and cleared. Perennial irrigation, supplied by a network of canals and barrages, replaced the reliance on the annual flood, and doubled production. By the mid-1860s foreign investment was growing, and foreign-owned banks sprang up to serve the new landed class. Alexandria boomed as the Mediterranean port city of the export economy. Railways were built. A European-style quarter was laid out in Cairo alongside the Nile, with a new royal palace, a stock exchange, an opera house, and sweeping boulevards on the Parisian pattern.[113] With its centralized bureaucracy, landowning elite, liberal property laws, and large foreign community (100,000 strong by the 1870s: by contrast, the number in Iran was much less than a thousand), Egypt seemed the model of a 'development' state, a triumph of reform, an Islamic Japan. It attracted the service of adventurous Europeans – like Charles 'Chinese' Gordon (the later Gordon 'of Khartoum'), sent to rule the Sudan and extirpate slavery (what better proof of the ruler's modernity?). By the 1870s, full independence seemed only a matter of time. Perhaps it would come by default in the next great crisis in Ottoman fortunes. Meanwhile Ismail (who had obtained the more dignified title of 'khedive' in 1867) was flatteringly described in an authoritative guide to the country: 'His Highness speaks French like a Parisian . . . Be you engineer, merchant, journalist, politician, practical agriculturalist, or almost no matter what else, you will soon feel that you have met your match in special intelligence and information.'[114]

For Said and Ismail, the Suez Canal was meant to crown their achievements.[115] The costs would be high, but the pay-off tremendous. Its income would bring them a new stream of wealth. Its Nile connection (the Sweetwater Canal) would bring a new tract of land into intense cultivation. It promised above all a huge geopolitical dividend. Once the ruler of Egypt had become the guardian of the world's most valuable seaway, the great powers of Europe would acknowledge the need to protect him against any threat of aggression, and would see the point of his independence. It was no wonder that Said was persuaded to take a large share in the company launched by de Lesseps to build the canal. When cotton prices soared up in the 1860s (when the American South was cut off by blockade and then wrecked by invasion), it was easy for Ismail to borrow in Europe until the national debt reached £100 million. But as the cotton price sank in the mid-1870s, and before the canal (opened in 1869) could show a return, speculative boom turned to financial bust. In 1875 Ismail had to sell his canal shares to the British government for £4 million – perhaps a quarter of their value. A year later he – and Egypt – was bankrupt.

Now the full price of the race against time began to be paid. The frantic change in Egypt's social order had piled up resentments. The landowning class was eager to check the authoritarian style of the ruler. The *ulama* (whose headquarters at al-Azhar in Cairo – part mosque, part university – was the most prestigious centre of learning

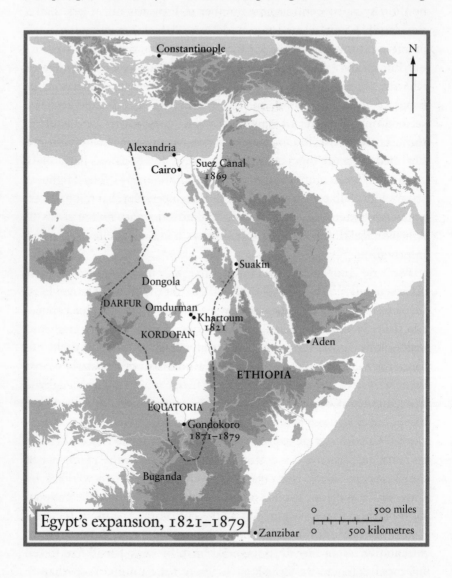

Egypt's expansion, 1821–1879

in the Islamic world) disliked the ruler's embrace of foreign infidel practices, his web of corruption, and his extravagant lifestyle. In the army and bureaucracy, the Arabic-educated class loathed the continued domination of the Turko-Circassian elite, restored to favour by Ismail after Said's flirtation with a more 'Arabic' policy. All these unresolved conflicts were charged with a sense of social malaise: fear and suspicion of European carpetbaggers; moral unease at the gross exploitation of the *fellahin* (rural cultivators) class, the principal victims of agrarian change.[116] The mood of revolt now had a new voice in the journalists and newspapers that began to appear. Thus the external crisis over foreign debts (and Europe's demand for effective control over Egypt's finances) quickly turned into a crisis at home over who would bear the real burden of the foreign demands. The Suez Canal – the booster rocket towards full independence – became the Trojan Horse of foreign control, and (quite literally) the invasion route for alien rule.

Iran was more fortunate, and its rulers less bold. They had anyway much less room for manoeuvre. Mehemet Ali had founded his state on the power of his army and the wealth to be gained by the export of cotton. The Qajar rulers, who entrenched their power at much the same time, lacked these resources. Creating an army that would deter external aggressors and internal dissent was far more difficult: indeed, they had to make do with an imperial bodyguard of 4,000 men.[117] The shahs faced the antipathy of the clerical elite – the Shi'a *ulama* – whose social power was much greater than that of the *ulama* in Egypt.[118] They had to base their authority to a crucial degree on an alliance of tribes, since pastoral nomads made up more than a third (and perhaps even half) of the whole population, and formed a mass of armies in being. They had no bank of 'new' land with which to reward a compliant elite or finance a larger bureaucracy. And, although the Iranian economy staged a major recovery from the chaos and disorder of the late eighteenth century, there was no bonanza from cotton to draw in foreign investment or pay for a programme of public improvements in irrigation, railways or roads. The country remained in a stage of acute localization, in which tribe and sub-tribe, village community, artisan guild, urban quarter or ward, sect, religion or language remained the main source of identity and the main cause of division. In short, the means to build a strong dynastic state upon the Egyptian model were almost entirely lacking.

Yet the Qajars were threatened by external dangers at least as acute as those that confronted the Ottoman Empire. Russia's expansion into the Caucasus had cost them dearly. By the treaties of Gulistan (1813) and Turkmanchai (1828) they had been forced to give up their claim on Georgia and Armenia and surrender much of Azerbaijan. The growth of Britain's sea power in the Persian Gulf was bound to make them uneasy. It encouraged the unruliness of the great southern tribes, and might snap the allegiance of its coastal communities, like Mohammerah, whose great sheikh was ethnically Arab. After all, even late in the century, it was much quicker to reach Tehran from the Gulf by ship through the Black Sea and the Caspian and then south to the capital, rather than directly by road. When Nasir al-Din seized Herat (in modern Afghanistan, but a prized possession of the Safavid shahs) in 1856, the British forced him to disgorge it by bombarding Bushire and sending troops to Mohammerah. No shah could ignore the risk that a foreign defeat, or the loss of a province, would smash his prestige and unravel the bonds that held his multi-ethnic empire together.

Under Nasir al-Din (r. 1848–96), some efforts were made to strengthen the shah's power. The Ottoman model of *Tanzimat* reform was influential.[119] A college was founded to diffuse Western knowledge and produce a new administrative class. But this brief phase of 'reform' coincided with the rise of the Babis, dissident Muslims, some of whom denounced the corruption of rule. When one of them tried to murder the shah, the movement was crushed: shah and *ulama* closed ranks. The reforming minister was dispatched to political and then physical oblivion. But, although the shah's authority was still bound to depend on the skilful manipulation of communities and interests, symptoms of a more unified polity slowly appeared. The border with the Ottomans was settled at last in 1847; Tehran's control over Sistan and Baluchistan was asserted in 1866; and the frontier with Afghanistan was agreed in 1872.[120] The influence of Shi'ite Islam – chief source of cultural identity – was strengthened, partly as a result of the struggle with the Babis.[121] The reach of the bureaucracy became gradually longer, and state law replaced the sharia in matters of property.[122] The telegraph linked Tehran to some of its provinces. The export of opium brought greater prosperity to the west of the country. By the 1870s, however, there were ominous signs that a crisis was coming.

Russia's advance was the obvious warning. By 1859–60 the tsar's army was in Turkestan. In 1866 Tashkent was annexed. By 1873 the Russians were in Khiva. They faced the north-eastern quarter of the shah's dominions, and the holy city of Meshed. Nasir al-Din had few means of resistance. His revenues were falling, while prices were gripped in an inflationary spiral. He set off for Europe to win fresh support. The quest for cash in the hand drove him to make a sensational bargain, the 'Reuter's Concession'. Under its terms, rights to the profits from any new enterprise anywhere in the country – railways, minerals, irrigation works, factories – were granted away to a foreign entrepreneur (Julius Reuter, founder of the news agency) in return for £40,000 down. The furore this caused, and its hasty withdrawal, showed how far the shah was from a timely reinforcement of Iran's defences. Instead, he pushed on down what came to seem later a risky if unavoidable path: allowing foreign commercial interests to enter the country. Perhaps he calculated that they would balance each other. It was certainly true that Anglo-Russian antagonism was the best guarantee that neither country would be able to dominate Iran. It was also the case that Iran's geostrategic position and decentralized politics, as well as the strength of its religious elite, made it a hard nut to crack. But whether the Qajars, and Iranian independence, could survive the stresses of foreign intrusion in a land where Westerners had scarcely been seen[123] would soon be revealed.

Many other Afro-Asian states faced the same challenge as China, Japan and the Ottoman Empire in the middle years of the nineteenth century, including Abyssinia (modern Ethiopia) and Siam (modern Thailand). They feared invasion and the loss of lightly ruled borderlands where their writ had run. They mistrusted the motives of European merchants. They were anxious to modernize their armies and (necessarily) their revenues. They hoped to play off the Europeans against each other, and preserve their freedom by indirect means. They toyed with methods of state-led growth, sometimes by licensing concessionaires from Europe, or encouraging immigrants. All faced the dilemma that drastic change in states where the central power was weak risked chaos and revolt, heightening the danger of outside intervention. All faced the reality that by the 1880s the gap between the technological, financial and demographic resources of Europe and those of Afro-Asia seemed to be widening rapidly. The race against time after 1880 had entered the home straight.

6

The Limits of Empire

6. French soldiers at Tientsin (Tianjin) in the Boxer Rebellion

After 1880 the frontiers of Greater Europe surged forward as if the final subjection of the non-Western world was only a matter of time. The most obvious sign of this was the rapid partition of those parts of the globe that had escaped the attention of European colonizers in earlier decades. The most famous case was Africa, shared out between Britain, France, Italy, Portugal, Spain, Germany and the Belgian king (who held his vast stake as a private fiefdom) in an astonishing series of bargains after 1884. But Africa was not unique. There were other partitions in South East Asia and the South Pacific. Nor was Greater Europe's advance just territorial. It rode upon a huge expansion of international trade and a dramatic increase (from small beginnings) in the amount of capital sent to regions previously dismissed as too risky or unprofitable. It coincided with a colossal rise in the flow of migrants out of Europe, most of them heading for North or South America, but with enough left over to provide a settler spearhead in tropical Africa and Asia, and a much larger bridgehead in Russian North Asia. It provoked, and drew strength from, a fiercer assertion than ever before of Europe's cultural mission to be the whole world's engine of material progress and also its source of religious and philosophical truth. Europeans were uniquely progressive, it was variously claimed, because of their physical, social or religious evolution. This was the charter of their 'race supremacy'. Last but not least, Greater Europe's expansion into Afro-Asian lands too remote or resistant in earlier times seemed a tribute to its scientific and technological primacy. The 'knowledge gap' between Europeans and (most) others looked wider, not narrower, at the end of the century. Parts of Europe were entering the second industrial revolution of electricity and chemicals before the non-Western world had exploited coal and steam.

The result was to impose, for the first time in world history, a global hierarchy of physical, economic and cultural power. It worked through a set of institutions, practices and conventional beliefs that largely held sway until the Second World War. To an extent inconceivable as late as 1860, the world of 1900 was an imperial world: of territorial empires spreading across much of the globe; and of informal empires of trade, unequal treaties and extraterritorial privilege (for Europeans) – and garrisons and gunboats to enforce it – over most of the rest. Concepts of international law (invented in Europe) dismissed claims to sovereignty (and justified foreign intervention) unless the state concerned met a 'standard of civilization' that was approved in Europe. In economic theory, and increasingly in practice, this imperial world implied a division of labour. The imperial powers were (in varying degrees) also industrial powers. They supplied (or tried to supply) manufactured goods, capital investment, technical know-how and skilled personnel. The role of the colonies, and of 'semi-colonial' lands (like China or Argentina), was to produce the foodstuffs, raw materials and commodities that the industrial world wanted and to take in return its manufactures and capital – an economic rule that meant enforcing free trade against local interests and their protected markets. Demographically, the imperial world was a white man's world. Europeans were more or less free (wars and depressions permitting) to migrate where they wished, or could make a living. Imperial rulers promoted Afro-Asian migrations to develop their colonies, and discounted the claims of local communities to keep their land to themselves. The cultural theory of this imperial world was perhaps its most pervasive feature. Europeans convinced themselves, and persuaded others, that, while non-European civilizations and cultures were exotic, fascinating, romantic or beautiful, they were at best a series of culs-de-sac. Only Europe's way was a proven path to 'moral and material progress' – the title of the annual report issued by the (British-run) government of India.

We know, of course, that this powerful system of European dominance was never completed and did not endure. A citizen of its strongest unit, the British Empire, who was born in 1890 might have lived to see it decay and collapse. One of the central questions in modern world history is why this happened. Much of the answer can be found in the great world crisis of 1914–45. But we can also find some important clues in the previous era. 'Global colonialism' was an impressive construct. But it was erected at speed, and its foundations were shallow. Perhaps more to the point, its equilibrium depended upon a set of conditions that could not remain stable. The diplomacy of imperialism, like its economics and ideology, turned out to contain a 'genetic flaw' that could not be cured.

VISIONS OF EMPIRE

After 1880, it became a commonplace that the world had shrunk. This was partly a reaction to the rapid spread of swift communications. Steamships, railways and the electric telegraph had been widely adopted in Europe and North America from the 1830s and '40s. By the 1870s they were colonizing vast new areas of the world, carving corridors of access into regions where travel had been difficult (and costly) and information scarce. The opening of the Suez Canal in 1869 meant the extension eastward of the steamship lines and their scheduled services, creating the great trunk road of merchant shipping all the way to Shanghai and Yokohama. Submarine cables and the overland telegraph could now bring commercial and political news from East Asia to Europe within days, and then hours. But most of all it was the railway that revolutionized thinking about distance. The late nineteenth century was the greatest age of railway imperialism. The British and French built colonial railways in West, East and Southern Africa to bind restless hinterlands to their coastal bridge-heads. The Trans-Caspian Railway (1880–88) carried Russian power into Central Asia. The Trans-Siberian Railway (1891–1904), the grandest of all these imperial projects, was meant to turn Russia's Wild East into an extension of Europe. Other lines were planned on a heroic scale but were left unfinished: the Bagdadbahn to connect Hamburg to Basra (and the Persian Gulf); a 'Trans-Persian' railway, linking Europe to India; and Cecil Rhodes's dream, a Cape to Cairo railway running all the way over a British-ruled Africa. The railway, thought the great British geographer Halford Mackinder, would change world history. The 'Columbian epoch', when sea power was everything, was about to give way to a new age of great land empires that commanded vast resources and were virtually impregnable.[1]

By the end of the century, no part of the world could be considered immune from the transforming effects of the communications revolution. In its strategic nature as well as in its economic relations, the world had become – or was rapidly becoming – a single space. The annihilation of distance became a late-Victorian cliché. The intimate jostling to which Europeans were accustomed on their own crowded continent would now be reproduced on a global scale. The quarrelsome tendencies with which Europeans were so familiar – commercial rivalry, diplomatic friction and cultural animosity – would require global, not merely continental, solutions. International society, a European concept, would have to be widened to embrace non-European states with whom contact was becoming more frequent and regular. In all these ways, it was easy to think that the trend of the times was towards the universal interdependence to which mid-century free-traders (like Richard Cobden) had looked as the best guarantee of general progress and peace. But cutting across this 'cosmopolitan' future (to which many liberal thinkers were deeply attached) was a contrary trend that came in retrospect to define the age.

We have already seen in previous chapters how the growing wealth and power of the Euro-American world had encroached on the sphere of many African and Asian societies. Some had been conquered, others disrupted, and still others put on notice that without swift renovation they had little chance of survival as autonomous states. But until the 1870s there was still room for doubt over the scale of the change and the speed of its happening. European resources were limited. Resistance or rebellion in their existing domains had made European governments hesitate to assume new liabilities. 'It is well for our countrymen in China to understand', remarked *The Times* in 1875, 'that we are not in the mood to undertake the responsibilities of another India.'[2] The restorative powers of Afro-Asian states were still regarded as plausible. The 1870s saw a sea change. By the end of the decade, a vast geopolitical crisis was unfolding across the still independent states of Afro-Eurasia: in the North African Maghrib; sub-Saharan Africa; the Ottoman, Egyptian and Iranian Middle East; the khanates of Central Asia; mainland South East Asia; and China. Here lay a mass of apparently failing states – what one contemporary statesman called 'dying nations' and another the 'outlived oriental states'. Their political systems seemed on the verge of collapse. Internal order was breaking down. Their finances were in chaos. They could not defend their frontiers, which were often ill-defined. They had no means of protecting foreign property or persons. Violence, banditry and religious fanaticism threatened their old social order. The question was: what would become of them?

It was this combination of a 'globalizing' world and the weakness or decay of non-European states that excited and alarmed contemporary opinion – of all races and cultures. It helps to explain the sense of urgency with which European politicians, diplomats, merchants, settlers and missionaries debated their 'imperial' futures. Their expectations were fashioned by three different scenarios. The world as a 'single system', bound ever more closely by the iron links of its railways and the invisible bonds of finance and commerce, was a vista of plenty. Trade would expand; investment would flourish; more land would be brought into commercial production. The sphere of European influence – not least its religious influence – would grow in proportion. It was little wonder that a rash of speculative enterprise broke out and special-interest lobbies appeared: to raise cash, make publicity, and press their governments for help. In the new world economy, there were fortunes to be made. But the second scenario was less reassuring. Accompanying the sense of an accessible world, no longer protected by the moat of distance, was the pervasive fear that it was 'filling up' fast. In 1893 the young American historian Frederick Jackson Turner famously declared that America's open frontier had been closed, and he was quickly followed by similar warnings in Australia and New Zealand.[3] With no 'empty lands' in the temperate world to absorb their energies, the Europeans would compete for control of the tropics and the lands and commerce of the 'dying nations'.[4] Here, where local order was weak, a forceful foreign presence would be all. A treaty, a railway, a bank or a base would create a virtual protectorate, a diplomatic client, an exclusive zone of trade. Opportunism and vigilance were the price of survival in this coming world order. But the result would be an ever-fiercer rivalry between the European powers, and the growing risk that they would come to blows.

There was a third scenario, and a third set of anxieties. To Japanese, Chinese, Indian, Middle Eastern and African observers, the danger seemed to lie in the arrogant ease with which European interference could wreck their social cohesion and cultural self-confidence. The more accessible their states were to European travel and trade, the easier it became for foreign interests and influence to rush their defences, insert new foreign enclaves, and subvert local authority. Even in East Asia it was easy to imagine a not-distant future in which Western trade, sea power, bases, treaty ports and missionaries had segmented the region, disrupted its culture, and parcelled it up for conquest at leisure. The world had grown small, said the Japanese historian and expert on China Naito Konan. Europe and America had surrounded East Asia, and a racial struggle was coming.[5] Among Euro-Americans, the prospect of closer socio-economic relations with large Afro-Asian societies produced a different kind of disquiet. The Europeans might be masters of the universe. But their drastic encroachment upon more 'backward' peoples had created a 'crisis in the history of the world' noted the historian-turned-politician James Bryce.[6] 'For economic purposes,' he thought, 'all mankind is fast becoming one people' in which the 'backward nations' would be reduced to an unskilled proletariat. It would not be easy to avoid the 'race antagonism' that would follow, since intermarriage (the best cure) was disliked by the whites.[7] In his highly influential book *Social Evolution* (1894), Benjamin Kidd (who combined social research with his career as a taxman) warned that Europeans could maintain their predominant position only by the arduous pursuit of 'social efficiency', since neither colour, descent nor intellectual ability was the key to their primacy. The mobility of labour in the new global economy was another source of worry. Fear of a flood of cheap Japanese, Chinese, Indian and African labour bred paranoid fantasies of a stealth invasion in many settler countries: in Canada, the Pacific states of America, Australia, New Zealand and South Africa.

Thus triumphalist predictions of Europe's global supremacy had a much gloomier accompaniment. Segregation would be needed to prevent persistent race friction; systematic exclusion (as in the 'White Australia' policy) to keep non-whites from swamping the temperate 'white man's countries'; and stringent control over new subject peoples, lest the sign of weakness provoked a revolt. Even so, mused Charles Pearson in his *National Life and Character* (1893), a reversal of fortune was still on the cards. Once all the temperate lands had been filled, and there were no further outlets for Europe's population surplus, he argued, economic stagnation was bound to set in. And, since the 'lower races' would increase in number much faster than the 'higher', Europe's hour of triumph was bound to be brief. 'The day will come, and perhaps is not far distant', he warned his readers,

when the European observer will look round to see the globe girdled with a continuous zone of the black and yellow races, no longer too weak for aggression or under tutelage, but independent, or practically so, in government, monopolizing the trade of their own regions, and circumscribing the industry of the European; when Chinamen and the nations of Hindostan, the states of Central and South America, by that time predominantly Indian, and ... the African nations of the Congo and the Zambesi, under a dominant caste of foreign rulers, are represented by fleets in the European seas invited to international conferences, and welcomed as allies in the quarrels of the civilized world ... We shall wake to find ourselves elbowed and hustled, and perhaps even thrust aside by peoples whom we looked down upon as servile, and thought of as bound always to minister to our need. The solitary consolation will be, that the changes have been inevitable.[8]

AFRICA AND THE GEOPOLITICS OF PARTITION

The scaling-up of the Europeans' intrusive power after 1880 was a worldwide phenomenon. But nowhere else was their imperial expansion so dizzyingly swift or so astonishingly complete as in sub-Saharan Africa – the 'dark continent', whose interior Europeans had been noticeably slow to claim. This is why the African case has so fascinated historians. More than a century later, the 'scramble' for Africa in the 1880s and the continent's 'partition' and 'conquest' evoke strong emotions and uneasy debate. This is partly because they offend contemporary notions of racial justice, and partly because Africa's postcolonial condition has made its colonial past seem more painfully real than has been the case in more fortunate regions. The drama and violence of Europe's takeover of Africa has also encouraged the idea that it was the 'classic' case of European imperialism. In fact tropical Africa was no more typical of European expansion than was the commercial imperialism practised in Latin America and China, the settler imperialisms of North America and Australasia, or the imperialism of rule fashioned by the British in the Indian subcontinent. Compared with the contest for imperial power across the vast tracts of Eurasia, Africa was a sideshow. But the African case does allow us to see with greater clarity than elsewhere some of the geopolitical conditions that favoured European primacy after 1870. It may also prompt us to ask why African societies were so much more vulnerable to external disruption (once Europeans had the will and the means to inflict it) than most of their counterparts in Asia.

What impelled the Europeans' great leap forward in Africa? Its origins lie in the gradual application to this least accessible continent of the means of entry already used elsewhere. The steamship and railway were the battering rams with which European traders could break the monopolies that African coastal elites and their inland allies had tried to maintain over their commercial hinterlands. In the west, the east and the south, the 1870s were a time when the Europeans were laying plans to push their operations deeper. Nor were they alone. Egyptians (in the south of modern Sudan) and Zanzibaris (in the Great Lakes region) also hoped to carve out new commercial empires. What made these ventures seem practical (and potentially profitable) was not just a convenient new transport technology. Three other factors were also at work. The first was the way in which the commercial 'trunk routes' around the African coast were becoming steadily busier – reducing the cost of connecting its trade to the main global circuits. This was particularly obvious in East Africa, where the Suez Canal and the much heavier traffic between Europe and Asia brought a commercial revolution to the Indian Ocean and the East African coast.[9] But it also applied in the west and the south. The second great factor was the supply of cash. By the 1870s the development of Europe's financial machinery (especially in London) was making it far easier than before to raise the sums needed to push a speculative advance into little-known terrain. The habit of foreign investment was becoming more deeply ingrained and more widely practised among Europe's propertied classes. The black arts of 'boosterism' – commercial propaganda, company promotion and insider dealing – enjoyed a heyday of freedom to talk up the prospects of the most unlikely eldorados and gull the greedy and innocent. Thirdly, what helped to give substance to these dreams of wealth was the actual fact of a mineral bonanza in parts of Africa. By the 1870s both diamonds and gold had been found in South Africa, a prelude to the great gold rush of the 1880s. This attracted a stream of speculative capital into the search for gold ever further north. Once Cecil Rhodes and his friends won control of the Kimberley diamond fields for their new conglomerate, De Beers Consolidated, they used its profits to fund the great filibustering expedition that turned modern Zimbabwe and Zambia into a huge private empire, the domain of their 'British South Africa Company'.[10] Many at home were eager to buy into Rhodes's grand enterprise.

But this is only a part of the story. The piecemeal invasion by European private interests – some commercial, some part philanthropic – and the careerist activism of officials and soldiers on the edge of the existing colonial zones would have created a slow-moving frontier of influence and authority. It would have been an untidy process. Failed advances, furious commercial rivalry, bankrupt ventures, acts of resistance and frontier wars would have delayed the progress of European occupation and made it far slower than the conquest of North America – if only because the demographic weight of the European incomers was infinitely smaller. But this was *not* the pattern of the African scramble. This was exceptionally rapid and (in cartographical terms) extraordinarily complete. Above all, it was a process in which European governments took an active part – if only by agreeing on the terms of the share-out, and accepting the obligation to impose their rule. The localized activity of European frontiersmen was suddenly caught up in a vast diplomatic arrangement. Why did this happen?

Much of the answer lies in the knock-on effects of events unfolding elsewhere. The 1870s were a time of crisis in several of the great non-European states spread across Eurasia, but nowhere more than in the Ottoman Empire, whose financial strains we have already noted. Between 1875 and 1881 this empire was in turmoil. It went bankrupt. It was invaded. Its territories were cut down in the peace conference that followed. For several years, even its survival was in doubt. Its

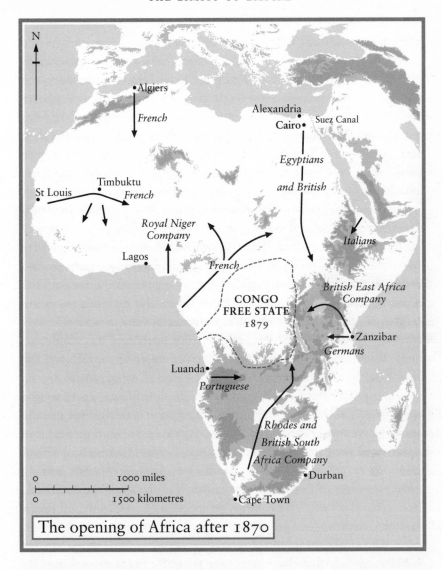

N

•Algiers

French

Alexandria
Cairo• Suez Canal

Egyptians

and British

St Louis•   Timbuktu•
             French

Royal Niger
Company

Lagos•

French

Italians

British East Africa
Company

CONGO
FREE STATE
1879

Zanzibar
Germans

Luanda•

Portuguese

Rhodes and
British South
Africa Company

•Durban

0   1000 miles

0   1500 kilometres

•Cape Town

The opening of Africa after 1870

bankruptcy (in 1875) helped to drag down its nominal dependency, the khedivate (or viceroyalty) of Egypt, whose go-ahead dynasty had tried to modernize the country with almost reckless haste around the grand centrepiece of the Suez Canal – one of the greatest engineering achievements of the nineteenth century. The ruler in Cairo had borrowed deeply from European lenders. But when his revenues sagged in the mid-1870s they refused to lend more, and without a flow of new cash the Cairo government defaulted.[11]

The Egyptian khedive Ismail dared not abandon his European creditors. He may well have feared that their governments would intervene. But he was also anxious, sooner or later, to resume the modernizing programme on which his dynasty was built. So he agreed to appoint two European watchdogs to supervise his finances and claw them back to solvency. It was a risky experiment. It was bound to annoy those who would suffer from the cuts. It would be resented by his officials and ministers. It would weaken his prestige. And it would rouse suspicion in a Muslim country (the site of Islam's greatest centre of learning was at al-Azhar) of an infidel plot to take political power. It was hardly surprising that the watchdogs soon found that their 'reforms' were ignored. Their complaints encouraged the governments in London and Paris to demand a tougher regime, the so-called 'Dual Control', on which their eye would be closer. But the main result was to provoke the growth of a popular national movement against foreign interference and against the authoritarian powers of the khedive as well. When the Dual Control tried to cut down the army, a revolt broke out in 1881 under a charismatic officer, Colonel Arabi.

London and Paris, not to mention the khedive, were now in a quandary. The khedive was forced to appoint Arabi to his government. But it was obvious that Arabi could keep his support only if he confronted the ruler and broke the Dual Control. British and French ministers came under pressure from their men-on the-spot and the lurid warnings of European journalists: *The Times* alone ran nearly 700 articles on the 'crisis' in Egypt in 1881–2. Arabi would lead a fanatical regime. Foreign property would be lost; loans never recovered. The Christian minority would be persecuted (or worse) by the Muslim mob. In London there were two other aspects that affected ministerial thinking. Though there was little evidence that the Suez Canal was directly at risk, its strategic value was already immeasurable as the vital route through which British troops could be sent to India if a second Mutiny broke out (and the memory of the first was still very fresh). Secondly, for the British officials who ran the government of India, and who regarded Islamic fanaticism as the most dangerous threat to their Anglo-Indian Raj, a successful revolt against European influence on the high road to India was an unacceptable challenge to their all-important prestige. It might light the fuse to a much larger conflagration.[12]

A cocktail of political, financial and strategic arguments pushed Gladstone's Liberal government first into the clumsy bombardment of Alexandria (to intimidate Arabi) and then into an outright invasion of Egypt in September 1882 (the French decided not to take part). Arabi was defeated and forced into exile. The khedive's authority was vindicated, although his wings were clipped. British advisers were installed, and a new constitution was drafted at British suggestion. In 1883 Evelyn Baring (of the banking family) arrived to oversee a British withdrawal as soon as conditions were stable. But by the end of the decade the British had made up their minds to stay on indefinitely, and Baring himself stayed for twenty-four years. Egypt had become a 'veiled protectorate', in which the British pretended that their occupation was temporary and that they were merely advising the Egyptian government. In fact their control was guaranteed by a garrison in Cairo and by their naval power in the eastern Mediterranean.

For the British government, being stuck in Egypt was a dangerous hostage to fortune – the main reason why the decision to stay was put off for so long. The other great powers fiercely resented the way that Britain had seized one of the largest provinces of the Ottoman Empire (Egypt's technical status). Isolation over Egypt risked major collateral damage to other British interests elsewhere. Nor was early withdrawal an easy solution. The British would need the active agreement of those European powers who had seats on the board that administered Egypt's debts. Without swift financial reform, Egypt's crisis would worsen. London would face an unpleasant dilemma: whether to abandon Egypt (and British interests there) or dig in regardless of the great powers' displeasure. To escape from their impending 'bondage in Egypt' (contemporaries revelled in the biblical references), the British adopted the path of appeasement. They offered concessions where it mattered least (to them). In parts of West, East and Southern Africa, where they had assumed by default an informal predominance, they accepted the claims of French and (especially) German interests. They also agreed to a new set of rules to decide the share-out of claims where they were in dispute. At the Berlin West Africa Conference in

1885 (the location is significant), provision was made for 'effective occupation' as the key criterion in the adjudication of rights. To reduce the risk of commercial conflict, a free-trade zone was declared in the Niger and Congo basins.[13]

The African 'deal' was enough to scale down the diplomatic row over Egypt and divide Britain's critics – though the occupation remained a source of British embarrassment until the French were bought off in 1904 when the British recognized their claim to predominance in Morocco. It seems very unlikely that its makers expected any drastic consequences, least of all in Africa. They may well have thought that by requiring 'effective occupation' they would delay indefinitely the formal extension of European rule in the African interior. In fact their formula became the starting gun to divide the continent. The reasons had little to do with any deliberate policy among the governments of Europe. Nothing much would have happened had there not already been would-be empire-builders on the spot, determined to find wealth, promotion or fame, regardless of the views of faraway officialdom. The one great exception to this was the king of the Belgians, Leopold II. But even his 'Congo Free State', whose claim to the Congo basin he had persuaded the powers to accept in 1884–5 (perhaps because it solved the problem of who else should have it), was a private empire that belonged to him, not the Belgian state. Elsewhere in Africa, the 'Berlin rules' became an open inducement to European adventurers to win their governments' backing for their territorial ambitions. Their logic was simple. Once other Europeans were excluded, it would be very much easier to enforce their will over the African communities whose lands, labour and trade they coveted. The real surprise was that it proved so easy to lobby governments at home to endorse their claims.

From the mid-1880s to around 1900, the 'scramble' – the term seems to have been coined by *The Times* in September 1884 – proceeded at breakneck speed. Across a huge swathe of West Africa between the desert and the forest, a group of French marine officers under Commandant Louis Archinard, and their black rank and file, created a military fiefdom that defeated or absorbed all the African states that stood in its path.[14] Ignoring the angry complaints from Paris, this military clique, the *officiers soudanais*, conquered first and sought permission later.[15] They challenged the politicians to disavow their gains. Reports of their heroism in the popular press and ministerial weakness in a fragmented National Assembly were enough to save them from recall and disgrace. Meanwhile, in the lower Niger valley, a tough British soldier-turned-businessman called George Goldie had changed a failing family firm into a new kind of enterprise. Intense competition (with the arrival of steamships) and a sharp fall in the price of the main West African export, palm oil (down by a third in the later 1880s), had made control over supply the key to survival.[16] In 1886, after ruthless lobbying, Goldie won a royal charter from the London government – in effect a licence to exercise a minimal form of administrative control in parts of southern Nigeria (as it later became) where his firm was trading. But Goldie turned his 'Royal Niger Company' into a regional power, with a private army, and light artillery brought over from England.[17] He could now impose taxes on rival African traders, and enforce a virtual monopoly in the palm-oil trade that was the regional staple. Before long the Company's army, under another ex-officer of wide African experience, Frederick Lugard, was beginning to spar with the *officiers soudanais* in the north-western districts of modern Nigeria.

In West Africa, the European intruders were able to muster just enough firepower to move in from the coast and defeat their local opponents, sometimes by only the narrowest margin. Their African foes were very adept in the use of fire in battle, Goldie warned his officers, and would burn them out if they had a chance.[18] Facing an African army of 30,000 men, 'the 12-pounder and 9-pounder [guns] alone saved us from annihilation,' he reported to London a few weeks later.[19] In East Africa (a much more isolated region before 1870), Europeans could exploit the fact that the Zanzibar sultanate (an Arab dynasty from the Gulf) was in the throes of political crisis just as the region itself became easier and cheaper to reach because of the new Suez route. The much publicized travels, and even more publicized death, of David Livingstone (the missionary saint of Victorian Britain) turned the humanitarian spotlight on the East African slave trade and its Arab practitioners. The Zanzibar sultan had been forced to outlaw it. In Scotland especially there was an ardent desire to honour Livingstone's memory by bringing 'Christianity, commerce and civilization' (his famous formula) to the scene of his last great journeys in modern Uganda and Malawi. A company was formed under a Bombay-based businessman called William Mackinnon, and lobbied successfully for a charter in 1888. Already, however, the dwindling power of the Zanzibar sultan had encouraged German traders, like Carl Peters, to get Bismarck's support for a 'zone of protection' – to which the British had agreed in 1884–5. Mackinnon's company tried and failed to make a profit in Uganda, where a civil war raged between Muslim converts and Christians. After more furious lobbying, helped in part by the British government's fear that the whole of Zanzibar's 'empire' would be lost to the Germans and French, two vast new protectorates, covering modern Uganda and Kenya, were declared British territory in 1895. East Africa was partitioned.

In South and Central Africa, the scramble was largely the work of two restless tycoons. In Leopold's Congo Free State a polyglot band of half-pay officers (mostly Belgian) and drifters set out to impose his rule across a colossal tract as large as Western Europe. To give his regime a respectable veneer, Leopold tried to hire as governor another Victorian celebrity, the evangelical soldier Charles 'Chinese' Gordon (who chose instead to go to Khartoum). But the real object of Leopold's shambolic 'government' was to coerce the population into collecting ivory and rubber (both highly profitable crops). It took over twenty years before the terrifying brutality that this regime unleashed with genocidal results (perhaps 10 million Congolese died from its direct and indirect effects)[20] forced the winding up of Leopold's private state and its reorganization as a colony under the Belgian government.[21]

Cecil Rhodes's aims were much more ambitious, and his methods less crude. Rhodes was more than willing to buy the influence he needed (the boards of his companies were crammed with cash-strapped peers), to dupe the investor, and to use brute force against any African community that resisted his power. His company fought wars against both Ndebele and Shona in what is now Zimbabwe, and seized African land for him and his followers (much of modern Zimbabwe was first shared out in this way).[22] But Rhodes's objective was not just a land-grab or his own enrichment. He was determined to unite almost the whole of Southern Africa in a single great state as 'British South Africa'. This was not simply for the sake of imposing

London's authority. For what Rhodes intended was that local white settlers of British origins and outlook should be in control, making the whole vast subcontinent into a 'white man's country' like Canada or (the grandest example, to which Rhodes was much attracted) the United States. But without London's help Rhodes ultimately lacked the strength to impose this plan on his local opponents: two Boer republics with the will and the means to make a fight for their freedom.

The extraordinary course of the African scramble raises a whole series of questions. Why in the first place did the European governments believe that they had the right to propose rules for the grand larceny of Africa? After all, they devised no similar programme for the Middle East, China or Latin America. Much of the answer must lie in their hostile view of African states and cultures. Little was known about the African interior, and most of what was reflected the self-serving bias of the missionaries, explorers and dubious business-men who had made a career there. A good case can be made that much of what was reported by travellers as fact about the 'dark continent' was the imaginary product of minds fuddled by drink, fuelled by drugs (the cocktail of medications to ward off disease) and filled with dreams of glory and gold.[23] No African ruler (with the possible exception of the Christian emperor of Ethiopia) was con-sidered capable of exercising all the functions of sovereignty. Instead, it was widely assumed that the interior states were a chaos of barbar-ism, where slavery thrived and civilization had stalled. Under the 'Berlin rules', the European powers that asserted a claim were expected to suppress the one and promote the other. But this does not explain why the European governments were willing to allow frontier mer-chants and soldiers to suck them into commitments that they usually disliked on grounds of (some) risk or expense.

Here the answer is threefold. Firstly, the frontier interests were extremely adept at the art of lobbying through their backers at home. They played upon religious and humanitarian feeling, as well as patri-otic emotion, and commercial greed. They touched a raw nerve of economic anxiety in an era of falling prices that lasted into the mid-1890s. They exploited to the full the new means of publicity in the popular press (like Le Petit Journal, with its 1 million readers).[24] Since they usually controlled what information there was, their version of events was often hard to challenge. In the hands of a master like Rhodes, all this was combined with a remarkable talent for co-opting support among the good and the great, often by a generous distribution of shares in his companies. The second factor is financial. It is doubtful whether even skilful lobbying would have loosened the purse strings of the governments at home. Had frontier expansion meant large sums of money at the taxpayers' expense, its benefits would have been questioned, the politicians would have been warier, and the controversy much greater. As it was, however, the occupation of Africa proved astonishingly cheap – one of the reasons why public enthusiasm waxed rather than waned in the 1890s. The private empires of Leopold and Rhodes cost the taxpayer nothing. The West African conquests of the *officiers soudanais* brought nearly 2 million square miles into France's empire for the sterling equivalent of £5 million.[25] Thirdly, much the same applies to the prospect of war. Despite the verbal aggression with which colonial claims were often publicly debated, it was well understood that they could never be pressed so far as to risk a European conflict. Even France's long struggle to oust the British from Egypt assumed a diplomatic solution: German support at an international conference to 'settle' the Egyptian question.[26] When this failed to happen, and a French expedition to the upper Nile met Kitchener's army at Fashoda in late 1898, the whiff of war was enough to bring a humiliating French climbdown.[27]

Both these latter points need examining further. Why was it so cheap to occupy the African interior? Why did African rulers not sell their independence more dearly? It is reckless to generalize, and we still know little about most of pre-colonial Africa. But historians broadly agree about one vital fact. Almost everywhere in sub-Saharan Africa people were in short supply, leaving vast tracts of land uninhabited or unused. This may have been due to an unusually harsh environment, the impact of the slave trades and the effects of disease. The result was critical. Building states in pre-colonial Africa was exceptionally arduous. Imposing taxes or duties on reluctant subjects was hard enough anywhere. But, where rebelling meant no more than walking away to found a splinter community, the odds were heavily stacked on the negative side. Except in certain favoured locations (as in parts of West Africa), where rulers could tighten their grip over trade, states in Africa remained small and weak by Eurasian standards. They were poorly placed to exploit the growth of international commerce. Hardly any had the means to buy modern weapons or raise a strong enough force to repel a determined European attack. Worst of all, perhaps, the typical lack of broader political or cultural unity exposed African rulers to an insidious weakness. In almost every struggle, it was all too easy for the European invaders to find local allies. In what became French West Africa, the *officiers soudanais* carved out their warrior state with an army of black soldiers who were paid in slaves. That was why it cost so little. In British East Africa it was Maasai fighters who helped coerce Kikuyu and Embu in return for a share of the captured cattle.[28] For African rulers, the most hopeful prospect was to keep some local autonomy. Their chances of this were greatly improved if they could keep the loyalty of their subjects and followers and strike a reasonable bargain with their new European 'sovereigns'. In the north and west of Nigeria, and in Buganda (part of modern Uganda), pre-colonial rulers did this with conspicuous success.

But why were the European powers so unwilling to fight each other for their African empires? The partition of Africa was (for the Europeans at least) a peaceful partition. There was bad-tempered diplomacy, furious argument in the press, and much jostling and fist-shaking by the men-on-the-spot. But the Europeans did not fight each other. Governments at home played a double game. They were nervous of offending the powerful colonialist lobbies or of being accused of weakness in the face of rival claims. There were always politicians who hoped to advance their careers by waving the imperial flag. There were some who believed that decline was certain without an adequate share of the coming global partition. But, for all the European governments, a far higher priority than any colonial adventure was the continental balance of power. Their view of Europe was profoundly conservative. They refused to believe that, if it came to a crisis, any African empire would be worth the risk of a European explosion, from which none of them thought they were likely to gain. They were willing to contemplate a colonial sphere in Africa, but on the strict understanding that it posed no threat to their safety in Europe. They were also determined that so far as possible the territorial squabbles of the men-on-the-spot should be settled peacefully in Europe and not by force on the ground. They succeeded because of the diplomats' consensus that, apart from Suez and the Cape (where only the British were prepared to fight), the African stakes were invariably low. It was chiefly a matter of squaring the lobbies. So, while the Europeans had fought wars to divide the Americas, and periodically threatened to do so over the Middle East, they shared out Africa with surprising bonhomie. This had two crucial results. It reduced the scope for African leaders to exploit European differences and so prolong their freedom. And it meant that, once they were demarcated, colonial borders could be left undefended (until the First World War) against any European foe.

The scramble for Africa was the most obvious case of Europe's growing appetite for global supremacy, and the irresistible strength it could bring to the task. But it was also a paradox. Firstly, European governments showed little enthusiasm for extending their control over the African interior. They responded grudgingly to the clamour of lobbies. Secondly, once their sphere was marked out, they were content with little more than a nominal control over the peoples and places on their treaty maps. They saw no immediate need to win African loyalty or build a colonial patriotism. The colonial state remained a shallow state: lightly governed by a handful of foreigners; heavily reliant upon local 'collaborators', whose abuses of power, if discovered at all, could rarely be checked. Thirdly, the 'civilizing mission' (the ideological banner waved over the scramble) had a strange double life. Its spirit (in Europe) may have been strong; its flesh in Africa was invariably weak. It was this careless indifference to the obligations of rule that explains in part why the African experience of global colonialism was exceptionally brutal. The case of the Congo may have been an extreme one, but there is plenty of evidence that Europeans were willing to use physical violence as a matter of course, and to treat African property as a contradiction in terms. Racial and cultural contempt was one of the causes. But so was the willingness of European governments to leave their African subjects to the mercy of commercial or settler interests, the offspring of the lobbies who had engineered the partition. In a hard environment, where people were scarce, no enterprise could survive without capturing and keeping the Africans' labour, by fair means or foul. There was thus a terrible symmetry in the reasons that had made Africa so vulnerable first to conquest and then to some of the harshest regimes that Europeans devised anywhere in the world.

There was one part of Africa in the age of partition where the rules were broken. In the South African War of 1899–1902, white men fought white men. Tens of thousands of whites, including women and children, died from violence or disease or the effects of imprisonment. White men destroyed other white men's property, burning their farms or stealing their animals. Black people too were caught up in this white man's war, and suffered in similar ways.[29] What had brought it about?

Southern Africa was (as it long remained) a strange mutation in sub-Saharan Africa's history. It was the one place where Europeans had established a permanent settlement long before the late nineteenth century. Since around 1700, Dutch-speaking farmers (Boers) had moved up from the Cape, slowly imposing their power on the African peoples they met. In the late 1830s they surged forward in a series of 'treks' to occupy the northern half of modern South Africa, the plains of the 'highveld'. After 1870 this localized brand of European colonialism was suddenly energized by new mineral wealth – first diamonds, then gold. To the British government, overlords of the Cape since 1815, it was the perfect chance to steer a backward region away from its cycle of costly frontier wars. They wanted South Africa to be like Canada: a federal dominion, economically progressive, 'British' in outlook, and loyal to the empire. British trade would flourish, and the Cape would be safe for Britain's Indian traffic. This was also the goal towards which Rhodes was manoeuvring, and the main reason why London was willing to back his claim to modern Zimbabwe and Zambia. 'He has laid the foundations of a splendid empire,' said an admiring Lord Salisbury.[30] But the breakaway Boers of the northern interior had other ideas. Since the 1850s, they had enjoyed almost complete independence. In the early 1880s the Transvaalers had defeated a clumsy British attempt to turn their ramshackle 'republic' into a colony proper. By the 1890s, with its soaring revenue from the goldfields of the Rand, the once-bankrupt Transvaal was becoming the dominant state in the whole of South Africa. Its doughty president, the old frontier fighter Paul Kruger, thwarted Rhodes's grand design and smashed his attempt at a *coup d'état* – the infamous Jameson Raid (1895). He showed considerable skill in dividing the immigrant (largely British) community that had flocked on to the Rand and in stalling London's demands that they be given full political rights. But when (in September 1899) he seemed to press openly for full independence (i.e. the right to have direct relations with foreign powers) he touched a raw nerve. Britain saw a threat to unravel its regional primacy, with disastrous consequences for its diplomatic prestige and strategic security. War followed within weeks. When it ground to a halt nearly three years later, the Boers of the Transvaal and the Orange Free State had been forced to acknowledge that they were British subjects. But whites still ruled blacks across the whole of South Africa.

COMPETITIVE COEXISTENCE

The partition of Africa was the most dramatic evidence that the world beyond Europe and the United States faced a colonial (or semi-colonial) future: occupation and rule or forms of economic dependence. There were other partitions in South East Asia and the South Pacific, extending French, British, Dutch, German and (after 1898) American rule across Eurasia's maritime rim. After 1900, the larger part of the globe had become politically and legally an extension of Europe. It seemed reasonable to expect that the rest of the world – especially continental East Asia and the Middle East – would follow sooner or later. Indeed, there were many warning signs that such a division was imminent – if only the great powers could agree on their shares.

But partition was not the only change in the political face of the late-century world. The generation after 1880 also saw the consolidation of four or five 'world states' that were expected to share global mastery between them. Two were newcomers to the imperial stage. The most remarkable was the United States (the other was Germany). Its symbiotic relations with the Old European world were growing closer and closer. An ever-increasing flow of European migrants poured across the Atlantic. Italians, Poles, Russians, Jews and many other nationalities built a transatlantic connection with almost every part of Europe, redoubling and diversifying the European influence in American society and culture. By 1900 the United States had the largest population of European origin (82 million out of a total, including African Americans, of 92 million) of any country except Russia. It had also become the largest industrial economy in the world, producing by 1910 more pig iron and steel than Britain, France and Germany combined. Thomas Jefferson's republic of independent yeoman farmers had become the scene of huge industrial plants: digging iron and coal; making textiles and steel; building locomotives, ships and even cars; processing food and drink. It had a large working class, some of it housed in slum conditions that bore close resemblance to Europe's, as the social investigator Jacob Riis revealed to a scandalized public.[31] Although living standards were higher, class relations less rigid, and mobility far greater than was usual in Europe, by the end of the century an upper social class had become clearly visible. It attended elite schools, aped the upper-class life style seen across the Atlantic, and bemoaned the populism and crudity of American politics. It also displayed an intriguing tendency to marry across the 'pond', creating family alliances with the British aristocracy, one of which was to produce the infant Winston Churchill.

America was still set apart by its democratic populism and by its open avowal of race segregation. But in other respects it now seemed to resemble more and more closely a 'normal' European state. By 1890 it was ceasing to be a frontier society with vast tracts of unclaimed or unoccupied land. A new sense of the limits on America's natural resources encouraged a more protective approach to a much-abused environment. The other side of the coin was the stronger sense of an imperial destiny. It was a source of irritation that the valuable lands on America's Caribbean doorstep should suffer the careless management of their Hispanic guardians, European Spanish in Cuba, or local Creoles elsewhere in Central America. On the Pacific coast (where there was an old connection with China and Japan) there were others who saw California as America's base in the struggle for East Asia, and San Francisco Bay as the springboard of empire.[32] The alacrity with which the United States used a supposed grievance against Spain to dispossess it of Cuba and the Philippine Islands in the 'splendid little war' of 1898 showed that this widening conception of American national interests had become politically viable. Under Theodore Roosevelt's presidency (1901–9) it was carried further. America's pre-eminence in the Caribbean Sea was bluntly announced in the 'Roosevelt Corollary'. This declared that, in the event of misdemeanour or default by the independent states in and around the Caribbean, the United States would act for the aggrieved foreign power, whose direct interference would be very unwelcome. And, at Roosevelt's urging, America was at last to act like a major naval power (the great prophet of sea power, Alfred T. Mahan, was an American admiral). In 1907 the United States Navy's 'Great White Fleet' (a reference to its paintwork) made a much publicized cruise all round the Pacific.[33]

In these various ways, America was asserting its status as a major world power, on terms of equality with the largest European states. As a colonial power (after 1898) with extraterritorial privileges in China, its interests and outlook seemed remarkably similar to Europe's. America, declared the influential historian Frederick Jackson Turner, was 'an imperial republic with dependencies and protectorates . . . a new world power'.[34] The Mexican revolution that broke out in 1910 pushed Washington further towards an imperial mentality. To force the removal of the dictator General Huerta, Mexico's chief port was occupied for eight months in 1914.[35] But the similarities and parallels should not be exaggerated. American attitudes towards Europe's global colonialism remained semi-detached. America had played no part in the partition of Africa, although an American representative had attended the Berlin African conference. Before the 1890s it had no possessions in Asia. The imperial role assumed in 1898 provoked a political controversy that was far more bitter than the colonial debates that sometimes erupted in Europe. Roosevelt's naval programme was stinted and stymied by the sceptics in Congress.[36] Roosevelt himself envisaged his new model navy as the junior partner in an informal alliance of 'Anglo-Saxon' sea powers. Britain's naval supremacy, he remarked, 'was the great guaranty of the peace of the world'.[37] On the economic front, there were still significant differences. There was almost no American capital invested abroad, with most of what there was across the border in Mexico. American industry catered mainly for the huge home demand and a vast farmer economy. Only 5 per cent of American output was actually sent abroad (the British figure was 25 per cent). The economic colonies of American business lay in the west and south of the United States, not overseas. There was no consensus for adopting the aggressive style or military preparedness of the other world states. But what turned out to be critical in shaping American views was the astonishing growth of the US industrial economy, setting off fears of exclusion from other world markets. With so small a share of imperial real estate, little prospect of increasing it, and (by 1913) much the largest manufacturing capacity in the world, it was hardly surprising that American leaders should come to regard any global partition as more and more harmful to American interests.

The three decades after 1880 were just as critical to Russia's prospects as a global power. Conventional histories of the late tsarist period like to emphasize the failures of the old regime. Peasant discontent, a weak middle class, over-hasty industrialization and an 'obsolete' autocracy are the usual culprits. Tsarism was a revolution waiting to happen. But too much emphasis upon decline and decay makes for a myopic view of Russia's modern history. Despite the catastrophic impact of war and revolution in the time of troubles between 1917 and 1921, the Russian Empire did not fall apart. Moreover, it was able to stage an astonishing recovery in the mid-1940s, to reach a zenith of power that the most visionary official would have dismissed as absurd in the tsarist era.

This is all the more surprising because so much of Russia's Eurasian empire was little more than a shell before 1880. The imperial conquest of Muslim Central Asia was only just under way. The Russian sphere in North East Asia had been greatly enlarged at China's expense by the Aigun and Peking treaties of 1858–60. But the Russian presence across most of this vast region was little more than notional. The 1860s reforms had made no immediate difference to Russia's material strength: indeed the setbacks abroad in 1877–8 (when Russian hopes of a quick military victory over the Ottoman Empire were thwarted) and political dissidence at home suggested quite the opposite. The modernization of the serf economy had hardly begun. Given the speed of change elsewhere in the world – the flows of investment, the rising volume of trade, the onward rush of technology – Russia's claim to remain in the front rank of powers looked precarious at best. Oppression and muddle seemed (to most foreign observers) the dominant feature of the tsarist system. The result was a policy of 'alternate bravado and vacillation', said a young George Curzon with all the confidence of an Indian-viceroy-to-be.[38]

Yet Russian power was growing all the same. Industrialization had been slow to arrive, but by the 1890s it was expanding fast. By the end of the century, Russia's output of coal was some fifty times greater than in 1860, the production of steel two thousand times greater.[39] Both had doubled again by 1913. Russian exports rose sharply – from around £55 million (the average for 1881–5) to almost £100 million (1901–6).[40] The Ukraine was developed as a great producer of wheat. Odessa, the city founded by Catherine the Great on the shores of the Black Sea, was the great emporium of this new grain trade. Once Russia's alliance with France had been formalized (by 1894), a tide of French loans poured in to modernize Russia.[41] The great railway projects to link Russia's heartland with Central Asia (the Orenburg–Tashkent Railway) and the Pacific (the Trans-Siberian) could now be completed. As the railways drove forward, behind them followed an army of settlers, land-hungry peasants from the overcrowded villages of European Russia. These Russian colonists, farmers and railwaymen, spread out south and east to form the most durable element of Russia's Asian power.[42] By 1914, more than 5 million Russians had crossed the Urals into Siberia, and thousands more had settled in the old Muslim khanates in Russian Central Asia.[43]

In this piecemeal way, the tsarist regime had put into place before the First World War almost all the key elements of Russia's modern imperial system. It had kept its grip on rebellious Poland, its salient in Europe, the defensive bastion of the Russian heartland and a lever of influence in great-power diplomacy. The Ukraine had been made into a milch cow of wealth, the engine of Russia's growing commercial influence in the Black Sea region, and the dynamo of the new wheat-export economy. Ukrainian prosperity, and the railway system, helped strengthen Russia's hold on the Caucasian borderlands, the road bridge to the Middle East, and (from the opposite point of view) the great defensive outwork of the Volga valley – Russia's Mississippi. Before 1914, the oilfields found round Baku on the Caspian had added a new dimension to the Caucasus's strategic value. With railways, settlers, a new cotton economy and a strong military presence, Central Asia had been firmly locked into its colonial role guarding the south-east door into Russia's Eurasian empire. Its trade was carefully sealed off and made a Russian monopoly.[44] And, as Siberia was colonized and its communications improved, Russia's fragile grasp on the Pacific coast was decisively strengthened.[45] Not even the disaster of the Russo-Japanese War (1904–5), when Russian designs on Korea and Manchuria were brutally crushed (there had been a plan to infiltrate Korea with Russian soldiers disguised as lumberjacks), could break Russia's claim to be a Pacific power or roll back its expansion into North East Asia.[46] Thus, for all the brittleness of its imperial system, its technical backwardness, economic fragility and weak cultural magnetism,[47] Russia had more than kept pace with the rival world states. It had followed its own distinctive trajectory into global colonialism.

In 1880, Britain had some claim to be the leading world state – perhaps the only one to have possessions and interests in every part of the world. Its huge archipelago of colonies and spheres ran from western Canada to South Africa, from Suez to Hong Kong. Much of this empire had been built up rapidly since the 1830s, and much was lightly peopled and barely developed. Across vast areas, British claims to influence existed only by default, since no other power had any presence at all. But after 1880, as the world 'filled up', influence by default was no longer an option. The British were pushed into formalizing their claims, and sometimes backing them up by displays of force. As ever more of the world was partitioned, they acquired fresh sets of potentially troublesome neighbours, new fences to maintain, and a new need for vigilance. The result was paradoxical. Although the British Empire became larger and larger, the diplomats and strategists charged with protecting it became more and more anxious. Because the British had so much territory scattered round the world, they seemed always at odds with everyone else. The British

Empire was like a huge giant, moaned a senior official, 'with gouty fingers and toes stretching in every direction'. The minute it was approached by anyone else, the giant would scream with fear at the expected pain.[48] It was a poor recipe for diplomatic harmony. The strategists were just as nervous. They saw Britain's naval power and small professional army as dangerously overextended. Some of the most acute observers wondered whether the spread of railways had turned the tables on the great sea power. Perhaps the balance of advantage now lay with the rulers of an impregnable land mass – like Russia, the 'inland tyranny' – safe from British chastisement.

Fears like these reached a pitch of intensity during the South African War, which exposed an embarrassing deficit in British military prowess. Even more worrying was the risk that Britain's great-power rivals would seize a golden opportunity to put a squeeze on British interests in other parts of the world: in the Middle East, in China, and perhaps even by threatening an invasion of India across its north-west frontier. This fearful prospect set off a frenzy in military planning, one of the conclusions of which was that the British army would need to buy every camel in Asia to supply the front line. For one of the reasons we have already considered – the fear of disturbing the European balance – the other great powers decided against an anti-British coalition. But the sense of crisis had been real in London. It produced a major rethink in naval strategy, and the decision to build a new modern fleet. It brought an alliance with Japan (in 1902) to help guard British interests in East Asia.[49] In 1904 and 1907 it led to ententes with first France and then Russia – agreements that drew Britain into an informal alliance in Europe's great-power politics.[50]

In the new era of 'world politics' after 1880, Britain seemed to have suffered a relative decline. But by any standard its overall position remained immensely strong. There were very few places where a single power could seriously damage its interests. The great exception (since an American invasion of Canada seemed no longer conceivable) was a Russian invasion of Afghanistan, and the threat that that would pose to British power in India. It was extremely unlikely that a combination of powers would be allowed by the others to aggrandize themselves at Britain's expense – even if they were to risk the attempt.

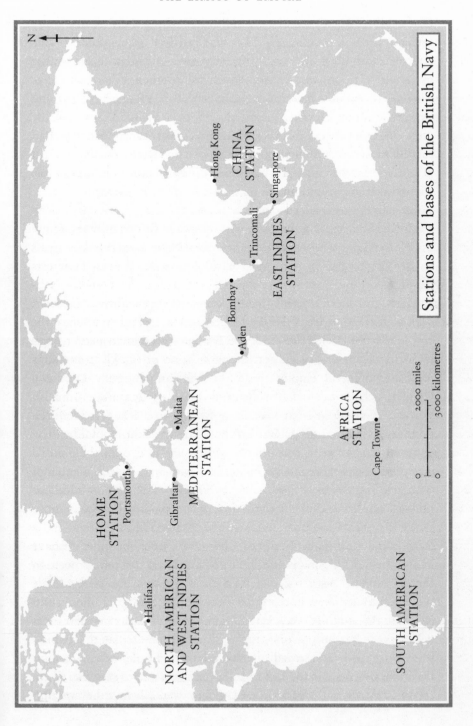

Stations and bases of the British Navy

HOME STATION
Portsmouth

NORTH AMERICAN AND WEST INDIES STATION
Halifax

MEDITERRANEAN STATION
Gibraltar
Malta

AFRICA STATION
Cape Town

SOUTH AMERICAN STATION

EAST INDIES STATION
Aden
Bombay
Trincomali

CHINA STATION
Hong Kong
Singapore

2000 miles
3000 kilometres
0

Furthermore, on several counts, the British themselves seemed to be getting richer and stronger. They had profited more than anyone else from the huge expansion of international trade. Their foreign investments alone were to double in size between 1900 and 1913. They had a massive balance-of-payments surplus from their invisible exports, and could easily afford the enormous cost of a huge new navy. Their settler colonies – a great manpower reserve of more than a million men of military age – were now growing rapidly. So also was India, the barrack and war chest of their empire in Asia. Their commercial imperium of overseas enterprises in banking, insurance, shipping, railways, telegraphs, mines and plantations dwarfed all its rivals. In the event of attack, the vast reserve power of their economic assets could be wheeled into action while the enemy was crushed by the constrictor-like grip of a naval blockade. That at least was the plan.

After 1904, it was mainly from Germany that the British expected such a threat to arise. Like the United States, Germany was a new-comer in great-power diplomacy, crashing on to the scene after 1870 with the defeat of France and the unification of the German states into a semi-federal 'empire' under the Prussian monarchy. Germany seemed to have both the means and, after 1900, the ambition to practise *Weltpolitik* – to become a world state. The platform for this was the rocketing growth of the German economy: Germany's national product grew threefold between 1873 and 1913.[51] Its indus-trial output was especially strong in the new manufacturing sectors of chemical and electrical goods. By 1900, Germany had an excellent railway system and the largest population of any European state except Russia.[52] Good communications, a great industrial base and a large population made Germany's conscript army the most efficient in Europe, and Germany itself Europe's greatest military power. In the mid-1880s, Bismarck had used these growing assets to collect some trophy colonies in the great African partition (and one or two others in the South Pacific). But all the signs are that he thought them worthless.[53] His successors after 1890 were not so sure. If China was partitioned (as seemed not unlikely), the Pacific boxed up into maritime spheres and the Ottoman Empire dismantled (another likely prospect by the mid-1890s), then Germany should claim a share that reflected its status and economic potential. If the future was to be a silent Darwinian struggle for survival or supremacy in a closed world system, any other course would be a virtual abdication.

The aggressive manner with which the Germans sought their 'place in the sun' has become a historical cliché. Yet what is really striking about the *Weltpolitik* they pursued from the late 1890s was how half-hearted it was.[54] In the various colonial squabbles in which they became embroiled – over Samoa, Morocco (twice), West Africa and the Baghdad railway to the Persian Gulf – the Germans backed off or accepted a compromise. There were good reasons for this. Although Germany's overseas trade was increasingly active (for example in Latin America),[55] its economic interests remained chiefly in Europe (as did German foreign investment). German military power was a European phenomenon. Without a deep-sea navy, it would have to stay that way. Yet when Berlin began building an ocean-going fleet, it immediately ran into the opposition of Britain. After 1909 it was crystal-clear that the British would out-build any German navy, no matter what the cost. And, from their great base in the Orkneys, they could bottle it up and prevent its escape from its North Sea ports.

There was a brutal logic to the German position. Germany's strength lay in Europe, where there were millions of ethnic Germans still beyond its frontiers, an old tradition of German commercial and financial pre-eminence in Eastern and Central Europe, and a set of would-be client states, including the Austro-Hungarian Empire, technically still one of the great powers of Europe. 'If the world across the seas should consolidate itself under England's hegemony,' said the colonial propagandist Carl Peters, 'there can be nothing but a United States of Europe to preserve for the old world its supremacy.'[56] Peters's meaning was clear. The achievement of a German hegemony in Europe (at the expense of Russia, France and Britain) would more than compensate for the lack of an empire on the British model. It would also smash the geopolitical props on which global colonialism had been built thus far, and open the way for a new global partition in Germany's favour. But to gain such a hegemony by force was much too dangerous a plan to be adopted lightly, or even debated openly by those who made policy (one of the reasons why the debate among historians over German war guilt has been so inconclusive). Up to

1914, it remained an imaginary prize that unforeseen circumstances might suddenly offer.

Superficially, France had the resources and skills to stand comparison with this world-power quartet. France was still a formidable power on land, and a major naval power (though in relative decline). It was second only to Britain as a foreign investor (with about half the investment), mainly to Europe, especially Russia. The global influence of French ideas and culture and the prestige of French writers, institutions and art were as great as ever. Since the 1870s, France's great-power status had been strikingly symbolized in its Afro-Asian empire. Between 1880 and 1910, France's overseas possessions grew by more than twelve times in area (from 350,000 square miles to 4.6 million) and more than sixteen times in population (from 3 to 50 million).[57] Much of North, West and Equatorial Africa, as well as Madagascar, Indochina and parts of the South Pacific, had come under French rule. France had fiercely asserted its claim to a generous share in the global partition. Yet this was not enough.

As an aspiring world power, France suffered from three disabling weaknesses. Domestically, its population was stagnant, and industrial development lagged far behind Germany's, let alone Britain's. Secondly, despite the vast scale of the French colonial empire, its economic potential was weak. France had no India to pay its imperial bills, and no settler countries to be its partners in trade and its allies in war. To make matters worse, much of this empire was a strategic hostage to fortune, since the naval power to defend it had been allowed to dribble away.[58] One school of thought, led by the great foreign minister Théophile Delcassé (1898–1905), dismissed French Indochina as practically valueless, and urged instead an Afro-Mediterranean empire based on Morocco and Algeria.[59] Thirdly, France's geographical position in Europe (with the loss of Alsace-Lorraine in 1871) made it much more vulnerable to a knockout blow than any other world power: no ocean barrier or masses of land lay between an invading army and the vital centres of government and industry. It was thus hardly surprising that French political opinion veered uneasily between closer friendship with Britain and reconciliation with Germany. The factional politics of the Third Republic, the rapid turnover of governments and the bitter divisions over religious and secular loyalties (brought to light in the Dreyfus affair) aggravated these uncertainties in French foreign policy.

There is an old tradition in historical writing in which rampant imperialism, red in tooth and claw, formed the anarchic prelude to the great conflagration of the First World War. But before 1914 there was little sign that the world's most powerful states intended to fight each other for global supremacy. Instead, they adopted a form of 'competitive coexistence' and recognized that, for the time being at least, a rough balance of power existed between them. Despite the jostling and friction in their mutual relations, they shared (along with the small colonial powers) a broadly similar view of how to behave towards the non-European peoples. To have backed a colonial movement against its imperial master, or espoused radical doctrines of national self-determination, would have seemed self-defeating at best. They took it for granted that their cultures were superior and that their 'standard of civilization'[60] justified intervention or colonization in 'less civilized' lands. A world divided up into great colonial empires seemed natural and inevitable under modern conditions. The progress of the colonized towards eventual self-rule – if it happened at all – would be painfully slow. Meanwhile, the greatest danger to international peace was thought likely to come from the 'dying empires' that had so far escaped partition. In the Ottoman, Iranian and Chinese empires, the stakes were higher and the chance of agreement was lower: over them the world powers might really fall out. It turned out, however, that there was a much more immediate danger. There was always the risk that the diplomatic rattling of sabres would get out of hand. A panicky ruler, an opportunist adviser, a rush of blood in the press, or simple miscalculation might tip the balance between peace and war. The fragile stability of global colonialism, and the peace of the world, really depended upon the mutual restraint of the main European states, and their respect for their own continent's uneasy balance of power. If that were to change, then the geopolitics of empire would be plunged into chaos.

GLOBAL ECONOMICS

Global colonialism was not simply a question of extending the area ruled by the European states. Such geopolitical change had an economic parallel. From the 1870s onward, a modern world economy emerged.[61] Of course, trade between continents had always existed. Indeed, as we saw in an earlier chapter, European access to American silver had created a system of global exchange in the sixteenth century, though one largely confined to bullion and luxuries. The eighteenth century saw a big expansion of seaborne trade, including the export of tea from China and of cotton fabrics from India to markets as faraway as America and West Africa. But much the heaviest intercontinental traffic was across the Atlantic. By the first half of the nineteenth century a high degree of economic integration had developed between North West Europe and the British Isles and North East America. The world economy of the later nineteenth century was partly the consequence of extending the dense commercial networks of the North Atlantic basin to new parts of the globe: South America, parts of Africa, India, South East Asia, Australasia, and East Asia. One of its distinguishing features was that, right across the world, the price not just of luxuries but of even quite common commodities (like food grains) was decided not by local or regional factors but by market forces on a global scale.[62] But it was not just a matter of there being more trade, although its value and volume continued to soar. It had reached nearly £3 billion by 1880, £4 billion by 1900, and then almost doubled between 1900 and 1913 to reach a pre-war figure of around £8 billion.[63] The great increase of trade was accompanied by – in fact depended upon – two further changes that bound together the commercial life of different world regions.

The first was the rise of an international payments 'circuit' into which any country could plug, and from which it could draw the foreign exchange needed to pay for its imports. It was no longer necessary to balance its books with every trading partner: as long as it had a surplus somewhere, it could use this credit in the payments circuit.[64] This relieved an important bottleneck that had obstructed commerce. The second was the growth after c.1870 of Europe's export of capital on a much vaster scale, and to far wider targets than in previous years. Though most was invested in the Americas and in other parts of Europe, with only a lesser share going to Asia and Africa (around 30 per cent of British foreign investment by 1913 was in Afro-Asia), the world had become a single market for capital. That placed a premium on rapid and accurate commercial information (the main function of the telegraph), but also on the closer conformity of financial and property practices. In effect, global colonialism in its commercial guise meant drawing the rest of the world into an economic system that was centred on Europe and its western extension in the United States. More to the point, it meant a global division of labour in which the manufactures, capital and credit of the industrial-imperial countries were exchanged for the raw products and commodities of the rest of the world.

Of course, this new global market was not just the result of purely commercial activity. Nor could it have been. In several crucial ways it depended upon the assertion of power, an expansion of empire both direct and indirect. In East Asia, for instance, the regime of free trade had been imposed by force and by the armed diplomacy of the 'unequal treaties'. It was maintained in India by the unequivocal insistence of the London government (against the doubts of local British officialdom). Secondly, the multilateral pattern of commercial payments that was centred on Britain would have functioned less smoothly – if it had functioned at all – had the British not enjoyed a favourable balance of payments with their Indian empire, secured as much by rule (Indians paid a 'service charge' to their foreign masters) as by commercial success.[65] Thirdly, in Australia, New Zealand, western Canada and Latin America, and more marginally in Africa, the global market was extended by Europe's demographic imperialism, the occupation of lands by European settlers, and the displacement (by agreement, force or fraud) of their indigenous owners. As the flows of trade and investment revealed, this form of 'empire' was much the most economically dynamic. Fourthly, in their colonial territories and in other countries as well, European governments promoted a property regime that would safeguard the interests of expatriate enterprise.[66] By local laws if possible, by extraterritorial privilege if necessary (as in the Ottoman Empire, Egypt, Iran, Siam, China and

Japan), the sphere of market institutions was to be steadily expanded.

The main driving force behind the new global economy was the great improvement in transport and its extension worldwide. Between 1869, when the Suez Canal opened, and 1914, when the Panama Canal was finished, much of the rest of the world was drawn into the nexus of communications that already existed between Europe and America. Steamships, railways and the electric telegraph, with its submarine cables, now girdled the earth. After 1900, the extension of this network to include every productive region seemed only a matter of time. The exchange of products on an ever-growing scale encouraged specialization and mutual economic dependence. As trade flows increased, they seemed to promote an inexhaustible appetite for more exotic products. So did the changing demands of industrial production in America and Europe. Rubber, tin, other base metals and fuel oil joined the older staples of international trade: cotton, wool, grain, timber, sugar, tea and coffee. From the 1880s, the new technology of refrigeration allowed an export trade in perishable produce from remote locations like Argentina and New Zealand to European consumers many weeks away. Nothing symbolized better the astonishing possibilities of a world economy than Britain's growing dependence upon basic foodstuffs carried by sea for more than 12,000 miles.

The growth of new trades and the expansion of old ones were plainly visible in the swelling size of the world's port cities. They were numerous enough in the North Atlantic world. But, in the late nineteenth century, new (or much larger) port cities appeared in the other continents. The population of Buenos Aires, the commercial hub for the newly conquered pampas, rose from 300,000 in 1880 to 1.3 million only thirty years later.[67] Cape Town grew rapidly to serve the up-country eldorados of diamonds and gold. Bombay took advantage of the Suez Canal to dominate India's westbound trade and extend its influence into the Persian Gulf.[68] Singapore continued its meteoric rise as the western gateway into the South China Sea and the grand entrepôt of South East Asian trade.[69] Shanghai strengthened its claim to be China's chief port and the commercial outlet of its most productive region in the Yangtze basin. Melbourne and Sydney (and remote Dunedin) connected Australasia's hinterlands with their suppliers and markets on the other side of the world.

Being a successful port city meant feverish activity to improve the harbour, to organize the docks, to build vast railyards and push the line of rail (or its riverine equivalent) ever further up-country.[70] The outward sign of commercial success was the rapid construction of customs houses, railways stations, banks and hotels, as well as lavish clubs and residences for the new merchant class. Bombay railway station, the Raffles' Hotel in Singapore, the 'Parisian' splendour of the new Buenos Aires, Cape Town's Standard Bank (where Rhodes had his account), the Shanghai Bund, Collins Street in Melbourne and the exuberant architecture of Sydney's leading banks (around Martin Place) showed the confidence and prosperity of this commercial world. It was served by a growing army of dockers, porters, railwaymen, packers, warehousemen and clerks. Its masters were a mobile and often cosmopolitan elite whose long-distance connections were frequently the key to their commercial success and to their credit rating. British, and especially Scottish, businessmen could be found on every continent. But there were many others who were just as enterprising. In the Near East and Black Sea, they were usually Greeks. The biggest merchants in Bombay were Parsis (originally from Iran) rather than Hindus. Parsis, Jews and Armenians (like the Sassoons) followed the trade routes east.[71] Their business houses could be found in Singapore (where there is still an Armenian church), Hong Kong and Shanghai. One of the largest shipowners in late-nineteenth-century Singapore was of Arab descent, part of a community of traders and seafarers long established in the Malay archipelago. Others were Chinese. The grandfather of Singapore's first prime minister, Lee Kuan Yew, owned a steamship line serving Singapore and Batavia (modern Jakarta).

In the late nineteenth century it was not unrealistic to think that, despite cultural differences, the members of this mercantile network had a great deal in common. They were economic liberals by instinct. They favoured easy movement across jurisdictions and frontiers. They disliked the interference of bureaucrats and officials. They wanted sympathetic governments who would invest in 'progress' (in its most concrete forms). They placed a high valuation on the keeping of contracts, and the rights of property. They needed reliable currencies and trustworthy banks. Their interests, in short, were against a global partition that would seal the world into closed imperial blocs. Still less did they want the kind of colonial regime that scorned business influence and practised exclusion by race. Resentment at this had made the Bombay Parsis among the earliest champions of Indian rights against the British Raj. On the other hand, even non-European merchants had nothing to gain if the world that commerce had made was divided into a patchwork quilt of fractious nation states whose rulers' aims were unlikely to chime with those of the chambers of commerce in the great port cities.

The merchants' interests could be briefly summed up as the 'open economy', with no barriers to trade, the flows of credit and capital, or the movement of people (especially labour). This was the 'empire of free trade' that the British had pursued since the 1840s, when they had tried to enforce it (with some degree of success) on Latin America and the Middle East as well as India and China. It had required the new transport technology to draw the rest of the world towards the high-pressure zone of Euro-American commerce. But that was not all. As we have seen, one of the main barriers to trade had been the difficulty of striking a balance between two different markets so that each could pay for the purchases that were made in the other. The solution was a multilateral system of foreign exchange to allow a country to buy goods for which it could not pay directly. But, to make that system work, there needed to be a form of 'common currency' in which most traders had confidence, to serve as a store of all their different claims. Secondly, there had to be a place where they could redeem their claims, or exchange them for goods that were of equal value.

Because it could meet these complex demands, London became the Queen City of the new world economy. Freely convertible gold-based sterling was the world's hardest currency, and the sterling 'bill on London' became the most reliable form of international exchange. As a free-trade port, centrally based in the Euro-American sphere, and the imperial capital of the Anglo-Indian 'system', London was the world's largest marketplace. Among the merchants and bankers crowded into the Square Mile of the 'City', there was no difficulty exchanging a sterling bill for another currency, finding a customer, or buying a cargo that could be sold elsewhere. London became the headquarters for a wide range of the commercial services on which trade depended. British overseas banks, insurance companies and shipping took the lion's share of the new traffic between continents. British shipping agents and steamers became ubiquitous. After 1870, London added foreign investment to its arsenal – a reaction to the fact that the British economy was now growing more slowly than the 'new' economies overseas. From then until 1914, London was the source of more than half the capital that was sent out of Europe. Much of it went into transport systems that would open new markets and connect new producers. By 1913, over 40 per cent of British capital abroad had gone into railways – state-controlled (as in Australia and India) or private.[72] The stream of sterling had other important effects. It smoothed the troughs and peaks of the commercial round, and encouraged monetary stability where this was otherwise hard.[73] It strengthened London's grip on the business capitals of the extra-European world, whose prosperity rested (it was easy to believe) on the flow of credits from the world's great lender of last resort. It helped to speed up the remarkable process by which more and more states adopted the 'gold standard': fixing their currency's value in gold to expand their trade and encourage inward investment.[74]

London's size and wealth thus grew in sympathy with the surging growth of international trade.[75] Among its merchants and bankers, it was an article of faith that what was good for London was good for the world. The idea of free trade and the open economy was adopted in Britain in the 1840s and '50s not just as a policy but as a total world-view, an ideology promoted with crusading passion. It imagined a world in which peoples would be freed from their bondage to rulers by the flood tide of commerce. Individual freedom and international trade would move forward together. Free trade was regarded as the key to British economic success, and to the economic progress of the rest of the world. (The alternative – protection – was rejected politically in Britain before 1914, and its supporters were divided over what to protect.) Its champions insisted that letting the market decide on what it made sense to produce was the most efficient way to use economic resources. Countries without capital or an industrial base should concentrate their efforts on the production of 'staples': the raw materials or foodstuffs for which a world demand existed. They should use the income that their staples earned to buy the manufactures they needed, and to pay back the interest on the capital they borrowed – since staple production could expand only if there were railways and harbours to bring the goods to market. Any other policy – for example building up industrial production behind a wall of tariffs – was not only inefficient (because industrial goods could be bought more cheaply abroad), it was also unjust. It meant that the consumer was taxed in favour of those who had gained the protection of tariffs, a political process that (so free-traders implied) was invariably corrupt. Enlightened colonial rule should thus enforce free trade (as the British did in India), just as a wise diplomacy should always encourage it. The great growth of exports in the late nineteenth century, including from India and (after 1890) China, seemed further proof of the universal validity of this economic prescription. Thus London's central role in the new world economy was not only profit-able, it was also benign. Even the export of capital could be plausibly described as providing a vital service. 'Canada' (perhaps the main recipient of British capital in 1900–1914), said the intellectual banker Robert Brand, 'has as much interest in maintaining unchecked the flow of capital from England as a city has in preventing its water supply from being cut off.'[76]

Free-trade theory saw commercial agriculture as the liberation of peasantries throughout the world. It conjured up visions of Indians and Chinese as satisfied customers, clad in Lancashire cottons. It extolled the peace-promoting virtues of economic interdependence. War was unthinkable, declared a famous tract of the time, because the powers that might wage it had too much to lose from the stoppage of trade.[77] But this constant harping upon the mutual benefits of the new world economy underrated its frictions and ignored its precarious stability. It was obvious that many of the new members of the econ-omic club had not been admitted on the same terms as the old. The new adherents to the world economy had to occupy the spaces not already taken. They had to produce the commodities that longer-established competitors did not wish to supply. They had to lower the cost of production to make up for the defects of their commercial machinery: their labour had to be very cheap. To make matters worse, it was often the case that the switch to cash-crop production threat-ened a social crisis. It was one thing to bring settlers into an empty land. It was quite another to produce cash crops for export in a densely crowded landscape where the right to cultivate and the demand for rent were the keys to social relations and status. Here 'clearing' the land of its 'surplus' peasantry to make room for efficient agricultural production would amount to social revolution. The prospect so frightened the British rulers of India that (from the 1870s onward) they progressively restricted the transfer of land from traditional cultivating castes to urban-based businessmen. In the African scenario, it was often the shortage of labour, not its over-supply, that stalled the kind of development that free trade recommended. It was the constant complaint of mining companies and settlers that the 'native was lazy', that he would not work for the minimal wages that were all they could afford in this marginal part of the capitalist world. Here the notion of mutual benefit was strained past its limit. To make Africans 'work' became the excuse for a colonial regime that turned them (at its worst) into a class of serfs. Coercive taxation (to make wage labour compulsory), a savage work discipline,[78] the ban on any form of labour organization, and the expropriation of land that had commercial value were part of the armoury of colonial capitalism in its African setting. It was hardly surprising that there and elsewhere the commercial economy was widely identified with white racial privilege.

Even in places where the new world economy was backed by local elites, who (like the Argentinian *estancieros*) expected to profit from the rising value of land and the new urban prosperity, support was much more conditional than free-traders liked to believe. To maintain the flow of credits, attract more capital, and take full advantage of the buoyant market for crops and commodities meant accepting disciplines that were often painful. To keep the currency stable, spending had to be curbed. To encourage trade, tariffs had to be low, and local industry sacrificed. To keep the foreign investor happy, his railway companies and banks had to be petted and courted. There were plenty of those in the extra-European world who thought the free-trade economy a one-sided bargain and resented the power exerted from London. In India and West Africa, where indigenous merchants tended to favour free trade, there were those who resented the favoured position of European business. While the value of trade was on a rising curve, these views were muted. But there could be no

guarantee that the commercial conditions that made the new international economy such a dynamic force would be stable or lasting. If
the boom in commodities turned into a bust, if the world market was
ruptured by a great-power conflict, or if London failed to meet the
demands of its role as the source of credit and capital, the enemies of
free trade would begin to gather. The other large economies of the
Euro-American world were more protectionist-minded. The rapid
growth of world trade had restrained this instinct – up to a point. But
if expansion was checked and the free-trading zone that was centred
on London contracted in area and declined in wealth, the most likely
alternative was a series of blocs controlled by the rival world states.
The mutual antagonisms of the great world powers would become
much fiercer without an 'open zone' where they had interests in
common. The economic regime that had helped to underwrite the
creation of global colonialism would have gone into reverse.

Indeed, before 1914 some symptoms of strain were already appear-
ing. The frantic expansion of trade began to ease off. The colossal
increase in the export of grain could not be kept up. Among the
industrial countries, it was the extraordinary growth of the American
economy that really stood out. But it was already a question whether
this industrial leviathan might not destabilize the new 'world economy' that was centred in Europe, and especially in London. America
had become a great industrial power, but it was largely self-reliant in
raw materials and foodstuffs. Its market for manufactures was found
mainly at home. It had little incentive to adopt free trade, and the
level of its tariffs was far higher than that of the European industrial
states, with the exception of Russia.[79] It had a huge hoard of gold
(almost one-third of the world's total supply in 1910),[80] and any
increase in its share (if gold was sucked in by a spurt in growth) could
create crisis conditions in other gold-based economies, because their
supply of money would shrink. Yet, if such a crisis arose, the vast size
and scale of the American economy, and the growing power of Wall
Street, would make it hard to enforce the 'advice' of the world's
bankers in London. If a fissure opened up between the two great
halves of the industrial world, the global economy that had just begun
to take shape might prove too discordant to manage.

CULTURE WARS

Global colonialism had brought a political hierarchy of imperial powers and colonial (or semi-colonial) dependencies. Across much of the world, the new commercial economy created a parallel universe of (European) industrial-capitalist masters alongside (mainly non-European) commodity-producing 'servants', who were poorly protected against the shifts and swings of international demand. Global colonialism had a third dimension. It projected a cultural hierarchy of astonishing force and pervasive influence. European cultural primacy was asserted more aggressively in this period than before or since. The sheer scale of Europe's physical predominance after 1880 across Asia, Africa and the Pacific meant that its cultural influence was disseminated more widely and authoritatively than in earlier times. European categories of thought, forms of scientific inquiry, interpretations of the past, ideas of social order, models of public morality, concepts of crime and justice, and modes of literary expression, as well as European recipes for health, notions of leisure, and even styles of dress, became the civilized 'standard' against which other cultures were measured and usually found wanting. Among the educated elites of the non-European world, who were increasingly exposed to the political authority of European rulers, the alarming disparity in knowledge and power was ruefully acknowledged. To Muslim thinkers it seemed especially dangerous. But how were they to challenge the cultural claims of an expanding Europe? Rejecting outright Europe's version of modernity would be a self-defeating call for a kind of cultural stasis. Such a cure would accelerate the disease that they had diagnosed. But the alternative course, of adapting European methods to their own cultural requirements – using new European engines to drive their own cultural revival – seemed almost as risky. It threatened to divide the local cultural elite, demoralize tradition, and pave the way by a different route for Europe's ultimate triumph.

The Europeans assumed that their sudden rise to such a dominant position among continents and cultures arose from their discovery of perpetual progress. They alone had broken out of the cycle of growth and decay to which all other civilizations were subject. They alone had discovered the secret of the wealth of nations. They had achieved an unequalled technological mastery. They had broken through the old barriers of superstition and myth to found their intellectual life on the rigorous collation of empirical knowledge. It was widely assumed that they had reaped this reward by the careful observance of four cardinal rules. The first was to encourage the free exchange of ideas and check the power of those (like priesthoods) who might try to restrain it. The second was to secure the right to individual property (and thus the motive for improvement) against ordinary crime or the predation of despots. The third was to construct a form of social order that would maintain moral, and especially sexual, discipline among those on whose labour material progress depended. The right treatment of women in their 'separate sphere' became the acid test of a developed society. The last was the promotion of physical vigour and courage, the 'manly' qualities to which Europeans abroad were inclined to attribute their military prowess and political dominance. But how and why these habits and attitudes had come to be adopted, and how securely fixed they were in European societies, remained deeply controversial.

Confidence in their unique command of progress explains in part the disconcerting arrogance that Europeans so often displayed towards other cultures. It has been plausibly claimed that the invention of an oriental 'other', sunk in the quagmires of moral and intellectual 'backwardness', was essential to the European self-image of progress. Only by insisting on the failings of the 'Orient' (in practice all non-Western peoples) could the Europeans be sure of their own progressive identity. This almost certainly exaggerates the intellectual interest that Europeans took in other parts of the world. Like most civilizations, they were obsessed not with others but with themselves. It was from viewing their own past that they derived the lesson that they had made astonishing progress, although there was no general agreement on how it had happened. They were also conscious that in many parts of Europe this progress had been slow, where it existed at all. The fiercest debates in European thought were not about non-Europe, but about how far it was safe to abandon the beliefs and values of Europe's pre-industrial past. Some of the sharpest exchanges between European intellectuals were over the place of religion, 'traditional' morality, 'folk' culture and language, and pre-modern social relations (social paternalism) in a modern society.[81] There was a pervasive sense that progress was fragile. It was threatened by 'reaction', especially, liberals thought, in the shape of the Church. It could be overthrown from below, by a popular revolt against its fierce economic discipline (the threat of socialism or anarchism). It might lead to 'degeneracy', the physical and moral consequence, so it was often claimed, of urban and industrial life. It could be self-destructive, by erasing the individual in favour of the mass, and replacing the spiritual with a crass material-ism. A sense of social panic infused these arguments with a mood of urgency.[82] Amid these introverted concerns, ignorance and indiffer-ence ruled European attitudes towards the non-Western world. Its peoples were bystanders in the great struggle of life. Interpreting them fell to a small minority. It was all too easy to explain their cultures in terms of a stagnant past from which only Europe (or its developed regions) had escaped.

This tendency was strongly reinforced by the circumstances in which much of non-Europe came to the attention of a European audience. Of course, a mass of literature introduced European readers to the Afro-Asian world. But most of it derived from the peculiar activities that Europeans pursued there. In the reportage of soldiers, explorers and missionaries, it was the violence, remoteness and superstition of Afro-Asian societies that received greatest emphasis. In existing colonies (the best example is India), ethnographic investigation was largely conducted by European officials.[83] It was hardly surprising that they deployed fashionable racial and physiological theories (like craniology), originally devised to explain differences within Europe,[84] to insist on the absence of those 'progressive' features that might set a term to their alien rule. Far from forging ahead in the wake of Europe, most Indians and Africans were portrayed as chained to traditions that made self-rule unthinkable, but which could be modi-fied only over an indefinite period. In the newly occupied zones of colonial rule, it was even easier to argue that the disorders occasioned by the European intrusion were positive proof of the chaos and bar-barity of the pre-colonial order. Far from plodding towards the distant goal of modernity, non-Western societies, if left to themselves, would follow a downward spiral of social and ethical decay. Where they faced the direct competition of European peoples, it might be their fate to die out altogether – the outcome often predicted for New Zealand Maori and Australian Aborigines.

By the end of the century, European commentators were increasingly inclined to see the 'stagnation' of non-European societies as a hereditary condition. Cultural differences, whatever their origin, became 'racial' differences, and cultural habits the product of racial 'instinct'.[85] Careless intervention, overhasty reform or irresponsible exploitation (the lofty official view of merchant and settler activity) could cause an explosion, and shatter the cohesion on which all order depended. Stability was the pressing need, and it was best promoted by favouring local customary law (rather than imported jurisprudence), and neo-traditional rulers (local dignitaries who accepted their colonial status) rather than the colony's Western-educated elite – a 'microscopic minority' in the dismissive phrase of an Indian viceroy.[86] In some cases, it was thought, stability was best secured by a deliberate policy of territorial segregation, the solution mooted by an official commission on South Africa's 'native affairs'.[87] Thus the Europeans had no single grand theory for their future relations with the non-Western world. The much-touted influence of Social Darwinism had no clear message of imperial expansion: indeed, many Social Darwinists were ardently opposed to the cultural and racial dilution they thought it would bring.[88] Just as they argued over the reasons for Europe's exceptional dynamism, Europeans disagreed sharply over the causes and effects of non-European 'stagnation'. India was variously interpreted as an immobile society of self-sufficient villages, a relic of medievalism, or as the unfortunate consequence of racial mixing between its original Aryan rulers and indigenous Dravidians.[89] Some European thinkers, disenchanted with industrialism, found much to admire in the 'spiritual' East: the survival of handicrafts, the lack of class conflict, or the 'closeness to nature' of non-Western societies.[90] Europeans struggled to categorize the bewildering variety of non-Western cultures. They acknowledged pragmatically the privileged status of the special groups on whom their rule depended: the 'martial races' needed for their colonial armies, or the Islamic elites in Nigeria and North India. They lacked the means, and also the nerve, to impose their own cultural blueprint (even if they had one). They were forced to rely upon local informants who supplied much of the data from which official histories, handbooks, law codes, gazetteers and ethnographies were compiled. It was thus not surprising that official wisdom in India decreed the traditional pre-eminence of the Brahmin castes, and affirmed caste as the basis of Indian society: it was from Brahmin scholars and pandits that the officials had derived much of their knowledge of the Indian past.[91]

The importance of this was that in most of the regions that fell under European dominance indigenous elites could still find the space for cultural resistance. We can see them waging three different kinds of cultural 'warfare'. The first drew heavily upon European models of cultural change. In Bengal, for example, the new literate class that sprang up to man the British administrative machine was quick to acquire an 'English' education. But it was also keen to equip Bengal itself with a cultural persona on the English model. Bengali should become a literary language. Poetry, fiction, history and journalism in the Bengali vernacular would create a new sense of Bengali identity.[92] Teachers and journalists would create a modern Bengali people. The embryonic institutions of the colonial regime would become a proto-parliament, a Westminster-to-be. The vital role of political leaders like Surendranath Banerjea, the uncrowned king of Bengal, was to build the framework of self-rule for a new Europe-style nation.[93] A similar pattern could be seen in Maharashtra in western India, where Western-style history in the vernacular language was consciously used to create political and cultural awareness.[94] Ambitions of this sort formed part of the fuel of early Indian nationalism. But as a cultural strategy they needed the presence of a strong literate elite to act as the intermediaries between the colonial power and the local society.

Partly for this reason, a commoner form of cultural resistance was found in religious revival. With few exceptions, Europeans were inclined to see Christianity's great Eurasian rivals like Islam or Hinduism as decadent or moribund. Islamic learning was dismissed as an obsolete scholasticism, with a glorious past but no intellectual future. Islamic scholars were chained to their classical texts, unable to acknowledge that the world had changed or to adapt their ideas to the flood of empirical data. It was this failure on the part of orthodox

343

scholars – the *ulama* or learned men – that gave so much scope to the Sufi 'brotherhoods' and their charismatic leaders, the sheikhs and marabouts. It opened up a space for 'fundamentalist' movements to wage jihad against infidels, pagans and corrupt fellow Muslims. Europeans reserved a particular loathing (and a special fear) for this Muslim 'fanaticism', symptomatic, they thought, of Islam's arrested development. Its most famous victory in the late nineteenth century was the Mahdist revolt against Egypt's colonial rule in the Nilotic Sudan, which culminated in 1885 with the capture of Khartoum and the death of General Gordon, the governor-general sent by the Egyptian government (under heavy British pressure) to stage an orderly retreat.[95] When the British re-entered the city thirteen years later, after defeating the Mahdist army at Omdurman, Kitchener ordered the bones of the first Mahdi ruler (Muhammad Ahmad, 1844–85) to be thrown in the Nile. A word from Queen Victoria was needed to stop him from using the Mahdi's skull as an ashtray.

In fact the general Muslim response to Europe's cultural expansion was much less sensational and a good deal more lasting. The Mahdi was a charismatic preacher on the outer margins of the Islamic world. The Muslim teachers at the main centres of learning were all too aware that their classical scholarship had become out of date. Ways had to be found to adapt orthodox learning to modern ideas. This was the project of the two great Muslim scholars of the late nineteenth century, Jamal al-Din al-Afghani (1839–97) and Muhammad Abduh (1849–1905). Both were at pains to master European thinking, and both studied in Paris. Both were committed to uphold Muslim solidarity in the face of Europe's advance, which they saw at first hand in the British occupation of Egypt, the home (in Cairo) of Islam's greatest centre of intellectual life at al-Azhar. The ultimate purpose was to revitalize the *umma*, the Muslim faithful around the world, and re-educate the *ulama*, their scholarly guides and advisers. That meant rooting out the superstitions, unorthodox beliefs, and syncretic practices adopted by Muslims from the widely varied cultures into which Islam had spread. It meant purification, but also a kind of modernization. A reformed *ulama* would be in closer touch with the main centres of scholarship. They would be properly trained in Muslim theology and history. They would be better equipped to counter European ideas with a convincing Islamic response. They would transmit Islam's message to the Muslim faithful with greater confidence and by more efficient means. Preaching, teaching and the diffusion of ideas would exploit the new media (the cheapness of print for newspapers and books), new kinds of education (using Western-style classrooms and schools) and the new ease of travel. The steamship and railway allowed many more Muslims than ever before to make the haj (the pilgrimage to Mecca), to sit at the feet of the leading scholars, and grasp the full scale of the Islamic world. Pan-Islamic solidarity, a more proficient elite, a more disciplined *umma*, and a much keener sense of Islam's special place in the modern world would be the promised reward.[96]

To many Muslim observers, it seemed that only limited progress towards this ideal had been made by 1914. The task of mobilizing an *umma* that was vast, scattered, and often illiterate and impoverished was a daunting one. The Islamic world was riven by political, ethnic and linguistic divisions. Modernizing Arabic, the classical language of Muslim science, law and theology, was a massive challenge. The principal Muslim states suffered (as we shall see) further defeats and humiliations at European hands. Indeed, in some Muslim communities, ethnic nationalism and the territorial state seemed a more promising basis for anti-colonial resistance than the remote ideal of pan-Islamic unity. There was sometimes fierce disagreement between those who insisted that Islam had no quarrel with Western science and politics and those who regarded the influence of these as corrupting. But there was also no doubt that the sharpening sense of Islamic identity that al-Afghani and Abduh had been so keen to promote had begun to energize a wide variety of Muslim societies. In West Africa, the Muslim religious elite consolidated their influence over the French authorities as well as tightening their grip on the community of faithful.[97] In Egypt, the epicentre of Islamic modernism, the Muslim concern for moral reform and greater social discipline extended the appeal of nationalist politics among the educated class.[98] In India, the new Muslim university founded at Aligarh (the 'Anglo-Oriental College') may have emphasized the value of the West's modern knowledge, but it was also a seminary of the 'Young Muslim' leaders who came to prominence after 1914.[99] In colonial South East

Asia, reformist movements and the new print media helped spread Islamic consciousness, and in the Dutch East Indies this took the form of a political movement, Sarekat Islam.[100]

In Hinduism, there was a similar trend towards cleansing and codifying religious practice. Reformist movements like the Arya Samaj implicitly acknowledged the spiritual appeal of Christian worship, with its stress upon the individual's relationship with God. At the popular level, this religious revival could be seen in campaigns for 'cow protection' and for encouraging the cult of the Hindu pantheon rather than local deities. Better means of travel encouraged more pilgrims to make their way to Benares and Mother Ganges, as well as other centres of Hindu devotion. Among the educated, the printed word in India's vernacular languages helped spread the influence of spiritual teachers and movements. But perhaps the most remarkable development before 1914 was Gandhi's manifesto for cultural resistance, published in 1909 under the title of *Hind Swaraj* ('Indian self-rule').[101] *Hind Swaraj* (composed while Gandhi travelled by sea between London and South Africa, where he lived and worked between 1893 and 1915) was a brilliant synthesis of religion, culture and politics. It set out a third grand strategy for cultural revival. It affirmed the value of a purified Hinduism as the moral base of society. It also adopted the European view of Indian society as a vast mosaic of 'village communities'. Gandhi's purpose was not to repeat the diagnosis of 'stagnation'. Instead he insisted on the moral superiority of the self-sufficing village over the artificial, exploitative and divisive civilization imposed by the West. Thus Indian self-rule would not be achieved by merely taking over the institutions of the colonial government – keeping the tiger's nature, while getting rid of the tiger, in Gandhi's colourful phrase. It meant repudiating everything that Western dominance had brought, including law and medicine, railways and telegraphs, and the Indian state itself. In Gandhi's formulation, religious reform merged into moral reform, moral reform into social reform, social reform into political struggle. Moral liberation would lead to political freedom, since once Indians rejected the mental hegemony on which British rule depended (the Indians, said Gandhi, had *allowed* the British to rule) they would revoke the collaboration on which the Raj was built. With astonishing skill (and in little more than a pamphlet) Gandhi had shown how a cultural movement could avoid direct confrontation with its colonial regime until the crucial moment. But when the process of (mental) liberation was complete, the final assault would be brief and bloodless.

Perhaps not surprisingly, *Hind Swaraj* was immediately banned as subversive by the government in India, and Gandhi himself was not to become an influential figure there until 1918. Some of the ideas he advanced – especially the need for cultural and economic self-sufficiency – were already at work in the so-called *swadeshi* campaign in Bengal after 1905, and in the polemical writing of the Congress politician Bal Gangadar Tilak. But they lacked the touch of political genius that Gandhi brought to them. It was the Gandhian model of political and cultural resistance, conceived at the high tide of Europe's imperial expansion, that was to turn Indian nationalism into a non-violent mass movement in the inter-war years.

It would be wrong to underestimate the enormous impact of Western ideas and the extent to which they penetrated the thinking of almost every society exposed to Euro-American influence. This often had the consequence – all the more powerful for being insidious – that non-European peoples began to see themselves (as well as Europeans) partly in terms of Western ideas and prejudices. But it would be equally wrong to deny that much of that impact sprang from attraction and sympathy, not forced imposition. Individual freedom, representative government, the nation-state ideal, empirical science and Christian doctrines all exerted an enormous appeal in the non-Western world. Nor could this cultural influence simply be harnessed to colonial rule or deployed in the interests of imperial dominance. Its content was pluralistic and sometimes contradictory. It evoked responses that were unpredictable and varied. It encountered local cultural networks that were deeply entrenched, and where cultural attitudes were closely bound up with religious identity. There were few colonial regimes that were able or willing to displace the cultural 'gatekeepers' of local society, whose cooperation had to be purchased by a form of cultural 'contract'. And exactly the weapons through which Western ideas were so widely diffused – the print media, cheap travel and educational institutions – could be turned to the tasks of cultural renovation and resistance.

This could even be seen in the use that was made of the idea of 'race', usually thought of as the heaviest weapon in Europe's cultural armoury. Although its basic assumption was that cultural differences were hereditary, European racism was an incoherent doctrine with no claim to precision. It blurred the distinction between cultural and physical attributes, despite the best efforts of its 'scientific' practitioners. It relied on a bank of stereotyped descriptions to cope with the differences within Europe itself, and the huge variation in the cultures and peoples of the non-Western world. However, it was 'vulgar' racism, not its 'intellectual' variant, that had the most impact. Europeans living in Asia and Africa knew perfectly well that their status and income depended on claims of insurmountable difference between themselves and the locals. It required little ingenuity to attach these claims to the story of Europe's material advancement and to reinvent themselves as the indispensable agents of civilization and progress. The need for security, fears of disease, and a pervasive suspicion that, left to their own devices, unattached Europeans would simply 'go native' (subverting the social and cultural order) encouraged varying degrees of segregation and separateness. Thus European racism often appeared less like a cultural theory than like a set of crude social attitudes, bluntly and often aggressively displayed.

But the idea of race did not remain a European (or Euro-American) monopoly. It was highly exportable. If being a 'race' was the secret of European power, then its attractions were obvious. By the end of the century, the new Chinese nationalism of Sun Yat-sen was deploying the notion of a distinctive Han race, the true Chinese nation. In colonial Bengal, where the Hindu *bhadralok* ('respectable people') resented exclusion from government and the disparaging language of their colonial masters, nationalist rhetoric turned the racial tables. The 'Hindu race' was much the most civilized. It shared its Aryan origins with the Europeans. It had a distinctive race mission – not political greatness or military power, but the exertion of 'spiritual energy'. By the deliberate emphasis upon cultural difference (wearing indigenous clothing), a cult of physical strength and courage, and the rediscovery of a heroic past, Bengalis could acquire all the hallmarks of a 'race', different from but as good as the European version.[102] 'A race that has a past . . . must also have a future,' remarked the magazine *Bharati* in 1904.[103]

Perhaps the most fascinating case of how the racial idea was adapted can be seen in the career of Edward Wilmot Blyden.[104] Blyden was born in the West Indies, and went first to America and then (in 1850) to Liberia, as part of the movement to bring freed slaves 'home' to West Africa. He became a Presbyterian minister. Blyden's conviction that racial boundaries were hardening led him to argue that what Africans needed was a stronger sense of their racial identity. 'We need some African power, some great centre of the race where our physical and intellectual strength may be collected,' he wrote. Blyden had in mind a West African nation, but it must, he insisted, be authentically African. Africans should avoid Western-style clothes.[105] They should preserve indigenous custom. They should also avoid interracial marriage.[106] (Blyden believed that only 'pure' blacks could foster African nationalism, and rejected the idea of 'race amalgamation'.)[107] In *Christianity, Islam and the Negro Race* (1887) he argued that Islam was more suited to Africa than the Christian religion. Intriguingly, Blyden, who served for a time as a colonial official in Sierra Leone, saw no conflict between his racial ideals and his project of building a West African nation under the auspices of British imperial power. But it was already apparent, before 1914, that the appeal to race could be used as much against Europe's hegemony as on its behalf.

UNFINISHED BUSINESS: EAST ASIA AND THE MIDDLE EAST 1880–1914

By the 1880s, Europeans and Americans had been probing the commercial promise of East Asia for more than a century. They had pushed commercial bridgeheads (the 'treaty ports') into China and Japan, and subjected both countries to 'unequal treaties' that gave extraterritorial privileges to foreign residents and property. They had enforced a low-tariff regime in the interests of their trade. They had fought two wars against China to assert these rights and extend them more widely. They had forced the Ch'ing emperor to admit the diplomatic equality of the Western states and adopt (in 1876) the

European practice of resident ambassadors.[108] But in 1880, despite the scale of the foreign presence, they were far from imposing on China as a whole (let alone on Japan) the kind of colonial subjection – or even semi-colonial dominance – that was fast becoming the rule elsewhere in Afro-Asia.

One reason for this was that East Asia was still comparatively remote from Europe, and the volume of trade between the two regions was considerably less than that between Europe and India (not to mention the Americas). But the Europeans' caution also reflected China's huge residual strength as a unified culture and a working political system. The adventurers and filibusters who shot their way into Africa, and carved out private empires with a handful of mercenaries, would have had short shrift in China. The cultural and political fragmentation that made it so easy for European intruders to pick up local allies in Africa had no counterpart here. There was a similar pattern on the commercial front. European merchants in their treaty-port godowns were in no position to control internal trade. They faced a highly organized commercial life, entrenched behind the barriers of language and China's complicated currency. They were forced by necessity to deal through the large Chinese merchants, who acted as 'compradors' (go-betweens) for the Western firms.[109] As late as 1893, this commercial relationship could still be portrayed on the Chinese side as one of mutual benefit, not foreign exploitation.[110] For all its travails in the middle years of the century, the imperial political structure was still in operation under the reformist rule of Li Hung-chang, the most powerful official for most of the period between 1870 and 1900. The ethnic consciousness of the Han majority had yet to be roused fully against the Manchu ruling caste who manned the inner citadel of the Ch'ing regime.[111] Not least, perhaps, the Ch'ing imperial government, with its tradition of parsimony, had studiously avoided incurring foreign debts, the Trojan Horse of outside interference. By the conciliatory treatment of the foreign enclaves and interests – and allowing expatriate management (under Chinese authority) in the sensitive sphere of maritime customs – Peking hoped to forestall a violent confrontation while China 'self-strengthened'.

Yet Manchu prestige and the stability of Ch'ing rule also depended upon China's central place in the East Asian 'world order'. The

Ch'ing's greatest achievement had been to attach the vast Inner Asian hinterland of Tibet, Sinkiang, Mongolia and Manchuria to the East Asian heartland of China proper. Foreign penetration of this imperial periphery threatened to unravel this far-flung network of power. In the 1880s the Europeans chipped away. The Russians pressed forward from Central Asia. The British conquered upper Burma. France forced Peking to abandon its claim to the suzerainty of Annam (much of modern Vietnam). But it was the fate of Korea that brought on the crisis. Korea was vulnerable to external pressure from Russia (which envied its ice-free ports) and Japan. Its Confucian polity had been badly shaken by domestic opponents, some of them Christians. Yet the Peking court could not run the risk that Korea might lean towards another power and cut its long-standing ties with China. The 'hermit kingdom' was the maritime gateway into Inner Asia. It was the springboard for advance into the empty space of Manchuria. Its loss might destabilize much of China's steppe diplomacy, turning Inner Asia into a hostile borderland. So when a Japanese-backed coup overthrew Korea's sinophile regime in 1894, Peking refused to back down. But, in the short war that followed between July 1894 and March 1895, it was China that suffered a humiliating defeat.

The Treaty of Shimonoseki (in April 1895) unleashed a whirlwind of change. It forced China to recognize the independence of Korea. Part of Manchuria was to be transferred to Japan, as well as Taiwan and the Pescadore islands. China had to pay a huge financial indemnity, equal to a year's worth of its public revenue. Among China's literate class – the provincial scholar-gentry on whose loyalty it depended – the Ch'ing dynasty suffered a devastating loss of prestige. To make matters worse, the imperial government was now forced to borrow abroad to help pay the indemnity and recoup its shattered military strength. Among the European powers, already alarmed by symptoms of impending collapse, this set off a race to lend China money, secured against the collateral of territorial and commercial rights. Russia led the way with a loan in return for Peking's permission to build a railway across Manchuria to its new eastern city at Vladivostok, along with an eighty-year lease to exploit the economic resources found along the line.[112] In 1898 Germany, Russia and Britain each acquired a naval base in North China near the maritime approach to

Peking. The great powers made agreements among themselves on the zones where they would have preference in the concessions for railways that the Ch'ing government now seemed poised to grant. In this feverish climate, the imperial court suddenly announced a long list of decrees to reform education, the army and the bureaucratic system along lines broadly similar to Meiji Japan. Before they could be implemented, the emperor's mother, the notorious dowager empress (Tz'u-hsi), staged a *coup d'état* and dismissed the reformers. Into the bitter atmosphere of political conflict burst the violent disorders aimed against Christian conversions in north-east China, the Boxer Rebellion of 1898–1900. With the complicity of the court, the Boxers (literally the 'Fists of Righteous Harmony', a fiercely anti-Christian movement) and their sympathizers occupied Peking, cut off the city, and besieged the foreign legations. If the aim was to enlist xenophobic mass feeling in defence of the dynasty (the Boxer slogan was 'Support the Ch'ing, exterminate the foreigner'), it backfired spectacularly. The foreign powers (the Europeans, Americans and Japanese) sent a large armed force (45,000 men) to rescue their diplomats and punish the Boxers. It seemed that China's rulers had blundered willy-nilly into an armed confrontation with the rest of the world.

The outcome inevitably was further humiliation. The dowager empress and her court fled the city. Another huge indemnity was imposed upon China. Under the terms of the Boxer settlement, the Chinese government was also forced to agree tariff reforms that would favour foreign trade. Browbeaten by the 'diplomatic body' – the collective weight of the foreign ambassadors – it seemed almost certain that Peking would yield railway concessions that extended foreign control deep into the Chinese interior. At the same time, there was every sign that the invading armies that had suppressed the Boxers would be slow to leave. More than two years later, despite a promise to go, Manchuria was occupied by nearly 150,000 Russian soldiers.[113] The momentum towards an economic share-out, or even a territorial scramble as the other powers reacted to Russia's aggrandizement, now seemed unstoppable.

Yet China escaped partition and the economic tutelage from which foreign commercial interests had hoped to profit. The reasons were complex. There was, in the first place, almost no chance that the great powers could agree on a share-out in the way they had just done in Africa. The Russians might have liked an empire in North China. But the British, whose commercial interest was much the largest, were determined not to agree on a split. This was partly because of the view in London that there should be 'no more Indias' – vast Asian possessions to defend and control – least of all a 'second India' with a Russian army on its doorstep.[114] That the Boxer crisis coincided with Britain's embarrassing difficulty in defeating the Boers, and growing war-weariness in public opinion at home, would have made any such scheme a form of political suicide. An undivided China, with a compliant government, was a much better prospect for both trade and investment. So the British and Americans (whose outlook was similar) encouraged Japan to oppose Russia's forward movement, and in 1902 the British concluded a regional pact, the Anglo-Japanese Alliance, promising military (i.e. naval) support if Japan came to blows with more than one great power – that is, if France, Russia's ally, were to enter the fray.[115] Neither France nor Germany, the remaining great powers with an interest in China, had sufficient incentive or adequate means to try to enforce a partition against London and Washington.

But it was not merely a question of what the imperialists wanted. Just as important was the tenacious resistance shown by the Chinese. It had always been difficult to break down the cohesion of Chinese authority, resting as it did on the self-interested loyalty of the scholar-gentry class to the dynastic regime that gave it employment. It might have been expected that the sequence of disasters since 1894–5 would have weakened the Ch'ing claim to the 'mandate of heaven'. And so it did. But the paradoxical result was a new political atmosphere much more fervently hostile to foreign interference. The 1890s had seen the rapid growth of a political movement that rejected the idea that Chinese unity depended on dynastic rule. Sun Yat-sen and his followers insisted that China was the nation state of the Han (Chinese-speaking) people and could be governed only by their chosen leaders.[116] The Ch'ing or Manchu dynasty was an alien tyranny.[117] Nor was Sun's nationalism the only form of Chinese political militancy. The new commercial life around the treaty-port towns created fresh social forms. Associations sprang up to serve the new urban middle class self-consciously creating a 'modern' Chinese society.[118]

Treaty-port industrialization produced a Chinese working class, a popular mass that could be used to intimidate foreign interests and enclaves. The provincial gentry, who had enjoyed increasing autonomy since the Taiping Rebellion, took over the role of defending China against the foreign threat from what increasingly seemed a corrupt and impotent dynasty. When Peking resumed the path of reform after the Boxer crisis, it played into their hands. The new army (modelled on those of Europe and Japan), the new bureaucracy, the new schools and colleges, and the abolition (in 1905) of the age-old examination system with its Confucian syllabus broke what remained of the old bonds of loyalty between the scholar-gentry class and the imperial centre. In the provinces, the scholar-gentry officials blocked every effort to use the railway concessions to extend foreign influence. 'Railways are making no progress in China,' the *Times* correspondent told his foreign editor.[119] To British financiers, like Charles Addis of the Hong Kong and Shanghai Bank, the Chinese demand for 'rights recovery' meant that, while foreigners could invest in the building of railways, they could not hope to control them.[120] When the Peking government, in a desperate effort to restore its dissolving authority and bolster its finances, proposed to take the new railways away from the provincial authorities (an imperial edict in May 1911 'nationalized' all trunk lines),[121] it triggered a revolt that brought down the dynasty. The end of Ch'ing rule in 1911 opened four decades of turmoil for the Chinese people. But it also signalled the end of the era when China's subjection to a *Eurocentric* world system might have been possible.

Japan had played a crucial role in checking the advance of European influence in East Asia after 1890. Ironically, it had been Japanese victory in the war of 1894–5 that had set off the race for bases and concessions among the European powers. But Japan did not play the part of 'little brother' to the Western imperialists. Japanese opinion remained deeply suspicious of European intentions, and deeply fearful of a combined Euro-American assault on Japan's precarious autonomy. The Europeans, remarked Ito Hirobumi on his 1882 tour of inquiry into Western constitutionalism, 'help and love their kith and kin and seek gradually to exterminate those who are remote and unrelated . . . The situation in the East is as fragile as a tower built of eggs . . . We have to do our utmost to strengthen and enlarge our armament.'[122] In *Datsua-ron* ('Leave Asia, enter Europe') (1885), the great prophet of modernization Yukichi Fukuzawa equated Asia with backwardness. But his aim was not that Japan should ally with the Western powers. Instead, Japan's manifest destiny was to assume the leadership of Asia to secure Asia's freedom. Indeed, Japanese thinking reflected a deep ambivalence towards China: contempt for Chinese 'backwardness'; desire for China's resources; fear that, without a pre-emptive move, much of China would fall under European control. There was a plenty of sympathy for Chinese nationalism, and many thousands of Chinese students spent time in Japan. In turn, Japan's striking success in reforming its government and keeping the foreign powers at bay made the Japanese model very influential in China.

Of course, Japan had done more than set an example. Since the 1870s, it had followed a policy of wary resistance to Russian expansion in North East Asia. By the 1890s this mutual suspicion was focused on Korea – in Japanese mythology 'the dagger pointing to our heart'. Russia deeply resented the rise of Japanese power there after 1895. A stand-off agreement in 1898 exchanging Russia's preponderance in Manchuria for Japan's in Korea broke down with the massing of Russian troops at the time of the Boxer Rebellion. When the Russians refused to withdraw from Manchuria or concede Japanese claims to pre-eminence in Korea (where Tokyo's control was far from secure), a resort to war became inevitable. The result was astonishing. When Russia's Baltic fleet sailed round the world to crush the new Japanese navy, it was annihilated in the Battle of Tshushima (May 1905) in the narrow seas between Korea and Japan. Soon afterwards a numerically inferior Japanese army defeated the Russians in the Battle of Mukden in the heart of Manchuria. In the peace treaty that followed, the Japanese took over Russia's bases on the Kwantung peninsula and its commercial concessions in southern Manchuria, and received the southern half of Sakhalin, the strategic island lying north of Hokkaido. The way was cleared for a protectorate over Korea, converted to full annexation in 1910. In a single blow, Japan had become the strongest naval and military power in the region; its consent would be needed before any outside power intervened in force.

Japanese strength should not be exaggerated. The struggle with Russia had tested Tokyo's financial resources to their limit. Japanese policymakers feared a Western backlash against their imperial expansion. 'Manchuria is not Japanese territory,' warned the veteran statesman Ito Hirobumi.[123] American antagonism became more explicit.[124] Nevertheless, Japan's ascent was remarkable. Japan had become a colonial power in East Asia. It had acquired a modern army and navy (most of the warships were built in Britain). It had defeated a great European state in war. It had cast off (by negotiation) the unequal treaties that granted Westerners extraterritorial privileges (China had to wait until 1943 to do likewise), and regained full tariff autonomy (in 1911). It had become a de facto great power, with a sphere of interest that was safely remote from the centre of gravity of its most likely rivals. Already it loomed over the Western commercial presence in China in a way that aroused mixed feelings of envy and alarm.[125] But how had Japan succeeded in this muted but highly effective challenge at a time when the European states were at the height of their power?

In part, perhaps, through Western observers persistently underestimating Japan's sources of strength. For obvious reasons, Japan was not well reported in the Western press, and even seasoned onlookers found Japanese politics very hard to explain. In Victorian Britain, it was Japanese quaintness that attracted most attention. Japan was an 'elf-land' ruled by a mikado (the Gilbert and Sullivan operetta opened in 1885).[126] A catastrophic miscalculation of Japanese strength and skill lay behind Russia's naval disaster in 1905. But Japan also enjoyed a unique geopolitical niche from which to defend its interests. It occupied a borderland zone between continental Eurasia and the Outer World. It lay at the furthest remove from the European maritime powers and European Russia, and was barely within reach of either. (Even in the steamship era, Tokyo was thirty-two days' sailing from the British ports, and lay 1,600 miles from the British base at Hong Kong, itself a far-flung outpost of British naval power.) From the 1870s, Japanese governments had skilfully exploited this benefit to consolidate their grip on the maritime and landward approaches to the Japanese archipelago. A treaty with Russia in 1875 had made the best of a bad job by exchanging Japan's claim to Sakhalin for the Kurile Islands. A few years later the Ryukyu Islands that stretched

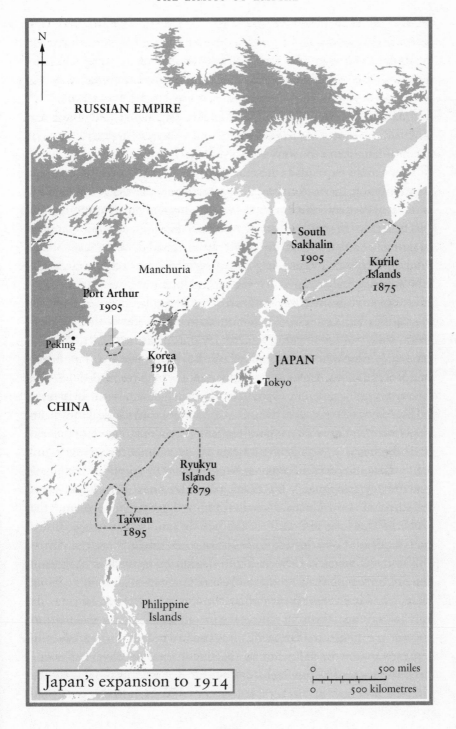

N

RUSSIAN EMPIRE

Manchuria

South
Sakhalin
1905

Kurile
Islands
1875

Port Arthur
1905

Peking

Korea
1910

JAPAN

Tokyo

CHINA

Ryukyu
Islands
1879

Taiwan
1895

Philippine
Islands

Japan's expansion to 1914

0   500 miles
0   500 kilometres

southward to Taiwan were absorbed into Japan.[127] Taiwan itself was a frontier society where Chinese control had never been thorough. It was one of the prizes the Japanese kept after their war with China in 1894–5. The penetration, occupation and eventual annexation of Korea, control of the Kwantung peninsula, and the recovery of southern Sakhalin completed the defensive ring surrounding the home islands. The risk of invasion – an age-old anxiety of Japanese governments – had been rendered almost null.

This would have counted for less had Japan's internal changes destabilized its politics, threatened foreign persons and property, and given scope for interference by the European great powers. The line-up of France, Russia and Germany to limit Japan's gains from China in 1895 showed that this threat could not be ignored. What was critical here was Japan's distinctive path of economic development. As we saw in a previous chapter, by the 1880s Japan was well on the way to competing successfully in international trade: not just in local specialities like raw silk, but in cotton yarn and cloth – perhaps the most widely traded manufactured product. But, crucially, Japan's trajectory towards industrialization did not depend upon heavy imports of capital, the most dangerous source of external dependence. Though 4 million people worked in industry by 1913, almost all were in workshops employing five people or fewer and using little or no machinery.[128] Very cheap labour (especially that of women), not mechanized efficiency, was Japan's ticket of entry into the global economy.[129] Imported technology was adapted and simplified, reducing both its cost and Japan's dependence upon foreign expertise and parts. And behind this industrial vanguard lay a huge agrarian sector that still employed the vast bulk of the population. As late as 1903, less than 8 per cent of Japanese were classified as urban.[130]

The result was a society in which foreign influence had been carefully filtered (not least by the barrier of language), and where social change had been sharply limited. In the countryside especially, the old rural hierarchy (requiring social inferiors to step aside for their betters and show exaggerated deference) was still in force. In more intellectual circles, support for political and cultural adaptation coexisted with a deep suspicion of *Oshu-shugi* – Europeanness – with its overt materialism, social divisions and cultural arrogance. Official attitudes to Christianity were also hostile. Mistrust of the foreign remained deeply ingrained. In a famous incident, the future Tsar Nicholas of Russia, while visiting Japan in 1891, was attacked and wounded by a policeman caught up, so he thought, in a Russian invasion. In such a climate, it is not difficult to see why the samurai statesmen of the Meiji era were able to impose such an authoritarian version of the modern state. The 1889 constitution, intended to crown Japan's acquisition of Western-style sovereignty, entrenched the power of the Satsuma–Choshu oligarchs, the *genro* or elders who chose the cabinet. Barely 1 per cent of the population had the vote. The Diet, or parliament, could not change the government. Control of the army and navy was carefully separated from the civilian ministers. An upper 'House of Peers' was filled with appointees from Satsuma and Choshu. And, to clothe this artful distribution of power with an aura of sanctity, it was shrewdly presented as the loyal application of 'imperial right'. The emperor and 'emperor-worship' became the focus of a patriotic cult to be promoted in schools alongside Western learning.

By these means, Japanese leaders had been able to fashion a uniquely favourable trajectory with which to enter a West-dominated world. But they were not invincible. The war against Russia forced them to turn to lenders abroad. The patriotic emotions it roused at home threatened the oligarchic tenor of Japanese politics. With its new burden of debt, the Japanese economy lurched into deficit. It risked the fate of other semi-industrial economies in the same position: monetary contraction (Japan was on the gold standard), a reduced demand for its domestic manufactures, and increased dependence upon raw-material exports.[131] Nor was the victory of 1905 secure beyond doubt. Russia was doubling the Trans-Siberian Railway, the iron artery of its eastern empire. In China, meanwhile, Yuan Shih-k'ai, a protégé of Li Hung-chang and an adversary of Japan since his days as China's emissary in Korea in 1884, had imposed his control as a 'strongman' president. By late 1913 he enjoyed the support of the leading Western powers as an effective ruler with whom to do business, a status that Japan had grudgingly to accept.[132] But timing is everything. Before these developments could undermine Japan's newfound regional pre-eminence, the European war upset all predictions.

*

East Asia was not the only 'unfinished business' of a Europe-centred global colonialism. In the Middle East, the Ottoman Empire had proved surprisingly resilient, despite its near-catastrophe in 1875–8. Sultan Abdul Hamid II pressed ahead with Ottoman self-strengthening, exploiting the great powers' inability to agree on a partition that might have felled his authority. State power grew wider and reached deeper. Schools and gendarmes carried it into the localities. An expanding bureaucracy drew in local elites.[133] Ottoman rule was gradually made more effective in the Arab provinces.[134] The Hejaz Railway between Aleppo and Medina tightened Ottoman control over the Red Sea coast and the great centres of pilgrimage. Along the 'Arab shore' of the Persian Gulf, Ottoman forces made their presence felt in the region of El Hasa, between Kuwait and Bahrein (where British influence was growing). Meanwhile the Ottoman economy was benefiting from the booming trade in raw materials after 1896.[135] Although modern mechanized factories were few and far between, the manufacture of cottons and carpets also grew steadily.[136]

As a purely Asian state, the Ottoman Empire might have been able to combine its diplomatic leverage and cultural cohesion to win the time it needed to build a stronger state structure and a stronger economy. But in its western half it was dangerously exposed to the unremitting pressure of local European nationalisms, directly expressed as religious and ethnic struggle. After 1878 the Ottomans had clung on to a substantial part of their European empire. Here, in Albania, Kosovo, Macedonia, Rumelia and Thrace, over half the population was Muslim.[137] But every attempt to consolidate Ottoman authority was bound to harden ethnic and religious divisions and redouble the antagonism of the subject peoples, both Christian and Muslim. Thus Muslim Albanians fiercely resisted their threatened loss of local autonomy. In the late 1890s, ethnic violence in Crete embroiled the Ottomans in war with Greece and, after great-power intervention, brought the practical end of their rule on the island. By 1908 it seemed that local revolt and foreign interference had brought the key region of Macedonia (the strategic pivot of Ottoman Europe) to the verge of independence. To militant 'Young Turks' in the Ottoman army and bureaucracy, 'Macedonia's independence means the loss of half of the Ottoman Empire and . . . its complete annihilation.'

It would drive the Ottoman frontier back to Constantinople, and force the capital out of Europe. 'The Macedonian Question is the Question of the Existence of the Turks.'[138] It was no coincidence that the political coup of 1908 to sideline the sultan and rebuild the empire round an ethnic Turkish core was launched from Salonica. In the short term at least, it did little good. Later that year, Bosnia (technically still an Ottoman territory) was annexed unilaterally by Austria–Hungary. By 1911 the Ottomans were at war with Italy in a hopeless struggle to keep control of Libya. The following year, Bulgaria, Serbia, Greece and Montenegro seized the chance to liquidate what remained of the Ottoman Europe. After a second war between the victor states, a fragile peace settled over the Balkans. The Ottoman government had kept control of the Straits (the site of its imperial capital). But its shattered prestige and signs of resistance in the Arab provinces to 'Turkification' made it seem more dependent than ever on the twists and turns of great-power diplomacy if it was to escape dissection.

By 1914, Iran (still usually called Persia) seemed still closer to the brink. Even under a forceful shah like Nasir al-Din, adept at managing the tribal, linguistic, religious and social divisions that seamed Iranian society, the goal of strengthening the state had been elusive. Granting foreign concessions to raise more revenue was deeply unpopular with bazaar merchants and *ulama*, the commercial and religious elites. After Nasir was murdered in 1896, his successor as shah, Muzaffar al-Din, pursued the search for new funds with even more urgency. He appointed a Belgian to take charge of the customs, the main source of state revenue. A large loan was contracted with Russia, secured on the customs revenues of the Caspian ports. A concession was granted to a British prospector searching for oil at the head of the Gulf: this was the D'Arcy concession, out of which grew the Anglo-Persian Oil Company, the parent of BP. But the shah was now being caught in a vice. As foreign interests grew larger, so did foreign influence. As more Iranians travelled abroad, or had contact with Europe, liberal, nationalist and even socialist ideas began to circulate among the elite. An extraordinary florescence of political activity in clubs and societies began to take shape. When Russia was plunged into revolutionary turmoil in 1905, choking off the main outlet for Iranian trade and creating commercial panic, a discontented elite joined forces with the merchants and clerics and the khans of the great Bakhtiari tribe to bring down the shah in the constitutional revolution of 1906.[139]

The results were dismaying. Although the shah was forced to accept the new constitution (which enshrined Shia Islam as the state religion, as well as creating a parliament), he did so on sufferance. When he staged a coup to recover his power, it badly misfired. But, although the constitution was saved, the damage was done. As rival factions struggled to control the government, the power of the centre began to dissolve. Provincial governors and tribal leaders, with their private armies, became the real source of authority. 'In modern Persia,' a Qashqai tribesman told a British consul, 'the rifle is the sceptre and ... every rifleman is a shah.'[140] It was only a short step to seek the protection of the chief foreign powers. After 1907, when Russia and Britain agreed to divide Iran between them into three spheres of influence – one Russian, one neutral, one British – this trend became stronger. Russian troops intervened in the north to stop the fighting between the shah's supporters and foes. In 1911 they forced the dismissal of the American expert hired to restore Iran's finances to order. Instead, under Russian protection, the provincial authorities diverted taxation and secured practical freedom from their nominal masters in Tehran. On the eve of the First World War, the British angrily complained that northern Iran had become a Russian 'political protectorate', enforced by a garrison of 17,000 men. 'Northern Persia was being governed as Russian province,' said the British ambassador.[141] The reply from St Petersburg was coldly dismissive. The Tehran government was made up of demagogues, with 'ultra-nationalist ideas not in accordance with the cultural or ethical level of these spheres'.[142]

Had Iran been strangled, as the dismissed American expert alleged?[143] Almost, but not quite. Despite the drastic decentralization of power that the revolution had brought, and which the foreign presence encouraged, it seems likely that the sense of Iran's national identity had actually been strengthened since the 1890s among the secular educated class as well as the clerics. Yet it was hard to see how an escape could be made from the virtual partition being imposed by the Russians with British complicity. Unless, that is, something happened to disturb the geopolitical setting and slacken the grip that the outside powers had fixed on the country.

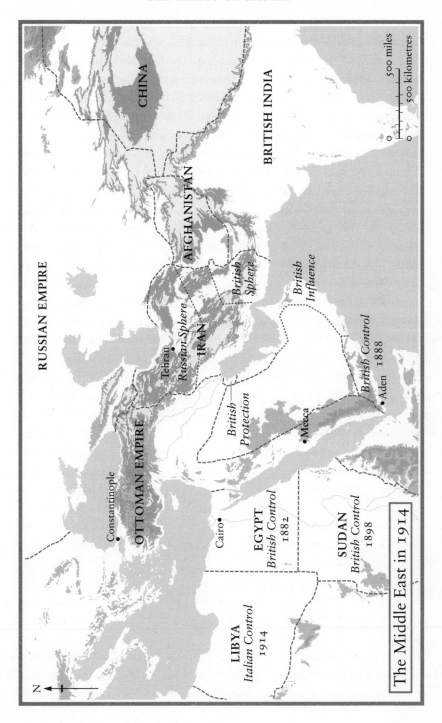

The Middle East in 1914

RUSSIAN EMPIRE

CHINA

BRITISH INDIA

AFGHANISTAN

OTTOMAN EMPIRE

Constantinople

IRAN

Tehran
Russian Sphere

British Sphere

British Influence

British Control 1888

Aden

British Protection

Meeca

Cairo

EGYPT
British Control
1882

LIBYA
Italian Control
1914

SUDAN
British Control
1898

N

500 miles

500 kilometres

These conditions in the 'Near East' (the European name for a vast region that also included Iran) and East Asia were the clearest evidence that a global order under the management of the European great powers, and designed to serve their imperial interests, remained at best a work in progress. In the Outer World beyond Eurasia, the Europeans had partitioned with gusto. Here it had proved relatively easy to attach – by coercion or cooperation – less-developed economies to the commercial and industrial heartland of the North Atlantic basin. Here too they had imposed their rule and fashioned 'neo-Europes' in an astonishing burst of demographic imperialism. But in the 'Old World' of Eurasia it had proved much harder to absorb Asian states and cultures into a European 'system', or even to agree upon a colonial share-out. This was the vast uneasy borderland of Europe's global colonialism. If the Europeans fell out among themselves, and their 'world economy' lost its magnetic power, they might face a rebellion against their worldwide pre-eminence. This test of their power was not long in coming.

7

Towards the Crisis of the World, 1914–1942

7. Gandhi's 'salt march' to the sea, 1930

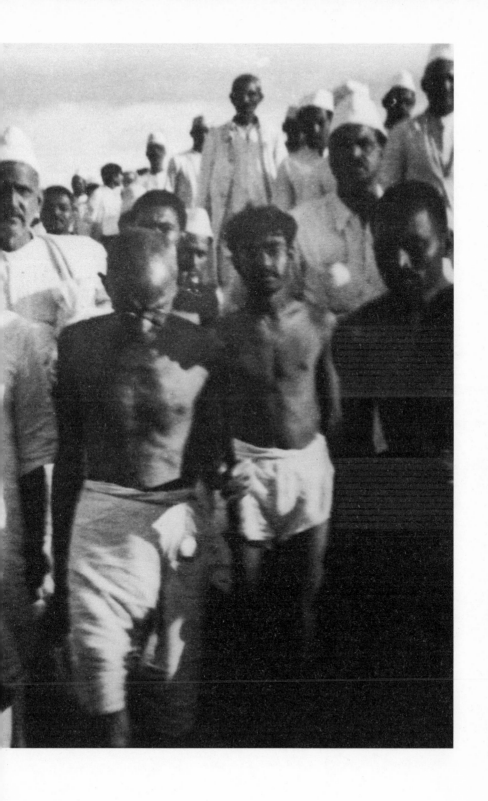

AN AGE OF DISORDER

Before 1914 there had been warning signs that a global imperial order offered no guarantee of universal peace and prosperity. East Asia's future as a sphere of Western influence was at best uncertain. The European great powers had squabbled irritably over the share-out of territory and influence in North Africa and the Middle East. The size and scale of the American economy raised awkward questions over how far American interests could be accommodated in a global economy centred on London and partitioned spatially between the European colonial powers. The frantic pace at which international trade and investment had been growing seemed to be easing off. Social unrest in Europe's industrial economies threatened to clip the wings of the great-power governments and to rein in their global ambitions and strategies. But, before the influence of any of these changes could be felt internationally, world politics were transformed by a volcanic explosion, beginning in Europe but rapidly spreading to engulf every important state across the breadth of Eurasia.

The First World War brought a violent end to the experiment in more or less cooperative imperialism among the six great powers (Britain, Russia, Germany, France, the United States and Japan). It reopened the question of a global partition half settled half shelved before 1914. It advanced a new conception of international society, theoretically (if not practically) at odds with the ever-wider extension of colonial rule. It opened a huge ideological fissure between one old imperial power, Russia, and the other great powers. It drove a massive wedge into the international economy: closing off trade routes, blocking currencies and payments, creating artificial shortages and siege-type economies. It forced a mobilization of colonial resources, including manpower, that bred a sharp reaction among colonial peoples, resentful of new burdens and rules that broke the old 'bargain' of colonial politics. It tore apart the myth of Europe's uniquely progressive culture, loosening the grip of older cultural elites and the ideas they had championed.

It was hardly surprising that there was no post-war return to pre-war 'normality'. There was no broad agreement on the rules of international order. The annexations and treaties that formed the 'legal' basis of the colonial system and its semi-colonial extensions in China and elsewhere were fiercely repudiated by the Bolshevik legatees of the tsarist empire. The United States rejected membership of the new League of Nations, a victors' club to police the post-war settlement. The economic recovery of Europe was heavily delayed by the bitter disputes over reparations for war damage. Europe's social and political stability suffered badly in consequence. Across much of Eurasia – in the Caucasus, Central Asia, the Middle East and parts of East Asia – the question of who would rule where had to be decided more by force, or the threat of it, than by diplomacy. In the colonial empires (the British Empire especially), nationalist demands for independence or self-rule showed unprecedented tenacity. Sinn Fein in Ireland, the Wafd movement in Egypt, and Gandhi's great 'non-cooperation' campaign in India (1920–22), with its large Muslim component, posed a ferocious challenge to British authority and exposed the limits of coercion as a method of rule. The mood of revolt was not simply political. There and elsewhere (most notably in China) it was also expressed in the demand for new cultures, authentically local but aimed (by mass consumption) to bind leaders and people in more intense solidarity against the outside (and imperial) world.

The massive aftershocks of the First World War had a collective significance. They marked the breakdown of the *ancien régime* across Eurasia. The war had become a graveyard of empires, European and Asian. The Hohenzollerns, the Habsburgs and the Romanovs had been dethroned (or worse) and their domains broken up. The Ottoman Empire had followed in their wake. The ill-fated attempt to revive Ch'ing imperial rule under a parvenu dynast collapsed in 1916. The vast centre of the world became a political cockpit in which movements, ideologies, religions, nationalities and interests struggled to build a new system of states, and the imperial powers (or what remained of them) manoeuvred to protect their claims and privileges. By the late 1920s an uneasy truce had settled over many of these conflicts. It did not last long. With the political fallout of the great depression after 1930, the post-war order dissolved in acrimony. By the middle of the decade it was openly flouted by the virulent new imperialisms of Germany, Italy and Japan – far more aggressive in style and far less modest in ambition than their European forerunners of the 1880s and '90s. Between 1937 and 1942 they set in motion a vast Eurasian crisis. In the global Armageddon that followed, it seemed almost inevitable that, whoever they might be, the winners would have no choice but to fashion a new world order.

WAR WITHOUT END?

The most vital prop of Europe's primacy in Eurasia, and of the powerful position of the great European states in the Outer World beyond, had been their collective determination not to fight each other. It had been this and the Atlantic peace between Europe and the Americas that had allowed the rapid growth of international trade, the steady extension of European influence and authority, and the ironic achievement of the African partition. The reluctance of European governments to upset their continental balance of power and risk the social and political upheaval that a general war would bring had restrained their pursuit of national and imperial advantage. Even where their interests seemed deeply engaged (as in the Ottoman Empire), or economic opportunities seemed especially promising (as in China), they acquiesced in makeshift arrangements that prolonged the old local regime rather than face the consequences of a 'final solution' by partition or conquest. Of course, to many observers, both then and subsequently, this untidy pattern seemed inherently unstable. Sooner or later an intense local crisis would become unmanageable by these hand-to-mouth methods. The balance of strength between the rival great powers might shift just enough to lessen their mutual restraint and create a sense of impatience with the existing share-out of spheres. The influence of lobbies, masquerading as 'public opinion' and projected through newspapers, threatened the cosmopolitan tradition of 'old' diplomacy, with its aristocratic disdain for the interests of mere 'business'. The imperial monarchies of Central and Eastern Europe, ruling uneasily over multi-ethnic empires (even the German Empire contained several million Poles), might be dangerously prone to treat dynastic prestige (rather than material interests) as a reason for war and be all too susceptible to the militarist ethos of their courts and armies.[1] Even the means that the great powers had used to deter each other's aggression – the build-up of armaments – might be the trigger for war if fear of future weakness encouraged a pre-emptive attack.

But up to 1914 the great European powers' competition in Africa, the Pacific, East Asia and the Middle East (including the Asian parts of the Ottoman and Iranian empires) showed little sign of creating an uncontrollable vortex of military conflict. In turn, this acted as a strong deterrent upon further Japanese expansion in North East Asia at the expense of either China or Russia. The critical breakdown of great-power relations occurred not over the powers' ambitions in the extra-European world but over their balance of influence in Europe's Balkan backyard. In reality, of course, the volatile politics of the Balkans arose directly from the progressive failure of the Ottoman Empire to contain the militant nationalisms of its Christian subjects. In the terrible crisis of 1911–13, the Ottomans were assailed first by the Italians (who seized modern Libya and parts of the Dodecanese) and then by a coalition of Serbia, Greece and Bulgaria which all but expelled the empire from Europe – the Turks clung on to a small part of Thrace. Unlike in previous crises, the great powers failed to prop up a vestige of Ottoman rule in Europe. The result was not to settle the politics of the region – indeed, the Balkan states promptly fought a second internecine war to divide the spoils. It merely posed much more starkly than before the question of which outside power would predominate there. For no one supposed that the Balkan governments could be trusted to honour their frontiers, restrain their militants, suppress inter-ethnic conflicts, or resist the temptation to exploit great-power intrigues for local advantage.

The shocking feature (as it seems in retrospect) was the failure of the great powers to agree on a peaceful partition of spheres in the way so familiar in their extra-European diplomacy. Yet it was never going to be easy to exert indirect control over an inaccessible region steeped in a tradition of localized ethnic violence, where governments were weak and the land awash with weapons. It was also the case that the geopolitical stakes in the Balkans seemed higher than anywhere else in Eurasia, let alone the Outer World. It was easy to imagine that a setback here might do irreparable damage to the long-term strategic interests (and hence political cohesion) of either Russia or Austria–Hungary – and by extension to the European alliances of which they were part. If the Balkans were consolidated as a virtual protectorate of the Habsburg monarchy and its great northern ally, then Austro-German influence would soon be supreme at the Straits as well, where a Turkish coup of 1913 had strengthened ties with Berlin. Germany and Austria–Hungary would have scored a smashing victory without firing a shot. A great swathe of their client states would fence Russia in, grasp its commercial windpipe between the Black Sea and the Mediterranean, and put out of reach for ever the cherished Russian goal of ruling Constantinople (today's Istanbul). The prestige of the Romanovs would fall like a stone. Alternatively, if the much-enlarged Serbia was allowed to foment anti-Habsburg nationalism among the monarchy's South Slavs with the protection of Russia, the triangular geometry of Austria–Hungary's politics (the mutual antagonisms of its Germans, Magyars and Slavs) might break up in chaos.[2] A vast zone of weakness in Eastern and Central Europe would wreck the balance of power and expose a weakened Germany to the darkest nightmare of strategic encirclement. The implications were breathtaking. The extraordinary events of 1911–13 had extended the old Balkan fault line in great-power diplomacy into the heart of Europe and drawn Asia Minor into the earthquake zone.

It would thus have required exceptional skill and goodwill to prevent the murder of the Habsburg heir by a Serb assassin in Bosnia from provoking an armed confrontation between the great powers. The July Crisis in 1914 grew out of the Austrian demand that, to make amends for hosting the assassin's secret society, the Serbs accept Austrian supervision of their internal security. Serbian rejection of this semi-colonial status relied on the diplomatic support of Russia. In 1908–9 the Russians had been forced into a humiliating climbdown after challenging the Austrian annexation of Bosnia. But in 1914 they could not back away without suffering a huge geopolitical defeat, with alarming domestic repercussions. Nor did they do so. As the Russians and Austrians began to mobilize their armies to show they meant business, the immediate question was whether the other European great powers would insist on a conference to settle the matter.

This was the crucial stage of the crisis. It was now that the Germans were forced to show their hand. Without their unqualified backing, the Vienna government – facing a war on two fronts, against Serbia and Russia – might be forced to retreat and let the Serbs escape. Russia's Balkan influence would recover sharply. Its growing military strength, to which German planners attached an exaggerated importance (Russia's 'grand programme' was expected to create an army three times as big as Germany's by 1917),[3] would further tilt the balance of power along the Balkan fault line. To stiffen the resolve of their weaker partner, the Germans gave Vienna carte blanche, effectively vetoing a conference. But the logic of this was to widen the crisis and reduce the chances of peace. For, if Germany was forced into a war against Russia, its strategic plan required that France, Russia's ally, should be defeated first or effectively neutralized. Only then could the full weight of German military power be safely deployed in the vast spaces of the east. To intimidate France and isolate Russia, Germany threatened the neutrality of Belgium (the invasion route to Paris) and demanded a promise from the British not to take sides. In little more than a month, Austria's attempt to coerce a disorderly Balkan state had grown into Germany's claim for a Europe-wide hegemony. It required little imagination to foresee the results if the Franco-Russian alliance broke up (the inevitable consequence of French neutrality) and the Anglo-French entente became a dead letter. With the British rejection of the German demand, an all-out European war became practically certain.[4]

The July Crisis revealed that the Achilles heel of Europe's global primacy was the underdevelopment of the European states system. It was Europe's sudden expansion on its Balkan doorstep, the brittle structure of its multinational empires, and the chaotic politics of its smallest states that turned a political murder into a general war. The European balance of power was unable to cope with the final collapse of Ottoman rule in the Balkans. To a shrewd insider just before the war, it seemed obvious enough that international peace must depend on the judgement and skill of statesmen and diplomats. Kurt Riezler (the private secretary of the German chancellor, Bethmann-Hollweg) argued that, in a closely interlocked world, the price of war was almost always too high. But he also assumed that states were bound to behave in an assertive way just because their interests had become so entangled (splendid aloofness was no longer an option), and to build up armaments to show their resolve. In the game of nations, it was often necessary to bluff: it was 'over-bluffing' that brought on the risk of war.[5] Riezler's theory was a persuasive account of great-power diplomacy since the 1870s. What it failed to predict was a European 'super-crisis', in which both sides believed that a compromise solution would mean a major defeat, and when (worse still) both sides thought that they had a good chance of winning. Still less did it allow for the effects of myopia: the inability of decision-makers to foresee all the ramifying consequences of a general war.

Indeed, the European war between the Triple Entente of Russia, France and Britain and the Central Powers (Germany and Austria–Hungary) quickly became global. At the end of October 1914 the Ottoman Empire (fearful of the results of an Entente victory) joined the Central Powers. That spread the war to the Caucasus, the Sinai border with British-ruled Egypt, and the Persian Gulf, then navally speaking a British lake. In East Asia, Japan joined the war as an ally of Britain, but with the obvious motive of seizing the Germans' Chinese base at Kiao-chao and their commercial rights in the nearby province of Shantung (Shandong). In West, East and South West Africa, colonial wars broke out between the British, French and Belgians on one side and the Germans on the other. And the war was oceanic. German surface-raiders and (increasingly) submarines waged war on the sea lanes radiating out from Britain, to choke off the supply of foodstuffs, raw materials and munitions on which the British war effort depended. The British in turn waged naval war by blockade to squeeze the German economy, and deny it overseas sources of food and strategic materials. Here was the proof that, with a world economy and a single system of world politics, there was no escape from the fallout of war, wherever it started.

But if Europe's war had become global, it had to be settled within Europe itself. By the end of 1915 an outright victory for either side seemed very unlikely. In the western war, the Germans had rapidly occupied parts of Belgium and France. The inconclusive campaigns of 1915 showed that, with the resort to trench warfare, a stalemate had set in. The French and British could not drive the Germans out; the

Germans in turn could not force them to give in. In the eastern war there was a similar pattern. By September 1915 the German and Austrian armies had forced the Russians back to a defensive line deep inside their empire (it ran from Riga to Czernowitz) and occupied a vast frontier zone that they called 'Ober-Ost'.[6] They swallowed Serbia, and, with Bulgarian help, controlled a wide Balkan corridor towards the Ottoman Empire. Yet without victory in the west they could hardly hope to muster all the men and materiel to overcome Russia, with its bottomless pit of military manpower. In the Entente camp, the resilience of the Ottomans in Anatolia, Mesopotamia and Palestine – and, worse still, at Gallipoli – was a crushing disappointment. The soft underbelly of the Central Powers proved as hard as nails. Yet neither side drew the conclusion that the war had confirmed a balance of military power. Neither side accepted the case that a diplomatic solution was necessary. Instead, both pinned their hopes on raising the odds: mobilizing more men and resources to achieve the break-through or to wear down the enemy by a war of attrition. Both assumed tacitly that the rupture of war had revealed the bankruptcy of the pre-war order.

As a result, the year 1916 marked the beginning of a new phase in the war, and, as it turned out, a new phase in world history. The commitment to win whatever the cost lay behind the terrible slaughter at Verdun, on the Somme, and in Brusilov's offensive on the eastern front, where Russia lost more than a million men. As the losses mounted, the preconditions for peace in a post-war world became more and more drastic. Britain, France and Russia agreed to partition the Ottoman Empire. The break-up of Austria–Hungary into nation states became an Allied war aim. The reconstruction of Germany to obliterate its 'militarism' was the best guarantee of 'never again'. On the German side, it was the Russian 'menace' that had caused all the trouble. The final destruction of the tsarist empire became the minimum needed for post-war security. In Germany, France and Britain, 1916–17 brought new leaders to power, committed to fight the war to a finish. But, long before there was any question of peace, the whole landscape of power was reshaped by the strains of fighting a total war. Germany's resort to unrestricted use of submarine war-fare, in a desperate effort to shorten the war, was the catalyst for the entry of the United States in April 1917. Any peace settlement would now have to square the territorial aims of the European powers with the American demand for an 'open door' to trade and American antagonism to European-style empires at home and abroad. But most dramatic of all was the sudden collapse of the Russian monarchy.

Of all the great powers, Russian had been the least well equipped for a total war. It lacked the industrial strength to sustain its vast armies. It needed the help of its Western allies. But there lay the problem. With the Straits closed by Turkey, the only accessible ports through which aid could be sent were Archangel in the far north and Vladivostok in the far east, both far from ideal. Much of it piled up uselessly. Even if more had been sent, it is doubtful whether it would have made any difference. Russia's railway system could not cope with the strain of supplying the fronts, or transporting the food and fuel that were needed to keep its war economy going. In all the countries at war, the combination of hardship, anxiety and dissatis-faction with leaders who failed to bring victory created political ten-sion. Russia's military failure – its huge losses of manpower, the vast loss of territory – was overwhelming. The desperate shortages in the main industrial cities – above all in Petrograd, the imperial capital – destroyed civilian morale and factory discipline. Setbacks on this scale would have shaken any government. But the tsarist regime was uniquely vulnerable. It had no political leader to direct the government with any shred of claim to popular backing. Its ministers were bureau-crats, answerable to the tsar, as much each other's rivals as political colleagues. The elected Duma could denounce and abuse, but had no power to remove them. The tsarist court was widely suspected of harbouring defeatists or traitors. As discontent mounted, the only available recourse was repression. The tsar's authority rested on police control of the crowd and (ultimately) the loyalty of the army. In the spring of 1917, amid a wave of popular disturbance in Petrograd, both broke down. It took barely a week to force the tsar's abdication and the end of a monarchy that was a thousand years old. The rising, remarked an English historian who spent the war in Russia, 'had been unorganized and elemental. It was if a corpse had lain on top of a passive people till with a single push from below it had rolled away of itself.'[7]

It seemed at first as if the new Russian state, with leaders answerable to the Duma, would have the patriotic drive, the public support and the political energy to rekindle the war effort and resume the offensive. But Russia's war economy was too badly damaged, and the organized discontent of the industrial workforce too deeply rooted, for any quick recovery. Perhaps only a German collapse could have saved the post-tsarist liberal state. After little more than six months it faced the same combination of popular discontent, economic disaster and military failure, but without the machine of repression on which the tsars had relied. Peasant hardship and land hunger dissolved the old rural order as the gentry were forced out (or murdered) and their estates divided up. (By 1914, peasant communities or individuals already owned three-quarters of arable land, and the consolidation of property in the hands of richer peasants may have sharpened the sense of land shortage.)[8] The Bolshevik coup in October 1917 brought to power a revolutionary government who knew that their own survival meant Russia's leaving the war. Indeed, it was their promise of peace and their apparent support for the peasants' revolt that ensured a precarious triumph in the struggle for power.

The price was paid in March 1918 at the town of Brest-Litovsk, where the peace treaty was signed. To buy peace from the Germans, the Bolsheviks were forced into concessions on a staggering scale. Most of western Russia, including Poland, the Baltic provinces and modern Belarus, had to be given up. The great salient that had made Russia a great power in Europe was simply wrenched away. But just as extraordinary was the loss of the Ukraine, where the invading Germans had promoted a separatist regime, the Rada. Russia's great grain basket (source of much of its export earnings before the war), its main source of coal, and its prime industrial centres were now controlled by a German client state. Indeed, the Brest-Litovsk treaty seemed only the prologue to a larger drama. German military power was set to extend all round the Black Sea, 'liberating' Russia's colonial territories in the Caucasus and perhaps beyond the Caspian. And, as civil war brewed in Russia's remaining lands, the grip of the centre on its old imperial periphery in Central Asia and the Far East provinces looked certain to fail. One great rivet that had clamped Eurasia together was breaking in half.

In fact the implosion of Russia opened the door to a vast reordering of the whole Eurasian land mass. Its immediate effect was to allow the Germans to transfer men from the east to knock out France and Britain before American help could become decisive. In the great offensive of March–June 1918, they came very close. As the armies of the Entente reeled under the blow, it seemed in London as if a catastrophic change in the shape of the war was about to unfold. France and Italy (after the disaster at Caporetto, in October 1917, when the Italian armies were thrown back by the Austrians) were on the verge of defeat. That would mean British (and American) withdrawal from the European mainland, where German control would become complete. What remained of Russia would be of no account: it is unlikely that the Bolshevik regime would have lasted long if Germany had won the war. With their Ottoman ally, and their newfound friends in the Ukraine and the Caucasus, the Germans would become the dominant power in the Near and Middle East. They would make Iran a client, and advance on the Gulf. British India would be in their sights. Nor could London be sure that, in this appalling scenario, its Japanese ally would not change sides, to protect the wartime gains it had made in North East Asia. Even if peace was made, under these conditions it was bound to be followed by a cold imperial war. So exposed in Europe, Britain would become much more dependent on its American ally. The 'Southern British World' (a contemporary phrase in British grand strategy) in Africa, India and Australasia would have to become a huge armed camp for an indefinite time, with unforeseeable consequences for its political future.[9]

The only safeguard against the global impact of German domination of Europe, reasoned British leaders, was to redouble efforts to control the crossroads of Eurasia in the Middle East. From March 1918, small British forces were dispatched to rally the resistance of the former Russian dependencies in the Caucasus and Central Asia against the German–Ottoman alliance. Another British unit, 'Norperforce', was sent to 'North Persia', to ensure a sympathetic regime in Tehran. A great new offensive was planned against the Ottoman army in Palestine as soon as men could be spared from the western front and new troops be raised in India. The absolute necessity to break up the Ottoman Empire and to impose a form of British paramountcy

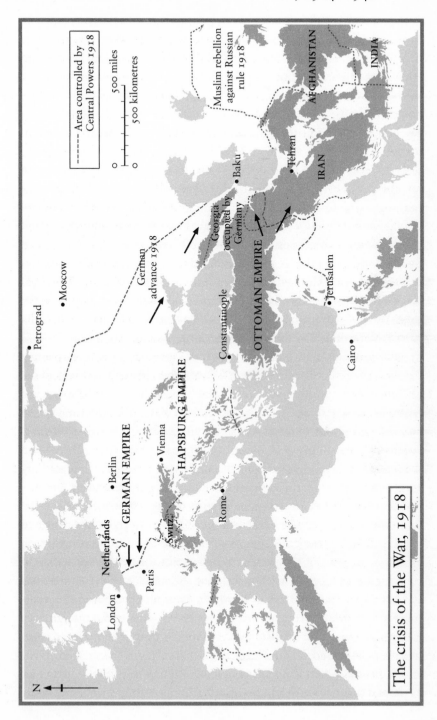

The crisis of the War, 1918

across the vast land area between Afghanistan and Greece became a radical new element in British foreign policy, inconceivable before 1914.[10] A British-controlled Middle East would join partitioned Africa as a dependant of Europe – though a Europe divided (as still seemed likely as late as July 1918) between a continental hegemon and an embattled offshore power. But before the realism of this amazing plan could be properly tested, the military tide began to turn in the west.

The Germans had tried to break the stalemate of trench war with an all-out offensive. But, like the British and French in 1916–17, they found it hard to maintain their momentum in a pattern of warfare that favoured defence. Despite an early breakthrough that nearly cut the Anglo-French armies in half, their advance had run out of steam by the middle of June. A well-organized counteroffensive began driving them back. The last hope of German victory before American manpower could make itself felt began to fade away. After heavy losses in early August, and the 'black day of the German army', the 'silent dictatorship' of Hindenburg and Ludendorff began to lose its nerve. Amid signs of social unrest at home, and with worsening news on the Balkan and Palestine fronts (where Allenby destroyed the Ottoman army at Megiddo), it decided to ask for an armistice. The Allied side, where the French and British had to count the cost of continuing the war in terms of an ever-increasing American influence, lacked the will to press on for an outright German surrender. When the armistice came, on 11 November, the German front line still lay across Belgium. The invasion of Germany would have taken the war into a further year. Here lay the origins of the pervasive myth of the inter-war years: that the German army had not been beaten, but had been 'stabbed in the back' by socialist treachery in domestic politics. Here lay the root of the persistent belief that the peace that followed took no account of the military balance sheet and was a cruel injustice to Germany's status as one of Europe's great powers. Because of that, the huge military struggle on the western front turned out to have settled nothing. The armistice was precisely that: a temporary truce in Europe's second Thirty Years War.

The peace conference that assembled in Paris in January 1919 had as its first priority drawing up the terms of a treaty between Germany and the four-power coalition that had forced it to abandon the war. These included the issue of Germany's boundaries, the demand for reparations for wartime damage, and (to justify reparations) an admission of German guilt for having started the conflict. But there was a huge extra agenda. The most pressing item was a new states system for Eastern, Central and South East Europe to replace the shattered imperial order of Romanovs, Habsburgs and Hohenzollerns. No less urgent was the political future of the former Ottoman Empire, and of the old tsarist borderlands in the Caucasus and Central Asia with their mixed populations of Christians and Muslims. In East Asia, where China had entered the war on the side of the Allies in 1917, the peacemakers were faced with the claims of Japan to the German sphere in Shantung (fiercely opposed in China). There was the awkward fact of Japan's growing power on the North East Asian mainland, where it had occupied Vladivostok in April 1918 – ostensibly as part of the Allied intervention to keep Russia from succumbing to German control. Both formed part of the larger question of whether Japan would be allowed to dominate post-imperial China. Taken together, this amounted to a programme for the political reconstruction of almost all of Eurasia. Compared with this, deciding which of the victor powers was to administer the Pacific and African colonies taken away from Germany, and under what terms, seemed a tiresome detail. Indeed, it was much the easiest issue to settle.[11]

On the greater issues, the odds against agreement were appallingly high. Quite apart from the rivalry of the victor powers, peacemaking was complicated by colossal uncertainties. Who would win the civil war between Reds and Whites that was now raging in Russia? Would Russia's revolutionary politics spread to the rest of Europe? Would the new nation states envisaged for Europe agree on their frontiers? Could the ethnic claims of Turks, Greeks, Armenians, Arabs and Jews be reconciled with each other and with the wartime agreements to partition the Ottoman Empire between Britain, France and Italy? What would happen if they could not? And who on the ground would emerge in control of Russia's former Asian empire? Had the victor powers enjoyed overwhelming military power and used it in unison they might have hoped to impose their favoured solutions (had they been able to agree on them). The reality was different. Demobilization was swift and war-weariness strong. Restless opinion at home made consistent policy hard. The result was a climate almost made for upheaval. On the one hand, local leaders had every incentive to recruit local armies and force through local solutions, presenting a fait accompli to faraway peacemakers and their underpowered agents. On the other, the new ideology of national self-determination, eagerly propagated as a weapon of war by the British and the Americans and upheld as the leitmotif of the peace conference in Paris, dangled hope of recognition to any plausible nationalism. Amid ample signs on all sides that Eurasia's old imperial order had been washed away by the flux of war, it was hardly surprising that revolutionary symptoms now appeared almost everywhere.

REVOLUTIONS AND EMPIRES

By March 1919 a general crisis of European control was well under way across much of Asia. On 10 March, British officials in Egypt reported riots in Cairo after the arrest of a leading nationalist, Saad Zaghlul. Within days the violence spread through the delta towns and into upper Egypt. A thousand Egyptians had died before the revolt was suppressed; the political unrest was much harder to quell. In early April there were violent disorders in British-ruled India. In the province of Punjab (the main recruiting ground for the Indian army), the British faced what they thought was an organized rising to smash their control. Their savage reaction reached a bloody climax in the events at Amritsar on 13 April, when nearly 400 protesters were shot by troops. In Anatolian Turkey, parts of which had been assigned by the peacemakers in Paris to an expansionist Greece, a national uprising began in May under Mustafa Kemal, a pre-war 'Young Turk' and a wartime general in the Ottoman army. In south-eastern Anatolia, a Kurdish revolt threatened the precarious grip of the British occupation in the province of Mosul. In the Arab Middle East, where Damascus was the epicentre of political action, the great powers' permission for a free Arab state was awaited impatiently, but with growing suspicion. In the old tsarist empire, the struggle for freedom by Bashkirs, Tatars, Kazakhs, Azerbaijanis and the Muslim peoples in Russian Central

Asia that had begun with the Russian Revolution of 1917 also hung in the balance. Most momentous of all, events in May 1919 showed that the Chinese revolution, apparently stalled since 1911, had at last taken off. The May Fourth demonstrations in Peking, whose immediate target was the decision in Paris that Japan should retain a sphere of influence in Shantung, signalled a far wider movement of national consciousness. That China must be a constitutional state, not a dynastic empire, now seemed accepted by all educated opinion. The restoration of full Chinese sovereignty, the end of foreign (especially British) enclaves and privileges, and China's acceptance as an equal member of the international community became the objectives of this new Chinese nationalism. The implications for East Asia, and for the colonial states that bordered China's territories or had Chinese minorities, were bound to be large.

Of course, these movements and others like them had not sprung from nowhere in 1918–19. In most cases they were built on older demands for nationhood, autonomy or at least recognition as a distinct community. Involuntary mobilization for war (as soldiers or suppliers), or the vicarious suffering of its hardships and losses, inflamed the grievances and widened the constituency of nationalist opposition. When the war ended or (as in Russia's case) imperial authority collapsed, the political climate soon reached fever heat. It was stoked by a mixture of fear and hope: fear that the repression of wartime would be continued indefinitely and the chance of freedom lost; hope that the cracking of Europe's imperial order and the promises of self-rule broadcast by the Allies in 1918 would mark the beginning of a new 'national' age. Gaining recognition for their cause in Paris, persuading the peacemakers to right historic wrongs, winning a licence for their separate existence were key objectives of nationalist leaders: in Egypt, Turkey, the Arab lands, Iran and China. When this gambit failed, or where it was hopeless, they pulled the trigger for more direct means.

The results were mixed. In Egypt, the brief explosion of popular violence left a bitter residue of political unrest. A British inquiry attributed much of its fury to wartime resentment: of inflation, shortages and the conscription of labour and animals for the imperial war effort against the Ottoman Empire. But the Egyptian elite were deeply suspicious that the British intended to absorb Egypt more fully into their imperial system at the end of the war (Egypt had never been formally annexed). The Wafd (or 'delegation') party was formed to take Egypt's case to the Paris peace conference and win international support for the virtual independence (or better) that the country had enjoyed before 1882. The brusque British refusal to permit this appeal, and the jailing of the Wafd leaders to pre-empt a popular campaign, produced the breakdown of order of March 1919 as strikes and demonstrations and the effects of rumour and fear fused with wider sources of social tension in a deeply stratified society. When the violence died down it was replaced politically by a climate of bitter resentment. The British controlled Egypt through Egyptian ministers and the Egyptian monarch (renamed the sultan in 1917). They preferred this indirect rule as a less confrontational way of securing what they wanted: a monopoly of foreign influence and absolute security for the Suez Canal, the lifeline of their empire in the East. Egypt, they argued, could never enjoy a 'real' independence. But after March 1919 no Egyptian minister would stay in office unless the British promised exactly that. Without Egyptian ministers, the British faced all-out opposition from every shade of local opinion: non-cooperation by officials; denunciation by teachers and clerics; strikes by key workers in transport and utilities; perhaps even recourse to the 'Irish' methods they feared the most – boycott, assassination and terror. Between March 1919 and February 1922 they struggled to find a formula that would appease a 'moderate' group of Egyptian leaders and split the nationalist coalition against them. It was only when they declared Egypt to be an independent state (but bound to follow British 'advice' in defence and foreign policy) that the fierce anti-British feeling began to die down.[12]

In the Arab lands the issue was more complex. The force behind demands for an Arab state was the alliance between Feisal and his Hashemite clan (the hereditary rulers of the holy places in Ottoman times) and the Syrian notables. It was Feisal, as the son of the sharif of Mecca, who had led the Arab revolt against the Ottoman Empire after 1916, with British help and encouragement, and who had extracted the notorious promise of an Arab state at the end of the war. The Syrian notables had taken the lead before 1914 in urging an Arab consciousness against Ottoman overrule – indeed Syria (Suriyya) had begun to be thought of as an Arab homeland from the 1860s.[13] Both Feisal and the Syrians had reason to be fearful. They knew that the Palestine district would be separately governed, partly to allow the creation of a 'national home' for Jews. They also knew that in 1916 the British and French had agreed a partition of the Arab lands, placing modern Syria and Lebanon under French supervision and most of modern Iraq under British. To make matters worse, it soon became clear that the new British regime set up in Baghdad regarded the idea of an Arab nation as at best irrelevant, and at worst absurd. It had no intention of allowing the Baghdadi notables to make common cause with their friends in Damascus. What Feisal hoped for was a British change of heart: a decision to repudiate the agreement with France and create an Arab state or states under a loose form of protection. The British had allowed him to head a provisional government in Damascus under their overall control. Feisal himself sought to buy off the French and to assure Jewish leaders that their 'national home' would be safe under an Arab government. But his hopes and diplomacy were both in vain. By the end of 1919 the British had agreed to pull their troops out of Syria and make way for the French. In the following spring the European victor powers (the United States had withdrawn into 'isolation') decreed (as the Supreme Council of the League of Nations) that the Arab lands would be divided up and governed as 'mandates', until each unit was deemed fit for self-rule. Palestine and Transjordan would be British. So would the new state of Iraq, an awkward combination of three disparate provinces: Mosul, with its large Kurdish population; Baghdad, which was dominated by a Sunni Muslim elite; and Basra in the south, which was overwhelmingly Shia. But Syria would be French and cut down to size, losing Lebanon (to be a separate French mandate) as well as the British mandates to the south. In a last act of defiance, a 'Syrian Congress' assembled at Damascus to denounce the mandates and call for Arab unity and independence under Feisal as king. With a makeshift army, Feisal tried to resist the French occupation. After a hopeless battle in July 1920 he fled into exile.

If the dream of 'Greater Syria' as a free Arab nation had been wiped from the slate, the Anglo-French partition was still far from secure. Defiance in Syria had spread to Iraq. The Baghdad notables, some of them linked through a secret society with Feisal's supporters, fiercely opposed the colonial-style rule the British had imposed at the end of the war. In June 1920 their political grievances found a massive echo. In the rural communities of the Euphrates valley, pent-up resentment at foreign rule and taxation set off an explosion of violence. As the British struggled to contain it, deploying more and more troops and spending more and more money, the case for installing a suitable Arab-led government became more and more urgent. It was Winston Churchill's idea (Churchill was colonial secretary with responsibility for the Arab Middle East, but not Egypt) that the now-exiled Feisal would be the best choice as leader, since only he, so it seemed, would have the skill and prestige to keep this ramshackle creation together in one piece. Yet whether even he could do so, and then on what terms, were still profoundly uncertain. For the fate of Iraq was only part of a larger question. By the end of 1920 it seemed more and more likely that a new Turkish state, hostile and aggressive, would rise from the ashes of the Ottoman Empire and claim its old place in the politics of the region. In 1921–2, Mustafa Kemal imposed the authority of his Turkish republic across most of Asia Minor, smashing both British hopes of a weak Turkish client state ruled by the sultan and the grand Greek project to turn much of western Anatolia into the 'Ionian' extension of a 'Greater Greece'.[14] In September 1922 he captured Smyrna (Izmir) and was marching on Constantinople, the old imperial capital, when he met a small British garrison stationed at Chanak to guard the Dardanelles. A vast crisis now loomed. If a new war began between the British and the Turks, the political future of the whole Middle East would be back in the melting pot.[15]

The actual outcome after months of tense diplomacy was a treaty of peace agreed at Lausanne in July 1923. It recognized Turkey as an independent republic. It restored Constantinople as a fully Turkish city. (It was officially renamed 'Istanbul' in 1930.) It voided the claims for European spheres in Turkey's Anatolian heartland. It scrapped the old system of foreign extraterritorial privilege (the 'Capitulations') and released Turkey from the thrall of the pre-war Debt Administration. It provided for an exchange of populations, clearing Turkey of 'Greek' Christians and Greece of Muslim 'Turks': a portent of things to come.[16] The Turks accepted the demilitarization of the

Straits, accepted the loss of their Arab empire, and agreed to arbitrate their special claim to Mosul. It was a remarkable compromise. It reflected the reluctance of both British and Turks to resume the armed struggle, the modest reassertion of Russian influence in the region after 1920 (see below), and the eagerness of Kemal to build his new Turkish state along the European lines favoured by pre-war reformers. It was the crucial stage in solidifying the grip of the British and French on their new Arab mandates. It allowed France a free hand to parcel up Syria and crush the great revolt that followed in 1925–7. It made a cheap British presence possible in Iraq, where the British traded air power (to help crush Feisal's opponents) for the bases they needed to guard the approach to the Gulf and reach India by air. Nevertheless, the scale of post-war resistance had left a deep mark on the Middle East's politics. In Syria and Palestine, Arab claims to self-rule had been roundly rejected. But in Egypt and Iraq the British had been forced to agree to wide local autonomy and acknowledge the claim of both states to independence – in 1922 to Egypt, a decade later to Feisal's Iraq – as a quid pro quo for Britain's control of their strategic zones, the Suez Canal especially. Even Transjordan had been given its own (Hashemite) king. Despite the trauma of partition, the Arab Middle East had not been transformed into a fully colonial region. The sense of pan-Arabness, awake before the war, had not been extinguished. There were many spaces left in which it could grow. European authority (it was mainly British) was shallowly rooted in social and cultural terms. It depended heavily on geopolitical contingency: the temporary easing of great-power rivalry with the eclipse of Germany and the isolation of Russia. In an age of depression, it gained little help from the spread of trade or the region's accession to the international economy. The growth of the oil industry was too long delayed (the Middle East produced only 1 per cent of world output in 1920, only 5 per cent in 1939, almost all of it from south-west Iran) to allow it to serve as a real Trojan Horse of European imperial influence. Once the brief excitement of war imperialism had passed, there was little enthusiasm for an Arab empire in either Britain or France – especially one that was going to cost money.[17] If the Middle East's partition was the high tide of empire, it was the tide that turned soonest, the imperial moment that was shortest.

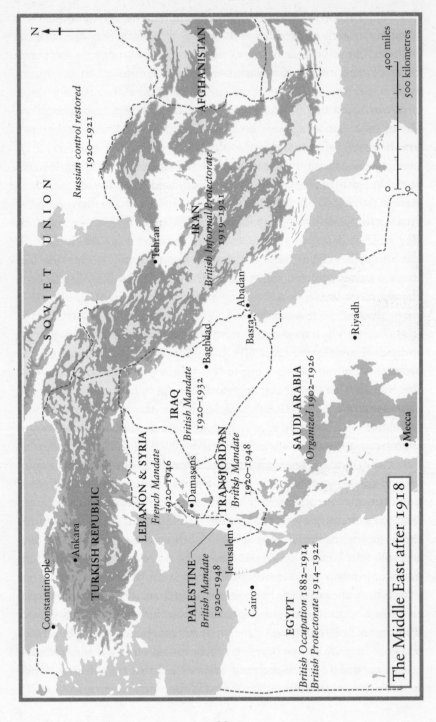

The Middle East after 1918

It was Turkey and Iran that seemed to gain most from the era of turmoil between 1918 and 1923. Both had been faced with humiliating relegation to protectorate status or worse: Turkey as the occupied rump of the Ottoman Empire; Iran as the client state of a victorious Britain. Both were to benefit from the dramatic easing of the external pressures that had been almost unbearable before 1914. Neither Russia nor Britain was eager to intervene actively in their internal affairs after 1923; each was preoccupied with domestic demands. The chance was seized by two remarkable state-builders to drive through the changes of which reformers had dreamed before 1914. Mustafa Kemal (later named 'Atatürk') assembled a Turkish republic in the Anatolian core of the ruined Ottoman Empire, largely 'cleansed' of its Christian minorities. In Kemal's republic, conservative Islam was the principal foe, the main obstruction to a modern state able to hold its own against ill-intentioned great powers. New laws about clothing (banning the brimless fez that allowed the Muslim faithful to touch their head to the ground), the alphabet (replacing the Arabic script with Latin-style letters), education (outlawing religious instruction in madrasas) and surnames (Turks were obliged to acquire Western-style family names) dramatized the conflict between a Muslim identity and the loyalty demanded by the secular state from its 'national' citizens.

Behind Kemal's success lay the 'national' movement created to win the war with the Greeks and restore Turkish independence. Kemal commanded an army that was (and remained) deeply committed to his national programme. He also inherited a recognizably modern administrative structure from the Ottoman reforms before 1914. In Iran the going was bound to be tougher. There the war and its aftermath had sharpened the conflicts within Iranian society, all but destroying the central government in Tehran. Foreign occupation (by British, Russian and then Soviet forces), breakaway governments, ethnic movements, social unrest and tribal self-assertion threatened to make the country ungovernable. In these desperate conditions, the military coup in February 1921 by Reza Khan, an officer in the Cossack Brigade (the only regular force under Tehran's nominal control), was widely supported, and Reza was able to negotiate a Soviet and British withdrawal. Once established in power, he quickly adopted a programme of change strikingly similar to Kemalist Turkey's. A large army was built up to crush provincial rebellions and tribal indiscipline. New railways and roads increased the government's reach. Laws about headwear (requiring caps or hats), on the adoption of surnames (Reza took the name 'Pahlevi'), on the treatment of women and outlawing the veil signalled Reza's main target: the influence of the mullahs. Faced with resistance, Reza became a virtual dictator: in April 1926 he crowned himself shah. Huge dynastic estates and extensive court patronage were added to the power supplied by the army and bureaucracy. Reza had fashioned a new imperial state far stronger than anything that the Qajars had hoped for. He was able to do so without the reliance upon foreign funds or concessions that had rallied the enemies of Qajar reform. The key reason for this was a new source of wealth. For, although Reza stopped short (as prudence dictated) of taking control of the oilfields just north of the Gulf from the British-owned company that held the concession (the Anglo-Persian Oil Company, of which the British government held 51 per cent of the shares), his revenues profited from the hundredfold increase in the income they earned after 1913. But for him, as for the republic that Atatürk (who died in 1938) had made, the real test would be felt when the geopolitical lull they had exploited so skilfully collapsed into war after 1939.[18]

In this phase of upheaval across so much of South West Asia, 'Islamic' politics had been a notable absentee. A sense of Muslim identity had undoubtedly played an important part in solidifying resistance to foreign control. But the nationalist movements in Turkey, Iran, Egypt and the Arab lands were strongly secular. In Syria especially, Christians had been among the most ardent promoters of an Arab nationalism whose bond of union was to be linguistic and cultural, not primarily religious. Where Islamic influence played a much larger part was further east, in India. Among Indian Muslims, the sense of their place in the larger Islamic world had been rising sharply before 1914. The shock of the war between the British and the Ottomans had been all the greater, for the Ottoman sultan was (if only in name) also the *khalifa*, the 'Commander of the (Muslim) Faithful'. With so many Muslim soldiers in its Indian army (much of which was sent to fight the Ottoman forces), the British Indian government was quick to repress even the mildest expression of pan-Islamic feeling by Muslim politicians and newspapers, and several leading Indian Muslims spent most of the war in jail. It was from this quarter particularly that there was strong resentment when the British promise of reform (a much larger share for elected Indian leaders in provincial affairs) was coupled with the threat that special wartime powers of arrest and detention under the so-called Rowlatt Act would be continued indefinitely.[19] It was the protest against this, orchestrated by Gandhi in his first great campaign as a political leader at the all-India level, that had helped set off the violence in 1919 and led indirectly to the Amritsar massacre – General Dyer's savage revenge for the killing of Europeans in the city.[20]

Gandhi at first sight was an unlikely ally for Indian Islam. He was a Hindu reformer who wanted to harness a simpler and more spiritual version of Hinduism to a programme of social and moral improvement. Temperance, chastity, self-restraint and modesty were all Gandhian ideals. But, as we saw in the last chapter, in his pre-war manifesto *Hind Swaraj* Gandhi had linked these virtues to Indian self-rule. They could only really be practised, so his argument ran, in the self-sufficient village communities of which India had once been made up. This was a fanciful version of the Indian past that owed something to the histories produced by British officials and a lot to the influence of later writing by Tolstoy (d. 1910) and his idealized view of the peasant commune in Russia. But in a country that was still overwhelmingly rural its appeal was enormous. Yet it was Gandhi's insistence that remoralizing India could begin only once British rule had ended that made his message so radical. British rule was the vehicle through which the West's alien culture had corrupted India. Its overthrow was urgent – though by moral pressure, not physical force. What Gandhi wanted was a vast campaign of psychological liberation to end Indian subjecthood. For it was Indians who *allowed* the British to rule, deferring to their systems of justice and law, adopting their ideas about economics and politics, copying their approach to education and culture. Breaking the grip of this mental servitude, asserting the freedom to think in Indian not British terms, using *satyagraha* ('truth-force') against physical power, was the surest, indeed only, way in which a real independence could be won quickly for India.

These ideas were a world away from those of the mainstream of Indian nationalist politics. The Indian National Congress had campaigned for self-rule since the 1880s. But its leaders wanted to take charge of the British Indian state, not destroy its authority over rural society or create an anarchist utopia. They admired British institutions like representative government and the civil service, and saw them as building blocks for a new Indian nation – built down from above, not up from below. Far from favouring a complete break with Britain, their aim was to be a self-governing dominion (like Canada), loyal to the Crown and inside the empire. They regarded Gandhi's ideas (all the more extraordinary in an English-educated lawyer who had spent twenty years of his life in Britain or South Africa – Gandhi was forty-six when he returned to India in 1915) as those of a crank, harmless or dangerous according to taste. The Congress leaders had hoped that India's loyalty in the war would earn a political reward. Up to a point it did. But the 'reforms' they were offered in 1918 were a big disappointment. They made almost no concession to the Congress demand for a parliamentary system with Indian ministers in the central government – on the 'white dominion' model. Instead, they made the province the main arena of politics, with the transparent purpose (many Congress leaders believed) of inflating the differences between India's regions and blocking the path to a true nation state. Frustration with reform made Gandhi's direct methods of political action look much more attractive – until they were discredited by the violence and disorder of 1919 (most Congress politicians were respectable property-owners). But in 1920 Gandhi discovered a different way of winning the Congress over.[21]

The secret lay in the rising anger among leading Muslims at the terms of peace imposed by the victor powers on the Ottoman Empire. Indian Muslims had been alarmed by Ottoman defeat and the break-up of the last great Islamic empire. They were concerned about the guardianship of Islam's holy places: indeed, those in Jerusalem had already fallen under British control. But they were incensed at the plans to deny Turkish rule in Constantinople, which they saw as a deliberate humiliation of the sultan/*khalifa* and a direct attack on the prestige of Islam as a world religion. To bring pressure to bear on the British government – the chief author of these plans – they launched a campaign to mobilize outrage among the Indian faithful against the Christian attack on the 'Khilafat' or caliphate, the sultan's hereditary office of Commander of the Faithful. Gandhi's response was inspired. He coupled the brutal repression of his Punjab *satyagraha* campaign (the 'Punjab wrong') with the 'Khilafat wrong', and called on Muslims and Hindus to support mass civil disobedience to achieve '*swaraj* [self-rule] in one year'. Muslims were encouraged to enter the Congress and elect the delegates sent to its annual conference. The result was a coup. With heavy Muslim backing, Gandhi forced the Congress old guard to back direct action. He turned what had been an elitist political club into a popular movement with a nominal membership fee and a real grass-roots presence. He transformed a political talking-shop into a fighting machine to harass the Raj, and to pose where it could as a parallel government.

From late 1920 until early 1922, with the Indian National Congress as his tool, Gandhi waged a form of pacific war against British colonial rule. Demonstrations and marches, boycotting government courts and schools, refusing to buy imported British goods and rejecting the reforms the government had offered (including a sharing of power at the provincial level) made up 'Non-Cooperation' – the withdrawal of consent to British authority. Coinciding as it did with so much disturbance elsewhere, and threatening to lapse into large-scale disorder, Non-Cooperation was a source of acute alarm to India's British masters. But what they feared most was the Islamic element in Gandhi's campaign, the religious appeal of the Khilafat cause to the Muslim masses, the influence of the imams, and a sudden upsurge of Islamic fervour that might spread unchecked to the police and army – both disproportionately Muslim.[22] In fact Gandhi's campaign reached a shattering climax. It began with the assault of poor Muslim tenants upon their Hindu landlords in part of South India – the 'Moplah' rising, which cost 10,000 lives – and ended with the burning of a North Indian police station by an angry mob, killing twenty-two men. Amid signs that Non-Cooperation had got out of control, Gandhi called off the struggle in March 1922, and was jailed soon after. Within a couple of years, the mass participation in Congress had dwindled away. The Khilafat campaign suffered a similar fate. In 1924 the office of *khalifa* was abolished not by the British but by

Mustafa Kemal's secular Turkish republic. The Muslim–Hindu alliance to win India self-rule lost its rhyme and reason. The great Gandhian experiment seemed to end with a whimper.

The British certainly hoped so. But the revolutionary phase in Indian politics left a powerful legacy. It showed for the first time how British rule could be challenged by an organized mass movement right across the subcontinent. Non-Cooperation's collapse had been a bitter blow to Gandhi's close disciples. Its obvious meaning was how hard it was to control such a movement and sustain its momentum. Yet, for their part, the British could now never be sure when they might have to face a new round of mass action to corrode their prestige and unravel the loyalty that bound Indian soldiers, policemen, public servants and local notables to their system of rule. Indeed, fear of a repeat dominated their policy for the next twenty-five years. Secondly, Gandhi's attack upon the British Raj had been an ideological triumph. Many Indian nationalists were still deeply attracted to the representative institutions the British had created. Gandhi's achievement was to persuade a huge new constituency of potential supporters that his version of nationalism, with its social and moral content, would meet the needs and wants of India's rural masses, and that Indian problems required Indian answers. He created, in short, an Indian rather 'British-Indian' nationalism. Thirdly (and partly in consequence), Gandhi made nationalism – and the Congress – a grass-roots movement, drawing in peasants, women, industrial workers, the 'tribal' peoples of the forests and hills, and the untouchables. Of course the level of popular interest and the scale of Congress membership could rise and fall (as they did after 1922). But the cadre of Gandhians pursuing 'village uplift', or promoting Gandhi's schemes of education and hygiene, formed a network of activists ready and waiting for the next *satyagraha* campaign. It remained to be seen when their chance would come.[23]

For the time being, however, even nominal self-rule of the kind granted to Egypt remained a distant prospect. Gandhi had shaken British self-confidence badly. But the 'steel frame' of Britain's Raj – the army, police and bureaucracy – with its tens of thousands of loyal Indian servants, was still in place. The religious and social divisions that Gandhi had been so anxious to bridge made a grand nationalist coalition against alien control something to hope for, not a practical basis for political action in the immediate future.

China was different. Between 1919 and 1922, against all the odds, Chinese leaders successfully asserted China's right to full sovereignty that had seemed at such risk after 1890. They won China a place on the new League Council, the steering committee of the League of Nations. By refusing to sign the Treaty of Versailles (because of the clause on Shantung), they eventually forced a new settlement for East Asia in the Washington treaties of 1921–2. They even secured what had seemed almost impossible before 1914: a programme to reverse the 'unequal treaties' – winning tariff autonomy, abolishing extraterritorial privilege, and shutting down (gradually) the numerous foreign enclaves on Chinese soil. China's revolt against a global order in which empire was the norm was far more complete than almost anywhere else in the Afro-Asian world.[24]

Of course, part of the reason was that, although the West had encroached upon China's independence in the nineteenth century (a number of Western countries enjoyed extraterritorial rights, including the USA, Brazil, Peru and Bolivia), the Chinese had fiercely resisted reduction to a form of semi-colonial dependence in the crucial decade before 1914. Instead, the need to turn China into a nation state (not a dynastic empire) with a republican government to express the popular will was accepted with astonishing rapidity among the educated class. The explosion of feeling in May 1919 when China's claim to Shantung was rejected in Paris showed that this new style of patriotism had not stopped there. The May Fourth movement began among students in Peking. But it quickly became a much wider protest, enlisting merchants and artisans in its demonstrations and boycotts, and spreading far beyond the capital. It was graphic proof that foreign business interests could be badly damaged by popular outrage, and that the angry crowds would take their cue from the nationalist rhetoric of the new literati. Yet this new popular mood was not translated into a strong national government. Between 1919 and 1922, China had a government in Canton as well as one in Peking. The Peking government was a cockpit of factions, and its writ hardly ran beyond the walls of the city.[25] Across much of China, the real voice of authority was the provincial *dujun*, the military commander or (a hostile translation) 'warlord'.[26] By 1922 the simmering hostility of these provincial bosses and their factional groupings had set off the civil wars that dominated China's politics until the capture of Peking by Chiang Kai-shek in 1928. The enthusiastic endorsement of China's sovereign statehood and the solemn promises to respect it in the Washington treaties are thus somewhat puzzling. If anything, the domestic turmoil of post-imperial China seemed to invite the interference of the foreign powers as much if not more so than before 1914.

It had certainly seemed so during the First World War. In January 1915, as soon as they grasped the gigantic scale of the European conflict, the Japanese presented their famous Twenty-One Demands to the Chinese government, on War Office paper 'watermarked with machine guns and dreadnoughts'.[27] They proposed the mother and father of unequal treaties. China was pressed to agree to a Japanese takeover of German claims in Shantung, to extend Japanese concessions and leases in Manchuria for the rest of the century, not to borrow foreign capital without Japan's permission to develop Fukien (a coastal province far to the south of Japan's usual sphere), and to take on Japanese advisers 'in political, financial and military affairs'.[28] To all intents, they proposed a virtual protectorate. Without allies or arms, the Chinese government gave in, and the treaty was signed. It opened the way for the rapid entrenchment of Japanese influence in the Chinese north, and the increasing dependence of the Peking government on loans from Tokyo. The fall of the tsar and the break-up of his empire ended the last real check upon Japanese dominance: neither Britain nor the United States was willing to challenge Tokyo at this stage of the war. When they did agree to intervene in Siberia to stop Russia falling under German control (the expected result of the Brest-Litovsk treaty in March 1918), it was Japan that supplied much the largest force, and expected to reap much the largest gain: extending its influence deep into Inner Asia. The Shantung decision in 1919 was thus of a piece with the massive shift of power in wartime East Asia. As China's unity fractured (the rival Canton government had appeared in 1917), and its provincial bosses took the Japanese shilling, it seemed that it might become part of a vast informal empire whose centre was Tokyo.

Yet this was not what happened. The explanation lies in a powerful convergence between China's politics and the conflictual relations of the great powers in East Asia. It was true that Peking could not impose its will on the provincial *dujuns*. But there was little doubt that on questions of 'rights recovery' the nationalist programme of its intellectual elite (centred in Peking's new university)[29] commanded mass support in the treaty-port cities of maritime China. That was the significance of the May Fourth movement. By the end of 1920, the Peking government had revoked the extraterritorial privileges of Germany and Austria–Hungary, its wartime enemies. The Bolshevik government had renounced Russia's claims. It seemed more than likely that Peking would go on to denounce the privileged status of the treaty powers that remained, including Britain, Japan and the United States.[30] It was easy to imagine the explosive effect of such a move in Shanghai and elsewhere, and the enormous difficulty of defending foreign interests and property against the mass demonstrations and boycotts that seemed certain to follow. It seemed safer by far to enlist Peking's support for a gradual change. The British and the Americans had an added reason to come to terms with Peking. They had watched with alarm the growing power of Japan, and mistrusted the 'militarist clique' that directed its policy.[31] Throughout 1920 they pressed the Japanese government to pool its commercial concessions in an international consortium, and opposed its claim to a special position 'beyond the Wall' in Manchuria.[32] This Anglo-American pressure was feared and resented in Tokyo, but Japanese leaders had other reasons to change course in East Asia. They faced domestic unrest, the outgrowth in part of the economic strains of wartime.[33] The Siberian expedition, with its costs and its losses, was deeply unpopular.[34] Without the old Russian threat, it was even harder to justify. In Korea, where an independence campaign had been brutally crushed in 1919, political tranquillity was urgently needed.[35] And the Japanese shared the Westerners' alarm that anti-foreign feeling might get out of hand in China and inflict big losses on their business interests, especially by Chinese boycott of their textile exports.[36] The case for conciliation had become overwhelming.

The upshot was the remarkable settlement embodied in the Washington treaties of 1921–2. The Western powers and Japan guaranteed the independence and integrity of the Chinese republic. Provision was made to reform the unequal treaties. No power was to seek any special concessions or make exclusive deals. China, it seemed, had recovered the national dignity painfully surrendered in the chaotic 1890s. But the status revolution was not the end of the story. From 1922 onward, foreign interests in China faced militant nationalism on a growing scale. A second revolution, social and political, made the Washington treaties' leisurely timetable for the recovery of China's full sovereignty look strangely complacent. The epicentre was Canton, the southern metropolis. Canton had been the centre of anti-Ch'ing politics. The Cantonese, said an old China-coast diehard, were the 'Irish of China' (it was not meant as a compliment).[37] Canton was less than eighty miles from Hong Kong, which served as its outport, and a safe haven for dissent in imperial times. It was where Sun Yat-sen had struggled before 1911 to build up his revolutionary party, later the Kuomintang, or Nationalist Party (KMT).[38] But, without a mass following, Sun was poorly placed to exploit the growing antagonism of merchants and artisans towards the exactions and oppressions of the new provincial rulers (many of them military) who had pushed aside the mandarin-scholars of the old imperial system. Nor could he appeal to the educated class (a category that included the young Mao Tse-tung), who bitterly resented their displacement from power by warlords and soldiers. In 1922 he was even chased out of Canton by a warlord faction. But the next three years brought an astonishing change. For in 1923 Sun made an epic compact with an agent sent from Bolshevik Russia. He accepted the offer of military aid and a corps of Soviet advisers[39] to rebuild the KMT on the Leninist model, in partnership with the infant Chinese Communist Party (CCP). The KMT–CCP began to build a mass base among peasants and town workers.[40] And with its own party army it at last had the means to defeat the warlords and build a new state.[41]

The revolutionary year was 1925. It started badly for the KMT, which lost control of Canton (briefly), and its leader Sun to a premature death. But on 30 May labour tension in Shanghai (where foreign enterprise was concentrated) burst into violence when the British police force in the International Settlement shot dead twelve Chinese during a large demonstration. A huge wave of protest swept up the Yangtze valley and along the coast to Hong Kong. On 23 June there was further shooting in the European enclave of Shameen in Canton. A general strike and boycott of British trade was organized in Hong Kong, in a direct challenge to the British authorities. The KMT now reaped the reward for its new credibility as a nationalist movement with the physical power to govern effectively. Soviet support, the anti-foreign mass movement and a bloody civil war between the warlords in the north suddenly opened the way to reunify China under a national government pledged to expel all foreign power.[42] In July 1926 the KMT army set off from Canton on the 'Northern Expedition', destination Peking. By the end of the year it had reached Wuhan, the great crossroads city in the middle of China. Nanking and Shanghai lay within its grasp. China's titular sovereignty – hailed with enthusiasm at the Washington conference – had become frighteningly real. For the British, whose stake in the old order was largest, there began a race to withdraw from the most vulnerable outposts before the shooting started.[43] What the future held for the large foreign presence (Japanese and Western) in Shanghai, the greatest treaty port of all, was anyone's guess.

There is a strange but important epilogue to this tale of revolution and empire in the aftermath of war. Across much of Northern Eurasia, what mattered most was the fate of imperial Russia, apparently dissolving in chaos in 1918. As tsarist rule collapsed, the subject peoples of what Lenin had called the 'prison of nations' had a glimpse of freedom. In the Ukraine, the Caucasus and Central Asia, and among the ethnic minorities of Russia proper (like the Bashkirs and Tatars), independent regimes made their bid for power. On the face of things, their chances were good. In 1918–19 the Bolsheviks were struggling to survive in a civil war. Moreover, the Bolshevik view had favoured liberation for Russia's subject nationalities, seeing them as allies against the tsarist autocracy. Lenin himself had proclaimed in his famous wartime manifesto *Imperialism: The Highest Stage of Capitalism* (1916) that colonial freedom was the crucial first step towards destroying capitalism in its European heartlands. In their state of siege after 1917, the Bolsheviks found that this revolutionary principle coincided with self-interest. They were anxious to pre-empt the threat of pan-Islamic sentiment among the Muslims of the Caucasus and

Central Asia. And, as we have seen, the fear of Japanese expansion and Anglo-American influence on its East Asian frontier had lain behind Moscow's intervention in 1922–3, first of all in North China and then, more profitably, in the nationalist south.[44]

Like the Romanovs before them, however, the Bolsheviks soon grasped that no Russian state was secure without the political mastery of Inner Eurasia and its strategic borderlands. To defeat the Whites in the civil war, they mobilized an army of over 5 million men.[45] The Red Army's attempt to carry revolutionary struggle into Central Europe was stopped by the Poles in 1920. But Moscow regained control over most of Belorussia and the Ukraine, which the Treaty of Brest-Litovsk had taken away. In the Volga region, where Moscow at first seemed to smile on an independent state for the Bashkirs and Tatars, the power of the centre was reasserted forcibly during 1920.[46] In Central Asia, the Russian settler community, many of them rail-waymen, resisted the attempt of the local Muslim elite to recover the freedoms lost forty years earlier. But the decisive factor was the Red Army's arrival to capture Khiva in February 1920 and Bukhara in September. Though 'Basmachi' fighters waged a guerrilla war on into 1921, their cause was lost. In the Caucasus, Moscow at first trod more carefully. It was anxious not to alienate either Turkey or Iran, both potential allies against British influence in the Middle East. It lacked the military power to subjugate a fractured region. It faced a tough Georgian government, whose independence it recognized in May 1920. But by the end of that year Russia's strategic position had become much more favourable. British power was ebbing from its high-water mark at the end of the war.[47] For fear of conquest by a resurgent Turkey, the Armenians abandoned independence in favour of Russian protection. The following year, for similar reasons, the Georgians did the same. By the end of 1921, Moscow was master of the tsar's old Caucasian provinces. Then in 1922 Japan's withdrawal from Siberia restored Russian control of the Pacific territories wrested from China after 1860. The empire was back.[48]

This astonishing recovery undoubtedly owed much to the military prowess of Trotsky's Red Army. It was also critical that, within the vast geographical realm that made up Inner Eurasia, no rival state could match the manpower and resources that Moscow could mobilize in European Russia. But, for all their triumph, the Bolsheviks lacked both the means and the will to revive the pre-war pattern of Russian imperial power. In the political trauma of 1918–23, amid civil war, foreign invasion, economic breakdown, peasant revolt, military disaster and the virtual collapse of the state apparatus, it could hardly be otherwise. Lenin was insistent that the loyalty of non-Russians in the old tsarist empire would have to be won by political concession and a display of sympathy for their national aspirations. The commissar of nationalities who applied this policy was a Georgian expatriate, Joseph Stalin. Stalin was the doyen of borderland warfare and the master of 'steppe politics'.[49] In his capable hands, nationality policy became the means to an end in the larger struggle. 'During four years of civil war,' he later told Lenin, 'given the foreign intervention, we were obliged to demonstrate Moscow's liberalism on the national question.'[50] Moscow's agents were ordered to restrain the chauvinist instincts of Russian settler communities like those in Central Asia.[51] As the borderland provinces (like the Ukraine and Belorussia) surrendered their brief independence, they were reinvented as soviet socialist republics under their own Bolshevik leaders. The smaller subject nations were also appeased by the promise to make them into separate republics and autonomous regions. Their leaders would be locals. They would enjoy 'cultural autonomy', to promote their own language, education and culture. They were free to build nations. Of course Stalin intended this offer of freedom to fall far short of sovereignty. The autonomous republics should have no foreign relations. The 'national Communists' would owe a higher allegiance to the Bolshevik cause. In effect, the Bolshevik party state would have a new 'party empire' until the Soviet nations eventually fused into a single Soviet people. In late 1922 he gave an angry warning that the borderland Communists were 'refusing to understand the game of independence as a game' and were trying to make it real (an echo of British complaints about Egypt).[52] They even wanted to have their own foreign policies. Stalin pressed the case for incorporating all the new soviet republics into a Russian federation. Lenin refused. The new Soviet constitution of 1924 preserved the legal fiction of a Soviet 'union' made up of equal states. The real guarantee of Moscow's authority over the member republics would be the invisible hand of the party's power. But the nationality principle, the child of a desperate crisis, was inscribed indelibly on the Soviet system.

A FRACTURED WORLD ORDER

By the mid-1920s, after the great phase of upheaval, much of the world seemed to be moving towards a more settled state. Those who looked back to the pre-war years as a form of 'international anarchy', or were scandalized by the predatory excesses of European imperialism, saw the League of Nations as a new beginning. The *ancien régime* of dynastic empires had become a 'world of nations'. The 'covenant' of the League, which bound its nation-state members, outlawed armed aggression and prescribed the peaceful resolution of international disputes. The age-old tradition that colonial conquests were legitimate spoils of war had been swept away. Germany's lost colonies, and the Ottomans' lost provinces, were to be international 'mandates', open to inspection by the League's officials, and open equally to the commerce of all. For some of them at least, there was a presumption in favour of early self-rule. The League itself held out a grander hope: that an international society sharing liberal values and a common framework of law would spread irresistibly from Europe to the 'neo-Europes' (like the Latin American states) and to the non-Western world beyond.[53]

The League was expected to act like the old Concert of Europe, but on a global scale and with liberal democracy as its ideological beacon. As in the Concert, its larger members would exert moral suasion over their more quarrelsome juniors. What made the League vital, in the eyes of its champions, was that international politics in future would be even more 'global' than before the war. The national interests of states would be interlocked more closely; the collective interest in non-aggressive behaviour would be felt more deeply; ideological influences (especially nationalism and democracy) would be diffused more widely. But, for the League to serve as the collective guardian of international peace, one thing was essential. All sovereign states had to enter its membership and acknowledge its rules. Of course, this never happened.

In fact the post-war world that took shape in the 1920s was divided from the start into four geopolitical zones. The largest of these was certainly the League zone. It formed a loose international confederation under the fractious leadership of Britain and France. Most of its members were European or Latin American. It included China and also Japan (until 1933). At first, neither Russia nor Germany was invited to join: both later became members, though not at the same time (Germany left in 1933; Russia joined in 1934). The United States rejected membership. Outside Europe, the sphere of the League was practically coextensive with the imperial systems of Britain and France and of lesser colonial powers like the Netherlands and Portugal. The Latin Americans remained semi-detached. The League's ability to deter aggression and uphold the post-war settlement depended heavily on the naval and military power of its two great principals. But they in turn needed stability in Europe – chiefly the promise of Franco-German friendship – to be free to act. The Treaty of Locarno of 1925, in which France and Germany gave mutual pledges to respect the border between them, seemed to mark a new age in which Europe's affairs would be managed amicably by its four great powers: Britain, France, Germany and Italy. A League that enjoyed their collective support would indeed have been a real power in the world, enabling the tacit revival of much of Europe's pre-war primacy. But in less than ten years the four were in bitter dispute, and the League zone itself had become a scene of upheaval. The League's failure to prevent Italy's conquest of Abyssinia, itself a League member, was the indirect consequence of Anglo-French fears about Germany. It marked the brutal collapse of the last Europe-centred experiment in maintaining global order.

American refusal to join the League was at first sight baffling, since the League seemed to embody so much of the vision of Woodrow Wilson, its most powerful proponent. The United States had also become a far greater international power since 1914. It had built, or was building, a much larger navy – at least as big as Britain's. The scale of its overseas economic interests had been vastly extended. In 1914, America's investments abroad stood at $4,820 million (about £1,000 million), slightly less than its overseas borrowings – around $5 billion. By 1919, in a huge reversal, the positive balance was more than $10 billion. Ten years later America had lent abroad the enormous figure of $35 billion, to overtake Britain as the world's largest creditor.[54] Much of this sum was invested in Europe. The United States played (as we have seen already) a crucial part in the East Asian settlement of 1921–2. To Woodrow Wilson's followers, it was glaringly obvious that American power should be used through the League to create a new global order. The progressive demolition of the European empires, universal free trade and the 'open door' to commerce, and a ban on alliance systems that could threaten American interests were the prizes they sought. But they were defeated by the fear that being part of the League would hamper American freedom or exploit American strength. The League would mean guaranteeing the British Empire, claimed Senator Borah: it was 'the greatest triumph of English diplomacy'. The Covenant would turn every future war into a world war said Senator Knox: 'We are thus thrust fully into the terrible cauldron of European politics.' America's fleets and armies could be ordered to war by other nations, warned Henry Cabot Lodge, Wilson's fiercest critic.[55]

Ironically, League membership was opposed by those (like Cabot Lodge) who wanted America to assert herself in the world, as well as by those (like Borah) who thought foreign entanglements a threat to democracy. For the 'great power' school the League was a shackle that would prevent America from using its real power, and bind it into a Europe-led system dominated by Britain. America's influence could be better applied from outside the League. If economic muscle had replaced territorial control as the test of world power, as many experts now claimed,[56] bankers in Wall Street, not diplomats at Geneva, would be the real engineers of America's future pre-eminence. Hence rejecting the League did not mean American withdrawal into isolation. American business was extremely active in Europe, in South America, and even in Asia. American culture, purveyed by Hollywood, spread even more widely.[57] American leaders promoted the idea of universal peace, and favoured cooperation with Britain against an arms race at sea. But American thinking was at heart unilateralist. It expected America to supersede the existing world order, not help to maintain it. It refused to see America as one of a group of great powers, on terms of equality. It reflected the suspicion of Middle

America that foreign commitments were risky, and foreign countries malign. Hence America dealt with the League as with a rival, sometimes friendly, power. At the first sign of danger it rebuilt the commercial walls of protection, with the Fordney–McCumber Tariff of 1922. In the Manchurian crisis of 1931–2 (see below, p. 407), Washington's instinct was against collective action.[58] Hence the inter-war years were not the prelude to an 'American century', but an age of impasse. American leaders were dissatisfied with the world as it was, and became very much more so when depression set in during the 1930s. But they had no practical idea how it could be remade, and could scarcely imagine any possible terms on which they might cooperate with another great power – not even with Britain.[59]

Much the same might be said of the ruling power in the third great zone. By 1922–3 the Bolshevik government had recovered control of the vast tsarist domain in Inner Eurasia except for the provinces lost to Poland, Finland and the Baltic states. As we have seen, the new 'Soviet Union' kept real control of all external relations firmly in Moscow's grip. Moscow was committed to promoting 'world revolution' in partnership with the Communist International organization (or Comintern), theoretically autonomous, but in reality an agency of the Soviet government. In the 1920s this effort was concentrated for good strategic reasons in China. At the same time, there was an opening to the West for the sake of economic recovery. Under Stalin's rule, the first five-year plan for swift industrialization (1928–32) meant a heavy reliance on imported machinery, and swelled foreign debts to their pre-war level. But there was no question at all of any real rapprochement between the Soviet world and the world of the League. The Soviet leadership regarded the great League states as ideological enemies, doomed to extinction sooner or later. In the meantime they posed a potentially deadly threat to the great socialist experiment. Stalin's five-year plan was not intended to enlarge the Soviet share of international trade: quite the reverse. Its double aim was to create the proletarian class as the foundation on which the Soviet party state would be built, and to supply the industrial means to defend the revolution. Indeed, after 1932 Russia retreated into an extreme form of autarky: foreign trade shrank to one-fifth of its value in 1913.[60]

Stalin's foreign policy was defensive in outlook to the point of paranoia. His paramount aim was to secure the huge Soviet zone. The Russian tsars did many bad things, he told a private dinner in 1937, 'But there's one good thing they did; they created an immense state from here to Kamchatka. We've been bequeathed this state. And for the first time we, the Bolsheviks, have rendered this state cohesive and reinforced it as a unitary and indivisible state.'[61] Yet its cohesion, as Stalin knew, could not be taken for granted. He was anxious to seal the Soviet Union's frontiers: after 1930, border populations with uncertain sympathies were brusquely relocated.[62] He feared an attack from the east by Japan, whom he sought to appease (by selling Russia's railway rights in Manchuria) while rebuilding his military and naval presence.[63] But he feared even more an attack from the west, where the loss of Poland and the Baltic provinces had drastically weakened Russia's strategic position, not least in relation to the doubtfully loyal Ukraine. Hence Soviet policy was above all to keep on good terms with Germany. Economic and (discreet) military cooperation had been close in the 1920s. Hitler's rise to power forced a reappraisal: Stalin entered the League (1934) and made a pact with France. His preference, however, was to guard Soviet safety by avoiding a break with the Nazi state. There was no serious intent to align with the League, whose motives he mistrusted. In Europe (by covert intervention in the Spanish Civil War, 1936–9) and in East Asia (by military help to the Kuomintang) Stalin played a lone hand.

The fourth zone was East Asia. Its post-war settlement was a tripartite arrangement between Britain, Japan and the United States. But it quickly became obvious that its fate was to be a contested sphere where neither the League nor any great power would have decisive authority. By the mid-1920s the British (who had the largest foreign stake in East Asia) were on the defensive, fearful that an insurgent nationalism would bundle them out of their treaty-port enclaves and make even Hong Kong a heavy liability. They sent a force to Shanghai in 1927, but were anxious to parley with the Kuomintang. The United States, with much less at stake (in 1931, American investment in China was only 6 per cent of the foreign total, far behind Britain with 37 per cent, Japan with 35 per cent, and even Russia with 8.4 per cent),[64] preferred to rely upon good relations with the Kuomintang regime, some of whose leading figures had strong American links. The Americans were keen to draw the Kuomintang away from its Russian connections. The same antipathy to Soviet influence made them reluctant to antagonize Japan, the Soviet Union's main enemy in North East Asia. When Japan occupied Manchuria in 1931, the United States expressed strong disapproval, but drew back from active opposition, hoping that the politicians in Tokyo would restrain the army.[65] The cooling of Anglo-American relations after 1931 – the result in part of economic friction – removed the main guarantee that the 'Washington system' would be upheld in East Asia.

After 1931, what mattered most was the triangular rivalry of the Kuomintang government, now based in Nanking, the Soviet Union, anxiously reinforcing its colonial presence, and imperial Japan. The Nanking government had emerged victorious from the civil wars of 1928–31 that combined with famine to cost the lives of 6 million people.[66] But it fell short of enjoying a monopoly of force (the acid test of effective rule) across China proper. It was powerless to prevent the savage Japanese attack on Shanghai in 1932, when Chinese anger at the occupation of Manchuria spilled over into violence against local Japanese interests. Under Chiang Kai-shek, in 1928 the Kuomintang leadership had broken decisively with the Communist elements of the party and had driven them out. But although the Kuomintang onslaught on the Kiangsi/Jiangxi 'soviet' forced Mao and his followers into an epic withdrawal, the 'Long March' to safe havens in north-west China in 1934–5, the Communists survived to fight another day under Soviet patronage. Soviet action in East Asia was designed to shore up Moscow's influence, prevent the destruction of the Chinese Communist Party, and check Japan's incursions into Inner Asia and its domination of China. But it was hampered by military and logistical weakness, Kuomintang animosity, and (as we have seen) fear of provoking a war on two fronts.

The initiative in East Asia was held by Japan. Japan's strength was disparaged by the Western powers in the 1920s: 'a weak rather than a strong Power' said the British ambassador in 1924.[67] In fact the Washington treaties, which forbade new fortifications in the western Pacific (including the British base at Hong Kong), had made Japan less vulnerable to a naval attack than before 1914. Tokyo's policy was to avoid confrontation with the British and Americans, but to consolidate its grip in Manchuria by a virtual protectorate over its warlord ruler.[68] Manchuria was the centrepiece of Japanese thinking. It obsessed the army, whose reputation had been made there. It was the great bastion against Russia's regional comeback. Its economic importance as a vast frontier region was taken for granted. After 1928, however, Japan's informal predominance came under growing pressure from a more assertive China. There was more and more friction with the South Manchurian Railway – Japan's commercial octopus – and with the Kwantung army that guarded the 'railway zone'. When the Kwantung army staged a violent incident and then occupied Mukden, the Manchurian capital, in September 1931, Tokyo gave its reluctant assent. The severity of depression and the united opposition of army and navy to the disarmament clauses that Japan had accepted at the London Naval Conference of 1930 had created a new political mood.[69] Japan left the League of Nations (in 1933), repudiated the Washington treaties by creating the puppet state of Manchukuo, and was drawn deeper and deeper into northern China. As the Kuomintang government prepared for the struggle,[70] the real uncertainties were when war would break out, who else would take part, how it would end, and what effects it would have on a fractured world order.

The failure to build a post-war system through which the most powerful countries could settle their differences and build coalitions against rule-breaking states might have been mitigated by economic good feeling. In the mid-1920s it looked as if the great commercial recovery would do this, and more. A dynamic world economy would draw America towards Europe, encourage liberalism in Germany, disarm Japanese fears, and keep the door ajar between the West and Russia. The fierce contraction of trade that had set in by 1930 had the reverse effect. Much the hardest hit were those who relied upon primary products as their main source of income: as their incomes collapsed, so did their buying. As markets slumped and prices fell (many by as much as 50 per cent), the main commercial states rushed to protect their stake. American tariffs, already high, rose by a quarter in 1930. To protect the value of sterling, the British abandoned free trade – for the time being at least – and built a tariff wall around their empire.[71] Soviet Russia all but withdrew from world trade altogether. The most obvious victims of this unfree trade (apart from the impoverished producers of raw materials and foods) were the industrial economies of Japan and Germany. German recovery after 1933 was based around production for internal demand, and strict exchange control to minimize imports. It also depended upon barter arrangements with Germany's South East European neighbours: by the mid-1930s, privileged access to raw materials in Eastern Europe – a de facto zone of German commercial control – had become an important part of the Nazi plan to retrieve Germany's status as a great world power.[72] In the Japanese case, the dilemma was even more acute. Japan had to import its raw materials and fuel (raw cotton from India and oil from America). It paid for them by exports, especially of textiles – exporting three times as much of its national output as did the United States.[73] Japan's main advantages were the low wages of labour, the remarkable efficiency of its large commercial firms, and the huge productivity gains made in cloth production.[74] These all helped Japan to achieve industrial growth in the 1930s when other industrial states were in serious difficulty. But it remained acutely exposed to the threat of trade barriers (like those that seemed likely in 1933–4 to close off its second-largest market, in India), price falls (like that for raw silk in the United States), boycotts (a recurrent menace in China) and the sudden dislocation of its whole economy – with terrifying consequences for social and political order. Fierce devaluation (by nearly 50 per cent), controls over imports, an aggressive diplomacy to win export quotas in overseas markets, and the attempt to build up a 'yen bloc' in East Asia were Tokyo's answer. It was symptomatic of a new global order. The politicization of trade, the growing belief that international trade was bound to decline further in relation to output, and the urgency of securing a political grip on key markets and supplies were the hallmarks of an age which had seen the 'globalization' of the late nineteenth century go into sharp reverse.[75]

Perhaps it was not surprising that geopolitical and economic cleavages should have found a loud cultural echo. Even before 1914 the Western liberals' programme for building a modern culture had not passed without challenge. Religious thinkers (in every part of the world) as well as educated elites (in some) treated its claims as a challenge to mobilize. While Western ideas about technological change, individual choice and the public sphere were drawn upon freely, new types of media and new forms of association were enrolled in the struggle to fashion distinctively national 'high cultures' out of older traditions. The First World War was a watershed. Its explosive impact on the mind and imagination gave a savage twist to the loss of liberal certainty. The extreme case was Russia. The survival of Bolshevism as the new ruling order demanded cultural no less than political revolution. The new Soviet culture was meant to reach technical modernity through collective proletarian effort, not bourgeois self-help. It was part of the vast campaign of 'de-peasantization'.[76] The new 'Soviet man' would embrace science and socialism in the certain belief that capitalist societies were on course to self-destruct. In Germany too the culture of liberalism came under heavier fire after 1918. This was no coincidence. There was long-standing antipathy on both Left and Right to the corrosive effect of laissez-faire capitalism on social cohesion. Part of the appeal of a German-led Mitteleuropa had been its offer of a middle way between the backward East and an over-commercialized West. The trauma of defeat, the 'loss' of millions of Germans permanently separated from the new German state, and the devastating impact of economic shocks from outside created a powerful sense of social and cultural crisis. Only a strong state could save the German *Volk* from being broken on the wheel of international capitalism, with its ruthless disregard for authenticity and belonging. These views, already widespread before 1929, acquired added authority with Hitler's accession to power in January 1933.[77]

Soviet and Nazi culture were agreed in offering alternative versions of modernity. Both insisted on their technological dynamism. Each claimed that technology was being made to serve a common social purpose. Both urged the need for cultural autarky to exclude foreign influence. Each denounced the West as corrupt and decadent and in steep decline. The failure of the leading capitalist states – the United States, Britain and France – even to agree upon a plan to save the international trading system, let alone act on it, seemed to vindicate these criticisms from the Left and the Right. Nor, of course, was the cultural attack on the West confined to Europe. In Japan, where industrialization accelerated sharply in the 1920s and '30s (with a heavy dependence upon female labour), the rush to the towns, the stresses on rural life, the impact of new media (especially American films) and fear of the break-up of old social disciplines produced symptoms of deep cultural anxiety.[78] Events after 1930 seemed to confirm the alienness and bankruptcy of the international order imposed by the West on a reluctant East Asia. In Kuomintang China, where hopes of Western support were dealt a heavy blow by the League's timid response to Japan's attack in Manchuria, and where the struggle with Communism was a vital concern, nationalist ideology stressed social discipline through the 'New Culture' movement and revived Confucian notions of communal duty. In British-ruled India, the Congress Party was the main nationalist vehicle. By the 1930s the intellectual loyalties of its 'high command' were divided between loyalty to the autarkic utopia of Gandhianism and loyalty to the Soviet-inspired socialism favoured by Gandhi's cerebral protégé Jawaharlal Nehru. Religious revivalism (among both Hindus and Muslims) and popular Gandhianism, which promoted the idea of a pristine, rural and godly India, formed a combined assault upon the cultural values of imperial rule, condemned as the alien violation of India's moral order. The same kind of objection was voiced in colonial Africa by Kikuyu notables who feared that the settler occupation in the Kenya colony would smash their social and ethical system.[79] In *Facing Mount Kenya* (1938), Jomo Kenyatta (who had trained in London as an anthropologist under the great Bronislaw Malinowski) denounced colonial rule as a vandal that had wrecked the material foundations of Kikuyu culture, destroying in the process a sense of freedom and responsibility of which the ignorant Europeans had no understanding.[80]

Against this lowering background, it is little wonder that the fate of Europe's overseas empires seemed at best uncertain. From their different angles, Marxists, imperialist diehards and even anxious liberals predicted the early demise of European imperialism.[81] Without drastic measures, it would soon be politically, economically and culturally bankrupt. Between these signs of glee on the Left and gloom on the Right, imperial rulers displayed periodically a crisis of confidence. Meanwhile, prophecies of downfall sharpened the anger of those who felt vulnerable to its immediate impact – like the white minorities in South and Central Africa, or the resident expatriates in treaty-port Shanghai.[82] But, like Tom Sawyer's obituary, earnest prognoses of a 'lost dominion' or 'the world revolt against Europe' were to be premature. The imperial systems of Europe's main colonial powers – Britain, France, the Netherlands, Portugal and Belgium – proved surprisingly resilient. On the eve of the Second World War they remained territorially intact. Even where nationalism had won the widest support, the breakthrough to freedom was tantalizingly elusive. In 1938, after two decades of struggle, Jawaharlal Nehru all but despaired of India's political prospects.[83] Real independence still seemed far in the future.

Imperial survival was partly the result of imperial pragmatism. Colonial policy rejected reliance on coercion as costly, clumsy and counterproductive. The post-war upheaval had hammered home that lesson. Finding local allies meant yielding more local power. The British practised this doctrine in earnest after 1920. In Iraq and Egypt they renounced direct supervision of internal affairs, preferring instead to base their claim to pre-eminence on the terms of a treaty.[84] This should not be mistaken for a tacit acceptance that imperial power was over. In India, especially, the British combined a gradual enlargement of Indians' political rights with constitutional changes that were carefully designed to make the province, not the nation, the focus of political life. As province-based leaders assumed full responsibility for provincial affairs, their electorates would expect them to concentrate on 'knife and fork' matters of development and welfare, not chase the wild goose of 'independence now'. Not only that. Provinces varied greatly in their religious and linguistic make-up. Their new leaders were unlikely to give all-out support to the Indian National Congress, the main antagonist of the British Raj, and dominated politically by North Indian Hindus. In two of the most important provinces, Bengal and the Punjab, provincial self-government had brought Muslims to office. In 1935 the British carried their Machiavellian liberalism to an even higher level. They promised India self-government as a federal dominion. But the constitutional rules, which assured a large quota of seats for Muslims and princes (the federation would unite 'British' and 'princely' India), seemed almost certain to keep Congress from power and might even ensure its eventual break-up.[85]

It would be wrong to exaggerate the cunning behind these imperial manoeuvres. What is striking, however, is the cool expectation that colonial politics could be 'managed' in ways that would leave the key imperial interests safe: strategic use of local resources and exclusive control over external relations. This was not irrational. Until the late 1930s the British, French and Dutch could assume that the risk of another great power daring to interfere in their empires' internal politics was practically nil. While that remained true, local nationalist leaders had no hope of playing off their imperial masters against another great patron. Nor could they hope to raise the price of their loyalty. Worse still, the virtual absence of an external threat left colonial rulers free to use coercive tactics against local oppositions they defined as 'extremist'. Armed with much better intelligence than before 1914, colonial regimes could now strike hard at 'subversive' movements: Communist rebellions in French Indochina and the Dutch East Indies were quite easily broken in the 1930s.[86] The other great lever that the rulers could wield was the divided nature of most colonial societies.

It was a crucial paradox in colonial politics that social and cultural change worked both for and against the cause of nationalism. In most parts of the world, colonial boundaries were essentially artificial. Colonial states Sellotaped together districts and regions that had little in common. Imperial frontiers and divisions were determined by administrative convenience, the pattern of conquest, or partition diplomacy, not a wish to preserve ethno-linguistic unity or old ties of trade and exchange. Of course, once the colonial state began to take shape and to assert its authority across the whole of its territory, it tended to stimulate a parallel growth among its colonial subjects. When even remote districts began to feel the demands of a faraway government and to sense the effects of 'policy' made in the colonial capital, their leaders and notables had a powerful motive to build supra-local alliances. Only a colony-wide movement could apply adequate pressure on the colonial officials and exert local influence at the point of decision – at the colonial centre. This kind of nationalism was given added impetus by two important trends. The first was the bonding together of different parts of the colony by speedier travel, the circulation of knowledge (often by newspapers) and new types of education (in European-style colleges and schools). The second was the adoption by the emergent native 'Western-educated elite' of the political ideology not of the colonial rulers but of their distant motherlands faraway in Europe. Legal equality, freedom of speech and the right to self-government became the battle cry of one of the first and greatest of these nationalist movements (and the model for many others), the Indian National Congress. In principle, the junction between a skilful, sophisticated and well-connected elite in the colonial capital, well versed in the rule books of colonial governance, and local district notables, anxious to influence the decisions of government – in finance, education, transport or agriculture – meant the moment of take-off for mass nationalism. All that was needed was to keep local resentments simmering at just the right heat while the nationalist elite squeezed successive instalments of political power from their baffled rulers.

That was the theory. The practice was usually different. Colonial rulers made it their business to deflate the claims of nationalist leaders, whose motives and authenticity were contrasted unfavourably with those of traditional authorities: princes, landlords, sheikhs and chiefs. In much of British-ruled Africa, the inter-war years saw the remorseless spread of 'indirect rule', which devolved local affairs not to elected bodies but to chiefs and their followers ('tribes').[87] By granting limited taxing powers and promoting the use of customary law (codified versions of local practice), indirect rule turned the colonial state into a loose confederacy of different ethnic units whose links and connections, whether horizontal or vertical, could be easily patrolled by the colonial officials.[88] That was one challenge to the advance of nationalist politics, but not the most dangerous. Far more serious was the rise of 'sub-nationalisms' – new solidarities based on language, religion, ethnicity or status that denied the reality of the colonial state as a cultural or political unit. It was easy to see how these had come about. The uneven spread of literacy and print, the differential impact of economic change, and the sharpening lines between religious faiths and creeds mobilized a succession of 'new' communities often antagonistic to the original nationalists. Here the classic case was India. 'Self-government within . . . or without the British Empire, the formation of a consolidated North-West Indian Muslim State appears to me the final destiny of the Muslims, at least of North-West India,' declared the poet-philosopher Muhammad Iqbal in his presidential address to the Muslim League in December 1930.[89] 'We Hindus are bound together not only by the tie of love . . . to a common fatherland . . . but . . . by the tie of the common homage we pay to our great civilization – our Hindu culture,' claimed V. D. Savarkar in his tract *Hindutva: Who is a Hindu?*,[90] dismissing the notion of a secular Indian nationalism. 'The British have an Empire,' exclaimed B. R. Ambedkar, the leader of the untouchables. 'So have the Hindus. For is not Hinduism a form of imperialism and are not the Untouchables a subject race, owing their allegiance and servitude to their Hindu Master?'[91] Gandhi's claim that the Congress was the sole representative of all Indian opinion had lost credibility by the 1930s. In other colonial regions, political or cultural awakening was the signal to demand separation from, or protection against, other indigenous groups whose past exploitation was resented or whose future dominance was feared. For Hill State peoples in Burma, or the Lao and Khmer in French Indochina, colonial rulers were far less threatening than ethnic Burmans or Vietnamese. There was no reason to think that, as time went on, the original nationalist movements would maintain their lead over the newer sub-nationalisms or survive the attempt to quash or contain them. It was fear that the Congress would succumb to the magnetic force of provincial, sectional, class or religious interests that so depressed Nehru in the late 1930s. If the chance of independence was missed, it might never recur, except in a form too limited to be real.

It was thus hard to envisage the early demise of the European empires. Indeed, the British, who had the largest, were tending if anything to strengthen their hold on those parts of their system that had (like Argentina) become more dependent upon the British market or (like Australia and New Zealand) felt more in need than ever of British strategic protection. Across the vast areas of Africa, Asia and the Middle East where European imperialism depended upon the grudging acquiescence of local allies and clients, what had really set in was a form of stalemate. The colonial impetus (never strong in most places) had been lost. The resources of power had run low. The sense of purpose had dissolved. But colonialism remained a 'going concern'. Its local enemies had yet to find a way out of the labyrinth it had built. It would take a huge external shock to help blast a path.

IMPERIALISMS AT WAR

Imperialism can be defined as the attempt to impose one state's predominance over other societies by assimilating them to its political, cultural and economic system. As we have seen already it was not just a European phenomenon, although Europeans had tended to carry it furthest. Nor was it practised in only one mode. Sometimes it relied upon the direct political control of the zone of expansion. But it was often convenient to defer or disguise the fact of foreign predominance by leaving in place a notionally sovereign government. Sometimes it led to the displacement of peoples by a mass of new settlers colonizing the land. But in Europe's advance into Afro-Asia this trend had been weak. Quite often its motive had been to delimit a sphere of economic exclusion, reserving trade and investment to the imperial power. But not invariably: the biggest empire of all, the British, had practised free trade until the 1930s. It was usually based upon an ideological claim (the 'civilizing mission') and an appeal to notions of a cultural hierarchy in which the colonizers' capacity for 'moral and material progress' was sharply contrasted with the regression of the colonized. However, for all its arrogance, this cultural imperialism lacked the brutal certainty of 'biological racism'. Belief in the limits set by ethnic descent on intellectual or moral development was far from uncommon among late-nineteenth-century imperialists, but it was not universal. In both the French and the British empires (by contrast with the United States) the potential for equality among persons of all races remained the formal position in law, in institutions and in official ideology.

Imperialism should thus be seen as a continuum with wide variation in its objects and methods. In a now famous argument, the greatest historians of British imperialism showed that its mode of expansion differed from place to place and was mainly determined by the scope for cooperating with local elites. Where British interests required more than these elites would deliver, 'formal' rule was imposed – but not otherwise.[92] This insight can be widened. States that cherished imperial ambitions varied considerably in their expansive capacities, in their notions of self-interest, and in the opportunities available. A shortage of capital and limited geopolitical leverage increased the appeal of an exclusive empire but reduced the chance of winning a large one. Coming late to the race might mean that the rich pickings had gone before there was time to stake a real claim. The costs and risks of expansion at a particular moment might seem much greater to the ruling group in the would-be imperial power than any possible benefit. It was partly this that ensured that the forward surge of empires after 1880 had passed off without a resort to arms between the European states. Partition diplomacy also reflected the fact that where the stakes were highest – in the Middle East and China – the existing order had yet to collapse and no single power had the motive or means to enforce a division.

Historians have been mesmerized by the imperial rivalries of the late nineteenth century. But the 'new imperialism' out of which they grew was a tepid affair: it had little in common with the brutal expansions of the 1930s and '40s. It was then that the struggle for empire, repressed by the outcome of the First World War, reached its savage climax. In these decades, the grab for territory by would-be imperial powers assumed an urgency that was infinitely greater than before 1914. The threat it posed to international order could not be defused – as in earlier times – by diverting its impact into the weakly ruled spaces of the Outer World. Three crucial conditions reinforced its ferocity and wrecked the chances of compromise. First was the depth of the economic crisis after 1930, and the fear it aroused of a vast social breakdown. Second was the violence of the ideological warfare that raged between states – communist, fascist and liberal – and the gulf of mistrust that this served to widen. Third was the fear of impending encirclement – economic, racial or geostrategic – in a world whose division into mutually antagonistic blocs was the most likely future. To make matters worse, the regimes that felt most at risk from these dangers – Germany and Japan – were the least inclined to prop up the balance of power or the old social order, the two great brakes on imperial adventurism before 1914. Still less were they likely to treat the world's existing borders as if they were legitimate. The new imperialism of the 1930s was the toxic product of an anxious, lawless, insecure world.

What form did it take? The prime mover was Germany. Once Hitler came to power, the German revolt against the leaders of the 'League

World' became unstoppable. By openly flouting the disarmament rules of the Versailles Treaty, militarizing the Rhineland, uniting with Austria (the *Anschluss*) and forcing Czechoslovakia's dismemberment with aggressive diplomacy, Hitler humiliated and demoralized the two guarantors of the post-war order, Britain and France. He encouraged the defection of their once junior partner, Italy, now also a rebel against the League World's rules. Hitler's imperialism – the quest for *Lebensraum* – targeted Eastern Europe, the Ukraine and Russia. It was meant to be built over the physical and ideological ruins of the Soviet empire. By contrast, he took little interest in the colonial empires of Britain and France, and regarded Germany's pre-1914 challenge to Britain as a catastrophic error.[93] But in 1939 he discovered that the two Western powers would not let him become the imperial hegemon of Eastern Europe without a fight. To win that war, the necessary prologue to the main struggle against Stalin, Hitler concluded the Nazi–Soviet pact of August 1939. Both partners bought time: time for Germany to win supremacy in Western and Central Europe; time for Stalin to prepare for the struggle that was bound to come. Of the two, it seemed for some months as if Hitler's gamble was bigger. After all, if the First World War was anything to go by, it was hardly likely that he would be able to defeat Britain and France in an all-out war, especially if he had to look over his shoulder at a hostile Russia. Even after the first phase of the war was over, and Poland was shared out between its two brutal neighbours, an unofficial armed truce – the 'phoney war' or *drôle de guerre* – reigned in the west. If Germany could not win quickly, it was widely assumed that its overstrained economy would collapse long before the economies of the British and French with their investments and empires.[94] After six months of 'war', maybe the Germans had lost their nerve. 'Hitler', said Neville Chamberlain, the British prime minister in April 1940, 'has missed the bus.'[95]

But in the lightning war of May–June 1940, and against all reasonable prediction, Hitler made himself master of most of continental Europe. From the Atlantic coast of France he could apply the tourniquet of submarine warfare to the sea lanes of Britain. Sooner or later he could begin the conquest of the Soviet Union and secure German domination from the Atlantic to the Urals. In the meantime, his dramatic defeat of the Western powers signalled the meltdown of the post-First World War order – and not just in Europe. Once France had fallen, Italy entered the war to seize a Mediterranean empire, attacking Greece and Egypt, the strategic bastion of British Middle Eastern power. If the British lost Cairo (the grand centre of their imperial communications) and the Suez Canal, the road would be open for an Axis advance to the Persian Gulf and (eventually) the frontiers of India. For Hitler, ironically, the Italian advance into Greece and Egypt was a damaging distraction. It delayed the grand assault on the Soviet Union, 'Operation Barbarossa', that he opened in June 1941. As the German armies tore into Russia and raced across the Ukraine, a huge geopolitical revolution was under way. There was every sign that within a year the Germans would control the Soviet land mass west of the Urals, as well as the Caucasus with its supplies of oil. They would have built an empire on the grandest of scales. They would command what Mackinder had called the 'heartland', and be the dominant power in continental Eurasia, driving Britain (and America) to its maritime fringes and the Outer World beyond. 'We should be the blockaded party,' declared an American expert.[96] It was inconceivable, if that happened, that much would survive of the old colonial order in Asia, Africa or the Middle East. Indeed, by mid-1941 the signs of a crisis were already apparent in the largest colony of all. Faced with German supremacy on the European mainland and the new Middle Eastern threat, the British had been forced (against their original plans) to mobilize Indian resources. Now they would have to pay the price demanded by Indian nationalists and Muslim sub-nationalists, or face a political revolt. They embarked upon the twisting path of concession that led by mid-1942 to the fateful promise of Indian independence at the end of the war.

At the eastern end of Eurasia, a second vast upheaval had already begun. After their conquest of Manchuria, the Japanese had continued the slow penetration of North China, and had dragged Inner Mongolia into their sphere of control by mid-1936. In July 1937 their army in China clashed with the forces of the Kuomintang government and began an all-out war. Tokyo's objective was to make China a part of its East Asian system, cutting off its connections with the West and Russia. Japan's imperialism was fuelled by a sense of cultural anxiety,

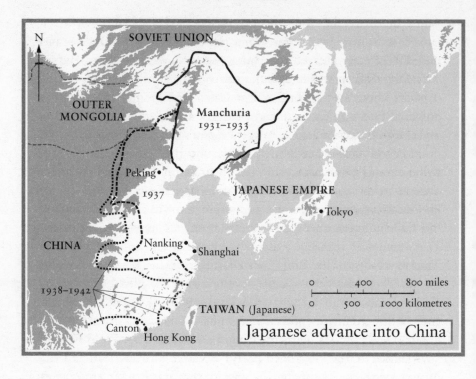

Japanese advance into China

by the ideological appeal of a 'pan-Asian' revolt against the colonialist West,[97] and by a growing belief that Europe's power in Asia was in steep decline.[98] Japan had enjoyed economic success in the 1930s, but its vital markets abroad were acutely dependent upon good relations with Britain (while the British ruled India) and the United States. Of all the great powers, Japan was most vulnerable to the external disruption of its industrial economy: a commercial empire of its own was the best guarantee against the catastrophic effects of this. Indeed, the high command of the army, the dominant force in the Tokyo government, assumed that the world would soon be divided into regional spheres and closed economic zones. In a future war, the Soviet Union and Britain could be expelled from East Asia. Meanwhile, so it reasoned, the gradual extension of Japanese power over China could be pushed ahead without the risk of war with the United States, whose acute hostility towards the Soviet Union would balance its dislike for Japan's empire-building.[99] The striking failure of the British and

Americans to agree a response to Japan's attack upon China, the 1938 United States Congress decision against building new battleships, and the defensive posture of the United States Navy in the Pacific all seemed to confirm this confident judgement.[100]

It turned out to be wrong. The British and Americans did not back down: both continued to send help to Chiang Kai-shek even after he was driven from Nanking to Chungking in the far west of China. But London and Washington also miscalculated. They discounted Japan's willingness to confront them militarily. After June 1940 and the fall of France, however, Japan's hand was much stronger. On 23 September, Hitler's client regime in France allowed the Japanese army into French Indochina. A few days later (on the 27th) the Japanese signed the Tripartite Pact with Germany and Italy, perhaps to deter more Anglo-American help to the Kuomintang government. The following April they made another bargain. In August 1939 the Japanese army had fought a crucial battle against Soviet forces at Nomonhan in Mongolia. The Red Army won. Both sides drew the moral that further fighting was pointless – for the time being at least. Both sides were anxious not to fight on two fronts. The Neutrality Pact of April 1941 formalized this position. It freed the Soviet army to fight in the west and the Japanese army to wage a new war in the south. In July 1941 it entered southern Indochina, the launch pad for the invasion of Thailand, Malaya and the Dutch East Indies, with its great reserves of oil. When Washington riposted with an oil embargo (80 per cent of Japanese oil still came from America), the decision was taken for a pre-emptive war. With the attack on Pearl Harbor on 7 December and the capture of Singapore just over two months later (victories as astonishing as Hitler's in the west) Japan became master of the Asian Pacific. Colonial South East Asia had fallen: the invasion of India seemed just a matter of time. By mid-1942 the Soviet empire was reeling; the British was on the ropes. Two new imperialisms were about to divide Eurasia, and then perhaps the world. A 'new order' was coming.

These amazing events marked the final collapse of the Europe-centred world order that had seemed so secure before 1914. They also revealed the terrifying fragility of the 'liberal world', whose post-war renewal had been loudly proclaimed. It was not just a matter of the end of free trade. The 1930s had seen a scale of political violence in both Europe and East Asia that defied past comparison. Thought-control, propaganda and physical force became the daily recourse of authoritarian governments. Ideological war was waged with uncompromising ferocity. Normal feelings of humanity gave way under the strain. Most terrible of all was the boiling up not just of racial antagonism but of programmatic racism. It reached its ghastly climax in 1942, perhaps the most critical year in modern world history. A bureaucrats' conference at Wannsee, near Berlin, signalled the moment at which the Holocaust became policy in the German government.[101] That year, 1942, was 'the most astounding year of the Holocaust, one of the most astounding years of murder in the whole history of mankind'.[102] Almost half of all the Jews who fell into Nazi hands were killed in the twelve months after March 1942. In this orgy of murder we might also see the end of a world. What had opened up this moral abyss?

It is tempting to dismiss the 1930s and '40s as a freakish era of fanatics and madmen. There is no warrant for this. The process is complex, but the main lines of causation seem clear enough. At the root of the violence, the hatred, the murders, the search for cultural seclusion and economic self-sufficiency lay the clash between the two great forces that had shaped the world after 1890. The first was the intense globalization that opened up cultures, economies and political systems to external influence on a massive scale and at tremendous speed. For all the attractions of this, it was hardly surprising that in many societies there were multiple symptoms of distress and alarm, including widespread movements for cultural and racial 'purification'. The second was state-building. State-building was stimulated by many of the forces that promoted globalization: improved communications, the rise of large-scale industry, and the growth of new communities. It could also exploit them to create new kinds of authority and new techniques of control. State-builders found that they could harness the fear of the foreign to strengthen their claim to patriotic obedience. Until 1914, globalization and state-building had advanced together in a precarious balance. But the great double crisis of the early twentieth century wrecked this uneasy equilibrium. The First World War and its outcome destroyed the legitimacy of international order, the political framework on which globalization depended. In Europe's largest states, Russia and Germany, the shock of defeat bred a violent reaction against economic and cultural openness. The great contraction of trade after 1930 gave a savage twist to the mood of revolt. The experiment in globalism had been a disaster, and its final demise could not be far off – a conviction shared by Communists, fascists and Japanese pan-Asianists. In the coming struggle for power, and perhaps survival, all that really mattered was the strength and cohesion of the nation state and the size and scale of its zone of expansion. In a fragmented world with no collective will, there were few restraints. The vast Eurasian war that filled the horizon by mid-1942 was the crisis of the world.

8

Empire Denied

8. The new face of war: nuclear test in the Marshall Islands, 1952

To those tossed about in its terrible wake, the Second World War was the end of the world. It smashed the flimsy structure of international society, already fractured after 1918. It tore down states or wrecked their workings. It blocked the channels of trade, and created new forms of economic dependence. It loaded peoples and governments with huge new burdens that they could barely carry either financially or physically. It fashioned new forms of coercive power through propaganda, policing and an intricate web of economic controls. It raised ideology to a screaming pitch as part of the struggle to motivate and mobilize. It spread a vast tide of violent disorder extending far beyond the zones of battle or the march of armies. It displaced, enslaved or murdered huge numbers of people, especially in Europe, South East Asia and China. However the war ended, it was bound to cast its shadow on the peace that followed. The massive task of reconstruction would fall on peoples and governments already exhausted and disoriented.[1] In the post-war world, social and political cohesion – or discipline – would be at a premium. Those states that maintained (or exceeded) their wartime production would be at a great advantage in any struggle for power. One thing was certain: there was no going back to the status quo, even if such a thing had existed in the turbulent 1930s. As much as the world before 1914, the pre-1939 world had gone for good.

Of course, this did not mean that the world was a moonscape in which everything would be new. For all the terrible stresses of the conflict, large areas of the globe – in the Americas and Africa – had preserved their social and political order. In much of the rest, the strongest wish of civilian populations was (almost certainly) to free themselves from the demands of authority and recover some shreds of normal domestic life. They would begrudge new rules, new calls on their labour, or new material hardships. The victor powers would bring to the peace many old aims and assumptions, however much modified by the war's extraordinary course. Wherever they could, they would harness the forces left behind by the war to build a new order in tune with their interests – if they could decide what they were. There was little chance in reality that they would all agree on a blueprint for peace (another legacy of the inter-war years), or have the will or the means to impose it globally. Hence the post-war world (whatever the dreams of prophets and planners) was not a new beginning or a cure for conflict. It was like a bombed-out city in which the most urgent need was to shore up the buildings that had survived the blast and divide up the remainder between rival contractors. But with little agreement on where to rebuild or what to demolish, and with competing claims to some of the grandest ruins, reconstruction was slow, conflictual and bitter. After 1949, this poisonous atmosphere became even more acrid, since both superpowers now possessed the means for massive destruction using atomic weapons. This was the setting in which old empires were broken and new ones assembled.

EURASIA PARTITIONED

The turning point in the global war came in 1942–3. At the Battle of Midway in June 1942, America destroyed the offensive power of the Japanese navy in the western Pacific. At Alamein in October–November 1942, the German–Italian effort to capture Egypt and break the British Empire in two suffered a decisive setback. Above all, at Stalingrad and the tank battle of Kursk, German hopes of defeating the Soviet Union were effectively shattered. Whatever successes they scored, after mid-1943 the Axis powers could not win outright and there could be no new world order designed in Tokyo and Berlin. What remained hugely uncertain was when and how the war would end, the state of the world when it did, and the balance of strength between the victorious powers when the shooting stopped. An Allied disaster in Normandy in June 1944, or a Japanese victory at Imphal on the frontier of India at much the same time, would have had drastic consequences.

Meanwhile, on the side of the 'United Nations', as the anti-Axis coalition began to style itself, the demise of the old colonial order was the public aim of its two strongest allies, the United States and the Soviet Union. In Moscow, hostility to empire (except of the Soviet variety) was axiomatic. Its destruction would herald the inevitable fall

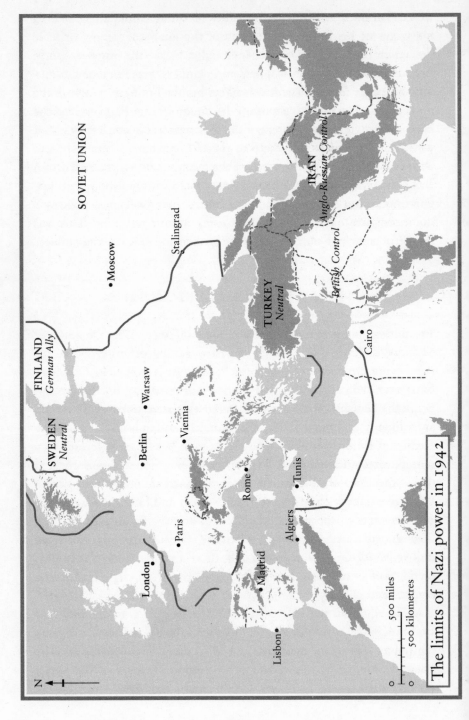

SOVIET UNION

• Moscow

Stalingrad

FINLAND
German Ally

SWEDEN
Neutral

Berlin • • Warsaw

Vienna •

Paris •

London •

Madrid •

Lisbon •

Rome •

Algiers • • Tunis

TURKEY
Neutral

IRAN
Anglo-Russian Control

British Control

Cairo •

N

500 miles
500 kilometres

The limits of Nazi power in 1942

of capitalism. The American president Franklin D. Roosevelt made no secret of his dislike for European colonial rule, though out of deference to Churchill he reserved much of his fire for the sins of French rather than British colonialism. But it was widely assumed among American policymakers that, for all the heroism of their island defence, the British were irredeemably decadent as an imperial power. Indeed, this view was echoed within Britain itself. The fall of Singapore, the loss of Malaya and Burma, the feeble performance of the British forces, and the lack of enthusiasm for the imperial cause by Britain's Asian subjects, notably in India, all seemed to show that Britain's century of dominance in South and South East Asia had come to an end. To cling to old-style imperialism would be futile and dangerous. In *Soviet Light on the Colonies* (a Penguin Special in 1944), one expert critic compared British colonial policy unfavourably with Soviet practice in the Central Asian republics.[2] The government itself, worried by the hostility of American public opinion, waged a charm offensive to present imperial rule as a beneficent partnership to promote democracy and development among 'backward' peoples.[3] Colonial governments were given the nod to widen political life and hold more elections. None of this was lost on colonial politicians. Whatever the outcome of the war, it seemed certain to break the pre-war stalemate in colonial politics. One grand symbol of change was already in evidence. In 1943 the remnants of China's unequal treaties were at last swept away when the British abandoned their surviving privileges there as so much useless lumber.

Yet the course of the war offered no reassurance that the world of empires would be smoothly transformed into a world of nations. The first region made secure by the Allied powers was the Middle East. The immediate effect was to restore the primacy that the British had enjoyed since 1918. Indeed, victory allowed them to entrench it more deeply – or so it appeared. They had made Cairo the centre of a huge operational sphere in the Mediterranean as much as in the Middle East. The 'Suez Canal Zone', demarcated in the Anglo-Egyptian treaty of 1936, was a great military enclave, housing thousands of troops, as well as workshops and stores, training areas and airfields. It was a bastion of power from which British military might could be dispatched in any direction. In fact the British showed little sign of believing that their Middle East imperium should be given away. They feared a revival of Soviet power, and suspected Stalin's designs on northern Iran (occupied during the war by Soviet troops) and the Turkish Straits. They were determined to protect their oil concessions in south-western Iran, and their refinery enclave at Abadan on the Gulf. They saw the Middle East as the vital platform from which to project their authority in the eastern half of the world. Their aim was not to impose old-style colonial rule, abandoned as impractical two decades before, but to reshape local politics in convenient ways. Their basic assumption was that 'moderate' nationalists in Egypt, Iran and the Arab countries would accept a more 'discreet' British presence in exchange for promises of protection against external attack and a generous package of economic aid. What they failed to foresee was how quickly the Arab–Jewish conflict in Palestine (governed by the British under an international mandate) would be intensified by the torrent of Jewish refugees who poured in at the end of the war, and how badly their influence would suffer from the Arab belief that the creation of Israel (and the Arab defeat in the Palestine war that followed British withdrawal in 1948) was an act of British betrayal. The end of empire in the Middle East was to be anything but a consensual transition to a nation-state age.

The question of Palestine, the risk of Anglo-Soviet rivalry and the growing importance of its oil reserves linked the future of the Middle East to the outcome of the war in Europe. In an ideal world, there would have been a European settlement to revive the pre-war states system, restore democratic self-government, and promote economic recovery. Had such a 'new Europe' emerged to balance the power of the United States and the Soviet Union, the general pattern of the post-war world would have been very different. But the course of the war made such an outcome impossible. The Allies' insistence on 'unconditional surrender' (partly from loathing of the Nazi regime, partly from fear that negotiation would split them), and Hitler's resolve to fight to the end, turned almost all of Europe into a vast battleground in 1944–5. Much of the continent had already become a colossal Nazi empire mobilized for war, obliterating pre-war states, uprooting pre-war communities, liquidating pre-war minorities. In the terrible death throes of Nazi imperialism in Eastern, Western and

Central Europe, the scale of the violence, ethnic and ideological divisions, and the stigma of collaboration, whether forced or not, were a fateful legacy. In the climate of fear, retribution and hate, the task of reviving democratic self-government (in Eastern Europe especially) was desperately vulnerable to social or racial conflict and external pressure. There could be no swift restoration of Europe's place in the world. What occurred instead was a succession struggle between the victor powers and their local allies to win control of the defunct Nazi empire.

The partition of Europe did not come immediately. The original expectation of Stalin, Roosevelt and Churchill seems to have been a rough division of interests that recognized Soviet predominance in Poland, Romania and Bulgaria but left a wide 'middle sphere' – including Austria, Hungary and Czechoslovakia – whose future would be settled by the European peace. But a real European peace could be made only if a solution was found to the problem of Germany. Fear of German recovery, a new German imperium or a second Nazi empire built on the wreckage of Eastern and Central Europe ruled Allied diplomacy. For obvious reasons, it was the dominant element in Soviet thinking. Hence the reconstruction of Europe was meant to proceed in a continent made safe from German aggression. A four-power commission (France would join the 'Big Three') was to dismantle permanently the apparatus and sources of German imperialism. Disarmed, denazified and deindustrialized, Germany could empire-build no more. But it was over this programme that the Allies fell out. To the Western powers economic recovery was paramount. They feared that its delay would spark mass unrest across Western Europe, and refused to postpone economic normalization in their part of Germany. When Stalin objected, they went ahead anyway. After the Berlin blockade in 1948 (Stalin's riposte), joint supervision of Germany was abandoned in favour of a de facto partition. Across Eastern and Central Europe, Soviet power helped install Communist-led governments subservient to Moscow (Yugoslavia was the exception). In the west, American financial aid (through the Marshall Plan) and the promise of protection against Soviet pressure shored up a mixed economy and democratic politics.

The division of Europe was a critical fact of the post-war world. It marked the final breakdown of the Allies' wartime unity. It affirmed Stalin's conviction that he faced an American onslaught[4] – since capitalism could not tolerate the Soviet experiment. When Soviet control over Poland, Romania and Bulgaria was followed by efforts to assert Soviet influence in Iran, Turkey and Greece, opinion in Washington began to shift rapidly. For this seemed to confirm the view, already propounded by the leading American expert on Soviet policy George Kennan, in his famous 'long telegram' from Moscow in 1946, that the Soviet Union was bent on expansion. Kennan seems to have argued both that Soviet expansion was ideology-driven and that it was the continuation of tsarist expansion under new management.[5] In American politics, the case for containing the Soviet threat and accepting a huge new commitment to defend Western Europe was fused with the paranoid fear of a Communist plot against American freedom – the nightmare vision that became McCarthyism. It entrenched an ideological vision of international rivalry, and laid down the theoretical grounds for American intervention anywhere in the world. When North Korea (the state formed out of the Soviet sphere in the Korean peninsula after Japan's eviction in 1945) attacked South Korea in June 1950, the conviction that America was engaged in a global cold war against Soviet expansion became the cardinal rule of American policy. Meanwhile, the division of Europe drove its western half into much deeper dependence on American power than anyone had envisaged at the end of the war – a pattern that was replicated in the Soviet-controlled east. For the world beyond Europe, the results of Europe's partition were even more surprising.

We have already seen that American leaders had a strong dislike for the colonial empires that were ruled from Europe. To their way of thinking, these empires were feudal survivals: bastions of privilege; negations of democracy; inefficient, unprogressive and clumsy. Worse still, they acted as zones of economic exclusion, barring the gate to American trade, hampering the growth of American exports. The fall of empires in French Indochina, the Dutch East Indies and British-ruled Malaya and Burma, and the impending withdrawal of the British from India, seemed positive results of the Pacific war. After a brief reoccupation to remove the Japanese armies, there was every reason for America to insist on the swift dissolution of colonial rule. Colonial states could then be reborn as ex-colonial nations, who would look for help and advice to the world's greatest ex-colony. In their weakened state, and with more urgent concerns much closer to home, the European colonial powers could be expected to take a similar view. Empire was a luxury they could ill afford – or so it might have been thought.

In one crucial case this is exactly what happened. The British had fought the war to save themselves from Hitler. Yet, at Churchill's insistence, the British war effort was also designed to preserve their imperial power. 'I have not become the King's First Minister', Churchill declared in a famous phrase, 'to preside over the liquidation of the British Empire.' But in the desperate crisis of 1942 even Churchill had been forced to agree that India's independence should follow soon after the war. For eighteen months after Japan's surrender, the Labour government in London struggled to find a political formula to give India freedom but keep it united. They resisted Muslim demands for an Indian partition, partly because the majority Congress Party refused to agree, and partly because they hoped that a united India would be Britain's willing partner in post-war Asia. But in early 1947, as their economic crisis grew deeper, and in fear of being trapped in an Indian civil war, they threw in the towel. A new viceroy was sent to wind up the Raj in just over a year. Lord Mountbatten exceeded his brief. After persuading the Congress that partition was the price of swift independence, and that to resist it further risked a descent into chaos, he staged a lightning retreat after six months of office in August 1947. Within less than a year, Ceylon (Sri Lanka) and Burma had gained independence as well.

The surprising thing was that this retreat from empire did not become general. It was true that the British also abandoned their mandate in Palestine. But that was mainly because they thought that further involvement in the Arab–Jewish conflict would wreck the Middle East primacy they were so keen to maintain. Far from drawing the lesson that their economic weakness and strategic exposure had made their overseas empires an unprofitable burden, Britain, France, the Netherlands and Belgium reached the opposite conclusion. To rebuild their war-shattered economies, they needed cheap raw materials and tropical commodities that they could resell for dollars

– the dollars to help pay for their essential imports from the United States. Their colonies now seemed the perfect source: they could be forced to accept payment at below the world price, and in Europe's soft currencies not hard American dollars. Cocoa from West Africa, copper from the Congo, tin and rubber from Malaya, sugar, coffee and oil from the Dutch East Indies would keep the wolf from the door until the metropolitan economies got back into balance. 'Indië verloren, ramspoed geboren' ('If the Indies are lost, ruin will follow') ran the saying in Holland. 'We are on the edge of the abyss,' said the Netherlands finance minister in April 1947, shortly before the Dutch 'police action' to regain control of key economic assets in Java.[6] It went without saying that Britain's concession for oil in south-western Iran was even more valuable.

The argument for empire was not solely economic. A crucial part of the British case for staying put in the Middle East was geostrategic. Soviet aggression in Central Europe, the strategists argued, could best be deterred by the use of air power – the huge bomber force the British had deployed against Nazi Germany. Russia's industrial cities were beyond the range of Britain's own airfields, but from its Middle East bases they could be bombed at will. The British imperium in the Middle East would make up for British weakness close to home in Europe. France's post-war leaders were also convinced that they needed their empire – as much if not more so. After France's defeat in June 1940, it had been the African colonies that had rallied to 'Free France'. Any hope of recovering France's pre-war status as one of the world's great powers seemed to depend on keeping the empire intact, not least as a source of military manpower.

But staying on was not an easy option. It was bound to cost money and divert precious resources from reconstruction at home. In South East Asia it meant rebuilding colonial power in the face of resistance movements that had originally sprung up against Japan's occupation. Leaning as they did on America's financial help, the unrepentant imperialists would scarcely have dared defy a veto from Washington. They had no need to fear. As Truman and his advisers grasped what they saw as the Soviet challenge, their view of Europe's colonialism turned almost full circle. It no longer seemed wise to force their European friends to abandon their assets. When the British sought help with the burden of military aid to Turkey and Greece, Washington responded with the Truman Doctrine, to share the burden of containment in the Mediterranean and Middle East. The American chiefs of staff urged 'all feasible political, economic and if necessary military support . . . to the United Kingdom and the communications of the British Commonwealth'.[7] At a billion dollars a year, the United States underwrote the costs of defending Britain's overseas empire, quietly approving Britain's imperial presence in the Middle East. By the late 1940s, large tranches of aid were propping up France's struggle to keep Indochina French. The astonishing outcome of the war in Europe had turned the United States into the patron and protector of the European empires – although a patron which expected that, sooner or later, their imperial economies would be opened up to its own.

Of course, it was not just the chain of events in Europe that produced this result. The collapse of Nazi imperialism on the European continent had its counterpart in East Asia. But, just as in Europe, the way the Asian war ended took an unpredictable turn and had unexpected results. In the fight with Japan, the Soviet Union was a neutral. Much of the Japanese army (more than a million soldiers) was stationed in China, to guard Japan's puppet regimes and grind down the resistance of the Kuomintang army. The American assault on Japan required a slow bloody progress from island to island, leading eventually (this was the plan) to a D-Day type landing on the main Japanese land mass. The part that China would play in the defeat of Japan and in the new peacetime order envisaged in Washington shifted dramatically in the last year of the war. By late 1944 the disastrous performance of Chiang Kai-shek's army in the 'Ichigo' campaign had convinced Roosevelt and Churchill that the Kuomintang would count for little in the assault on Japan. They turned their attention to persuading Stalin to attack Japan as soon as war ended in Europe. At the Yalta Conference in February 1945, they agreed in return that Russia should take back the territory lost in 1905 (the Kurile Islands and northern Sakhalin), its old railway rights in Manchuria, and (most astonishing of all) its old naval base at Port Arthur (now called Lüshun) guarding the maritime entry into northern China. In this unceremonious way, the previous assumption that, in the post-war world, Kuomintang China would be one of the 'Four Policemen' (alongside the United States, the Soviet Union and the British Empire/Commonwealth), and America's great partner in the Asian Pacific, was quietly downgraded. The urgency of forcing Japan to surrender, the terrible toll in American lives that a seaborne invasion was expected to take, and the vital necessity of Soviet help imposed a new set of priorities.

As it turned out, the defeat of Japan was achieved not with Soviet aid but by use of the A-bomb on Hiroshima and Nagasaki. But the collapse of the Japanese Empire and of its far-reaching claims over 'Greater East Asia' brought no advantage to the Kuomintang state. In the 1930s Chiang Kai-shek might have hoped that, if Japan were crushed, the new nationalist China would win a dominant place in the East Asian order. A renascent China would play off the powers and reclaim the vast sphere where Ch'ing influence had ruled: Sinkiang, Tibet, Mongolia, Manchuria, Korea, Vietnam and perhaps even Burma.[8] For a few months after the end of the war, the KMT government still seemed an irresistible force: even Stalin discounted the chances of Mao's Communist followers.[9] In fact the eight-year-long war of resistance (1937–45) had sapped much of the Kuomintang's strength. With only a dribble of aid from abroad (only 3 per cent of America's Lend Lease programme was directed to China), it had been a hopeless task to create a war economy in the parts of China outside the occupied zone. There was no income from exports. The domestic commercial economy, based on the exchange of agricultural produce between China's different regions, was wrecked by the war and the fragmentation it brought. As China sank into a subsistence economy, there was nothing to back the Kuomintang currency, which became virtually worthless. The extraction of taxes from rural producers became more and more brutal and more and more difficult.[10] So, when the Kuomintang government tried at the end of the war to destroy the parallel Communist state under Mao Tse-tung, it faced an uphill struggle. Mao's version of Communism appealed to peasant hostility against landlords and towns – the administrative base of the tax-gathering government. It promised rural self-help and the redistribution of land as an immediate cure for the desperate poverty of peasant communities.[11] Mao's Communist armies received crucial assistance from the prompt Soviet entry into Manchuria, and had access to the stockpile of Japanese arms. When Chiang Kai-shek rushed north to seize control of Manchuria's industrial assets – southern Manchuria was China's richest and most industrialized region[12] – he overstrained the resources of his weakened regime. In 1949 Kuomintang resistance was broken. In October that year the People's Republic of China was proclaimed in Beijing (Peking).

The implications were seismic. At each end of Eurasia the war had created a divided subcontinent. Just as there was no agreed post-war order to settle the future in Europe, so there would be no general peace settlement to end the war in East Asia. As Washington took stock of the Kuomintang's failure, a surge of Communist influence in the war-shattered societies from Korea to Java (and not excluding Japan) seemed increasingly likely. Yet any new commitment on the mainland of Asia, to add to the burden of defending Europe, seemed out of the question. It was this dilemma that pushed American policy in its new direction. It strengthened the argument for backing British and French colonialism against Communist-led movements in Vietnam and Malaya. It weakened the case for supporting the Dutch against Indonesian nationalists who, to Washington's delight, crushed a Communist uprising in 1948. It reversed the plan to neuter Japan's industrial muscle (Japan would become the 'Switzerland of Asia' had been General Macarthur's prediction) in the interests of China. Instead, Japan would become America's Asian ally, offering unlimited use of its national territory in return for American protection. This remarkable bargain seemed to some observers to be in the grand tradition of Asia's unequal treaties.

'We are living in a revolutionary age of transition,' Jawaharlal Nehru told a group of Asian leaders in January 1949.[13] It was a shrewd piece of analysis. The effects of the war and the turmoil that followed it broke the habit of obedience in many parts of the world. The first three or four years after the Second World War are usually portrayed by historians as the prelude to cold war, first in Europe then in Asia. And so they turned out to be. But the drift to cold war is only part of the story, and in many parts of the world not the most important part. Nor was it obvious what its impact would be on all the other upheavals produced by the war. For the conflicts ignited at each end of Eurasia had detonated a chain of further explosions right around the world. Under their battering, the established order – often recent and fragile – buckled, bent and in some places broke. Those excluded from power before the outbreak of war – whether Communists, socialists, nationalists, Zionists, Islamists or separatists – relished the chance to break the political mould. Local parties and interests scrambled to influence the dominant regional power and mobilized furiously to raise their strength on the ground. But every move they made reflected a state of extreme uncertainty. Would the victor powers impose a set of collective decisions – as Mao still expected in 1946?[14] Would they quarrel irreconcilably? Would America drift into isolation once more, as in 1919? Would the global economy slip back into slump? Would the devastation of war exclude much of the world from engaging in trade? Would state-controlled autarky be the only practicable means of economic recovery? Had the assault on property under wartime conditions (by taxation, confiscation or destruction) and the general retreat of individual rights erased old social differences and levelled society for good? Was a new mass culture now certain to triumph over pre-industrial 'high' cultures and folk ways alike? Was the coming era to see a world of great states and great continental conglomerates, or a loose confederacy of free nation states?

In the first half-decade of peace, the signs were conflicting. Many smaller states invested high hopes in the United Nations Organization, set up in 1945 as a more potent successor to the League of Nations. But would it be a counterweight to the dominant powers, or merely the arena for their competition and conflict? The Bretton Woods agreements in 1944–5 set up new machinery to prevent the return of catastrophic slump. The International Monetary Fund allowed states to meet a temporary crisis in their balance of payments without a resort to the controls on trade and exchange that had shrivelled the world economy in the 1930s. With the zeal of new converts, the Americans demanded the scrapping of tariffs and other restraints on trade. But, in face of the huge imbalance in productive capacity between the United States and the rest of the world and the shortage of dollars with which to buy American goods, the new era of free trade soon became a dead letter. The Sterling Area (comprising Britain, its colonial territories, independent Commonwealth countries, including India, and certain Middle East countries like Egypt and Iraq) formed a separate trade and currency zone, whose dollar purchases were strictly controlled. It was far from clear – even with Marshall Aid dollars from the United States – how fast Western Europe would recover as producer or market. The Soviet bloc moved back towards autarky. In such austere conditions, it was hard to imagine an age of growth and prosperity and wider private choice. The priority was to expand production at almost any cost. Whether this was compatible with a rapid advance in political freedom was an interesting question. Whether small states were viable outside a larger bloc (or empire) or without adequate access to scarce supplies of capital seemed at best uncertain.

It was hardly surprising, then, that there was no consensus on the likely shape of a new world order. In the old colonial powers, most informed opinion believed that keeping empire going wherever conditions allowed was the safest option – even if it were best to liberalize colonial rule. Empire could be plausibly justified as being in the material interest of colonial peoples in a disordered world. Anti-colonial nationalists could take heart from the sudden retreat of British imperial power from its *raj* in South Asia. But there was no reason to think that the fall of colonial empires would be universal, or would take place quickly. It seemed almost as likely that in much of the world colonial rulers would recover their nerve and rebuild their colonial states (in a modified form) with American backing. Nehru's revolutionary age was still in the making.

DECOLONIZATION

We know, of course, that the colonial revival was limited in scope and very short-lived. Instead, decolonization became the overwhelming political fact across most of Asia, Africa and the Middle East, and its effects reverberated ideologically in Latin America as well. Decolonization is often equated with the end of colonial *rule*, but this is much too narrow. It is far more useful to think of it as the demolition of a Europe-centred imperial order in which territorial empire was interlocked with extraterritorial 'rights'. The bases, enclaves, garrisons, gunboats, treaty ports and unequal treaties (as in Egypt or China) that littered the Afro-Asian world were as much the expression of this European imperialism as were the colonies and protectorates coloured red, blue, yellow or green on the old imperial maps. So was the assumption that intervention was justified by the general failure of non-European states to reach the civilizational standard that European visitors were entitled to expect. This imperial 'order' imagined a cultural hierarchy in which the progressive capabilities of North West European (and Euro-American) societies were contrasted with the (sometimes picturesque) 'stationary state' in which non-Western cultures were presumed to be stuck. It also expected, and where possible enforced, an economic division of labour in which the capital, manufactures and technical skills of the imperial-industrial world were exchanged for the raw materials and foodstuffs of the non-Western countries.

Most, if not all, of this global 'regime' was quickly demolished in the two decades that followed the Second World War. A Europe-centred world order was no longer sustainable. Indeed, the effort to maintain it by Britain and France in regions that they ruled or where their influence had been dominant evoked the very resistance that forced their departure. They might have stayed longer as subcontractors of American influence. But their transatlantic patron had lost faith in their methods by the mid-1950s. The climate had changed. The language of empire and colonial rule had lost almost all its legitimacy in international affairs. The world's two largest powers had long since denounced it. There was already a large group of ex-colonial states (India was the most prominent) for whom demolishing colonialism was the most urgent priority, and for whose goodwill and favour both superpowers were competing. Both the institutions and the charter of the United Nations – the main arena where the superpowers contended for influence – envisaged a world in which the free nation state had become the ideal and the norm. The prop was pulled from under colonial power.

Decolonization had very striking results. It brought an explosion in the number of sovereign states, almost quadrupling the total of the inter-war years. It demolished the apparatus of European privilege in some non-European states that had been only technically sovereign. It shattered the legitimacy of imperial rule and ridiculed the ethos of imperial 'service'. It opened the way for post-imperial governments to expropriate foreign-owned property, control external trade, and reach a (sometimes profitable) accommodation with multinational firms. It was the vital stimulus for a great reappraisal of cultural values, and for the rejection – or questioning – of those that were seen as European in origin. What was much less clear (as we will see in what follows) was whether the collapse of a Europe-dominated imperial order would mean a real transition to a 'world of nations'. Or whether the partition of Eurasia (as the vital context in which decolonization occurred) would encourage the rise of new kinds of empires, reliant much less on colonial rule than on forms of influence that might be just as effective.

The end of British rule in India in 1947 and the withdrawal two years later of Europe's navies from China marked the end of the 'Vasco da Gama epoch' in Asian history. The age of European dominance was over. This was the verdict of an Indian historian a few years later.[15] Of course the weight of the European presence should not be exaggerated. The Europeans had assembled grand colonial empires, in Southern Asia especially: in the Malay archipelago, in Indochina, above all in India. They commanded the seaways to East Asia after c.1840, and were firmly lodged in maritime China by the 1860s. But Japan had resisted subordination to Europe and more than preserved its autonomy. The European effort after 1890 to drive deeper into China's society and economy was scarcely under way before it was choked off by the geopolitical changes of the First World War. Europe's colonization of Asia had been a patchy affair, only shallowly rooted in much of South East Asia (where colonial rule had gained limited purchase before the 1890s). It was much more impressive on the continent's maritime fringes than it was inland. (In this respect, as in others, India was different.) It was partly this that explained why it fell apart so quickly in 1941–2, and staged only a brief recovery after 1945.

Yet change after 1945 was real enough. Less than ten years later, colonial rule had all but vanished from South, East and South East Asia. Where it still persisted, the timetable for independence was already drawn up, or the territory concerned was of trivial importance. The exception was Hong Kong. But Hong Kong remained a colony by grace and favour of the Chinese government, and for its convenience.[16] Contemplating a divided and war-shattered Europe, it was hardly surprising that a new generation of Asian political leaders were struck by the difference that a few years had made. The simultaneous crash of a Europe-centred world order and the sudden revival of independent statehood across most of Asia promised a new beginning. Asian conceptions of race and culture, Asian indifference to Europe's fratricidal quarrels, the interests of Asia's impoverished millions could now find a voice.

This was the spirit of the 'Asian–African' conference held at Bandung in Indonesia in May 1955. The host was Sukarno, the Indonesian president and hero of its anti-colonial revolution. Delegates came from more than twenty-five countries, including the Gold Coast and Cyprus, then both still colonies.[17] Egypt was represented by Gamal Abdel Nasser. The presence of Nehru and of Chou En-lai, the prime ministers of India and China, lent an added authority to the conference proceedings. The meeting had no formal agenda, but its implicit purpose was to assert the claims of the non-Western world in international politics. Conference resolutions called for more Afro-Asian members in the United Nations Security Council, denounced all forms of race discrimination, and declared colonialism an evil 'which should speedily be brought to an end'. In a notably conciliatory speech, Chou En-lai insisted that China had no expansionist aims and was ready to negotiate with the United States. Nehru denounced entry into an alliance with the West as 'an intolerable humiliation for an Afro-Asian country', and NATO as 'one of the most powerful protectors of colonialism'. Africa and Asia should remain neutral in the conflict of East and West: 'why should we be dragged into their quarrels and wars?'[18]

Behind the speeches of Nehru and Chou En-lai was a vision of an Asia and Africa in which outside influence would exist only on sufferance. It was a heroic conception of decolonization that rejected any vestige of post-imperial attachment. The Asian states would take up the struggle to free the remaining colonized peoples. Cultural cooperation between Asians and Africans would replace the old deference to Europe's civilizational claims. These ideas remained powerful. The possibilities of a non-aligned 'Third World', independent alike of the East and the West, exerted enormous appeal. Third World solidarity against colonialism, forcefully displayed at the United Nations, helped to accelerate the end of European rule, especially in Africa after 1960. But, for all its attractions, the post-colonial future imagined at Bandung was doomed from the outset. Decolonization was not just a matter of demolishing colonial rule or excluding European influence. Even at Bandung, a rift appeared between those Afro-Asian states that favoured Nehru's 'neutralist' line and the sizeable group that was openly pro-Western. Part of the reason lay in the nervous apprehension (despite Chou En-lai's reassurance) of Sino-Soviet intentions. But a deeper cause lay in the complex tensions evoked by Asia's escape from empire. For it was not the case that a family of new nations emerged fully formed from Asia's *ancien régime*. Where empires had caved in or had been overthrown, what followed instead were struggles for succession between rival claimants to their title deeds. Since imperial rule had often strung together different ethnic groups and ridden roughshod over old ethno-cultural boundaries, neither new national identities nor their territorial rights could be taken for granted. It might have been simpler if this had been true only of the colonial empires the Europeans had made. But by the 1950s Asia was littered with the wreckage of other empires as well. The imperial ambitions of Britain, France, Russia, the Netherlands and Portugal had their Asian counterparts in the vast Inner Asian dominion built up by the Ch'ing, Japan's abandoned colonies in Korea and Taiwan, and the South East Asian empires whose Thai, Burmese and Vietnamese masters had been caged and cramped in the colonial era. Kashmir, Tibet, Korea, the Taiwan straits, Vietnam, Sumatra and the Hill States of Burma were the open sores of this painful transition from empire to nation, the glaring evidence that post-imperial state-making was only rarely consensual. Asia's immersion in the expanding Cold War masked the bitter reality of these local and regional conflicts.

As so often before in Eurasian history, China's role was crucial. By the end of 1950 its mainland had been unified under Communist rule. Mao's remarkable victory may have owed much to the 'peasant nationalism' of China's rural masses (kindled by hatred of Japan's occupation),[19] as well as to the appeal of the party's land reform programme. The proportions are still disputed.[20] But there was no doubt that China had once more resumed a premier place in East Asia, with a huge battle-hardened army. Under certain conditions, this might have resulted in an inward-looking policy of domestic reform that left China's Asian neighbours to their own devices. In the actual climate of the early 1950s, such an outcome was unlikely. Instead, the new regime's leaders adopted the view of their republican predecessors, and the Ch'ing before them, that their rule would be safe only if the landward approaches to China were in trustworthy hands. They forcefully reasserted Beijing's authority in Tibet. When it seemed likely that northern Korea might fall under non-Communist control, they intervened massively in the Korean War. Two million Chinese served in Korea, and more than 150,000 died there.[21] Mao took a similar view of China's frontier in the south. At the critical stage of the struggle between the Viet Minh and the French in northern Vietnam, Chinese military help and strategic 'advice' played a crucial part in France's crushing defeat at Dien Bien Phu in May 1954, the prelude to the end of its colonial power in Indochina.[22] Beijing's fear of encirclement sprang from the fact that its Kuomintang enemies had survived (on Taiwan) and with American help might resume the political struggle. For, despite the scale of their victory, Mao and his colleagues were all too aware that it had not been total. They faced the challenge of building a new industrial state on China's agrarian base – which would have to pay the bill. They had to anchor their power in a new social order – which would have to be fashioned. They had to defend a revolution.

The sense of threat from without as well as within precluded retreat into the splendid seclusion favoured by new dynasts in previous eras. It was dramatically symbolized by the denial of membership of the United Nations, instigated by America and reversed only in 1971. At first Chinese policy mixed caution and hope. The obvious urgency of an industrial programme, as well as the need to balance American help to the Kuomintang foe, drove the People's Republic into alliance with Stalin. In Korea and Vietnam in 1953–4, Beijing accepted a compromise peace of partition. After France's defeat in the First Indochina War, Chou En-lai sought to disarm regional fears (and stifle

American influence) by soft-voiced diplomacy. But by the late 1950s Mao was convinced that harsher methods were needed. He mistrusted Moscow's call for coexistence with capitalism, and saw the Soviet leader Nikita Khrushchev's summit diplomacy as a betrayal of China. Sino-Soviet solidarity lasted barely a decade. Faced with the hardening of American support for the Taiwan regime, Mao raised the military stakes by bombarding Quemoy, a close-in offshore island under Kuomintang rule. He countered the loss of momentum in China's transformation at home with an aggressive new strategy of rural collectivization, the so-called 'Great Leap Forward'. The redistribution of land from landlords to peasants turned out (as in Russia) to be only the prelude to the state's taking control. And in 1960 he approved Hanoi's insistent demand to resume the armed struggle (suspended since 1954) for a Communist victory in South Vietnam.[23] Mao's new course was to make China the sponsor of revolutionary violence against surviving colonial states, or those successor regimes that colluded with capitalism. His message was simple. Imperialism's overthrow was far from complete. Decolonization must come – if it was to be real – by a great rural revolt of impoverished peasants: a global 'people's war' against the world's bourgeoisie.[24]

Mao's drastic programme for a post-imperial world aroused wide enthusiasm, intellectual and political, not least among those who hoped to savour its victory from a comfortable distance. In the 1960s and '70s it offered a hopeful alternative to the failures and compromises of post-colonial regimes. It attracted those who still hoped to reverse capitalism's unexpected revival in the post-war world. As we shall see in a moment, it achieved its most striking success in the special conditions of South East Asia. But on a wider view it was the containment of China and Maoist anti-imperialism that was really significant. In part this arose from the disruptive effects of Mao's political doctrines – especially his 'Cultural Revolution', a form of massive purge – on the Chinese economy. In part it reflected the revival of tension with China's great northern neighbour. But the most serious obstacle to Mao's ambitions grew out of the dramatic divergence between East Asia's two great states.

If China's turn towards Communism confounded most wartime predictions, no less surprising was the readiness of Japan (in John

Dower's striking phrase) to 'embrace defeat'.[25] At the end of the war, Japan had been occupied by a large American garrison, military and civilian, nearly a million strong.[26] For more than six years, an American viceroy (for most of that time General Douglas MacArthur) held executive power, and his approval was needed for any major decision. Japan's sovereignty was suspended; Japanese were forbidden to travel abroad; no criticism was allowed of the occupation regime. A raft of reforms was designed to root out what were seen as the sources of Japan's militaristic imperialism. Women were enfranchised and the voting age was lowered, more than doubling the electorate. A new constitution prescribed by the occupiers barred the armed forces from a seat in the government and renounced war as an instrument of national policy. The great family-ruled business combines or *zaibatsu* were broken up. Land reform reduced the power of the landlords and doubled the proportion of those who farmed their own land to some 60 per cent.[27] Trade unions were encouraged. New textbooks were written, and the educational syllabus was democratized.[28] So fierce an assault upon the pre-war order might have provoked a hostile reaction, since the civilian elite with whom the Americans dealt remained deeply conservative. In fact it formed part of a remarkable bargain. When their fears about China led them to 'reverse course', the Americans accepted the need for a strong Japanese state with an industrial economy. They made their peace with the powerful bureaucracy. They had the tacit support of the Japanese emperor, whose role as a figurehead had been carefully preserved. Amid the growing turmoil in mainland East Asia and the outbreak of war on the Korean peninsula in June 1950, Japan's conservative leaders also had little room for manoeuvre. They were anxious to end the American occupation and restore Japanese sovereignty. But an open challenge to Washington's policy might anger the American public and delay independence. It might encourage the Left, who commanded a third of Japanese votes, and induce more radical change.

The result was to give the Americans an extraordinary leverage over the shape and direction of the new Japanese state. The peace treaty signed in San Francisco in 1951 returned Japanese sovereignty, though neither the Soviet Union nor China was a signatory. America's terms were stiff. Japan was required to accept a mutual-security pact that allowed American forces to use any part of the country and exempted their personnel from Japanese jurisdiction. The island of Okinawa, annexed by Japan in 1879 and the scene of an epic battle in the Pacific War, became a great American base, no longer administered as part of Japan. The Japanese economy was linked to America's through a fixed exchange rate, while its old market in China was closed in deference to America's trade embargo. At the critical stage of East Asia's post-war formation, Japan had become the indispensable bulwark of America's regional power, the great offshore platform from which its economic weight and military muscle could be used as a check on the resurgence of China. American influence was also strongly felt in Japanese popular culture. Ironically, in decolonized East Asia, the influence of the West (not merely of Europe) was asserted more forcefully than before the Second World War.

Asia's third great state was India. India enjoyed the prestige of being Asia's largest democracy. Under Nehru's leadership, it might have expected to play a prominent part in settling the shape of post-colonial Asia.[29] Indeed, Nehru may have hoped to partner Beijing to exclude outside influence from the continent's politics – as he had urged at Bandung. But the odds were against it. India's influence was hobbled by its own post-colonial inheritance. Its independence had come with a traumatic partition and left an unresolved conflict to poison relations. It was a further misfortune that the question of Kashmir (claimed by Pakistan but largely held by India) soon became linked to the highly charged issue of Tibetan autonomy. China's brutal suppression of Tibet's traditional government after 1950 was achieved in part by cutting its links through the Himalayas. The two main routes between India and Tibet lay through Sikkim to the south and Leh in Kashmir to the west.[30] Military activity on an ill-defined border was a source of Sino-Indian tension, and eventually war.[31] India's defeat (in 1962) was aptly symbolic of Nehru's grander ambitions. India's political system (which dispersed considerable power and resources to its state-level governments), the threat 'at home' of war with Pakistan, and the lacklustre progress of the Indian economy (India's share of world trade fell by two-thirds in the 1950s and 1960s)[32] conspired to frustrate India's claim, at this stage, to be an Asian 'great power'.

In its widest sense, the course of Asia's decolonization was powerfully shaped by the limitations and weaknesses of its largest states. Neither singly nor in combination could they hope to resolve the succession disputes that arose from Asia's imperial past or the ideological conflicts of its revolutionary present. That left the door open for the outside powers whom Nehru had wanted to banish. It was China's subservience that let Stalin unleash the North Korean attack in June 1950.[33] It was control of Japan that allowed the deployment of a huge American army to defend South Korea. But the main theatre of conflict where external power played a critical part was in South East Asia.

This was no coincidence. Here the end of colonialism was a much more ragged affair than in South Asia (where British rule had collapsed) or East Asia (where the Japanese empire was shattered by war). This was partly because of American help to both Britain and France (though not to the Dutch). But it was also a product of ethnic and religious division, a fragmented geography, and the limited progress that state-building had made in the colonial era. It had appeared at first as if wartime occupation by Japan had broken the back of European colonial rule across the whole of the region. It had given local political leaders just enough freedom (and just enough time) to build new political loyalties and smash the old colonial machine. In Burma, Indochina and the Dutch East Indies (Indonesia), new 'national' governments appeared. When the Allied troops of South East Asia Command (mainly British and Indians) returned in the wake of the Japanese retreat, they found in place new claimants to power. The result was a stand-off. The colonial powers' tactic was to co-opt the new leaders by promising the devolution of power but not real independence. But both local politics and the international scene were much too unstable for any bargain to hold. In Burma, the British were quickly forced out by the obvious cost of reimposing control and the negligible benefit of trying to do so.[34] In Indonesia, Indochina and British Malaya the struggle was more protracted.

The Dutch hoped in Indonesia to exploit the fact that nationalism enjoyed only limited backing across much of the archipelago, where fear of Javanese domination and (in some cases) anti-Islamic feeling made Dutch colonial rule the lesser of two evils. But the reality was that overall Dutch control, even under a Netherlands–Indonesia 'commonwealth', could not be maintained without the backing of Java, the most developed part of the island complex, with five-eighths of its population. It was Dutch failure to achieve this, and the American refusal to back a prolonged guerrilla war in Sumatra and Java (which might have wrecked the Indonesian economy and widened support for Communism), that forced the Dutch out in 1949–50.[35]

In Indochina the outcome was different. Here the French were able to reinsert themselves in both the north (Tonkin) and the south (Cochin China). They faced a formidable movement, the Viet Minh, under Ho Chi Minh, based upon peasant support in the north and in Cochin China's plantation economy. What allowed the French to hang on for a time was a crucial advantage. Ho's brand of Vietnamese nationalism (Ho himself was a Marxist and a veteran of the inter-war Communist International) was disliked by large sections of Vietnamese society: the propertied classes, much of the urban population, Catholics (who formed up to 20 per cent of Tonkin's population), and followers of the sects Cao Dai and Hoa Hao, as well as some in the upland ethnic minorities.[36] Many of these remained uncommitted, or backed the attempt of the Vietnamese monarch, Bao Dai, to gain Vietnamese autonomy within the 'French Union'. This was the platform for France's military struggle to destroy the Viet Minh and for the massive American aid to keep Vietnam out of the hands of (in the graphic language of the US Secretary of State) 'Chi commie hatchet men and armed forces'.[37] By mid-1953, however, Bao Dai's credibility had come to depend overwhelmingly on French military prestige. When that was shattered at Dien Bien Phu the following year, his position, and France's, became untenable. Yet the result was not an easy triumph for Ho.

The reason was not simply American eagerness to confront the expansion of the Communist sphere, which had led Washington to consider an all-out war against China – Ho's principal backer – in 1954. A second crucial ingredient was the skill with which Ngo Dinh Diem, a well-connected Catholic notable, built a strong enough network to hold much of the south. Diem was a nationalist. He had been shrewd enough to cultivate American sympathy and reject the semi-independence on offer from France. He was later to be vilified as an American lackey, but his original aim was to cut Ho Chi Minh down and build a Vietnamese state after his own design.[38] Thirdly, the Viet Minh were restrained by their Chinese ally – partly from fear of American firepower, but partly because China did not want to drive either Laos or Cambodia into American arms. (In return, Laos and Cambodia pledged neutrality; Thailand had already joined the West's Manila Pact of South East Asian states.) In mainland South East Asia, much of the friction turned on the state-building projects of Burmese, Thais, Vietnamese, Laos and Khmers: it was largely the conflicts among and between them that drew the outsiders into the region and made it hard to resist foreign offers of aid. Much the same was true in the case of Malaya. Malay political leaders viewed the Communist insurrection after 1948 as a local Chinese challenge to a future Malay state as much as a threat to British colonial rule. To keep it at bay and ward off the bear hug of their Malay 'big brother' – Sukarno's Indonesia – they combined independence (in 1957) with a British alliance, not non-alignment or neutralism.[39]

The critical phase of decolonization in Asia between 1945 and 1960 thus followed a course very different from the hopes and dreams that had been aired at Bandung. Far from disdaining as futile the game of Cold War diplomacy – as Nehru had urged – many Asian leaders had accepted the reality of a 'bipolar' world. Far from maintaining a proud independence, they hoped to turn the Cold War to their local advantage. In reality, perhaps, they had little choice. Economic and military weakness, internal division, social unrest and the century-old habit of looking beyond Asia for the route to modernity were all bound to deflect Asia's post-colonial trajectory. It remained to be seen how far they would drag the continent into the orbit of a new imperial system.

Decolonization in the Middle East was no less tortuous, embittered and conflict-ridden. The end of the Second World War was greeted there, as much as in the rest of Asia, as a new beginning. With peace came the promise of an end to the vast military machine that the British had built all across the region – a super-imperialism that had turned the Arab states and Iran (also partially occupied by Russian troops) into mere auxiliaries of the imperial war effort. Once that had gone, political life might begin again. Better still, the British had decided (for their own convenience) to lever the French out of Syria and the Lebanon, France's pre-war mandates, and secure their independence (1946). This was a promising start. They had also encouraged the formation of the Arab League in 1944–5. The British intended the League to be a channel of their influence, a way of keeping the Arab states together under a British umbrella. But it might also serve as a vehicle for Arab cooperation to exclude or contain the influence of outside powers. The new geopolitical scene in which Soviet and American power was seen to balance (if not outweigh) that of Britain made this far less unlikely than it would have been before 1939. To many young Arabs, there seemed reason to hope that the post-war world would be a new 'national age'. The false dawn of freedom from Ottoman power after 1918 – which had led instead to Britain's regional overrule – might at last give way to the glorious morning of full Arab nationhood.

Almost immediately the barriers piled up. The British rejected the 'logic' of withdrawal: instead they dug themselves in.[40] Arguments of strategy (as we have seen) and heavy dependence on oil (still mainly from Iran) made retreat unthinkable. The strategic vulnerability and economic weakness with which Britain had entered the peace (London hoped they were temporary) ruled out the surrender of imperial assets unless (as in India) they had become untenable. In the Middle East, the British still believed that they had a strong hand. Their position was founded on their alliance with Egypt, the region's most developed state, with more than half the population of the Arab Middle East – 19 million out of some 35 million.[41] The long-standing conflict between the Egyptian monarchy and the landlord class gave them enormous leverage in the country's politics. If more 'persuasion' was needed, they could send troops into Cairo from their Canal Zone base in a matter of hours. To improve relations after the strains of war, they now dangled the promise of a smaller military presence. They assumed that sooner or later the Wafd or the king would want to come to terms, because Egypt's regional influence, like its internal stability, needed British support. So, when negotiations stalled, the British stayed put, intending to wait until things 'calmed down'. They could afford to do so – or so they thought. For they could also count on their political friendship with the Hashemite monarchies in Iraq and Jordan. It was well understood that the cohesion of both states (demarcated by the British in the early 1920s) and the survival of their monarchs (installed by the British at much the same time) rested on the promise of British assistance against internal revolt as much as external attack. To the south and east lay the Persian Gulf, still a 'British lake'. Along its Arab shore lay a string of small states from Kuwait to Oman bound to the British by the promise of protection against their potentially predatory neighbours. At Arabia's southern tip lay an old British base at Aden, and a coastal strip under loose British rule. As if all this was not enough, the British were laying plans for bases in Libya, taken from the Italians and scheduled for self-rule under a British-backed king. It went without saying that the British exerted a prescriptive right to *regulate* the politics of the whole Middle East region. Diplomatic support in a quarrel between states, the offer of aid, and refusal to do business with an 'unfriendly' government were the classic techniques of quasi-imperial control. The British had played this game for a generation or more. Driving them out was bound to be difficult, divisive and perhaps even bloody.

To more radical Arabs the solution was obvious. The imperial juggernaut could be beaten only by the collective force of pan-Arab nationalism. A vision of shared Arab nationhood would discredit the bargains the British had made with the rulers and 'big men' in the Arab states. It would challenge the complacency of the landed elite and improve the social conditions that kept Arab life expectancy on a level with Indian. But as yet Arab unity was a distant dream. Ethnic, religious and social divisions – the legacy in part of Ottoman and European rule – were deeply entrenched. Pan-Arab nationalism had to compete with the endemic hostility between the region's ruling elites. Nationalists in Egypt felt little in common with the other Arab states ('a collection of zeroes,' sneered Saad Zaghlul in the 1920s).[42] They dwelt on Egypt's pharaonic glory (encouraged by the great Tutenkhamun finds in the 1920s) and regarded themselves as the true custodians of Arab nationalism and culture in their highest form. Egyptian opinion dismissed the Hashemite rulers in Iraq and Jordan as puppets and parvenus, and their claims to leadership of the Arab world as absurd and impudent. The Hashemite kings were equally certain of their historic claim to head the Arab cause: it was they, after all, who had led the rising after 1916 and proclaimed an Arab nation. Their long-standing ambition was a great Hashemite state uniting Syria (lost to the French in 1920) and Palestine with Iraq and Jordan. Their fiercest enmity, returned with interest, was towards the house of Saud. It was the Saudi monarch who had seized the holy places of Mecca and Medina from their Hashemite guardian, and turned Hashemite Hejaz into a province of what became 'Saudi' Arabia. Much of the rivalry between Egypt, the Hashemites and the Saudis was focused on Syria, whose religious and regional conflicts made it a fertile ground for influence from outside.[43]

This rough equilibrium of political forces in the post-war Middle East was quickly upset by the volcanic impact of the Palestine question. The British had planned to keep their regional imperium by a smooth transition. All the Arab states would be independent; some would be bound by treaty to Britain; the rest would acknowledge its de facto primacy as the only great power with real strength on the ground. It was always going to be difficult to manage this change in the case of Palestine, ruled directly by Britain under a League of Nations mandate since the First World War. Reconciling the promise of a Jewish 'national home', in which Jews could settle, with the rights of the Arabs who were already there had been hard enough in the 1920s. The flood of refugees from Nazi oppression in the 1930s made it all but impossible. London's pre-war plan was to appease the anger of the Palestine Arabs at the growing Jewish migration by fixing a limit to ensure a permanent Arab majority. With its future settled as an Arab state, Palestine could be edged towards a form of self-rule. After 1945 this ingenious solution was soon blown to pieces. The practical difficulty and political embarrassment of excluding Jewish refugees, diplomatic pressure from the United States against the attempt to do so, and the scale and ferocity of the terrorist campaign waged by Jewish settlers destroyed any semblance of British authority by mid-1948.[44] The result was the worst of all colonial worlds: an ungovernable territory whose control was disputed between two seemingly irreconcilable foes; outside encouragement that hardened the resolve of both contending parties; and the absence of either the means or a method to impose any decision. The partition proposed by the

United Nations could not be enforced. The war that followed between the Jews and Arabs (local Palestinians and the contingents sent by the Arab states) brought a Jewish victory. The new state of Israel was strong enough to impose a second and more favourable territorial partition. But it was not strong enough to force the Arab states to accept this outcome as a permanent condition.

The Arab catastrophe marked a crucial stage in the end of empire in the Middle East. It galvanized the sentiment of pan-Arab nationalism and gave it a cause and a grievance. It was a crushing humiliation for the ruling regimes in the main Arab states, where post-war inflation and hardship were fostering mass discontent: the violent demonstrations of the Wathbah (the 'Leap') in Baghdad in January 1948 had already stopped the renewal of the Anglo-Iraqi treaty.[45] It provoked bitter resentment in the ranks of the armies, who blamed their defeat on their civilian leaders. The impact on Egypt was the greatest of all. The king had insisted on sending an army, to boost his domestic prestige and assert Egypt's first place among the Arab states.[46] The shock of defeat was felt all the more deeply. To make matters worse, he could make little progress towards evicting the British from their massive Canal Zone, the great visible symbol of Egypt's subaltern status. Nor indeed could his old political foes, the leaders of the Wafd. Where diplomacy failed, direct action stepped in. The struggle with the British became increasingly violent. Strikes, assassination and other acts of terror exploited British dependence upon Egyptian labour and the vulnerable state of British installations and personnel. Retaliation and revenge spread to Egypt's main cities. As the sense of order broke down, the king planned a putsch to purge discontent in the army. Before he could act, the 'Free Officers' movement seized control of the government in July 1952, and forced him into exile.

The effects at first seemed far from radical. The new regime set out to restore order. It crushed the Muslim Brotherhood, an Islamist movement that enjoyed mass support. It accepted the loss of Egyptian influence in the upper Nile when the British-ruled Sudan was promised independence as a separate state (the British rejected Cairo's demand to respect the 'unity of the Nile valley'). Above all, it secured British agreement to leave the Canal Zone base by conceding a right of return if its use were needed to repel an outside attack (code for a Soviet invasion) on the Middle East region. The British had concluded that, with a nuclear deterrent that they could deliver by air, the base was redundant in its present form as well as politically costly.[47] What they probably hoped was that the new Nasser regime would turn its attention to internal reform. Egypt, they thought, would exert limited influence in the Arab world.[48] Meanwhile they would remodel their imperium around a closer alliance with the Hashemite states and a new military pact. American influence, helpful in making the Suez agreement, would be thrown on their side. Egypt would be isolated and on its best behaviour. But Nasser's response was not to comply. Instead, his astonishing revolt against the British 'system' was the central event in the Middle East's decolonization.

As an Egyptian nationalist (one of the first acts of the new officers' government was to bring a statue of Ramses II to Cairo), Nasser had every reason to mistrust the British and plot their departure from the Middle East as a whole. He was also influenced by pan-Arab feeling and the Palestine war. He wanted a cleansing tide of revolutionary politics to smash the old regime of landlords and kings, left over from the Middle East's colonial era. He also feared that time was against him. Any ruler in Cairo would have faced much the same dilemma. The Sudan was lost. There was high tension with Israel. The Arab East (the Mashreq) was being closed to Egyptian influence and perhaps even its trade. Without markets or oil, he faced stagnation at home and growing social unrest. He would be dangerously dependent on economic aid from the West. His regime was untried. His critics would multiply. His revolution would fail. So, as the British assembled their 'Baghdad Pact' (with Turkey, Iraq and – they hoped – Jordan: Syria was next on the list),[49] Nasser launched a counter-attack. He embraced pan-Arabism. With Saudi support, he backed the anti-Iraqi faction in Syrian politics. He encouraged opposition in Jordan to joining the pact. Then in September 1955 came a spectacular coup. Nasser broke free from the embargo on arms imposed by the West and arranged a supply from the Soviet bloc. Egypt would now be a real military power. By early 1956 he had declared an open political war on Britain's Middle East influence. The rising level of violence along the borders with Israel played into his hands. With what seemed amazing ease, he had seized the initiative in regional politics. He had made

Egypt the champion of the pan-Arab cause, and pan-Arab feeling into a dynamic force. The reaction in London was one of panic and rage.

The Suez Crisis in 1956 grew directly out of this confrontation. When a loan to pay for Egypt's Aswan High Dam was stalled in Washington, there was no going back. Nasser expropriated the Suez Canal, then jointly owned by Britain and France. It seemed an act of bravado. But perhaps Nasser guessed that the British would find it hard to defeat him. They no longer had troops in the old Suez base. An open attack would enrage all Arab opinion. International pressure (through the United Nations) was unlikely to bring what they really wanted: his political downfall. Nasser may also have sensed that London's relentless hostility was not shared fully in Washington. Indeed, the riposte, when it came, revealed Britain's political weakness. Thinly disguised as an intervention between the forces of Egypt and Israel (in whose invasion they colluded), Anglo-French occupation of the Suez Canal was meant to humiliate Nasser and ensure his collapse. The key to Nasser's survival was the enormous appeal of his act of defiance to patriotic Arab opinion. It convinced President Eisenhower that allowing the British their victory would unite Arab feeling against the West as a whole, throw open the door to more Soviet influence, and wreck American interests into the bargain. By a painful irony, the economic fragility that had helped spur the British into their struggle with Nasser – fear that his influence would damage their vital sources of oil – now proved decisive. Without Washington's nod, they faced financial collapse. The British withdrew, and ate humble pie. Nasser kept the canal.[50] It was not he who fell through the political trapdoor, but the British prime minister, Sir Anthony Eden.[51]

Suez signalled the end of British ambition to manage the politics of the whole Arab world. It created a vacuum of great-power influence. It was the moment to forge a new Middle East order. Nasser stood forth as an Arab Napoleon. His prestige was matchless: he was the *rais* (boss). With its large middle class, its great cities and seaports, its literature and cinema, its journalists and teachers, Egypt was the symbol of Arab modernity. Nasser's pan-Arab nationalism (formally inscribed in Egypt's new constitution) chimed with a phase of sharp social change in most Middle Eastern states. To the new urban workers, the growing number of students, the expanding bureaucracy, the young officer class, it offered a political creed and a cultural programme. It promised an end to the Palestinian grievance, through the collective effort of a revitalized nation. Within less than two years of his triumph at Suez, Nasser drew Syria into political union, to form the United Arab Republic. The same year (1958) saw the end of Hashemite rule in Iraq. Nasser still had to reckon with American power (the United States and Britain intervened jointly to prevent the overthrow of Jordan and Lebanon by pro-Nasser factions). But American fears of rising Soviet influence and Nasser's opposition to Communism allowed a wary rapprochement. It looked indeed as if Nasser had achieved a stunning double victory. He had displaced the British as the regional power in favour of a looser, more tolerant American influence. He had made himself and Egypt the indispensable partners of any great power with Middle East interests. Pan-Arab solidarity under Egyptian leadership (the new Iraqi regime with its Communist sympathies had been carefully isolated) opened vistas of hope. It could set better terms with the outside powers. It could use the oil weapon (oil production was expanding extremely rapidly in the 1950s). It might even be able to 'solve' the question of Palestine.

But, as it turned out, the Middle East's decolonization fell far short of this pan-Arab ideal. Nasser might have hoped that the oil-rich sheikdoms of the Persian Gulf (especially Kuwait) would embrace his 'Arab socialism' and throw off their monarchs. But the British hung on in the Gulf and backed its local rulers against Nasser's political challenge. Secondly, the pan-Arab feeling on which Nasser relied faced a powerful foe. In the early post-war years the new Arab states seemed artificial creations. The educated Arab elite moved easily between them. So did their ideas. State structures were weak, and could be easily penetrated by external influence. By 1960 this had begun to change. New 'local' elites began to man the states' apparatus. Every regime acquired its *mukhabarat* – a secret police. The sense of national differences between the Arab states became clearer and harder: the charismatic politics of Nasser's pan-Arabism faced an uphill struggle. His union with Syria broke up after three years.[52] Thirdly, the Israeli state proved much more resilient than might have been hoped, and its lien on American sympathy showed no sign of failing: if anything, it was growing steadily stronger by the early 1960s.[53] Fourthly (and largely in consequence), the pan-Arabist programme could not be achieved without help from outside. The search for arms, aid and more leverage against Israel (and their own local rivalries) drew the Arab states into the labyrinth of Cold War diplomacy. Lastly, a twist of geological fate placed the oil wealth of the region in the states least inclined to follow Cairo's ideological lead: Saudi Arabia, Iraq, and Britain's Gulf protectorates. Nor did oil become (as coal had once been for Britain) the dynamo of social and industrial change. In fact Arab prosperity (or the prospect of it) seemed grossly dependent on an extractive industry over which real control lay in foreign hands – the 'seven (multinational) sisters' who ruled the world of oil.[54] The second catastrophe of the 1967 Six Day War, fought between Israel and Egypt, Jordan and Syria, was a savage reminder that mineral wealth was not the same as power, and that oil dollars did not mean industrial strength. By 1970, the year of Nasser's premature death, the promise of post-imperial freedom had become the 'Arab predicament'.[55]

The three largest states in the Middle East were Egypt, Turkey and Iran (each of which was to reach a population of 66 million in 2001). With the failure of Nasser's struggle to make Egypt the centre of an Arab revolution, his successor, Anwar Sadat, turned back (like Mehemet Ali in the 1840s) towards an accommodation with the West. By the late 1970s Egypt had become the second largest recipient (after Israel) of American aid.

Turkey, under Atatürk's shrewd former lieutenant Ismet Inonu, remained carefully neutral during the Second World War. But the huge forward movement of Soviet power at the end of the war, and Stalin's open avowal of his designs on the Straits – 'It was impossible to accept a situation where Turkey has a hand on Russia's windpipe,' he declared at Yalta – pushed Ankara firmly towards the Western camp. Under the Truman Doctrine (1947), Turkey was included in the sphere of American help and protection, however vague at this stage. By 1955 it had become a full member of NATO. In a way that Kemal Atatürk could hardly have dreamed of, the pattern of Cold War conflict had opened the door for Turkey's acceptance as a part of the West, with, by the end of the century, a widely recognized claim to enter the European Union. Tensions with Greece and over the future of Cyprus (which Turkey invaded and partitioned in the 1970s) made relations fretful at times. Within Turkey itself, the key question for much of the half-century after 1945 was how far Atatürk's grand project of a strong bureaucratic state, with a modern industrial base and a secular culture, was compatible with representative democracy (Atatürk's Turkey had been a one-party state) and an open (not state-dominated) economy.

The case of Iran is the most intriguing of all. Iran had been jointly occupied by Soviet and British forces in 1941, partly to block Reza Shah's approaches to Germany, mainly to secure free passage for supplies from Britain to an embattled Russia. Reza Shah abdicated and was sent off into exile. The result was to unravel his authoritarian state. Resentful notables (the powerful landowning class), radical movements in the towns (like the Tudeh Party), tribal leaders (of the Qashgai and Bakhtiari) and ethnic minorities (Kurds, Arabs and Azerbaijanis) challenged the new young shah's authority and scrambled for favour from the occupying powers. At the end of the war, this instability grew. The Red Army stayed on in Iranian Azerbaijan until 1946. The effects of wartime inflation ravaged the economy. The supporters of the shah struggled with the radicals and notables for control of the Majlis, or parliament. The government faced increasing resistance from tribal, provincial and ethnic groups. By 1949, however, the shah was close to reasserting control, perhaps because the alternative seemed a further fragmentation of the Iranian state and a deepening cycle of social unrest.

Before this could happen, a huge crisis broke out. To restore his position, the shah had been anxious to swell Iran's revenue from its main source of wealth, the vast oilfields in the south-west of the country, controlled by the British-owned Anglo-Iranian Oil Company (today's BP). In July 1949 a so-called 'supplemental agreement' proposed to increase the royalty that the company paid from 15 to 20 per cent, with further increases envisaged. But this agreement ran foul of two massive obstructions. The first was the fear among the shah's opponents that this newfound wealth would seal the revival of his power along pre-war lines. The second was the much wider hostility across Iranian opinion against continued foreign control of Iran's key resource and against the influence the company was believed to exert. To make matters worse, while the matter was debated in the Majlis, it became known that Aramco, the Arab-American Oil Company, had offered a 50 per cent share of profits to its host government in Saudi Arabia. As negotiations with Anglo-Iranian ground on, the political temperature rose and in March 1951 the Majlis passed a law to nationalize the company. A few days later Mohamed Mossadeq, a veteran antagonist of the shah and his father, took office as prime minister.[56]

The result was a stand-off. British talk of armed intervention was vetoed in Washington, where London's approach was regarded as reckless and retrograde.[57] Instead, the large British staff was withdrawn from the fields and the Abadan refinery. The major oil companies, fearing that others might follow the Iranian example, imposed an international boycott on Iranian oil that was very effective. Mossadeq had seemed on the brink of achieving a constitutional revolution, but his support – never very cohesive – now began to break up. In the West he was suspect as a dangerous demagogue, paving the way for Communist rule. In August 1953 he was overthrown by a military coup, aided and part-funded by American agents with some British support, and replaced by a premier who was loyal to the shah. Under a new oil agreement, Iran's oil was sold through a cartel of British and American companies. The shah's oil income rose spectacularly: tenfold between 1954–5 and 1960–61, to $358 million; and a further fifteenfold by 1973–4. So did his military and political power. By the early 1960s he was firmly established as a major ally of the West, whose value as a bulwark against a Soviet southward advance was offset periodically by the fear that his drive to be master of the Gulf would set off a conflict with the Arab states of the region.

In Cold War terms, the shah's triumph over Mossadeq seemed a victory for the West. In fact his success owed as much to the divisions and mistakes of his opponents and to the deep-dyed conservatism of a landlord-dominated society as it did to the machinations and manoeuvres of the CIA.[58] From another point of view, the shah and Mossadeq between them had wrought a remarkable change in Iran's general position. The semi-colonial status which even Reza Shah had not entirely thrown off, the Company's privileges as almost a state within the state, and the pervasive influence that the British exerted over Iranian officialdom and through their provincial allies had all been swept away in the humiliating retreat into which Anglo-Iranian was forced. To an extent that no other Middle East ruler could rival, the shah could assert not only Iran's independence but also its claim to be the one great power of the region. It was a signal irony that those who eventually inherited the state he had built were the bitterest enemies of the changes it imposed on Iranian society.

It was events in East Asia, South Asia and the Middle East that destroyed the Europeans' illusion that their colonial empires could be revived in the post-war world. For a while at least, Africa seemed different. Even well-informed observers doubted that Africa could follow in the wake of Asia, or would be allowed to do so without a bitter struggle. In the Maghrib countries (Morocco, Algeria, Tunisia), the power of France remained deeply entrenched. The French idea of a Mediterranean 'destiny' precluded real separation from lands thought so vital to France's place in the world. With 1 million settlers in Algeria (all with a voice in France's parliamentary system) and an Armée d'Afrique (mainly recruited in North Africa) that filled a crucial place in their military system, post-war French governments were doubly disinclined to see a North African lesson in their forced withdrawal from Indochina. In sub-Saharan Africa, the British, French, Portuguese and Belgians saw even less reason to prepare for an early withdrawal.

Sub-Saharan Africa had felt indirectly some of the fallout of war: inflation, shortages, the recruitment of soldiers, localized industrialization, the screech of propaganda. But (except briefly in Ethiopia) no real war was fought on its soil, and no invasion had disrupted the colonial regime. Linguistic, ethnic and religious diversity seemed to rule out the danger that African nationalism would ever become as potent as pan-Arab, mobilizing mass support within (let alone across) colonial boundaries. For similar reasons, the prospect that African leaders could create political movements on the model of Indian nationalism seemed very remote. The vast subcontinental coalition created by Gandhi was a world away from the localized nature of Africa's colonial politics. Indeed, far from evolving into African nations, the colonial states of sub-Saharan Africa seemed to be moving in the opposite direction. 'Tribal' Africa was still being invented, in part at least as the African response to the forms of 'indirect rule' the Europeans had imposed. Creating 'tribes' (some, like the Yoruba, on a very large scale) still seemed the optimum way for African elites to exert their influence and build their power. Lastly, in the 'White South', it was white settler nationalism, not black African nationalism, that mobilized most aggressively after 1945. Enforcing apartheid (literally 'separation') and fortifying white political supremacy was the political programme in 1950s South Africa. Building and defending a white-ruled Central African state was the settlers' aim in Northern and Southern Rhodesia (modern Zambia and Zimbabwe).[59] The entrenchment of white power had a further dimension. With the rediscovery of its colonial mission after 1945, Salazarist Portugal embarked on the systematic colonization of its two great African territories in Angola and Mozambique.[60]

Ironically, then, while the old colonial powers were struggling to hang on in Asia, they thought in Africa that they had time to play with. Bureaucratic blueprints for the transfer of power in the indefinite future and after a series of stages (like a dunce's progress from the first form to the sixth) flowed from the pens of colonial planners. The real imperative was the urgent need to make the colonies produce: cocoa, vegetable oil, cotton, sisal, tobacco, copper, gold, uranium, cobalt, asbestos and aluminium. Dollar shortage and Cold War tension turned Africa from the derelict of the inter-war years into Europe's Aladdin's cave. The 'nightwatchman' state, which let sleeping dogs lie, had to be made into the 'developmental' state, which interfered everywhere. White settler communities in East and Central Africa, typically regarded by pre-war colonial officials as a redundant nuisance, had now to be petted and their expansion encouraged. In colonial West Africa, where there were no white settlers, colonial administrators looked for support to the educated elite of the coastal towns. Coldly regarded before the war, they were now to help energize the drive for growth. With curious optimism, more romantic than rational, the makers of policy in London and Paris assumed that the promise of ultimate self-government would soothe the irritation of a much more intrusive colonial presence and lay the foundations of

'Eurafrican' partnership when colonial rule was eventually relinquished.

What they failed to allow for was the rickety condition of the colonial state. Across much of Africa, it had always been feeble. In the age of partition and conquest before 1914, it sought little more than a rough colonial pax and relied on settlers and concession-holders to create a taxable revenue. In the inter-war years, the prevailing dogma of indirect rule (based on fear of destabilizing 'traditional' African society) and depression-hit revenues favoured a shoestring regime that delegated power to so-called 'native authorities' at the local level. More perceptive governors were all too aware that, without a change of direction, it would get harder and harder to hold their colonies together or to win general assent for any central initiative.[61] It was only the war (with its demand for more action and spending) and its aftermath that made reform seem urgent. But what the policymakers intended as a consensual advance towards a louder African voice and a more proactive state held a different meaning for African opinion. Amid post-war austerity, colonial governments had to regulate prices, hold down wages, quash labour unrest, and limit local consumption. They had to force through improvements in agricultural practice – like cattle-dipping, anti-erosion measures and burning diseased cocoa trees – that aroused intense animosity and relied on compulsion. With the swarm of alien experts and (in some places) new settlers, colonial Africa experienced what some historians have called its 'second colonial occupation'.[62] It was hardly surprising that this sudden spasm of activity by the colonial regime provoked suspicion and resistance. Within a short space of time, colonial governments had to choose between two alternative courses. They could devolve more quickly to African leaders and try to win the state more popular backing (the option pursued by the British in Ghana after the 1948 disturbances). Or they could turn instead to a regime of repression, in the hope that forceful action would discourage 'extremism' (the term reserved for those who refused to cooperate with colonial governments) and refill the ranks of those (called 'moderates') who were willing to accept a leisurely timetable of political change and an indefinite period before African majority rule.[63]

The first preference of governments in London and Paris (and even in Brussels), once the scale of African resentment was clear, was to avoid confrontation and strike a new bargain with African leaders. But in Kenya and Central Africa this solution was barred by the vocal presence of white settler communities. When settlers became a target for African attack in Kenya (though very few indeed were actually murdered), the demand for an 'emergency' became irresistible. The result was to unleash a huge cycle of violence. For in Kenya the 'Mau Mau' insurgency among the Kikuyu people was fuelled as much by resentment against fellow Kikuyu as by hatred of settlers. Economic change had allowed many Kikuyu notables and their followers to increase their wealth at the expense of the poor – the landless or less well connected. Older notions of a 'moral economy' and social reciprocity had broken down.[64] When the settler panic jerked the colonial state into repression, it turned these tensions into a social war, as 'loyal' chiefs harried those suspected of Mau Mau sympathies, and these reacted in kind or fled to the forests, the base for guerrilla war. The back of Mau Mau resistance was broken by 1956. But even in Kenya, the cost of a prolonged security operation, the need to rally African communities to the government side, and embarrassment over the atrocities and brutalities of the repression apparatus (especially the camps where Mau Mau suspects were 'rehabilitated')[65] had made devolution unavoidable by 1960. By that date, indeed, independence under governments chosen and led by Africans had become the accepted policy of all the colonial powers, with the exception of Portugal. But what they hoped and intended was to control the time-table of change, to install 'moderate' regimes with whom relations would be cordial, and to maintain close supervision over the foreign relations and internal development of the ex-colonial territories. Since sub-Saharan Africa still seemed an international backwater, remote from the front line of cold war, they thought they had time in hand for a post-colonial transition.

This illusion was shattered by the crisis in the Congo. The Belgian government had granted independence in June 1960 on the premise of minimal change in its role and influence in the Congo's affairs.[66] It was a catastrophic misjudgement. Within a matter of days the army had mutinied, spreading panic and terror among the large expatriate community. The charismatic new premier, Patrice Lumumba, rejected a close post-colonial partnership. The mineral-rich provinces of South Kasai and Katanga seceded unilaterally from the new Congo republic, in Katanga's case with the connivance of Brussels, perhaps with the aim of destroying Lumumba. By August 1960 Lumumba had appealed for aid to the Soviet Union, and Soviet arms and personnel began to arrive on the scene. A United Nations force of 10,000 men was sent to hold the country together. But, with the rise of new separatist regimes, the escalation of violence as rival armies battled for control, the murder of Lumumba by Katangan (and perhaps Belgian) soldiers,[67] and international differences over the purpose of the UN force, the country portrayed only three years before as a model colony had become the 'Congo disaster'.[68] Although a semblance of order had returned by 1964–5, the Congo's tragedy transformed the meaning of decolonization in Africa. It revealed the unexpected hazard of a Cold War competition between East and West for African allegiance. It confirmed the wisdom (as it seemed in London) of an early withdrawal from Britain's remaining colonial burdens in East and Central Africa before they were afflicted by the contagion of disorder. And, most decisively of all, it entrenched the suspicion of whites south of the Zambezi that anarchy and barbarism were the inevitable product of concession to African nationalists. As progress towards complete independence became more and more hectic in the rest of Africa (even Algeria, despite its million '*pieds-noirs*' – white settlers – had thrown off French rule in 1962), in the 'southern third' white control tightened to form a solid bloc that also included the Portuguese colonies in Angola and Mozambique. Here was a new and peculiar 'partition' of Africa.

As much as in the Middle East or the rest of Asia, decolonization in Africa was not a clean break with the imperial past, or a ticket of entry into a 'world of nations'. The new African states inherited the weaknesses of their colonial forerunners – into whose shoes they had stepped after the briefest transition. Regional or local ethnicity was much stronger than nationalism. Building national identities without common vernacular languages presented an enormous challenge. The 'tribal' legacy of colonial rule was deeply embedded: indeed, in many parts of Africa, creating new forms of 'tribal' ethnicity was the usual means of adjusting to the larger scale of economic and social life.

Meanwhile, the pressure to expand the state's role was acute, whether in social services or economic development. The imperative need for any new regime was to find external sources of financial and often military aid, before it lost its claim on the loyalty of its followers.[69] It was a scene ready-made for the growth of external influence in a novel post-colonial form. If the world's greatest powers had a motive to do so, the means to build new empires of influence lay all around.

UNDECLARED EMPIRES

Decolonization is best understood as the dissolution of the distinctive global order – geopolitical, legal, economic, cultural and demographic – that had made an appearance by the 1840s, was consolidated in the 1890s, and staggered on into the 1940s and '50s where conditions still favoured its survival. The ability of the surviving colonial powers to preserve this old imperial system faded rapidly after 1945. That, as we have seen, was one key element of the new post-war international landscape. The other, just as critical, was the bloody collapse of the war imperialisms of the Nazis and Japan. It was the near simultaneous fall of both these imperial regimes – the 'old colonial' and the 'new imperialist' – that cleared a space for the emergence of new world empires, with new ideologies, new methods, and new aims and objects.

Even so, the breakneck expansion of American power was somewhat surprising. Accepting obligations outside the North American continent or Central America had always been contentious in American opinion. Fear of foreign entanglements ran very deep. American freedom was widely thought to derive from a deliberate rejection of the atavistic mentality and warlike spirit of a decadent Old World, and to be gravely threatened by too much contact with it. The American political system seemed poorly equipped for the formulation and conduct of foreign policy, the continuity of which was easily wrecked on the shoals of domestic controversy. American attitudes tended to be strongly unilateralist, scorning the need for the coalitions and compromises that were part and parcel of an active diplomacy. They were powerfully reinforced by the legalist tradition that viewed external relations as something best regulated by judicial decision and solemn binding agreements.[70] By contrast, diplomacy in the European mode – the opportunistic pursuit of the national interest – appeared cynical, self-destructive and futile. These traits had contributed to the notorious American refusal to join the League of Nations or to cooperate in the containment of Nazi expansion before 1939. Yet after 1945 American governments assumed huge new burdens all around the world, and wove a web of alliances to help in their upkeep. What had changed?

Two factors transformed the American outlook. The first was the extraordinary gap that had opened up between America's material strength and that of any other state. In 1950, five years after the war, the American economy produced twice as much as the economies of Britain, France and Germany combined (compared with a rough equality in 1913).[71] This economic advantage was dramatically re-inforced by the possession of nuclear technology and the unique capacity to deploy atomic weapons. By themselves, perhaps, these new sources of power might have promoted an even more isolationist mood than in the inter-war years. But they were coupled with aware-ness that the defensive perimeter of America's safety had been hugely extended by advances in air transport and the need to manage the international economy to avoid a post-war depression. 'Fortress America' was no longer invulnerable. Instead, American leaders now enjoyed the margin of power to make alliances on terms that secured American primacy. The fear of returning to the strategic nightmare of 1941–2 gave them the motive to do so.

The result was the creation of an American 'system' imperial in all but name. In 1946 plans were laid for a naval command in the Mediterranean. In 1947 the Truman Doctrine promised military help to Turkey and Greece against Soviet pressure, and Marshall Aid pledged the means to restore the battered West European economies. In early 1948 Washington signalled its readiness to negotiate an Atlan-tic pact that would commit it to the defence of Western Europe, and the Vandenberg Resolution gave the Senate's blessing. In April 1949 the North Atlantic Treaty was signed, and two years later American troops were deployed for the landward defence of Western Europe. There were parallel commitments in Canada (over which ran the shortest air route to the Soviet Union) and East Asia, where the mutual security pact with Japan was signed in 1951. By that year, in fact, the system's main elements had been put in place. It was not symmetrical. It comprised a close alliance with Britain, the key European member of the North Atlantic pact, and a defensive partnership with the other West European states. West Germany (whose army was under effective American command) and Japan (where America enjoyed far-reaching extraterritorial rights) were semi-protectorates. The Philippines (technically independent from 1946) granted America control over some twenty-three bases, and undertook not to grant them to anyone else without American agreement; it was a real (if not nominal) protectorate.[72] Micronesia was retained under Washington's direct supervision for the sake of its bases, especially Guam, America's fortress in the western Pacific, guarding its route to Japan and the Philippines.[73] We could add to this list America's vast sphere of 'informal empire' in Latin America, where the war had brought the final extinction of Britain's commercial presence. The Rio treaty of 1947 (the 'Inter-American Treaty of Reciprocal Assistance') provided for military aid from the United States against both armed attack and other forms of aggression (code for Communist 'subversion') towards the Latin American states. In the 1950s only three Latin American governments maintained diplomatic relations with the Soviet Union.

This colossal imperium was on an unprecedented scale. No previous world power had entrenched itself at both ends of Eurasia, or had had the power to do so. What made it possible was partly the eagerness with which America's friendship was sought and its leadership welcomed. The Anglo-American alliance was a remarkable example of cooperation between a declining imperial power (which expected to recover) and its most obvious successor. For a crucial period, both parties accepted the myth of equality and practised a form of co-dominium. In Western Europe, America built an empire 'by invitation' – in the striking phrase coined by Geir Lundestad.[74] In Japan, as we saw, the political elite preferred the onerous terms of the security pact to the risk of a leftward lurch in public opinion. Whether real or imaginary, the fear of Communism and of Soviet expansion was the catalyst of collaboration abroad and fuelled American readiness at home to assume the burdens of power. In no other circumstances could America have won such wide acquiescence in its new world role.

By the early 1950s, geopolitics and ideology had been powerfully reinforced by the third component of American influence. With the gradual recovery of the European and Japanese economies, the pump-priming effect of American Marshall Aid, and the further boost of military spending during the Korean War, international trade burst out of the long stagnation of 1913–50. Exports worldwide doubled in value between 1953 and 1963, and almost doubled in volume.[75] The United States had played the most important part in creating the conditions for this extraordinary boom. The International Monetary Fund (to promote exchange-rate stability) and the General Agreement on Tariffs and Trade (to liberalize trade) would have come to nothing without its support. Above all, perhaps, it was the American dollar, convertible into gold, which supplied the universally accepted reserve currency on which trade expansion depended. America, of course, was perfectly placed to reap the rewards of the new commercial economy. Between 1939 and 1950 the value of American investment abroad had more than doubled. American industry reached its competitive peak in the 1950s. In dynamic sectors like air transport and mass entertainment, American products were almost unbeatable. The 'soft power' of economic and cultural influence underwrote the 'hard power' of strategic might. No country that relied on a trading currency could risk Washington's displeasure, lest in moments of strain the support of the dollar might be withheld.

The huge zone where America provided – or imposed – its strategic protection (by 1955 the United States had 450 bases in 36 countries) overlapped with the sphere of the new international economy of which America was the pivot. Together they formed the Pax Americana. In the 1950s it was consolidated rapidly, though not without friction. A critical year was 1956. Washington's refusal to help the Hungarian revolt against Soviet hegemony marked a tacit acceptance of the European partition of 1945–8. Almost simultaneously, by forcing the British and French (through financial pressure) to abandon their effort to destroy Nasser's regime, Washington served notice that its European allies must manage what remained of their imperial space in ways that conformed with its grand design. The general return to convertibility among the Western currencies in 1958 signalled the end of 'emergency economics' and the normalization of the global trading economy.[76] In the Middle East and South East Asia, it seemed that limited intervention was enough to forestall the expansion of Soviet influence and stabilize the frontier between the superpower spheres. With the line of 'containment' now tightly drawn across much of Eurasia, and the strategic means (by a nuclear onslaught) to deter a Soviet breakout into Western Europe, the global balance now looked firmly tilted towards American primacy.

In fact the global effects of Eurasia's division were not so easily confined. The main reason lay in the astonishing trajectory of Soviet power. In three years of war between 1942 and 1945, the Soviet Union recovered from the brink of catastrophic defeat to play the largest part in the victory over Germany. The reward for this was the massive extension of the sphere of Soviet predominance in East and Central Europe and, above all, a practical veto on the reunification of Germany. This great triumph in the west was the main foundation of Soviet world power. Perhaps the crucial element in the post-war strength of the Soviet imperial system was its geopolitical vantage. Its military salient in eastern Germany threatened the heartlands of Western Europe and neutralized America's lead in high-technology weapons. Its South East European satellites guarded the low road to the Ukraine and South Russia which the Wehrmacht had followed with such devastating consequences in 1941–2. While this *limes* remained in place, the Soviet Union was almost invulnerable in a conventional war. Two things had made it much easier than it might have been to rivet Soviet control over so much of occupied Europe in 1945–8. The first was the lack of any serious threat from post-war East Asia remotely comparable to that of Japan before 1941. Indeed the victory of Mao Tse-tung in the Chinese Civil War was an unexpected bonus. Moscow's whole strength could be turned to the west. The second was the legacy of Nazi imperialism, which had virtually decapitated the political elites of pre-war Eastern Europe (a task the NKVD – Stalin's secret police – eagerly finished off) while sowing bitter divisions between the social, religious and ethnic groups it had favoured or spurned during a desperate conflict.

Even so, the dramatic enlargement of the Soviet sphere into Eastern and Central Europe was a colossal burden, not least in manpower. It fell on a country that had lost in war some 14 per cent of its population (the staggering figure of 27 million people – the United States lost some 400,000) and perhaps a quarter of its physical assets.[77] Harvest failure in 1946 brought large-scale famine. Economic recovery was the final achievement of Stalin's industrial order. Ferocious work discipline, conscripted labour, and the heavy reliance on slave or semi-slave labour were used even more widely than before the war against a cowed, ill-fed and exhausted population.[78] Perhaps 10 per cent of industrial output came from the Gulag.[79] By the time of Stalin's death, in 1953, the wartime losses had been made good and the Soviet Union reached levels of economic growth that were exceeded only by the 'miracle' economies of Germany and Japan.[80] This was the platform on which Khrushchev would build a further expansion of Soviet influence.

Khrushchev embodied a new Soviet confidence that it could compete with the West upon equal terms, and not just in Europe – a striking change from the 'bunker' mentality of the Stalinist period. Soviet space scientists were the first to launch an orbiting space vehicle (the 'Sputnik') in 1957, a hugely prestigious assertion that they had more than caught up with their Western competitors. Khrushchev authorized the expansion of Soviet sea power under the redoubtable Admiral Gorshkov. By the late 1950s its huge submarine force made the Soviet navy the world's second largest,[81] designed to shadow America's fleets and deny them 'command of the sea' – defined as unchallenged control of the world's seaways. Khrushchev was also determined to force Western agreement to the permanent division of Germany – the cause of the Berlin crisis in 1961. The Berlin Wall (which followed Western refusal) signalled the Soviet will to rule over its European *raj* for the foreseeable future. But the most radical feature of Khrushchev's approach was his canny appraisal of what decolonization offered. The cracking of Britain's Middle Eastern hegemony, the rush to independence in colonial Africa, and signs of social unrest in Latin America promised ways of escape from Eurasian containment, a Soviet breakthrough into the Outer World. What the Soviet Union lacked in economic inducements it might hope to make up with the ideological appeal of 'Soviet modernity'. In many new states, the Soviet model of industrial growth, the strength and efficiency (so it seemed) of the Soviet party state, and the dazzling alchemy of

authoritarian rule and egalitarian values that Marxism–Leninism proclaimed were deeply attractive. Here was a route to the modern world
(tried and tested) which did not lie through continued subservience to
the foreign business interests that had ruled the roost in the colonial
(or semi-colonial) era.

Khrushchev's aim (we may surmise) was to exploit the new fluidity
in global politics before American power and the West-centred economy could become the dominant influence in the post-colonial world.
Like the German Empire before 1914, the Soviet Union sought a
'place in the sun' and the right to shape the emerging world order. By
1960 the signs of rivalry were coming thick and fast. When Washington tried to crush Castro's revolution in Cuba by barring the import
of Cuban sugar (a proven tactic), Khrushchev promised to buy it
instead. When the Congo exploded, he denounced the failure to support Lumumba's government and portrayed the UN as a tool of the
West needing drastic reform. In London and Washington there was
deep alarm.[82] In 1961 a new front opened in South East Asia when
Ho Chi Minh launched the struggle against the Diem regime in South
Vietnam. The Yemen revolution in 1962, and the civil war that followed, made it seem likely that Nasser (who intervened massively on
the revolutionary side) would become much more dependent upon
Soviet aid and that the Yemeni war would unsettle Saudi Arabia. With
great reluctance, the Americans promised their help against any attack
on the Saudi state by Nasser's Yemeni clients.[83] Most dramatic of all,
was the dispatch of Soviet missiles to Khrushchev's new ally in Latin
America. The Cuban Missile Crisis in October 1962 was resolved in
the end by the removal of the Soviet weapons, in return for a similar
concession over American missiles to be deployed in Turkey and
(perhaps) an American promise not to invade Cuba. But, although
the outcome seemed to be a Soviet climbdown, the crisis revealed the
widening scope of Soviet–American rivalry. It confirmed the view of
the Kennedy White House that more resolute methods were needed
to block the expansion of Soviet influence in the 'Third World' of
Africa, Asia and Latin America. This was the climate in which the
threatened collapse of Diem's South Vietnamese government took on
what seemed a more than local importance.

*

For the next twenty years the superpower struggle for influence was the dominant feature of global politics. The prize was not (as in the 1890s) a great territorial domain, but an informal empire of clients and allies, glued together by arms supplies and military missions, 'development' aid and commercial credits. In what became a fluctuating, unpredictable contest, five aspects are striking. The first was the reluctance of either power after 1962 to pose a direct challenge in the other's 'backyard', reinforced by the fact of nuclear parity by the late 1960s. American occupation of the Dominican Republic in 1965, like the Soviet invasion of Czechoslovakia three years later, drew no riposte. The détente diplomacy of the 1970s acknowledged the permanence of Europe's divisions: the Helsinki 'Final Act' in 1975 was to all intents a European peace treaty by which the European states (including the Soviet Union) bound themselves to accept their existing frontiers. The second was the relative mismatch in the economic strength of the two contestants. Despite the triumphs of its military-industrial complex, the Soviet economy remained smaller and weaker than its American counterpart. Between 1960 and 1975 its share of world exports never rose above 4 per cent.[84] America's share of the world's manufactured exports was 13 per cent in 1976.[85] The free-market economy of which it formed the pivot took the lion's share of international commerce. The third was the persistent instability of the large 'frontier' zone where the two world powers strove to assert their claims. This turbulence sprang from the travails of state-building in ex-colonial lands, anti-colonial conflicts in parts of Africa, and economic upheaval in the 1970s (the 'oil shock' of 1973 and the drastic rise in the price of fuel). It created a hunger for arms and aid by regimes and their rivals. It ensured a constant demand for superpower sponsors, and fed the domino mentality of superpower strategists. It created an ever-widening sphere in the Outer World where they waged war by proxy. By the mid-1970s Soviet military aid and political influence were reaching deep into the Horn of Africa and the southern third of the continent. The fourth aspect was the consequence (in part) of this instability: the exposure of both superpower competitors to great reversals of fortune. The humiliating defeat of America's effort to preserve South Vietnam as a non-Communist state was the most crushing example. But the sudden

disavowal of its Soviet alliance by the Egyptian government in the
following year (1976), and the expulsion of an army of Soviet advisers,
was, in geostrategic terms, of hardly less significance.[86] Fifth and last,
as we might deduce from this, for all the plenitude of their military
muscle, there were drastic limits to the control that either superpower
could exert over its restless, unruly and self-willed clients. Both ran,
as a result, the serious risk of overcommitting themselves to unreliable
allies, of being dragged willy-nilly towards confrontation. And, just
as it had in the late nineteenth century, China resisted assimilation
into any imperial system.

To many contemporary analysts, there seemed no reason why the
ebb and flow of this superpower imperialism should not continue
indefinitely. To the 'declinologists' in the United States, the lesson
of Vietnam was that American power had been overstretched. The
financial strain of the Vietnam War and the sudden rise in the price
of oil (part of the Arab states' attempt to apply indirect pressure on
Israel) checked the rapid growth of the market economies after 1970.
The mighty dollar had to go off gold. Marxists daydreamed of a
capitalist meltdown and a 'world revolution'. Schemes were projected
for a 'new international economic order' to stage the transfer of
technology and capital to the developing states. The fear in the West
was of a radical turn in the ex-colonial world. With global strength
becoming more evenly balanced and the developing states making
larger demands, the pursuit of influence in the zones of contest looked
certain to grow increasingly arduous. The struggle over Angola, where
a civil war raged between Marxist and anti-Marxist factions, revealed
how quickly such a 'proxy war' could embroil a whole subcontinent.[87]
In the Horn of Africa, large-scale Soviet aid to Ethiopia's Marxist
leaders was countered by American help to its neighbour, Somalia.[88]
But direct action was even more alarming. The Soviet invasion of
Afghanistan in late 1979 was seen in the West as the opening salvo of a
'new' Cold War, a fresh advance by the 'evil empire' (Ronald Reagan's
memorable phrase) that was ruled from Moscow. Containment had
failed, the Secretary of State told the American Senate in June 1983.
'Soviet ambitions and capabilities have long since reached beyond the
geographical bounds that this doctrine took for granted.'[89] Far from
heralding a 'world of nations', decolonization's unexpected course

seemed to have set the scene for new kinds of empire. Indeed, it could have been argued that the collateral damage of late-twentieth-century imperialism – the destabilizing effects of covert intervention, the financial succour lent to authoritarian rulers, and the militarization of politics encouraged by the vast traffic in weapons[90] – was at least as great as that of its late-nineteenth-century version. It certainly seemed that the dangerous uncertainty of 'competitive coexistence' (with the appalling prospect of 'mutually assured destruction' in an atomic exchange) was the inevitable price of a bipolar world. But it did not turn out like that.

The reversal was astounding. In the mid-1980s the scope of Soviet ambition seemed greater than ever. From a forward base at Camranh Bay in southern Vietnam, the Soviet navy could make its presence felt across the main sea lanes running through South East Asia and in the Indian Ocean, a 'British lake' until the 1950s.[91] By laying down huge new aircraft carriers like the *Leonid Brezhnev*, Moscow now aimed to rival the Americans' capacity to intervene around the globe. But then in less than half a decade this vast imperial structure – the ruling power across Northern Eurasia; the tenacious rival in Southern Asia, Africa and the Middle East – simply fell to pieces. By 1991 it was an empire in ruins. There was no 'silver age' or phase of decline: just a calamitous fall.

The explanation may lie in the converging pressures for internal reform and the ill-fated schemes of the Soviet leaders to escape from the vice they thought was closing upon them. The basic failing of the Soviet system was economic. After 1970, the rapid growth of previous decades could not be sustained. The extra production to improve living standards and fund the apparatus of military power eluded the Soviet planners. Without the sanction of terror, the command economy that Stalin had fashioned lost its grip on the workforce.[92] The lack of a price mechanism to direct investment and select innovation became more and more costly. To make matters worse, the setbacks affecting the market economies in the 1970s proved very short-lived. In the G-7 countries (Germany, Italy, France, Britain, Canada, Japan and the United States) that made up the core of the capitalist world, the 1980s saw extremely rapid movement towards the characteristic forms of commercial globalization: ever-greater dependence upon exports and trade; bank activity across national borders; the flow of capital into foreign investment; the large-scale buying and selling of currencies.[93] America's corporate economy staged a major recovery in the 1980s.[94] The spectacular growth of so-called 'newly industrialized countries', like Singapore, Malaysia, Thailand, Taiwan and, above all, South Korea (the world's tenth largest producer of steel by 1989), most of which had sheltered under American strategic protection, erased the fear that they would be hollowed out by Marxist liberation movements. In South East Asia, the 'South Korean' road to industrial prosperity, not the 'Vietnamese' road to peasant revolution, exerted the stronger appeal. But in the Soviet empire the burden of military spending became more and more crushing, while the satellite economies of Communist Eastern Europe looked increasingly westward for investment and trade.

Gorbachev's 'perestroika' was a last-ditch effort of imperial reform by a new Soviet leader.[95] Its principal aim was to 'Westernize' both the 'domestic' economy of the Soviet Union and the 'imperial' economy of the 'outer empire': to make them more responsive to consumer demand and technological innovation. The logic of this was very far-reaching. It meant promoting 'new' men and weakening the grip of the party bureaucracy on the command economy. It meant freeing up resources previously committed to the military effort. It meant loosening the 'discipline' that Moscow imposed on the satellite governments in Eastern Europe, to permit 'moderate' change. It meant negotiating access to Western investment and Western new technologies. And, because none of this was possible without easing the tensions of the 'new Cold War', it meant shrinking the scale of the Soviet military presence: in Eastern and Central Europe; in the spheres of intervention across Asia and Africa; above all in Afghanistan. Yet it is most unlikely that Gorbachev intended to surrender the claim of the Soviet Union to be a global power – indeed, the second great power. What he sought was a breathing space. His détente diplomacy was designed to protect Eastern Europe's delicate transition from a Soviet sphere of control to an 'informal empire' of fraternal influence. The Soviet empire would be modernized under Western eyes in a congenial climate of 'cooperative coexistence'. Revived and rejuvenated, it would still claim to offer a 'parallel modernity'.

But Gorbachev found (like the old colonial powers before him) that informal imperialism was not an easy option. To give up control and the threat of coercion was to take a big risk. Without other means to keep old clients loyal, it might even prove fatal. What Moscow could offer by way of economic inducements was paltry indeed compared with the West: this could already be seen in the slackening grip of Soviet power on Poland in the 1980s. So, with dizzying speed, East European reform turned into East European revolt. In November 1989 the Berlin Wall came down, pro-Soviet governments collapsed, the East European 'outer empire' vanished. This disaster devastated the authority and legitimacy of the Soviet regime. The command economy broke down at home. In the following year (1990) the revolt spread quickly across the 'inner empire' of the Soviet Union. The Soviet republics – including Russia itself, under Boris Yeltsin – now demanded their freedom. The abortive attempt by Gorbachev's colleagues to stem the political tide by a military coup and a state of emergency was the final straw. The Treaty of Alma Ata in December 1991 dissolved the Soviet Union into fifteen new states. It acknowledged the end of the Soviet *raj* in the Baltic, in the Trans-Caucasus and in Central Asia. Perhaps most telling of all, even the Ukraine, the vital auxiliary of Russian imperial power since the 1650s, voted for full independence. Post-Soviet Russia remained a colonial power with a huge domain. But, with a crippled economy and growing American influence in Inner Eurasia, its prospects might have daunted even Peter the Great.

UNLIMITED EMPIRE?

The empire-building of the bipolar age had been the other face of decolonization. Two great imperial systems had struggled to contain each other's expansion (real or imagined) and stabilize the wide zone of post-colonial instability to their own advantage. In fact stabilization had proved a mirage. There was even less chance than before 1914 that the rivals could agree on a global partition, or enforce its terms if they did. Firstly, the new norm of sovereignty inscribed in the charter of the United Nations ruled out recourse to overt territorial control – as did the domestic ideology of both contending powers. Secondly, with the exception of Europe, neither was willing to concede the permanent loss of any world region where hope still remained of political change. On that point, too, domestic ideology was firm. Thirdly, the legacy of empire to the post-colonial world had been anything but a smooth start in life. Geopolitical disputes between successor states, unresolved religious and ethnic conflicts, the use of state power to amass private wealth, and the vulnerability of weak states to economic shocks from outside were among the bitter fruits of colonial freedom. They hugely increased both the risk of upheaval and the scope for outside interference, by invitation or not. Fourthly, even if the two superpowers had settled the limits of their imperial spheres, they faced the irreconcilable enmity of the excluded other. Courted or quarrelled with, China was the joker in superpower politics. Neither side could be sure when or how it might change the game. Indeed, China's turn towards capitalism in the late 1970s, and the extraordinary growth of its hitherto closed economy, injected a large new factor of uncertainty in the last decade of superpower rivalry.

But what would happen once the Soviet collapse brought an end to competition? It was immediately clear that there would be no American retreat into hemispheric isolation. The great forward movement of American power and influence after 1945 would not be reversed. The Cold War had been the great age of American expansion. The vast new scale of American trade and investment, and America's dependence upon imported products (especially oil), made it just as important as at the end of the Second World War to have a dominant voice in shaping the rules of the world economy. The geostrategic revolution brought about by air power, satellite technology and nuclear weapons affirmed even more forcefully that American security was a global, not a hemispheric, matter. Thus the American response to the end of the Cold War was to see it not as the chance to lay down an imperial burden, but as a metahistoric opportunity to shape the course of world history.[96] This was the moment to complete the permanent transformation of the global economy, already under way in the 1970s and '80s. Closed economies should be opened up; state monopolies be broken down; the open door be enforced; private property – especially foreign private property – be made safe. Wood-row Wilson's prescription for international peace – long obstructed by Marxism–Leninism, Nazism and old-fashioned European col-onialism – could at last be administered right around the world. Political differences, the scars of nationalism, the wounds of class warfare, even the horrors of race hatred, would be washed away by the cleansing tide of free economic exchange and its cultural by-products. For the market economy would bring in its train an irresist-ible demand for democratization. Freed from the tyranny of the command economy and the spiritual oppression of ideological war-fare, hitherto subject peoples would naturally choose liberal democ-racy. The vital corollary for this global task was geostrategic. No state could be allowed to frustrate its achievement by the use of force. No state should be able to threaten its neighbours and carve out a regional 'empire' designed to exclude the global economy and its liberal culture. The enormous military lead that the United States had built up by the end of the Cold War must now be deployed to freeze the global balance of power, where it mattered most. To the veteran grand strategist Zbigniew Brzezinski the logic was obvious. American policy had no choice but to play a managing role in the geopolitics of Eurasia.[97]

It was hardly surprising that the seemingly unlimited scope of American ambition bred a mixed reaction. Unrestrained by the need to solicit goodwill, no longer in need of its Cold War alliances, and riding the wave of ideological triumph, America seemed free to use its economic and military muscle against all opposition, and the oppo-sition of all. Talk of an American 'empire', previously confined to the rhetoric of the Left, became increasingly common. A universal empire, in which one state imposed its domestic laws upon all the others, was the polar opposite of the long tradition of international law that had evolved in Europe since the seventeenth century. In that tradition, it was the need to respect the sovereignty of states that was constantly stressed, and the requirement to seek the agreement of all (in the nineteenth century it had been all 'civilized' states) when framing the rules of international conduct.[98] Unease on the Left was fused with the suspicion of many post-colonial states that the freedoms they had enjoyed under bipolar conditions were about to be lost, and with the wider complaint that building decolonized cultures – in which the 'normality' of the West was no longer assumed – was an impossible task in the face of 'globalization' under American auspices.

These fears were sharpened at the end of the century. For it was then that the easy assumptions of a post-Cold War world began to unravel. In the Middle East, in East Asia and in sub-Saharan Africa the conflict and instability of the Cold War era showed a stubborn persistence. History had not come to an end. Decolonization, in its larger sense, remained incomplete. The response in America was to assert much more bluntly that American power should be used to secure the gains and advance the programme of the new world order after 1989. The ensuing debate made still more explicit the question of whether the United States was an empire, or should embrace the role of an imperial power. What the critics perceived was the aggressive revival of two deep-rooted attitudes towards the rest of the world. The first was unilateralism: the reluctance to be bound by rules made for others. It sprang from beliefs about America's 'exceptional' origins as a democratic society in a world ruled by despots or the feudal detritus of the European nobility. The second was universalism: what was good for America was good for the world. Democratic institutions on the American model, America's version of the market economy, and a commercial culture made for mass consumption were the best guarantees of wealth and stability. To refuse to adopt them was a hostile act against progress and peace. Unilateralism and universalism were harmless foibles in an isolationist power. In the world's only superpower they became the chief elements of an imperial outlook. Wedded to the use of a coercive diplomacy or armed intervention, they were the high road to 'empire' in which perpetual war abroad would subvert democracy at home.[99]

It is pointless to debate whether America should be seen as an imperial power: the case has already been made. After 1990 it became the only world empire. A state with the means to intervene forcibly in almost any part of the world, with such a massive advantage in military power over any possible rival, and with an advanced economy more than twice the size of its nearest competitor was such an empire de facto. That America was without the colonial possessions that contributed *partly* to the global pre-eminence of Victorian Britain is of trivial importance. Victorian Britain was widely different in its public ideology, economic objectives and political methods from first-century Rome, but both ruled empires. Empires exist to accumulate power on an extensive scale; the form that they take reflects prevailing conditions, not unthinking adherence to an obsolete model. The interesting question about America's empire is not its existence (which we may take as read) but the limits to which it (like all previous empires) may be subject (or not).

The elements of its power can be briefly listed. In 2003 the United States possessed more than 700 bases (and 234 military golf courses) in 130 countries, not counting a number of 'temporary' installations. More than 250,000 uniformed personnel served overseas in the huge regional commands ('Pacom', 'Southcom', 'Centcom' etc.) that divided the globe between them. With fifty-four nuclear attack submarines, twelve aircraft carriers, a dozen helicopter carriers and a huge fleet of support vessels, the United States holds command of the sea. In space, in the air and in modern warfare on land, American superiority is all but unchallengeable. In economic terms, the scale of American wealth is just as astounding. The United States accounted for nearly one-third of the world's gross production in 1999;[100] its gross national product is five times that of China. As a buyer and seller on a massive scale, as the loudest voice in the organizations that regulate the world's trade and finance, and as the home of many of the world's largest business corporations, the United States can wield enormous 'soft power'. Thirdly, economic success and the prestige and appeal of American-style democracy have combined to create new bridgeheads of influence all over the world. The cavernous purse from which to reward cooperation and friendship, and the social networks built by educational links and by migrations and diasporas whose richest members reside in America, offer the means to drive them wider and deeper. For the American empire (like the British before it) is not the preserve of governments and policymakers. Much of the energy that fuels American expansion is unofficial and private.

But it might be argued that these 'imperial' assets have been overvalued, will gradually shrink, and are easily wasted. American military power, suggests a shrewd observer, can easily dominate the common spaces of the globe. But it is poorly adapted to irregular warfare in densely occupied lands, in great urban complexes or in terrain un-suited to using mechanized firepower. Here sheer weight of numbers may count for much more, and also the willingness to take heavy losses.[101] Shoring up friendly regimes or coercing resistance might prove no easier in the future than it had been in Vietnam. Military failure would sap prestige and morale, and encourage further recalci-trance. American economic power might face a similar attrition as East and Southern Asia become the world's most productive regions. The dollar's value already depends upon the inflow of savings from Japan and China, and would suffer badly if these savings changed direction. With the worldwide diffusion of American business prac-tices, the competitive advantage that they once conferred is now widely shared with other advanced economies.[102] There is a powerful argument that, for all the weight that America carries, it can no longer resist (or not without heavy cost) the mass of rules, regulations, customs and conventions that govern global affairs, and which depend on consensus. Nor should a tame acquiescence in American popular culture be taken for granted. Cultural resistance, most vividly seen in Islamic fundamentalism, might spread more quickly as the guardian elites of vernacular cultures come to fear for their influence. And as the costs of greatness rise, and its benefits fall, the American taxpayer might come to resent the burden of empire and lose heart in the effort to preserve American power in its lonely pre-eminence. The cycle of change would start once again.

All these in theory could correct the imbalance of a unipolar world. They may actually do so. But it is hard to be sure. American military power may lack the means to win wars in the 'contested zone' where the fighting is 'low tech' and casualties are high. But it may find allies willing (for a price) to bear the cost of fighting such 'dirty wars'. American industry may become uncompetitive, and America's balance of trade even more unfavourable. But America's role as the monetary pivot of the global economy, and the complex link between the value of the dollar and American military power, may command a large 'rent' that others will pay until the distant day when a substitute is found. Thirdly, it is far from clear that cultural resistance – except in very localized forms – will set effective limits to the spread of America's 'Anglo' culture, with its massive arsenal of media output, educational provision and research activity. In the early twenty-first century, most of the evidence points in the opposite direction. Fourthly, although the collaboration of political elites in different parts of the world will certainly fluctuate, resisting American influence may prove increasingly difficult. The borders of states (especially weak states) will become more and more porous, and the leverage within them of transnational enterprise (whether commercial companies or non-governmental organizations) looks certain to grow. Rallying 'nationalism' against the external oppressor may become even less easy. Other forms of resistance are as likely to be directed against America's client states and allies as against America itself. And, without another great 'sponsor' promising international support, the cost of more than local resistance may be unreasonably high. Fifthly, for all the prognoses that new rivals will appear (China is the usual suspect), it is at least as likely that the internal stresses of socio-political change will abort their advance towards superpower status. Lastly, the chances of a domestic revolt against America's imperial burden will depend very heavily on the costs it imposes. For all the reasons above, these are very hard to predict.

This is not to say that no limits exist to America's power. But, on almost any criterion, this now transcends the limits of empire that we have observed in force since the early fifteenth century. Those writers who have likened America's 'hegemonic' status to that of Victorian Britain betray a staggering ignorance of the history of both. Whether this power will be used to make the world safer, or to sharpen its conflicts by ill-managed interventions, is a different question entirely. No prediction is safe. Like all previous generations, we face the future with little more than guesswork on which to build our plans. Were the frantic pace of economic integration (what we call 'globalization') to slow down sharply, or go into reverse, the previous paragraph would lose much of its force. And our view of the past, as well as the future, would be altered once more.

9
Tamerlane's Shadow

9. Tiananmen Square: the empire continues

At the start of this book it was argued that the shape of today's world cannot be explained away as the product of a global economy and its political and cultural side effects. Behind the variations of wealth and power, the divergence of institutions and values, and the differences in cultural and religious attachment that are still so visible in the twenty-first century world lies a much more complex history of competitive empire-, state- and culture-building. But this is not a history that is easy to trace. It remains deeply controversial. It is sometimes portrayed as the brutal saga of predatory imperialism, the West's invasion of the hapless non-West. The opposite view is just as stark: the history of the world becomes the long march to modernity, with the West as a guide, and using its template. Since neither version can win more than partisan support, it is easy to see the attractions of retreat into geographical determinism. But even if it is true that a larger supply of plants and animals for domestication explains why Eurasia conquered the 'Outer World' and not the other way round,[1] that cannot unravel the problem with which this book is concerned: the shifting balance of power and wealth within Eurasia itself in the last half-millennium.

For all the passions that they arouse, the evidence of this book is that histories founded on the rival grand narratives of 'exploitation' and 'modernization' have limited value as a guide to the Eurasian past. That is not because we cannot find plentiful evidence of both phenomena in action. But neither had a free rein. Each became entangled in the politics and culture of the states and regions where its influence was felt. Each was forced into compromise to win over the local allies and agents without which it was (usually) hamstrung. Both were dependent on the fluctuating conditions that favoured or deterred imperial ambition, commercial expansion and cultural assertion in different parts of the world. Both were 'projects' that could be hollowed out, taken over or paralysed by sophisticated forms of resistance and adaptation. There is no neat chronology of imperial rise and fall; no neat geography of European mastery over the rest of Eurasia. Nor indeed did the 'empire' of the West come to an end in the bonfire of colonial vanities that we call decolonization.

We need, in short, a more realistic view of this contentious past to make sense of our times – and to begin to see them not as an everlasting 'present', but as a historical 'period', condemned like all others to change and decay. In earlier parts of this book, much stress has been laid on the tortuous route by which the contemporary world came into existence. The account that they give has little in common with those road maps of history on which ideologues (of every persuasion) draw their straight lines. It suggests, nonetheless, that a number of grand themes form the heart of the story – and offer a glimmer of insight into the fate of Eurasia, and thus of the world. To these we now turn.

IMPERIAL HISTORIES

The history of the world, it is tempting to say, is an imperial history, a history of empires. It would be easy to think from much historical writing that empires are abnormal: unwelcome intrusions in a non-imperial world. Their rise is credited to exceptional circumstances, or the manic energy of a unique personality. Their fall is predictable, because the exceptional circumstances that permitted their rise have a limited life. This view is appealing, but has little else to commend it. A glance at world history suggests on the contrary that, for most of the time, the default position so far as politics went was imperial power. Empires were systems of influence or rule in which ethnic, cultural or ecological boundaries were overlapped or ignored. Their ubiquitous presence arose from the fact that, on a regional scale, as well as a global, the endowments needed to build strong states were very unequally distributed. This was a question not just of cultivable plains or navigable rivers, but of social and cultural solidarity and the relative ease with which both manpower and goods could be mobilized by the state. It was this kind of 'modernity' that allowed the creation of a huge Chinese empire by 200 BC. Against the cultural attraction, or physical force, of an imperial state, resistance was hard, unless reinforced by geographical remoteness or unusual cohesion. Even those states that escaped subjugation had to manoeuvre their way between imperial powers to avoid being trampled beneath their elephants' feet.

If empires were common, they were also diverse. Most empires in history would strike us today as modest affairs, with small populations and limited reach. Even if we confine our attention to the grander empires discussed in this book, we find wide variations. What are sometimes called the 'classical' empires were great agrarian bureaucracies. Their essential feature was control of the land and the surplus it yielded. A more or less centralized officialdom, organized and recruited to enforce the power of the emperor against localized interests or landholding aristocrats, collected the revenue and dispensed imperial justice. The prestige of the emperor was a vital resource, to be carefully guarded by seclusion, ritual and ceremony. After the fall of the Roman Empire in the West, China was the best model of how such an advanced empire should work. Elsewhere, conditions were usually less favourable: religion, ecology or the geopolitical setting precluded imperial rule along Chinese lines. In Middle Eurasia, rulers turned instead to the device of military slaves, the Mamluks, recruited from the margins of empire. As aliens dependent on the amir's favour, or as converts to Islam, they had no local connections, no clan or kin to taint their allegiance. They formed the counterpoise to the local solidarity of towns, tribes and entrenched rural elites. Both these kinds of empire were very different indeed from the overseas empires that Europeans began to construct in the late fifteenth century.

Of course, these 'colonial' empires came in multiple versions. They were usually carved out not by government action, but by private adventurers enjoying a licence or charter from the government at home. Some depended on seizing the labour of those whom they conquered; some on the purchase of slave labour from Africa. Some tried to replicate (or even improve on) the kind of society left behind in Europe. These were the true settler societies, from which both slaves and indigenous peoples were largely excluded. Needless to say, these colonial forms made little headway in Asia. For almost two hundred years, Europe's invasion of Asia was limited to bases and depots, footholds and outposts that faced out to sea, not towards the interior: Bombay, Goa, Pondicherry, Madras, Calcutta, Batavia and Macao. They were part of mercantile, maritime empires that skirted the rim of Asia's great states. Their power was felt, where it was felt at all, on the uninhabited wastes of the sea. When Europeans began to amass territorial dominions from the late eighteenth century (and mainly in South Asia), they preferred to fill the shoes of previous Asian rulers rather than fashion a new order on 'European' lines. It was the Mughals' revenue system, tightened up and screwed down, that gave the British East India Company the financial means to build a subcontinental *raj* in the century after the Battle of Plassey (1757).

It would be a mistake to draw too sharp a distinction between 'European' methods and 'Asian'. But in the long nineteenth century (1815–1914) the scene was transformed by industrial power. Industrial technique allowed Europeans to colonize far faster and on a far larger scale than was previously possible. It gave them the means to penetrate new markets and crush old competition. It enlarged their ability to collect information and exploit it efficiently. Above all, it enhanced their capacity to project their physical power over far greater distances and at much lower cost. In the age of the steamship and later the railway, strategic remoteness lost much of its meaning. When a European army could advance on Nanking (as the British were to do in the First Opium War of 1839–42), no part of Asia seemed safe. One result was to permit many more 'little Indias': the colonies of rule that began to spread across Asia and between which Africa was divided after 1880. The other was to forge a third kind of empire, of 'invisible sway':[2] the systematic accumulation of predominant influence over regions and states whose rulers were left with a purely technical sovereignty. Where European bankers, diplomats, merchants and missionaries enjoyed privileged status, managed the bulk of overseas trade, had their hands on the tap of foreign investment, and could threaten blockade or bombardment if their interests were challenged, the labour of ruling could seem redundant or futile. 'Informal empire' – if costs and benefits were to be the criterion – was imperialism at its highest stage.

In theory, all kinds of empire were unavoidably subject to great stresses and strains, spasms of crisis, and an ultimate fall. It was a historical truism that no empire was permanent. Collapse could be triggered by a wide range of causes. Where an empire depended on the cooperation or loyalty of subject elites, rebellion or resistance at an inconvenient time could inflict irreparable damage on its prestige and authority. The need to appease its recalcitrant allies might cause a slower, but fatal, erosion of the means of control. If exerting imperial power required the approval of public opinion in the imperial 'homeland', or inflicted new burdens on its manpower or wealth, a revolt at the centre and not the periphery might be decisive in bringing an empire down. New ideologies (or religions) might destroy the moral and political credit on which empires could base their claim to legitimacy – the sense that they were part of the natural order of things. Just as common a danger was becoming unwieldy: when the weight of commitments became too much to bear, but the pain of disposal was too much to take. Imperial obesity was a drain on physical strength and a temptation to rivals. Empires were also exposed to the hazards of economic and environmental change. The resources and technologies on which their power had been built might begin to dry up or become obsolete. Material wealth and technical prowess might dribble away, or shift elsewhere to more favoured locations. Worst of all, perhaps, empires might be driven into wars of mutual destruction, in which the pursuit of limited ends could unleash willy-nilly a world-changing upheaval. Even without such a doomsday scenario, an insidious danger lurked inside most imperial systems. It was almost inevitable that their commanding heights would fall into the hands of well-connected elites who would dig themselves in. By degrees they would turn the imperial structure into a semi-private domain, geared to promoting their sectional interests. They would enlist the support of other factions and groupings to form a grand coalition, to defend a status quo from which they were the chief gainers. But this reluctance to change was a fatal mistake, since the price of empire was the constant adjustment to domestic, colonial and external pressures, and the swift exploitation of innovations in culture or economic activity.[3]

In the late nineteenth century it did indeed seem as if these multiple sources of decay and collapse would reshape the world. To most Western observers the conclusion was obvious. The remaining indigenous empires in Asia and Africa, large and small, could not survive long. The period during which they had coexisted uneasily with the European empires was reaching an end. Economic stagnation, cultural senescence and systemic corruption had destroyed their political will. They lacked the means to guard their frontiers. They faced the revolt of their ethnic minorities. Their economic failure sharpened social conflict. Cultural stasis encouraged the hunger for foreign ideas, but bred an angry reaction, xenophobic or fanatical. Chaos and ruin awaited: these were 'dying nations', defunct empires. By contrast, so it seemed, Europe's colonizing powers and their North American cousins had discovered the secret of perpetual progress and eternal empire – the hubris against which Kipling famously warned.[4] They had broken the cycle of imperial decline. Industrialization, inorganic fuel (coal) and a far-flung resource base, drawing on produce from thousands of miles away, made old environmental limitations irrelevant. Their commerce and culture would attract a mass of new subjects, or at least their elites, whose loyalty (or collaboration) would keep the costs of empire low. The situation at 'home' had also changed for the better. Empire 'on the cheap' and the sense of growing dependence on faraway markets were much more favourable conditions to promote an 'imperial' ideology. The increasing power of the 'state nation' over domestic society was strengthening the idea of a 'national' community, willing if need be to sustain empire abroad. Perhaps most potent of all, the adoption of 'liberal' politics – more or less free competition in economic and political life – seemed a sure guarantee against the corrupt privatization of political power and rigid resistance to change. This progressive mentality was supposedly rooted in 'race' – an incoherent amalgam of physical, social and cultural characteristics. That was why Europeans – or some of them – had discovered the secret of social evolution. The reward, they assumed, would be permanent mastery of the rest of the world.

The likeliest outcome – or so it appeared – was a new global order in which power was concentrated among a handful of 'world states'. The remaining states and empires of the non-Western world would be parcelled out, or, if kept in existence, turned into semi-protectorates under close supervision. Support would be given to their 'reformers' and 'progressives', to break the resistance of their vast backward hinterlands. The price would be a willing acceptance of European rules: an open door to commerce and culture, and new legal norms to protect foreign persons and property. This era of tutelage was expected to be long, perhaps infinitely so, with many failures and relapses. But it did not turn out like that.

Part of the reason was geopolitical. The key precondition of Europe's advance into Asia had been European peace, the avoidance of general war. Fierce as they sounded, Europe's imperial rivalries in the mid and late nineteenth century had been artfully managed: croaking and crowing replaced actual conflict. But in 1914 this long interregnum of competitive coexistence was broken for good: the post-war efforts to revive it came to little or nothing. The Europe-centred world order was aborted almost before it began. Key parts of Eurasia kept the West at bay at a critical stage. Geopolitics, however, was only part of the story.

THE PATTERN OF PERSISTENCE

Most histories of 'empire' after the mid eighteenth century share a common assumption: the only empires that matter are the colonial empires of the Europeans – until Japan starts to borrow the colonial idea at the turn of the twentieth century. The drama of the African scramble has led to a distorted image of a rampant imperialism that nothing could stop. But if we look closer at Asia we get a different impression. For all their nibbling at its maritime fringes and their halting inland advance at the end of the century, with the grand exception of India the Europeans' domination of Asia was very partial at best. The case could be made that the real story in Asia in the long nineteenth century was one of Asian persistence and not of Asian defeat. The great example was China. Despite the ravages of dynastic conflict, civil war and revolution, China preserved an astonishing unity up to 1914. The idea of China survived both the end of the imperial monarchy in 1911 and the forty years of turmoil, occupation and war that followed soon after. More surprising, perhaps, was China's retention of its huge Inner Asian empire: Manchuria, Mongolia, Sinkiang and Tibet. Despite the desperate crisis of the 1930s and '40s, all were held on to (except Outer Mongolia). China today has much the same frontiers as the vast Ch'ing Empire into which Europe had crashed in the 1830s. Japan's perseverance in the face of the European challenge was even more striking. Its monarchy was reinvented to supply the ideological glue for a new political order.

The result was a state that was strong enough to withstand the opening up to the West and soon to embark on an imperial career of its own.

A similar pattern can be seen in parts of Middle Eurasia. Exposed as they were to Europe's commercial and physical power, the main Muslim states in West Asia did not succumb to colonialism. Shorn though it was of its European provinces by 1913, and then forced to surrender its Arab dominions after 1918, the Anatolian core of the Ottoman Empire escaped the partition that the peacemakers intended, to become a new 'Turkish' state. The territorial extent of the Iranian Empire had waxed and waned under Safavids and Qajars. But the area now ruled by the Islamic Republic comprises most of 'historic' Iran, including the four great cities of Tabriz, Isfahan, Tehran and Mashad. And even those parts of Middle Eurasia (like Egypt or India) whose political shape was drastically altered by Europe's intervention retained or constructed a distinctive identity that transcended the limits of a colonized culture.

What made this possible? Part of the answer, as we saw in an earlier chapter, was that Europeans lacked the resources and sometimes the motive to make global empire complete. Their imperial diplomacy baulked at the task of partitioning China, Iran or the Ottoman Empire before 1914. After 1918, their divisions were greater and the task even harder. But this is only one side of a complex equation. Just as important were the tenacious traditions of political and cultural autonomy in the great Asian states, which hemmed in outsiders like an invisible wall. These were strengthened and deepened by the state-building drive in early modern Eurasia, whose effects were felt right across the Old World and not just in Europe. The Ming renovation, the Tokugawa peace, the Safavid compromise and the Ottoman transition from a warrior state into an Asian, African and European empire were all achievements as striking as the new model monarchies being fashioned in Europe. They created forms of government that proved remarkably durable even under stressful conditions. Dynastic change in China (from Ming to Ch'ing) and Iran's time of troubles in the eighteenth century might have uprooted less entrenched political systems – not least in Iran, with its linguistic divisions and great tribal confederacies.

These early-modern reconstructions had a lasting importance. They helped to preserve a continuous practice of statecraft through into the time when the pressure from Europe became much more intense. The states that the Europeans faced were *anciens régimes* in need of renewal, not broken-backed states that had fallen to pieces. Those who had served them were often aware of their weakness and the need for 'reform'. But that meant the grafting of new political methods on to the original stock, not imposing an alien blueprint to which no one was loyal. It was a crucial distinction. Kemal's republic in Turkey was built on the foundations of Ottoman reform, not conjured from thin air. Its 'official' version of history proclaimed not Turkey's subservience to Europe, but the world-historical significance of the Turkish people.[5] Its political godfather (however quietly disowned) was Sultan Abdul Hamid II (r. 1876–1909), under whose rule state control of society was pressed forward vigorously.[6] Reza Shah Pahlevi (r. 1921–41) could invoke Iran's ancient monarchial tradition to assert his authority over rebellious regions and tribes and strengthen the state. The emperor's charter oath was the warrant to impose a much more centralized rule in Meiji Japan, and deny its opponents an ideological base. Even in China, where the end of the Ch'ing dynasty signalled a more complete break with the past, the new nationalism laid claim to the Inner Asian patrimony bequeathed by the Ch'ing, and revived the old system of household surveillance to regain social control in the turbulent 1920s.

Persistence was cultural as well as political. The role of religion, language and literature in creating national identities in Europe is a familiar story. There were several reasons why the nation-state idea developed more intensely in Europe than in other parts of Eurasia before 1914, not least the effects of the revolutions and wars that raged across much of the continent between 1789 and 1815. Across most of Eurasia (and including much of Eastern Europe), the link between culture and state had not followed the model that appeared in Western Europe. Absolute loyalty to a territorial state and its ruler conflicted with notions of an Islamic community of believers – the *umma* – and the autonomous authority of those who interpreted the Koran and the sharia. In the vast subcontinental empire of China, with its periphery of smaller, weaker or dependent states, the cockpit mentality of dynastic conflict and state-building that shaped European nationalism was conspicuously lacking. In Japan, two centuries of seclusion reinforced an intense suspicion of outsiders. But little need had arisen to identify Japaneseness with a strong central state. Yet, if the European obsession with the nation state as a union of culture and politics had little meaning elsewhere, the effort to bind society together with common values and practices (from diet and dress through to history and cosmology) was taken just as seriously. Across the rest of Eurasia, just as in Europe, traditions of learning were maintained and transmitted by teachers and texts. Around them were gathered the educated elites who enjoyed social prestige and exerted cultural authority. In Iran and China, this class was closely identified with the idea of the state. From Safavid times onward, the *ulama* asserted the claim that the Iranian state's first duty was to protect Shia Islam from the assaults of its enemies. The minority status of Shia in the Islamic world made this all the more urgent. In China, the scholar-gentry formed the administrative cadre as well as the cultural elite of the imperial system – a role, it seems likely, that they continued to fill in the 'nationalist' era that followed. Even in India, where British rule was gradually imposed from the mid eighteenth century, pre-colonial traditions survived, because they were already deeply embedded in vigorous vernacular cultures. Regional patriotisms, ideas of just government, and alternative visions of history coexisted uneasily with the cultural apparatus of the colonial regime.[7] In the late nineteenth century, when the Indian vernaculars were being transformed into ordered literary languages, regional sentiment acquired a powerful new means to express social and political concerns. Without this foundation, it seems very unlikely that the movement through which Gandhi was able to make Indian nationalism into a popular cause would have gathered strength so quickly after 1914.

The importance of all this is that when Europe's cultural impact on the rest of the world reached a peak of intensity, in the late nineteenth century, it faced an increasingly well-organized resistance. Yet, to the guardians and 'gatekeepers' of other Eurasian cultures, the struggle for survival appeared a closely fought contest. They dreaded the outright collapse of their cultural tradition amid the tidal surge of a Western modernity. They were oppressed by the fear that they would lose their authority over their own lower orders, for whose moral and cultural

welfare they saw themselves as responsible. They grasped the significance of Europe's technological lead, and the social and cultural
innovations that helped to sustain it, but were deeply ambivalent
about the moral and social effects of those. Hence they were strongly
attracted to versions of modernity that, while framed in the West,
were bitterly hostile to its liberal capitalist values and imperial claims.
Gandhi's campaign to awaken the masses took its original cue from
Tolstoy's conception of a self-sufficient rural utopia. The appeal of
Marxism–Leninism lay in its promise of industrial progress without
the social conflict that seemed inherent in capitalism. Both seemed to
offer a path to modernity that could be controlled. In the regimes that
emerged after 1918 in Iran, Turkey and nationalist China, in the
political leadership that was to govern India after 1947, and (more
emphatically still) in Communist-ruled China after 1949, the strict
supervision of foreign cultural imports seemed just as essential as the
building of barriers against foreign industrial power. The growing
reach of the state through education, broadcasting, propaganda and
censorship was harnessed to the task. If this came to resemble a
cultural 'siege mentality', this was hardly surprising. The intense ideological storms that swept over the world for most of the twentieth
century made an open society into a gamble with fate.

THE TERMS OF CONVERGENCE

This pattern of political and cultural persistence makes little sense on
its own. It would be hard to explain without some account of the
material conditions in which rulers and elites in different parts of
Eurasia pursued their objectives. The prospects of maintaining cultural autonomy and political freedom depended in part upon economic success. They were also bound to be influenced by the magnetic
attraction of external trade, and by the appeal, or otherwise, of what
outsiders were selling. At all times in world history (and no less today),
the rewards of commercial exchange, opening the door to foreign
products and business, have been matched by the cultural and political
risks. The fear of domination or absorption by commercial 'great
powers', and of being invisibly colonized by foreign-owned enterprise

and its local collaborators, has rarely been far from the surface. Nor has anxiety that new kinds of production or new forms of consumption would induce damaging social and cultural disturbance. Hence the rules of engagement in economic relations – the conditions of entry into the global economy – have always been critical.

A strong case can be made that a global economy of sorts came into existence in the sixteenth century.[8] Once the Americas had been connected to Eurasia and Africa, a whole new set of exchanges began to develop. American silver helped Europe to buy much larger amounts from South and East Asian producers of textiles, ceramics and tea. American sugar paid for the import of (eventually) millions of African slaves, and increased indirectly the consumption by Africans of the trade goods for which the slaves were exchanged. American foodstuffs, like cassava, maize, beans and potatoes, transformed (in places) the agrarian potential of Europe, Asia and Africa. A profitable network of long-distance sea lanes helped to turn Europe into a great maritime entrepôt ruling the oceans. But this early-modern world economy (1500–1750) gave Europe no decisive advantage over the rest of Eurasia. It increased Europe's dependence on the produce of Asia, but offered few means of enlarging its share of Asian consumption.[9]

After 1750 this pattern altered dramatically, but not all at once. The opportunistic seizure of the Bengal economy gave the British the chance to change the terms of their trade with China. India was the source of the opium supply with which and the military base from which they made their forced entry into East Asian trade. However, the critical change was the advent of mechanized production in Europe. Within a few decades, Asia's export market in textiles had been lost to European competition, and European cloth was even pushing its way into the textile economies of India and China. The volume of world trade now began to grow rapidly – by some twenty-five times in the long nineteenth century. But the terms on which Asia now traded with Europe gave it much less room for manoeuvre. Europeans controlled the networks of long-distance commerce, as well as supplying its most valuable items. To enter this trade and pay for Europe's manufactures, Asian economies were forced to rely on exports of raw materials and foodstuffs. To make matters worse, from an Asian standpoint, they had to compete with the commodity producers of the Atlantic economy as well as with each other. American cotton and wheat rivalled Indian; Indian tea replaced China tea in the British market. With their command and control of Asia's seaborne trade, their newfound access to the Asian consumer (by conquest in India, by forced treaty in China) and their big industrial lead, the Europeans seemed to have drawn the Asian economies into a globalized market at the moment of greatest divergence in their relative strengths. The numbers are telling. Whereas in 1820 India and China had a gross domestic product per head around one half of the level in Western Europe, by 1913 it was more like one seventh.[10]

This gloom-laden picture is not the whole story. Asia became part of a new global economy in which the volume of goods that was traded was enormously greater than before 1750. But the Europeans' control over the Asian economies was far from complete – for a number of reasons. They had too little capital to 'colonize' Asian producers fully. They were baffled by the problems of penetrating deeper into Asia's largest economy. China's language, currency and domestic mercantile networks kept them at bay. Nor was time on their side. It was well after mid-century before railway construction, the Suez Canal, the steamship and the telegraph brought even maritime Asia into the same proximity as transatlantic economies had long had with Europe. The timing was especially significant in the case of Japan, where industrialization was well under way by the 1880s. Far from East Asia being reduced to a subaltern region, Japan's export trade to the West and the income it brought triggered a rapid expansion of trade *within* Asia and *between* Asian economies. It was soon Japanese industrialists (often in partnership with Chinese merchants) and Indian mill-owners who were meeting the region's demand for more consumer goods. By 1914 Asia's trade with Asia was growing more quickly than its trade with the West.[11]

The hundred years that led up to 1914 could thus be described as an age of 'semi-globalization'. They had seen the emergence of a single world market for primary and industrial goods as well as for capital and financial services. In a number of states (though not the majority) the volume of trade compared with the state's total output had grown very significantly. The level, however, was still far below what it had reached by the end of the twentieth century.[12] And, except for East Asia, manufacturing industry had been heavily concentrated in Atlantic Europe and the Old Northeast of the United States. No other part of the world could compete in those markets with industrial goods. Semi-globalization was all but stopped in its tracks by the outbreak of war in Europe. In the age of disruption that followed, the economic integration of the pre-1914 world went into reverse. After a short-lived recovery in the late 1920s, the global economy shrank. Its main entrepôt, Britain, abandoned the policies that had smoothed its exchanges: a gold-backed world currency and the commitment to free trade. The world's largest economy, the United States, retreated deeper into its cave of protection. Much of the rest of the world was divided between blocs: each under its hegemon; each aiming to shrink its trade with the others. The Soviet Union withdrew into virtual isolation. Smaller states struggled to reduce their external dependence. Primary producers saw their incomes collapse. The East Asian economy, within which China had been industrializing swiftly, was now cut in half, first by Japan's 'yen bloc' and then (in 1937) by its invasion of China. By the time the world mobilized for a new total war, the great trade expansion of the previous century could no longer be seen as a guide to the future. The closed economy, self-reliance and internal development – not the promotion of trade – had become the price of survival in a segmented world.

Nor was this view to be dispelled completely after the Second World War. The post-war recovery, when it eventually came, mirrored the divisions that peace left unsolved. The vision of global free trade that had inspired the creation of the International Monetary Fund, the World Bank and the General Agreement on Tariffs and Trade had to face the reality of global cold war. The autarkic empire of the Soviet Union was hugely expanded in Eastern and Central Europe. The Communist triumph in China entrenched even more deeply the pre-war partition of the East Asian economy. China, like Stalinist Russia, withdrew into planned isolation. South Korea, Taiwan, Hong Kong and Singapore followed Japan's path and became its trade partners. The European Community, the vehicle for Western Europe's recovery, formed a protectionist bloc. Its economic arrangements reflected its primary purpose: to secure a permanent end to Franco-German antagonism, not to promote an open global economy. When the European overseas empires broke up into a mass of new states, most favoured a closed, state-managed, economy in their drive to build an industrial base, and leveraged diplomatic alignment against aid and investment from the superpower rivals. But perhaps the most significant feature of this age of recovery was the scale of American power. It was the Second World War that made the United States not just the world's largest economy, but also its strongest. It was the global cold war that made it the world's greatest military power. These were the assets with which America entered the 'globalized' world at the end of the century.

Perhaps enough has been said to make an obvious point. The economic regime to which we have grown used in the last decade and a half represents an extraordinary moment in the turbulent history of the global economy. It was produced by an earthquake as dramatic as anything in the world's modern history. It required the combination of geopolitical change – the sudden collapse of Soviet power and China's decision to embrace a market economy – and a technological revolution in communications and transport. The turn to the market in the People's Republic and the former Soviet bloc brought a massive enlargement of productive capacity and an enormous new market. It coincided with the growth of much cheaper air travel, the 'container revolution' in the shipment of goods, and, above all, the commercial application of Internet technology. Hard on the heels of the financial 'liberalization' of the 1980s that brought much greater freedom for financial services and capital transfers between Western countries, the conditions were met for a phase of exceptional growth in the volume of trade and an intense integration of economic activities on a global scale far beyond the limited promise of the pre-1914 world. The 'great divergence' in wealth and economic performance between the Euro-Atlantic West and most of the rest of Eurasia has given way instead to the 'great convergence', which should, if it continues, restore the balance to the rough equilibrium of half a millennium ago in the next fifty years.

Yet the world that 'globalization' is in process of remaking has largely been formed under very different conditions. For most of the period covered in this book, economic relations between different parts of the world have done little to hinder (and quite a lot to encourage) the building of empires, states and cultures with distinctive values, attitudes, institutions and ideologies. Economic interdependence, the main constraint upon cultural diversity, has been too short-lived, too quickly aborted and too blunt in its impact to reverse this trend. It is widely assumed that this long era is ending: that vernacular cultures and the nation state cannot withstand the invasive effects of the world of free movement in information, people and goods. So far the run of free movement has been short. We will have to see.

TAMERLANE'S SHADOW

Perhaps this is the point. It might well be true that we are now on the brink of a great transformation – in geopolitics, economics and culture – at least as far-reaching as the Eurasian Revolution of the late eighteenth century. If this is so, it can hardly be doubted that its impacts in different parts of the world will vary enormously. The history of Eurasia suggests that, while new methods of warfare and government, new techniques of production, new cultural practices and new religious beliefs were diffused from one end of the Old World to the other (and from every direction), they failed to induce a common view of modernity or of what it was to be 'modern'. The past patterns of trade and conquest, diaspora and migration that have pushed and pulled distant regions together and shaped their cultures and politics have been exceptionally complex. Their effect has been not to homogenize the world, but to keep it diverse. By contrast, the magnetic force of the global economy has been too erratic thus far, and too unevenly felt, to impose the cooperative behaviour and cultural fusion to which theorists of free trade have often looked forward. What we call globalization today might be candidly seen as flowing from a set of recent agreements, some tacit, some formal, between the four great economic 'empires' of the contemporary world: America, Europe, Japan and China. For them, and for all other states and societies, the challenge will be to reconcile their internal cohesion with the disturbing effects of free competition. The strain will be great; the outcome uncertain. But if there is one continuity that we should be able to glean from a long view of the past, it is Eurasia's resistance to a uniform system, a single great ruler, or one set of rules. In that sense, we still live in Tamerlane's shadow – or, perhaps more precisely, in the shadow of his failure.

Notes

PREFACE

1. Frederick Teggart, *Rome and China* (Berkeley, 1939), p. 245.

CHAPTER 1: ORIENTATIONS

1. For Ibn Khaldun, Y. Lacoste, *Ibn Khaldun* (Paris, 1969); *Encylopaedia of Islam* (Leiden, 1999).
2. The authoritative study is B. F. Manz, *The Rise and Rule of Tamerlane* (Cambridge, 1989).
3. For a recent study stressing the exchanges across Mongol Eurasia, Thomas T. Allsen, *Culture and Conquest in Mongol Eurasia* (Cambridge, 2001). See also John Masson Smith, 'The Mongols and the Silk Road', *Silk Road Foundation Newsletter* vol. 1, no. 1 at http://www.silkroadfoundation.org/newsletter/volumeonenumberone/mongols.html.
4. Karl Marx, 'The British Rule in India' (1853), repr. in E. Kamenka (ed.), *The Portable Karl Marx* (Harmondsworth, 1983), pp. 334–5.
5. Lenin's *Imperialism: The Highest Stage of Capitalism* was published in Zurich in 1916.
6. See I. Wallerstein, *Historical Capitalism* (London, 1983) for an elegant outline of this school of thought.
7. M. Weber, *The Sociology of Religion* (1922; Eng. trans. London, 1965), p. 270. Weber also stressed the effects of the caste system and hostility of the Confucian literati to innovation. See H. H. Girth and C. Wright Mills (eds.), *From Max Weber: Essays in Sociology* (pbk edn, London, 1974), chs. 16, 17.
8. For an excellent survey of 'subaltern' history, V. Chaturvedi (ed.), *Mapping Subaltern Studies and the Postcolonial* (London, 2000), 'Introduction'.
9. J. C. van Leur, *Indonesian Trade and Society: Essays in Asian Social and Economic History* (The Hague, 1955), p. 261.

10. For an account of van Leur, J. Vogel, 'A Short Life in History', in L. Blussé and F. Gaastra (eds.), *The Eighteenth Century as a Category in Asian History: Van Leur in Retrospect* (Aldershot, 1998).

11. S. Subrahmanyam, 'Connected Histories: Notes towards a Reconfiguration of Early Modern Eurasia', *Modern Asian Studies* 31, 3 (1997), pp. 734–62.

12. See the discussion of 'Monsoon' and 'Arid' Asia in J. Gommans, 'Burma at the Frontier of South, East and Southeast Asia: A Geographic Perspective', in J. Gommans and J. Leider (eds.), *The Maritime Frontier of Burma: Exploring Political, Cultural and Commercial Interaction in the Indian Ocean World* (Leiden, 2002), pp. 1–7.

13. A powerful statement of this view can be found in Kenneth Pomeranz, *The Great Divergence: China, Europe and the Making of the Modern World Economy* (Princeton, 2000), from where the phrase 'surprising resemblances' comes (p. 29).

14. E. Said, *Orientalism* (London, 1978).

15. S. L. Eisenstadt, 'Multiple Modernities', *Daedalus* 129, 1 (2000), pp. 1–29.

16. Some writers claim that caste was all but imposed by the British; a more balanced view ascribes a major role to Indian informants. For the extreme position, N. Dirks, *Castes of Mind* (Princeton, 2001).

17. T. Spear, 'Neo-Traditionalism and the Limits of Invention in British Colonial Africa', *Journal of African History* 44 (2003), pp. 2–27.

18. See below, ch. 5; also J. Belich, *The New Zealand Wars* (Auckland, 1986).

19. Originally in his paper for the Royal Geographical Society entitled 'The Geographical Pivot of History', *Geographical Journal* 23, 4 (1904), pp. 421–37.

20. The best discussion remains D. Hay, *Europe: The Emergence of an Idea* (Edinburgh, 1957).

21. For Russia's place in a European 'cultural gradient', see Catherine Evtuhov and S. Kotkin (eds.), *The Cultural Gradient: The Transmission of Ideas in Europe 1788–1991* (Oxford, 2003).

22. For a recent review of the debate, P. K. O'Brien, 'Metanarratives in Global Histories of Material Progress', *International History Review* 22, 2 (2001), pp. 345–67.

23. See Book 1, Chapter 2.

24. A. de Tocqueville, *Democracy in America* (1835; Everyman edn, London, 1994), vol. 1, p. 332.

25. See Eisenstadt, 'Multiple Modernities'.

26. D. Obolensky, *The Byzantine Commonwealth* (London, 1971) and M.

Whittow, *The Making of Orthodox Byzantium 600–1025* (London, 1996) offer the best general accounts.

27. The classic account is G. Duby, *The Early Growth of the European Economy* (1973; Eng. trans. Ithaca, NY, 1974). It should now be compared with C. Wickham, *Framing the Early Middle Ages* (Oxford, 2005).

28. See M. Lombard, 'La Chasse et les produits de chasse dans le monde musulman VIIIe–XIe siècles', in M. Lombard, *Espaces et réseaux du Haut Moyen Age* (Paris, 1972), pp. 176–204. When that demand was reduced by disruption in the Near East, the effects were felt severely. See R. Hodges and D. Whitehouse, *Mahomet, Charlemagne and the Origins of Europe* (London, 1983).

29. See A. Lewis, *The Sea and Mediaeval Civilisation* (London, 1978), ch. 14; K. Leyser, 'Theophanus divina gratia imperatrix Augusta', in his *Communications and Power in Medieval Europe: The Carolingian and Ottoman Centuries*, ed. Timothy Reuter (London, 1994).

30. For the Christian conversion of Vladimir of Kiev in the 980s, S. Franklin and J. Shepard, *The Emergence of Rus 750–1200* (London, 1996), ch. 4.

31. For a brilliant discussion, R. Bartlett, *The Making of Europe: Conquest, Colonisation and Cultural Change 950–1350* (London, 1993).

32. See R. Fletcher, *The Conversion of Europe* (London, 1997); E. Christiansen, *The Northern Crusades* (London, 1980).

33. Duby, *Early Growth*, pp. 257–62.

34. See E. Ashtor, *Levant Trade in the Later Middle Ages* (Princeton, 1983), pp. 462, 469, 512.

35. R. Fletcher, *Moorish Spain* (London, 1992), ch. 7.

36. A. Wink, *Al-Hind: The Making of the Indo-Islamic World*, vol. 1: *Early Mediaeval India and the Expansion of Islam, 7th–11th Centuries* (Leiden, 1996), p. 23.

37. See A. M. Watson, *Agricultural Innovation in the Early Islamic World: The Diffusion of Crops and Farming Techniques 700–1100* (Cambridge, 1975).

38. See P. Ratchnevsky, *Genghis Khan: His Life and Legacy* (1983; Eng. trans. Oxford, 1991).

39. Ibn Khaldun, *The Muqadimmah: An Introduction to History*, trans. F. Rosenthal (London, 1967). The *Muqadimmah* was translated into French in the 1860s. The first full version in English, of which this volume is an abridgement, appeared in 1958.

40. The classic analysis is P. Crone, *Slaves on Horses: The Evolution of the Islamic Polity* (Cambridge, 1980).

41. See D. Pipes, *Slave Soldiers and Islam* (New Haven and London, 1981).

42. M. G. S. Hodgson, *The Venture of Islam* (3 vols., Chicago, 1974) is a brilliant analytical survey.

43. R. R. Di Miglio, 'Egypt and China: Trade and Imitation', in D. S. Richards (ed.), *Islam and the Trade of Asia* (Oxford, 1970), pp. 106–22.

44. I. M. Lapidus, *Muslim Cities in the Later Middle Ages* (Cambridge, 1967), p. 9.

45. See J. Abu-Lughod, *Before European Hegemony: The World System 1250–1350* (New York, 1989), pp. 230ff.; C. Cahen, 'Quelques mots sur le déclin commercial du monde musulman à la fin du moyen âge', in C. Cahen, *Les Peuples musulmans dans l'histoire medievale* (Damascus, 1977), pp. 361–5.

46. M. Elvin, *The Pattern of the Chinese Past* (London, 1973), p. 205. The quotation is from a thirteenth-century writer.

47. C. P. Fitzgerald, *The Southern Expansion of the Chinese People* (London, 1972), ch. 7.

48. For this suggestive view, see A. Waldron, *The Great Wall: From History to Myth* (Cambridge, 1990), pp. 190–92.

49. For a recent authoritative assessment of Elvin's thesis, R. von Glahn, 'Imagining Pre-Modern China', in P. J. Smith and R. von Glahn (eds.), *The Song–Yuan–Ming Transition in Chinese History* (Cambridge, Mass., 2003), pp. 35–70.

50. Elvin's key ideas can be followed in his *The Pattern of the Chinese Past* (London, 1973), chs. 14, 17, and in 'The High Level Equilibrium Trap', in *Another History: Essays on China from a European Perspective* (Sydney, 1996), ch. 2.

CHAPTER 2: EURASIA AND THE AGE OF DISCOVERY

1. See F. Fernandez-Armesto, *Before Columbus* (London, 1987), pp. 216–20.

2. See P. Chaunu, *European Expansion in the Later Middle Ages* (1969; Eng. trans. London, 1979), pp. 95–7.

3. See A. Hamdani, 'An Islamic Background to the Voyages of Discovery', in S. K. Jayyusi (ed.), *The Legacy of Muslim Spain* (Leiden, 1994), pp. 286–7.

4. J. Phillips, *The Mediaeval Expansion of Europe* (Oxford, 1988), pp. 251ff.

5. For a recent study, S. Subrahmanyam, *Vasco da Gama* (Cambridge, 1997).

6. J. Vogt, *Portuguese Rule on the Gold Coast 1469–1682* (Athens, Ga., 1979), p. 89.

7. M. N. Pearson, *The Portuguese in India* (Cambridge, 1987), p. 43.

8. A. Das Gupta, 'The Maritime Merchant of Medieval India', in *Merchants of Maritime India* (Aldershot, 1994), p. 8; Pearson, *Portuguese in India*, p. 56.

9. S. Subrahmanyam and L. F. F. R. Thomaz, 'Evolution of Empire: The

Portuguese in the Indian Ocean in the Sixteenth Century', in J. D. Tracy (ed.), *The Political Economy of Merchant Empires: State Power and World Trade 1350–1750* (Cambridge, 1991), p. 318.

10. For the significance of Brazilian trade, J. C. Boyajian, *Portuguese Trade in Asia under the Habsburgs* (Baltimore and London, 1993).

11. G. B. Souza, *The Survival of Empire: Portuguese Trade and Society in China and the South China Sea, 1630–1754* (Cambridge, 1986), p. 229.

12. Hamdani, 'Islamic Background'.

13. Chaunu, *European Expansion*, p. 170.

14. R. Hassig, *Mexico and the Spanish Conquest* (London, 1994), p. 146.

15. See T. Todorov, *La Conquête de l'Amérique* (Paris, 1982).

16. These figures have been debated by historians for decades. For a recent survey, Linda A. Newson, 'The Demographic Collapse of Native Peoples in the Americas, 1491–1650', in W. Bray (ed.), *The Meeting of Two Worlds: Europe and the Americas, 1492–1650*, published in *Proceedings of the British Academy* 81 (1993), pp. 249–77. For the estimate of a 90 per cent die-off in Peru, D. N. Cook, *Demographic Collapse: Indian Peru 1520–1620* (Cambridge, 1981), p. 116.

17. P. Calvasco, 'The Political Economy of the Aztec and Inca States', in G. Collier, R. Rosaldo and J. D. Wirth (eds.), *The Inca and Aztec States, 1400–1800: Anthropology and History* (New York, 1982).

18. B. A. Tenenbaum (ed.), *Encyclopedia of Latin American History and Culture* (New York, 1996), vol. 4, p. 435.

19. See G. L. Villena, *Les Espinosa* (Paris, 1968) for Gaspar Espinosa, the Panama-based merchant.

20. See G. W. Conrad and A. A. Demarest, *Religion and Empire: The Dynamics of Aztec and Inca Expansionism* (Cambridge, 1984).

21. This is the theme of S. Gruzinski, *The Conquest of Mexico* (1988; Eng. trans. London, 1993).

22. H. S. Klein and J. J. TePaske, 'The Seventeenth-Century Crisis in New Spain: Myth or Reality?', *Past and Present* 91 (1981), pp. 116–35.

23. J. I. Israel, *Race and Class in Colonial Mexico 1610–1670* (Oxford, 1975), p. 8.

24. Gruzinski, *Conquest*, p. 152.

25. F. F. Berdan, 'Trauma and Transition in Sixteenth-Century Central Mexico', in Bray (ed.), *The Meeting of Two Worlds*, p. 187.

26. See A. Hennessy, 'The Nature of the Conquest and the Conquistadors', in Bray (ed.), *The Meeting of Two Worlds*, p. 23.

27. Gruzinski, *Conquest*, pp. 176–87.

28. Berdan, 'Trauma and Transition', p. 190.

29. J. Lockhart, *Spanish Peru 1532–60: A Colonial Society* (Madison, 1968).

30. Hennessy, 'Nature of the Conquest', p. 19.

31. Ortega y Gasset, quoted in R. H. Billington, *The Icon and the Axe: An Interpretive History of Russian Culture* (pbk edn, New York, 1970), p. 71.

32. H. Birnbaum, 'The Balkan Slavic Component of Medieval Russian Culture', in H. Birnbaum and M. S. Flier (eds.), *Medieval Russian Culture* (London, 1984), pp. 3–30.

33. R. O. Crummey, *The Formation of Muscovy 1301–1617* (London, 1987), pp. 36, 41.

34. Ibid., pp. 36ff.

35. See W. H. Parker, *An Historical Geography of Russia* (London, 1968) for Moscow's position.

36. See N. Davies, *God's Playground: A History of Poland*, vol. 1: *The Origins to 1795* (Oxford, 1981), pp. 148–52, for the Polish Renaissance.

37. D. Obolensky, 'Russia's Byzantine Heritage', in his *Byzantium and the Slavs: Collected Studies* (London, 1971), p. 99; N. Andreyev, *Studies in Muscovy: Western Influence and Byzantine Inheritance* (London, 1970), pp. 14, 21; R. Wortman, *Scenarios of Power: Myth and Ceremony in Russian Monarchy*, vol. 1: *From Peter the Great to the Death of Nicholas I* (Princeton, 1995), p. 24.

38. Billington, *Icon*, p. 64.

39. Ibid., p. 90.

40. G. V. Lantzeff and R. A. Pierce, *Eastward to Empire* (Montreal and London, 1973), pp. 72, 107, 109.

41. J. L. Wieczynski, *The Russian Frontier: The Impact of Borderlands upon the Course of Early Russian History* (Charlottesville, Va., 1976), p. 77.

42. See the lyrical description of the steppe in Nikolai Gogol's story, 'Taras Bulba' (1835), in N. Gogol, *Village Evenings near Dikanka* and *Mirgorod* (Eng. trans. Oxford, 1994), p. 257.

43. The difficulties of Russian military advance into the southern steppes are explained in W. C. Fuller, *Strategy and Power in Russia, 1600–1914* (New York, 1992).

44. See E. Keenan, 'Muscovy and Kazan: Some Introductory Remarks on the Pattern of Steppe Diplomacy', *Slavic Review* 26, 4 (1967), p. 553. Also A. S. Donnelly, *The Russian Conquest of Bashkiria 1552–1740* (New Haven and London, 1968) for a general account of Russia's steppe expansion.

45. For a suggestive parallel, F. Barth, *Nomads of South Persia* (Oslo, 1964), pp. 106–11.

46. Keenan, 'Muscovy and Kazan', p. 555.

47. See the cautious conclusions in P. Bushkovitch, *The Merchants of Muscovy 1580–1650* (Cambridge, 1980), pp. 93–101.

48. M. Khodarkovsky, *Where Two Worlds Meet* (Ithaca, NY, 1992), ch. 3.

49. See W. D. Allen (ed.), *Russian Embassies to the Georgian Kings (1589–1605)*, Hakluyt Society, 2nd Series, 138 (2 vols., Cambridge, 1970), vol. 1, pp. 69–71.

50. For this interpretation, R. Hellie, *Enserfment and Military Change in Muscovy* (Chicago and London, 1971) and J. H. L. Keep, *Soldiers of the Tsar* (Oxford, 1985), pp. 47–8.

51. Hellie, *Enserfment*, p. 164.

52. Billington, *Icon*, pp. 102–4.

53. E. S. Forster (ed.), *The Turkish Letters of Ogier Ghiselin de Busbecq* (Oxford, 1927), pp. 111–12.

54. For the background to this conflict, Shai Har-El, *The Struggle for Domination in the Middle East: The Ottoman–Mamluk War 1485–1491* (Leiden, 1995).

55. Forster, *Turkish Letters*, p. 112.

56. By 1528 the Ottomans had a standing army of some 87,000. See H. Inalcik, 'The Ottoman State: Economy and Society 1300–1600', in H. Inalcik with D. Quataert (eds.), *An Economic and Social History of the Ottoman Empire 1300–1914* (Cambridge, 1994), p. 88.

57. For Ottoman sea power, P. Brummett, *Ottoman Sea Power and Levantine Diplomacy in the Age of Discovery* (Albany, NY, 1994).

58. Ibid., p. 174; A. Hess, 'The Evolution of the Ottoman Seaborne Empire in the Age of Oceanic Discoveries, 1453–1525', *American Historical Review* 75, 7 (1970), pp. 201–22.

59. P. F. Sugar, *Southeastern Europe under Ottoman Rule 1354–1804* (London, 1977), p. 109.

60. P. Mantran, *La Vie quotidienne à Constantinople au temps de Soleiman le Magnifique et ses successeurs* (Paris, 1965), p. 295.

61. See C. Kafadar, *Between Two Worlds: The Construction of the Ottoman State* (Berkeley, Los Angeles and London, 1995), p. 153.

62. Forster, *Turkish Letters*, pp. 111–12.

63. The relative success of the Ottoman economy has been much debated. The gloomier views in D. Goffman, *Izmir and the Levantine World, 1550–1650* (Seattle, 1990) and B. Masters, *The Origins of Western Economic Dominance in the Middle East: Mercantilism and the Islamic Economy in Aleppo* (New York, 1988) can be compared with those in S. Faroqhi, 'In Search of Ottoman History', in H. Berktay and S. Faroqhi (eds.), *New Approaches to State and Peasant in Ottoman History* (London, 1992), and the discussion in S. Faroqhi, 'Crisis and Change, 1590–1699', in Inalcik with Quataert (eds.), *Ottoman Empire*, pp. 474–531.

64. H. Islamoglu-Inan, *State and Peasant in the Ottoman Empire* (Leiden, 1994) for the link between tax-farming and commercialization.

65. See Rifa'at Ali Abou El-Haj, *The Formation of the Modern State: The Ottoman Empire, Sixteenth to Eighteenth Centuries* (Albany, NY, 1991), p. 10.

66. These conflicts are brilliantly surveyed in W. D. Allen, *Problems of Turkish Power in the Sixteenth Century* (London, 1963).

67. For the general setting, W. Barthold, *An Historical Geography of Iran* (Princeton, 1984).

68. P. Jackson and W. Lockhart (eds.), *The Cambridge History of Iran*, vol. 6: *The Timurid and Safavid Periods* (Cambridge, 1986), pp. 227–8.

69. For Shia Islam in Iran, H. Halm, *Shiism* (Edinburgh, 1991), pp. 91ff.

70. See J. J. Reid, 'Tribalism and Society in Islamic Iran, 1500–1629', PhD thesis, University of California at Los Angeles, 1978.

71. Jackson and Lockhart, *Cambridge History of Iran*, pp. 246, 263. See also the chapter by R. M. Savory on Safavid administration in the same volume.

72. D. Navridi, 'Socio-Economic and Political Change in Safavid Iran in the Sixteenth and Seventeenth Centuries', PhD thesis, Vanderbilt University, 1977, pp. 71ff.

73. J. B. Tavernier, *Voyages en Perse* (Paris, 1970), pp. 251–2. Tavernier made his first visit in 1639. His *Voyages* was originally published in 1670.

74. Navridi, 'Safavid Iran', p. 168.

75. J. Fryer, *A New Account of East India and Persia, Being Nine Years' Travels, 1672–1681*, ed. W. Crooke (3 vols., London, 1909–15), vol. 2, pp. 246–50.

76. Even in the nineteenth century, between a third and one-half of Iran's population were nomadic and tribal. A. Wink, *Al-Hind: The Making of the Indo-Islamic World*, vol. 2: *Slave Kings and the Islamic Conquest, 11th–13th Centuries* (Leiden, 1997), p. 15.

77. Halm, *Shiism*, pp. 94–8.

78. For Babur's origins and early career, S. A. M. Adshead, *Central Asia in World History* (London, 1993), pp. 131ff.

79. J. F. Richards, *The Mughal Empire* (Cambridge, 1993), p. 6.

80. S. F. Dale, *Indian Merchants and Eurasian Trade 1600–1750* (Cambridge, 1994), pp. 6–7.

81. *Baburnama (Memoirs of Babur)*, trans. A. S. Beveridge (Delhi, 1921, 1989), pp. 531–2.

82. Richards, *Mughal Empire*, p. 2.

83. R. M. Eaton, *The Rise of Islam and the Bengal Frontier 1204–1760* (London, 1993), p. 36.

84. For the amirs, Richards, *Mughal Empire*, p. 19. In 1595, two-thirds of Akbar's nobility were of Turkic or Iranian origin. See Eaton, *Bengal Frontier*, p. 165.

85. T. Raychaudhuri and I. Habib (eds.), *The Cambridge Economic History of India*, vol. 1: *c.1200–1750* (Cambridge, 1982), p. 184; Richards, *Mughal Empire*, p. 66.

86. Raychaudhuri and Habib (eds.), *Economic History*, vol. 1, p. 266.

87. D. Streusand, *The Formation of the Mughal Empire* (Delhi, 1989), p. 71.

88. Ibid., p. 130.

89. Ibid., p. 131.

90. See F. C. R. Robinson, 'Perso-Islamic Culture in India from the 17th to the Early 20th Centuries', in R. L. Canfield (ed.), *Turko-Persia in Historical Perspective* (Cambridge, 1991), pp. 110–11.

91. Adshead, *Central Asia*, p. 131.

92. Dale, *Indian Merchants*, pp. 15, 21; Raychaudhuri and Habib (eds.), *Economic History*, vol. 1, for a survey of the Mughal economy.

93. As safe as France or Italy, noted Tavernier. Raychaudhuri and Habib (eds.), *Economic History*, vol. 1, p. 353.

94. For these aspects, see ibid., pp. 288–301.

95. I owe this suggestion to an unpublished paper by David Washbrook.

96. E. L. Farmer, *Early Ming Government: The Evolution of Dual Capitals* (Cambridge, Mass., 1976), p. 19.

97. J. Dardess, 'The End of Yuan Rule in China', in H. Franke and D. Twitchett (eds.), *The Cambridge History of China*, vol. 6: *Alien Regimes and Border States, 907–1368* (Cambridge, 1994), pp. 581–2.

98. See R. Huang, *Taxation and Governmental Finance in Sixteenth-Century Ming China* (Cambridge, 1974), p. 55.

99. Huang, *Taxation and Finance*, p. 310.

100. For Ming relations with Tamerlane and his successors, Joseph E. Fletcher, 'China and Central Asia, 1368–1884', in J. K. Fairbank (ed.), *The Chinese World Order: Traditional China's Foreign Relations* (Cambridge, Mass., 1968).

101. A. Waldron, *The Great Wall: From History to Myth* (Cambridge, 1990) provides an excellent account of the strategic debates under the later Ming emperors.

102. S. Jagchid and V. J. Symons, *Peace, War and Trade along the Great Wall* (Bloomington, Ind., 1989), p. 86.

103. See D. O. Flynn, 'Comparing the Tokugawa Shogunate and Hapsburg Spain', in J. D. Tracy (ed.), *The Rise of Merchant Empires* (Cambridge, 1990).

104. See J. E. Wills, 'Maritime China from Wang Chih to Shih Lang', in J. Spence and J. E. Wills (eds.), *From Ming to Ch'ing* (New Haven, 1979), p. 211.

105. See A. Reid, 'An Age of Commerce in Southeast Asian History', *Modern Asian Studies* 24, 1 (1990), pp. 9–10.

106. See R. von Glahn, *Fountain of Fortune: Money and Monetary Policy in China 1000–1700* (Berkeley, 1997); F. W. Mote and D. Twitchett (eds.), *The Cambridge History of China*, vol. 7: *Ming Dynasty 1368–1644*, pt 1 (Cambridge, 1988), pp. 587–8; Reid, 'Age of Commerce', pp. 10, 21–3.

107. J. W. Hall (ed.), *The Cambridge History of Japan*, vol. 4: *Early Modern Japan* (Cambridge, 1991), p. 321.

108. See M. Jansen, *China in the Tokugawa World* (Cambridge, Mass., 1992).

109. See Wills, 'Maritime China'.

110. Ibid., p. 244.

111. P. Burke, *Tradition and Innovation in Renaissance Italy* (pbk edn, London, 1974), p. 306.

112. In his hugely influential *The Civilization of the Renaissance in Italy*, published in Basle in 1860. However, the book did not become widely known until the 1880s.

113. See Jacob Burckhardt, *The Civilization of the Renaissance in Italy* (Eng. trans. London, 1944), pt 1.

114. F. Braudel, *The Mediterranean and the Mediterranean World in the Age of Philip II* (1966; Eng. trans. 2 vols., London, 1972–3), vol. 2, p. 913.

115. See G. Parker, *The Grand Strategy of Philip II* (London, 1998).

116. See G. Muto, 'The Spanish System', in R. J. Bonney (ed.), *Economic Systems and State Finance* (Oxford, 1995), pp. 246, 248.

117. See A. Peroton-Dumon, 'The Pirate and the Emperor', in Tracy (ed.), *Political Economy of Merchant Empires*, pp. 196–227.

118. See D. F. Lach, *Asia in the Making of Europe*, vol. 1: *The Century of Discovery* (Chicago, 1964), ch. 4.

119. A. R. Mitchell, 'The European Fisheries in Early Modern History', in E. E. Rich and C. H. Wilson (eds.), *The Cambridge Economic History of Europe*, vol. 5: *The Economic Organisation of Early Modern Europe* (Cambridge, 1977), pp. 157–8.

120. W. L. Schurz, *The Manila Galleon* (New York, 1939); H. Kamen, *Spain's Road to Empire: The Making of a World Power* (London, 2002).

121. For Philip's 'messianic imperialism', G. Parker, *Grand Strategy*, ch. 3.

122. For the effects of America, see J. H. Elliott, 'Final Reflections', in K. O. Kupperman (ed.), *America in European Consciousness 1493–1750* (Chapel Hill, NC, and London, 1995), p. 406.

123. See J. de Vries, *The European Economy in the Age of Crisis 1600–1750* (pbk edn, Cambridge, 1976), p. 130.

124. See A. W. Crosby, *The Columbian Exchange* (Westport, Conn., 1972); A. J. R. Russell-Wood, *A World on the Move* (New York, 1992).

125. See B. Lewis, *Cultures in Conflict* (Oxford, 1995) for Ottoman indifference to the Americas.

CHAPTER 3: THE EARLY MODERN EQUILIBRIUM

1. J. B. Brebner, *The Explorers of North America* (pbk edn, New York, 1955), p. 255.

2. Ibid., p. 255.

3. Ibid., p. 299.

4. The classic study is J. Baker, *History of Geographical Exploration* (London, 1931).

5. See J. C. Beaglehole, *The Life of Captain James Cook* (London, 1974).

6. See R. Law, ' "Here is no resisting the country": The Realities of Power in Afro-European Relations on the West African Slave Coast', *Itinerario* 17, 2 (1994), pp. 56–64.

7. For the *bandeirantes*, C. R. Boxer, *The Golden Age of Brazil 1695–1750* (London, 1962), pp. 31–2.

8. N. Canny, *Europeans on the Move* (Oxford, 1994), p. 265.

9. F. Jennings, *The Invasion of America* (pbk edn, London, 1976), pp. 30, 178–9, 300.

10. T. Burnard, 'European Migration to Jamaica, 1655–1780', *William and Mary Quarterly*, 3rd Series, 52, 4 (1996), pp. 769–96.

11. B. Bailyn, *Voyagers to the West* (London, 1986), p. 24.

12. D. Eltis, 'Free and Coerced Transatlantic Migration: Some Comparisons', *American Historical Review* 88, 2 (1983), pp. 252–5.

13. R. S. Dunn, *Sugar and Slaves: The Rise of the Planter Class in the English West Indies 1624–1713* (Chapel Hill, NC, 1972).

14. P. R. P. Coelho and R. A. McGuire, 'African and European Bound Labour: The Biological Consequences of Economic Choice', *Journal of Economic History* 57, 1 (1997), p. 108.

15. B. Solow, 'Slavery and Colonization', in B. Solow (ed.), *Slavery and the Rise of the Atlantic System* (Cambridge, 1991), p. 29.

16. I. Blanchard, *Russia's Age of Silver* (London, 1989).

17. For sugar consumption in Europe, S. Mintz, *Sweetness and Power* (pbk edn, London, 1986), p. 67.

18. K. N. Chaudhuri, *The Trading World of Asia and the East India Company 1660–1750* (Cambridge, 1978), pp. 7–10; L. Dermigny, *La Chine et l'Occident: Le Commerce à Canton 1719–1833* (3 vols., Paris, 1964), vol. 2, p. 691.

19. See R. Davis, 'English Foreign Trade 1660–1700', *Economic History Review*, New Series, 7, 2 (1954), pp. 150–66; R. Davis, 'English Foreign Trade, 1700–1774', *Economic History Review*, New Series, 15, 2 (1962), pp. 285–303.

20. N. Zahedieh, 'Trade, Plunder and Economic Development in Early

English Jamaica, 1655–1689', *Economic History Review*, New Series, 39, 2 (1986), pp. 205–22; K. Glamann, 'The Changing Pattern of Trade', in E. E. Rich and C. H. Wilson (eds.), *The Cambridge Economic History of Europe*, vol. 5: *The Economic Organisation of Early Modern Europe* (Cambridge, 1977), p. 191.

21. See J. de Vries, *The European Economy in the Age of Crisis 1600–1750* (pbk edn, Cambridge, 1976).

22. Ibid., p. 116.

23. Ibid., p. 125.

24. Ibid., p. 181.

25. See for example J. H. Plumb, 'The Commercialization of Leisure', in Neil McKendrick, John Brewer and J. H. Plumb, *The Birth of a Consumer Society: The Commercialization of Eighteenth-Century England* (London, 1982).

26. For this argument, I. Wallerstein, *The Modern World System* (2 vols., London, 1974, 1980).

27. De Vries, *Crisis*, p. 142.

28. For the Royal Africa Company, K. G. Davies, *The Royal Africa Company* (London, 1962). For the South Seas Company, J. Carswell, *The South Sea Bubble* (Stanford, 1960). The declining profitability of the Dutch East India Company and the failure of the two Dutch West India Companies are discussed in J. de Vries and Ad van der Woude, *The First Modern Economy: Success, Failure and Perseverance of the Dutch Economy, 1500–1815* (Cambridge, 1997), pp. 463–4, 468.

29. See Holden Furber, *Rival Empires of Trade in the Orient 1600–1800* (Minneapolis, 1976; repr. New Delhi, 2004), pp. 334–9.

30. See M. Korner, 'Expenditure', in R. J. Bonney (ed.), *Economic Systems and State Finance* (Oxford, 1995), pp. 393–422.

31. See N. Henshall, *The Myth of Absolutism* (London, 1992).

32. See J. Berenger, *Finances et absolutisme autrichiens dans la seconde moitié du xviime siècle* (2 vols., Paris, 1975), vol. 2, p. 662; R. J. W. Evans, *The Making of the Habsburg Monarchy* (Oxford, 1979), pp. 96–9.

33. E. Le Roy Ladurie, *L'Ancien Régime* (2 vols., Paris, 1991), vol. 2, p. 26.

34. The phrase comes from J. Henretta, *'Salutary Neglect'* (Princeton, 1972).

35. J. H. Parry, *The Spanish Seaborne Empire* (London, 1966), ch. 14.

36. D. Ogg, *Europe of the Ancien Régime 1715–83* (London, 1965), pp. 41–4, citing J. H. Bielefeld's *Institutions politiques* (1760).

37. Parry, *Empire*, pp. 202–5.

38. E. S. Morgan, *American Slavery, American Freedom: The Ordeal of Colonial Virginia* (New York, 1975), ch. 13.

39. D. Baugh, 'Maritime Strength and Atlantic Commerce', in L. Stone (ed.), *An Imperial State at War* (London, 1994), pp. 185–223.

40. B. Bailyn, *The Origins of American Politics* (pbk edn, New York, 1968), pp. 72–4.

41. Korner, 'Expenditure', p. 416.

42. R. J. Bonney, 'The Eighteenth Century II: The Struggle for Great Power Status and the End of the Old Fiscal Regime', in Bonney (ed.), *Economic Systems*, pp. 322ff.

43. M. Anderson, *The War of the Austrian Succession 1740–48* (London, 1995), pp. 25ff.

44. See B. Lenman, *Britain's Colonial Wars, 1688–1783* (London, 2001).

45. For campaigning in 'Danubia', J. Stoye, *Marsigli's Europe* (London, 1994).

46. See W. C. Fuller, *Strategy and Power in Russia, 1600–1914* (New York, 1992).

47. T. Smollett, *The Adventures of Roderick Random* (1748; Everyman edn, London, 1927), ch. 34, p. 191.

48. G. W. Forrest, *The Life of Lord Clive* (2 vols., London, 1918), vol. 1, pp. 26–30.

49. A. Osiander, *The States System of Europe 1640–1990* (Oxford, 1994), pp. 78–81.

50. For the Spanish 'system', R. A. Stradling, *Europe and the Decline of Spain* (London, 1981).

51. Anderson, *Austrian Succession*, p. 58.

52. W. Goetzmann, *New Lands, New Men: America and the Second Great Age of Discovery* (pbk edn, London, 1987), pp. 62–4.

53. J. Tully, *An Approach to Political Philosophy: Locke in Contexts* (Cambridge, 1993), ch. 5.

54. See J. Harrison and P. Laslett, *The Library of John Locke* (Oxford, 1965).

55. Dermigny, *La Chine*, vol. 1, pp. 19–22.

56. Montesquieu, *Lettres persanes* (1721), letter 121.

57. Montesquieu, *The Spirit of the Laws* (1748; Eng. trans. New York, 1949), vol. 1, pp. 301–4.

58. Ibid., p. 368.

59. Quoted in N. A. M. Rodger, *The Command of the Ocean: A Naval History of Britain 1649–1815* (London, 2004), p. 235.

60. J.-P. Rubiès, 'New Worlds and Renaissance Ethnology', *History and Anthropology* 6, 2–3 (1993), pp. 157–97.

61. M. J. Anderson, *Britain's Discovery of Russia 1553–1815* (London, 1958), p. 98.

62. See Wallerstein, *Modern World System*, vol. 2.

63. J. Billington, *The Icon and the Axe: An Interpretive History of Russian Culture* (London, 1970), pp. 146, 154, 166.

64. J. M. Letiche and B. Dmytryshyn, *Russian Statecraft: The* Politika *of Iurii Krizhanich* (Oxford, 1985), p. xlvii.

65. G. V. Lantzeff and R. A. Pierce, *Eastward to Empire* (Montreal and London, 1973), pp. 139ff.

66. Blanchard, *Russia's Age of Silver*, p. 90.

67. For this process, A. S. Donnelly, *The Russian Conquest of Bashkiria 1552–1740* (New Haven and London, 1968).

68. The best account of Peter's policies is now L. Hughes, *Russia in the Age of Peter the Great* (London, 1998). For the senate pronouncement, p. 296.

69. O. Subtelny, *Ukraine: A History* (Toronto, 1988), p. 182.

70. S. H. Baron, 'Who were the *Gosti*?', in his *Muscovite Russia: Collected Essays* (London, 1980).

71. Blanchard, *Russia's Age of Silver*, pp. 218ff. By 1710 the tax burden was equal to 64 per cent of the grain harvest, a rough approximation to the national product. See R. Hellie, 'Russia', in R. J. Bonney (ed.), *The Rise of the Fiscal State in Europe c.1200–1815* (Oxford, 1999), p. 497.

72. Hughes, *Russia*, chs. 7, 9.

73. B. H. Sumner, *Peter the Great and the Emergence of Russia* (London, 1951), pp. 55, 72.

74. Kliuchevskii cited in 'The Weber Thesis and Early Modern Russia', p. 333, in Baron, *Muscovite Russia*.

75. Letiche and Dmytryshyn, *Russian Statecraft*, pp. lviii–lix.

76. S. A. M. Adshead, *China in World History* (3rd edn, London, 1995), p. 243.

77. 'Ch'ing' meant 'pure'.

78. L. D. Kessler, *Kang-hsi and the Consolidation of Ch'ing Rule 1661–1684* (Chicago, 1976), p. 10.

79. See J. E. Wills, 'Maritime China from Wang Chih to Shih Lang', in J. Spence and J. E. Wills (eds.), *From Ming to Ch'ing* (New Haven, 1979), p. 226.

80. Kessler, *Kang-hsi*, p. 86.

81. V. S. Miasnikov, *The Ch'ing Empire and the Russian State in the 17th Century* (1980; Eng. trans. London, 1985), p. 183.

82. Wills, 'Maritime China', p. 228.

83. J. E. Wills, 'Ch'ing Relations with the Dutch 1662–1690', in J. K. Fairbank (ed.), *The Chinese World Order: Traditional China's Foreign Relations* (Cambridge, Mass., 1968), p. 245.

84. See Joseph E. Fletcher, 'China and Central Asia, 1368–1884', in Fairbank (ed.), *Chinese World Order*.

85. J. Spence, *Emperor of China: Self-portrait of K'ang-hsi* (New York, 1974), p. 9.

86. Miasnikov, *Ch'ing Empire*, p. 94.

87. Ibid., p. 286.

88. Pei Huang, *Aristocracy at Work: A Study of the Yung-cheng Period* (Bloomington, Ind., 1974), p. 181.

89. Huang, *Aristocracy*, p. 160; generally, B. Bartlett, *Monarchs and Ministers* (Berkeley and Los Angeles, 1991).

90. Adshead, *China*, p. 253.

91. P. C. Perdue, *Exhausting the Earth: State and Peasant in Hunan 1500–1850* (Cambridge, Mass., 1987), p. 10.

92. Ibid., p. 22.

93. M. Elvin, *The Pattern of the Chinese Past* (London, 1973), p. 248.

94. For the Kiangnan region and its cotton trade, M. Elvin, 'Market Towns and Waterways: The County of Shanghai from 1480 to 1910', in M. Elvin, *Another History: Essays on China from a European Perspective* (Sydney, 1996), p. 109.

95. For comparisons between the early modern economies of China and Europe, K. Pomeranz, *The Great Divergence: China, Europe and the Making of the Modern World Economy* (Princeton, 2000), pp. 106–7.

96. Spence, *Emperor of China*, p. 78.

97. Ibid., p. 83.

98. R. J. Smith, *China's Cultural Heritage: The Ch'ing Dynasty 1644–1911* (Boulder, Colo., and London, 1983), pp. 190ff.

99. Ibid., p. 108.

100. C. P. Fitzgerald, *The Southern Expansion of the Chinese People* (London, 1972), pp. 152–5.

101. Peng Yoke, 'China and Europe: Scientific and Technological Exchanges', in T. H. C. Lee (ed.), *China and Europe: Images and Influence in Sixteenth to Eighteenth Centuries* (Hong Kong, 1991), p. 196.

102. F. H. Bray, 'Some Problems Concerning the Transfer of Scientific and Technological Knowledge', in Lee (ed.), *China and Europe*, p. 16.

103. Smith, *Cultural Heritage*, pp. 185–7.

104. For two highly suggestive views of the long-run tendencies in Chinese political organization, J. A. Fogel, *Politics and Sinology: The Case of Naito Konan, 1866–1934* (Cambridge, Mass., 1984) and J. Schrecker, *The Chinese Revolution in Historical Perspective* (New York, 1991).

105. C. Totman, *Early Modern Japan* (London, 1993), p. 140.

106. Edo was the first city to reach a population of a million: see H. Jinnai, 'The Spatial Structure of Edo', in C. Nakane and S. Oishi (eds.), *Tokugawa Japan: The Social and Economic Antecedents of Modern Japan* (Tokyo, 1990).

107. Totman, *Early Modern Japan*, p. 149.

108. S. Nakamura, 'The Development of Rural Industry', in Nakane and Oishi (eds.), *Tokugawa Japan*, pp. 81–5.

109. See E. Kato, 'The Early Shogunate and Dutch Trade Policies', in L. Blussé and F. Gaastra (eds.), *Companies and Trade* (Leiden, 1981).

110. A. Reid, 'An Age of Commerce in Southeast Asian History', *Modern Asian Studies* 24, 1 (1990), pp. 10, 21.

111. M. Jansen, *China in the Tokugawa World* (Cambridge, Mass., 1992), p. 16.

112. Ibid., p. 7.

113. Ibid., p. 8.

114. Totman, *Early Modern Japan*, p. 138; Jansen, *Tokugawa World*, p. 35.

115. See Y. Yonezawa and C. Yoshizawa, *Japanese Painting in the Literati Style* (Eng. trans. New York, 1974).

116. Jinnai, 'The Spatial Structure of Edo', p. 148.

117. Totman, *Early Modern Japan*, p. 261.

118. A. Reid, *Southeast Asia in the Age of Commerce, 1450–1680* (2 vols., New Haven, 1988, 1993), vol. 2, ch. 3.

119. J. S. Trimingham, *A History of Islam in West Africa* (pbk edn, Oxford, 1970), pp. 131–6.

120. Ibid., p. 122.

121. B. Lewis, *The Muslim Discovery of Europe* (London, 1982), p. 237; H. A. R. Gibb and H. Bowen, *Islamic Society and the West: A Study of the Impact of Western Civilisation on Moslem Culture in the Near East*, vol. 1: *Islamic Society in the Eighteenth Century*, pt 1 (London, 1950), p. 214.

122. See J. Mokyr, *The Lever of Riches: Technological Creativity and Economic Progress* (Oxford, 1990), ch. 4.

123. Trimingham, *Islam*, pp. 141–2.

124. For a recent study of this period, I. Parvev, *Habsburgs and Ottomans between Vienna and Belgrade (1683–1739)* (New York, 1995).

125. B. Masters, *The Origins of Western Economic Dominance in the Middle East: Mercantilism and the Islamic Economy in Aleppo* (New York, 1988); D. Goffman, *Izmir and the Levantine World, 1550–1650* (Seattle, 1990).

126. Lewis, *Discovery*, p. 296.

127. *Memoirs of the Baron de Tott on the Turks and the Tartars* (Eng. trans., 2 vols., 1785), vol. 2, p. 15; Lewis, *Discovery*, p. 153.

128. P. Goubert, *Cent mille provinciaux au XVIIe siècle: Beauvais et les Beauvaisis de 1600 à 1750* (pbk edn, Paris, 1968), pp. 172–3.

129. Rifa'at Ali Abou El-Haj, *The Formation of the Modern State: The Ottoman Empire, Sixteenth to Eighteenth Centuries* (Albany, NY, 1991), p. 10.

130. Carol B. Stevens, 'Modernising the Military: Peter the Great and Military Reform', in J. Kotilaine and M. Poe (eds.), *Modernising Muscovy: Reform and*

Social Change in Seventeenth-Century Russia (London, 2004), pp. 247–62, esp. pp. 258–9.

131. See L. Valensi, *Le Maghreb avant la prise d'Algers (1800–1830)* (Paris, 1969); A. C. Hess, 'The Forgotten Frontier: The Ottoman North African Provinces', in T. Naff and R. Owen (eds.), *Studies in Eighteenth-Century Islamic History* (Carbondale, Ill., 1977), pp. 71–83.

132. H. Inalcik, 'Centralization and Decentralization in Ottoman Administration', in Naff and Owen (eds.), *Islamic History*, pp. 38–46.

133. See B. McGowan, 'The Age of the Ayans, 1699–1812', in H. Inalcik with D. Quataert (eds.), *An Economic and Social History of the Ottoman Empire 1300–1914* (Cambridge, 1994), pp. 664–76.

134. For Cairo's coffee trade, A. Raymond, *Artisans et commerçants au Caire au XVIIIe siècle* (Damascus, 1972), p. 144. For the rapid growth of Izmir, S. Faroqhi, *Towns and Townsmen of Ottoman Anatolia* (Cambridge, 1984), p. 6.

135. J. Carswell, 'From the Tulip to the Rose', in Naff and Owen (eds.), *Islamic History*, pp. 328–9.

136. See S. Faroqhi, 'Crisis and Change, 1590–1699', in Inalcik with Quataert (eds.), *Ottoman Empire*, p. 526, and McGowan, 'The Age of the Ayans', p. 724.

137. S. Blake, *Shahjahanabad: The Sovereign City in Mughal India 1639–1739* (Cambridge, 1991).

138. R. M. Eaton, *The Rise of Islam and the Bengal Frontier 1204–1760* (pbk edn, London, 1996), pp. 228ff.

139. C. A. Bayly, *Rulers, Townsmen and Bazaars: North Indian Society in the Age of British Expansion 1770–1870* (Cambridge, 1983), p. 155.

140. T. Raychaudhuri and I. Habib (eds.), *The Cambridge Economic History of India*, vol. 1: *c.1200–1750* (Cambridge, 1982), p. 396; J. R. McLane, *Land and Local Kingship in Eighteenth Century Bengal* (Cambridge, 1993), p. 31.

141. Raychaudhuri and Habib (eds.), *Economic History*, vol. 1, pp. 400–402.

142. Ibid., p. 417.

143. See the brilliant essay by F. Perlin, 'Commercial Manufacture and the "Protoindustrialisation" Thesis', in F. Perlin, *Unbroken Landscape: Commodity, Category, Sign and Identity: Their Production as Myth and Knowledge* (Aldershot, 1994), esp. pp. 81–2.

144. E. Maclagan, *The Jesuits and the Great Moghul* (London, 1932), p. 268.

145. Ibid., p. 269.

146. Ibid., pp. 243ff.

147. L'Escaliot to Sir T. Browne, 28 Jan. 1664, in N. C. Kelkar and D. V. Apte (eds.), *English Records on Shivaji* (Poona, 1931), p. 73.

148. Ibid., p. 374.

149. S. Gordon, *Marathas, Marauders and State Formation in 18th Century India* (New Delhi, 1994), p. 28.

150. Ibid., ch. 2.

151. A. Wink, *Land and Sovereignty in India: Agrarian Society and Politics under the Eighteenth-Century Maratha Svarajya* (Cambridge, 1986), p. 40.

152. See ibid., pp. 7, 34.

153. M. Alam, *The Crisis of Empire in Mughal North India: Awadh and the Punjab 1707–1748* (Delhi, 1986), p. 241.

154. W. Irvine, *The Later Mughals*, vol. 2: *1719–1739* (Calcutta, 1922), p. 360.

155. For the 'nuclear zones' of the Mughal Empire, Jos Gommans, *Mughal Warfare: Indian Frontiers and the Highroads to Empire 1500–1700* (London, 2002), p. 18.

156. D. Ludden, *Peasant History in South India* (New Delhi, 1989), p. 74.

157. See Perlin, 'Commercial Manufacture'.

158. For White's career, M. Collis, *Siamese White* (London, 1936).

159. Forrest, *Lord Clive*, vol. 1, p. 26.

160. G. R. G. Hambly, 'The Emperor's Clothes', in S. Gordon (ed.), *Robes of Honour* (New Delhi, 2003), pp. 31–49, esp. p. 43.

161. See the remarkable study by J. J. L. Gommans, *The Rise of the Indo-Afghan Empire, c.1710–1780* (Leiden, 1995).

162. For a fascinating insight into Georgian politics, W. E. D. Allen, *Russian Embassies to the Georgian Kings (1589–1605)*, Hakluyt Society, 2nd Series, 138 (2 vols., Cambridge, 1970), vol. 1, 'Introduction'.

163. L. Lockhart, *Nadir Shah* (London, 1938), p. 268.

164. Ibid., p. 268; P. Sykes, *A History of Persia* (3rd edn, 2 vols., London, 1951), vol. 2, pp. 241ff.

165. Gommans, *Indo-Afghan Empire*, pp. 55ff.

166. Ibid., pp. 26–7.

167. R. L. Canfield, *Turko-Persia in Historical Perspective* (Cambridge, 1991), p. 22.

168. Lockhart, *Nadir Shah*, pp. 212ff.

169. Gommans, *Indo-Afghan Empire*, p. 177.

170. De Vries and van der Woude, *The First Modern Economy*, p. 693.

CHAPTER 4: THE EURASIAN REVOLUTION

1. S. F. Dale, *Indian Merchants and Eurasian Trade 1600–1750* (Cambridge, 1994).

2. P. C. Perdue, *China Marches West* (Cambridge, Mass., 2005).

3. For the politics of the upper Nile in the mid eighteenth century, J. J. Ewald,

Soldiers, Traders and Slaves: State Formation and Economic Transformation in the Greater Nile Valley 1700–1885 (Madison, 1990).

4. The classic study is P. J. van der Merwe, *The Migrant Farmer in the History of the Cape Colony, 1657–1842* (1938; Eng. trans. Athens, O., 1995).

5. W. P. Cumming, S. Hillier, D. B. Quinn and G. Williams, *The Exploration of North America 1630–1776* (London, 1974), pp. 233–4.

6. Quoted in R. J. Bonney, 'The Eighteenth Century II: The Struggle for Great Power Status and the End of the Old Fiscal Regime', in R. J. Bonney (ed.), *Economic Systems and State Finance* (Oxford, 1995), p. 315.

7. The best introduction to this region remains W. H. McNeill, *Europe's Steppe Frontier* (London, 1974).

8. According to a French inquiry in 1763, French revenues at 321 million *livres tournois* were well ahead of Britain's on 224, with the Netherlands in third place on 120, and Austria fourth on 92. See Bonney, 'The Struggle for Great Power Status', p. 336.

9. W. Goetzmann, *New Lands, New Men: America and the Second Great Age of Discovery* (New York, 1986), pp. 69–73.

10. For the power of the assemblies, B. Bailyn, *The Origins of American Politics* (pbk edn, New York, 1968).

11. T. Schieder, *Frederick the Great* (1983; Eng. trans. London, 2000), pp. 116–17.

12. For Frederick's fears of Russian expansion, ibid., pp. 151–8.

13. Mainly to recover Silesia, lost to Prussia in 1740.

14. See S. Sebag-Montefiore, *Potemkin* (London, 2000); N. K. Gvosdev, *Imperial Policies and Perspectives towards Georgia, 1760–1819* (London, 2000), ch. 4.

15. P. Mackesy, *The War for America* (London, 1964) remains the standard account.

16. G. Nobles, *American Frontiers: Cultural Encounters and Continental Conquest* (London, 1997), chs. 2, 3, for a recent overview.

17. Cook's instructions, quoted in J. C. Beaglehole (ed.), *The Journals of Captain James Cook. The Voyage of the Endeavour, 1768–1771* (Cambridge, 1957), p. cclxxxii.

18. A. Wink, *Land and Sovereignty in India: Agrarian Society and Politics under the Eighteenth-Century Maratha Svarajya* (Cambridge, 1986).

19. This description was in a letter published in the *London Chronicle* in July 1757. S. C. Hill (ed.), *Indian Records Series: Bengal in 1756–1757* (3 vols., London, 1905), vol. 3, p. 85.

20. Vivid contemporary accounts of the crisis can be followed in ibid., appx 2 and 3.

21. Clive to his father, 19 Aug. 1757, in ibid., p. 360.

22. Clive to William Pitt, 7 Jan. 1759, in W. K. Firminger (ed.), *Fifth Report . . . on the Affairs of the East India Company 1812* (1917; repr. New York, 1969), p. clvi.

23. Clive to the East India Company, 16 Jan. 1767, in ibid., p. clix.

24. See B. Stein, 'State Formation and Economy Reconsidered', *Modern Asian Studies* 19, 3 (1985), pp. 387–413; K. Brittlebank, 'Assertion', in P. Marshall (ed.), *The Eighteenth Century in Indian History: Evolution or Revolution* (New Delhi, 2003), pp. 269–92.

25. R. Callahan, *The East India Company and Army Reform* (Cambridge, Mass., 1972), p. 6.

26. For an account of this trade, E. H. Pritchard, *The Crucial Years of Anglo-Chinese Relations 1750–1800* (Pullman, Wash., 1936); Holden Furber, *Rival Empires of Trade in the Orient 1600–1800* (Minneapolis, 1976; repr. New Delhi, 2004).

27. A. Sorel, *Europe and the French Revolution: The Political Traditions of the Old Regime* (1885; Eng. trans. London, 1969), p. 119.

28. R. J. Bonney, 'France 1494–1815', in R. J. Bonney (ed.), *The Rise of the Fiscal State in Europe c.1200–1815* (Oxford, 1999), pp. 148–50.

29. For a recent account, M. Price, *The Fall of the French Monarchy* (London, 2002).

30. A Sorel, *L'Europe et la Révolution française: La chute de la royauté* (10th edn, Paris, 1906), p. 458.

31. Bonney, 'The Struggle for Great Power Status', p. 360.

32. F. de Bourrienne, *Memoirs of Napoleon Bonaparte* (1836; Eng. trans. ed. E. Sanderson, London, n.d.), p. 68.

33. F. Charles-Roux, *Bonaparte: Governor of Egypt* (1936; Eng. trans. London, 1937), p. 2.

34. See J. B. Kelly, *Britain and the Persian Gulf 1795–1880* (Oxford, 1968), ch. 2.

35. Bourrienne, *Bonaparte*, p. 328.

36. The best account of the settlement is now P. W. Schroeder, *The Transformation of European Politics 1763–1848* (Oxford, 1994), ch. 12. See also E. V. Gulick, *Europe's Classical Balance of Power* (London, 1955), pt 2 – a brilliant study.

37. See Kenneth Pomeranz, *The Great Divergence: China, Europe and the Making of the Modern World Economy* (Princeton, 2000).

38. P. Bairoch, *Victoires et déboires: Histoire économique et sociale du monde du xvi siècle à nos jours* (3 vols., Paris, 1997), vol. 2, p. 852. For the dramatic falls in the price of cotton yarn and cloth in Britain, C. Knick Harley, 'Cotton Textile Prices and the Industrial Revolution', *Economic History Review*, New Series, 51, 1 (1998), pp. 49–83.

39. See N. F. R. Crafts, *British Economic Growth during the Industrial Revolution* (Oxford, 1985).

40. See E. L. Jones, *The European Miracle: Environments, Economies and Geopolitics in the History of Europe and Asia* (Cambridge, 1981).

41. This is the central argument of Pomeranz, *Great Divergence*.

42. See the suggestive remarks in D. Washbrook, 'From Comparative Sociology to Global History: Britain and India in the Pre-History of Modernity', *Journal of the Economic and Social History of the Orient* 40, 4 (1997).

43. Pomeranz, *Great Divergence*, p. 85.

44. Ibid., p. 138.

45. For the Ottoman economy, B. McGowan, 'The Age of the Ayans, 1699–1812', in H. Inalcik with D. Quataert (eds.), *An Economic and Social History of the Ottoman Empire 1300–1914* (Cambridge, 1994), pp. 703, 724, 727.

46. W. Floor, *The Economy of Safavid Persia* (Wiesbaden, 2000), pp. 161, 331.

47. J. E. Inikori, *Africans and the Industrial Revolution in England: A Study in International Trade and Economic Development* (Cambridge, 2002), p. 443. Indian cottons 'completely dominated' the West African market in the early eighteenth century.

48. C. A. Bayly, *Rulers, Townsmen and Bazaars: North Indian Society in the Age of British Expansion 1770–1870* (Cambridge, 1983), p. 194.

49. Pomeranz, *Great Divergence* for the analysis that follows.

50. Ibid., pp. 290, 325.

51. Crafts, *British Economic Growth*, p. 138. Strictly, 2.7.

52. Harley, 'Cotton Textile Prices', pp. 50ff.

53. M. W. Flinn, *The History of the British Coal Industry*, vol. 2: *1700–1830: The Industrial Revolution* (Oxford, 1984), p. 114.

54. From 68,000 tons to 240,000. T. S. Ashton, *Iron and Steel in the Industrial Revolution* (Manchester, 1924), p. 99.

55. See G. N. von Tunzelman, *Steam Power and British Industrialization to 1860* (Oxford, 1978), pp. 46, 224, 295.

56. D. A. Farnie, *The English Cotton Industry and the World Market 1815–1896* (Oxford, 1979), pp. 96–7.

57. J. A. Mann, *The Cotton Trade of Great Britain* (1860; repr. edn, London, 1968), table 25. After 1840, India took first place.

58. P. Hudson, *The Industrial Revolution* (London, 1992), p. 183.

59. R. Davis, 'English Foreign Trade, 1700–1774', *Economic History Review*, New Series, 15, 2 (1962), pp. 285–303.

60. Hudson, *Industrial Revolution*, 197–8.

61. P. Mantoux, *The Industrial Revolution in the Eighteenth Century* (rev. edn, London, 1961), p. 199.

62. Ibid., p. 203.

63. G. Unwin, *Samuel Oldknow and the Arkwrights: The Industrial Revolution in Stockport and Marple* (Manchester, 1924), p. 44.

64. Ibid., p. 62.

65. The Company was accused of selling Indian goods cheaply to meet its costs at home. A. Redford, *Manchester Merchants and Foreign Trade 1794–1858* (London, 1934), pp. 122–3.

66. Unwin, *Samuel Oldknow*, p. 98.

67. Farnie, *English Cotton Industry*, p. 96.

68. A. Feuerwerker, *State and Society in Eighteenth Century China* (Ann Arbor, 1976), p. 111.

69. J. Spence, *In Search of Modern China* (London, 1990), pp. 112–14.

70. M. L. Cohen, 'Souls and Salvation', in J. L. Watson and E. Rawski (eds.), *Death Ritual in Late Imperial China* (Berkeley, 1988), pp. 200–201.

71. P. Kuhn, *Soulstealers: The Chinese Sorcery Scare of 1768* (Cambridge, Mass., 1990), pp. 43–4.

72. C. A. Ronan (ed.), *The Shorter Science and Civilisation in China: An Abridgement of Joseph Needham's Original Text* (Cambridge, 1978), vol. 1, p. 305.

73. R. J. Smith, 'Mapping China's World: Cultural Cartography in Late Imperial Times', in Wen-hsin Yeh (ed.), *Landscape, Culture and Power in Chinese Society* (Berkeley, 1998), p. 75.

74. See J. Spence, *Treason by the Book* (London, 2001).

75. E. Rawski, 'The Qing Formation and the Early Modern Period', in L. Struve (ed.), *The Qing Formation in World Historical Time* (Cambridge, Mass., 2004), p. 234.

76. Perdue, *China Marches West*, p. 456.

77. Smith, 'Mapping China's World', pp. 85ff.

78. Quoted in A. Singer, *The Lion and the Dragon* (London, 1992), p. 99.

79. An anxiety felt as far away as Mosul. A. Hourani, *Islam in European Thought* (Cambridge, 1991), p. 138.

80. B. Lewis, *The Muslim Discovery of Europe* (London, 1982), pp. 81–3.

81. Ibid., p. 157.

82. G. Goodwin, *Islamic Architecture: Ottoman Turkey* (London, 1977), pp. 21, 161–78.

83. For his career and ideas, Gulfishan Khan, *Indian Muslim Perceptions of the West in the Eighteenth Century* (Oxford, 1998), pp. 100ff.

84. Thus many 'Greek' Christians in Anatolia used Turkish written in Greek script. See B. Lewis, *Multiple Identities in the Modern Middle East* (London, 1998), p. 8.

85. H. Algar, *Religion and State in Iran 1785–1906* (Berkeley and Los Angeles, 1969), ch. 1.

86. Ibid., p. 78.

87. R. M. Eaton, *The Rise of Islam and the Bengal Frontier 1204–1760* (London, 1993), p. 282; M. Laffan, *Islamic Nationhood and Colonial Indonesia* (London, 2003), pp. 20, 23–4.

88. The role of the Sufis is discussed in H. A. R. Gibb and H. Bowen, *Islamic Society and the West: A Study of the Impact of Western Civilisation on Moslem Culture in the Near East*, vol. 1: *Islamic Society in the Eighteenth Century*, pt 2 (London, 1957), pp. 187–97, and in Hourani, *Islam in European Thought*, pp. 156–63. The Ottoman provincial boss Ali Pasha carefully patronized the Bektashi dervishes to strengthen his power. See F. W. Hasluck, *Christianity and Islam under the Sultans* (2 vols., Oxford, 1929), vol. 2, p. 537.

89. Khan, *Indian Muslim Perceptions*, p. 375.

90. See Abd al-Rahman al-Jabarti, *Chronicle of the First Seven Months of the French Occupation of Egypt*, ed. and trans. S. Moreh (Leiden, 1975); S. Moreh, 'Napoleon and the French Impact on Egyptian Society in the Eyes of al-Jabarti', in I. Bierman (ed.), *Napoleon in Egypt* (Reading, 2003).

91. See J. S. Trimingham, *A History of Islam in West Africa* (Oxford, 1962), ch. 5; G. Robinson, *Muslim Societies in African History* (Cambridge, 2004), ch. 10.

92. J. Israel, *The Radical Enlightenment: Philosophy and the Making of Modernity 1650–1750* (Oxford, 2001), p. 10. The main burden of this study is the radical intellectual influence exercised by the materialist philosophy of Spinoza.

93. N. Hampson, *The Enlightenment* (London, 1968), p. 131.

94. For Locke's ideas, M. Cranston, *John Locke* (London, 1957), ch. 20; Hampson, *Enlightenment*, pp. 38–9.

95. J. Tully, *An Approach to Political Philosophy: Locke in Contexts* (Cambridge, 1993), pp. 200–201.

96. Most recently in Israel, *Radical Enlightenment*.

97. J. Locke, *Two Treatises on Civil Government* (1690), ed. J. W. Gough (Oxford, 1946), sect. 49.

98. For a recent study, see A. Pagden, *European Encounters with the New World* (London, 1993).

99. For Hume, N. Phillipson, *Hume* (London, 1989), pp. 32–4.

100. See H. Reiss (ed.), *Kant's Political Writings* (Cambridge, 1970), p. 106.

101. J. W. Burrow, *Evolution and Society* (Cambridge, 1970), p. 39.

102. Ibid., p. 47.

103. E. Stokes, *The English Utilitarians and India* (Oxford, 1959), p. 53.

104. Quoted in Spence, *In Search of Modern China*, p. 123.

105. S. Drescher, *Capitalism and Anti-Slavery: British Mobilization in Comparative Perspective* (London, 1986).

106. U. Heyd, 'The Ottoman 'Ulema and Westernization in the Time of Selim

III and Mahmud II', in A. Hourani, P. S. Khoury and M. C. Wilson (eds.), *The Modern Middle East* (London, 1993), pp. 29–59.

107. R. Owen, *The Middle East in the World Economy 1800–1914* (London, 1981), pp. 65–72.

108. Ewald, *Soldiers, Traders and Slaves*, pp. 152–65.

109. For a recent analysis of Mehemet Ali's state, K. Fahmy, *All the Pasha's Men: Mehmed Ali, his Army and the Making of Modern Egypt* (Cairo, 2002).

110. J. R. Perry, *Karim Khan Zand* (Chicago, 1979).

111. An entertaining description of Tehran's dealings with the Bakhtiari of south-western Iran in the 1840s is in H. Layard, *Early Adventures in Persia, Susiana and Babylonia* (2 vols., London, 1887), vol. 2, chs. 11–16.

112. Algar, *Religion and State*, pp. 45–7.

113. V. Lieberman, 'Reinterpreting Burmese History', *Comparative Studies in Society and History* 29, 1 (1987), p. 179; Thant Myint-U, *The Making of Modern Burma* (Cambridge, 2001), chs. 1, 2.

114. For this pattern, V. Lieberman, 'Local Integration and Eurasian Analogies: Structuring Southeast Asian History, *c*.1350–*c*.1830', *Modern Asian Studies* 27, 3 (1993), pp. 475–572; and V. Lieberman, *Strange Parallels: Southeast Asia in Global Context c.800–1830*, vol. 1: *Integration on the Mainland* (Cambridge, 2003), chs. 2, 3, 4.

115. For the rise of Zanzibar, M. V. Jackson Haight, *The European Powers and Southeast Africa* (rev. edn, London, 1967), pp. 99–141.

116. Lord Auckland's dispatch, 28 Feb. 1842, in Kelly, *Britain and the Persian Gulf*, p. 449.

117. For this account, see C. Totman, *Early Modern Japan* (London, 1993), chs. 15–21, and M. Jansen, *The Making of Modern Japan* (Cambridge, Mass., 2000), chs. 8, 9.

CHAPTER 5: THE RACE AGAINST TIME

1. T. R. Malthus, *Principles of Political Economy* (1820), variorum edn, ed. J. Pullen (Cambridge, 1989), p. 234.

2. See R. E. Cameron, *France and the Economic Development of Europe 1800–1914* (Princeton, 1961).

3. For this argument, the centrepiece of his account, P. W. Schroeder, *The Transformation of European Politics 1763–1848* (Oxford, 1994).

4. See P. E. Moseley, *Russian Diplomacy and the Opening of the Eastern Question in 1838–1839* (Cambridge, Mass., 1934); B. H. Sumner, *Russia and the Balkans, 1870–1880* (Oxford, 1937); R. W. Seton-Watson, *Disraeli, Gladstone and the Eastern Question* (London, 1935), esp. pp. 194–5.

5. See E. D. Steele, *Palmerston and Liberalism 1855–1865* (Cambridge, 1991) for the domestic constraints on Palmerston's diplomacy.

6. See C. J. Bartlett, *Great Britain and Seapower 1815–1853* (Oxford, 1963); G. S. Graham, *The Politics of Naval Supremacy* (Cambridge, 1965); P. Kennedy, *The Rise and Fall of British Naval Mastery* (London, 1976), ch. 6.

7. The exception being the North's four year blockade of the South during the American Civil War.

8. The protracted debate over Napoleon's reputation and legacy is the subject of the brilliant study by P. Geyl, *Napoleon: For and Against* (London, 1949).

9. The ideas of Constant (1767–1830) can be followed in his essays *De l'esprit de conquête et de l'usurpation* (1814), *Principes de politique* (1815), and *Mélanges de littérature et de politique* (1829) in Benjamin Constant, *Ecrits politiques*, ed. M. Gauchet (Paris, 1997).

10. See A. S. Kahan, *Aristocratic Liberalism* (London, 1992) for a study of Tocqueville, J. S. Mill and the Swiss historian Jacob Burckhardt.

11. For a study of Burckhardt, L. Gossman, *Basel in the Age of Burckhardt* (Chicago, 2000), chs. 5, 10, 11.

12. O. Figes, *Natasha's Dance: A Cultural History of Russia* (London, 2002), p. 76.

13. Ibid., ch. 2.

14. H. Seton-Watson, *The Russian Empire 1801–1917* (Oxford, 1967), p. 355.

15. B. Eklof, J. Bushnell and L. Zakharova (eds.), *Russia's Great Reforms 1855–1881* (Bloomington, Ind., 1994), pp. 214, 233.

16. Ibid., p. 249.

17. G. Hosking, *Russia: People and Empire 1552–1917* (London, 1997), p. 333.

18. For Kliuchevskii, N. V. Riasonovsky, *The Image of Peter the Great in Russian History and Thought* (Oxford, 1985).

19. E. G. Wakefield, *A Letter from Sydney* (1829; Everyman edn, London, 1929), p. 47.

20. For the increasingly unfavourable view of the United States in France after *c*.1830, R. Remond, *Les Etats-Unis devant l'opinion française 1815–1852* (Paris, 1962), pp. 675, 731, 740, 863.

21. See D. Potter, *The Impending Struggle* (New York, 1976), p. 244; D. W. Howe, *The Political Culture of the American Whigs* (Chicago, 1974). Andrew Jackson was president in 1828–36.

22. A. J. H. Latham and L. Neal, 'The International Market in Rice and Wheat, 1868–1914', *Economic History Review*, New Series, 36, 2 (1983), pp. 260–75.

23. C. Jones, *International Business in the Nineteenth Century* (Brighton, 1987);

G. Jones, *Merchants to Multinationals: British Trading Companies in the Nineteenth and Twentieth Centuries* (Oxford, 2000); D. R. SarDesai, *British Trade and Expansion in Southeast Asia, 1830–1914* (New Delhi, 1977).

24. A. G. Kenwood and A. L. Lougheed, *The Growth of the International Economy 1820–1980* (London, 1983), pp. 90–91. For economic integration in the Atlantic – a sphere that they extend as far as Australia – K. H. O'Rourke and J. G. Williamson, *Globalization and History: The Evolution of a Nineteenth-Century Atlantic Economy* (Cambridge, Mass., 1999).

25. Kenwood and Lougheed, *International Economy*, p. 93.

26. W. Schlote, *British Overseas Trade from 1700 to the 1930s* (Oxford, 1952), pp. 156–8.

27. B. R. Mitchell, *Abstract of British Historical Statistics* (Cambridge, 1962), p. 317.

28. P. Bairoch, *Victoires et déboires: Histoire économique et sociale du monde du xvi siècle à nos jours* (3 vols., Paris, 1997), vol. 2, p. 34.

29. Ibid., p. 18.

30. B. H. Sumner, *A Survey of Russian History* (London, 1944), pp. 356–7.

31. Bairoch, *Victoires et déboires*, vol. 1, p. 467.

32. S. L. Engerman and R. E. Gallman (eds.), *The Cambridge Economic History of the United States*, vol. 2: *The Long Nineteenth Century* (Cambridge, 2000), p. 713.

33. Mitchell, *Abstract*, pp. 315, 318. Northern = Russia, Sweden, Norway, Denmark. Western = France, Belgium, Netherlands.

34. See Cameron, *France and the Economic Development of Europe*.

35. Engerman and Gallman (eds.), *Economic History*, vol. 2, p. 696; L. E. Davis and R. J. Cull, *International Capital Markets and American Economic Growth 1820–1914* (Cambridge, 1994), p. 111. The figure for Australia after 1860 was nearer to 50 per cent, with half of capital needs being supplied from Britain. See N. J. Butlin, *Australian Economic Development 1861–1900* (Cambridge, 1964), pp. 28–30.

36. R. G. Albion, *The Rise of New York Port 1815–1860* (New York, 1939); S. Beckert, *The Monied Metropolis: New York City and the Consolidation of the American Bourgeoisie* (Cambridge, 2001).

37. Bairoch, *Victoires et déboires*, vol. 1, p. 410.

38. Engerman and Gallman, *Economic History*, vol. 2, p. 50; P. Mathias, *The First Industrial Nation* (London, 1969), p. 243.

39. S. Bruchey, *Enterprise: The Dynamic Economy of a Free People* (London, 1990), p. 237.

40. Mitchell, *Abstract*, p. 318.

41. Engerman and Gallman, *Economic History*, vol. 2, p. 700.

42. See S. Ambrose, *Undaunted Courage* (New York, 1996).

43. John Langdon, 'Three Voyages to the West Coast of Africa *1881–1884*', ed. M. Lynn, in B. Wood and M. Lynn (eds.), *Travel, Trade and Power in the Atlantic 1765–1884* (Cambridge, 2002).

44. See S. Bard, *Traders of Hong Kong: Some Foreign Merchant Houses 1841–1899* (Hong Kong, 1993).

45. B. S. A. Yeoh, *Contesting Space–Power Relations and the Urban Built-Environment in Colonial Singapore* (Kuala Lumpur, 1996), p. 35.

46. J. Conrad, *The End of the Tether* (London, 1902), p. 168.

47. J. Forbes Munro, *Maritime Enterprise and Empire: Sir William Mackinnon and his Business Network* (Woodbridge, 2003), chs. 5, 6, 7, 8.

48. R. Giffen, 'The Statistical Century', in his *Economic Inquiries and Studies* (2 vols., London, 1904), vol. 2, pp. 270, 273.

49. R. C. Wade, *The Urban Frontier: Pioneer Life in Early Pittsburgh, Cincinnati, Lexington, Louisville and St Louis* (Chicago, 1964), p. 341.

50. For a discussion of the contrast between an 'enterprise' economy and one in which the state played a larger role (the cases being the USA and Canada), W. T. Easterbrook, *North American Patterns of Growth and Development: The Continental Context* (Toronto, 1990).

51. G. Blainey, *The Tyranny of Distance* (Melbourne, 1966).

52. For a brilliant discussion of this, G. Raby, *Making Rural Australia* (Oxford, 1996).

53. G. Brechin, *Imperial San Francisco: Urban Power, Earthly Ruin* (Berkeley, Los Angeles and London, 1999).

54. W. Issel and R. W. Cherny, *San Francisco 1865–1932* (London, 1986), ch. 2.

55. Elliott West, *The Contested Plains: Indians, Goldseekers and the Rush to Colorado* (Lawrence, Kan., 1998).

56. For the significance of the revolver in allowing the white American conquest of the Plains Indians, Walter Prescott Webb, *The Great Plains* (New York, 1936), pp. 167–79: 'It enabled the white man to fight the Plains Indians on horseback.'

57. D. Robinson, *Paths of Accommodation: Muslim Societies and French Colonial Authorities in Senegal and Mauretania, 1880–1920* (Athens, O., and Oxford, 2000), p. 59.

58. *The Heart of Darkness* was published in 1902. This reference comes from the Everyman edition (London, 1974), p. 62.

59. R. Ileto, 'Religion and Anti-Colonial Movements', in N. Tarling (ed.), *The Cambridge History of Southeast Asia*, vol. 3: *From c.1800 to the 1930s* (pbk edn, Cambridge, 1999), p. 216.

60. See C. H. Ambler, *Kenyan Communities in the Age of Imperialism* (New Haven, 1988) for a study of the Embu.

61. Winwood Reade, *The Martyrdom of Man* (London, 1872), p. 242. Reade's purpose, in what became by the 1920s a very widely read (as well as extraordinarily original) book, was to insist that Africa did not lie apart from world history, but had played a central role in it.

62. M. Osborne, *The River Road to China* (London, 1975), p. 186.

63. L. Subramanian, 'Banias and the British: The Role of Indigenous Credit in . . . Imperial Expansion in Western India', *Modern Asian Studies* 21 (1987), pp. 473–510.

64. Twenty years later, the armies of British India's three 'presidencies', Bengal (covering much of North India), Bombay and Madras, amounted to more than 270,000 men. M. K. Pasha, *Recruitment and Underdevelopment in the Punjab* (Karachi, 1998), p. 32.

65. The best short study of the age of Company rule is D. A. Washbrook, 'India, 1818–1860: The Two Faces of Colonialism', in A. Porter (ed.), *The Oxford History of the British Empire*, vol. 3: *The Nineteenth Century* (Oxford, 1999), pp. 395–421. See also his 'Economic Depression and the Making of "Traditional" Society in Colonial India 1820–1855', *Transactions of the Royal Historical Society*, 6th Series, 3 (1993), pp. 237–63.

66. Thornton's *Gazetteer of India 1857* (London, 1857), pp. 136, 175.

67. S. David, *The Indian Mutiny* (London, 2002), p. 397.

68. Ibid., p. 346.

69. For aspects of the Mutiny and its causes, R. C. Majumdar, *The Sepoy Mutiny and the Revolt of 1857* (Calcutta, 1968); C. A. Bayly, *Empire and Information* (Cambridge, 1996), ch. 9; E. T. Stokes, *The Peasant and the Raj* (Cambridge, 1978); C. A. Bayly, 'Two Colonial Revolts: The Java War and the Indian "Mutiny" of 1857–59', in C. A. Bayly and D. A. Kolff (eds.), *Two Colonial Empires* (Dordrecht, 1986); F. Robinson, 'The Muslims of Upper India and the Shock of the Mutiny', in his *Islam and Muslim History in South Asia* (New Delhi, 2000), pp. 138–55.

70. Stokes, *Peasant*, p. 150, footnote.

71. See E. Stokes, *The English Utilitarians and India* (Oxford, 1959).

72. 'T'ung-chih' was the reign-name of the Chinese emperor of 1862–75; 'Meiji' that of the Japanese emperor of 1868–1912.

73. The classic account remains M. Greenberg, *British Trade and the Opening of China* (Cambridge, 1951).

74. See J. K. Fairbank, *Trade and Diplomacy on the China Coast* (Cambridge, Mass., 1953).

75. Feng's essays, written in 1860–61, were presented to his patron, Tseng Kuo-fan, a key figure in the T'ung-chih restoration. See S. Teng and J. K. Fairbank (eds.), *China's Response to the West* (Cambridge, Mass., 1979), pp. 50–53.

76. See J. Spence, *God's Chinese Son: The Taiping Heavenly Kingdom of Hong Xinquan* (New York, 1996) for the best recent history.

77. Between 1853 and 1863 the Nien controlled an area larger than the UK. See S. Y. Teng, *The Nien Army and their Guerilla Warfare* (The Hague, 1961), pp. 219ff.

78. For a recent survey, J. Lee, 'Trade and Economy in Pre-Industrial East Asia *c.*1500–*c.*1800: East Asia in the Age of Global Integration', *Journal of Asian Studies* 58, 1 (1999), pp. 2–26.

79. Opium consumption increased sevenfold between the 1810s and 1850s. See Y. P. Hao, *The Commercial Revolution in Nineteenth-Century China: The Rise of Sino-Western Mercantile Capitalism* (Berkeley and London, 1986), p. 69.

80. P. Richardson, *Economic Change in China c.1800–1950* (London, 1999), p. 21.

81. See Mary C. Wright, *The Last Stand of Chinese Conservatism: The T'ung-chih Restoration 1862–1874* (Stanford, 1957).

82. For this incident, H. B. Morse and H. F. MacNair, *Far Eastern International Relations* (2nd edn, Cambridge, Mass., 1931), p. 352.

83. Wright, *Last Stand*, p. 195.

84. Ibid., pp. 52, 55; E. J. Rhoads, *Manchus and Han* (Seattle, 2000) argues for the persistence of ethnic and cultural differences until after 1900.

85. Y. P. Hao, *The Comprador in Nineteenth-Century China* (Cambridge, Mass., 1970) is the standard account.

86. Hao, *Commercial Revolution*, p. 340; for the merchants' difficulties, F. E. Hyde, *Far Eastern Trade 1860–1914* (London, 1973), ch. 5.

87. Hao, *Commercial Revolution*, pp. 338–9.

88. For an excellent description, Albert M. Craig, *Choshu in the Meiji Restoration* (Cambridge, Mass., 1961), pp. 17ff.

89. See C. Totman, *Early Modern Japan* (London, 1993), pp. 242–5.

90. Craig, *Choshu*, pp. 26, 53–70; C. L. Yates, *Saigo Takamori* (London, 1995), p. 19.

91. For these events, Craig, *Choshu*, chs. 8, 9.

92. For the powers' declaration of neutrality, E. Satow, *A Diplomat in Japan* (London, 1921), p. 303; Morse and MacNair, *Far Eastern International Relations*, p. 325.

93. The best introduction to this process remains E. H. Norman, *Japan's Emergence as a Modern State* (New York, 1940), a brilliant study now curiously ignored in the specialist literature whose arguments and ideas it largely anticipates.

94. *The Autobiography of Fukuzawa Yukichi* (Tokyo, 1981), p. 227.

95. See Roger F. Hackett, *Yamagata Aristomo in the Rise of Modern Japan* (Cambridge, Mass., 1971).

96. For this process, see T. Fujitani, *Splendid Monarchy: Power and Pageantry in Modern Japan* (London, 1998).

97. G. C. Allen and A. Donnithorne, *Western Enterprise in Far Eastern Economic Development: China and Japan* (London, 1954), p. 202.

98. C. Howe, *The Origins of Japanese Trade Supremacy* (London, 1996), p. 250.

99. E. S. Crawcour, 'Economic Change in the Nineteenth Century', in M. B. Jansen (ed.), *The Cambridge History of Japan*, vol. 5: *The Nineteenth Century* (Cambridge, 1989), p. 616.

100. This may in part have been induced by financial need. See T. Suzuki-Morris, *A History of Japanese Economic Thought* (London, 1989), p. 57.

101. See Herbert P. Bix, *Peasant Protest in Japan 1590–1884* (New Haven, 1986), pp. 210–12; G. Roznan, 'Social Change', in Jansen (ed.), *Cambridge History of Japan*, vol. 5, p. 525.

102. See ch. 4.

103. D. Quataert, 'The Age of Reforms, 1812–1914', in H. Inalcik with D. Quataert (eds.), *An Economic and Social History of the Ottoman Empire 1300–1914* (Cambridge, 1994), p. 881.

104. Xavier de Planhol, *L'Islam et la mer: La Mosque et le matelot* (Paris, 2000), pp. 270–71. In fact the Turkish navy was the third largest in Europe, but performed very poorly.

105. M. Todorova, 'Midhat Pasha's Governorship of the Danubian Provinces', in C. E. Farah (ed.), *Decision-Making and Change in the Ottoman Empire* (Kirksville, Mo., 1993), pp. 115–23.

106. See J. McCarthy, *Death and Exile: The Ethnic Cleansing of Ottoman Muslims 1821–1922* (Princeton, 1995), pp. 37ff.

107. C. Clay, 'The Financial Collapse of the Ottoman State', in D. Panzac (ed.), *Histoire économique de l'Empire Ottoman et de la Turquie (1326–1960)* (Aix, 1992), pp. 119, 124.

108. C. Issawi, 'Middle East Economic Development 1815–1914', in A. Hourani, P. S. Khoury and M. C. Wilson (eds.), *The Modern Middle East* (London, 1993), p. 183.

109. Thus Izmir (Smyrna) enjoyed easier links with Europe and America than with the Anatolian interior. See A. J. Toynbee, *The Western Question in Greece and Turkey* (London, 1922), p. 125.

110. Issawi, 'Middle East Economic Development', p. 190.

111. See K. Fahmy, *All the Pasha's Men: Mehmed Ali, his Army and the Making of Modern Egypt* (Cairo, 2002).

112. C. Issawi, *Egypt: An Economic and Social Analysis* (London, 1947), p. 14.

113. See J. Berque, *Egypt: Imperialism and Revolution* (London, 1972), pp. 88–94.

114. J. R. McCoan, *Egypt* (New York, 1876), p. 91.

115. The best modern study is D. A. Farnie, *East and West of Suez: The Suez Canal in History, 1854–1956* (Oxford, 1969).

116. For the best study of Egypt's social and political crisis, A. Schölch, *'Egypt for the Egyptians': The Socio-Political Crisis in Egypt, 1878–1882* (London, 1981).

117. E. Abrahamian, *Iran between Two Revolutions* (Princeton, 1982), p. 28.

118. See H. Algar, *Religion and State in Iran 1795–1906* (Berkeley and Los Angeles, 1969), ch 1.

119. H. Algar, *Mirza Malkum Khan* (Berkeley and Los Angeles, 1973), pp. 24ff.

120. A. K. S. Lambton, *Qajar Persia* (London, 1987), pp. 20, 21, 44.

121. P. Avery, G. R. G. Hambly and C. Melville (eds.), *The Cambridge History of Iran*, vol. 7: *From Nadir Shah to the Islamic Republic* (Cambridge, 1991), p. 726.

122. Lambton, *Qajar Persia*, p. 292.

123. Perhaps 150 Europeans lived in Iran in the mid nineteenth century; still only 800 in 1890. Ibid., p. 207.

CHAPTER 6: THE LIMITS OF EMPIRE

1. See H. J. Mackinder, 'The Geographical Pivot of History', *Geographical Journal* 23, 4 (1904), pp. 421–37.

2. *The Times*, 15 Sept. 1875, quoted in N. Pelcovits, *Old China Hands and the Foreign Office* (New York, 1948), p. 101.

3. Frederick Jackson Turner, 'The Significance of the Frontier in American History' (1893), reprinted in his *The Frontier in American History* (New York, 1920).

4. For a characteristic statement, B. Kidd, *The Control of the Tropics* (London, 1898).

5. Naito Konan's article 'Shosekai' ('Small World') was published in 1888. For a study of his views, J. Fogel, *Politics and Sinology: The Case of Naito Konan, 1866–1934* (Cambridge, Mass., 1984), pp. 41, 50.

6. J. Bryce, *The Relations between the Advanced and Backward Peoples* (Oxford, 1902), pp. 6–7.

7. Ibid., p. 13.

8. C. N. Pearson, *National Life and Character* (London, 1893), pp. 89–90.

9. See J. Forbes Munro, *Maritime Enterprise and Empire: Sir William Mackinnon and his Business Network, 1823–1893* (Woodbridge, 2003), ch. 7.

10. For Rhodes's business empire, C. W. Newbury, *The Diamond Ring* (Oxford, 1989).

11. For the crisis in Egypt, R. E. Robinson and J. A. Gallagher, *Africa and the Victorians* (London, 1961), chs. 4, 5; A. Schölch, *'Egypt for the Egyptians': The Socio-Political Crisis in Egypt, 1879–1882* (London, 1981); J. R. I. Cole, *Colonialism and Revolution in the Middle East: The Social and Cultural Origins of the 'Urabi Movement* (Princeton, 1993).

12. For a fierce statement of this view by an ex-viceroy and British cabinet minister, B. Mallett, *Thomas George, Earl of Northbrook: A Memoir* (London, 1908), pp. 169–70.

13. For a brilliant review of the conference and its significance, J.-L. Vellut, *Un centenaire 1885–1985: Les Relations Europe–Afrique au crible d'une commemoration* (Leiden, 1992).

14. M. Klein, *Slavery and Colonial Rule in French West Africa* (Cambridge, 1998), pp. 78–93.

15. See A. S. Kanya-Forstner, *The Conquest of the Western Sudan* (Cambridge, 1969).

16. See J. F. Munro, *Africa and the International Economy 1880–1960* (London, 1976), p. 67.

17. For Goldie's career and the Royal Niger Company, J. Flint, *Sir George Goldie and the Making of Nigeria* (London, 1960); D. Wellesley, *Sir George Goldie: A Memoir* (London, 1934).

18. Note by Goldie, 1 Jan. 1897, Rhodes House Library, Oxford, MSS Afr. S. 88, Scarbrough MSS 4.

19. Goldie to Royal Niger Company council, 6 Feb. 1897, ibid.

20. A. Hochschild, *King Leopold's Ghost* (London, 1999), p. 23, for this calculation and its basis.

21. S. H. Nelson, *Colonialism in the Congo Basin, 1880–1940* (Athens, O., 1994), pp. 112–16. The new regime retained Leopold's practice of parcelling out the Congo among concessionaire companies.

22. D. Beach, *War and Politics in Zimbabwe 1840–1900* (Harare, 1986); A. Keppel-Jones, *Rhodes and Rhodesia: The White Conquest of Zimbabwe* (Montreal, 1983).

23. For a brilliant discussion of the disorienting effects of African travel on Europeans, J. Fabian, *Out of Our Minds: Reason and Madness in the Exploration of Central Africa* (London, 2000).

24. William H. Schneider, *An Empire for the Masses: The French Popular Image of Africa, 1870–1900* (Westport, Conn., and London, 1982), pp. 6–7.

25. Kanya-Forstner, *Conquest*, p. 263. Calculated at FF25=£1.

26. C. M. Andrew, *Théophile Delcassé and the Making of the Entente Cordiale* (London, 1968), pp. 94–8.

27. Ibid., p. 92.

28. R. Waller, 'The Maasai and the British: The Origins of an Alliance, 1895–1905', *Journal of African History* 17, 4 (1976), pp. 529–53.

29. Bill Nasson, *The South African War 1899–1902* (London, 1999) and his *Abram Esau's War: A Black South African War in the Cape 1899–1902* (Cambridge, 1991); P. Warwick, *Black People and the South African War 1899–1902* (Cambridge, 1983).

30. *Parliamentary Debates, Lords*, 4th Series, vol. 30, p. 701 (14 Feb. 1895).

31. J. Riis, *How the Other Half Lives* (New York, 1890).

32. G. Brechin, *Imperial San Francisco: Urban Power, Earthly Ruin* (Berkeley, Los Angeles and London, 1999), ch. 3.

33. See N. Harper, *A Great and Powerful Friend* (St Lucia, 1987), ch. 1.

34. Address as president of the American Historical Association, 1910, *American Historical Review* 16, 2 (1911), pp. 217–33.

35. R. E. Quirk, *An Affair of Honor: Woodrow Wilson and the Occupation of Vera Cruz* (New York, 1962).

36. H. and M. Sprout, *Towards a New Order of Sea Power* (Princeton, 1940), p. 288.

37. W. Tilchin, *Theodore Roosevelt and the British Empire* (New York, 1997), p. 236.

38. G. N. Curzon, *Russia in Central Asia in 1889* (London, 1889), p. 316.

39. B. H. Sumner, *A Survey of Russian History* (London, 1944), p. 362.

40. G. Chisholm, *Handbook of Commercial Geography* (4th edn, London, 1908), pp. 583, 609.

41. By 1914, 25 per cent of French foreign investment had been placed in Russia. R. E. Cameron, *France and the Economic Development of Europe 1800–1914* (Princeton, 1961), p. 486.

42. D. Moon, 'Peasant Migration and the Settlement of Russia's Frontiers, 1550–1917', *Historical Journal* 40, 4 (1997), pp. 859–93, esp. pp. 867–8.

43. D. W. Treadgold, *The Great Siberian Migration* (Princeton, 1957), p. 13. By 1917 the figure was 7 million.

44. M. Joffe, 'Diamond in the Rough: The State, Entrepreneurs and Turkestan's Hidden Resources in Late Imperial Russia', in M. Siefert (ed.), *Extending the Borders of Russian History* (London, 2003), p. 185.

45. The Russian population of the Russian Far East was 10,000 in 1860 and 300,000 by 1900. D. Dallin, *The Rise of Russia in Asia* (London, 1949), p. 14.

46. See J. J. Stephan, *The Russian Far East: A History* (Stanford, 1996).

47. Brilliantly discussed in A. Rieber, 'Persistent Factors in Russian Foreign Policy', in H. Ragsdale (ed.), *Imperial Russian Foreign Policy* (Cambridge, 1993).

48. Observations by Lord Sanderson, 21 Feb. 1907, in G. P. Gooch and H.

Temperley (eds.), *British Documents on the Origins of the War, 1898–1914* (12 vols., London, 1927–38), vol. 3, p. 430.

49. I. H. Nish, *The Anglo-Japanese Alliance* (London, 1966).

50. The classic analysis is still G. Monger, *The End of Isolation* (London, 1963).

51. P. Mathias and M. M. Postan (eds.), *The Cambridge Economic History of Europe*, vol. 7: *The Industrial Economies: Capital, Labour and Enterprise*, pt 1: *Britain, France, Germany and Scandinavia* (Cambridge, 1978), p. 555.

52. Germany's population in 1911, 65 million; Russia-in-Europe, 136 million.

53. For Bismarck's views on colonial expansion, O. Pflanze, *Bismarck and the Development of Germany*, vol. 3: *The Period of Fortification, 1880–1898* (Princeton, 1990), ch. 5.

54. For official uncertainty about what Germany's world interests really were, W. Mommsen, *Imperial Germany 1867–1918* (1990; Eng. trans. London, 1995), p. 82.

55. See I. L. D. Forbes, 'German Informal Imperialism in South America before 1914', *Economic History Review*, New Series, 31, 3 (1978), pp. 396–8.

56. C. Peters, *England and the English* (Eng. trans. London, 1904), p. 388.

57. J. Marseille, *Empire coloniale et capitalisme française* (Paris, 1984), p. 40.

58. E. H. Jenkin, *A History of the French Navy* (London, 1973), pp. 307–9.

59. Andrew, *Delcassé*, pp. 105ff.

60. See G. W. Gong, *The 'Standard of Civilisation' in International Society* (Oxford, 1984).

61. See W. Fischer and R. M. McInnis (eds.), *The Emergence of a World Economy 1500–1914*, pt 2: *1850–1914* (Wiesbaden, 1986).

62. A. J. H. Latham and L. Neal, 'The International Market in Wheat and Rice, 1868–1914', *Economic History Review*, New Series, 36, 2 (1983), pp. 260–75.

63. W. Woodruff, *The Impact of Western Man: A Study of Europe's Role in the World Economy 1750–1960* (London, 1966), p. 313. Woodruff's estimate of £7.6 billion may be compared with one of £8.3 billion in C. Issawi, 'Middle East Economic Development 1815–1914', in A. Hourani, P. S. Khoury and M. C. Wilson (eds.), *The Modern Middle East* (London, 1993), p. 183.

64. For a lucid explanation, S. B. Saul, *Studies in British Overseas Trade 1870–1914* (Liverpool, 1960), ch. 3, 'The Pattern of Settlements'.

65. Ibid., pp. 203–7.

66. C. Lipson, *Standing Guard: Protecting Foreign Capital in the Nineteenth and Twentieth Centuries* (London, 1985), ch. 2.

67. J. R. Scobie, 'Buenos Aires as a Commercial-Bureaucratic City', *American Historical Review* 77, 4 (1972), p. 1045.

68. R. Chandarvarkar, *The Origins of Industrial Capitalism in India* (Cambridge, 1994), p. 23.

69. C. Trocki, *Singapore: Wealth, Power and the Culture of Control* (London, 2006), chs. 1, 2.

70. O. Ruhen, *Port of Melbourne 1835–1876* (North Melbourne, 1976); F. Broeze, *Island Nation* (London, 1998).

71. See S. Jackson, *The Sassoons* (London, 1968).

72. See I. Stone, *The Global Export of Capital from Great Britain, 1865–1914: A Statistical Survey* (Basingstoke, 1999).

73. League of Nations, *The Network of World Trade* (Geneva, 1942), p. 84.

74. See M. de Cecco, *Money and Empire* (Oxford, 1974).

75. For the best description, R. Michie, *The City of London: Continuity and Change, 1850–1990* (Basingstoke, 1992); D. Kynaston, *The City of London: Golden Years 1890–1914* (London, 1995).

76. Speech in Canada (?1913). Bodleian Library, Robert Brand Papers, box 26.

77. N. Angell, *The Great Illusion* (London, 1911).

78. See I. Phimister, *Wangi Kolia* (Johannesburg, 1994) for a graphic account of labour conditions on the Wankie coalfield in Southern Rhodesia (Zimbabwe).

79. Revenue from customs duties equalled 27.6 per cent of the value of imports in the United States in 1900. The figure for Britain, France and Germany was between 5 and 8.8 per cent. See A. Stein, 'The Hegemon's Dilemma: Great Britain, the United States and the International Economic Order', *International Organization* 38, 2 (1984), pp. 355–86.

80. R. Lindert, *Key Currencies and Gold, 1900–1930* (Princeton, 1969), p. 121.

81. See J. W. Burrow, *The Crisis of Reason* (London, 2000), ch. 3.

82. Ibid., p. 96.

83. See, for example, H. H. Risley, *The People of India* (London, 1908). By the time this was published Risley was one of the most senior officials in the government of India. For the Russian case, A. Jersild, *Orientalism and Empire* (Montreal, 2002).

84. Burrow, *Crisis*, p. 103.

85. G. W. Stocking, *Victorian Anthropology* (New York, 1987), p. 236.

86. For the use of this expression by British officialdom, A. Seal, *The Emergence of Indian Nationalism* (Cambridge, 1968), p. 15.

87. See S. Dubow, *Racial Segregation and the Origins of Apartheid in South Africa 1919–1936* (London, 1989), pp. 22–3.

88. Greta Jones, *Social Darwinism and English Thought* (London, 1980), p. 150.

89. See T. Metcalf, *Ideologies of the Raj* (Cambridge, 1995), ch. 3.

90. See the argument in J. MacKenzie, *Orientalism: History, Theory and the Arts* (Manchester, 1995).

91. S. Bayly, *Caste, Society and Politics in India* (Cambridge, 1999), p. 101; for a contrary view that holds the British responsible for entrenching caste in modern India, N. Dirks, *Castes of Mind* (Princeton, 2001).

92. See T. Raychaudhuri, *Europe Reconsidered: Perceptions of the West in Nineteenth Century Bengal* (Oxford, 1989).

93. For an autobiographical account, S. Banerjea, *A Nation in Making* (London, 1925).

94. The key work here was M. G. Ranade, *The Rise of the Maratha Power* (Eng. trans. Bombay, 1900).

95. See P. M. Holt, *The Mahdist State in the Sudan 1881–1898* (Oxford, 1958).

96. For a discussion of these themes, A. Hourani, *Arabic Thought in the Liberal Age 1798–1939* (London, 1962; repr. Cambridge, 1983); F. Robinson, *Islam and Muslim History in South Asia* (New Delhi, 2000), pp. 59–78 and ch. 11; M. F. Laffan, *Islamic Nationhood and Colonial Indonesia* (London, 2003).

97. D. Robinson, *Paths of Accommodation: Muslim Societies and French Colonial Authorities in Senegal and Mauretania, 1880–1920* (Athens, O., and Oxford, 2000), pp. 231–3.

98. Hourani, *Arabic Thought*, pp. 200–203.

99. See D. Lelyveld, *Aligarh's First Generation: Muslim Solidarity in British India* (Princeton, 1978).

100. See Laffan, *Islamic Nationhood*, ch. 7.

101. The original English version has been reprinted in A. J. Parel (ed.), *Gandhi: 'Hind Swaraj' and Other Writings* (Cambridge, 1997).

102. A. Chowdhury, *The Frail Hero and Virile History: Gender and the Politics of Culture in Colonial Bengal* (New Delhi, 2001), pp. 14, 17, 40, 44–5.

103. Ibid., p. 152.

104. For Blyden's career, H. R. Lynch, *Edward Wilmot Blyden: Pan-Negro Patriot* (Oxford, 1967).

105. Ibid., p. 219.

106. Ibid., p. 216.

107. For Blyden's rejection of Booker T. Washington as a 'race amalgamator', L. R. Harlan (ed.), *The Booker T. Washington Papers*, vol. 3: *1889–1895* (London, 1974), p. 497.

108. See J. D. Frodsham (ed.), *The First Chinese Embassy to the West: The Journals of Kuo Sung-T'ao, Lin His-hung and Chan Te-yi* (Oxford, 1974), p. xxvi.

109. Y. P. Hao, *The Commercial Revolution in Nineteenth-Century China: The Rise of Sino-Western Mercantile Capitalism* (Berkeley and London, 1986), p. 355.

110. See the fascinating account of the Shanghai 'jubilee' procession in B. Goodman, 'Improvisations on a Semi-Colonial Theme, or How to Read a Celebration of Transnational Urban Community', *Journal of Asian Studies* 59, 4 (2000), pp. 889–926.

111. For Manchu–Han relations, E. J. Rhoads, *Manchus and Han* (Seattle, 2000).

112. R. K. I. Quested, *'Matey' Imperialists?: The Tsarist Russians in Manchuria, 1895–1917* (Hong Kong, 1982), pp. 21–2.

113. Ibid., p. 59.

114. See L. K. Young, *British Policy in China, 1895–1902* (Oxford, 1970).

115. Nish, *The Anglo-Japanese Alliance.*

116. For Sun's career, H. Z. Schiffrin, *Sun Yat-sen: Reluctant Revolutionary* (Boston, 1980).

117. See E. Rawski, 'Re-envisioning the Qing: The Significance of the Qing Period in Chinese History', *Journal of Asian Studies* 55, 4 (1996), p. 839.

118. R. Bin Wong, *China Transformed: Historical Change and the Limits of European Experience* (Ithaca, NY, 1997), p. 163.

119. George Morrison to Valentine Chirol, 8 Sept. 1906, in Lo Hui-min (ed.), *The Correspondence of G. E. Morrison* (2 vols., Cambridge, 1976), vol. 1, p. 375; J. O. P. Bland, *Recent Events and Present Policies in China* (London, 1912).

120. F. H. H. King, *The Hong Kong Bank in the Period of Imperialism and War, 1875–1918* (Cambridge, 1988), p. 348.

121. C.-K. Leung, *China: Railway Patterns and National Goals* (Hong Kong, 1980), p. 39.

122. C. Tsuzuki, *The Pursuit of Power in Modern Japan 1825–1995* (Oxford, 2000), p. 104.

123. P. Duus, R. Myers and M. Peattie (eds.), *Japanese Informal Empire in China, 1895–1937* (Princeton, 1989), p. xxxiii.

124. A. Iriye, *Pacific Estrangement: Japanese and American Expansion, 1897–1911* (Cambridge, Mass., 1972), p. 221.

125. J. O. P. Bland to C. Addis, 23 Sept. 1907, Thomas Fisher Library, University of Toronto, J. O. P. Bland MSS, box 23.

126. T. Yokoyama, *Japan in the Victorian Mind* (Basingstoke, 1987), ch. 8.

127. A. Iriye, 'Japan's Drive to Great Power Status', in M. B. Jansen (ed.),

The Cambridge History of Japan, vol. 5: *The Nineteenth Century* (Cambridge, 1989), pp. 738ff.

128. A. Waswo, *Modern Japanese Society, 1868–1994* (Oxford, 1996), p. 60.

129. See K. Sugihara, 'Patterns of Asia's Integration into the World Economy, 1888–1913', in Fischer and McInnis (eds.), *World Economy*, pt 2.

130. Tsuzuki, *Pursuit of Power*, p. 195.

131. C. Howe, *The Origins of Japanese Trade Supremacy* (London, 1996), pp. 148, 157, 197–9, for Japan's pre-war difficulties.

132. J. Ch'en, *Yuan Shih-kai, 1859–1916* (London, 1961), ch. 9.

133. M. E. Meeker, *A Nation of Empire: The Ottoman Legacy of Turkish Modernity* (Berkeley, Los Angeles and London, 2002), pp. 276–7.

134. See Eugene Rogan, *Frontiers of the State in the Late Ottoman Empire: Transjordan 1850–1921* (Cambridge, 1999).

135. See D. Quataert, 'The Age of Reforms, 1812–1914', in H. Inalcik with D. Quataert (eds.), *An Economic and Social History of the Ottoman Empire 1300–1914* (Cambridge, 1994), p. 872.

136. Ibid., pp. 910–28.

137. J. McCarthy, *Death and Exile: The Ethnic Cleansing of Ottoman Muslims, 1821–1922* (Princeton, 1995), pp. 135–6.

138. Quoted in M. S. Hanioglu, *Preparations for a Revolution: The Young Turks, 1902–1908* (Oxford, 2001), p. 65.

139. This account is based on E. Abrahamian, *Iran between Two Revolutions* (Princeton, 1982), pp. 57–111.

140. A. T. Wilson, *South West Persia: Letters and Diary of a Young Political Officer, 1907–1914* (London, 1942), p. 189.

141. Memo by Sir E. Grey to Russian ambassador, 10 June 1914, in Gooch and Temperley (eds.), *British Documents*, vol. 10, pp. 798–800; Buchanan to Grey, 21 June 1914, ibid., pp. 804–5.

142. Memo by Sazonov, ibid., pp. 816–20.

143. W. M. Shuster, *The Strangling of Persia: A Record of European Diplomacy and Oriental Intrigue* (London, 1912).

CHAPTER 7: TOWARDS THE CRISIS OF THE WORLD, 1914–1942

1. The classic diagnosis of this atavistic ethos was by the Austrian economist J. A. Schumpeter, in his essay on the 'Sociology of Imperialism' (1919). See the English translation in F. M. Sweezy (ed.), *Imperialism and Social Classes* (London, 1951).

2. The best contemporary analysis is H. Wickham Steed, *The Hapsburg*

Monarchy (London, 1913). Steed spent ten years in Austria–Hungary as *The Times*'s correspondent, and was later foreign editor and editor of the paper.

3. H. Strachan, *The First World War: To Arms* (Oxford, 2001), p. 62.

4. The literature on the outbreak of the war is colossal. The calculations of the great-power governments can be followed in V. Berghahn, *Germany and the Approach of War in 1914* (London, 1974); J. Keiger, *France and the Origins of the First World War* (London, 1983); D. Lieven, *Russia and the Origins of the First World War* (London, 1983); S. Williamson, *Austria–Hungary and the Origins of the First World War* (London, 1991); Z. Steiner, *Britain and the Origins of the First World War* (London, 1977). I. Geiss, *The July Crisis: The Outbreak of the First World War: Selected Documents* (London, 1967) provides a detailed account of the final approach to war. Strachan, *The First World War* offers a superb synthesis.

5. Riezler's *Grundzüge der Weltpolitik in der Gegenwart* was published in Munich in 1914.

6. See V. G. Liulevicius, *War Land on the Eastern Front: Culture, National Identity and German Occupation in the First World War* (Cambridge, 2000); A. Zweig, *The Case of Sergeant Grischa* (Eng. trans. New York, 1928) is a fascinating semi-fictional portrait of 'Ober Ost'. For a general account of the eastern war, N. Stone, *The Eastern Front 1914–1917* (London, 1975).

7. B. Pares, *The Fall of the Russian Monarchy: A Study of the Evidence* (New York, 1939), p. 476.

8. H. Seton-Watson, *The Russian Empire 1801–1917* (Oxford, 1967), p. 653.

9. How real these fears were can be seen from the correspondence of Lord Milner, then the chief director of British grand strategy. The similarity with the 'heartland' ideas of Halford Mackinder (set out after the war in his *Democratic Ideals and Reality* (London, 1919)) was not accidental: Mackinder was part of Milner's circle.

10. The deliberations of the War Cabinet's Eastern Committee can be followed in J. Darwin, *Britain, Egypt and the Middle East: Imperial Policy in the Aftermath of War* (London, 1981), ch. 6.

11. The details can be followed in W. R. Louis, *Great Britain and Germany's Lost Colonies* (Oxford, 1967).

12. For the crisis in Egypt and its outcome, E. Kedourie, 'Saad Zaghloul and the British', in his *The Chatham House Version* (London, 1970); Darwin, *Britain, Egypt and the Middle East*, chs. 3, 4, 5; J. Beinin and Z. Lockman, '1919: Labour Upsurge and National Revolution', in A. Hourani, P. S. Khoury and M. C. Wilson (eds.), *The Modern Middle East* (London, 1993), pp. 395–428.

13. A. Hourani, *Arabic Thought in the Liberal Age 1798–1939* (London, 1962; repr. Cambridge, 1983), p. 276.

14. See M. Llewellyn Smith, *Ionian Vision: Greece in Asia Minor 1919–1922* (London, 1973).

15. For an account of the crisis, D. Walder, *The Chanak Affair* (London, 1969).

16. The human consequences of the war and the treaty are discussed in J. McCarthy, *Death and Exile: The Ethnic Cleansing of Ottoman Muslims 1821–1922* (Princeton, 1995), ch. 7.

17. A British withdrawal from Iraq altogether was actively debated in the cabinet in 1923. The prime minister of the day, Andrew Bonar Law, was in favour of going.

18. For Atatürk's state-building, B. Lewis, *The Emergence of Modern Turkey* (London, 1961); A. Mango, *Atatürk* (London, 1999); M. E. Meeker, *A Nation of Empire: The Ottoman Legacy of Turkish Modernity* (Berkeley, Los Angeles and London, 2002). For Reza Shah's reconstruction of Iran, E. Abrahamian, *Iran between Two Revolutions* (Princeton, 1982), pp. 118–65. See A. T. Wilson, *Persia* (London, 1932), p. 307, for the huge increase in the value of oil exports. M. E. Yapp, *The Near East since the First World War* (London, 1991) is an excellent general account.

19. For the intensification of Indian Muslim resentment, F. C. R. Robinson, *Separatism among Indian Muslims: The Politics of the United Provinces Muslims, 1860–1923* (Cambridge, 1974); Jacob M. Landau, *The Politics of Pan-Islam: Ideology and Organization* (Oxford, 1990), pp. 182–215; M. Hasan, *Mahomed Ali: Ideology and Politics* (Delhi, 1981). Mahomed Ali was interned for sedition by the British until 1919.

20. The best account of Amritsar is now N. Collet, *The Butcher of Amritsar* (London, 2006) – despite its colourful title, a subtle and scholarly study.

21. For Gandhi's early political career, and the movement of 1919, J. M. Brown, *Gandhi's Rise to Power* (Cambridge, 1972); R. Kumar (ed.), *Essays in Gandhian Politics* (Oxford, 1971).

22. D. A. Low, 'The Government of India and the First Non-Cooperation Campaign, 1920–22', in Kumar (ed.), *Gandhian Politics*; D. Page, *Prelude to Partition: The Indian Muslims and the Imperial System of Control 1920–1932* (Delhi, 1982).

23. These nervous manoeuvrings can be followed in B. R. Tomlinson, *The Indian National Congress and the Raj* (London, 1976).

24. See Zhang Yongjin, *China in the International System, 1918–1920: The Middle Kingdom at the Periphery* (London, 1991).

25. A. J. Nathan, *Peking Politics 1918–1923* (London, 1976).

26. A. Waldron, 'The Warlord: Twentieth Century Chinese Understandings of Violence, Militarism and Imperialism', *American Historical Review* 96, 4 (1991), pp. 1073–1100; for an overview, Hsi-Sheng Ch'i, *Warlord Politics*

in China (Stanford, 1976); for a provincial case study, Angus W. McDonald, *The Urban Origins of Rural Revolution: Elites and the Masses in Hunan Province, China, 1911–1927* (Berkeley, Los Angeles and London, 1978).

27. H. B. Morse and H. F. MacNair, *Far Eastern International Relations* (2nd edn, Cambridge, Mass., 1931), p. 581.

28. Ibid., pp. 581–3.

29. See Jerome B. Grieder, *Intellectuals and the State in Modern China* (New York, 1981), pp. 214–26.

30. Yongjin, *China in the International System*, p. 184.

31. For a classic expression of this view, see memo by Sir B. Alston (British minister in Peking), 1 Aug. 1920, in R. Butler, J. P. T. Bury and M. Lambert (eds.), *Documents on British Foreign Policy 1919–1939*, 1st Series, vol. 14 (London, 1966), pp. 81–6.

32. Y. T. Matsusaka, *The Making of Japanese Manchuria 1904–1932* (Cambridge, Mass., 2001), pp. 242ff.

33. C. Tsuzuki, *The Pursuit of Power in Modern Japan 1825–1995* (Oxford, 2000), pp. 210, 217.

34. Matsusaka, *Japanese Manchuria*, p. 206.

35. Tsuzuki, *Pursuit of Power*, pp. 206, 236–7.

36. See C. Howe, *The Origins of Japanese Trade Supremacy* (London, 1996), p. 381, for the effects of Chinese boycotts on Japan's textile exports.

37. J. O. P. Bland, *China: The Pity of It* (London, 1931), p. 40.

38. For Sun's career, H. Z. Schiffrin, *Sun Yat-sen: Reluctant Revolutionary* (Boston, 1980).

39. For the dangerous lives of these 400 '*sovietniki*', see D. N. Jacobs, *Borodin: Stalin's Man in China* (Cambridge, Mass., 1981).

40. For an account of this that stresses the limited influence of the Communist Party, Ming K. Chan, 'The Realpolitik and Legacy of Labour Activism and Popular Mobilisation in 1920s Greater Canton', in M. Leutner, R. Felber, M. L. Titarenko and A. M. Grigoriev (eds.), *The Chinese Revolution in the 1920s: Between Triumph and Disaster* (London, 2002), pp. 187–221.

41. For an outstanding study of this process, Hans van der Ven, *War and Nationalism in China 1925–1945* (London, 2003), ch. 2.

42. Ch'i, *Warlord Politics*, pp. 223–4; Waldron, 'The Warlord', pp. 1075ff.

43. For British policy towards the challenge posed by Chinese nationalism, E. K. S. Fung, *The Diplomacy of Imperial Retreat* (Hong Kong, 1991); Chan Lan Kit-Ching, *China, Britain and Hong Kong 1895–1945* (Hong Kong, 1991). Not for the last time, there was friction between the views of the colonial governor in Hong Kong and his diplomatic colleagues in Peking and London.

44. Van der Ven, *War and Nationalism*, ch. 2.

45. R. Overy, *The Dictators: Hitler's Germany, Stalin's Russia* (London, 2004), p. 445.

46. Jeremy Smith, *The Bolsheviks and the National Question 1917–1923* (London, 1999), p. 98.

47. See R. Ullman, *The Anglo-Soviet Accord* (London, 1972), chs. 10, 11.

48. The classic account of this process is R. Pipes, *The Formation of the Soviet Union: Communism and Nationalism 1917–1923* (rev. edn, Cambridge, Mass., 1964).

49. For a description of this phase of his career, see R. Service, *Stalin* (London, 2004).

50. Stalin to Lenin, 22 Sept. 1922, in J. Smith, *Bolsheviks and the National Question*, p. 183.

51. Ibid., pp. 93–4.

52. Stalin to Lenin, 22 Sept. 1922.

53. See F. P. Walters, *The History of the League of Nations* (London, 1952) for a general account of the League.

54. B. Eichengreen, 'Twentieth-Century US Foreign Financial Relations', in S. L. Engerman and R. E. Gallman (eds.), *The Cambridge Economic History of the United States*, vol. 3: *The Twentieth Century* (Cambridge, 2000), pp. 476–7.

55. See D. F. Fleming, *The United States and the League of Nations 1918–1920* (New York, 1932), pp. 122–43.

56. For the views of the highly influential political geographer Isaiah Bowman, N. Smith, *American Empire: Roosevelt's Geographer and the Prelude to Globalization* (London, 2003), pp. 184–8.

57. See A. Iriye, *The Cambridge History of American Foreign Relations*, vol. 3: *The Globalising of America* (Cambridge, 1995).

58. See C. Thorne, *The Limits of Power: The West, the League and the Far Eastern Crisis of 1931–1933* (London, 1972).

59. See B. McKercher, *Transition of Power: Britain's Loss of Global Pre-eminence to the United States 1930–1945* (Cambridge, 1999).

60. Overy, *Dictators*, p. 398.

61. Service, *Stalin*, p. 325.

62. Overy, *Dictators*, p. 561.

63. J. Haslam, *The Soviet Union and the Threat from the East* (London, 1992), p. 28: the USSR had 200,000 troops in eastern Siberia by 1933.

64. J. Spence, *In Search of Modern China* (London, 1990), p. 382.

65. American policy can be followed in S. K. Hornbeck, *The Diplomacy of Frustration: The Manchurian Crisis of 1931–1933 as Revealed in the Papers of Stanley K. Hornbeck* (Stanford, 1981).

66. Van der Ven, *War and Nationalism*, p. 131.

67. A. Best, *British Intelligence and the Japanese Challenge in Asia 1914–1941* (Basingstoke, 2002), p. 89.

68. See Matsusaka, *Japanese Manchuria*, pp. 281–8.

69. For a recent analysis, ibid., pp. 378–9.

70. See Van der Ven, *War and Nationalism*, pp. 188ff.

71. See Tim Rooth, *British Protectionism and the International Economy: Overseas Commercial Policy in the 1930s* (Cambridge, 2002).

72. For the German *Grossraumwirtschaft* in Eastern Europe after 1934, A. Basch, *The Danube Basin and the German Economic Sphere* (London, 1944), chs. 11, 16; E. A. Radice, 'The German Economic Programme in Eastern Europe', in M. Kaiser (ed.), *The Economic History of Eastern Europe 1919–1975* (Oxford, 1986), vol. 2, pp. 300–301.

73. Cotton and silk goods made up over half of Japan's exports. Howe, *Trade Supremacy*, p. 121.

74. Ibid., pp. 215–18; I. Inkster, *Japanese Industrialisation: Historical and Cultural Perspectives* (London, 2001), pp. 97–116.

75. For a general study, H. James, *The End of Globalisation* (London, 2001).

76. See L. Viola, *Peasant Rebels under Stalin: Collectivization and the Culture of Peasant Resistance* (New York, 1996).

77. See J. Z. Muller, *The Other God that Failed* (Princeton, 1987); H. Lehmann and J. J. Sheehan (eds.), *An Interrupted Past: German-Speaking Refugee Historians in the United States after 1933* (Cambridge, 1991) for the intellectual career of the sociologist Hans Freyer; H. Lehmann and J. van H. Melton, *Paths of Continuity: Central European Historiography from the 1930s to the 1950s* (Cambridge, 1994) for Nazi sympathies among historians; M. Malia, *Russia under Western Eyes* (Cambridge, Mass., 1999), pp. 325ff.

78. See H. Harootunian, *Overcome by Modernity: History, Culture and Community in Inter-war Japan* (Princeton, 2000) for a fascinating study of these anxieties.

79. These ideas are the subject of John Lonsdale's essay 'The Moral Economy of Mau Mau: Wealth, Poverty and Civic Virtue in Kikuyu Political Thought', in B. Berman and J. Lonsdale, *Unhappy Valley: Conflict in Kenya and Africa*, book 2: *Ethnicity and Violence* (London, 1992).

80. J. Kenyatta, *Facing Mount Kenya* (London, 1938), p. 318.

81. See for example, M. J. Bonn, *The Crumbling of Empire: The Disintegration of World Economy* (London, 1938).

82. For the mood of the 'Shanghailanders', R. Bickers, *Empire Made Me: An Englishman Adrift in Shanghai* (London, 2003), chs. 7, 9.

83. See his letter to Gandhi, 28 Apr. 1938, in J. Nehru, *A Bunch of Old Letters* (Bombay, 1958), pp. 276–7.

84. An Anglo-Egyptian treaty on these lines was eventually signed in 1936.

85. The tortuous movements of British policy and Indian politics can be followed in Page, *Prelude to Partition* and Tomlinson, *The Indian National Congress and the Raj*.

86. N. Tarling (ed.), *The Cambridge History of Southeast Asia*, vol. 3: *From c.1800 to the 1930s* (pbk edn, Cambridge, 1999), pp. 269–70, 276. For 'political' policing in India, D. Arnold, *Police Power and Colonial Rule: Madras 1859–1947* (Delhi, 1986), ch. 6.

87. A. D. Roberts, 'The Imperial Mind', in A. D. Roberts (ed.), *The Cambridge History of Africa*, vol. 7: *From 1905 to 1940* (Cambridge, 1986), pp. 24–76.

88. For this approach at work in inter-war Nigeria, see the memorandum of September 1939 by its governor, Sir Bernard Bourdillon, in A. F. Madden and J. Darwin (eds.), *The Dependent Empire 1900–1948*, vol. 7: *Colonies, Protectorates and Mandates: Select Documents on the Constitutional History of the British Empire and Commonwealth* (Westport, Conn., 1994), pp. 705–9.

89. L. A. Sherwani, *Speeches, Writings and Statements of Iqbal* (Lahore, 1944), pp. 3–26.

90. Published in 1923. Savarkar became president of the Hindu Mahasabha in 1937.

91. S. Bayly, *Caste, Society and Politics in India* (Cambridge, 1999), p. 262, n. 65.

92. This idea was first set out in a famous essay by J. Gallagher and R. Robinson, 'The Imperialism of Free Trade', *Economic History Review*, New Series, 6, 1 (1953), pp. 1–15.

93. This point is made clear in *Mein Kampf*.

94. This judgement was made in the authoritative journal of American business. See *Fortune*, July 1940, p. 136.

95. Quoted in G. L. Weinberg, *A World at War: A Global History of World War Two* (Cambridge, 1994), p. 118.

96. E. Staley, 'The Myth of the Continents', published in *Foreign Affairs*, Apr. 1941; repr. in H. Weigert and V. Stefansson (eds.), *The Compass of the World* (London, 1943).

97. See A. Iriye, *China and Japan in the Global Setting* (Cambridge, Mass., 1992), pp. 78–80.

98. Y. Kibata, *Anglo-Japanese Relations in the 1930s and 1940s* (London, 1982).

99. A Iriye, 'The Failure of Military Expansionism', in S. Large (ed.), *Showa Japan: Political, Economic and Social History 1926–1989*, vol. 1: *1926–1941* (London, 1998), pp. 213–15, 223, 226–7.

100. I. Cowman, *Dominion or Decline: Anglo-American Naval Relations in the Pacific 1937–1941* (Oxford, 1996), pp. 85, 88, 93–4.

101. M. Roseman, *The Villa, the Lake, the Meeting: Wannsee and the Final Solution* (London, 2004), p. 107.

102. Ibid., p. 101.

CHAPTER 8: EMPIRE DENIED

1. The disorientation is brilliantly evoked in Czeslaw Milosz, *The Captive Mind* (1953; pbk edn Harmondsworth, 1980), pp. 26–7.

2. L. Barnes (Harmondsworth, 1944).

3. This was the object of W. K. Hancock, *Argument of Empire*, published as a paperback in both Britain and America in 1942. For the wider scene, Suke Wolton, *Lord Hailey, the Colonial Office and the Politics of Race and Empire in the Second World War: The Loss of White Prestige* (London, 2000).

4. See O. A. Westad, *Cold War and Revolution: Soviet–American Rivalry and the Origins of the Chinese Civil War* (New York, 1993), pp. 177–8.

5. See D. C. Engerman, *Modernization from the Other Shore* (Cambridge, Mass., 2003), pp. 262–9.

6. See H. W. van den Doel, *Het Rijk van Insulinde* (Amsterdam, 1996), pp. 284, 286.

7. Quoted in Wm Roger Louis and Ronald Robinson, 'The Imperialism of Decolonisation', *Journal of Imperial and Commonwealth History* 22, 3 (1994), p. 468.

8. For British anxiety at the prospect of 'Modern China's Asiatic Empire' – the subject of an India Office memorandum – Lanxin Xiang, *Recasting the Imperial Far East: Britain and America in China 1945–1950* (Armonk, NY, 1995), p. 32.

9. Westad, *Cold War and Revolution*, pp. 173–4.

10. For the best discussion of these issues, Hans van der Ven, *War and Nationalism in China 1925–1945* (London, 2003), ch. 7.

11. Under the 'May 4th directive' in 1946, land was to be confiscated from landlords and distributed to the peasants. See *Selected Military Writings of Mao Tse-tung* (Peking, 1963), pp. 322–4.

12. C. Howe, *The Origins of Japanese Trade Supremacy* (London, 1996), p. 403.

13. D. Norman (ed.), *Nehru: The First Sixty Years* (2 vols., London, 1965), vol. 2, p. 452.

14. Westad, *Cold War and Revolution*, p. 167.

15. 'The Vasco da Gama epoch' was the striking phrase of K. M. Pannikar. See his *Asia and Western Dominance* (London, 1953), pp. 13–17.

16. See R. Foot and J. Brown (eds.), *Hong Kong's Transitions* (London, 1997).

17. For the full list, *Keesing's Contemporary Archives, 1955*, p. 14181.

18. For the text of these speeches, *Keesing's Contemporary Archives 1955*, pp. 14181ff.; G. Kahin, *The Asian–African Conference at Bandung, Indonesia, April 1955* (Ithaca, NY, 1956).

19. The influential thesis of Chalmers Johnson, *Peasant Nationalism and Communist Power* (Stanford, 1962).

20. See S. Pepper, 'The Political Odyssey of an Intellectual Construct: Peasant Nationalism and the Study of China's Revolutionary History – a Review Essay', *Journal of Asian Studies* 63, 1 (2004), pp. 105–25.

21. O. A. Westad, *Decisive Encounters: The Chinese Civil War 1946–1950* (Stanford, 2003), p. 323.

22. Qiang Zhai, *China and the Vietnam Wars 1950–1975* (Chapel Hill, NC, 2000), pp. 20, 43–9.

23. Ibid., pp. 82–3.

24. Mao's thinking is examined in J. D. Armstrong, *Revolutionary Diplomacy: Chinese Foreign Policy and the United Front Doctrine* (Berkeley and London, 1977), ch. 3.

25. John Dower, *Embracing Defeat: Japan in the Aftermath of World War Two* (Harmondsworth, 1999).

26. Ibid., p. 206.

27. C. Tsuzuki, *The Pursuit of Power in Modern Japan 1825–1995* (Oxford, 2000), p. 357.

28. Dower, *Embracing Defeat*, pp. 249, 560.

29. For a recent study, J. M. Brown, *Nehru* (London, 2004).

30. See J. Rizvi, *Trans-Himalayan Caravans: Merchant Princes and Peasant Traders in Ladakh* (New Delhi, 1999), ch. 1.

31. The standard account is N. Maxwell, *India's China War* (London, 1970).

32. D. Kumar (ed.), *The Cambridge Economic History of India*, vol. 2: *c.1757–c.1970* (Cambridge, 1982), pp. 972–3.

33. Westad, *Decisive Encounters*, p. 320.

34. The course of British policy can be followed in the documents published in H. Tinker (ed.), *Constitutional Relations between Britain and Burma: The Struggle for Independence 1944–1948* (2 vols., London, 1983–4).

35. American policy towards Indonesian nationalism can be followed in *Foreign Relations of the United States [FRUS] 1948*, vol. 6: *The Far East and Australasia* (Washington, 1974), especially Acting Secretary of State to US ambassador in Moscow, 30 Dec. 1948, pp. 613ff; and *FRUS 1949*, vol. 7: *The Far East and Australasia* (Washington, 1975), especially Acting Secretary of State, conversation with Dutch ambassador, 11 Jan. 1949 (threatening end of American economic aid), p. 139.

36. See S. Tonnesson, 'National Divisions in Indochina's Decolonization', in

P. Duara (ed.), *Decolonization: Perspectives from Now and Then* (London, 2004), p. 262; E. Miller, 'Vision, Power and Agency: The Ascent of Ngo Dinh Diem, 1945–54', *Journal of Southeast Asian Studies* 35, 3 (2004), pp. 437–40.

37. Note by Dean Acheson, 20 May 1949, in *FRUS 1949*, vol. 7, p. 29.

38. For analysis of Diem, Miller, 'Vision, Power and Agency'; Tonnesson, 'Indochina's Decolonization'; D. Duncanson, *Government and Revolution in Vietnam* (London, 1968), ch. 5.

39. For Malayan–Indonesian tensions before and after independence, Joseph Chinyong Liow, 'Tunku Abdul Rahman and Malaya's Relations with Indonesia 1957–1960', *Journal of Southeast Asian Studies* 36, 1 (2005), pp. 87–109.

40. For the best account of British policy, W. R. Louis, *The British Empire in the Middle East 1945–1951: Arab Nationalism, the United States, and Postwar Imperialism* (Oxford, 1984).

41. For this estimate, W. B. Fisher, *The Middle East: A Physical, Social and Regional Geography* (London, 1950), p. 249.

42. Ghada Hashem Talhani, *Palestine and Egyptian National Identity* (New York, 1992), p. 9.

43. P. Seale, *The Struggle for Syria: A Study of Post-War Arab Politics 1945–1958* (London, 1966); A. Rathmell, *Secret War in the Middle East: The Covert Struggle for Syria 1949–1961* (London, 1995); P. Seale, 'Syria', in Y. Sadiqh and A. Shlaim (eds.), *The Cold War and the Middle East* (Oxford, 1997); M. Ma'oz, 'Attempts to Create a Political Community in Syria', in I. Pappe and M. Ma'oz, *Middle East Politics and Ideas: The History from Within* (London, 1997).

44. M. J. Cohen, *Palestine and the Great Powers 1945–1948* (Princeton, 1982) is the standard account.

45. H. Batatu, *The Old Social Classes and the Revolutionary Movements of Iraq* (Princeton, 1978), pp. 470–72, 545–66, 680.

46. Talhani, *Palestine*, pp. 48–50.

47. For a recent discussion, see R. McNamara, *Britain, Nasser and the Balance of Power in the Middle East 1952–1967* (London, 2003), ch. 3.

48. This was the judgement of the British ambassador in Cairo in July 1954. See James Jankowski, *Nasser's Egypt, Arab Nationalism and the United Arab Republic* (Boulder, Colo., 2002), p. 56.

49. Rathmell, *Secret War*, ch. 4.

50. The standard account is K. Kyle, *Suez* (London, 1991).

51. For Eden's political fate, D. Carlton, *Anthony Eden* (London, 1981).

52. See Rathmell, *Secret War*, pp. 160–62; Abdulaziz A. al-Sudairi, *A Vision of the Middle East: An Intellectual Biography of Albert Hourani* (London,

1999), pp. 98–100; Fouad Ajami, 'The End of Pan-Arabism', *Foreign Affairs*, winter 1978/9.

53. For the intensification of America's 'special relationship' with Israel from the late 1950s, D. Little, 'The Making of a Special Relationship: The United States and Israel 1957–1968', *International Journal of Middle East Studies* 25, 4 (1993), pp. 563–85; G. M. Steinberg, 'Israel and the United States: Can the Special Relationship Survive the New Strategic Environment?', *Middle East Review of International Affairs* 2, 4 (1998).

54. See A. Sampson, *The Seven Sisters: The Great Oil Companies and the World They Made* (London, 1975).

55. The title of the influential study by Fouad Ajami (London, 1981).

56. For the onset of the crisis, E. Abrahamian, *Iran between Two Revolutions* (Princeton, 1982), ch 5. For Anglo-Iranian, J. Bamberg, *The History of the British Petroleum Company*, vol. 2: *The Anglo-Iranian Years 1928–1954* (Cambridge, 1994).

57. For the American view, see for example Rowntree to McGhee, 20 Dec. 1950, in *FRUS 1950*, vol. 5: *The Near East, South Asia and Africa* (Washington, 1978), p. 634. For British policy, Louis, *The British Empire in the Middle East*, pp. 632–89.

58. For a recent study of the 1953 coup, M. J. Gasiorowski and M. J. Byrne (eds.), *Mohammad Mosaddeq and the 1953 Coup in Iran* (Syracuse, NY, 2004), 'Conclusion'. For landlord dominance and its impact, Abrahamian, *Iran*, pp. 378–82.

59. J. R. T. Wood, *The Welensky Papers* (Durban, 1982) remains the best account.

60. The number of white settlers in Portugal's main African territories in Angola and Mozambique increased from 67,000 in 1940 to 300,000 by 1960. See A. J. Telo, *Economia e Imperio no Portugal Contemporanea* (Lisbon, 1994), p. 267.

61. See the memo by the governor of Nigeria in September 1939, CO 583/244/30453, printed in A. F. Madden and J. Darwin (eds.), *The Dependent Empire 1900–1948*, vol. 7: *Colonies, Protectorates and Mandates: Select Documents on the Constitutional History of the British Empire and Commonwealth* (Westport, Conn., 1994), pp. 705ff.

62. For the origins of this view, D. A. Low and J. Lonsdale, 'Towards the New Order', in D. A. Low and A. Smith (eds.), *History of East Africa*, vol. 3 (Oxford, 1976), pp. 1–63.

63. For the strategies open to colonial governments, J. Darwin, 'The Central African Emergency, 1959', in R. F. Holland (ed.), *Emergencies and Disorders in the European Colonial Empires after 1945* (London, 1994).

64. See J. Lonsdale, 'The Moral Economy of Mau Mau: Wealth, Poverty and Civic Virtue in Kikuyu Political Thought', in B. Berman and J. Lonsdale,

Unhappy Valley: Conflict in Kenya and Africa, book 2: *Ethnicity and Violence* (London, 1992), pp. 265–504.

65. For a recent study of the workings of the Kenya emergency, D. Anderson, *Histories of the Hanged* (London, 2005). C. Elkins, *Britain's Gulag* (London, 2005) offers a more vehement account.

66. The best account remains Crawford Young, *Politics in the Congo: Decolonization and Independence* (Princeton, 1965).

67. For the circumstances, see Ludo de Witte, *The Assassination of Lumumba* (Eng. trans. London, 2001).

68. See Colin Legum, *Congo Disaster* (published as a Penguin Special, Harmondsworth, 1961).

69. The dilemmas confronting post-colonial governments in Africa are brilliantly evoked in two recent studies: P. Chabal and J.-P. Daloz, *Africa Works: Disorder as Political Instrument* (Oxford, 1999); J.-F. Bayart, S. Ellis and B. Hibou, *The Criminalization of the State in Africa* (Oxford, 1999).

70. See J. Zasloff, 'Law and the Shaping of American Foreign Policy: From the Gilded Age to the New Era', *New York University Law Review* 78, 30 (2003), pp. 101–288. I owe this reference to Andrew Hurrell.

71. D. Lake, *Entangling Relations: American Foreign Policy in its Century* (Princeton, 1999), p. 102.

72. For this analysis, ibid., p. 193.

73. Without control of the rest of Micronesia, Guam's value was nullified. See W. Price, *Japan's Islands of Mystery* (London, 1944), pp. 46–54.

74. See G. Lundestad, *The American 'Empire'* (London, 1990).

75. H. van der Wee, *Prosperity and Upheaval: The World Economy 1945–1980* (London, 1986), table 30.

76. Ibid., p. 451.

77. For these estimates, D. Filtzer, *Soviet Workers and Late Stalinism: Labour and the Restoration of the Stalinist System after World War Two* (Cambridge, 2002), p. 13.

78. Ibid., p. 246.

79. Ibid., p. 25.

80. See P. Gregory, *The Political Economy of Stalinism: Evidence from the Soviet Secret Archives* (Cambridge, 2004), pp. 243–4.

81. L. Sondhaus, *Navies in the Modern World* (London, 2004), p. 242.

82. See memo by Secretary of State Rusk for President Kennedy, 1 Feb. 1961, in *FRUS 1961–63*, vol. 20: *The Congo Crisis* (Washington, 1994).

83. D. Holden and R. Johns, *The House of Saud* (London, 1981), pp. 232–41.

84. B. Pockney, 'Soviet Trade with the Third World', in E. J. Feuchtwanger and P. Nailor (eds.), *The Soviet Union and the Third World* (London, 1981), pp. 70, 72–3.

85. S. Bruchey, *Enterprise: The Dynamic Economy of a Free People* (London, 1990), p. 509.

86. For an account of this K. Dawisha, 'The Soviet Union in the Middle East', in Feuchtwanger and Nailor (eds.), *The Soviet Union and the Third World*, pp. 123–6.

87. See C. Legum, *After Angola: The War over Southern Africa* (London, 1976).

88. *The Times*, 10 October 1980.

89. P. Lettow, *Ronald Reagan and his Quest to Abolish Nuclear Weapons* (New York, 2005), p. 127. The speaker was George Shultz, Secretary of State 1982–9.

90. Military spending in sub-Saharan Africa was 0.7 per cent of GNP in 1960, but five times higher by 1990 (*The Times*, 28 June 1993, p. 42). For a more general discussion, W. J. Foltz and H. Bienen, *Arms and the African: Military Influences on Africa's International Relations* (New Haven, 1985).

91. See 'Britain Joins SE Asia Exercise as Fears of Soviet Naval Power Grow', *The Times*, 7 May 1985; Sondhaus, *Navies in the Modern World*, p. 262.

92. See G. I. Khanin, 'The 1950s – the Triumph of the Soviet Economy', *Europe–Asia Studies* 55, 8 (2003), pp. 1187–1218; H. Ticktin, 'Soviet Studies and the Collapse of the USSR: In Defence of Marxism', in M. Cox (ed.), *Rethinking the Soviet Collapse* (London, 1998), p. 89.

93. See Robert J. Art, *A Grand Strategy for America* (London, 2003), pp. 20–26.

94. S. L. Engerman and R. E. Gallman (eds.), *The Cambridge Economic History of the United States*, vol. 3: *The Twentieth Century* (Cambridge, 2000), pp. 959–60.

95. Gorbachev's programme can be followed in the series of speeches published as *Perestroika* (English trans. London, 1987).

96. A sentiment expressed at its bluntest in F. Fukuyama's *The End of History and the Last Man* (New York, 1993), the core of which had been published as an article in 1989.

97. See Z. Brzezinski, *The Grand Chessboard: American Primacy and its Geostrategic Implications* (New York, 1997). The influence of earlier writers, especially the British geographer Halford Mackinder, is patent.

98. See Martin Koskenniemi, *The Gentle Civiliser of Nations: The Rise and Fall of International Law 1870–1960* (Cambridge, 2002).

99. For a representative example of this 'anti-empire' literature, see Chalmers Johnson, *The Sorrows of Empire: Militarism, Secrecy and the End of the Republic* (New York, 2004).

100. Actually 29.5 per cent. Japan's share was 14 per cent, China's 3.4. See B. Posen, 'Command of the Commons: The Military Foundations of US Hegemony', *International Security* 28, 1 (2003), p. 10, n. 14.

101. The principal argument of Posen, 'Command of the Commons'.
102. See V. De Grazia, *Irresistible Empire: America's Advance through Twentieth-Century Europe* (Cambridge, Mass., 2005).

CHAPTER 9: TAMERLANE'S SHADOW

1. This is the argument in J. Diamond, *Guns, Germs and Steel* (London, 1997).
2. The idea of 'informal empire' was developed by J. Gallagher and R. Robinson in a famous essay, 'The Imperialism of Free Trade', *Economic History Review*, New Series, 6, 1 (1953), pp. 1–15.
3. The role of vested interests in producing stagnation is set out by M. Olson in *The Rise and Fall of Nations: Economic Growth, Stagflation and Social Rigidities* (New Haven, 1982).
4. R. Kipling, 'Recessional' (1897).
5. See B. Ersanli, 'The Empire in the Historiography of the Kemalist Era', in F. Adanir and S. Faroqhi (eds.), *The Ottomans and the Balkans: A Discussion of Historiography* (Leiden, 2002), pp. 115–54.
6. See S. Deringil, *The Well-Protected Domains: Ideology and the Legitimation of Power in the Ottoman Empire, 1876–1909* (London, 1999).
7. C. A. Bayly, *Origins of Nationality in South Asia: Patriotism and Ethical Government in the Making of Modern India* (New Delhi, 1998), chs. 1–4.
8. The leading exponents of this view are D. O. Flynn and A. Giraldez. See their 'Path Dependence, Time Lags and the Birth of Globalisation', *European Economic History Review* 8 (2004), pp. 81–108.
9. For the insistence upon the nineteenth-century origins of globalization, K. H. O'Rourke and J. G. Williamson, 'Once More: When Did Globalisation Begin?', *European Economic History Review* 8 (2004), pp. 109–17.
10. See 'Growth and Development Trends 1960–2005', in *United Nations World Economic and Social Survey 2006*, p. 5, consulted at http://www.un.org/esa/policy/wess/wess2006files/chap1.pdf.
11. See K. Sugihara (ed.), *Japan, China, and the Growth of the Asian International Economy, 1850–1949* (Oxford, 2005), 'Introduction', p. 5.
12. See R. Findlay and K. H. O'Rourke, *Commodity Market Integration, 1500–2000*, National Bureau of Economic Research Working Paper (Boston, 2001), table 3.

Further Reading

This is not intended as a full bibliography of the sources used in this book. The details of these can be found in the notes and references that accompany each chapter. What is offered here is a selection of the books and articles that I have found especially useful, or interesting, and which will allow the interested reader to pursue further the ideas and topics that I have discussed all too briefly.

1. GENERAL

W. H. McNeill, *The Rise of the West* (Chicago, 1964) remains the grandest attempt thus far to write a history of the world in a single huge volume. Much of it deals with the world before 1500. It abounds with insights, and its conclusions remain thought-provoking. Some of McNeill's key ideas can be followed in his *Europe's Steppe Frontier* (London, 1974) and *Plagues and Peoples* (London, 1976), which analyses the importance of epidemic disease as a historical force. Fernand Braudel, *Civilisation and Capitalism 15th to 18th Century*, in three volumes (Eng. trans. London, 1981–4), is a panoptic view of economic and social patterns across the early modern world. E. L. Jones, *The European Miracle: Environments, Economies and Geopolitics in the History of Europe and Asia* (Cambridge, 1981) and Kenneth Pomeranz, *The Great Divergence: China, Europe and the Making of the Modern World Economy* (Princeton, 2000) present (partly) conflicting explanations of Europe's economic primacy. Marshall G. S. Hodgson, *The Venture of Islam* (3 vols., Chicago, 1974) and his *Rethinking World History: Essays on Europe, Islam and World History* (Cambridge, 1993), both published posthumously, offer a perspective on world history with the Islamic world, not Europe, at the centre.

Owen Lattimore, *The Inner Asian Frontiers of China* (New York, 1940) replaced an oceanic, maritime and Western view of Chinese history with one that emphasized its Inner Asian imperatives. Like Hodgson and McNeill, Lattimore stresses the interaction of settled and nomadic peoples, a theme most brilliantly analysed by the Islamic historian Ibn Khaldun (1332–1406), whose *Muqadimmah: An Introduction to History* was written in 1377 and translated into English in 1958 (there was an earlier translation into French). P. S. Khoury and J. Kostiner (eds.), *Tribes and State Formation in the Middle East* (London, 1990) applies Khaldunian ideas to modern Middle East history.

Amid a mass of writing on the impact of Europe's expansion on other cultures and peoples, Eric Wolf's *Europe and the Peoples without History* (London, 1982) stands out, partly for the anthropological insights that inform it. Readers in search of a general account of European imperialism will find nothing to equal the ideas contained in J. Gallagher and R. Robinson, 'The Imperialism of Free Trade', *Economic History Review*, New Series, 6, 1 (1953), pp. 1–15.

2. MEDIEVAL EURASIA

A dazzling account of the origins of medieval Eurasia is P. Brown, *The World of Late Antiquity* (London, 1971). R. W. Southern, *The Making of the Middle Ages* (London, 1953) remains the most entrancing introduction to the history of early medieval Europe. G. Duby, *The Early Growth of the European Economy* (1973; Eng. trans. Ithaca, NY, 1974) should now be compared with C. Wickham, *Framing the Early Middle Ages* (Oxford, 2005). R. Bartlett, *The Making of Europe: Conquest, Colonisation and Cultural Change 950–1350* (London, 1993) and R. Fletcher, *The Conversion of Europe* (London, 1997) describe the making of Christian Europe. J. Abu-Lughod, *Before European Hegemony: The World System 1250–1350* (New York, 1989) and Marshall G. S. Hodgson, *The Venture of Islam* (3 vols., Chicago, 1974) present non-Eurocentric views of medieval Eurasia. A. Wink, *Al-Hind: The Making of the Indo-Islamic World*, vol. 1: *Early Mediaeval India and the Expansion of Islam, 7th–11th Centuries* (Leiden, 1996), A. Hourani, *A History of the Arab Peoples* (London, 1991) and D. Pipes, *Slave Soldiers and Islam* (New Haven and London, 1981) examine the world of medieval Islam. M. Elvin, *The Pattern of the Chinese Past* (London, 1973), A. Waldron, *The Great Wall: From History to Myth* (Cambridge, 1990) and J. A. Fogel, *Politics and Sinology: The Case of Naito Konan, 1866–1934* (Cambridge, Mass., 1984) offer key insights. E. O. Reischauer and J. K. Fairbank, *East Asia: The Great Tradition* (Boston, 1958) is still a good starting point. V. Lieberman, *Strange Parallels: Southeast Asia in Global*

Context c.800–1830 (Cambridge, 2003) is a fascinating exercise in comparative history.

3. EURASIA AND THE ERA OF DISCOVERIES

F. Braudel, *The Mediterranean and the Mediterranean World in the Age of Philip II* (1966; Eng. trans. 2 vols., London, 1972–3) is a work of astonishing artistry, a revelation of how history can be written. C. Cipolla, *European Culture and Overseas Expansion* (London, 1970) examines a key issue. J. D. Tracy (ed.), *The Political Economy of Merchant Empires: State Power and World Trade 1350–1750* (Cambridge, 1991) contains a number of fascinating essays. For Portuguese expansion, S. Subrahmanyam, *Vasco da Gama* (London, 1997), and the same writer's *The Portuguese Empire in Asia 1500–1700* (London, 1993); for Spanish, H. Kamen, *Spain's Road to Empire: The Making of a World Power* (London, 2002). The less familiar story of Russian expansion can be followed in G. V. Lantzeff and R. A. Pierce, *Eastward to Empire* (Montreal and London, 1973), W. C. Fuller, *Strategy and Power in Russia, 1600–1914* (New York, 1992), M. Khodarkovsky, *Russia's Steppe Frontier: The Making of a Colonial Empire 1500–1800* (Bloomington, Ind., 2002) and A. S. Donnelly, *The Russian Conquest of Bashkiria 1552–1740* (New Haven and London, 1968).

For the Islamic world of 'Middle Eurasia', H. Inalcik with D. Quataert (eds.), *An Economic and Social History of the Ottoman Empire 1300–1914* (Cambridge, 1994), H. Inalcik, *The Ottoman Empire: The Classical Age, 1300–1600* (London, 1973), C. Kafadar, *Between Two Worlds: The Construction of the Ottoman State* (Berkeley, Los Angeles and London, 1995), M. Kunt and C. Woodhead, *Suleiman the Magnificent and his Age* (London, 1995), P. Jackson and W. Lockhart (eds.), *The Cambridge History of Iran*, vol. 6: *The Timurid and Safavid Periods* (Cambridge, 1986), J. F. Richards, *The Mughal Empire* (Cambridge, 1993) and S. A. M. Adshead, *Central Asia in World History* (London, 1993).

A. Reid, *Southeast Asia in the Age of Commerce, 1450–1680* (2 vols., New Haven, 1988, 1993) integrates environmental, economic and political history somewhat in the spirit of Braudel. D. Twitchett and F. Mote (eds.), *The Cambridge History of China*, vol. 8: *The Ming Dynasty, 1368–1644*, pt 2 (Cambridge, 1998) and P. J. Smith and R. von Glahn (eds.), *The Song–Yuan–Ming Transition in Chinese History* (Cambridge, Mass., 2003) present recent work on China.

4. EARLY MODERN EURASIA

R. J. Bonney (ed.), *Economic Systems and State Finance* (Oxford, 1995) deals with a fundamental aspect of *ancien régime* Europe. A. Sorel, *Europe and the French Revolution: The Political Traditions of the Old Regime* (1885; Eng. trans. London, 1969) is a brilliant, if cynical, introduction to eighteenth-century European diplomacy. J. de Vries and Ad van der Woude, *The First Modern Economy: Success, Failure and Perseverance of the Dutch Economy, 1500–1815* (Cambridge, 1997) explains the limits of growth in Europe's most successful pre-industrial economy. L. Hughes, *Russia in the Age of Peter the Great* (London, 1998) assesses the impact of Peter's reforms.

The context of European commercial activity in Asia can be followed in Holden Furber, *Rival Empires of Trade in the Orient 1600–1800* (Minneapolis, 1976; repr. New Delhi, 2004). J. E. Wills, 'Maritime Asia, 1500–1800: The Interactive Emergence of European Domination', *American Historical Review* 98, 1 (1993), pp. 83–105, is a useful survey of more recent writing. S. F. Dale, *Indian Merchants and Eurasian Trade 1600–1750* (Cambridge, 1994) is a reminder of the continuing importance of overland trade. The classic study of change in the Ottoman Empire is H. A. R. Gibb and H. Bowen, *Islamic Society and the West: A Study of the Impact of Western Civilisation on Moslem Culture in the Near East*, vol. 1: *Islamic Society in the Eighteenth Century* (2 pts, London, 1950, 1957). The disorder that followed the fall of the Safavids in Iran is described in J. R. Perry, *Karim Khan Zand* (Chicago, 1979). For the growth of Mughal power, J. F. Richards, *The Mughal Empire* (Cambridge, 1993), Jos Gommans, *Mughal Warfare: Indian Frontiers and the Highroads to Empire 1500–1700* (London, 2002) and R. M. Eaton, *The Rise of Islam and the Bengal Frontier 1204–1760* (London, 1993).

J. Spence, *Treason by the Book* (London, 2001) and P. C. Perdue, *China Marches West* (Cambridge, Mass., 2005) deal with different aspects of China's great age of success. L. Struve (ed.), *The Qing Formation in World Historical Time* (Cambridge, Mass., 2004), despite a forbidding title, contains a valuable selection of recent work in Chinese history.

For Japan, C. Totman, *Early Modern Japan* (London, 1993) and M. Jansen, *China in the Tokugawa World* (Cambridge, Mass., 1992).

5. THE EURASIAN REVOLUTION

P. W. Schroeder, *The Transformation of European Politics 1763–1848* (Oxford, 1994) and C. A. Bayly, *Imperial Meridian* (London, 1988) help to set the geopolitical scene. R. J. Bonney (ed.), *The Rise of the Fiscal State in Europe c.1200–1815* (Oxford, 1999) discusses a crucial element of Europeans' capacity to project their power.

P. Bairoch, *Victoires et déboires: Histoire économique et sociale du monde du xvi siècle à nos jours* (3 vols., Paris, 1997), as yet untranslated, provides a panoptic account of economic change. The debate over economic change in Britain can be followed in P. Hudson, *The Industrial Revolution* (London, 1992), J. Mokyr, *The Lever of Riches: Technological Creativity and Economic Progress* (Oxford, 1990), E. A. Wrigley, *Continuity, Chance and Change: The Character of the Industrial Revolution in England* (Cambridge, 1988), N. F. R. Crafts, *British Economic Growth During the Industrial Revolution* (Oxford, 1985) and J. E. Inikori, *Africans and the Industrial Revolution in England: A Study in International Trade and Economic Development* (Cambridge, 2002). An important reassessment, based on quantitative evidence, of the economic performance of Europe and Asia is R. C. Allen, 'Real Wages in Europe and Asia: A First Look at the Long-Term Patterns', in R. C. Allen, T. Bengtsson and M. Dribe (eds.), *Living Standards in the Past: New Perspectives on Well-Being in Asia and Europe* (Oxford, 2005).

R. Owen, *The Middle East in the World Economy 1800–1914* (London, 1981), Kenneth Pomeranz, *The Great Divergence: China, Europe and the Making of the Modern World Economy* (Princeton, 2000) and C. A. Bayly, *Rulers, Townsmen and Bazaars: North Indian Society in the Age of British Expansion 1770–1870* (Cambridge, 1983) deal with the economic history of the Middle East, China and India respectively.

P. Marshall (ed.), *The Eighteenth Century in Indian History: Evolution or Revolution* (New Delhi, 2003) collects much of the recent research on Indian history in the period of British expansion. J. J. L. Gommans, *The Rise of the Indo-Afghan Empire, c.1710–1780* (Leiden, 1995) adds an important dimension to the history of political change in North India. P. Kuhn, *Soulstealers: The Chinese Sorcery Scare of 1768* (Cambridge, Mass., 1990) and J. M. Polachek, *The Inner Opium War* (Cambridge, Mass., 1991) open up aspects of Chinese politics and culture. For cultural and intellectual life, A. Hourani, *Islam in European Thought* (Cambridge, 1991), B. Lewis, *The Muslim Discovery of Europe* (London, 1982), A. Pagden, *European Encounters with the New World* (London, 1993), N. Hampson, *The Enlightenment* (London, 1968), Gulfishan Khan, *Indian Muslim Perceptions of the West in the Eighteenth Century* (Oxford, 1998) and R. Drayton, *Nature's Government: Science, Imperial Britain and the 'Improvement' of the World* (London, 2000).

6. THE LONG NINETEENTH CENTURY

R. E. Robinson and J. A. Gallagher, *Africa and the Victorians* (London, 1961) is a brilliant evocation of the psychology behind British imperial policy in the age of expansion. D. K. Fieldhouse, *Economics and Empire 1830–1914* (London, 1973) is an unrivalled survey of the economic and non-economic influences on European empire-building. W. Woodruff, *The Impact of Western Man: A Study of Europe's Role in the World Economy 1750–1960* (London, 1966) provides much hard information. C. A. Bayly, *The Birth of the Modern World 1780–1914: Global Connections and Comparisons* (Oxford, 2004) emphasizes the parallels in social, cultural and political change across much of the world. D. Abernethy, *The Dynamics of Global Dominance: European Overseas Empires 1415–1980* (New Haven, 2000) covers a longer period, and is packed with analytical ideas. K. H. O'Rourke and J. G. Williamson, *Globalization and History: The Evolution of a Nineteenth-Century Atlantic Economy* (Cambridge, Mass., 1999) is a sweeping interpretation of the emergence of a world economy in the nineteenth century. The importance of East Asian trade is emphasized in K. Sugihara (ed.), *Japan, China, and the Growth of the Asian International Economy, 1850–1949* (Oxford, 2005). European thought is surveyed in J. W. Burrow, *The Crisis of Reason* (London, 2000). The ambivalence of European responses to the 'Orient' is convincingly stressed in J. MacKenzie, *Orientalism: History, Theory and the Arts* (Manchester, 1995).

For Russia, there is nothing to match the fizz of M. Malia, *Russia under Western Eyes* (Cambridge, Mass., 1999), but D. Lieven, *Russia's Rulers under the Old Regime* (London, 1989) gets under the skin of the tsarist regime to show how it really worked – or not. The best introduction to African history is J. Iliffe, *Africans: The History of a Continent* (Cambridge, 1995); the best account of an African region is A. G. Hopkins, *An Economic History of West Africa* (London, 1973). For the Ottoman Middle East, S. Deringil, *The Well-Protected Domains: Ideology and the Legitimation of Power in the Ottoman Empire, 1876–1909* (London, 1998), A. Hourani, *Arabic Thought in the Liberal Age 1798–1939* (London, 1962; repr. Cambridge, 1983) and A. Hourani, 'Ottoman Reform and the Politics of Notables', in A. Hourani, P. S. Khoury and M. C. Wilson (eds.), *The Modern Middle East* (London, 1993), pp. 83–109. For Iran, H. Algar, *Religion and*

State in Iran 1785–1906 (Berkeley and Los Angeles, 1969) is fundamental. K. Fahmy, *All the Pasha's Men: Mehmed Ali, his Army and the Making of Modern Egypt* (Cairo, 2002) reverses much myth-making about nineteenth-century Egypt. A. Seal, 'Imperialism and Nationalism in India', in J. Gallagher, G. Johnson and A. Seal (eds.), *Locality, Province and Nation* (Cambridge, 1973), offers what is still the most compelling account of how colonial rule provoked a nationalist response. R. Bin Wong, *China Transformed: Historical Change and the Limits of European Experience* (Ithaca, NY, 1997) is an especially stimulating account of Chinese experience. J. Hevia, *English Lessons: The Pedagogy of Imperialism in Nineteenth-Century China* (London, 2003) examines European efforts to force China into a colonial mould. E. H. Norman, *Japan's Emergence as a Modern State* (New York, 1940) is a neglected classic.

Much American history remains stubbornly resistant to external comparison, and America's relations with Europe (and the rest of the nineteenth-century world) have been curiously neglected by an introverted historiography. But the series of books by D. W. Meinig on 'The Shaping of America: A Geographical Perspective on 500 Years of History', especially his *Continental America, 1800–1867* (New Haven, 1993), is a wonderful stimulus to comparative thinking. And the most influential of all American historians, Frederick Jackson Turner, whose 'The Significance of the Frontier in American History' was originally published in 1893, continues to provoke comparative study. See M. Bassin, 'Turner, Solov'ev and the "Frontier Hypothesis": The Nationalist Significance of Open Spaces', *Journal of Modern History* 65, (1993), pp. 473–511. J. C. Malin was a Kansas maverick. His 'Mobility and History: Reflections on the Agricultural Policies of the United States in Relation to a Mechanised World', *Agricultural History* 17, 4 (1943), pp. 177–91, debunks many of the myths of the American frontier.

7. THE CRISIS AGE

H. Strachan, *The First World War: To Arms* (Oxford, 2001) is the first of three projected volumes. It is especially good on the approach to war and on the Middle East and African theatres, as well as on the economics and financing of the war. Z. Steiner, *The Lights That Failed: European International History, 1919–1933* (Oxford, 2005) provides an authoritative account of post-war diplomacy. M. Mazower, *The Dark Continent: Europe's Twentieth Century* (London, 2000) brings fresh insight to Europe's modern 'dark age'. For the breakdown of the world economy, H. James, *The End of Globalisation* (London, 2001). The three volumes of Robert Skidelsky's biography of John Maynard Keynes – *John Maynard Keynes: Hopes Betrayed 1883–1920* (London, 1983), *John Maynard Keynes: The Economist as Saviour 1920–1937* (London, 1992) and *John Maynard Keynes: Fighting for Britain 1937–1946* (London, 2000) – are a superb introduction to the economic history of the first half of the twentieth century.

American attitudes and policy are discussed in A. Iriye, *The Cambridge History of American Foreign Relations*, vol. 3: *The Globalising of America* (Cambridge, 1995), N. G. Levin, *Woodrow Wilson and World Politics: America's Response to War and Revolution* (Oxford, 1968) and M. J. Hogan, *Informal Entente: The Private Structure of Cooperation in Anglo-American Economic Diplomacy* (Columbia, Mo., 1977). For Soviet Russia, R. Overy, *The Dictators: Hitler's Germany, Stalin's Russia* (London, 2004), R. Pipes, *The Formation of the Soviet Union: Communism and Nationalism 1917–1923* (rev. edn, Cambridge, Mass., 1964), M. Malia, *Russia under Western Eyes* (Cambridge, Mass., 1999), and L. Viola, *Peasant Rebels under Stalin: Collectivization and the Culture of Peasant Resistance* (New York, 1996).

For the Middle East, B. Lewis, *The Emergence of Modern Turkey* (London, 1961), A. Mango, *Atatürk* (London, 1999) and M. E. Meeker, *A Nation of Empire: The Ottoman Legacy of Turkish Modernity* (Berkeley, Los Angeles and London, 2002) explain Turkey's post-imperial transition. E. Abrahamian, *Iran between Two Revolutions* (Princeton, 1982) is the indispensable account of Iran's modern history. M. E. Yapp, *The Near East since the First World War* (London, 1991) is a superb general survey.

For Indian politics in the last phase of colonial rule, D. Hardiman, *Peasant Nationalists of Gujarat* (Delhi, 1981) offers a fascinating close-up. S. Bose and A. Jalal, *Modern South Asia: History, Culture, Political Economy* (London, 1998) is a lively treatment. Gandhi's autobiography can be read alongside the modern biography by J. M. Brown, *Gandhi: Prisoner of Hope* (London, 1991). B. Parekh, *Colonialism, Tradition and Reform* (London, 1989) explains Gandhi's ideas. For the growth of Muslim politics, D. Page, *Prelude to Partition: The Indian Muslims and the Imperial System of Control 1920–1932* (Delhi, 1982).

For the links between Japan's domestic history and its career of expansion, P. Duus, R. Myers and M. Peattie (eds.), *Japanese Informal Empire in China, 1895–1937* (Princeton, 1989), W. G. Beasley, *Japanese Imperialism 1894–1945* (Oxford, 1991) and H. Harootunian, *Overcome by Modernity: History, Culture and Community in Inter-war Japan* (Princeton, 2000). Hans van der Ven, *War and Nationalism in China 1925–1945* (London, 2003) is now essential for understanding the most violent phase of China's history. R. Mitter, *A Bitter Revolution: China's Struggle with the Modern World* (Oxford, 2004) brings out the later significance of the May Fourth movement.

B. Berman and J. Lonsdale, *Unhappy Valley: Conflict in Kenya and Africa,* book 2: *Ethnicity and Violence* (London, 1992) brilliantly explores the tensions within a colonized African society. G. L. Weinberg, *A World at War: A Global History of World War Two* (Cambridge, 1994) is the best modern one-volume study.

8. EMPIRE DENIED

For the Cold War setting in Europe and beyond, J. L. Gaddis, *We Now Know: Rethinking Cold War History* (Oxford, 1997), O. A. Westad, *Cold War and Revolution: Soviet–American Rivalry and the Origins of the Chinese Civil War* (New York, 1993) and O. A. Westad, *The Global Cold War* (Cambridge, 2005). For a general account of decolonization, R. F. Holland, *European Decolonisation 1918–1981* (London, 1985) and J. Darwin, *Britain and Decolonisation: The Retreat from Empire in the Post-War World* (London, 1988). The underlying strategy behind the transfer of power in colonial states is exposed in Wm Roger Louis and Ronald Robinson, 'The Imperialism of Decolonisation', *Journal of Imperial and Commonwealth History* 22, 3 (1994). For the Chinese Revolution and after, Westad, *Cold War and Revolution*, Chalmers Johnson, *Peasant Nationalism and Communist Power* (Stanford, 1962) and two books by S. Schram, *Mao Tse-tung* (London, 1967) and *The Political Thought of Mao Tse-tung* (London, 1971). The Cultural Revolution is the subject of a trilogy by R. MacFarquhar, *The Origins of the Cultural Revolution*, vol 1: *Contradictions among the People 1956–57* (London, 1974); vol 2: *The Great Leap Forward 1958–1960* (London, 1983); vol 3: *The Coming of the Cataclysm 1961–1966* (London, 1999). For Japan, John Dower, *Embracing Defeat: Japan in the Aftermath of World War Two* (Harmondsworth, 1999) is essential.

For the Middle East, W. R. Louis, *The British Empire in the Middle East 1945–1951: Arab Nationalism, the United States, and Postwar Imperialism* (Oxford, 1984) is a detailed study of the policy and planning in the two Western powers most involved in the region. M. J. Cohen, *Palestine and the Great Powers 1945–1948* (Princeton, 1982) explains the geopolitical circumstances in which Israel came into existence. R. McNamara, *Britain, Nasser and the Balance of Power in the Middle East 1952–1967* (London, 2003) and K. Kyle, *Suez* (London, 1991) examine the rise and fall of Nasser and the Arab nationalism he championed. E. Abrahamian, *Iran between Two Revolutions* (Princeton, 1982) analyses the post-war turbulence in Iran and the consolidation of the shah's power in the 1950s and '60s. M. E. Yapp, *The Near East since the First World War* (London, 1991) remains invaluable.

A. Sampson, *The Seven Sisters: The Great Oil Companies and the World They Made* (London, 1975) is an accessible account of the international oil industry.

D. Anderson, *Histories of the Hanged* (London, 2005) is a forensic examination of the realities behind the Mau Mau emergency in Kenya, and reveals in the process the stresses that helped wreck the late colonial state. P. Chabal and J.-P. Daloz, *Africa Works: Disorder as Political Instrument* (Oxford, 1999) and J.-F. Bayart, S. Ellis and B. Hibou, *The Criminalization of the State in Africa* (Oxford, 1999) are a fascinating discussion of the post-colonial state. For the growth of America's 'empire', D. Lake, *Entangling Relations: American Foreign Policy in its Century* (Princeton, 1999) and G. Lundestad, *The American 'Empire'* (London, 1990).

The sources of Soviet economic power are explained in D. Filtzer, *Soviet Workers and Late Stalinism: Labour and the Restoration of the Stalinist System after World War Two* (Cambridge, 2002). The international economy in its 'pre-globalization' phase is described in H. van der Wee, *Prosperity and Upheaval: The World Economy 1945–1980* (London, 1986). Some of the debate over the use and abuse of American power can be followed in Robert J. Art, *A Grand Strategy for America* (London, 2003) and Chalmers Johnson, *The Sorrows of Empire: Militarism, Secrecy and the End of the Republic* (New York, 2004).

Index